A HISTORY OF WESTERN SOCIETY

Volume A: From Antiquity to the Reformation

A HISTORY OF WESTERN SOCIETY

Volume A: From Antiquity to the Reformation

JOHN P. McKAY

BENNETT D. HILL

JOHN BUCKLER

UNIVERSITY OF ILLINOIS, URBANA

HOUGHTON MIFFLIN COMPANY

BOSTON

DALLAS   GENEVA, ILLINOIS

HOPEWELL, NEW JERSEY   PALO ALTO

LONDON

TEXT CREDITS

Excerpts from S. N. Kramer, *The Sumerians* (Chicago: University of Chicago Press, 1964), copyright © by the University of Chicago. Reprinted by permission. Excerpts from "Sumerian Myths and Epic Tales," trans. S. N. Kramer; "Akkadian Myths and Epics," trans. E. A. Speiser; "Laws from Mesopotamia and Asia Minor," trans. S. N. Kramer; and "Sumarian Wisdom Text," trans. S.N. Kramer; in *Ancient Near Eastern Texts Relating to the Old Testament* by James B. Pritchard (ed.), 3rd ed. with Supplement (copyright © 1969 by Princeton University Press), pp. 44–590 (passim). Reprinted by permission of Princeton University Press. Riddle No. 44 from Michael Alexander, trans., *The Earliest English Poems* (London: Penguin Books Ltd, 1966), p. 99. Copyright © Michael Alexander, 1966. Reprinted by permission of Penguin Books Ltd.

COVER PHOTOGRAPH

Peter Breughel the Elder. The Four Seasons: Spring, 16th century, the Netherlands. Courtesy, Museum of Fine Arts, Boston

CHAPTER OPENING PHOTOGRAPHS

Chapter 1: From the photographic collections of the University Museum, University of Pennsylvania *Chapter 2:* Photo: Caroline Buckler *Chapter 3:* Courtesy, World Heritage Museum. Photo: Caroline Buckler *Chapter 4:* Alinari/Scala *Chapter 5:* Vatican Museum, Alinari/Scala *Chapter 6:* Courtesy, World Heritage Museum. Photo: Caroline Buckler *Chapter 7:* Yale Medical Library *Chapter 8:* Courtesy, World Heritage Museum. Photo: Caroline Buckler *Chapter 9:* Bibliothèque Publique de Dijon *Chapter 10:* Bildarchiv Preussischer Kulturbesitz *Chapter 11:* Archives Nationales, Paris/Giraudon *Chapter 12:* Radio Times Hulton Picture Library

Printed in the U.S.A.

Library of Congress Catalog Card Number: 78-69593

ISBN: 0-395-27272-6

CONTENTS

PREFACE

History is the study of change over time and historians have seen many changes in their own discipline in recent years. Imaginative questions and innovative research have opened up vast new areas of interest and increased historical knowledge rapidly. The pushing back of the frontiers of knowledge has been especially dramatic in European social history, where the history of population, women, the family, and popular culture—to name only four important components—have emerged as major fields of inquiry on both sides of the Atlantic. Similar if less well-publicized advances have been made in economic and intellectual history and the history of science and technology. New research and fresh interpretations have also revitalized the study of the traditional mainstream of political, diplomatic, and religious development.

Yet while new historical interest and knowledge have grown, the broad public has paradoxically appeared to become less interested in history in general and in more distant European history in partic-

ular. Appreciation for the study of the past often seems quite limited among the intelligentsia as well. A distinguished mathematical economist of our acquaintance smugly quips "What's new in history?"—confident that the answer is nothing and that historians are as dead as the events they examine.

It has been our conviction, based on the experience of a dozen years of introducing large numbers of students to the broad sweep of Western civilization, that the books currently available for this purpose, some of which are fine works, do not adequately incorporate the new areas of interest and discovery within the profession. We feel that a book which reflects these current trends can be exciting and can inspire a new interest in history and a new curiosity about our Western heritage.

Our basic strategy has been twofold. First, we have made social history the core element of our work. Not only is this perhaps the first serious introduction to Western civilization to incorporate much recent research by social historians on such topics as population, women, and the family, but it also re-creates the life of ordinary people in human, understandable terms. It is our expectation that the social element will appeal strongly to instructors as well as students, in part because today's readers can easily identify with the common man and woman and can become genuinely interested in European history with this approach.

At the same time we have been equally determined to write a balanced history of the Western world. We have given the great economic, political, intellectual, and cultural developments the attention they unquestionably deserve. And we have tried hard to show connections and interactions between different aspects of the human experience. Ours is not a narrow, eccentric book. Indeed, we are convinced that a book which barely mentions Alexander the Great or deals superficially with the ideas of the Enlightenment would be just as incomplete as those which ignore women and the family, or diet and medicine, or the social setting of political and intellectual history. With such a balanced integrated framework, individual readers and instructors will have a good general perspective. They will be free to pursue on their own or in the classroom those themes and problems that they find particularly appealing and significant.

Our book has other notable features. Readers with little background in history are often frustrated by the mass of material they encounter. We sympathize. To help guide the reader toward understanding what is important we have posed specific historical questions at the beginning of each chapter. These questions are then answered in the course of the chapter, which normally concludes with a succinct summary of the chapter's findings.

We have also tried to suggest how historians actually work and think. We have quoted rather extensively from a wide variety of primary sources and have demonstrated in our use of these quotations how historians sift and weigh evidence. We want the reader to realize that history is neither a list of cut-and-dried facts nor a senseless jumble of conflicting opinions.

Each chapter concludes with several carefully selected suggestions for further reading. These suggestions are briefly described, in order to help readers know where to go to continue thinking and learning about the Western world. For the sake of convenience, books in paperback, which are starred, have been selected when possible.

The geographical focus of *A History of Western Society* is upon Europe. But we have taken pains to show how Western society expanded and how that expanding society has influenced and been influenced by non-Western peoples. Contemporary world history—a complex interactive process of different continents and civilizations—is basically a product of Western development, and we believe therefore that our book will make an excellent core text for a realistic study of world history. By the same token, we deal with North America at various points, gladly placing American history within the broad framework of Western civilization where it is best understood.

The illustrations in *A History of Western Society* have been carefully selected to re-enforce both the book's social theme and its balanced treatment of all aspects of Western history. Artwork is an integral part of our book, for the past can speak in pictures as well as words. Maps and line drawings are also a fundamental part of the book and, as with illustrations, they normally carry captions to enhance their value.

Western civilization courses differ widely in chronological structure from one campus to another. To accommodate the various divisions of historical time into intervals that fit a two-quarter, three-quarter, or two-semester period, *A History of Western Society* is being published in three paperbound versions, each set embracing the complete work:

One volume, A HISTORY OF WESTERN SOCIETY; two-volume, A HISTORY OF WESTERN SOCIETY *Volume I: From Antiquity to the Enlightenment* (Chapters 1–16), *Volume II: From Absolutism to the Present* (Chapters 15–30); three-volume, A HISTORY OF WESTERN SOCIETY *Volume A: From Antiquity to the Reformation* (Chapters 1–12), *Volume B: From the Renaissance to 1815* (Chapters 12–20), *Volume C: From the Revolutionary Era to the Present* (Chapters 20–30).

Note that overlapping chapters in both the two- and the three-volume sets permit still wider flexibility in matching the appropriate volume with the opening and closing dates of a course term. Furthermore, for courses beginning with the Renaissance rather than antiquity or the medieval period, the reader can begin study with Volume B.

A History of Western Society also has a study guide for students, as well as an instructor's manual. Both of these excellent aids have been written by Professor James Schmiechen of Illinois State University. Professor Schmiechen read all our drafts, from the first prospectus to the final typescript, and he gave us many valuable suggestions in addition to his enthusiastic and warmly appreciated support. His *Study Guide* contains chapter summaries, chapter outlines, study questions, self-check lists of important concepts and events, and a variety of other aids and activities. We believe that Professor Schmiechen's *Study Guide*, which takes the reader through the book step by step, will be very useful to many students.

It is also a pleasure to thank Roger Schlesinger, Washington State University; Charles Rearick, University of Massachusetts at Amherst; Donald Buck, DeAnza College; James Powell, Syracuse University; John M. Riddle, North Carolina State University; Laurence Lee Howe, University of Louisville; and Archibald Lewis, University of Massachusetts at Amherst, who read and critiqued the manuscript through its development.

Many of our colleagues at the University of Illinois kindly provided information and stimulation for our book, often without even knowing it. N. Frederick Nash, Rare Book Librarian, gave freely of his time and made many helpful suggestions for illustrations. Georgette Meredith, Director of the World Heritage Museum at the University, allowed us complete access to the sizable holdings of the museum. James Dengate kindly supplied information on objects from the museum's collection. Caroline Buckler took many excellent photographs of the museum's objects and generously helped us at crucial moments in production. Such wide-ranging expertise was a great asset for which we are very appreciative. We also acknowledge a special debt of gratitude to John R. Dahl. Professor Dahl started us on the undertaking, and he read and commented helpfully on all our efforts.

Each of us has benefited from the generous criticism of his co-authors, although each of us assumes responsibility for what he has written. John Buckler has written the first five chapters; Bennett Hill has continued the narrative through Chapter 15; and John McKay has written Chapters 16 through 30. Finally, we warmly welcome any comments or suggestions for improvements from our readers.

JOHN P. MCKAY

BENNETT D. HILL

JOHN BUCKLER

A HISTORY OF WESTERN SOCIETY

Volume A: From Antiquity to the Reformation

Chapter 1

NEAR EASTERN ORIGINS

The culture of the modern Western world has its origins in places as far away as modern Iraq, Iran, and Egypt. In these areas human beings first abandoned their life of roaming and hunting to settle in stable agricultural communities. From these communities developed the first cities and the first civilizations, societies that invented concepts and techniques that have become integral parts of contemporary life. Fundamental in this respect is the invention of writing by the Sumerians in Mesopotamia, an invention that enables knowledge of the past to be preserved and facilitates the spread and accumulation of learning, lore, literature, and science. Mathematics, astronomy, and architecture were all innovations of the ancient Near Eastern civilizations. So too were the first law codes and religious concepts that still permeate daily life.

How did human beings go from wild hunters to urban dwellers? How did the roots of Western culture establish themselves in far-off Mesopotamia, and what caused Mesopotamian culture to become predominant throughout most of the ancient Near East? What part did the Egyptians play in this vast story? What contributions to Western culture did the ancient Hebrews make? These are the questions this chapter will explore.

On December 27, 1831, young Charles Darwin stepped aboard H.M.S. *Beagle* to begin a voyage to South America and the Pacific Ocean. In the course of that five-year voyage he became convinced that species of animals and human beings had evolved from lower forms. At first Darwin was reluctant to make public his theories because they ran counter to the biblical account of creation, which claimed that God had made Adam in one day. Finally, however, in 1859 he published *On the Origin of Species*. In 1871 he followed it with *The Descent of Man,* in which he argued that human beings and apes are descended from a common ancestor. Even before Darwin had proclaimed his theories, evidence to support them had come to light. In 1856, the fossilized bones of an early form of man were discovered in the Neander valley of Germany. He became known as Neanderthal Man, after the place of his discovery. He was physically more primitive than and anatomically a bit different from modern man (*Homo sapiens,* or thinking man), but he was clearly a human being and not an ape. He offered proof of Darwin's theory that *Homo sapiens* had evolved from less-developed forms.

The theories of Darwin, supported by the evidence of fossilized remains, ushered in a new scientific era, an era in which scientists and scholars have re-examined the very nature of human beings and their history. Men and women of the twentieth century have made new discoveries, solved some old problems, and raised many new ones. Since 1959, the anthropologists Louis and Mary Leakey and their son, Richard, working in the Olduvai Gorge in East Africa, have uncovered fossilized bones of several very early types of human beings as well as species of advanced apes. The work of the Leakeys alone demonstrates how complex the course of human evolution has been.

Why did some human types become extinct while others thrived? More importantly, what are the links among the fossilized remains? The answers to these questions lie in the future. For the moment, perhaps the wisest and most humble answer is the observation of Loren Eiseley, a noted American anthropologist: "The human interminglings of hundreds of thousands of years of prehistory are not to be clarified by a single generation of archaeologists."[1]

Despite the enormous uncertainty surrounding human development, a reasonably clear picture can be had of two important early periods: the Paleolithic, or Old Stone Age, and the Neolithic, or New Stone Age. The Paleolithic Age (ca 400,000–7000 B.C.) takes its name from the crude stone tools the earliest hunters chipped from flint and obsidian, a black volcanic rock. The Neolithic Age (7000–3000 B.C.) saw the making of new types of stone tools and the introduction of agriculture.

THE PALEOLITHIC AGE

Life in the Paleolithic Age was perilous and uncertain at best. Survival depended on the success of the hunt, but the hunt often brought sudden and violent death. In some instances, Paleolithic peoples were their own worst enemies. At times they fought each other for control of hunting grounds, and some early hunters played an important part in wiping out less aggressive peoples. On occasion Paleolithic peoples seem to have preyed on one another. One of the grimmest indications that Neanderthal Man was at times cannibalistic comes from a cave in Yugoslavia, where investigators found human bones burned and split open.

On the other hand, the peoples of the Paleolithic Age were responsible for some striking accomplishments. Most obvious is the use of the stone implements that gave the period its name. The ability to make and use tools gave Paleolithic peoples the means to change their environment. They could compete with larger and stronger animals and could hunt animals faster and more ferocious than themselves. In the frozen wastes of the north, they hunted the mammoth, the woolly rhinoceros, and the reindeer. In milder southern climates, they hunted deer, badgers, squirrels, and rabbits. The demands of the hunt sharpened their wits. They supplemented their diet by collecting fruits, nuts, and seeds, and in the process they discovered the plant world around them. Paleolithic peoples learned to control fire and to make clothes from the skins of their prey.

Paleolithic peoples were also world travelers. Before the dawn of history bands of *Homo sapiens* flourished in Europe, Africa, and Asia, and they had crossed into the continents of North America and South America and had landed in Australia. By the end of the Paleolithic Age, there were very few "undiscovered" areas in the world.

The most striking accomplishments of Paleolithic peoples were intellectual. The development of the human brain made possible thought and symbolic logic. An invisible world opened up to *Homo sapiens.* Unlike animals, whose behavior is the result of instinct, Paleolithic peoples used reason to govern their actions. Thought and language permitted the lore and experience of the old to be passed on to the young. The Neanderthalers developed the custom of burying their dead and of placing offerings with the dead, perhaps in the belief that in some way life continued after death.

Paleolithic peoples produced the first art. They decorated the walls of their caves with paintings of animals and scenes of the hunt. They also began to fashion clay models of pregnant women and of animals. These first examples of art illustrate the way in which early men and women communicated to others their experience of the past and hope for the future. Many of the paintings, such as those at Altamira in Spain and Lascaux in France, are found deep in the caves, in areas not easily accessible. These areas were probably places of ritual and initiation, where young men were taken when they joined the ranks of the hunters. They were also places of magic. The animals depicted on the walls were either those hunted for food or those feared as predators. Many are shown wounded by spears or arrows; others are pregnant. The early artists may have been expressing the hope that the hunt would be successful and game plentiful. By portraying the animals as realistically as possible, the artists and hunters may have hoped to gain power over them. The statuettes of pregnant women seem to express a wish for fertile women to have babies and thus insure the group's survival. The wall paintings and statuettes show human beings' earliest yearnings to control their environment.

THE NEOLITHIC AGE

Hunting is at best a precarious way of life, even when the diet is supplemented by the gathering of seeds and fruits. During the long, hard years of various ice ages, the periods when huge glaciers covered vast parts of Europe, small bands of hunters were at the mercy of the elements. If the climate changed even slightly, the all-important herds might move to new areas. In that case tribes either moved with the herds or adapted themselves to new circumstances. Yet toward the end of the last Ice Age, around 10,000 B.C., some hunters and gatherers began to learn the secrets of agriculture and the domestication of animals. This discovery was the beginning of the Agricultural Revolution — a discovery that changed the course of history. The Agricultural Revolution is the great achievement of the Neolithic Age.

How and why farming began is still unknown. Quite probably, the discovery of agriculture was accidental. Paleolithic hunters had long gathered seeds for food. In the process, some seeds were probably lost and sprouted naturally. Or Paleolithic peoples may have noticed that stored seeds sometimes sprouted, and they may have come to realize that seeds could be planted. The crucial step toward the Agricultural Revolution was taken when nomads decided to settle down to grow crops and raise animals rather than follow the herds. Between 8000 and 6500 B.C., groups of people in places as far apart as Jarmo in modern Iraq, Jericho in Palestine, and Hacilar in Anatolia (see Map 1.1) turned to farming, which included the domestication of wild animals. Although the dog was the first animal to be tamed, the sheep and the goat proved more important because they supplied fleeces and food.

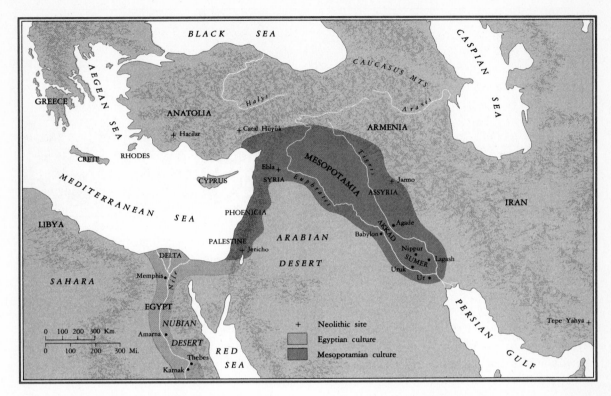

MAP I.I   THE SPREAD OF EARLY NEAR EASTERN CULTURES

The first farmers gathered and then planted the seeds of wild wheat and barley. Later farmers learned to improve their cereals. In 1976, the excavators of Tepe Yahya in modern Iran demonstrated how specialization in farming could have led to a new species of grain. In the first place, the Neolithic farmers of Tepe Yahya preferred a particular species of wheat to others, and they planted only that species. Meanwhile, wild grasses in the area fertilized the wheat naturally and gave rise to a new species, a hybrid. Interesting also is the excavators' conclusion that the community at Tepe Yahya tightly controlled the circulation of seeds. The seeds were stored in large jars to be doled out only for human consumption or for planting the

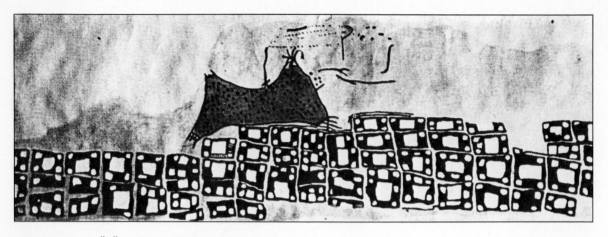

TOWN OF CATAL HÜYÜK.   This unusual drawing is a modern reconstruction of a Neolithic wall-painting found at Catal Hüyük. A volcano smokes in the background. At its foot are blocks of houses, laid out on terraces. (Courtesy, James Mellaart)

next year's crop. Farming was a group effort and demanded the cooperation of the entire community.

Once people began to rely on farming for their livelihood, they settled in permanent villages and built houses. The location of the village was crucial. Early farmers chose places where the water supply was constant and adequate for their crops and flocks. At first, the villages were small, consisting of a few households. As the population expanded and prosperity increased, villages usually developed into towns. Between 8000 and 7000 B.C., the community at Jericho grew to include at least two thousand people. They lived in mud-brick houses built on stone foundations, and they surrounded their town with a massive fortification wall. The Neolithic site of Catal Hüyük in Anatolia covered thirty-two acres. The outer houses of the settlement formed a solid wall of mud brick, which served as a bulwark against attack. This practice is repeated at Tepe Yahya, where the Neolithic farmers surrounded their town with a wall.

Walls offered protection and permitted a more secure and stable way of life than that of the nomad. They also prove that towns grew in size, population, and wealth, for these fortifications were so large that they could have been raised only by much labor and a large labor force. In addition, they indicate that towns were developing social and political organization. The fortifications were the work of the whole community, and they would have been impossible without central planning.

One of the major effects of the Agricultural Revolution was a dramatic increase in population. No census figures exist for this period, but the number and size of the towns prove that Neolithic society was expanding. Early farmers found that agriculture provided a larger and much more dependable food supply than had hunting and gathering. No longer did the long winter months carry the immediate threat of starvation. Farmers actually raised more food than they could consume, and they learned to store the surplus for the winter. Because the farming community was better fed than ever before, it was also more resistant to diseases that kill people who are suffering from malnutrition. Thus, these people were healthier and longer-lived than their predecessors. All these factors explain the growth of towns like Jericho and Jarmo.

The surplus of food had two other momentous consequences. First, grain became an article of commerce. The farming community traded surplus grain for items it could not produce itself. The community thus obtained raw materials, such as precious gems and metals. In Mesopotamia the early towns imported copper from the north until eventually copper replaced stone for tools and weapons. Trade also brought Neolithic communities into touch with one another, making possible the spread of ideas and techniques.

Second, agricultural surplus made possible the division of labor. It freed some members of the community from the necessity of raising food. Artisans and craftsmen devoted their attention to making the new stone tools farming demanded — hoes and sickles for the field work and mortars and pestles for grinding the grain. Other artisans began to shape clay into pottery vessels, which were used to store grain, wine, and oil, and which served as kitchen utensils. Still other artisans wove baskets and cloth. People who could specialize in particular crafts produced more and better goods than any single individual could.

Prosperity and stable conditions nurtured other innovations and discoveries. Neolithic farmers improved their tools and agricultural techniques. They domesticated bigger, stronger animals, such as the bull and the horse, animals that could work for them. To harness the power of these animals they invented tools like the plow, which came into use by 3000 B.C. The first plows had wooden shares and could break only light soils, but they were far more efficient than stone hoes. Also, by 3000 B.C. the wheel was invented, and farmers devised ways of hitching bulls and horses to wagons. These developments let Neolithic farmers raise more food more efficiently and easily than ever before, simply because animals and machines were doing a greater proportion of the actual work.

In areas like Mesopotamia and Egypt, farmers learned to irrigate their land. By diverting the waters of large rivers, they were able to open new land to cultivation. River waters flooding the fields deposited layers of rich mud, which increased the fertility of the soil. Thus, the rivers, together with the manure of domesticated animals, kept replenishing the land. One result was a further increase in population and wealth. Irrigation, especially on a large scale, demanded group effort. The entire community had to plan which land to irrigate and how to lay out the canals. Then everyone had to help dig the canals. The demands of irrigation underscored the need for strong central authority within the community. Successful irrigation projects in turn strengthened the central authority by proving it effective and beneficial. Towns evolved a corporate spirit and forms of government, to which individuals were subordinate. Here were the makings of urban life.

The Agricultural Revolution was a fundamental turning point in the history of Western civilization. Farming made possible an enormous increase in population. It gave rise to stable societies, which experienced considerable prosperity. Some members of the budding towns turned their attention to the production of goods that made life more comfortable. Settled circumstances and a certain amount of leisure made the accumulation and spread of knowledge easier. Finally, the Agricultural Revolution led to the rise of towns and prepared the way for urban life.

ENVIRONMENT AND MESOPOTAMIAN CIVILIZATION

Mesopotamia is the Greek name for the land between the Euphrates and Tigris rivers. Both rivers have their headwaters in the mountains of Armenia in modern Turkey. Both are fed by numerous tributaries, and the entire river system drains a vast, mountainous region. Overland routes in Mesopotamia usually follow the Euphrates, because the banks of the Tigris are frequently steep and difficult. North of the ancient city of Babylon the land levels out into a barren expanse. In 401 B.C., the Greek writer and adventurer Xenophon gave a vivid description of this area:

In this area the land is a level plain just like the sea, full of wormwood. If there was any brush or reed there, it was invariably fragrant, like spices. Trees there were none, but wild animals of all sorts — a great many wild asses and many ostriches. There were also bustards and gazelles.[2]

Immediately south of Babylon the desert continues, and in 1857 the English geologist and traveler W. K. Loftus depicted it in grim terms:

There is no life for miles around. No river glides in grandeur at the base of its [the ancient city of Uruk] mounds; no green date groves flourish near its ruins. The jackal and the hyena appear to shun the dull aspect of its tombs. The king of birds never hovers over the deserted waste. A blade of grass or an insect finds no existence there. The shrivelled lichen alone, clinging to the weathered surface of the broken brick, seems to glory in its universal dominion upon those barren walls.[3]

Farther south the desert gives way to a six-thousand square-mile region of marshes, lagoons, mud flats, and reed banks. At last, in the extreme south the Euphrates and the Tigris unite and empty into the Persian Gulf.

This forbidding area became the home of many folk and the land of the first cities. Bands of Semitic nomads occupied the region around Akkad (modern Baghdad). Into the south came the Sumerians, a people who probably migrated from the east. The Sumerians were farmers and city builders. By 3000 B.C. they had established a number of cities in the southernmost part of Mesopotamia, a region that became known as Sumer. As the Sumerians pushed north, they came into contact with the Semites, who readily adopted Sumerian culture, and turned to urban life. The Sumerians soon changed the face of the land and made Mesopotamia the "cradle of civilization."

From the outset geography had a profound effect on the evolution of Mesopotamian civilization. The growing of crops within this region is possible only through irrigation. Consequently, the Sumerians and later the Akkadians built their cities along the Tigris and Euphrates and their branches. The rivers supplied the urban dwellers with fish, a major element of their diet. The rivers also provided them with reeds and clay, which they used as building materials. Since this entire area lacks stone, mud brick became the primary building block of Mesopotamian architecture.

Although the rivers sustained life, they simultaneously acted as a powerful restraining force, especially on Sumerian political development. They cut Sumer up into a geographical maze. Between the rivers, streams, and irrigation canals stretched either open desert or swamp. Nomadic tribes roamed the wastes. Communication between cities was difficult and at times dangerous. City was separated from city, each isolated in its own locale. Sumerian cities became states, each independent of the others and jealous of its independence. They resisted the efforts of any city that tried to unify the country. As a result, the political history of Sumer is one of almost constant warfare. The experience of the city of Nippur is an example of how bad conditions could become. At one point in its history Nippur was conquered eighteen times in twenty-four years. Although Sumer was eventually unified, unification came late and was always tenuous.

The harsh environment fostered a grim, even pessimistic, spirit among the Mesopotamians. They especially feared the ravages of flood. The Tigris can bring quick devastation, as it did to Baghdad in 1831, when floodwaters destroyed seven thousand homes in a single night. The same tragedy often happened in antiquity. The chronicle of King Hammurabi recorded years in which floods wiped out whole cities. Such natural phenomena affected Mesopotamian religious beliefs.

The Mesopotamians thought that natural catastrophes were the work of the gods. At times the Sumerians described their chief god, Enlil, as "the raging flood which has no rival." Occasionally, the gods might even use nature to punish the Mesopotamians. The myth of the Deluge, which gave rise to the biblical story of Noah, tells of the god Enki warning Ziusudra, the Sumerian Noah:

A flood will sweep over the cult-centers;
To destroy the seed of mankind . . .
Is the decision, the word of the assembly of the gods.[4]

The myth of Atrahasis describes the gods' annoyance at the prosperity of mankind and tells how Enlil complained to the other gods:

Oppressive has become the clamor of mankind.
By their uproar they prevent sleep.
Let the flour be cut off for the people,
In their bellies let the greens be too few.[5]

Enlil and the other gods decide to send a drought and then a flood to destroy human life. In the face of such harsh conditions the Mesopotamians considered themselves weak and insignificant as compared to the gods. This feeling was particularly strong among the Sumerians, and it shaped the way their cities developed.

SUMERIAN SOCIETY

The Sumerians sought to please and calm the gods, especially the patron deity of the city. In the center of each city the people erected a shrine and then built their houses around it. The best way to honor the god was to make the shrine as grand and impressive as possible, for a god who had a splendid temple might think twice about sending floods to destroy the city.

The temple had to be worthy of the god, a symbol of his power, and it had to last. Special skills and materials were needed to build it. Only stone was suitable for its foundations and precious metals for its decoration. Since the Mesopotamians had to import both stone and metals, temple construction encouraged trade. Architects, engineers, craftsmen, and workers had to devote a great deal of thought, effort, and time to build the temple. The result was the world's first monumental architecture — the ziggurat, a massive, stepped tower that dominated the city. Once the ziggurat was built, a professional priesthood was needed to run it and to perform the god's rituals. The people of the city met the expenses of building and maintaining the temple and its priesthood by setting aside extensive tracts of land. The priests took charge of the produce of the temple lands and the sacred flocks. Part of the yield went to the feeding and clothing of the priests and the temple staff, or for offerings to the gods. Part was sold or bartered to obtain goods, such as precious metals or stone, needed for construction, maintenance, or ritual.

Until recently, the importance and the wealth of the temple had led historians to consider the Sumerian city-state an absolute theocracy, government by an established priesthood. According to this view, the temple and its priests owned the city's land and controlled the economy. Newly discovered documents and recent works, however, have resulted in new ideas about the city and its society. It is now known that the temple owned a large fraction, but not all, of the city's territory, and it did not govern the city. Instead, a king, or *lugal,* exercised political power, and most of the city's land was the property of individual citizens. Society was a complex arrangement of freedom and dependence and was divided into four categories: nobles, free clients of the nobility, commoners, and slaves.

The nobility consisted of the king and his family, the chief priests, and high palace officials. The king originally rose to power as a war leader, elected by the citizenry, who established a regular army, trained it and led it into battle. The might of the king and the frequency of warfare in Mesopotamia quickly made him the supreme figure in the city, and kingship soon became hereditary. The symbol of his status was the palace, which rivaled the temple in grandeur.

The king and the lesser nobility held extensive tracts of land that, like the estates of the temple, were worked by slaves and clients. The clients were free men and women who were dependent on the nobility. In return for their labor the clients received small plots of land to work for themselves. Although this arrangement assured the clients of a livelihood, the land remained the possession of the

MAP OF NIPPUR.   The oldest map in the world, dating to ca 1500 B.C., shows the layout of the Mesopotamian city of Nippur. Inscribed on a clay tablet, the map has enabled archaeologists to locate ruined buildings: (A) the ziggurat, (B) canal, (C) enclosure and gardens, (D) city gates, and (E) the Euphrates River. (From the photographic collections of the University Museum, University of Pennsylvania)

nobility or the temple. Thus, not only did the nobility control most — and probably the best — land, they also commanded the obedience of a huge segment of society. They were the dominant force in Mesopotamian society.

The commoners were free citizens. They were independent of the nobility; however, they could not match the nobility in social status and political power. Commoners were organized in large patriarchal families that owned land in their own right. Commoners could sell their land, if the family approved, but even the king could not legally take their land without their approval. Commoners had a voice in the political affairs of the city and full protection under the law.

Until comparatively recent times, slavery was a fact of life throughout the history of Western society. Some Sumerian slaves were foreigners and prisoners of war. Some were criminals, who had lost their freedom in punishment for their crimes. Still others served as slaves in repayment of debts. These were more fortunate than the others, because the law demanded that they be freed after three years of slavery. But all slaves were subject to whatever treatment their owners might mete out. They could be beaten and even branded. Yet they were not considered dumb beasts. They engaged in trade and made profits. Indeed, many slaves bought their freedom. They could borrow money, and they received at least some protection under the law.

THE SPREAD OF MESOPOTAMIAN CULTURE

The Sumerians established the basic social, economic, and intellectual patterns in Mesopotamia, but the Semites played a large part in spreading them far beyond the boundaries of Mesopotamia.

Despite the cultural ascendancy of the Sumerians, their unending wars wasted their strength. In 2331 B.C., the Semitic chieftain Sargon conquered Sumer and created a new empire. The symbol of his triumph was a new capital, the city of Agade. Sargon, the first "world conqueror," led his armies to the Mediterranean Sea. Although his empire lasted only a few generations, it spread Mesopotamian culture throughout the Fertile Crescent, the belt of rich farmland that extends from Mesopotamia in the east up through Syria in the north and down to Egypt in the west.

The impact of Sargon's work and the extent of Mesopotamian influence even at this early period were dramatically revealed at Ebla in modern Syria. In 1964, archaeologists unearthed there a once-flourishing Semitic civilization that had assimilated political, intellectual, and artistic aspects of Mesopotamian culture. In 1976, the excavators uncovered thousands of clay tablets, which proved that the people of Ebla had learned the art of writing from the Mesopotamians. Eblaite artists borrowed heavily from Mesopotamian art but developed their own style, which in turn influenced Mesopotamian artists. Thus, the Eblaites transmitted the heritage of Mesopotamia to other Semitic centers in Syria. In the process, a universal culture developed in the ancient Near East, a culture basically Mesopotamian but fertilized by the traditions, genius, and ways of many other peoples.

The clay tablets of Ebla will have a tremendous impact on biblical scholarship. Although linguists have read very little of the many documents found in 1976, they have already recognized place names, such as Jerusalem and the "Five Cities of the Plain," which included the biblical Sodom and Gomorrah. This discovery seems to support the findings of recent scholars who have recognized the heavy Mesopotamian influence on the Bible.

The Old Testament itself retains a memory of its Mesopotamian background. Genesis recalls that the patriarch Abraham came from the Sumerian city of Ur, "Ur of the Chaldees." The Ebla tablets prove the existence of and will one day shed light on the importance of direct contact between Mesopotamia and Syria as early as the third millenium B.C. Eventually, the Ebla tablets will probably clarify the connection between Mesopotamian literature and religion and the theology of the Old Testament. Already they demonstrate the early and widespread influence of Mesopotamian civilization.

The Triumph of Babylon

Although the empire of Sargon was extensive, it was also short-lived, and it was the Babylonians (not the Akkadians) who united Mesopotamia politically as well as culturally. The Babylonians were Amorites, a Semitic people who migrated from Arabia and settled in the Sumerian city of Babylon. Babylon enjoyed an excellent geographical position, and it was ideally suited to be the capital of Mesopotamia. It dominated trade on the Tigris and Euphrates rivers, so that all commerce coming from Sumer and Akkad had to pass by its walls. It also looked beyond Mesopotamia. By following the Tigris, Babylonian merchants traveled north to Assyria and Anatolia. The Euphrates led the merchants to Syria, Palestine, and the Mediterranean. The city grew great because of its commercial importance and because its power was soundly based.

Babylon was also fortunate in its king Hammurabi (1792–1750 B.C.). Hammurabi set out to do three things: to make Babylon secure, to unify Mesopotamia, and to win for the Babylonians a place in Mesopotamian civilization. He accomplished the first two by conquering Assyria in the north and Sumer and Akkad in the south. Then he attacked his third goal.

Politically, Hammurabi combined in his kingship the Semitic concept of the tribal chieftain and the Sumerian idea of urban kingship. Culturally, he encouraged the creation of myths that explained how Marduk, the god of Babylon, was elected king of the gods by the Mesopotamian deities. Hammurabi succeeded in making Marduk the god of all Mesopotamians, and Marduk's city became the religious center of Mesopotamia. Through Hammurabi's genius the Babylonians made their own contribution to Mesopotamian culture, a culture vibrant enough to maintain its identity even while assimilating the new and different. Because of Hammurabi's conquests and the activity of Babylonian merchants, this enriched culture spread north to Anatolia and west to Syria and Palestine.

The Invention of Writing and the First Schools

In large part, Mesopotamian culture spread so rapidly because of the Sumerian invention of writing, which the Akkadians and Babylonians adopted. By around 3000 B.C., the Sumerians had developed a system of writing called cuneiform — from the Latin words meaning wedge-shaped, which describe the appearance of this script. The Mesopotamians wrote on wet clay. When the clay tablet dried, nothing could be added to it. The tablet was very durable; and if it was baked, it became rock hard.

The cuneiform system was originally pictographic; that is, each sign was a picture of an object. If a scribe wanted to indicate a star, he simply drew a picture of it (see line A of Figure 1.1). Anyone looking at it would know what he meant and would think of the word for star. This complicated and laborious system had serious limitations. It would not represent abstract ideas or relationships. For instance, how could a scribe draw a picture of a slave woman?

The solution came when the scribe discovered that he could combine signs to express meaning. To refer to a slave woman he used the sign for woman (line B) and the sign for mountain (line C) — literally, "mountain woman" (line D). Since the Sumerians regularly obtained their slave women from the mountains, this combination of signs was easily understandable.

The next step was to simplify the system. Instead of drawing pictures, the scribe made conventionalized signs. Thus, the signs became ideograms: they symbolized ideas. The sign for star could also be used to indicate heaven, sky, or even god.

The real breakthrough came when the scribe learned to use signs to represent sounds. For instance, the scribe drew two parallel wavy lines to indicate the word *a,* or "water" (see line E). Besides water, the word *a* in Sumerian also meant "in." The word "in" expresses a relationship that is very difficult to represent pictorially. Instead of trying to invent a sign to mean "in," some clever scribe used the sign for water, because the two words sounded alike. The phonetic use of signs made possible the combining of signs to convey abstract ideas. By the use of writing, merchants could keep long and complicated business records, inventories, and bills of lading. More importantly, the learning, lore, history, and philosophy of a culture could be recorded and preserved for unborn generations.

The Sumerian system of writing was so complicated that only professional scribes mastered it, and even they had to study it for many years. By 2500 B.C., scribal schools flourished throughout Sumer. Most students came from wealthy families, and it was entirely a male profession. Each school had a master, teachers, and monitors. Discipline was strict, and students were caned for sloppy work and misbehavior. One graduate of a scribal school had

	Meaning	Pictograph	Ideogram	Phonetic sign
A	Star			
B	Woman			
C	Mountain			
D	Slave woman			
E	Water In			

FIGURE I.I SUMERIAN WRITING (Excerpted from S. N. Kramer, *The Sumerians: Their History, Culture and Character,* University of Chicago Press, Chicago, 1963, pp. 302–306)

few fond memories of the joy of learning. He told of a typical day:

My headmaster read my tablet, said:
"There is something missing," caned me.

. . . .

The fellow in charge of silence said:
"Why did you talk without permission," caned me.
The fellow in charge of the assembly said:
"Why did you stand at ease without permission,"
    caned me.[6]

The boy was so lax at his work that he was expelled. Only when his father wined and dined the headmaster was he allowed to return to school.

The Sumerian system of schooling set the educational standards of Mesopotamian culture, and the Akkadians and the Babylonians adopted its practices and techniques. Students began by learning how to prepare clay tablets and to make signs. They studied grammar and word lists, and they solved simple mathematical problems. Mesopotamian education always had a practical side, because of the economic and administrative importance of scribes. Most scribes took administrative positions in the temple or palace, where they kept records of business transactions, accounts, and inventories. But scribal schools did not limit their curriculum to business affairs. They were also centers of culture and learning. Topics of study included mathematics, botany, and linguistics. Advanced students copied and studied the "classics" of Mesopotamian literature. Talented students and learned scribes wrote compositions of their own. As a result of this work many literary, mathematical, and religious texts are extant today, giving a surprisingly full picture of Mesopotamian intellectual and spiritual life.

Intellectual and Religious Thought

The Mesopotamians made significant and sophisticated advances in mathematics, in which they used a numerical system based on units of sixty. For practical purposes they also used factors of ten and six. They developed the concept of place value — that the value of a number depended on where it stood in relation to other numbers. Mesopotamian mathematical texts are of two kinds: tables and problems. Scribes compiled tables of squares and square roots, cubes and cube roots, and reciprocals. They wrote texts of problems, which dealt with equations and pure mathematics. And some texts dealt with concrete problems, such as how to plan irrigation ditches. The Mesopotamians did not consider mathematics purely a theoretical science. The building of cities, palaces, temples, and canals demanded a knowledge of geometry and trigonometry. The Mesopotamians solved the practical problems involved, but they did not turn their knowledge into theories. In this respect, they were quite different from the Greeks, who enjoyed theorizing.

Mesopotamian medicine was a combination of magic, prescriptions, and surgery. Mesopotamians believed that demons and evil spirits caused sickness, but that incantations and magic spells could drive them out. Or, they believed, the physician could force the demon to leave by giving the patient a foul-tasting prescription. As medical knowledge grew, some prescriptions were found to work and thus were true medicines. The physician relied heavily on plants, animals, and minerals for his recipes, and he often mixed them with beer to cover their unpleasant taste. Surgeons practiced a dangerous occupation, and the penalties for failure were severe. One section of Hammurabi's law code decreed: "If a physician performed a major operation on a seignor with a bronze lancet and has caused the seignor's death, or he opened up the eye-socket of a seignor and has destroyed the seignor's eye, they shall cut off his hand."[7] No wonder that one medical text warned a physician to have nothing to do with a dying person.

The areas in which Mesopotamian thought had its profoundest impact were theology and religion. The Sumerians originated many beliefs, and the Akkadians and Babylonians added to them. The American journalist H. L. Mencken once suggested that "the theory that the universe is run by a single God must be abandoned and . . . in place of it we must set up the theory that it is actually ruled by a board of gods all of equal puissance and authority."[8] The Mesopotamians would have smiled at Mencken's suggestion. They would have agreed that many gods run the world, but they did not consider all the gods and goddesses equal to one another. Some deities had very important jobs, such as taking care of music, law, sexual intercourse, and victory, while others had lesser tasks, such as overseeing leatherworking and basket weaving. The god in charge of metalworking was hardly the equal of the god of wisdom.

Divine society was a hierarchy. According to the Sumerians the air-god Enlil was the king of the gods, and he laid down the rules by which the universe was to be run. Enki, the god of wisdom, put Enlil's plans into effect. The Babylonians believed that the gods elected Marduk as their king, after which he gave the lesser gods various duties to perform. Once the gods received their tasks, they carried them out forever.

Mesopotamian gods lived their lives much as human beings lived theirs. The gods were anthropomorphic, or human in form. Unlike men and women, they were powerful and immortal and could make themselves invisible. Otherwise, the gods and goddesses were very human: they celebrated with food and drink, and they raised families. They enjoyed their own "Garden of Eden," a place filled with water, trees, and plants. They could be irritable, and they were not always holy. Even Enlil received punishment from other gods because he had once raped the goddess Ninlil.

The Mesopotamians did not worship their deities because the gods were holy. Human beings were too insignificant to pass judgment on the conduct of the gods, and the gods were too superior to honor human morals. Rather, the Mesopotamians worshiped the gods because they were mighty. Likewise, it was not the place of men and women to understand the gods. The Sumerian Job once complained to his god:

The man of deceit has conspired against me,
And you, my god, do not thwart him,
You carry off my understanding.[9]

The motives of the gods were not always clear. In times of affliction one could only pray and offer sacrifices to appease them.

The Mesopotamians had many myths and epics to account for the creation of the universe. According to one Sumerian myth, only the primeval sea existed at first. (This is precisely what is said in Genesis, the first book of the Old Testament.) The sea produced heaven and earth which were united. Heaven and earth gave birth to Enlil, who separated them and made possible the creation of the other gods.

Babylonian beliefs were similar. In the beginning was the primeval sea, the goddess Tiamat, who gave birth to the gods. When Tiamat tried to destroy the gods, Marduk killed her and divided her body:

He split her like a shellfish into two parts:
Half of her he set up and ceiled as sky,
Pulled down the bar and posted guards.
He bade them not to let her waters escape.[10]

These myths are the earliest known attempts to deal with the question "how did it all begin?" The Mesopotamians obviously thought about these matters, as about the gods, in human terms. They never organized their beliefs into a philosophy, but their myths gave understandable explanations of natural phenomena. They were emotionally satisfying, and that was their greatest appeal.

The Mesopotamians also had myths to explain the origin of human beings. In one myth the gods decided to make their lives easier by creating servants, which they wanted made in their image. Nammu, the goddess of the watery deep, brought the matter to Enki. After some thought, Enki instructed Nammu and the others:

Mix the heart of the clay that is over the abyss.
The good and princely fashioners will thicken the
*   clay.*
You, do you bring the limbs into existence.[11]

In Mesopotamian myth, just as in Genesis, men and women were made in the divine image. Even though they were fashioned in the divine image, however, human beings did not have godlike powers. The myth "The Creation of the Pickax" gives an excellent idea of their insignificance. According to this myth, Enlil drove his pickax into the ground, and out of the hole crawled the Sumerians, the first people. Enlil stood looking at them, while some of his fellow gods approached him. They were so pleased with Enlil's work that they asked him to give them some people to serve them. Consequently, the Mesopotamians believed it their duty to supply the gods with sacrifices of food and drink and to house them in fine temples. In return, they hoped that the gods would be kind.

These ideas of the creation of the unvierse and of human beings are part of the Mesopotamian legacy to Western civilization. They spread throughout the ancient Near East and found a home among the Hebrews, who adopted much of Mesopotamian religious thought and made it part of their own belief. Biblical parallels to Mesopotamian literary and religious themes are many. Such stories and concepts as the creation of Adam, the Deluge, the Garden of Eden, and the tale of Job go back to Mesopotamian originals. Through the Bible, Mesopotamian as well as Jewish religious concepts influenced Christianity and Islam. Thus, these first attempts of women and men to understand themselves and their world are still alive today.

Daily Life in Mesopotamia

Along with the intellectual and the spiritual went the daily cares of the Mesopotamians. A wealth of information about daily life comes from the law code of King Hammurabi. Hammurabi issued his code to "establish law and justice in the language of the land, thereby promoting the welfare of the people." His code may seem harsh, but it was no more harsh than the Mosaic law of the Hebrews, which it heavily influenced. Hammurabi's code inflicted such penalties as mutilation, whipping, and burning. Today in parts of the Islamic world these punishments are still in use. Despite its severity, a spirit of justice and a sense of responsibility pervade the code. Hammurabi genuinely felt that his duty was to govern the Mesopotamians as righteously as possible. He tried to regulate the relations of his people so that they could live together in harmony.

Two things mark Hammurabi's code. First, the law differed according to the social status of the offender. Aristocrats were not punished as harshly as commoners, nor commoners as harshly as slaves. Even slaves had their rights, however, and received some protection under the law. Second, the code demanded that the punishment fit the crime. Like the Mosaic law of the Hebrews, it called for "an eye for an eye, and a tooth for a tooth," at least among equals. However, if an aristocrat destroyed the eye of a commoner or slave, he could pay a fine instead of losing his own eye. Otherwise, as long as the criminal and the victim shared the same social status, the victim could demand exact vengeance for his injury.

LAW CODE OF HAMMURABI. Hammurabi ordered his code to be inscribed on a stone pillar and set up in public. At the top of the pillar Hammurabi is depicted receiving his laws from the god of justice. (Clichés des Musées Nationaux, Paris)

Hammurabi's code began with legal procedure. There were no public prosecutors or district attorneys, so individuals brought their own complaints before the court. Each side had to produce written documents or witnesses to support its case. In cases of murder, the accuser had to prove the defendant guilty. Any accuser who failed to do so was put to death. This strict law was designed to prevent people from lodging groundless charges. The Mesopotamians were very worried about witchcraft and sorcery. Anyone accused of witchcraft, even if the charges were not proved, still underwent an ordeal by water. The gods themselves would decide the case. The defendant was thrown into the Euphrates, which was considered the instrument of the gods. A defendant who sank was guilty; a defendant who floated was innocent. (In medieval Europe and colonial America accused witches also underwent an ordeal by water, but they were considered innocent only if they sank.) Another procedural matter covered the conduct of judges. Once a judge had rendered a verdict, he could not change it. If he did, he was fined heavily and deposed from his position. In short, the code tried to guarantee a fair trial and a just verdict.

Hammurabi expected his officials to do their duty and to protect his subjects. Governors and city officials were required to wipe out crime, and they paid for their failure to protect the innocent. If a person was robbed and the robber was not caught, the officials had to repay the victim. This law encouraged officials to keep order. Soldiers either carried out the king's command or faced dire consequences. Any soldier, whether officer or private, who tried to shirk his duty by hiring a substitute was put to death, as was any officer who illegally forced men to serve in the army. The law protected soldiers from abuse from their officers. Any officer who wronged a soldier or stole his property was put to death.

Consumer protection is not a modern idea; it goes back to Hammurabi's day. Merchants and businessmen had to guarantee the quality of their goods and services. A boatbuilder who did sloppy work had to repair the boat at his own expense. The first duty of a boatman was to navigate safely. If he lost the owner's boat or sank someone else's boat, he replaced it and its cargo. Housebuilders guaranteed their work with their lives. Careless work could result in the collapse of a house and the death of the owner. If that happened, the builder himself was put to death. A merchant who tried to increase the interest rate of a loan forfeited the entire amount. A farmer who hired an overseer to cultivate his land expected the overseer to know his business. He had the right to order an incompetent overseer to be dragged through the fields. Hammurabi's laws tried to insure that consumers got what they paid for and paid a just price.

Crime was a feature of Mesopotamian urban life just as it is in modern cities. Burglary was a serious problem, and one hard to control. Because houses were built of mud brick it was easy for an intruder to dig through the walls. Hammurabi's punishment for burglary matched the crime. A burglar caught in the act was put to death on the spot, and his body was walled into the breach he had made. The penalty for looting was also grim. Anyone caught looting a burning house was thrown into the fire.

Mesopotamian cities had breeding places of crime. Taverns were notorious for being the haunts of criminals, especially since they often met at taverns to make their plans. Tavern keepers were expected to keep order and arrest anyone overheard planning a crime. Taverns were normally run by women, and they also served as houses of prostitution. Prostitution was disreputable but not illegal, and the law did not regulate it. Despite their social stigma, taverns were popular places, for the Mesopotamians were fond of beer and wine. Drinks were expensive, and tavern keepers made a nice profit.

Some of them increased their profits by watering drinks; but if they were caught, they were drowned.

In all these statutes the aim of Hammurabi was to punish the criminal for the specific crime. Exact retribution gave the victim or the victim's family legal satisfaction and was intended to end the matter. To some degree the code protected society by removing a person who had committed a serious crime. Beyond that it did not go.

Because farming was essential to Mesopotamian life, Hammurabi's code dealt extensively with agriculture and the maintenance of irrigation canals. Tenant farming was widespread, and tenants rented land on a yearly basis. Instead of money they paid a proportion of their crops as rent. Unless the land was carefully cultivated, it quickly reverted to wasteland. Therefore, tenants faced severe penalties for neglecting the land or for not working it at all. Since irrigation was essential for the growing of crops, tenants had to keep the canals and ditches in good repair. Otherwise, the land would be subject to floods and farmers to serious losses. So anyone whose neglect of the canals resulted in damaged crops had to bear all the expense of the lost crops. If the tenant could not pay the costs, he was sold into slavery.

Farmers used oxen and asses for plowing and for threshing grain. Oxen were allowed to roam the streets and were liable to gore passers-by. Once an ox had gored a person, its owner had to pad its horns or tie it up or else bear the responsibility for future damages. Cattle and goats provided milk, butter, and cheese, and the code indicates that sheep raising was a major industry. (Sheep raising was very lucrative because textile production was a major Mesopotamian industry — Mesopotamian cloth was famous throughout the Near East.) The shepherd was a hired man with considerable responsibility. He was expected to protect the flock from wild animals, which were a standing problem, and to keep the sheep out of the crops. Date palms were the only source of wood in Mesopotamia, and wanton destruction of trees was a serious offense. This strict regulation of agriculture paid rich dividends. The Mesopotamians usually raised more than they could consume, and consequently they exported their surplus for luxury items and raw materials.

Hammurabi gave careful attention to marriage and the family. As so often in the Near East, marriage took on the aspect of a business agreement. The prospective groom and the father of the future bride took care of all the arrangements. The man offered the father a bridal gift, usually a sum of money. If the man and his bridal gift were acceptable, the father provided his daughter with a dowry. The dowry always belonged to the woman (although the husband normally administered it) and was a means of protecting her rights and status. Once the two men agreed upon financial matters, they drew up a contract. No marriage was considered legal without one. Either party could break off the marriage, but not without paying a stiff penalty. Fathers often contracted marriages while the children were still young. Either the girl continued to live in her father's house until she reached maturity, or she went to live in the house of her father-in-law. During this time she was legally considered a wife. Once she and her husband became of age, they set up their own house.

The wife was expected to be rigorously faithful. The penalty for adultery was death. According to Hammurabi's code: "If the wife of a man has been caught while lying with another man, they shall bind them and throw them into the water."[12] The husband had the power to spare his wife by obtaining for her a pardon from the king. A man could accuse his wife of adultery, even if he had not caught her in the act. In that case she cleared herself

by swearing an oath that she was innocent. A wife actually faced greater danger when someone other than her husband accused her of adultery. Even if the accuser had no proof, she was considered guilty until proven innocent. She cleared herself of suspicion by throwing herself into a river. Like the suspected sorcerer, she was innocent only if she floated. A wife who floated received some satisfaction, however, because her accuser was publicly humiliated by having half of his hair and beard shaved.

Although the wife had to be faithful, the husband did not. A man might also have children by a slave woman and raise her children in his house. In such cases the man could legally recognize the children as legitimate and make them his heirs. Even if he did not, the slave woman and her children became free after his death. In homes where the husband had a slave family, the position of the wife and her children was secure, and only she was responsible for the management of the household.

The husband could obtain a divorce rather easily. In Mesopotamia the purpose of marriage was solely to produce children, and a man could divorce his wife for barrenness. In that case he gave her the equivalent of the marriage price and returned her dowry. This law was designed to provide the wife with support. The financial settlement probably discouraged divorce for trivial reasons. If a wife caught a disease that prevented her from having children, her husband could take another wife, but his first wife had the right to full support as long as she lived. A man could get a divorce if his wife wanted to go into business. He could let her go without paying her anything, or he could marry another woman and keep his first wife in the house as a servant. A wife could be drowned for gossiping about her husband, for causing the neighbors to gossip, or for wasting his money. A woman could get a divorce only by refusing intercourse with her husband. Her husband then brought the matter before the city council, which investigated. As long as she had been a dutiful wife, she could take her dowry and leave her husband. If she decided to take the direct approach and kill her husband, she was impaled.

The husband had virtually absolute power over his household. Like the later Roman *paterfamilias*, (see Chapter 4) he could sell his wife and children into slavery to pay his debts. Sons did not lightly oppose their fathers, and any son who struck his father could have his hand cut off. A father was free to adopt children and include them in his will. Artisans sometimes adopted children to teach them the family trade. Although a father's power was great, he could not disinherit a son without just cause. Cases of disinheritance became matters for the city to decide, and the code ordered the courts to forgive a son for his first offense. Only if a son wronged his father a second time could he be disinherited.

Law codes are always concerned with the problems of society, and they often give a bleak view of things. Other Mesopotamian documents give a happier glimpse of life. Hammurabi's code dealt with marriage shekel by shekel, yet a Mesopotamian poem told of two people meeting secretly in the city. Their parting is delightfully modern:

Come now, set me free, I must go home,
Kuli-Enlil . . . set me free, I must go home.
What can I say to deceive my mother![13]

Countless wills and testaments prove that husbands habitually left their estates to their wives, who in turn willed the property to their children. All this suggests happy, normal family life. Hammurabi's code restricted married women from commercial pursuits, but financial documents prove that many women engaged in business without hindrance. Some carried on the family business, while others became wealthy landowners in their own right. All Mesopotamians found their lives lightened by holidays and religious festivals. Traveling merchants brought news of the outside world, and

swapped tall tales and marvelous stories. Despite their pessimism, the Mesopotamians enjoyed a vibrant and creative culture, a culture that left its mark on the entire ancient Near East.

THE LAND OF THE PHARAOHS
(3100–1800 B.C.)

The Greek historian and traveler Herodotus in the fifth century B.C. called Egypt the gift of the Nile River. No other geographical factor had such a fundamental and profound impact on the shaping of Egyptian life, society, and history as the Nile. The broad river was primarily a creative force, and unlike the rivers of Mesopotamia it rarely brought death and destruction. Its waters, even in flood times, seem almost tame when compared to the rampaging Tigris. The Egyptians never feared the Nile in the way that the Mesopotamians feared their rivers. Rather, the Nile was the supreme fertilizer and renewer of the land. Each September the Nile floods its valley, transforming it into a huge area of marsh or lagoon. By the end of November the water retreats, leaving behind a thin covering of fertile mud, which is ready to be planted with crops.

The annual flood made the growing of abundant crops simple and almost effortless, especially in southern Egypt. Herodotus, who was used to the rigors of Greek agriculture, was amazed by the ease with which the Egyptians raised their crops:

For indeed without trouble they obtain crops from the land more easily than all other men. . . . They do not labor to dig furrows with the plough or hoe or do the work which other men do to raise grain. But when the river by itself inundates the fields and the water recedes, then each man, having sown his field, sends pigs into it. When the pigs trample down the seed, he waits for the harvest. Then when the pigs thresh the grain, he gets his crop.[14]

As late as 1822, John Burckhardt, an English traveler, watched nomads sowing grain by digging large holes in the mud and throwing in seeds. The extraordinary fertility of the Nile valley made it easy to produce an annual agricultural surplus, which in turn sustained a growing and prosperous population.

Whereas the Tigris and Euphrates and their many tributaries carved up Mesopotamia into isolated areas, the Nile served to unify Egypt. The river was the principal highway, and it made communication throughout the valley simple and convenient. As individual bands of settlers moved into the Nile valley, they created stable agricultural communities or districts. By about 3100 B.C. there were some forty of these communities, and they were in constant contact with one another. This contact, encouraged and facilitated by the Nile, almost assured the early political unification of the country.

Egypt was fortunate because it was nearly self-sufficient. Besides the fertility of its soil, Egypt possessed enormous quantities of stone, which served as the raw material of architecture and sculpture. Abundant clay was available for pottery and gold for jewelry and ornaments. The raw materials that Egypt lacked were close at hand. The Egyptians could obtain copper from Sinai and timber from Lebanon. They had little reason to look to the outside world for their essential needs, which helps to explain the insular quality of Egyptian life.

Geography further encouraged isolation by closing Egypt off from the outside world. To the east and west of the Nile valley stretched grim deserts. The Nubian Desert and the cataracts of the Nile discouraged penetration from the south. Only in the north did the Mediterranean Sea leave Egypt exposed. Thus, geography shielded Egypt from invasion and from extensive immigration. Unlike the Mesopotamians, the Egyptians enjoyed centuries of peace and tranquillity, and during these years they developed their own unique and distinctive civilization.

Yet Egypt was not completely sealed. As early as 3250 B.C., Mesopotamian influences, including architectural techniques and materials and perhaps even writing, made themselves felt in Egyptian life. Still later, from 1680 to 1580 B.C., northern Egypt was ruled by foreign invaders, the Hyksos. Infrequent though they were, such periods of foreign influence fertilized Egyptian culture without changing it in any fundamental way.

The God-King of Egypt

The natural unity of Egypt quickly gave rise to the political unification of the country under the authority of a king, whom the Egyptians called "pharaoh." The details of this process are now lost, but the Egyptians themselves told of a great king, Menes, who united Egypt into a single kingdom around 3100 B.C. Thereafter, the Egyptians divided their history into dynasties, or families of kings. A broader and more useful division of Egyptian history is into periods. The political unification of Egypt gave rise to the period known as the Old Kingdom, an era remarkable for its prosperity and artistic flowering.

The focal point of all life in the Old Kingdom was the pharaoh, who commanded the wealth, the resources, and the people of all Egypt. He was a very powerful figure, so powerful that the Egyptians considered him to be the sun-god Horus in human form. The surroundings of the king had to be worthy of a god. Only a magnificent palace was suitable for his home; in fact, the very title "pharaoh" means "great house." The king's tomb also had to reflect his might and exalted status. To this day the great pyramids at Giza near modern Cairo bear silent but magnificent testimony to the god-kings of Egypt. The mere ability of the pharaoh to command the resources and labor to build a huge pyramid proves that the god-king was an absolute ruler.

PERIODS OF EGYPTIAN HISTORY

Period	Dates	Significant Events
Archaic	3100–2660 B.C.	Unification of Egypt
Old Kingdom	2660–2180 B.C.	Construction of the pyramids
First Intermediate	2180–2080 B.C.	Political chaos
Middle Kingdom	2080–1640 B.C.	Recovery and political stability
Second Intermediate	1640–1570 B.C.	Hyksos "invasion"
New Kingdom	1570–1075 B.C.	Creation of an Egyptian empire Akhenaten's religious policy

THE PYRAMIDS AT GIZA. Giza was the burial place of the pharaohs of the Old Kingdom and of their aristocracy, whose rectangular tombs are visible behind the middle pyramid. The small pyramids at the foot of the foremost pyramid probably belong to the pharaoh's wives. (Courtesy, Museum of Fine Arts, Boston)

The religious significance of the pyramid is as awesome as the political. The pharaoh as a god was the earthly sun, and the pyramid, which towered to the sky, helped the dead king to ascend the heavens. The pyramid provided the dead king with everything that he would need in the afterlife. His body had to be preserved from decay if his *ka,* an invisible counterpart of the body, was to live on. So the Egyptians developed an elaborate process of embalming the dead pharaoh and wrapping his corpse in cloth. As an added precaution, they carved a statue of the pharaoh out of hard stone, a statue that looked like him. If anything happened to the fragile mummy, the pharaoh's statue would help keep his ka alive. The need for an authentic likeness accounts for the naturalism of Egyptian portraiture. The artistic renderings of the pharaohs combine the real and the abstract as the sculptor tried to capture the essence of the living person. This approach produced that haunting quality of Egyptian sculpture — portraits of lifelike people imbued with a solemn, ageless, and serene spirit.

To survive in the spirit world the ka needed everything that the pharaoh needed in life: food and drink, servants and armed retainers, costly ornaments, and herds of animals. In Egypt's prehistoric period, the king's servants and herdsmen and their flocks were slaughtered at the tomb to provide for the ka. By the time of the Old Kingdom, artists had substituted statues of scribes, officials, soldiers, and servants for their living counterparts. To remind the ka of daily life, artists covered the walls of the tomb with paintings of ordinary scenes, everything from views of agricultural routines to banquets and religious festivities, from pictures of hunting parties to drawings of gardens and ponds. Designed to give joy to the ka, these paintings, models of furniture, and statuettes today give an intimate picture of Egyptian life 4,500 years ago.

The humor and vivacity of Egyptian tomb paintings are striking, especially when they depict everyday scenes. For instance, the scene on page 26, which dates to about 2400 B.C., is remarkable chiefly because it is typical. In the top band, men with sickles reap the standing grain, while the song of a piper and singer provide them with a rhythmical cadence. In the second band, two men bundle the cut grain, as others drive in donkeys to haul away the sheaves. The third band displays the warmth and humor so often found in Egyptian art. The donkey on the left is obviously reluctant to be loaded and is putting up "passive resistance," and two men make no progress in changing his mind. At the far right a gang of men load another donkey, and again they do not find it an easy job. One man has to hold the donkey's tail, while another has a hammerlock on the donkey's head. But if scenes such as these, and the countless others that have survived, give a warm and pleasant view of Egyptian daily life in the Old Kingdom, other sources of information portray gloomy aspects.

The Pharaoh's People

Because the common folk stood at the bottom of the social and economic scale, they were always at the mercy of grasping officials. The arrival of the tax collector was never a happy occasion. One Egyptian scribe described the worst that could happen:

And now the scribe lands on the river-bank and is about to register the harvest-tax. The janitors carry staves and the Nubians rods of palm, and they say, Hand over the corn, though there is none. The cultivator is beaten all over, he is bound and thrown into a well, soused and dipped head downwards. His wife has been bound in his presence and his children are in fetters.[15]

That was an extreme situation. Nonetheless, taxes might amount to 20 percent of the harvest, and the collection of taxes could often be brutal.

On the other hand, everyone, no matter how lowly, had the right of appeal, and the account of one such appeal, "The Tale of the Eloquent Peasant," was a favorite Egyptian story. The hero of the tale, Khunanup, was robbed by the servant of the high steward, and Khunanup had to bring his case before the steward himself. When the steward delayed his decision, Khunanup openly accused him of neglecting his duty, saying, "The arbitrator is a spoiler; the peace-maker is a creator of sorrow; the smoother over of differences is a creator of soreness."[16] The pharaoh himself ordered the steward to give Khunanup justice, and the case was decided in the peasant's favor.

Egyptian society seems to have been a curious mixture of freedom and constraint. Slavery did not become a common institution until the New Kingdom. There was neither a caste system nor a color bar, and humble people could rise to the highest positions if they possessed talent. The most famous example of this fact (which, however, dates to the New Kingdom) is the biblical story of Joseph, who came to Egypt as a slave and rose to be second only to the pharaoh. On the other hand, most ordinary folk were probably little more than serfs, people who could not easily leave the land of their own free will. Peasants were also subject to forced labor, just

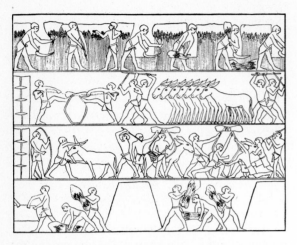

HARVESTING SCENE. This drawing, taken from an Egyptian relief, depicts the harvesting of the grain crop from the time it is reaped to the time it is stored in the granary. (From *Art Through the Ages,* 3rd ed., by Helen Gardner, ©1948 by Harcourt Brace Jovanovich, Inc., and reproduced with their permission)

as they were in early modern France, and this labor included work on the pyramids and canals. Young men were drafted into the pharaoh's army, which served both as a fighting force and as a labor corps.

The vision of thousands of people straining to build the pyramids and of countless artists adorning the pharaoh's tomb brings to the modern mind a distasteful picture of oriental despotism. Yet H. Frankfort, one of the most perceptive historians of ancient Egypt, has treated the matter in a purely Egyptian context:

Nothing would be more misleading than to picture the Egyptians in abject submission to their absolute ruler. . . . Their polity was not imposed but evolved from immemorial predilections and was adhered to, without protest, for almost three thousand years. . . . If a god had consented to guide the nation, society held a pledge that the unaccountable forces of nature would be well disposed and bring prosperity and peace. . . . Truth, justice, were "that by which the gods live," an essential element in the established order. Hence, Pharaoh's rule was not tyranny, or his service slavery.[17]

The Egyptian view of life and society is alien to those raised on the Western concepts of individual freedom and human rights. To the Egyptians the pharaoh embodied justice and order — harmony among men and women, nature, and the divine. For these reasons the pharaoh stood at the very center of Egyptian life. If the pharaoh was weak, or if he allowed anyone to challenge his unique position, he opened the way to chaos. Twice in Egyptian history the pharaoh failed to maintain this rigid centralization. During those two eras, which are known as the First and Second Intermediate periods, Egypt was exposed to civil war and invasion. Yet even in the darkest times the monarchy survived, and in each period a strong pharaoh arose to crush the rebels or expel the invaders and restore order.

MASS MIGRATIONS
(2000–1200 B.C.)

While Egyptian civilization flourished behind its bulwark of sand and sea, momentous changes were taking place in the ancient Near East, changes that would leave their mark even on rich and insular Egypt. These changes involved enormous and remarkable movements of peoples, especially of peoples speaking Semitic and Indo-European languages.

The original home of the Semites was probably the Arabian peninsula. Some tribes moved into northern Mesopotamia, others into Syria and Palestine, and still others into Egypt. Shortly after 1800 B.C., people whom the Egyptians called Hyksos, which means "Rulers of the Uplands," began to settle in the Nile Delta. Although the Egyptians portrayed the Hyksos as a conquering horde, they were probably no more than nomads looking for good land. Their entry into the delta was probably gradual, generally peaceful, and much like that of the Hebrews, who did not arrive until around 1500 B.C. Indeed, the Hebrews are typical of the Semitic movement. They were a pastoral people, organized in large tribes whose chiefs and patriarchs directed the life of the community.

The Hyksos "invasion" was one of the fertilizing periods of Egyptian history; it introduced new ideas and techniques into Egyptian life. The Hyksos brought with them the method of making bronze and casting it into tools and weapons. They thereby brought Egypt fully into the Bronze Age culture of the Mediterranean world, a culture in which the production and use of bronze implements became basic to society. Bronze tools made farming more efficient than ever before because they were sharper and more durable than the copper tools they replaced. The Hyksos' use of bronze armor and weapons as well as horse-drawn chariots and the composite bow, which was made of laminated wood and horn and which was far more powerful than the simple wooden bow, revolutionized Egyptian warfare.

Even more dramatic and extensive than the Hyksos invasion were the movements of the Indo-Europeans. The term "Indo-European" properly refers to a large family of languages that includes English, most of the languages of modern Europe, Greek, Latin, Persian, and Sanskrit, the sacred tongue of ancient India. During the eighteenth and nineteenth centuries, European scholars learned that peoples speaking related languages had spread themselves as far west as Ireland and as far east as central Asia. In the twentieth century, linguists deciphered the language of the Hittites, a mysterious people who lived in Anatolia, and the Linear B script of Mycenaean Greece. When both languages proved to be Indo-European, scholars were able to form a clearer picture of these vast movements. Archaeologists were able to date them and put them into their historical context.

The original home of the Indo-Europeans remains to be identified. Judging primarily from the spread of the languages, linguists have suggested that the migrations started from central Europe. Although two great waves began around 2000 B.C. and 1200 B.C., these migrations were usually sporadic and extended over long periods of time. For instance, the Celtic-speaking Gauls did not move into modern France, Belgium, and Germany until the seventh century B.C., long after most Indo-Europeans had found new homes. Around 2000 B.C., however, Indo-Europeans were on the move on a massive scale. Peoples speaking the ancestor of Latin pushed into Italy, while Greek-speaking Mycenaeans settled in Greece. The Hittites arrived in Anatolia, and other folk thrust into Iran, India, and central Asia. At first the waves of Indo-Europeans and others disrupted existing states, but in time the newcomers settled down.

For the civilization of the ancient Near East the most important of these migrations were those of the Hittites and two unrelated groups, the Hurrians and Kassites. Neither the Hurrians nor the Kassites were Indo-Europeans, but both worshiped gods with Indo-European names. Indo-European or not, all three peoples were barbarians by Near Eastern standards, and their arrivals were marked by destruction. Around 1595 B.C., the Kassites brought down the Babylonian kingdom and established their own rule there, while the Hurrians created the kingdom of Mitanni in the upper reaches of the Euphrates and Tigris. The Hittites settled in central Anatolia and soon spread their influence south to Syria. The Hittite king Telipinus chronicled the early wars of his people:

And the land was small; but on whatever campaign he [the first Hittite king] went, by his strength he kept the hostile country in subjection. And he kept devastating countries, and he made the countries tremble; and he made them boundaries of the sea.[18]

In all three instances the superior culture of Mesopotamia withstood the invaders. This development is most clearly seen among the Hittites. The Hittites adopted the cuneiform script for their own language. Hittite kings published law codes, just as Hammurabi had done. Royal correspondence followed Mesopotamian forms. The Hittites delighted in Mesopotamian myths, legends, and epics. Of Hittite art one scholar has observed that "there is hardly a single Hittite monument which somewhere does not show traces of Mesopotamian influence."[19] To the credit of the Hittites one must add that they used these Mesopotamian borrowings to create something of their own. Nonetheless, the huge debt of the Hittites and the other invaders brilliantly illustrates the great attraction and strength of Mesopotamian culture.

THE NEW KINGDOM IN EGYPT

In Egypt too the old and impressive culture of the pharaohs civilized the Hyksos, who eagerly and quickly adapted many aspects of it. They worshiped Egyptian gods and modeled their monarchy on the pharaoh's. Whereas the Babylonian kingdom succumbed to the newcomers, Egypt did not. A remarkable line of kings, the pharaohs of the Eighteenth Dynasty, arose to meet the Hyksos challenge. The pharaoh Thotmes III (1490–1436 B.C.) conquered Palestine and Syria and fought with the kingdom of Mitanni. These warrior-pharaohs inaugurated a new period in Egyptian history, the New Kingdom — a period of enormous wealth and conscious imperialism. These kings created the first Egyptian empire, and they celebrated accordingly. They built monuments on a scale not seen since the pharaohs of the Old Kingdom had built the pyramids. Even today the colossal granite statues of these pharaohs and the rich tomb objects of Tutankhamen ("King Tut") testify to the might, the wealth, and the splendor of the New Kingdom.

Akhenaten and Monotheism

One of the most extraordinary of this unusual line of kings was Akhenaten (1367–1350 B.C.), a pharaoh whose thoughts dwelt on religion rather than conquest. Nefertiti, his wife and queen, encouraged his religious bent. They were monotheists who believed that the sun-god Aton, whom they worshiped, was universal, the only god. All other Egyptian gods and goddesses were frauds, and the royal pair forbade their worship.

The religious notions and the actions of Akhenaten and Nefertiti were in direct opposition to traditional Egyptian beliefs. The Egyptians had long worshiped a host of gods, chief of whom was Amon-Re. Originally, Amon and Re had been two distinct sun-gods, but the Egyptians merged them and worshiped Amon-Re as the king of the gods.

THE TOMB OF "KING TUT." The pharaoh Tutankhamun was buried in three coffins, one inside the other. Shown here is the removal of the second coffin from the outer coffin. The innermost coffin was made of gold. (The Metropolitan Museum of Art. Photograph by Harry Burton)

Besides Amon-Re, the Egyptians honored other deities, such as Osiris, Osiris's wife Isis, and his son Horus. Indeed, Egyptian religion had room for many gods and an easy tolerance for new gods. Herodotus once remarked that the Egyptians "are excessively religious, more so than other men."

Akhenaten's attack on the old gods affected all Egyptians, for the old gods were fundamentally important to the afterlife of human beings. Over the centuries the Egyptians had developed complex and often contradictory concepts of an afterlife. These beliefs were all rooted in the environment of Egypt itself. The climate of Egypt is so stable that change is cyclical and dependable: even though the heat of summer bakes the land, the Nile always floods and replenishes it. The dry air preserves much that would decay in other climates. Thus, there was an air of permanence about Egypt; the old lived on and became a part of the present.

This natural rhythm was reflected in Egyptian religious beliefs. Each year, according to the Egyptians, the god Osiris, a fertility god associated with the Nile, dies, and each year Isis brings him back to life. Osiris became king of the dead, a god who weighed the hearts of human beings to determine whether they had lived justly enough to acquire everlasting life. Osiris's care for the dead was shared by Anubis, the jackal-headed god who annually helped Isis resuscitate Osiris. Anubis was the god of mummification, which was essential to Egyptian funerary rites.

Naturally, then, many Egyptians viewed Akhenaten's attack on Osiris, Isis, Anubis, and other gods as a threat to their own chances of gaining immortality. Others were sincerely devoted to the old gods for different reasons. After all, had Amon-Re not driven out the Hyksos and brought Egypt a new era of happiness? To these genuine religious sentiments were added the motives of the traditional priesthood. Although many priests were devout and truly scandalized by Akhenaten's monotheism, many others were more concerned about their own narrow welfare. What were the priests of the outlawed gods to do? Akhenaten had destroyed their livelihood and their reason for existence. On grounds of pure self-interest the established priesthood opposed Akhenaten. Opposition in turn drove the pharaoh to intolerance and persecution. With a vengeance he tried to root out the old gods and their rituals.

Akhenaten celebrated his break with the past by building a new capital, Akhetaten, the modern El-Amarna. There Aton received an immense temple and proper worship. That worship involved "truth" (as Akhenaten defined it) and a desire for the natural. The pharaoh and his queen demanded that the "truth" be carried over into art. Instead of the "classical" Old Kingdom Egyptian painting and sculpture, which combined the actual and the abstract, the art of this period became relentlessly realistic. Sculptors molded exact likenesses of Akhenaten, despite his ugly features and misshapen body. Artists portrayed the pharaoh in intimate family scenes, playing with his infant daughter or showing affection to members of his family. On one relief Akhenaten appears gnawing a cutlet of meat, while on another he lolls in a chair. Akhenaten was being protrayed as a mortal man, not as the dignified pharaoh of Egypt.

Akhenaten's monotheism was imposed from above, and it failed to find a place among the people. One of the major reasons for Akhenaten's failure is that his god had no connection with the past of the Egyptian people, who trusted the old gods and felt comfortable in praying to them. Average Egyptians were no doubt distressed and disheartened when their familiar gods were outlawed, for they were the heavenly powers that had made Egypt powerful and unique. The fanaticism and persecution that accompanied the new monotheism were in complete defiance of the Egyptian tradition of tolerant polytheism, the worship of several gods. Thus, when Akhenaten died, his religion died with him.

The Fall of Empires

While Akhenaten had concentrated on religion, the Egyptian empire was crumbling. The Hittites had consolidated their power in Anatolia, and they began to threaten Syria and Palestine. The letter of an Egyptian vassal, the king of Byblos in Syria, to the pharaoh warned of danger: "My lord should hasten the dispatch of the archers or else we are as good as dead. . . . Would that Your Majesty come out and inspect the lands and take all of them over again."[20] His plea went unheard, and Syria fell to the Hittites.

After Akhenaten's death in 1350 B.C., subsequent pharaohs fought to keep Palestine and to regain Syria. At the battle of Kadesh (ca 1288 B.C.) the Egyptians fought the Hittites to a standstill; and rather than continue a futile war, the two empires concluded peace with one another (ca 1280 B.C.). To maintain the peace they formed an alliance and supported each other politically. The result was a period of international tranquillity.

This situation endured until the cataclysm of the thirteenth century B.C., when the Hittite and Egyptian empires both fell to marauders whom the Egyptians called "the Sea Peoples." These Sea Peoples remain one of the puzzles of ancient history. Modern archaeology has been unable to identify them, but it is known that they were a symptom of even larger movements of peoples.

In 1200 B.C., as earlier, Indo-European and Semitic-speaking peoples were on the move. They brought down the old centers of power and won new homes for themselves. In Mesopotamia the Assyrians destroyed the kingdom of Mitanni and struggled with the Kassites; the Hebrews moved into Palestine; and another wave of Indo-Europeans penetrated Anatolia. But once again their victory was political and military, not cultural. The old cultures — especially that of Mesopotamia — im-

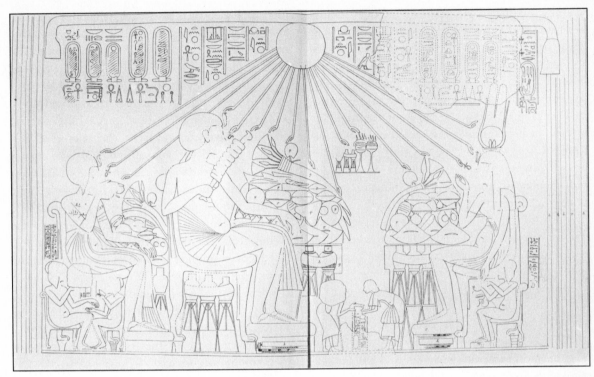

AKHENATEN AT DINNER.   This sculptured scene is a fine example of the stark realism of the art of the Amarna period. Akhenaten digs into a huge cutlet, while Nefertiti, seated behind him, attacks a whole roasted bird. In front of Akhenaten is his mother Tyi, who like the king and queen is confronted by a mound of food. (Photo: Caroline Buckler)

pressed their ideas, values, and ideals on the newcomers. Although the chaos of the thirteenth century B.C. caused a serious material decline throughout the ancient Near East, the old cultures lived on through a dark age.

THE RISE OF THE ASSYRIANS AND THE PERSIANS

Out of the political disintegration of the thirteenth century B.C. came two broad developments: the growth of petty kingdoms and the rise of the Assyrian and then the Persian empires. No longer crushed between the Hittites in the north and the Egyptians in the south, a number of small kingdoms sprang up in the Near East, especially in Syria, Phoenicia, and Palestine. One of the sturdiest of these new growths was that of the Phoenicians, a

Semitic-speaking people who became outstanding merchants and explorers. Phoenician culture was urban, based on the prosperous commerical centers of Tyre, Sidon, and Byblos. The most important cultural achievement of the Phoenicians was the invention of an alphabet, which they passed on to the Greeks sometime in the late eighth century B.C. In their trading ventures they sailed as far west as North Africa, where in 813 B.C. they founded the city of Carthage, which would one day struggle with the city of Rome for the domination of the western Mediterranean.

South of the Phoenician cities the Hebrews established a political union in Palestine, where they turned from a pastoral life to agriculture. The need to defend themselves from attack encouraged them to create a monarchy. In the eleventh century B.C., Saul, a noted warrior, was made king, but he was unable to unify his people politically. More successful was King David, who defeated the Philistines, the most powerful Hebrew enemy, and built a state with its capital at Jerusalem. David's son Solomon (ca 965–925 B.C.) extended Hebrew power, but at his death the kingdom split into a northern half, Israel, with its capital at Samaria, and a southern half, Judah, with its capital at Jerusalem.

Small kingdoms such as those of the Phoenicians and the Hebrews could exist only in the absence of a major power. The beginning of the ninth century B.C. saw the rise of such a power, the Assyrians in northern Mesopotamia. The Assyrians were a Semitic-speaking people heavily influenced by the Mesopotamian culture of Babylon to the south, another example of the pervasive influence of that fertile culture. The Assyrians were one of the most warlike people in history, in large part because throughout their history they were threatened by neighboring folk. The constant threat to their survival caused them to strengthen their political cohesion and organize their military might.

From the ninth century B.C. until 612 B.C., the Assyrians struggled to dominate the Near East.

They extended their sway over Babylon, Phoenicia, and Israel, and twice invaded Egypt. From their capital at Nineveh, located north of Babylon on the eastern side of the Tigris, they ruled a vast empire. In the process they became notorious for their harsh methods. With grim efficiency they sacked rebellious cities, leaving forests of impaled prisoners or piles of severed heads to signal their victory. Their severity terrorized their subjects and bred a vast hatred among them. At last, in 626 B.C., Babylon won its independence and joined forces with a new people, the Medes, an Indo-European–speaking folk from Iran. Together the Babylonians and the Medes destroyed the Assyrian Empire in 612 B.C. The Hebrew prophet Nahum no doubt echoed the sentiments of many when he proclaimed: "Nineveh is laid waste: who will bemoan her?"[21] When, in 401 B.C., the Greek adventurer Xenophon passed by the ruins of Nineveh, he marveled at their extent but knew nothing of the Assyrians, the glory of their empire forgotten.

The overthrow of the Assyrian Empire cleared the way for the triumph of the Persians (see Map 1.2). The Persians were Indo-Europeans who lived in Iran and were closely related to the Medes. In 550 B.C., Cyrus the Great became king of the Persians, and by the time of his death in 530 B.C. he had made his people the rulers of the entire ancient Near East. The empire he created stretched from the shores of the Mediterranean to the mysterious land of India, from the Caucasus Mountains to southern Egypt and the Persian Gulf. The Persian Empire was easily the greatest of the Eastern monarchies, and in sheer size it can be compared only to the Roman Empire.

The Persians assumed many aspects of Mesopotamian culture, including the cuneiform script, which they adapted for their Indo-European language. They also derived their astronomy and mathematics from the Mesopotamians. The most lasting cultural legacy of the Persians was an aspect

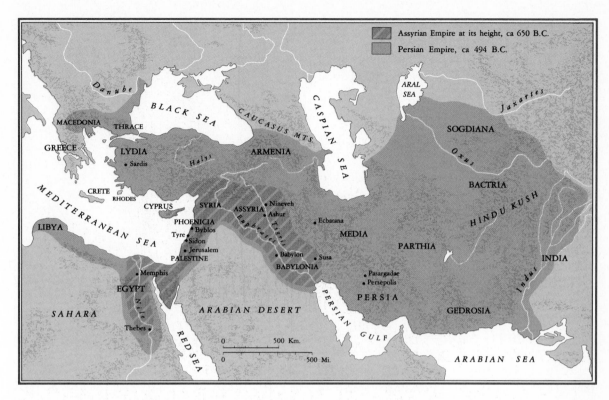

MAP 1.2   THE ASSYRIAN AND PERSIAN EMPIRES

of their religion, Zoroastrianism, which taught that the Persian god Ahura-Mazda, the god of light and truth, fought against the forces of darkness and evil. The Persians believed that this struggle was eternal and that only the constant efforts of Ahura-Mazda kept evil from conquering the world. Despite their fervent faith in their own religion, the Persians were very tolerant of foreign religions, and even helped their subjects rebuild shrines and temples to their local gods.

For over two hundred years the Persians gave the ancient Near East political unity to match the cultural unity that was the enduring gift of Mesopotamia. The Persians organized their empire into large provinces, called satrapies, and they ruled their subjects mildly. By governing wisely and by protecting the Near East from barbarian invasions, the Persians made possible a long period of peace, a period in which various Eastern peoples prospered materially and further developed their individual talents. Thanks to the Persians the achievements of the ancient East survived to fertilize the classical world of the Greeks and Romans.

THE CHILDREN OF ISRAEL

While the Assyrians and the Persians struggled for empire, the Hebrews, or ancient Jews, evolved spiritual concepts that still permeate Western society. Although the Hebrews were politically and culturally unimportant, a people who produced neither art nor science, their chief literary product, the Old Testament, has fundamentally influenced both Christianity and Islam and still exerts a compelling force on the modern world.

A crucial figure in the development of Jewish religious concepts is Moses, a figure so shrouded in legend that many have doubted his existence. Yet the legend is important, and strikingly similar to that concerning Romulus, the founder of Rome. According to the two legends, both Moses and Romulus were abandoned as infants and set adrift on rivers. Both were recovered — Moses by the pharaoh's daughter, Romulus by a she-wolf. Both grew to be leaders of their people — Moses a great religious leader, Romulus the king of a city destined to rule the ancient world.

These two legends were both attempts to put profound philosophical concepts into human terms. From the time human beings began to express their ideas, they have struggled with the unknown. They have believed in unseen, unknowable, and unprovable things, but they have also tried to understand these things. These two legends, like legend and myth in general, are important because they try to reduce the cosmic to a scale comprehensible to human beings. But whereas Romulus is purely legendary, most scholars consider Moses a

IN THE BEGINNING, BY ABRAHAM RATTNER. This lithograph depicts Yahweh, whose hand is visible in the upper right corner, giving Moses the stone tablets. This is the moment when in Jewish and Christian tradition Yahweh made his covenant with Moses and the children of Israel. (Photo: Caroline Buckler)

historical figure and see no real reason to doubt that he was responsible for a religious revolution.

According to Jewish tradition, Yahweh — or Jehovah as he is called in the Bible — appeared to Moses in a burning bush and commanded Moses to be his spokesman. He ordered Moses to tell the Jews that Yahweh promised to watch over them and considered them his people. In return, the Jews were to worship Yahweh and no other god.

Yahweh was unique because he was a lone god, although at first he was not considered the only god. Unlike the gods of Mesopotamia and Egypt, Yahweh was not the son of another god, nor did he have a divine wife or family. He was considered the creator of all things; the name Yahweh itself means "he causes to be." He governed the cosmic forces of nature, including the movements of the sun, moon, and stars. He was the god of storms, and his presence filled the universe.

At the same time Yahweh was a personal god. Despite his awesome power, he was not too mighty or aloof to care for the individual. The Jews even believed that he intervened in human affairs. Yahweh was an anthropomorphic god. According to a story in Exodus, the second book of the Old Testament, Yahweh allowed Moses to see his back, but not his face. Although Yahweh could assume human form, he was not to be depicted in any form. Consequently, the Jews considered graven images — statues or other representations — idolatrous.

The original form of Yahweh's covenant with the Jews was the Ten Commandments. These laws dealt with specific religious matters and embodied an ethical code of conduct. They forbade the Jews to steal, murder, lie, and commit adultery. In return for living by Yahweh's commandments, the Jews became his chosen people. No matter what calamities befell them, Yahweh would always protect his people. The covenant was a constant force in Jewish life, and the Old Testament records one occasion when the entire nation formally reaffirmed it:

And the king [of the Jews] stood by a pillar, and made a covenant before the lord, to walk after the lord, and to keep his commandments and his testimonies and his statutes with all their heart and all their soul, to perform the words of this covenant that were written in this book [Deuteronomy]. And all the people stood to the covenant.[22]

At first Yahweh was probably no more than the god of the Jews, not the god of the Mesopotamians or Egyptians. Enlil, Amon-Re, and the others sufficed for the foreigners. In time, however, the Jews conceived of Yahweh as universal, as the only god who existed. Here were the beginnings of true monotheism. Unlike Akhenaten's monotheism, Jewish monotheism was not an unpopular religion imposed from above. Rather, it was a religion of the whole people, a religion to be cherished and revered. Yet the Jews did not feel that they had the duty to spread the belief in the one god. The Jews rarely proselytized, as later the Christians did. As the chosen people, the chief duty of the Jews was to maintain the worship of Yahweh as he demanded.

From the Ten Commandments evolved Jewish law, a code of law and customs originating with Moses and built upon by many peoples — priests, holy men and women, and self-proclaimed prophets. The earliest part of this code, the Torah or Mosaic law, was harsh, often harsher than Hammurabi's code, which had a powerful impact upon it. Later tradition, largely the work of prophets who lived from the eleventh to the fifth centuries B.C., tended to be humanitarian. The work of the prophet Jeremiah (ca 626 B.C.) can be taken as typical of this gentler spirit.

According to Jeremiah, Yahweh demanded righteousness from his people and protection for the weak and helpless:

For if ye thoroughly amend your ways and your doings; if ye thoroughly execute judgment between a man and his neighbor; if ye oppress not the stranger, the fatherless, and the widow, and shed not innocent blood in this place, neither walk after other gods to your hurt: then I will cause you to dwell in this place, in the land that I gave your fathers, for ever and ever.[23]

Here the emphasis is on mercy and justice, on avoiding wrongdoing to others because it is displeasing to Yahweh. These precepts replaced the demand of the old law for "an eye for an eye." This passage is representative of a subtle and positive shift in Jewish thinking. Jeremiah proclaimed that the god of anger was also the god of forgiveness: "Return, thou backsliding Israel, saith the lord; and I will not cause mine anger to fall upon you; for I am merciful, saith the lord, and I will not keep anger forever."[24] Although Yahweh would punish wrongdoing, he would not destroy those who repented. One generation might be punished for its deeds, but Yahweh's mercy was a promise of hope for future generations.

The uniqueness of this entire phenomenon can be seen by comparing the essence of Hebrew monotheism with the religious outlook of the Mesopotamians. Whereas the Mesopotamians considered their gods capricious, the Jews knew what Yahweh expected of them. The Jews believed that their god would protect them and make them prosper if they obeyed his commandments. The Mesopotamians thought human beings insignificant as compared to the gods, so insignificant that the gods might even be indifferent to men and women. The Jews too considered themselves puny in comparison to Yahweh. Yet they were Yahweh's people, and he had promised never to abandon them. Finally, the Mesopotamians believed that the gods generally preferred good to evil, but their religion did not demand ethical conduct. The Jews could please their god only by living up to high moral standards in addition to worshiping him.

The evolution of Hebrew monotheism resulted in one of the world's greatest religions, which deeply influenced the development of two others. Judaism and many parts of the Old Testament show obvious debts to Mesopotamian culture. Nonetheless, to the Jews goes the credit for developing a religion so emotionally satisfying and ethically grand that it has not only flourished but has also profoundly influenced Christianity and Islam. Without Moses there could not have been Jesus or Mohammed. The religious standards of the modern West are deeply rooted in Judaism.

NOTES

1. L. Eiseley, *The Unexpected Universe,* Harcourt Brace Jovanovich, New York, 1969, p. 102.

2. Xenophon, *Anabasis* 1.5.1.

3. W. K. Loftus, *Travels and Researches in Chaldaea and Susiana,* R. Carter & Brothers, New York, 1857, p. 163.

4. J. B. Pritchard, ed., *Ancient Near Eastern Texts,* Princeton University Press, Princeton, 3rd ed., 1969, p. 44. Hereafter called *ANET.*

5. Ibid., p. 104.

6. Quoted in S. N. Kramer, *The Sumerians,* University of Chicago Press, Chicago, 1964, p. 238.

7. *ANET,* p. 175.

8. H. L. Mencken, *A Mencken Chrestomathy,* Knopf, New York, 1949, p. 67.

9. *ANET,* p. 590.

10. Ibid., p. 67.

11. Kramer, p. 150.

12. *ANET,* p. 171.

13. Kramer, p. 251.

14. Herodotus, *The Histories* 2.14.

15. Quoted in A. H. Gardiner, "Ramesside Texts Relating to the Taxation and Transport of Corn," *Journal of Egyptian Archaeology* 27 (1941): 19–20.

16. A. H. Gardiner, "The Eloquent Peasant," *Journal of Egyptian Archaeology* 9 (1923):17.

17. H. Frankfort, *The Birth of Civilization in the Near East,* Doubleday, New York, 1956, pp. 119–120.

18. E. H. Sturtevant and G. Bechtel, *A Hittite Chrestomathy,* Linguistic Society of America, Philadelphia, 1935, p. 183.

19. M. Vieyra, *Hittite Art* 2300–750 B.C., Alec Tiranti Ltd., London, 1955, p. 12.

20. A. Leo Oppenheim, *Letters from Mesopotamia,* University of Chicago Press, Chicago, 1967, pp. 131–132.

21. Nahum 3.7.

22. 2 Kings 23.3.

23. Jeremiah 7.5–7.

24. Ibid., 3.12.

SUGGESTED READING

The continuing research on the evolution of mankind makes any book quickly outdated, but one of the most informative and best illustrated is R. Leakey and R. Lewin, *Origins* (1977). G. Clark, *Archaeology and Society: Reconstructing the Prehistoric Past* (3rd ed., 1957), is a study in methodology, and his *The Stone Age Hunters** (1967) describes life and society in the Paleolithic Age. A convenient general treatment is G. Clark and S. Piggott, *Prehistoric Societies* (1965).

For the societies of Mesopotamia, see A. Leo Oppenheim, *Ancient Mesopotamia* (rev. ed., 1977); M. E. L. Mallowan, *Early Mesopotamia and Iran** (1965); and H. W. F. Saggs, *The Greatness That Was Babylon* (1962). E. Chiera, *They Wrote on Clay** (1938), gives a delightful glimpse of Mesopotamian life, as does H. W. F. Saggs, *Everyday Life in Babylonia and Assyria* (1965).

C. Aldred, *The Egyptians* (1961), provides a good, readable survey of Egyptian developments. More detailed is A. Gardiner, *Egypt of the Pharaohs* (1961). See also J. M. White, *Everyday Life in Ancient Egypt** (1963).

A solid introduction to the Hebrews and their neighbors is S. Moscati, *Ancient Semitic Civilization** (1960), and more recently, R. R. Wilson, *Genealogy and History in the Biblical World* (1977). M. Pearlman, *In the Footsteps of Moses* (1974); J. Van Seters, *Abraham in History and Tradition* (1975); and E. W. Heaton, *Solomon's New Men: The Emergence of Israel as a National State* (1974), give the current views of Jewish political and religious development.

For other Near Eastern peoples, see O. R. Gurney, *The Hittites** (2nd ed., 1954), a fine introduction by an eminent scholar. Good also is J. G. MacQueen, *The Hittites and Their Contemporaries in Asia Minor* (1975). D. Harden, *The Phoenicians* (1971), treats the life, history, and art of the Phoenicians. R. N. Frye, *Heritage of Persia* (1963), written in lucid prose, surveys the importance of the Persians. A. T. Olmstead, *History of the Persian Empire** (1948), covers the history, thought, and religion of the Persians in great detail. See also R. Collins, *The Medes and the Persians: Conquerors and Diplomats* (1974).

For Near Eastern religion and mythology, good introductions are S. N. Kramer, ed., *Mythologies of the Ancient World** (1961); E. O. James, *The Ancient Gods: The History and Diffusion of Religion in the Ancient Near East and the Eastern Mediterranean* (1960); and J. Gray, *Near Eastern Mythology* (1969).

Surveys of Near Eastern art include H. Frankfort, *The Art and Architecture of the Ancient Orient** (1954), old but still very useful; R. D. Barnett and D. J. Wiseman, *Fifty Masterpieces of Ancient Near Eastern Art** (1969); and J. B. Pritchard's delightful *The Ancient Near East in Pictures* (2nd ed., 1969). For literature, see S. Fiore, *Voices from the Clay: The Development of Assyro-Babylonian Literature** (1965); W. K. Simpson, ed., *The Literature of Ancient Egypt* (1973); and, above all, J. B. Pritchard, ed., *Ancient Near Eastern Texts* cited frequently in the Notes.

*Available in paperback.

Chapter 2

THE LEGACY OF HELLENIC GREECE

he ancient Near East was the seat of old cultures and rich empires, but the rocky peninsula of Greece was the home of the civilization that fundamentally shaped Western civilization. The history of the Greeks is divided into two broad periods: the Hellenic, roughly the time between the arrival of the Greeks and the triumph of Philip of Macedon (the subject of this chapter), and the Hellenistic, the age beginning with Alexander the Great and ending with the Roman conquest (the subject of Chapter 3).

The Greeks first explored most of the problems that continue to concern Western thinkers to this day. Going beyond mythmaking and religion, the Greeks strove to understand, in logical, rational terms, the universe and the position of men and women in it. The result was philosophy and science, which were far more important to most Greek thinkers than religion. The Greeks speculated on human beings and society and created the very concept of politics.

While the scribes of the ancient Near East produced king lists, the Greeks invented history to record, analyze, and understand how people and states functioned in time and space. In poetry, the Greeks spoke as individuals, expressing their dreams, aspirations, loves, fears, and hatreds. In drama, they dealt with the grandeur and the weakness of humanity and with the demands of society on the individual. The greatest monuments of the Greeks were not enormous buildings, huge statues, or gigantic tombs, but profound thoughts set down in terms as fresh and as immediate today as they were some 2,400 years ago.

How did the Greeks grapple with the fundamental problems of life and society? Where did they succeed and where did they fail? These are the questions this chapter will attempt to answer.

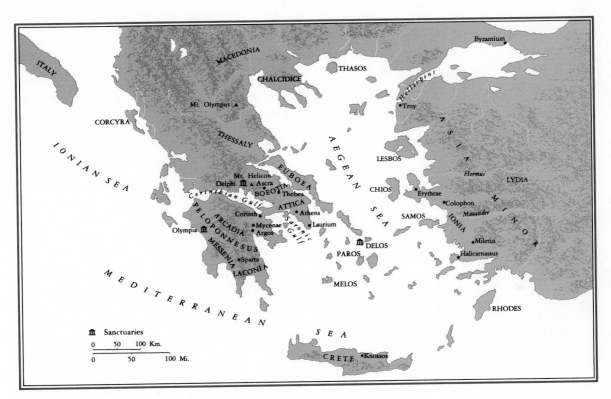

MAP 2.1   THE AEGEAN BASIN

THE LAND AND THE POLIS

Hellas, as the ancient Greeks called their land, included the Aegean Sea and its islands as well as the Greek peninsula (see Map 2.1). By 1000 B.C., Greeks from the peninsula had settled along the coastline of Asia Minor, with the heartland of the eastern Greeks centered in Ionia. The Greek peninsula itself forms an extension of the Balkan system of mountains, and it stretches in the direction of Egypt and the Near East. Greece is mountainous; its rivers are never more than creeks, and most of them go dry in the summer. It is, however, a land blessed with good harbors, and the most important of them look to the east. The islands of the Aegean continue to sweep to the east, and they act as steppingstones between the peninsula and Anatolia. Thus, geography alone encouraged the Greeks to turn their attention to the old civilizations of Asia Minor and Egypt.

Despite the poverty of its soil, Greece is strikingly beautiful, as was observed by the eminent historian K. J. Beloch:

Greece is an alpine land, which rises from the waters of the Mediterranean sea, scenically probably the most beautiful region in southern Europe. The noble contours of the mountains, the bare, rocky slopes, the dusty green of the conifer forests, the white cover of snow which envelops the higher summits for the greatest part of the year, added to which is the profound blue surface of the sea below, and above everything the diffused brightness of the southern sun; this gives a total picture, the charm of which impresses itself unforgettably on the soul of the observer.[1]

The Greeks themselves gloried in the beauty of their land, and this sense of beauty was one of the factors that bound their loyalty to the soil of this hard peninsula. In addition, the climate of Greece is mild; though hot in summer, the air is dry and stirred by breezes. In winter snow may blanket the mountain slopes, but it rarely covers the lowlands.

Simultaneously, geography acted as an enormous divisive force in Greek life. The mountains of Greece dominate the landscape. They cut the land into many small pockets, and isolate areas of inhabitation from one another. Innumerable peninsulas open to the sea, which is dotted with islands, most of them small and many uninhabitable. The geographical fragmentation of this region encouraged political fragmentation. The small physical units of Greece discouraged the growth of great empires. As in Sumer, so too in Greece the typical political unit was the city-state, which the Greeks called the polis.

Rarely in Greece was there the combination of extensive territory and geographical unity that allowed one polis to rise above others. Only three city-states were able to muster the strength of a large area or a whole region behind them (see Map 2.2):

Sparta, which dominated the regions of Laconia and Messenia; Athens, which united the large peninsula of Attica under its rule; and Thebes, which in several periods marshaled the resources of the fertile region of Boeotia. Otherwise, the political pattern of ancient Greece was one of many small city-states, few of which were much stronger or richer than their neighbors.

Physically, the term "polis" designated a city or town and its surrounding countryside. The typical polis consisted of people living in a compact group of houses within the city. The city contained a point, usually elevated, called the acropolis, and a public square or marketplace (agora). The city derived its water supply from public fountains and cisterns. By the fifth century B.C., the city was generally surrounded by a wall. On the acropolis, which in the early period was a place of refuge, stood the temples, altars, public monuments, and various dedications to the gods of the polis. The agora was originally the place where the warrior assembly met, but it became the political center of the polis. In the agora were porticoes, shops, and public buildings, such as council and administrative buildings and courts.

The unsettled territory of the polis formed the usual basis of its wealth. This territory consisted of arable land, pastureland, and wasteland. Farmers left the city each morning to work their fields or tend their flocks of sheep and goats, and they returned to the city at night. On the wasteland men often quarried stone, mined for precious metals, or at certain times of the year obtained small amounts of fodder. Thus, the polis encompassed a combination of urban and agrarian life.

Regardless of its size or wealth, the polis was fundamental to Greek life, as the English scholar H. D. F. Kitto forcefully pointed out:

The city-state . . . became the focus of a man's moral, intellectual, aesthetic, social and practical life, developing and enriching these in a way which no form of society

MAP 2.2   PHYSICAL GREECE AND ITS REGIONS

MACEDONIA

CHALCIDICE

▲ Mt. Olympus

Mt. Ossa ▲

THESSALY

AEGEAN SEA

🏛 Dodona

EPIRUS

Mt. Pelion ▲

ACHAEA PHTHIOTIS

Cape Artemisium

LEUCAS

ACARNANIA

Mt. Oita ▲

MALIS

Thermopylae

✕

Mt. Dirphys ▲

DORIS

LOC

RIS

EUBOEA

AETOLIA

▲ Mt. Parnassus

ITHACA

PHOCIS

LOCRIS

🏛
Delphi

Chaeronea

•Chalcis
•Eretria

Mt. Helicon ▲ •Ascra •Thebes

BOEOTIA

KEPHALLENIA

Leuctra ✕ ✕Plataea

Mt. Parnes ▲

✕

Mt. Cithaeron ▲

ATTICA

Marathon •
▲ Mt. Pentelicus

ACHAEA

Sicyon •

Mt. Gerania ▲

Megara ▲

🏛 Eleusis

•Athens

• Elis

Mt. Erymanthus ▲

Corinth •

SALAMIS

✕

▲ Mt. Hymettus

Mt. Kyllene ▲

ELIS

ARCADIA

Olympia 🏛

Mt. Maenalus ▲

AEGINA

Cape Sounion

ZACYNTHUS

Mantinea •

Mycenae •
Argos •
Tiryns •

ARGOLIS

•Thoricus

CEOS

Tegea •

Mt. Ithome ▲

Mt. Parnon ▲

MESSENIA

Mt. Taygetus ▲

• Sparta

• Pylos

LACONIA

MEDITERRANEAN SEA

Cape Malea

🏛 Sanctuaries

✕ Major battle

0   25   50 Km.

0   25   50 Mi.

CYTHERA

had done before or has done since. Other forms of political society have been, as it were, static; the city-state was the means by which the Greek consciously strove to make the life both of the community and that of the individual more excellent than it was before.[2]

Aristotle, perhaps Greece's greatest thinker, could not envisage civilized life apart from the polis. "The polis," he wrote, "exists by nature, and man is by nature a being of the polis." Aristotle was summing up the Greek view that the life of men and women in the polis was the only way to live according to nature.

The polis was far more than a political institution. Above all, it was a community of citizens, and the affairs of the community were the concern of all citizens. The intimacy of the polis was an important factor, and one hard for modern city dwellers to imagine. The philosopher Plato thought that five thousand citizens constituted the right population for an ideal polis. Though utopian, Plato was not in this case being unrealistic. Although population figures for Greece are mostly guesswork, because most city-states were small enough not to need a census, the polis of Thebes in Boeotia stands as a useful illustration of how small a Greek state was. When Alexander the Great destroyed Thebes in 336 B.C., he sold thirty thousand people into slavery. Some six thousand people had died in the fighting, and many others he spared. The free population of Thebes had numbered between thirty and forty thousand at most, and Thebes was a large polis, a major power. Most city-states were far smaller then Thebes.

The mild climate of Greece meant that much of Greek life was spent outdoors. In a polis, just as in a modern Greek village, a person might easily see most other citizens in the course of the day. Nearly everything that happened within a polis was known immediately and discussed at length. Any stranger who arrived with news from abroad found a large and talkative audience at once. Similarly, the citizen would normally see the public buildings and the temples of the polis daily. The monuments of past victories, the tombs of dead warriors, all these would be personal and familiar. In short, life in the polis was very public. The smallness of the polis enabled Greeks to see how the individual fitted into the overall system — how the human parts made up the social whole.

The customs of the community were at the same time the laws of the polis. Whereas Rome created a single magnificent body of law, the Greeks had as many law codes as they had city-states. Even though the laws of one polis might be roughly similar to those of another polis, the law of any single polis was unique simply because the customs and the experience of each polis had been unique.

The polis also included a religious aspect. Although all Greeks customarily worshiped the great deities — Zeus, Hera, Apollo, Athena, and others, who supposedly lived on Mount Olympus — the citizens of each polis had their own specific and particular cults for these gods. Besides the Olympian gods, each polis had its own minor deities, each with his or her own local cult. Participation in the cults and rituals was a civic duty. By honoring the gods and goddesses of the polis, the citizens honored the polis itself. But this civic religion, unlike the religion of the Hebrews, did not entail religious belief. What individuals believed was their own business. Citizens could be total atheists, but they were still expected to participate in the religion of the polis. Their participation did not brand them as hypocrites, but rather as loyal citizens.

The polis could be governed in several ways. First, it could be a monarchy, a term derived from the Greek that means "the rule of one man." A king could represent the community, reigning according to law and respecting the rights of the citizens. Second, the aristocracy, those who owed their position to birth, could govern the state. Third, the running of the polis could be the duty and prerogative of an oligarchy, which literally means "the rule of a few" — a small group of wealthy citizens. Last, the polis could be governed by a democracy, the rule of the people, which in Greece meant that all the citizens, without respect to birth or wealth, administered the workings of government.

Ironically, the very integration of the polis proved to be one of its weaknesses. Because the bonds that held the polis together were so intimate, the Greeks were extremely reluctant to allow foreigners to share fully in its life. An alien, even someone Greek by birth, could almost never expect to be made a citizen. Nor could women play a political role in the polis. Women participated in the civic cults, and they served as priestesses, but the polis had no room for them in state affairs. Thus, the exclusiveness of the polis doomed it to a limited horizon.

The individualism of the polis proved to be another serious weakness. The citizens of each polis were determined to remain free and autonomous. Rarely were the Greeks willing to unite in political bodies larger than the polis. When they did, they preferred leagues or confederations in which each polis insisted on its autonomy. The political result in Greece, as in Sumer, was almost constant warfare. The polis could dominate, but unlike Rome, it could not incorporate.

THE BRONZE AGE (2000-1100 B.C.)

Greek-speaking peoples did not enter the peninsula of Greece until the Bronze Age. Of these early years the ancient Greeks themselves remembered almost nothing. One of the sterling achievements of modern archaeology was the discovery of this lost past. In the nineteenth century, Heinrich Schliemann, a German businessman turned archaeologist, excavated the site of Mycenae in Greece and the site of Troy in Asia Minor. He discovered the lost past of the Greek people, and to this past he gave the name "Mycenaean."

The Mycenaeans entered Greece around 2000 B.C. and settled in central Greece and in the Peloponnesus, the peninsula that forms the southernmost part of Greece. Mycenaean civilization was utterly unlike anything the later Greeks evolved. The political unit of the Mycenaeans was the kingdom, not the polis. The king and his warrior-aristocracy stood at the top of society. The symbol of the king's power and wealth was the palace, which was also the economic center of the kingdom. Within its walls royal craftsmen fashioned jewelry and rich ornaments, made and decorated fine pottery, forged weapons, prepared hides and wool for clothing, and manufactured the goods needed by the king and his retainers. In the palace scribes kept account of taxes and drew up inventories of the king's possessions. From the palace the king directed the lives of his subjects, and he tightly controlled society. About the king's subjects, almost nothing is known.

The Mycenaean kingdoms were in touch with each other and with the Bronze Age culture of the Minoans in Crete, but these contacts were usually violent. The Minoans had established a vibrant and artistically gifted civilization, from which the Mycenaeans derived much of their art. The wealth of the Minoans tempted Mycenaean greed and ambition, and in about 1450 B.C., a band of Mycenaean raiders conquered Knossus, the most important and the richest Minoan site. This attack was typical of the Mycenaeans, who were consistently a warlike and restless people.

Indeed, the entire history of Mycenaean Greece is a dreary tale of warfare. During the years 1300-1100 B.C., kingdom after kingdom suffered attack

PERIODS OF GREEK HISTORY

Period	Major Writers	Significant Events
Bronze Age 2000–1100 B.C.		Arrival of the Greeks in Greece Rise and fall of the Mycenaean kingdoms
Dark Age 1100–800 B.C.	Homer Hesiod	Greek migrations within the Aegean basin Social and political recovery Evolution of the polis Rebirth of literacy
Lyric Age 800–500 B.C.	Archilochus Sappho Tyrtaeus Solon Anaximander Heraclitus	Rise of Sparta and Athens Colonization of the Mediterranean basin Flowering of lyric poetry Development of philosophy and science in Ionia
Classical Age 500–338 B.C.	Herodotus Thucydides Aeschylus Sophocles Euripides Aristophanes Plato Aristotle	Persian wars Growth of the Athenian empire Peloponnesian War Rise of drama and historical writing Flowering of Greek philosophy Spartan and Theban hegemonies Conquest of Greece by Philip of Macedon

and destruction. Not one alien artifact has been found on any of these sites. There are no traces of invading peoples, nothing to suggest that these kingdoms fell to foreign invaders. Instead, the legends preserved by later Greeks, such as the poets Homer and Hesiod, told of grim wars between kingdoms and of the fall of great royal families. Mycenaean Greece destroyed itself in a long series of internecine wars and thereby set a pattern that would be followed by Greeks of later ages.

The fall of the Mycenaean kingdoms had far-reaching repercussions on society. A period of such poverty, disruption, and backwardness began that historians usually call it the "Dark Age" of Greece (1100–800 B.C.). Yet even this period was important to the development of Greek civilization. It was a time of widespread movements of Greek-speaking peoples. Some Greeks sailed to Crete, where they established new communities. A great wave of Greeks spread eastward through the Aegean and over the coast of Asia Minor. These immigrations turned the Aegean into a Greek lake. In Greece itself a number of people stayed behind and rebuilt society. They thus provided an element of continuity, a link between the Mycenaean period and the Greek culture that emerged from the Dark Age.

The movement of Greek-speaking peoples was not confined to the descendants of the Mycenaeans.

During the Dark Age the last groups of peoples who would help create Greek civilization of the historical period moved into Greece. The Boeotians entered Greece from Thessaly and settled in Boeotia. The Dorians, who were nomads, followed the Boeotians and settled in the Peloponnesus. The common language of these peoples, newcomers and survivors alike, was a bond between them.

HOMER, HESIOD, AND THE HEROIC PAST (1100–800 B.C.)

The Greeks, unlike the Hebrews, had no sacred book that chronicled their past. Instead, they had the *Iliad* and the *Odyssey,* the epic poems created by Homer (eighth century B.C.) to describe a time when gods still walked the earth. And they learned the origin and the descent of the gods from the *Theogony,* an epic poem by Hesiod (ca 700 B.C.). For all their importance to Greek thought and literature, Homer and Hesiod were shadowy figures. Later Greeks knew little about them and were not even certain when they had lived. Although some later Greeks thought they had flourished in the tenth century B.C., the historian Herodotus (484–425 B.C.) gave a more accurate date:

It seems to me that the age of Hesiod and Homer was no more than 400 years earlier than my time. They are the poets who gave the Greeks the genealogy of the gods, and they distributed to the gods their honors and acts, and they declared their forms.[3]

This uncertainty over the poets' dates is significant. It indicates that the Greeks remembered very little of their own past, especially the time before they entered Greece. It also shows that they had forgotten a great deal about the Bronze and Dark ages.

Instead of authentic history the poems of Homer and Hesiod presented to the Greeks an ideal past, a "Heroic Age" largely legendary though partly factual. In terms of pure history these poems contain scraps of information about the Bronze Age, much about the early Dark Age, and some about the poets' own days. Chronologically, then, the "Heroic Age" falls mainly in the years between the collapse of the Mycenaean world and the rebirth of literacy. Yet it is a mistake to treat the *Iliad* and the *Odyssey* as history; rather, they are magnificent blendings of legend, myth, and a little authentic tradition.

In the *Iliad* Homer told of an expedition of Mycenaeans, whom he called Achaeans, to besiege the city of Troy in Asia Minor. The heart of the *Iliad,* however, is the quarrel between Agamemnon, the king of Mycenae, and Achilles, the tragic hero of the poem, and how their quarrel brought suffering to the Achaeans. Only when Achilles put away his anger and pride did he consent to come forward, face, and kill the Trojan hero Hector. The *Odyssey* narrates the adventures of Odysseus, one of the Achaean heroes who fought at Troy, during his return home from the fighting.

The splendor of these poems does not lie in their plots, even though the *Odyssey* is a marvelous adventure story. Rather, both poems deal with engaging, but often flawed, characters who are larger than life and yet typically human. Achilles, the hero of the *Iliad,* is capable of mastering Trojan warriors but can barely control his own anger. Agamemnon is the commander of kings, yet is a man beset by worries. Hector, the hero of the Trojans, is a formidable, noble, and likable foe. Odysseus, the hero of the *Odyssey,* trusts more to his wisdom and good sense than to his strength. Odysseus' wife, Penelope, faithfully endures the long years of war and separation, patiently waiting for her beloved husband to return from Troy.

Homer was strikingly successful in depicting the deeds of the great gods, who sit on Mount Olympus and watch the fighting at Troy as though they were spectators at a modern baseball game. Homer's deities are reminiscent of the Mesopotamian gods

FIGHTING AT TROY. The sweep of combat at Troy shows Achilles killed by arrows. Over him, the hero Ajax kills a Trojan who is trying to drag off Achilles' body as spoils of war. The figure carrying the shield with the pinwheel design is the Trojan Aeneas, whom the Romans later considered their heroic founder. (Photo: Caroline Buckler)

and goddesses. The Olympians are hardly a decorous lot. They are raucous, petty, deceitful, and splendid. In short, they are human. Zeus, the king of the gods, favors the Trojans, but Hera, his wife and queen of the gods, supports the Achaeans. To distract Zeus so that she can aid her favorites, Hera seduces him with wine and sex. Athena, the gray-eyed goddess of wisdom, squabbles with human beings as though she were a fishwife. In the *Odyssey,* Hephaestus, the god of fire, uses an invisible net to catch his wife, Aphrodite, the goddess of love, sleeping with Ares, the god of war. When Hephaestus summons the other gods to witness the scene, they laugh and joke about his catch. One god even wishes that someday he could be as unlucky as Ares.

Homer at times portrayed the gods in a serious vein, but he never treated them in a systematic fashion, as did Hesiod. Hesiod's epic poem, the *Theogony,* traces the descent of Zeus. Hesiod was influenced by Mesopotamian myths, which the Hittites had adopted and spread to the Aegean. Hesiod's poem claims that in the beginning there was chaos, the "yawning deep." From chaos came Gaea (Earth), who gave birth to Uranus (Heaven). Gaea and Uranus then gave birth to Cronus (Ocean, the deep-swelling waters). Cronus, the son of Earth and Heaven, like the Mesopotamian Enlil, separated the two and became king of the gods.

Like the Hebrews, Hesiod envisaged his cosmogony — the way in which the universe developed — in moral terms. Zeus, the son of Cronus, defeated his evil father and took his place as the king of the gods. He then sired Lawfulness, Right, Peace, and other powers of light and beauty. Thus, in Hesiod's conception, Zeus was the god of righteousness, a god who loved justice and hated wrongdoing.

In another epic poem, *Works and Days,* Hesiod wrote of his own time. He lived in the village of Ascra in Boeotia, a scenic place set between beautiful mountains and fertile plains, but he was a grim pessimist and did not think highly of his village: "Ascra, bad in winter, uncomfortable in summer, never good." Although sometimes portrayed as a common man, Hesiod was a wealthy farmer, though not an aristocrat. His social standing makes him unique, for all the other great writers of Greece — and Rome — were members of the aristocracy. Naturally, then, the themes of ancient Greek and Roman literature always reflected the values, cares, and ambitions of the aristocracy. That alone is why the common man in Greco-Roman culture is largely unknown to the modern world. Hesiod affords a rare glimpse of the nonaristocratic side of life.

Hesiod was the victim of injustice. In his will, Hesiod's father had divided his lands between Hesiod and his brother Perses. Perses bribed the aristocratic lords to give him the larger part of the inheritance and then squandered his wealth. Undaunted by the injustice of the powerful, Hesiod thundered back with a voice reminiscent of Khunanup, the "Eloquent Peasant" (see Chapter 1):

Bribe-devouring lords, make straight your decisions,
Forget entirely crooked judgments.
He who causes evil to another harms himself.
Evil designs are most evil to the plotter.[4]

He warned that Zeus would see that justice was done and that injustice was punished. He spoke of Zeus as Jeremiah had spoken of Yahweh. Hesiod cautioned his readers that Zeus was angered by those who committed adultery and those who harmed orphans and offended the aged. Hesiod's ethical concepts and his faith in divine justice were the product of his belief that the world was governed by the power of good.

Hesiod then went on to advise Perses how to become a prosperous farmer. Hesiod's agricultural year was determined by the stars and the seasons. He advised Perses to plow when the constellation Pleiades set and to harvest when it rose. Wood was best cut in autumn, and then the farmer should begin building his plows and wagons and fashioning his tools. When the star Arcturus rose at dusk, it was time to prune the vines. Hesiod warned against doing field work during the time of biting cold, when

all the immense wood roars;
Wild animals shiver and put their tails between their
    legs,
Even those whose hide is covered with fur.
For now the cold wind blows through animals even
    though they be shaggy-breasted.[5]

In the heat of the summer, however, when the crops were stored in the barn, the farmer rested, sitting in the shade and sipping his wine.

In *Works and Days* Hesiod also gave some hardheaded advice on how to live. Although his pessimism was ever-present, his advice was very practical. Hesiod was not theorizing; he was giving his readers tips on how to survive in a hard world. He recommended that a man get a house, an ox, and a slave woman to help with the field work. A man should not take a wife until he was around thirty years old. Then he should be very careful about his prospective bride: "He who trusts women trusts deceivers." Beware of the flirt because "she wants your barn." Marry, he advised, a fine maiden, "for a man gains nothing better than a good wife." Hesiod warned that a couple should have only one son, but if they are to have a second, to have him late in life. He insisted upon the importance of good neighbors, because neighbors will help each other in times of trouble. The constant theme of Hesiod's philosophy is to live justly and uprightly, but never trust anyone.

THE LYRIC AGE
(800–500 B.C.)

Hesiod stood on the threshold of one of the most vibrant periods of Greek history, a period of extraordinary expansion geographically, artistically, and politically. In terms of geography, the Greeks spread themselves as far east as the Black Sea and as far west as Spain (see Map 2.3). This period was also one of tremendous literary flowering, as poets broke away from the heroic tradition and wrote of their own lives, loves, hopes, and sorrows. The individualism of the poets typifies this age of adventure and exploration, and the term "Lyric Age" strikingly conveys the spirit of these years. Politically, these were the years in which Sparta and Athens — the two poles of the Greek experience — rose to prominence.

Overseas Expansion

During the years 1100–800 B.C., the Greeks not only recovered from the breakdown of the Mycenaean world, but they also increased in wealth and numbers. This new prosperity brought with it new problems. Greece is a small and not especially fertile country. The increase in population meant that many men and their families had very little land or none at all. The land hunger of the Greeks drove

them to seek new homes. Other factors, largely intangible, played their part as well: the desire for a new start, a love of excitement and adventure, and natural curiosity about what lay beyond the horizon.

The Mediterranean offered the Greeks an escape valve, for they were always a seafaring people. To them the sea was a highway, not a barrier. Through their commercial ventures they had long been familiar with the rich areas of the western Mediterranean. Moreover, the geography of the Mediterranean basin favored colonization. The land and the climate of the Mediterranean region are remarkably uniform. Greeks could travel to new areas, whether to Cyprus in the east or to Malta in the west, and establish the kind of settlement they had had in Greece. They could also raise the same crops that they had raised in Greece. The move to a new home was not a move into totally unknown conditions. Once the colonists had established themselves in their new homes, they continued life essentially as they had lived it in Greece.

From about 750 to 550 B.C., Greeks from the mainland and from Asia Minor poured onto the coasts of the northern Aegean, the Ionian Sea, and the Black Sea, and into North Africa, Sicily, southern Italy, southern France, and Spain (see Map 2.3). Just as the migrations of the Dark Age had turned the Aegean into a Greek lake, so too did this later wave of colonization spread the Greeks and their culture throughout the Mediterranean. Colonization on this scale had a profound impact on the course of Western civilization. It meant that the prevailing culture of the Mediterranean basin would be Greek, and to this heritage Rome would later fall heir.

One man can in many ways stand as the symbol of the vital and robust era of colonization. Archilochus was born on the island of Paros, the bastard son of an aristocrat. He knew that because of his illegitimacy he would never inherit his father's land,

MAP 2.3   GREEK COLONIZATION OF THE MEDITERRANEAN BASIN

and this knowledge seems to have made him self-reliant. He was also a poet of genius, the first of the lyric poets who left an indelible mark on this age. Unlike the epic poets, who portrayed the deeds of heroes, Archilochus sang of himself. He knew the sea, the dangers of sailing, and the price that the sea often exacted. He spoke of one shipwreck in grim terms and even treated the god of the sea with irony: "Of fifty men gentle Poseidon left one, Koiranos, to be saved from shipwreck."

Together with others from Paros he took part in the colonization of Thasos in the northern Aegean. He described the island in less than glowing terms: "Like the spine of an ass it stands, crowned to the brim with a wild forest." His opinion of his fellow colonists was hardly kinder; about them he commented: "So the misery of all Greece came together in Thasos." Yet at Thasos he fell in love with a woman named Neoboule. They did not marry because her father opposed the match. In revenge, Archilochus seduced Neoboule's younger sister, railed at the entire family, and left Thasos to live the life of a mercenary.

His hired lance took him to Euboea, and he left a striking picture of the fighting there:

Not many bows will be strung, nor bullets be slung
When Ares begins battle in the plain.
There will be the mournful work of the sword:
For in this kind of battle are the spear-famed
Lords of Euboea experienced.[6]

Through it all, however, he kept his sardonic humor. Commenting on the death of a relative, for example, he remarked, "I won't cure anything by weeping or make it worse by pursuing pleasures and festivities." For Archilochus the adventure of colonization had a happy, if unusual, ending. The people of Paros, overlooking his waywardness because of his poetic genius, welcomed him back. Later he was killed defending his homeland.

Archilochus exemplifies the energy, restlessness, self-reliance, and sense of adventure that characterizes this epoch. People like him broke old ties, faced homelessness and danger, and built new homes for themselves. They made the Mediterranean Greek.

Lyric Poets

Archilochus the colonist and adventurer is not nearly as important as Archilochus the lyric poet. His individualism set a new tone in Greek literature. For the first time in Western civilization, men and women began to write of their own experiences. Their poetry reflected their belief that they had something precious to say about themselves.

To them poetry did not belong only to the gods or to the great heroes on the plain of Troy. Some lyric poets, like the Spartan Tyrtaeus and the Athenian Solon, used their literary talents for the good of their city-states. They stood forth as individuals and in their poetry they urged their countrymen to be patriotic and just.

One of the most unforgettable of these writers is the poet Sappho. Unlike Archilochus, she neither braved the wilds nor pushed into the unknown, yet she was no less individual than he. Sappho was born in the seventh century B.C. on the island of Lesbos, a place of sun, sea, and rustic beauty. Her marriage produced a daughter to whom she wrote some of her poems. Her poetry is personal and intense. She delighted in her surroundings, which were those of aristocratic women, and she celebrated the little things around her. Hers was a world of natural beauty, of sacred groves, religious festivals, weddings, and noble companions. She fondly remembered walks with a girlfriend:

There was neither a hill nor a sanctuary
Nor a stream of running water
Which we failed to visit;
Nor when spring began any grove
Filled with the noise of nightingales.[7]

The rising of Hesperus, the evening star, prompted her to welcome it:

Hesperus, bringing back all things
  Which light-giving dawn disperses,
You bring back the sheep, you bring back the goat,
  You bring the child back to its mother.[8]

The wedding of a girlfriend inspired a poem laced with a little good fun at the expense of the best man:

The doorkeeper's feet are seven fathoms long.
Ten shoemakers used up five ox-hides
To make his sandals.[9]

She treated a tall groom more gently:

Up with the roofbeam.
Sing the wedding song!
Carpenters, raise it up.
Sing the wedding song!
The groom comes like Ares,
Much taller than a tall man.[10]

Sappho is best known for erotic poetry, for she expressed her love frankly and without shame. She was bisexual, and much of her poetry dealt with her homosexual love affairs. In one of her poems she remembered the words of her lover:

Sappho, if you don't come out,
Surely I will no longer love you.
O come to us and free your lovely
Strength from your bed.
Lifting off your Chian robe,
Bathe in the waters like a
Pure lily beside a spring.[11]

In another poem she described Aphrodite appearing to her in answer to her prayers. The goddess advised Sappho to be patient: the girl she loved would return her love soon enough.

In antiquity Sappho's name became linked with female homosexual love. Today, the English word "lesbian," referring to a female homosexual is derived from Sappho's island home. Yet to see Sappho as a licentious pervert is to misunderstand her and her world completely. The Greeks accepted bisexualism — that men and women could enjoy both homosexual and heterosexual lovemaking. Homosexual relationships normally carried no social stigma. In her mature years Sappho was courted by a younger man who wanted to marry her. By then she had already proclaimed her love for several girls, yet the young man did not consider these affairs abnormal. As it turned out, Sappho refused to marry in her maturity because she was past childbearing age.

MOSAIC PORTRAIT OF SAPPHO. The Greek letters in the upper left corner identify this idealized portrait as that of Sappho. The mosaic, which was found at Sparta, dates to the late Roman Empire and testifies to Sappho's popularity in antiquity. (Photo: Caroline Buckler)

Through their poetry Archilochus and Sappho present two sides of Greek life in this period. Archilochus exemplifies the energy and adventure of the age, while Sappho reveals the intensely personal side of life. As will be seen later, Tyrtaeus and Solon devoted their talents to politics, and have thus illuminated for posterity the political difficulties of the age. The common link among them all is their individualism, their faith in themselves, and their desire to reach out to other men and women in order to share their experiences, thoughts and wisdom.

The Growth of Sparta

During the Lyric Age the Spartans expanded the boundaries of their polis and made it the leading power in Greece. Like other Greeks, the Spartans faced the problems of overpopulation and land hunger. Unlike other Greeks, the Spartans solved these problems by conquest, not by colonization. To gain more land the Spartans set out in about 735 B.C. to conquer Messenia, a rich and fertile region in the southwestern Peloponnesus. This conflict, known as the First Messenian War, lasted for twenty years, and ended in a Spartan triumph. The Spartans appropriated Messenian land and turned the Messenians into Helots, or state serfs.

In about 650 B.C., Spartan exploitation and oppression of the Messenian helots led to a Helot revolt so massive and stubborn that it became known as the Second Messenian War. The Spartan poet Tyrtaeus, a contemporary of these events, vividly portrayed the ferocity of the fighting:

For it is a shameful thing indeed
*   When with the foremost fighters*
An elder falling in front of the young men
*   Lies outstretched,*
Having white hair and grey beard,
Breathing forth his stout soul in the dust,
Holding in his hands his genitals stained with blood.[12]

Confronted with horrors such as this, Spartan enthusiasm for the war waned. To rally his countrymen Tyrtaeus urged the warriors to face the Messenians:

And let each man coming near
*   With his great spear or sword,*
Wounding his man cut him down and take him;
And putting foot against foot and leaning shield
*   against shield,*
Crest upon crest and helmet upon helmet,
And chest to chest, drawing near, let him fight his
*   man,*
Taking him with the hilt of his sword or with his
*   Great spear.*[13]

Finally, after some thirty years of fighting, the Spartans put down the revolt. Nevertheless, the political and social strain caused by this war led to a transformation of the Spartan polis.

It took the full might of the Spartan people, aristocrat and commoner alike, to win the Second Messenian War. After the victory, the nonnobles, who had done much of the fighting, demanded rights equal to those of the nobility. Their agitation disrupted society, until the aristocrats agreed to remodel the state. Although the Spartans later claimed that the changes brought about by this compromise were the work of Lycurgus, a legendary, semidivine lawgiver, they were really the work of the entire Spartan people.

The "Lycurgan regimen," as these reforms were called, was a new political, economic, and social system. Political distinctions among the Spartans were eliminated, and all citizens became equal to one another. In effect, the Lycurgan regimen abolished the aristocracy and made the government an oligarchy. The actual governance of the polis was in the hands of two kings, who were primarily military leaders. The kings and twenty-eight elders made up a council that deliberated on foreign and domestic matters and prepared legislation for the assembly, which consisted of all Spartan citizens. The real executive power of the polis was in the hands of five *ephors,* whose name means "overseers." The ephors were elected from and by all the people.

To provide for their economic needs the Spartans divided the land of Messenia among all the citizens. Helots worked the land, raised the crops, and provided the Spartans with their living. The Spartans kept the Helots in line by systematic terrorism, hoping to beat them down and keep them quiet. Spartan citizens were supposed to devote their time exclusively to military training.

In the Lycurgan system every citizen owed primary allegiance to Sparta. The suppression of the individual, together with the emphasis on military prowess, led to a barracks state. Family life itself was sacrificed to the polis. If an infant was deformed or handicapped at birth, the polis could demand that the parents expose it and leave it to die. In this respect the Spartans were no better or worse than other Greeks. Infanticide was common in ancient Greece and Rome, and many people resorted to it as a way of keeping numbers down. The only difference is that in other Greek states the decision to kill a child belonged to the parents, not to the polis.

Once a Spartan boy reached the age of seven, he lived in barracks with other boys his age. Spartan youth all underwent rugged physical and military training until they reached twenty-four, when they became front-line soldiers. For the rest of their lives, Spartan men kept themselves prepared for combat. Their military training never ceased, and the older men were expected to be models of endurance, frugality, and sturdiness to the younger men.

When in battle Spartans were supposed to stand and die rather than retreat. An anecdote about one Spartan mother sums up Spartan military values. As her son was setting off to battle, the mother, "having handed her son his shield and advising him, said: 'Son, either this [that is, shield] or on it'" — come back either victorious carrying the shield or dead being carried on it.[14] In short, in the Lycurgan regimen Spartans were expected to train vigorously, disdain luxury and wealth, do with little and like it.

The Evolution of Athens

Like Sparta, Athens too faced pressing social and economic problems during the Lyric Age, but the Athenian response to them was far different from that of the Spartans. Instead of creating an oligarchy, the Athenians extended to all citizens the rights and duties of governing the polis. Indeed, the Athenian democracy was one of the most thorough-going in Greece.

In the seventh century B.C., however, the aristocracy governed Athens, and they were as oppressive as the "bribe-devouring lords" against whom Hesiod had railed. The aristocrats owned the best land, they met in an assembly to govern the polis, and only they interpreted the law. Noble landowners were forcing small farmers into economic dependence. Many families were being sold into slavery, others exiled and their land pledged to the rich. Poor farmers who borrowed from their wealthy neighbors put up their land as collateral. If a farmer was unable to repay the loan, his creditor put a stone on the borrower's field to declare his indebtedness and thereafter took one-sixth of the annual yield until the debt was paid. If the farmer had to borrow again, he pledged himself and at times his family. If he was again unable to repay the loan, he became the slave of his creditor. Because the harvests of the poor farmer were generally small, he normally raised enough to live on but not enough to repay his loan.

STATUE OF "LEONIDAS." Found at Sparta, this statue is thought by some to represent Leonidas, the Spartan king who was killed at Thermopylae. The statue, with its careful rendering of the muscles and the face, reflects the Spartan ideal of the strong, intelligent, and brave warrior. (Photo: Caroline Buckler)

The peasants, however, were strong in numbers, and they demanded reforms. They wanted the law to be published so that everyone would know its contents. Under pressure, the aristocrats relented and turned to Dracon, a fellow aristocrat, to codify the law. In 621 B.C., Dracon published the first law code of the Athenian polis. His code was thought harsh, but it nonetheless embodied the ideal that the law belonged to all citizens. The aristocrats hoped that Dracon's law code would satisfy the peasants, but it did not. Many of the poor began demanding redistribution of the land, and it was obvious that broader reform was needed. Unrest among the peasants continued.

In many other city-states conditions such as those in Athens led to the rise of tyrants. The word "tyrant" brings to mind a cruel and bloody dictator, but the Greeks at first used the word to denote a leader who gained power without legal right. Many of the first tyrants, though personally ambitious, were men who kept the welfare of the polis in mind. They usually enjoyed the support of the peasants because they reduced the power of the aristocrats. Later tyrants were often harsh and arbitrary — hence the Greeks began to use the word "tyrant" in the modern sense — and when they were, peasants and aristocrats alike suffered.

Only one person in Athens had the respect of both aristocrats and peasants: Solon, himself an aristocrat and poet but a man opposed to tyrants. Like Hesiod, Solon used his poetry to condemn the aristocrats for their greed and dishonesty. He stormed against

those citizens who are persuaded
to destroy this great city
because they desire reckless wealth.[15]

Solon recited his poems in the Athenian agora, where everyone could hear his relentless call for justice and fairness. The aristocrats realized that Solon was no crazed revolutionary, and the common people trusted him. Around 594 B.C., the aristocrats elected him *archon,* chief magistrate of the Athenian polis, and gave him extraordinary power to reform the state.

Solon immediately freed all people enslaved for debt, recalled all exiles, canceled all debts on land, and made enslavement for debt illegal. He divided society into four legal groups on the basis of wealth. In the most influential group were the wealthiest citizens, but even poor people in the least powerful group enjoyed certain rights. Solon allowed them into the old aristocratic assembly, where they could take part in the election of magistrates.

In all his work, Solon gave thought to the rights of the poor as well as the rich. He gave the commoners a place in government and a voice in the political affairs of Athens. His work done, Solon insisted that all swear to uphold his reforms. Then, since many were clamoring for him to become tyrant, he left Athens to travel.

Although Solon's reforms solved some immediate problems, they did not bring peace to Athens. Some aristocrats attempted to make themselves tyrants, while others banded together to oppose them. In 546 B.C., Pisistratus, an exiled aristocrat, returned to Athens, defeated his opponents, and became tyrant. Pisistratus reduced the power of the aristocracy while supporting the common people. Under his rule Athens prospered, and his building program began to transform it into one of the splendors of Greece. His reign as tyrant helped the growth of democratic ideas by arousing in the Athenians rudimentary feelings of equality.

Athenian acceptance of tyranny did not long outlive Pisistratus, for his son Hippias ruled harshly, and his excesses led to his overthrow. After a brief period of turmoil between factions of the nobility, Cleisthenes, a wealthy and prominent aristocrat, emerged triumphant in 508 B.C., largely because he won the support of the people. Cleisthenes created the Athenian democracy, and he did so with the full knowledge and approval of the Athenian people.

He reorganized the state completely, but he presented every innovation to the assembly for discussion and ratification. All Athenian citizens had a voice in Cleisthenes' work.

Cleisthenes created a new local unit, the deme, and made it the basis of his political system. Citizenship was tightly linked to the deme, for in each deme was the roll of those admitted to citizenship. Cleisthenes also created ten new tribes as administrative units. All the demes were grouped in tribes, which thus formed the link between the demes and the central government. The central government included an assembly of all citizens and a new council of five hundred members. The council prepared legislation for the assembly to consider, and it handled diplomatic affairs. The result of Cleisthenes' work was to make Athens a democracy with a government efficient enough to permit effective popular rule.

Athenian democracy was to prove vitally important in Western civilization. It proved that a large group of people, and not just a few, could efficiently run the affairs of state. By paying attention to the opinions, suggestions, and wisdom of all the citizens the state enjoyed the maximum amount of good counsel. Since all citizens could speak their minds, they did not have to resort to rebellion or conspiracy to express their desires.

Athenian democracy, however, must not be thought of in modern terms. In Athens democracy meant a form of government in which poor men as well as rich enjoyed political power and responsibility. In practice, however, most important offices were held by aristocrats. Furthermore, Athenian democracy denied political rights to many people, including women and slaves. Foreigners were seldom admitted to citizenship. Unlike modern democracies, Athenian democracy did not mean that the citizen would merely vote for others who would then run the state. Instead, every citizen was expected to be able to perform the duties of most magistrates. In Athens citizens voted and served. The people were the government. It is this union of the individual and the state — the view that the state exists for the good of the citizen and the duty of the citizen is to serve it well — that has made Athenian democracy so compelling an ideal.

THE CLASSICAL PERIOD
(500–338 B.C.)

In the years 500–338 B.C., Greek civilization reached its highest peak in politics, thought, and art. In this period the Greeks beat back the armies of the Persian Empire. Then, turning their swords against one another, they destroyed their civilization in a century of warfare. These events prompted some thoughtful Greeks to record events and to analyze them; the result was the creation of history. This era saw the flowering of philosophy, as thinkers in Ionia and on the Greek mainland began to ponder the meaning of the universe. Not content to ask "why," they used their intellects to explain the world around them and to determine humanity's place in it. In art, the Greeks invented drama, and the Athenian tragedians Aeschylus, Sophocles, and Euripides explored themes that still inspire audiences today. Greek architects reached the zenith of their art and created buildings whose very ruins still inspire awe. Because Greek intellectual and artistic works attained their fullest and finest expression in these years, this age is called the Classical Period. Few periods in the history of Western society can match this period in sheer dynamism and achievement.

The Deadly Conflicts
(499–404 B.C.)

One of the hallmarks of the Classical Period was warfare. In 499 B.C., the Ionian Greeks, with the feeble help of Athens, rebelled against the Persian Empire. In 490 B.C., the Persians struck back at Athens but were beaten off at the battle of Marathon, a small plain in Attica. This failure only prompted the Persians to try again. In 480 B.C., the Persian king Xerxes led a mighty invasion force into Greece. In the face of this emergency the Greeks united and pooled their resources to resist the invaders. The Spartans provided the overall leadership and commanded the Greek armies. The Athenians, led by the wily Themistocles, provided the heart of the naval forces.

The first confrontation between the Persians and the Greeks came at the pass of Thermopylae and in the waters off Artemisium in northern Greece. At Thermopylae the Greek hoplites, the heavy-armed troops, showed their mettle. Before the fighting began, a report came in that when the Persian archers shot their bows the arrows darkened the sky. One gruff Spartan merely replied, "Fine, then we'll fight in the shade." The Greeks at Thermopylae fought to the last man, but the Persians took the position. In their next two battles, the Greeks fared better. In 480 B.C., the Greek fleet smashed the Persian navy at Salamis, an island south of Athens. In the following year, the Greek army destroyed the Persian forces at Plataea, a small polis in Boeotia.

The significance of the Greek victories is nearly incalculable. By defeating the Persians, the Greeks were able to develop their peculiar genius in freedom. These victories meant that Greek political forms and intellectual concepts would be the heritage of the West. By repelling the Persian forces, the Greeks insured that oriental monarchy would not stifle the Greek achievement.

After turning back the invasion, the Greeks took the fight to the Persian Empire. In 478 B.C., the Greeks decided to continue hostilities until they had liberated the Ionians from Persian rule, but for that goal a strong navy was essential. The Greeks turned to Athens, the leading naval power in the Aegean, for leadership. Athens and other states, especially those in the Aegean, established the Delian League. Athens was in control of the Delian League, providing most of the warships for operations and determining how much money each member should contribute to the league's treasury.

During the next twenty years the Athenians drove the Persians out of the Aegean and turned the Delian League into their own empire. Athenian rule became severe, and the Athenian polis became openly imperialistic. Although all members of the Delian League were supposed to be free and independent states, Athens reduced them to the status of subjects. Some idea of the harshness of Athenian rule can be gained from the regulations the Athenians imposed on their subject allies. After the Athenians had suppressed a revolt in Euboea, they imposed an oath on the people:

I will not revolt from the people of Athens either by any means or devices whatsoever or by word or deed, nor will I be persuaded by anyone who does revolt. And I will pay the tribute to the Athenians that I can persuade the Athenians [to levy]. I will be to them the best and truest ally possible. I will help and defend the people of Athens if anyone wrongs them, and I will obey the people of Athens.[16]

The Athenians dictated to the people of Erythrae, a polis on the coast of Asia Minor, their form of government:

There will be a council of 120 men chosen by lot. . . . The [Athenian] overseers and garrison commander will choose the current council by lot and establish it in office. Henceforth the council and the [Athenian] garrison commander will do these things thirty days before the council goes out of office.[17]

The Athenians also interfered with the economic affairs of the allies and decreed that they use Athenian coins, weights, and measures. The lengths to which the Athenians could go can be seen in the oath they forced on the people of Colophon, another polis in Asia Minor: "And I will love the Athenian people, and will not desert them . . . " The Athenians were willing to enforce their demands by armed might, and they were ready both to punish violations and to suppress discontent.

The expansion of Athenian power and the aggressiveness of Athenian rule alarmed Sparta and its allies. While relations between Athens and Sparta cooled, Pericles (ca 494–429 B.C.) became the leading statesman in Athens. An aristocrat of solid intellectual ability, he turned Athens into the wonder of Greece. But like the democracy he led, Pericles was aggressive and imperialistic. He made no effort to allay Spartan fear and instead continued Athenian expansion. At last, in 459 B.C., Sparta and Athens went to war over conflicts between Athens and some of Sparta's allies. The war ended in 445 B.C. with no serious damage to either side and nothing settled. Worst of all, this war had divided the Greek world between two great powers.

During the 440s and 430s, Athens continued its severe policies toward its subject allies and came into conflict with Corinth, one of Sparta's leading allies. Once again Athens and Sparta were drifting toward war. In 432 B.C., the Spartans convened a meeting of their allies, who complained of Athenian aggression and demanded that Athens be stopped. With a show of reluctance, the Spartans agreed to declare war. The real reason for war, according to the Athenian historian Thucydides, was very simple:

"The truest explanation, though the one least mentioned, was the great growth of Athenian power and the fear it caused the Lakedaimonians [Spartans], which drove them to war."[18]

At the outbreak of this, the Peloponnesian War, a Spartan ambassador said to the Athenians: "This day will be the beginning of great evils for the Greeks." Few men have ever spoken more truthfully. The Peloponnesian War, which lasted a generation (431–404 B.C.), brought in its wake fearful plagues, famine, civil wars, widespread destruction, and huge loss of life. Thucydides, the historian who was also a general who fought in the war, described its cataclysmic effects:

For never had so many cities been captured and destroyed, whether by the barbarians or by the Greeks who were fighting each other. . . . Never had so many men been exiled or slaughtered, whether in the war or because of civil conflicts.[19]

As the war dragged on, old leaders like Pericles died and were replaced by men of the war generation. In Athens the most prominent of this new breed of politicans was Alcibiades, an aristocrat, a kinsman of Pericles, and a student of the philosopher Socrates. Alcibiades (ca 450–404 B.C.) was brilliant, handsome, and charming, all of which made him popular with the people. He was also self-seeking and egotistical; a shameless opportunist, his first thoughts were always for himself.

Alcibiades' schemes helped bring Athens down in defeat. He planned an invasion of Sicily, which ended in disaster. He deserted to the Spartans and plotted with the Persians, who had sided with Sparta, against his homeland. When his policies had brought the Athenians to the brink of defeat, he struck a bargain with them. He promised to persuade Persia to throw its support to Athens, if the Athenians would allow him to return home. When they agreed, he cheerfully double-crossed the Spartans and led the Athenians against Sparta's forces.

In the end, all of Alcibiades' intrigues failed. The Spartans defeated the Athenian fleet in the Aegean and blockaded Athens by land and sea. Finally, in

MOSAIC PORTRAIT OF ALCIBIADES. The artist has caught all the craftiness, intelligence, and quickness of Alcibiades, who became a romantic figure in antiquity. Besides the artistic merit of the portrait, the mosaic is interesting because Alcibiades' name in the upper right corner is misspelled. (Photo: Caroline Buckler)

404 B.C., the Athenians surrendered and watched helplessly while the Spartans and their allies destroyed the walls of Athens to the music of flute girls. The Peloponnesian War lasted twenty-seven years, and it dealt Greek civilization a mortal blow.

One positive development grew out of the Persian and Peloponnesian wars: the beginnings of historical writing. The "Father of History," Herodotus, was born at Halicarnassus in Asia Minor. As a young man he traveled widely, visiting Egypt, Phoenicia, and probably Babylon. Later he migrated to Athens, which became his intellectual home, and he participated in the colonization of Thurii in southern Italy, where he died.

Herodotus gave his reasons for writing history in the first lines of his book, *The Histories:*

This is the publication of the researches of Herodotus of Halicarnassus — so that past deeds will not be forgotten by men through lapse of time — which points out the great and admirable achievements, both those of the Greeks and those of the barbarians, lest they be uncelebrated, and which points out why they waged war against each other.[20]

This introduction reads much like that which Homer used in the *Iliad,* and indeed *The Histories* has been called a prose epic. The basic difference, however, is that Herodotus dealt with the real and factual, not with legend. He even gave history its name; his word *historia* originally meant "investigation." Only after his book appeared did the word *historia* gain its modern meaning.

Herodotus chronicled the rise of the Persian Empire, sketched the background of Athens and Sparta, and described the land and customs of the Egyptians and the Scythians, who lived in the region of the modern Crimea. The sheer scope of this work is awesome. Lacking newspapers, sophisticated communications, and easy means of travel, he nevertheless wrote a history that covered the major events of the Near East and Greece.

Perhaps the chief characteristic of Herodotus is his curiosity. He loved to travel, and like most travelers he accumulated a stock of fine stories. He was an excellent storyteller, and the customs of non-Greek peoples fascinated him. But he never let tales and digressions mar the theme of his work. He diligently questioned everyone who could tell him anything about the Persian wars. The confrontation between East and West, as it appears in *The Histories,* unfolds relentlessly and reaches its climax in the great battles of Salamis and Plataea.

In Herodotus' opinion the victory of the Greeks was due to their ability to live life simply, without luxury or wealth. He emphasized this point when he described a meeting between the Persian king Xerxes and a Greek deserter. Xerxes was about to invade Greece, so he questioned the deserter about the Greeks and their land. The deserter told him that

"in Greece poverty is ever-present, but excellence is acquired, attained from wisdom and hard law. By making use of them Greece wards off both poverty and despotism."[21]

Herodotus turned to this thought again when he concluded his history with a moral: "Those accustomed to soft lands are themselves soft."

The outbreak of the Peloponnesian War prompted Thucydides (ca 460–ca 400 B.C.) to write a history of its course in the belief that

it would be great and more noteworthy than previous wars, considering that both states were in the prime of all their preparations and seeing that the other Greeks were taking sides with one or the other, some immediately, others intending to do so. For this was the greatest movement among the Greeks and some of the barbarians, and so to speak among most of mankind.[22]

A politician and a general, Thucydides saw action in the war until he was exiled for a defeat. His exile gave him the time and the opportunity to question eyewitnesses about the details of events and to visit battlefields. Since he was an aristocrat and a prominent man, he had access to the inner circles, to the men who made the decisions.

Thucydides was intensely interested in human nature and how it manifested itself during the war. In 430 B.C., a terrible plague struck Athens. Thucydides described both the symptoms caused by the plague and the reactions of the Athenians to the epidemic in the same clinical terms. He portrayed the virtual breakdown of a society beset with war, disease, desperation, and despair. Similarly, he chronicled the bloody civil war on the island of Corcyra. Instead of condemning the injustice and inhumanity of the fighting, as citizen turned on citizen and as people ruthlessly betrayed their friends, he observed that such things are normal as long as human nature is what it is.

Thucydides saw the Peloponnesian War as highly destructive to Greek character. He noted — with a visible touch of regret — that the old, the noble, and the simple fell before ambition and lust for power. Thucydides interpreted the war and its effects in purely human terms. He firmly rejected any notion that the gods intervened in human affairs. In his view, men and women could be unfortunate, but even so their fate was in their own hands.

Athenian Arts in the Age of Pericles

In the last half of the fifth century B.C. (ca 449–408 B.C.), Pericles turned Athens into the show place of Greece. He appropriated Delian League funds to pay for a huge building program. The new temples and other buildings he planned were to honor Athena, the patron goddess of the city, and they would display to all Greeks the glory of the Athenian polis. Pericles also pointed out that his program would employ a great many Athenians and would bring economic prosperity to the city.

Thus began the program that turned the Acropolis into a monument for all time. Work on the Parthenon began in 447 B.C., followed by that on the Propylaea, the temple of Athena Nike (Athena the Victorious), and the Erechtheion. Even today in their ruined state they still evoke awe. Plutarch, a Greek writer who lived in the first century A.D., observed:

In beauty each of them was from the outset antique, and even now in its prime fresh and newly made. Thus each of them is always in bloom, maintaining its appearance as though untouched by time, as though an ever-green breath and undecaying spirit had been mixed in its construction.[23]

Even the pollution of modern Athens, although it is destroying the ancient buildings, cannot rob them of their splendor and charm.

The planning of the architects and the skill of the workmen who erected these buildings were both very sophisticated. Visitors approaching the Acropolis first saw the Propylaea, the ceremonial gateway, a building of complicated layout and grand design. Its Doric columns seem to hold up the sky. As visitors walked through the central passageway, they got their first good view of the Parthenon, Erechtheion, and the other buildings.

On the right was the small temple of Athena Nike, the dimensions of which harmonize with those of the Propylaea. The temple was built to commemorate the victory over the Persians, and the Ionic frieze, the band of sculpture over the columns, depicted the battle of the Greeks and the Persians. Here for all the world to see was a tribute to Athenian and Greek valor — and a reminder of Athens' part in the victory.

THE ATHENIAN ACROPOLIS. This quaint print shows the Acropolis during the early nineteenth century, when traditional Greek costumes were still common. Today the plain has fallen victim to urbanization, and the ancient buildings themselves are endangered by pollution. (Photo: Caroline Buckler)

Ahead of the visitors as they stood in the eastern face of the Propylaea was the huge statue of Athena Promachus (the Front-Line Fighter), which was so gigantic that the crest of the helmet and the point of the spear could be seen by sailors entering the harbor of Athens. This statue celebrated the Athenian victory at the battle of Marathon, and was paid for by the spoils taken from the Persians. To the left stood the Erechtheion, an Ionic temple that housed several ancient shrines. On its southern side is the famous Portico of the Caryatids, a porch whose roof is supported by statues of Athenian maidens. The graceful Ionic columns of the Erechtheion provide a delicate relief from the prevailing Doric order of the massive Propylaea and Parthenon.

THE PARTHENON.   Stately and graceful, the Parthenon symbolizes the logic, order, and sense of beauty of Greek architecture. The Parthenon was also the centerpiece of Pericles'
plan to make Athens the artistic showcase of the Greek world
(Photo: Caroline Buckler)

As visitors walked on they obtained a full view of
the Parthenon, thought by many to be the perfect
Doric temple. The Parthenon was the chief monument to Athena and her city. The sculptures that
adorned the temple portrayed the greatness of
Athens and its goddess. The figures on the eastern
pediment depicted Athena's birth, those on the west
the victory of Athena over the god Poseidon for the
possession of Attica. The frieze along the cella (the
chamber containing the cult statue) represented the
Panathenaic procession, the chief Athenian religious
festival.

The Parthenon appears to be all rectangle and
triangle, yet it is a structure of curves. The stylobate
(the pavement that supports the columns) and the
architrave (the beam above the columns) are curved
to avoid the illusion of flatness. The columns

themselves are gently curved from bottom to top. The Parthenon also appears rigorously regular, but it is a collection of irregularities, all of them intended to eliminate the defects of optical illusion. For instance, the columns are not regularly spaced, and they are inclined inward; those at the rear are stockier than those at the front end. In all these refinements the Athenian architect showed his knowledge of mathematics, optics, and design. The impression left by the Parthenon is one of perfection. Well might all Athenians, no matter how humble, feel a great burst of pride in themselves, their goddess, and their polis when they gazed on the Parthenon.

In many ways the Athenian Acropolis is the epitome of Greek art and its spirit. Although the buildings were dedicated to the gods and most of the sculptures portrayed the gods, these works are nonetheless human and rational. Because Greek deities were anthropomorphic, Greek artists portrayed them as human beings. While honoring the gods, Greek artists were celebrating the importance of human beings. In the Parthenon sculptures it is visually impossible to distinguish the men and women from the gods and goddesses. This aspect of Greek art made a powerful impression on the American novelist Mark Twain, who visited the Acropolis at night:

As we wandered thoughtfully down the marble-paved length of this stately temple [the Parthenon] the scene about us was strangely impressive. Here and there in lavish profusion were gleaming white statues of men and women, propped against blocks of marble, some of them armless, some without legs, others headless — but all looking mournful in the moonlight and startlingly human![24]

Even in religious art, the Greek sculptor dealt with men and women.

The Acropolis also exhibits the rational side of Greek art. Greek artists portrayed action in a balanced, restrained, and sometimes even serene fashion. There is no violent emotion in this art, but instead a quiet intensity. Likewise, there is nothing excessive, for "nothing too much" was the canon of the artist and philosopher alike. Greek artists succeeded in capturing the noblest aspects of human beings: their reason, dignity, and promise.

Other aspects of Athenian cultural life were as bound to the polis as were the architecture and sculpture of the Acropolis. The development of drama was tied to the religious festivals of the city. The polis sponsored the production of the plays and required that wealthy citizens pay the expenses of their production. At the beginning of the year dramatists submitted their plays to the archon. He chose those he considered the best and assigned a theatrical troupe to each playwright. Although most Athenian drama has perished, enough has survived to prove that the archons had good taste. Many plays were highly controversial, but the archons neither suppressed nor censored them. Rather, the archons honestly tried to see that the best plays were performed.

The Athenian dramatists were the first artists in Western society to examine such basic questions as the rights of the individual, the demands of society on the individual, and the working out of good and evil. The element of conflict is a constant force in Athenian drama. The dramatists used their art to present life's basic conflicts, understand, and then resolve them.

Aeschylus (525–456 B.C.), the first of the great Athenian dramatists, was also the first to express the agony of the individual caught in conflict. In his trilogy of plays, *The Oresteia,* Aeschylus deals with the themes of betrayal, murder, and reconciliation. *The Agamemnon,* the first play of the trilogy, depicts Agamemnon's return from the Trojan War and his murder by his wife Clytemnestra and her lover Aegisthus. In the second play, *The Libation Bearers,*

Orestes, the son of Agamemnon and Clytemnestra, avenges his father's death by killing his mother and her lover. His act of vengeance is the work of a dutiful son, but the murder of his mother is a sin against his own blood.

The last play of the trilogy, *The Eumenides,* works out the atonement and absolution of Orestes. The Furies, goddesses who avenged murder and unfilial conduct, demand Orestes' death. At Athens, Orestes stands trial with Athena as judge and Apollo as counsel for the defense. When the jury casts six votes to condemn Orestes and six to acquit him, Athena casts the deciding vote in favor of mercy and compassion. Aeschylus used *The Eumenides* to urge reason and justice to reconcile fundamental conflicts. The play concludes with a prayer that civil dissension never be allowed to destroy the city and that the life of the city be one of harmony and grace.

Sophocles (496–406 B.C.), too, dealt with matters personal and political. In *Antigone* he examined the relationship between the individual and the state, exploring a conflict between the ties of kinship and the demands of the polis. In the play Polynices has attacked Thebes, his state, and has fallen in battle. Creon, the Theban king, refuses to allow Polynices' body to be buried. Polynices' sister Antigone is appalled by Creon's action because custom demands that she bury her brother's corpse. Creon is right in refusing to allow Polynices' body to be buried in the polis, but wrong in refusing any burial at all. He continues in his misguided and willful error. As the play progresses, Antigone comes to stand for the precedence of divine law over human defects. Sophocles touches upon the need for recognition of the law and adherence to it as a prerequisite for a tranquil state.

Sophocles' masterpieces have become classics of Western literature, and his themes have inspired generations of playwrights. Perhaps his most famous plays are *Oedipus the King* and its sequel, *Oedipus at Colonus. Oedipus the King* is the ironic story of a man doomed by the gods to kill his father and

marry his mother. Try as he might to avoid his fate, Oedipus' every action brings him closer to its fulfillment. When at last he realizes that he has carried out the decree of the gods, Oedipus blinds himself and flees into exile. In *Oedipus at Colonus* Sophocles dramatizes the last days of the broken king, whose patient suffering and uncomplaining piety win for him an exalted position, as the gods in the end honor him for his virtue. Although the interpretation of these two plays has been hotly debated, Sophocles seems to be saying that human beings should do the will of the gods, even without fully understanding it, for the gods stand for justice and order.

Euripides (ca 480–406 B.C.), the last of the three great dramatists, also explored the theme of personal conflict within the polis and sounded the depths of the individual. With him drama entered a new, and in many ways more personal, era. To Euripides the gods are far less important than human beings. Euripides viewed the soul as a place where opposing forces struggle with each other, a place where strong passions, such as hatred and jealousy, come into conflict with reason. The essence of Euripides' tragedy is the flawed character — the men and women who bring disaster on themselves and their loved ones because their passions master reason. Although Euripides' plays were not as popular in his own lifetime as were those of Aeschylus and Sophocles, Euripides was a dramatist of genius, and his work had a significant impact on Roman drama.

Writers of comedy treated the affairs of the polis in a bawdy and often coarse fashion. Nevertheless, their plays too were performed at religious festivals. The comic playwrights dealt primarily with the political affairs of the polis and the conduct of its leading politicians. The comedies of Aristophanes (ca 445–386 B.C.) are the best known. He was an ardent lover of his city and a merciless critic of cranks and quacks. He lampooned eminent generals and at times depicted them as morons. He commented snidely on Pericles, poked fun at Socrates and derided Euripides. He saved some of his best venom for Cleon, a prominent politician. It is a tribute to the Athenians that such devastating attacks could openly and freely be made on the city's leaders and foreign policy. Even during the worst days of the Peloponnesian War, Aristophanes proclaimed that peace was preferable to the ravages of war. Like Aeschylus, Sophocles, and Euripides, Aristophanes used his art to present his ideas on the right conduct of the citizen and the value of the polis.

Perhaps never were art and political life so intimately and congenially bound together as at Athens. Athenian art was the product of sincere and genuine love of the polis. It aimed at bettering the lives of the citizens and the quality of life in the state.

Daily Life in Periclean Athens

Contrasted with the rich intellectual and cultural life of Periclean Athens is the simple material life. The Athenians — and they are typical of Greeks in general — lived very happily with comparatively few material possessions. In the first place, there were very few material goods to own. The thousands of machines, tools, and gadgets considered essential for modern life had no counterpart in Athenian life. Enlightening in this respect is the inventory of Alcibiades' goods, which the Athenians confiscated after his desertion. His household possessions consisted of chests, beds, couches, tables, screens, stools, baskets, and mats. Other necessities of the Greek home included pottery, metal utensils for cooking, tools, luxury goods such as jewelry, and a few other things. These items they had to buy from craftsmen. Whatever else they needed, such as clothes and blankets, they produced at home.

The Athenian house was rather simple. Whether large or small, the typical house consisted of a series of rooms built around a central courtyard, with doors opening onto the courtyard. Many houses had bedrooms on an upper floor. Artisans and craftsmen often set aside a room to use as a shop or work area. The two principal rooms were the men's dining room and the room where the women worked wool. Other rooms included the kitchen and bathroom. By modern standards there was not much furniture. In the men's dining room were couches, a sideboard, and small tables. Cups and other pottery were often hung on the wall from pegs. Other household furnishings included items such as those confiscated from Alcibiades.

In the courtyard was the well, a small altar, and a washbasin. If the family lived in the country, the stalls of the animals faced the courtyard. The countryman kept oxen for plowing, pigs for slaughtering, sheep for wool, goats for cheese, and mules and donkeys for transportation. Even in the city chickens and perhaps a goat or two roamed the courtyard together with dogs and cats.

Cooking, done over a hearth in the house, provided welcome warmth in the winter. Baking and roasting were done in ovens. Food consisted of various grains, especially wheat and barley, as well as lentils, olives, figs, and grapes. Garlic and onion were popular garnishes, and wine was always on hand. These foods were stored at home in large jars, and with them the Greek family ate fish, chicken, and vegetables. Women ground wheat into flour at home, baked it into bread, and on special occasions made honey or sesame cakes. The Greeks used olive oil for cooking, as families still do in modern Greece. They also used it as an unguent and as fuel for lamps.

By American standards the Greeks did not eat much meat, but they did so on special occasions, such as important religious festivals. The family ate the animal sacrificed to the god and gave the god the exquisite delicacy of the thighbone wrapped in fat. The only Greeks who consistently ate meat were the Spartan warriors. They received a small portion of meat each day, together with the infamous Spartan black broth, a ghastly concoction of pork cooked in blood, vinegar, and salt. One Greek, after tasting the broth, commented that he could understand why the Spartans were so willing to die.

Most Athenians supported themselves by agriculture, but unless the family were fortunate enough to possess holdings in a plain more fertile than the rest of the land, they found it difficult to get a good crop from the soil. The plow, though wooden, sometimes had an iron share, and it was pulled by oxen. Attic farmers were free men. Hardly prosperous, they were by no means destitute. Greek farmers could usually expect yields of five bushels of wheat and ten of barley per acre for every bushel of grain sown. A bad harvest meant a lean year. In many places farmers grew more barley than wheat because of the nature of the soil. Wherever possible farmers also cultivated vines and olive trees. Wealthy landowners sold their excess produce in the urban marketplace, but many people must have consumed nearly everything they raised.

For sport both the countryman and the city dweller often hunted for rabbits, deer, or wild boar. A successful hunt supplemented the family's regular diet. Wealthy men hunted from horseback; most others hunted on foot with their dogs. Hunting was a social pastime, and several men would gather for an outing. Hunting also allowed a man to display to his fellows his bravery and prowess in the chase. If wild boar were the game, the sport could be dangerous, as Odysseus discovered when a charging boar slashed open his foot.

In the city a man might support himself by being a craftsman, a potter, bronzesmith, sailmaker, or tanner. Or he could contract with the polis to work on public buildings, such as the Parthenon and Erechtheion. Men without skills worked as paid laborers but competed with slaves for work. Slaves were paid as much for their labor as were free men.

Slavery was common in Greece, as it was throughout the ancient world. In its essentials Greek slavery resembled Mesopotamian slavery. Slaves received some protection under the law and could buy their freedom. On the other hand, masters could mistreat or neglect their slaves short of killing them, which was illegal. The worst-treated slaves were those who worked the silver mines at Laurium. These slaves lived, worked, and died under wretched conditions. Otherwise, Greek slavery was rather humane. One crusty aristocrat complained that in Athens one could not tell the slaves from the free. Most slaves in Athens served as domestics and performed light labor around the house. Nurses for children, teachers of reading and writing, and guardians for young men were often slaves. The lives of these slaves were much like those of their owners.

Other slaves were skilled workers, who could be found working on public buildings or in small workshops. Yet the importance of slavery must not be exaggerated. Apart from the slave owners who ran the Laurium mines, Athenians did not own huge gangs of slaves as did Roman owners of large estates. Slave labor competed with free labor and kept wages down, but it never replaced free labor, which was the mainstay of the Athenian economy.

The social condition of Athenian women has been the subject of much debate and little agreement. One thing, however, is certain: the status of a free woman of the citizen class was strictly protected by law. Only her children, not those of foreigners or slaves, could be citizens. Only she was in charge of the household and the family's possessions. Yet the law protected her primarily to protect her husband's interests. Raping a free woman was a lesser crime than seducing her because seduction involved the winning of her affections. In this instance the law was not concerned with the husband's feelings. Rather, it was meant to insure that a husband have no doubt about the legitimacy of his children.

Ideally, respectable women lived a secluded life in which the only men they saw were relatives. How far this ideal was actually put into practice is impossible to say. At least Athenian women seem to have enjoyed a social circle of other women of their own class. They also attended public festivals, sacrifices, and funerals. Nonetheless, prosperous and respectable women probably spent much of their time in the house. A white complexion — a sign that a woman did not have to work in the fields — was valued highly.

A woman's main functions were to raise the children, oversee the domestic slaves and hired labor, and together with her maids work wool into cloth. The women washed the wool in the courtyard and then brought it into the women's room, where the loom stood. They spun the wool into thread and wove the thread into cloth. They also dyed wool at home and decorated the cloth by weaving in colors and designs. The woman of the household either did the cooking herself or directed her maids. Poor women lived a freer life than did wealthier women. They performed manual labor in the fields or sold goods in the agora. They went about their affairs much in the way that men did.

An important factor in Athenian life, as well as in Greek life in general, was homosexuality. No one has satisfactorily explained how the Greek attitude toward homosexual love developed, or how common homosexual behavior was. Homosexuality was probably far more common among the aristocracy than among the lower classes. It is impossible to be sure simply because most of what the modern world knows of ancient Greece and Rome comes from the writings of aristocrats. Since aristocratic boys and girls were often segregated and brought up separately, the chances of homosexual relationships were very great. This style of life was impossible for the common folk because every member of the family — husband and wife, son and daughter — got out and worked. Among the poorer classes the sexes mingled freely.

Even among the aristocracy attitudes toward homosexuality were complex and sometimes conflicting. Most people saw homosexual love affairs among the young as a development toward a mature heterosexual life. Yet in Athens some aristocrats held homosexual practices up to ridicule. Comic writers habitually made fun of "boy-crazy men" and "effeminate youths." Others, such as the Spartans and the philosopher Plato, saw in homosexual relationships the opportunity for older men to train their juniors in practical wisdom. For them, the sexual element was supposed to give way to the benefits of education. In Sparta, just as in Sappho's Lesbos, noble women loved girls for the same reasons. Warrior-aristocracies generally emphasized the physical side of the relationship in the belief that warriors who were also lovers would fight all the harder to impress each other. They would also be less likely to desert their lovers in battle.

Despite the emphasis on the intellectual and the educational, homosexual love affairs always contained a sexual element. Men and boys, women and girls enjoyed each other physically; they took their lovers to bed, fondled them, and reached orgasm.

What effect did homosexual love affairs have on the Greeks? An American psychologist has concluded that the "Greek adolescent . . . ended up as a non-neurotic, completely (or predominantly) heterosexual adult."[25] Most of Sappho's young lovers went on to marry and raise families. They never regretted the homosexual loves of their past or thought them unusual. Their previous relationships did not prevent them from devoting their primary affection to their new mates. For many Greeks, homosexuality was a normal practice, and they treated it as straightforwardly and honestly as they did heterosexual love and other aspects of life.

Despite some modern doubts to the contrary, relations between Athenian husbands and wives were probably close and normal. The presence of female slaves in the home could be a source of trouble; men were always free to resort to prostitutes; and some men and women engaged in homosexual love affairs. But basically husbands and wives depended on each other for mutual love and support. The wife's position and status in the household were guaranteed by her dowry, which came from her father and which was her property throughout her married life. If the wife felt that her marriage was intolerable, she could divorce her husband far more easily than could a Mesopotamian wife.

To judge by the evidence of funerary reliefs, Athenian wives and husbands got along as well as people have always done. One scholar has noted that funerary reliefs show the sorrow of the entire household — husband, children, and slaves — at the death of a wife. The following is an epitaph of the fourth or third century B.C.:

Chaerestrate lies in this tomb. When she was alive her husband loved her. When she died he lamented.[26]

In short, there seems to have been nothing radically odd about the typical Athenian family.

The Flowering of Philosophy

The myths and epics of the Mesopotamians are evidence that speculation about the origin of the universe and of mankind did not begin with the Greeks. The signal achievement of the Greeks, however, was their willingness to treat these topics in rational rather than mythological terms. Although the full flowering of Greek philosophy occurred only in the Classical Period, this entire development began in the Lyric Age, when Ionian thinkers began to ask what the universe was made of. These men are usually called the Pre-Socratics, for their work preceded the philosophical revolution begun by the Athenian Socrates. The Pre-Socratics were born observers, even though they rarely experimented. They took individual facts and wove them into general theories. They believed that despite appearances the universe was actually simple and subject to natural laws. Drawing upon their observations, they speculated about the basic building blocks of the universe.

The first of the Pre-Socratics was Thales (ca 600 B.C.). He learned mathematics and astronomy from the Babylonians and geometry from the Egyptians. Yet there was an immense and fundamental difference between Near Eastern thought and the philosophy of Thales. The Near Eastern peoples considered such events as eclipses to be evil omens. Thales considered them natural phenomena that could be explained in natural terms. He believed that the basic element of the universe is water. Even though he was wrong, the way in which he had asked the question was important: it was the beginning of the scientific method.

Thales' follower Anaximander (first half of the sixth century B.C.) continued his work. Anaximander was the first to use general concepts, which are essential to abstract thought. One of the most brilliant of the Pre-Socratics, a man of striking originality, Anaximander devised the theory that the basic element of the universe is "the boundless" or "endless"—something infinite and indestructible. In his view, the earth floats in a void, held in balance because of its distance from everything else in the universe.

Anaximander even concluded that mankind had evolved naturally from lower organisms: "In water the first animals arose covered with spiny skin, and with the lapse of time some crawled onto dry land and breaking off their skins in a short time they survived."[27] This, in crude form, corresponds to Darwin's theory of the evolution of the species.

Another Ionian, Heraclitus (ca 500 B.C.) stated that the primal element is fire. He also declared that the world had neither beginning nor end: "This world, the world of all things, neither any god nor man made, but it always was and it is and it will be: an everlasting fire, measures kindling and measures going out."[28] Although the universe in his view was eternal, it changed constantly.

An outgrowth of this line of speculation was the theory of Democritus (mid-fifth century B.C.) that the universe is made of invisible, indestructible atoms. The culmination of Pre-Socratic thought was the theory that four simple substances make up the universe: fire, air, earth, and water.

With this impressive heritage behind them, the philosophers of the Classical Period reached into new areas of speculation. In part this development was due to the work of Hippocrates (second half of the fifth century B.C.), the father of medicine.

Like Thales, Hippocrates sought natural explanations for natural phenomena. He based his opinions on empirical knowledge, not on religion or magic. He taught that natural means could be employed to fight disease. In his treatise *On Airs, Waters, and Places,* he noted the influence of climate and environment on health. He and his followers put forth a theory that would prevail in medical circles until the eighteenth century. He said that the human body contained four humors, or fluids: blood, phlegm, black bile, and yellow bile. In a healthy body the four humors are in perfect balance; too much or too little of any one humor causes illness. Hippocrates also broke away from the mainstream of Ionian speculation. He declared that medicine was a separate craft — just as ironworking was a craft — and that it had its own principles. Yet Hippocrates and his pupils shared the Ionian belief that they were dealing with phenomena that could be explained purely in natural terms.

In the separation of natural science and philosophy, upon which Hippocrates insisted, the sophists, who traveled the Greek world teaching wealthy young men, also played an important part. Despite differences of opinion on philosophical matters, the sophists all agreed that human beings were the proper subject of study. They also believed that excellence could be taught, and they used philosophy and rhetoric to prepare young men for life in the polis. The sophists laid great emphasis on the meaning of words and on logic. They criticized traditional beliefs, religion, rituals, and myth, and they even questioned the laws of the polis. In essence they argued that nothing is absolute, and that everything — even the customs and constitution of the state — is relative. Hence, many Greeks of more traditional inclination considered them wanton and harmful, men who were interested in "making the worse seem the better cause."

One of those whom his contemporaries thought a sophist was Socrates (ca 470–399 B.C.), who sprang from the class of small artisans. Socrates spent his life in investigation and in definition. Not, strictly speaking, a sophist, because he never formally taught or collected fees from anyone, Socrates shared the sophists' belief that human beings and their environment are essential areas of philosophical inquiry. Like the sophists, Socrates thought that excellence could be learned and passed on to others. His approach when posing ethical questions and defining concepts was to start with a general topic or problem and to narrow the matter to its essentials. He did so by continuous questioning, a running dialogue. Never did he lecture.

Socrates thought that by constantly pursuing excellence, an essential part of which was knowledge, human beings could approach the supreme good and thus find true happiness. Yet, in 399 B.C., Socrates himself was brought to trial, convicted, and executed on charges of corrupting the youth of the city and introducing new gods.

Socrates' student Plato (427–347 B.C.) carried on his master's search for truth. Unlike Socrates, Plato wrote down his thoughts and theories and founded a philosophical school, the Academy. Plato developed the theory that all visible, tangible things are unreal and temporary. They are instead only copies of "forms" or "ideas" that are constant and indestructible. Only the mind — not the senses — can perceive the eternal forms. In Plato's view the highest form is the idea of good.

In *The Republic* Plato applied his theory of forms to politics in order to determine the ideal polis. His perfect polis is utopian; it aims at providing the greatest good and happiness to all its members. Plato thought that the ideal polis could exist only when its rulers were philosophers. He divided society into rulers, guardians of the polis, and workers. The role of people in each category is decided by the education, wisdom, and ability of the individual. In Plato's republic men and women are equal to one another, and women can become rulers. The utopian polis is a balance, with each individual doing what he or she can to support the state and with each receiving from the state his or her just due.

In a later work, *The Laws,* Plato discarded the ideal polis of *The Republic* in favor of a second best state. The polis of *The Laws* is grimly reminiscent of the modern dictatorship. At its head is a young tyrant, who is just and good. He meets with a council that sits only at night, and together they maintain the spirit of the laws. Nearly everything about this state is coercive; the free will of the citizens counts for little. The laws take care of every aspect of life; their sole purpose is to make people happy.

Aristotle (384–322 B.C.) carried on the philosophical tradition of Socrates and Plato. A student of Plato, Aristotle went far beyond his teacher in his efforts to understand the universe. The very range of Aristotle's thought is staggering. Everything within human experience was fit subject for his inquiry. In his *Politics* Aristotle followed Plato's example by writing about the ideal polis. Yet Aristotle approached the question more realistically than Plato, and he criticized *The Republic* and *The Laws* on many points. In the *Politics,* as elsewhere in his thought, Aristotle stressed moderation and concluded that the balance of his ideal state depended on people of talent and education who could avoid extremes.

Aristotle was not content to examine old questions. Instead, he opened up whole new fields of inquiry. He tried to understand the changes of nature—what caused them and where they led. In the *Physics* and *Metaphysics* he evolved a theory of nature in which he developed the notions of matter, form, and motion. He attempted to bridge the gap between abstract truth and concrete perception that Plato had created.

Aristotle took up the thread of Ionian speculation in his book *On the Heaven.* He proposed a theory of cosmology in which he added ether to air, fire, water, and earth as a building block of the universe. He concluded that the universe revolved and that it was spherical and eternal. He wrongly thought that the earth is the center of the universe, with the stars and other planets revolving around it. The Hellenistic scientist Aristarchus of Samos later realized that the earth revolves around the sun, but Aristotle's view was accepted until the time of the astronomer Nicolaus Copernicus (A.D. 1473–1543).

Aristotle's other scientific interests included zoology. In several works he describes various animals and includes observations on animal habits, animal anatomy, and how animals move. He also explored the process of reproduction. He intended to examine the entire animal kingdom and assigned the world of plants to his follower Theophrastus (see Chapter 3).

Not content with examining the physical world, Aristotle dealt also with Greek literature. He discussed Greek drama and comedy in the *Poetics,* in which he investigated their origins and nature. As in his study of the polis, Aristotle reduced drama to its essentials and sought to explain its function in and impact on human perception.

Aristotle possesed one of the keenest and most curious philosophical minds of Western civilization. While he took up old topics, such as those explored by the Pre-Socratics, he also created whole new areas of study. In short, he tried to learn everything possible about the universe and everything in it. He did so in the belief that all knowledge could be synthesized to produce a simple explanation of the universe and of humanity.

The Final Act
(403–338 B.C.)

The end of the Peloponnesian War punctuated a century of nearly constant warfare that lasted from 431 to 338 B.C. With Athens humbled, Sparta strove for empire over the Greeks. The arrogance and imperialism of the Spartans turned their former allies against them. Even with Persian help Sparta could not maintain its hold on Greece. In 371 B.C., the Spartans met their match on the plain of Leuctra in Boeotia. A Theban army under the command of

COINS OF PHILIP II. Philip of Macedonia ordered these designs for his coins to publicize his wealth and honors. The gold coin above depicts Philip's prize chariot team, while the coin below portrays the horse and rider which won for Philip the race at the Olympic Games of 356 B.C. (Courtesy, World Heritage Museum, Photos: Caroline Buckler)

Epaminondas, one of Greece's most brilliant generals, destroyed the flower of the Spartan army on one summer day. The victory of Leuctra left Thebes the most powerful state in Greece. Under Epaminondas the Thebans destroyed Sparta as a first-rate power, but they were unable to bring peace to Greece. In 362 B.C., Epaminondas was killed in battle, and a period of stalemate set in. The Greek states were virtually exhausted.

The man who turned this situation to his own advantage was Philip II, king of Macedonia (359–336 B.C.). Throughout most of Greek history Macedonia had been a backward and disunited kingdom, but the genius, courage, and drive of Philip turned it into a major power. Philip's ambition was not limited to Macedonia. By clever use of his wealth and his superb army he won control of the northern Aegean and awakened the fear of Athens, which had recovered from the Peloponnesian War. In Athens, Demosthenes, a great patriot and a fine orator, warned the Athenians against Philip:

Most of all there is this to fear. This cunning and terrible man makes use of his accomplishments, yielding on points when he must, threatening (and he certainly appears to mean it) on others. He slanders us and our inactivity. He fosters and takes for himself anything of value.[29]

Others too saw in Philip a threat. A comic playwright depicted one of Philip's ambassadors warning the Athenians:

*Do you know that your battle will be with men
Who dine on sharpened swords,
And gulp burning firebrands for wine?
Then immediately after dinner the slave
Brings us dessert—Cretan arrows
Or pieces of broken spears.
We have shields and breastplates for
Cushions and at our feet slings and arrows,
And we are crowned with catapults.*[30]

Finally, the Athenians joined forces with Thebes to stop Philip. In 338 B.C., the combined Theban-Athenian army met Philip's veterans at the Boeotian city of Chaeronea. Philip's army won a hard-fought victory: he had conquered Greece and put an end to Greek freedom. Because the Greeks could not put aside their quarrels, they fell to an invader.

NOTES

1. K. J. Beloch, *Griechische Geschichte,* K. J. Trübner, Strasbourg, 1912, vol. 1, pt. 1, p. 49.

2. H. D. F. Kitto, *The Greeks,* Penguin Books, Baltimore, 1951, p. 11.

3. Herodotus, *The Histories* 2.53.

4. Hesiod, *Works and Days* 263–266.

5. Ibid., 511–514.

6. F. Lasserre, *Archiloque,* Société d'Edition "Les Belles Lettres," Paris, 1958, frag. 9, p. 4.

7. W. Barnstable, *Sappho,* Anchor Books, Garden City, N.Y., 1965, frag. 24, p. 22.

8. Ibid., frag. 132, p. 106.

9. Ibid., frag. 61, p. 52.

10. Ibid., frag. 58, p. 50.

11. Ibid., frag. 23, p. 20.

12. J. M. Edmonds, *Greek Elegy and Iambus,* Cambridge, Mass., Harvard University Press, 1931, 1.70, frag. 10.

13. Ibid., frag. 11, p. 72.

14. Plutarch, *Moralia* 241F.

15. Edmonds, *Greek Elegy and Iambus,* frag. 4, p. 118.

16. R. Meiggs and D. Lewis, *A Selection of Greek Historical Inscriptions,* Clarendon Press, Oxford, 1969, no. 52, lines 21–32.

17. Ibid., no. 40, lines 9–11.

18. Thucydides, *History of the Peloponnesian War* 1.23.

19. Ibid.

20. Herodotus, *The Histories* 1.1.

21. Ibid., 7.102.

22. Thucydides, *The Peloponnesian War* 1.1.

23. Plutarch, *Life of Pericles* 13.5.

24. Mark Twain, *The Innocents Abroad,* Signet Classics, New York, 1966, p. 249.

25. G. Devereux, "Greek Pseudo-Homosexuality and the 'Greek Miracle,'" *Symbolae Osloenses* (1968): 70.

26. S. B. Pomeroy, *Goddesses, Whores, Wives and Slaves,* Schocken, New York, 1975, p. 92.

27. E. Diels and W. Krantz, *Fragmente der Vorsokratiker,* Weidmannsche Verlagsbuchhandlung, Berlin, 8th ed., 1960, Anaximander frag. A30.

28. Ibid., Heraclitus frag. B30.

29. Demosthenes, *First Olynthiac* 3.

30. J. M. Edmonds, *The Fragments of Attic Comedy,* E. J. Brill, Leiden, 2. 366–369, Mnesimachos frag. 7.

SUGGESTED READING

Translations of the most important writings of the Greeks and Romans can be found in the volumes of the Loeb Classical Library, published by Harvard University Press. Paperback editions of the major Greek and Latin authors are available in the Penguin Classics. Recent translations of documents include those by N. Lewis, *Greek Historical Documents: The Fifth Century B.C.** (1971); J. Wickersham and G. Verbrugghe, *Greek Historical Documents: The Fourth Century B.C.** (1973); and C. Fornara, *Translated Documents of Greece and Rome,* vol. 1: *Archaic Times to the End of the Peloponnesian War** (1977).

Among the many general treatments of Greek history, H. D. F. Kitto, *The Greeks** (1951), is a delightful introduction. V. Ehrenberg in two works, *From Solon to Socrates** (2nd., ed., 1973) and *The Greek State** (1960), covers major areas of Greek history.

For early Greece the most recent treatments include R. J. Hopper, *The Early Greeks* (1976), and L. H. Jeffery, *Archaic Greece* (1976). No finer introduction to the Lyric Age can be found than A. R. Burn's *The Lyric Age** (1960) and its sequel, *Persia and the Greeks** (1962). A good recent survey of work on Sparta is P. Oliva, *Sparta and Her Social Problems* (1971). Sound discussions of Athenian democracy are available in A. H. M. Jones, *Athenian Democracy* (1957), and C. Hignett, *History of the Athenian Constitution* (1952).

A. J. Graham, *Colony and Mother City in Ancient Greece* (1964), gives a good account of Greek colonization. Athens in the fifth century and the outbreak of the Peloponnesian War are covered in G. E. M. de Ste Croix, *The Origins of the Peloponnesian War* (1972), and R. Meiggs, *The Athenian Empire* (1972).

Daily life, the family, women, and homosexuality receive treatment in Pomeroy's book cited in the Notes; T. B. L. Webster, *Life in Classical Greece** (1969); M. and C. H. B. Quennell, *Everyday Things in Ancient Greece** (1954); and a special issue of the journal *Arethusa* 6 (1973).

For Greek literature, culture, and science, see A. Lesky, *A History of Greek Literature* (English trans., 1963): W. Jaeger, *Paideia,** 3 vols., (English trans., 1944–1945); H. C. Baldry, *The Greek Tragic Theater** (1971); J. Burnet, *Early Greek Philosophy* (4th ed., 1930) and *Greek Philosophy, Thales to Plato* (1914); M. Clagett, *Greek Science in Antiquity* (1971); and E. R. Dodds, *The Greeks and the Irrational** (1951).

The classic treatment of Greek architecture is W. B. Dinsmoor, *The Architecture of the Ancient Greeks* (3rd ed., 1950). More recent (and perhaps more readable) is A. W. Lawrence, *Greek Architecture* (3rd ed., 1973). J. Boardman, *Greek Art** (rev. ed., 1973), is both perceptive and sound, as is J. J. Pollitt, *Art and Experience in Classical Greece** (1972).

J. Pinsent, *Greek Mythology* (1969), is a handy introduction. M. P. Nilsson, *Cults, Myths, Oracles and Politics in Ancient Greece* (1951), examines Greek religion and myth in the contemporary context. See also G. S. Kirk, *The Nature of Greek Myths** (1974).

*Available in paperback.

Chapter 3

HELLENISTIC DIFFUSION

*I*n 336 B.C., *Philip of Macedon, the conqueror of Greece,* fell victim to an assassin's dagger. Philip's twenty-year-old son, known to history as Alexander the Great (336–323 B.C.) assumed the Macedonian throne. This young man, one of the most remarkable personalities of Western civilization, was to have a profound impact on history. "For in twelve years having conquered not a small part of Europe and nearly all of Asia, he was justly famous and his glory was equal to that of the heroes of old and of the demigods."[1] Although the ancient world marveled at Alexander's many victories, modern historians, such as U. Wilcken, are more deeply struck by other features of his achievement:

The permanent result of his life, however, was not the empire which he won by hard fighting, but the development of Greek civilisation into a civilisation which was world-wide. It is in this way that his influence has affected the history of mankind even down to our own time.[2]

By overthrowing the Persian empire and by spreading Hellenism — Greek culture, language, thought, and the Greek way of life — as far as India, Alexander was instrumental in creating a new period, a period traditionally called Hellenistic to distinguish it from the Hellenic. As a result of Alexander's exploits, the individualistic and energetic culture of the Greeks came into intimate contact with the far older and venerable culture of the Near East.

What did the spread of Hellenism mean to the Greeks and the peoples of the Near East? What did the meeting of West and East hold for the development of philosophy, religion, science, medicine, and economics? These are the questions this chapter will explore.

ALEXANDER AND THE GREAT CRUSADE

In 336 B.C., Alexander inherited not only Philip's crown but also his policies. After his victory at Chaeronea, Philip had organized the states of Greece into a huge league under his leadership, and he had announced to the Greeks his plan to lead them and his Macedonians against the Persian Empire. Fully intending to carry out Philip's designs, Alexander proclaimed to the Greek world that the invasion of Persia was to be a great crusade, a mighty act of revenge for the Persian invasion of Greece in 480 B.C.

Despite his youth, Alexander was well prepared to lead the attack. Philip had groomed his son to become king, and therefore had given him the best education possible. In 343 B.C., Philip invited the philosopher Aristotle to tutor his son. From Aristotle Alexander learned to appreciate Greek culture and literature, and the teachings of the great philosopher left a lasting mark on him. Alexander must have profited from Aristotle's practical knowledge, but he never accepted Aristotle's political theories. At the age of sixteen Alexander became regent of Macedonia, and two years later at the battle of Chaeronea he took his place in the battle in which the Greeks were defeated. By 336 B.C., Alexander had both the theoretical and the practical knowledge to rule peoples and lead armies.

In 334 B.C., Alexander led an army of Macedonians and Greeks into Asia Minor. He had with him a staff of philosophers and poets, scientists whose job was to map the country and to study strange animals and plants, and the historian Callisthenes, who was to write an account of the campaign. Alexander planned not only to conquer the Persians but to lead an expedition of discovery to open up the East to Greek knowledge.

In the next three years Alexander won three major battles: the Granicus River, Issus, and Gaugamela (see Map 3.1), which stand almost as road

COIN OF ALEXANDER. The head on this coin is that of the demigod Heracles, whom Alexander admired and imitated. Alexander claimed that he was descended from Heracles, and on several occasions he even dressed like Heracles. (Courtesy, World Heritage Museum. Photo: Caroline Buckler)

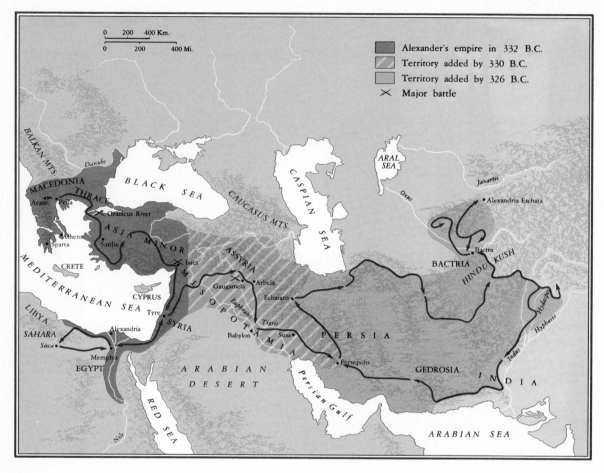

MAP 3.1   ALEXANDER'S CONQUEST OF THE PERSIAN EMPIRE

signs marking his march to the East. After his victory at Gaugamela in 331 B.C., Alexander captured the principal Persian capital of Persepolis, where he performed a symbolic act of retribution by burning the buildings of Xerses, the invader of Greece. In 330 B.C., he took Ecbatana, the last Persian capital, and he pursued the Persian king to his death.

The Persian Empire had fallen, and the war of revenge was over, but Alexander had no intention of stopping. He dismissed his Greek troops, but permitted many of them to serve on as mercenaries. Alexander then began his personal odyssey. With his Macedonian soldiers and Greek mercenaries he set out to conquer the rest of Asia. He plunged

ALEXANDER AT THE BATTLE OF ISSOS. At the left, Alexander the Great, bareheaded and wearing a breastplate, charges King Darius, who is standing in a chariot. This moment marks the turning point of the battle, as Darius turns to flee from the attack. (Museo Nazionale, Naples. Alinari/Scala)

deeper into the East, into lands completely unknown to the Greek world. Alexander's way was marked by bitter fighting and bloodshed. It took four more years to conquer Bactria and the easternmost parts of the now defunct Persian Empire, but still Alexander was determined to march on.

In 326 B.C., he crossed the Indus River and entered India. There too he saw hard fighting, but finally at the Hyphasis River his troops refused to go farther. Alexander was enraged by the mutiny, for he believed that he was near the end of the world. Nonetheless, the army stood firm, and Alexander had to relent. Still eager to explore the limits of the world, Alexander turned south to the Indian

Ocean. Even though the tribes in the area did not oppose him, he waged a bloody, ruthless, and unnecessary war against them. After reaching the Indian Ocean and then turning west, he led his army through the grim Gedrosian Desert, apparently to punish his troops for their mutiny at the Hyphasis. The army suffered fearfully, and many men died along the way, but in 324 B.C. Alexander reached Susa. The great crusade was over.

ALEXANDER'S LEGACY

The figure of Alexander loomed over the Hellenistic period and still casts its shadow today. Of Alexander the man history knows little: he too quickly became a figure of legend, a figure larger than life. Of Alexander's plans and intentions history likewise knows little. Although some scholars have seen him as a high-minded philosopher, his bloody and savage campaigns in the East seem rather the work of a ruthless and callous conqueror. Yet for the Hellenistic period and for Western civilization in general what Alexander intended was less important than what he actually did.

Alexander was instrumental in changing the face of politics in the eastern Mediterranean. His campaign swept away the Persian Empire, which had ruled the East for over two hundred years. In its place he established a Macedonian monarchy. More important in the long run was his foundation of cities and military colonies, for he scattered Greeks and Macedonians throughout the East. Thus, the practical result of his campaign was to open the East to the tide of Hellenism.

The Political Legacy

In 323 B.C., Alexander the Great died at the age of thirty-two. The main question at his death was whether his vast empire could be held together. The answer became obvious immediately (see Map 3.2). Within a week of Alexander's death began a round of fighting that would continue for forty years. No single Macedonian general was able to replace Alexander as emperor of his domain. By 275 B.C., three of Alexander's officers had divided it into large monarchies. Antigonus Gonatas became king of Macedonia and established the Antigonid dynasty, which ruled until the Roman conquest in 168 B.C. Ptolemy Lagus made himself king of Egypt, and his descendants, the Ptolemies, assumed the powers and the position of the pharaohs. Seleucus, founder of the Seleucid dynasty, carved out a kingdom that stretched from the coast of Asia Minor to India. In 263 B.C., Eumenes, the Greek ruler of Pergamum, a city in western Asia Minor, won his independence from the Seleucids and created the Pergamene monarchy.

The political face of Greece itself changed during the Hellenistic period. The day of the polis was over, and in its place arose leagues of city-states. The two most powerful and most extensive were the Aetolian League in western and central Greece, and the Achaean League in the Peloponnesus. Once powerful city-states like Athens and Sparta sank to the level of third-rate powers.

The political history of the Hellenistic period was dominated by the great monarchies and the Greek leagues. The political fragmentation and the incessant warfare that marked the Hellenic period continued on an even wider and larger scale during the Hellenistic period. Never did the Hellenistic world achieve political stability or lasting peace. Hellenistic kings never forgot the vision of Alexander's empire, spanning Europe and Asia, secure under the rule of one man. Try as they did, they were never able to re-create it. In this respect, Alexander's legacy fell not to his generals but to the Romans, who consolidated the East and gave it the *pax Romana,* the Roman peace.

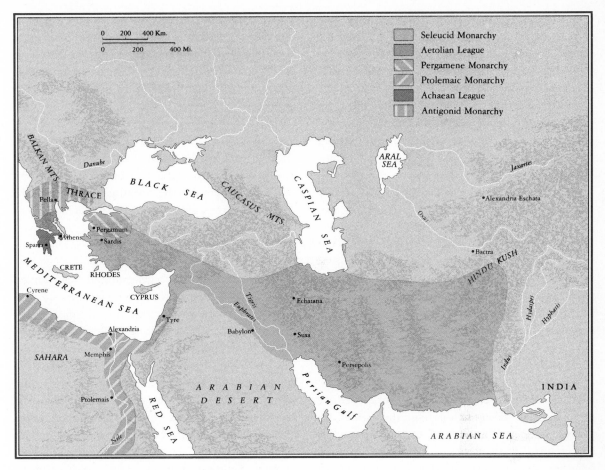

MAP 3.2   THE HELLENISTIC STATES AFTER ALEXANDER'S DEATH

The Cultural Legacy

As Alexander waded ever deeper into the East, distance alone presented him with a serious problem: how was he to retain contact with the Greek world behind him? Communications with Greece and Macedonia were vital, for he drew supplies and reinforcements from the West. He had to be sure that he was never cut off and stranded far away from the Mediterranean world. His solution was to plant cities and military colonies in strategic places in order to secure his communications with the Mediterranean. In his settlements Alexander left Greek mercenaries and Macedonian veterans no longer up to active campaigning. Besides keeping the road open to the West, these settlements dominated the countryside around them.

Their military significance aside, Alexander's cities and colonies became powerful factors in the spread of Hellenism throughout the East. Plutarch described Alexander's achievement in glowing terms: "Having founded over 70 cities among barbarian peoples and having planted Greek magistracies in Asia, Alexander overcame its wild and savage way of life."[3] Alexander had indeed opened the East to an enormous wave of immigration, and his successors continued his policy by inviting Greek colonists to settle in their realms. For seventy-five years after Alexander's death, Greek immigrants poured into the East, until at least 250 new Hellenistic colonies were established. The Mediterranean world had seen no comparable movement of peoples since the days of Archilochus, when wave after wave of Greeks had turned the Mediterranean basin into a Greek-speaking region.

The overall result of Alexander's foundations and those of his successors was the spread of Hellenism as far east as India. Throughout the Hellenistic period Greeks and Easterners became familiar with and adapted themselves to each other's customs, religions, and ways of life. Although Greek culture did not completely conquer the East, it at least gave the East a vehicle of expression that linked it to the West. Hellenism became a common bond among the East, peninsular Greece, and the western Mediterranean. This cultural unity was to be of supreme importance to Rome, itself heavily influenced by Hellenism, for Rome eventually gave political unity to a world already united by Hellenistic culture.

THE SPREAD OF HELLENISM

When the Greeks and Macedonians entered Asia Minor, Egypt, and the farther East, they encountered civilizations older than their own. In some ways the Eastern cultures were more advanced than the Greek, in others less so. Thus, this third great tide of Greek immigration differed from preceding waves, for the earlier waves had spread over land that was uninhabited or inhabited by less-developed peoples.

What did the Hellenistic monarchies give Greek immigrants both politically and materially? More broadly, how did Hellenism, on the one hand, and the cultures of the East, on the other, affect one another? What did the meeting of the East and West entail for the history of the world?

Cities and Kingdoms

Although Alexander's generals had created huge kingdoms, the concept of monarchy never replaced the ideal of the polis. Consequently, the monarchies never won the deep, emotional loyalty that the Greeks once felt for the polis. Hellenistic kings needed large numbers of Greeks to run their kingdoms. Otherwise, royal business would come to a halt, and the conquerors would soon be swallowed up by the far more numerous conquered population. Obviously, then, the kings had to encourage Greeks to immigrate and build new homes. To the Greeks monarchy was something from the heroic past, something found in Homer's *Iliad* but not in daily life. The Hellenistic kings were confronted with the problem of how to make life in the new monarchies nearly identical to the traditional Greek way of life. Since Greek civilization was urban, the kings continued Alexander's policy of establishing cities throughout their kingdoms in order to entice Greeks to immigrate. Yet the very creation of these cities posed a serious problem, which the Hellenistic kings failed to solve.

To the Greeks civilized life was impossible without the polis, which meant far more than merely "city." The Greek polis was by definition sovereign, an independent, autonomous state run by its citizens free from any outside power or restraint. Hellenistic kings, however, refused to grant sovereignty to their cities. In effect, kings willingly built cities, but they refused to build a polis. Instead, they attempted a compromise that ultimately failed.

Hellenistic monarchs gave to their cities all the external trappings of a polis. Each had an assembly of citizens, a council to prepare legislation, and a board of magistrates to conduct the political business of the city. Yet these communities, similar to the Greek city-state though they might be, could not engage in diplomatic dealings, make treaties, pursue their own foreign policy, or wage their own wars. None could govern its own affairs without interference from the king, who, even if he stood in the background, was the real sovereign. In the eyes of the king the cities were important parts of the kingdom, but the welfare of the kingdom as a whole came first. The cities had to follow royal orders, and the king often placed his own officials in the cities to see that his decrees were carried out.

A new Hellenistic city differed from a Greek polis in other ways as well. The Greek polis had enjoyed political and social unity even though it was normally composed of citizens, slaves, and resident aliens. The polis had one law and one set of customs. In the Hellenistic city the Greeks formed an elite citizen class. The natives and non-Greek foreigners who lived in Hellenistic cities usually possessed lesser rights than those of the Greeks and often had their own law. In some instances the disparity spurred natives to assimilate Greek culture in order to rise both politically and socially. In other instances, some peoples, such as the Jews, firmly resisted the essence of Hellenism. The Hellenistic city was not homogeneous, and it could not spark the intensity of life that marked the polis.

In many respects, the Hellenistic city resembled the modern city. It was a cultural center with theaters, temples, and libraries. It was the seat of learning, the home of poets, writers, scholars, teachers, and artists. It was the place where people could find amusement. The Hellenistic city was also an economic center that provided a ready market for the grain and produce raised in the surrounding countryside. The city was an emporium, the scene of trade and manufacturing. In short, the importance of the Hellenistic city was primarily cultural and economic.

There were no constitutional links between the city and the king. The city was simply his possession. It and its citizens had no voice in how the kingdom was run. The city had no rights except for those the king granted, and even these he could summarily take away. Ambassadors from the city could entreat the king for favors and petition him on such matters as taxes, boundary disputes, and legal cases. But the city had no right to advise the king on royal policy, and it enjoyed no political function within the kingdom.

Hellenistic kings tried to make the kingdom the political unit toward which citizens directed their allegiance. If the king could fix solidly the frontiers of his kingdom, he could give it a geographical identity. He could hope that his subjects would then place their primary loyalty with the kingdom rather than with individual cities. However, the efforts of the kings to fix their borders led only to sustained warfare. Once Alexander's successors began to divide up his empire, they carved out kingdoms for themselves by force. Their boundaries were determined by their military power, and rule by force became the chief political principle of the Hellenistic world.

Border wars were frequent and exhausting. The Seleucids and the Ptolemies, for instance, waged five wars for the possession of southern Syria. Other kings refused to acknowledge any boundaries at all. These men followed the example of Alexander and waged wars to reunify his empire under their own authority. By the third century B.C., a weary balance of power was reached, but only as the result of stalemate. It was not maintained by any political principle.

The Hellenistic kings failed to create in their kingdoms a political unit to replace the polis. Even the Hellenistic city, despite its beauty and its Hellenic trappings, failed to win the devotion and love that the Greeks had readily and enthusiastically given the polis. Nor did the Hellenistic kings ever give the Greeks anything else to which to attach their political loyalty.

The Greeks and the Opening of the East

If the Hellenistic kings failed to give the Greeks anything politically, they nonetheless succeeded in giving them unequaled economic and social opportunities. The ruling dynasties of the Hellenistic world were Macedonian, and Greeks filled all important political, military, and diplomatic positions. These people constituted an upper class that sustained Hellenism in the barbarian East. Besides building Greek cities Hellenistic kings offered the Greeks land and money as a lure to further immigration.

The more splendid, prestigious, and famous the kingdom was, the easier it was to attract settlers. Each kingdom strove to be more philhellenic — more Greek-like and more appreciative of Greek culture — than the others. Each claimed the ability to provide Greeks with the necessities of Greek life. The burden of these policies fell upon the native population of the various kingdoms. The Easterners paid for these enticements through heavy taxation.

The opening of the East provided the Greeks with the possibility of well-paying jobs and economic success. The Hellenistic monarchy, unlike the Greek polis, did not depend solely on its citizens to fulfill its political needs. Newly arrived, ambitious, and talented Greeks could expect to rise quickly within the governmental bureaucracy. Since these administrators were appointed by the king, they did not have to stand for election each year, as had many of the officials of a Greek polis. They held their jobs year after year, and they had ample time to evolve new administrative techniques. Naturally, they became more efficient than the amateur officials common in the Greek city-states of the Hellenic period. Thus, the needs of the Hellenistic monarchy and the opportunities it offered gave rise to a professional corps of Greek administrators.

Greeks and Macedonians also found ready employment in the armies and navies of the Hellenistic monarchies. Alexander had proved that the Greco-Macedonian style of warfare was far superior to that of the Easterners, and Alexander's successors, themselves experienced officers, realized the importance of trained Greek and Macedonian soldiers. Moreover, Hellenistic kings were extremely reluctant to arm the native population or to allow them to serve in the army, simply because they feared military rebellions among their conquered subjects. The result of this situation was the emergence of professional armies and navies consisting entirely of Greeks and Macedonians.

Greeks were able to dominate other professions as well. Architects, engineers, and skilled craftsmen found their services in great demand because of the building policies of the Hellenistic monarchs. If Hellenistic kingdoms were to have Greek cities,

THE CITADEL OF PERGAMUM.   The shape of Hellenistic cities is obvious in this model of the citadel of Pergamum. The citadel, which is surrounded by a wall, was filled with temples to various gods, palaces, military buildings, and a magnificent theater. The kings of Pergamum used their city to proclaim to the world that they too were Greeks and that their city was a Greek polis. (Staatliche Museen zu Berlin)

those cities needed Greek buildings — temples, porticoes, gymnasia, theaters, fountains, and houses. Architects and engineers were sometimes commissioned to design and build whole cities, which they laid out in regular checkerboard fashion and filled with typical Greek buildings. A truly enormous wave of construction took place during the Hellenistic period. In order to be really philhellenic the kingdoms and their cities also needed Greek writers and artists to create Greek literature, art, and culture on Asian soil.

Despite the opportunities they offered, the Hellenistic monarchies were hampered by their artificial origins. Their failure to win the political loyalty of their Greek subjects and their policy of wooing Greeks with lucrative positions encouraged a feeling of uprootedness and individualism among Greek immigrants. Once a Greek had left home to take service with, for instance, the army or the bureaucracy of the Ptolemies, he had no incentive beyond his pay or the comforts of life in Egypt to keep him there. If the Seleucid king offered him more money or a promotion, he might well accept it and take his talents to Asia Minor. Why not? In the realm of the Seleucids he, a Greek, would find the same sort of life and environment that the kingdom of the Ptolemies had provided for him. Thus, professional Greek soldiers and administrators were highly mobile and prone to look to their own interests, not to those of the kingdom they joined.

Further, the Hellenistic monarchies could not keep recruiting Greeks forever in spite of their wealth and their willingness to spend lavishly to attract and keep the Greeks coming. As long as Greeks continued to replenish their professional ranks, the kingdoms remained strong. In the process they drew an immense amount of talent from the Greek peninsula, draining the health and vitality of the Greek homeland. In time, however, the great surge of immigration slowed greatly. Even then the Hellenistic monarchs were reluctant to recruit Easterners to fill posts normally held by Greeks. The result was at first the stagnation of the Hellenistic world and finally, after 202 B.C., collapse in the face of the young and vigorous Roman Republic.

Greeks and Easterners

Even though the Greeks in the East were a minority, and Hellenistic cities were islands of Greek culture in an Eastern sea, Hellenism thrived in the Near East. Hellenistic monarchies were remarkably successful in at least partially hellenizing Easterners and in spreading a uniform culture throughout the East, a culture to which Rome eventually fell heir. The prevailing institutions, laws, and language of the East became Greek. Indeed, the Near East had seen nothing like this development since the days when Mesopotamian culture had spread itself through the area.

Yet the spread of Greek culture was wider than it was deep. At best it was a veneer, thicker in some places than in others. Thus, Hellenistic kingdoms were never entirely unified in language, customs, and thought. Greek culture took firmest hold along the shores of the Mediterranean, but in the Far East, in Persia and Bactria, it eventually gave way to Eastern cultures.

The Ptolemies in Egypt made no effort to spread Greek culture, and unlike other Hellenistic kings, they were not city builders. Indeed, they founded only the city of Ptolemais near Thebes. At first, the native Egyptian population, the descendants of the pharaoh's people, retained their traditional language, outlook, religion, and way of life. Initially untouched by Hellenism, the natives continued to be the foundation of the state: they fed it by their labor in the fields, and they financed its operations by their taxes.

Under the pharaohs, talented Egyptians had been able to rise to high office, but during the third century B.C. the Ptolemies cut off this avenue of advancement. Ever more tightly they tied the natives to the land and made it nearly impossible for them to leave their villages. The bureaucracy of the Ptolemies was so ruthlessly efficient that the native population was viciously and cruelly exploited. Even in times of hardship the king's taxes came first, despite the fact that payment might mean starvation for the natives. The desperation of the native population was summed up by one Egyptian, who scrawled the notice: "We are worn out; we will run away."[4] To many Egyptians revolt or a life of brigandage was far better than working the land under the Ptolemies.

Throughout the third century B.C., the Greek newcomers had little to do with the native populaton. In contrast to the natives, Greek immigrants formed a favored upper class. Many Greeks established homes in Alexandria and Ptolemais and entered the bureaucracy. They managed finances, served as magistrates, and administered the law.

Other Greeks settled in military colonies and supplied the monarchy with fighting men.

In the second century B.C., Greeks and native Egyptians began to intermarry and share their cultures. The language of the native population influenced Greek, and many Greeks adopted Egyptian religion and way of life. Simultaneously, natives adopted Greek customs and language, and began to play a role in the administration of the kingdom and even to serve in the army. Even though many Greeks and Egyptians remained aloof from each other, the overall result was the evolution of a widespread Greco-Egyptian culture.

The Seleucid kings established many cities and military colonies in western Asia Minor and along the banks of the Tigris and Euphrates rivers in order to nurture a vigorous and numerous Greek population. Especially important to the Seleucids were the military colonies, for they depended on Greeks to defend the kingdom. The Seleucids had no elaborate plan for hellenizing the native population, but the arrival of so many Greeks was bound to have an impact. Seleucid military colonies were generally founded near native villages, thus exposing Easterners to all aspects of Greek life. Many Easterners found Greek forms, both political and cultural, attractive, and they imitated them. Thus, in Asia Minor and Syria, for instance, numerous native villages and towns developed along Greek lines, and some of them became hellenized cities.

To the Easterners there were several advantages to adopting Greek forms. The Greek language became the common speech of the East. Indeed, a common dialect, called koine, even influenced the speech of peninsular Greece itself. Greek was the speech of the royal court, the bureaucracy, and the military. It was also the speech of commerce: any Easterner who wanted to compete in business had to learn Greek. Greek law also had an impact on the East, and natives adopted many aspects of it. As early as the third century B.C., some Greek cities were giving citizenship to natives who assumed Greek culture.

The vast majority of hellenized Easterners, however, took only the externals of Greek culture while retaining the essentials of their own way of life. There was never a true fusion of cultures, even though Greeks and Easterners adapted themselves to each others' ways. Nonetheless, each found useful things in the civilization of the other, and the two fertilized each other. This fertilization, this mingling of Greek and Eastern elements, is what makes Hellenistic culture unique and distinctive.

Hellenism and the Jews

One way of observing how the East took what it wanted from Hellenism while remaining true to itself is to examine the impact of Greek culture on the Jews. At first Jews in Hellenistic cities were treated as resident aliens. As they grew more numerous, they received permission to form a political corporation, a *politeuma,* which gave them a great deal of autonomy. The right to form a *politeuma* meant that the Jews could attend to their religious and internal affairs without interference from the Greek municipal government. The Jewish politeuma had its own officials, the leaders of the synagogue. In time the Jewish politeuma gained the special right to be judged by its own law and by its own officials, thus becoming in effect a Jewish city within a Hellenistic city.

The Jewish politeuma, like the Hellenistic city, obeyed the commands of the king, but there was virtually no royal interference with the Jewish religion. Indeed, the Greeks were always very reluctant to tamper with anyone's religion. Only the Seleucid king Antiochus Epiphanes (175–ca 164 B.C.) tried to suppress the Jewish religion in Judaea.

He did so not because he hated the Jews (who were a small part of his kingdom), but because he was trying to unify his realm culturally to meet the threat of Rome. Apart from this instance, Hellenistic Jews suffered no religious persecution. Some Jews were given the right to become full citizens of the Hellenistic city, but few exercised that right. Citizenship would have allowed them to vote in the assembly and serve as magistrates, but it would also have obliged them to worship the gods of the city — a practice few Jews chose to follow.

Jews living in Hellenistic cities often embraced a good deal of Hellenism. So many Jews, especially those in Alexandria, learned Greek that the Old Testament was translated into Greek, and services in the synagogue came to be conducted in Greek. Jews often took Greek names, and they copied Greek practices by forming their own trade associations, using Greek political forms, putting inscriptions on graves just as the Greeks did, and much else. Yet no matter how much of Greek culture or its externals the Jews might assume, they normally remained true to their religion. Their ideals and those of the Greeks were different. The exceptions were some Jews in Asia Minor and Syria who adopted Greek or local Eastern cults as part of their worship. To some degree this development was due not only to the strength and attraction of these cults but also to the growing belief among Greeks and Easterners that all peoples, despite differences in cult and ritual, actually worshiped the same gods.

Thus, in spite of their Hellenistic trappings, hellenized Jews remained Jews at heart. The value of Hellenism both to Jews and to other Easterners was its gift of a common cultural background and means of expression. It was an effective way to bridge the gap between Greeks and natives.

Women During the Hellenistic Period

With the growth of monarchy in the Hellenistic period came a major new development: the importance of royal women, many of whom played an active part in political and diplomatic life. In the Hellenic period the polis had replaced kingship, except at Sparta, and queens were virtually unknown, apart from myth and legend. Even in Sparta queens did not participate in politics. Hellenistic queens, however, did exercise political power, either in their own right or by manipulating their husbands. Many Hellenistic queens were depicted as willful or ruthless, especially in power struggles over the throne, and in some cases those charges are accurate. Other Hellenistic royal women, however, set an example of courage and nobility. This is especially true of Cratesiclea, mother of the Spartan king Cleomenes.

In 224 B.C., Cleomenes was trying to rebuild Sparta as a major power, but he needed money. King Ptolemy of Egypt promised to help the Spartans because doing so would further his own diplomatic ends. In return for his support Ptolemy demanded that Cleomenes give him his mother, Cratesiclea, as a hostage. Ptolemy's demand was an insult and a grave dishonor to the Spartan lady, yet Cleomenes' plans could not succeed without Ptolemy's money. Reluctant to agree to Ptolemy's terms, Cleomenes was also reluctant to mention the matter to his mother. Plutarch related her reaction:

Finally, when Cleomenes worked up his courage to speak about the matter, Cratesiclea laughed aloud and said: "Is this what you often started to say but flinched from? Rather put me aboard a ship and send me away, wherever you think this body of mine will be most useful to Sparta, before sitting here it is destroyed by old age."[5]

Cratesiclea's selflessness and love of her state became legendary. Other Hellenistic queens and women of royal blood demonstrated the same qualities of self-sacrifice and devotion to duty.

The example of the queens had a great effect on Hellenistic attitudes toward women in general. Women began to participate in politics on at least a limited basis. Often they served as priestesses, as they had in the Hellenic period, but they also began to serve in civil capacities. For their services to the state they received public acknowledgment. Women sometimes received honorary citizenship from foreign cities because of aid given in times of crisis. Few women achieved these honors, however, and those who did were from the upper classes.

This major development was not due to male enlightenment. Although Hellenistic philosophy addressed itself to many new questions, the position of women was not one of them. The Stoics, in spite of their theory of the brotherhood of man, thought of women as men's inferiors. Only the Cynics, who waged war on all accepted customs, treated women as men's equals. The Cynics were interested in women as individuals, not as members of a family or as citizens of the state. Their view did not make much headway. In this matter, as with much of Cynic philosophy, more was admired than followed.

The new prominence of women was, instead, due largely to their increased participation in economic affairs. During the Hellenistic period some women took part in commercial transactions. Nonetheless, they still lived under legal handicaps. In Egypt, for example, a Greek woman needed a male guardian to buy, sell, or lease land, to borrow money, and to do much else for her. Yet in a number of cases the guardian was present only to fulfill the letter of the law. The woman was the real agent, and she handled the business being transacted. In Hellenistic Sparta women accumulated large fortunes and vast amounts of land. Even by the beginning of the Hellenistic period women owned two-fifths of the land of Laconia.

STATUE OF A PRIESTESS. Women in the Hellenistic period continued to play an important part in society and religion by serving as priestesses. Here the young priestess holds a tray, on which she carries the cult objects used in the god's ritual. (Museo Nazionale Romano)

Women also found it easier to obtain education during this period, including that involving athletics. More important was the increased possibility of intellectual training. More women learned to read and write during the Hellenistic period than during the Hellenic period. Some even studied with philosophers. As a rule, these developments touched only wealthier women, however. Poor women, and probably the majority of women, were barely literate, if literate at all.

These changes do not amount to a social revolution, but women had begun to participate in business, politics, and legal activities. They worked under handicaps that men did not have, and few of them were involved in these matters. But it was a start.

Religion in the Hellenistic World

In religion Hellenism gave the Easterners far less than the East gave the Greeks. In material terms the Hellenistic period saw the spread of Greek religious cults throughout the East. When Hellenistic kings founded cities, they also built temples and established new cults and priesthoods for the old Olympian gods. The new cults enjoyed the prestige of being the religion of the conquerors, and they were supported by public money.

The most attractive aspects of the Greek cults were their rituals and their festivities. Greek cults included literary, musical, and athletic contests. They fostered Greek culture and traditional sports, and thus they were a splendid means of displaying Greek civilization in the East. Contests connected with the cults were staged in beautiful surroundings among impressive Greek buildings. In short, the cults involved bright and lively entertainment, both intellectual and physical, and they provided a good show.

Despite various advantages, Greek cults suffered from some severe drawbacks. They were primarily concerned with ritual. Participation in the civic cults did not even involve belief. Greeks and others could observe the rituals without believing in the existence of the deities being worshiped. Nor did civic cults impose an ethical code of conduct. Greeks did not have to follow any particular rule of life, practice certain virtues, or even live decent lives in order to participate in the cults. On the whole, the civic cults neither appealed to religious emotions nor embraced matters such as sin and redemption. Greek mystery religions helped fill this gap, but the centers of these religions were in old Greece. Although the new civic cults were lavish in pomp and display, they could not satisfy deep religious feelings or spiritual yearnings.

Even though the Greeks participated in the new cults for cultural reasons, they felt little genuine religious attachment to them. In comparison to the emotional and sometimes passionate religions of the East, the Greek cults seemed sterile. Greeks increasingly sought solace from other sources. The educated and serious turned to philosophy as a guide to life, while others turned to superstition, magic, or astrology. Still others might shrug and speak of *Tyche,* which meant Fate or Chance.

In view of the spiritual decline of Greek religion, it is surprising that Eastern religions did not make more immediate headway among the Greeks, but at first they did not. Although Hellenistic Greeks clung to their own cults as expressions of their Greekness rather than for any ethical principles, they did not rush to embrace native religions. Only in the second century B.C., after a century of exposure to Eastern religions, did the Greeks begin to adopt them.

Nor did Hellenistic kings make any effort to spread Greek religion among their Eastern subjects.

The Greeks always considered religion as a matter best left to the individual. Greek cults were attractive only to those socially aspiring Easterners who adopted Greek culture for personal advancement. Otherwise, Easterners were little affected by Greek religion. Nor did native religions suffer from the arrival of the Greeks. Some Hellenistic kings limited the power of native priesthoods, but they also subsidized some Eastern cults with public money. Alexander the Great actually reinstated several Eastern cults that the Persians had suppressed.

The only significant place where Greek and Eastern religious aspirations met was in the growth and spread of new mystery religions, so called because they featured a body of ritual not to be divulged to those not initiated in the secret of the cult, and which incorporated aspects of both Greek and Eastern religions. A leading aspect of the new mystery cults was their broad appeal to both Greeks and Easterners who yearned for personal immortality. Since the Greeks were already familiar with old mystery cults, such as the Eleusinian mysteries in Attica, the new cults did not strike them as alien or barbarian. Familiar too was the concept of preparation for an initiation. Devotees of the Eleusinian mysteries and other such cults had to prepare themselves mentally and physically before entering the presence of the gods. Thus, the new mystery cults fit well with traditional Greek usage.

The new religions enjoyed one tremendous advantage over the old Greek mystery cults. Whereas old Greek mysteries were tied to particular places, such as Eleusis, the new religions spread their centers throughout the Hellenistic world. People did not have to undertake long and expensive pilgrimages just to become members of the religion. In that sense, the new mystery religions came to the people, for temples of the new deities sprang up wherever Greeks lived.

The mystery religions all claimed to save their adherents from the worst that Tyche could do, and they promised life for the soul after death. They all had a single concept in common: the belief that by the rites of initiation the devotees became united with the god, who had himself died and risen from the dead. The sacrifice of the god and his victory over death saved the devotee from eternal death. Similarly, all mystery religions demanded of the devotees a period of preparation in which the convert strove to become holy — that is, to live by the precepts taught by the religion. Once the aspirants had prepared themselves, they then went through the initiation, in which they learned the secrets of the religion. The initiation was usually a ritual of great emotional intensity, a baptism into a new life.

The Eastern mystery religions that took the Hellenistic world by storm were the Egyptian cults of Isis and Serapis. Isis, the wife of Osiris, claimed to have conquered Tyche, and she promised to save any mortal who came to her. She became the most important goddess of the Hellenistic world, and her worship was very popular among women. Serapis was the invention of King Ptolemy, who combined elements of the Egyptian god Osiris with aspects of the Greek god Zeus, Pluto, the prince of the underworld, and Asclepius, the god of healing. Serapis was believed to be the judge of souls, who rewarded virtuous and righteous people with eternal life. Like Asclepius he was a god of healing. Serapis became an international god, and many Hellenistic Greeks thought of him as Zeus. Associated with Isis and Serapis was Anubis, the old Egyptian god, who, like Charon in the Greek pantheon, guided the souls of the initiates to the realm of eternal life.

STATUE OF ISIS. Though originally Egyptian, Isis became a Greek goddess during the Hellenistic period. Her cult spread throughout the Hellenistic world, and she became identified with many purely Greek goddesses. Still popular in the Roman period, her cult profoundly influenced the Christian cult of Mary, the mother of Jesus. (Museo Nazionale, Naples. Mansell Collection [Brogi])

The cult of Isis had even wider appeal than that of Serapis. Her priests claimed that she bestowed upon humanity the gift of civilization and that she founded law and literature. She was the goddess of marriage, conception, and childbirth, and like Serapis a deity who promised to save the souls of her believers.

There was neither conflict between Greek and Eastern religions nor wholesale acceptance of one or the other. Nonetheless, an important development was slowly taking place in the Hellenistic world, a development toward the belief in a single god who ruled over all people. Greeks and Easterners alike noticed similarities among one another's deities and assumed that they were worshiping the same gods in different garb. This tendency toward religious universalism and the desire for personal immortality would prove significant when the Hellenistic world came under the rule of Rome, for Hellenistic developments paved the way for the spread of Christianity.

Philosophy and the Common Man

Philosophy during the Hellenic period was an interest of the wealthy, for only they had leisure enough to pursue philosophical studies. During the Hellenistic period, however, philosophy reached out to touch the lives of more men and women than ever before. The reasons for this development were several. Since the ideal of the polis had declined, politics no longer offered people an intellectual outlet. Moreover, much of Hellenistic life, especially in the new cities of the East, seemed unstable and without venerable traditions. Greeks were far more mobile than they had ever been before, but their very mobility left them with a sense of being uprooted. Many people, in search of something permanent, something unchanging in a changing world, turned to philosophy. Another reason for the increased influence of philosophy was the decline of traditional religion and a growing belief in Tyche. Tyche was more than Fate—it was Chance and Doom, capricious and sometimes malevolent. To protect against the worst that Tyche could do many Greeks looked to philosophy.

Philosophers themselves became much more numerous, and several new schools of philosophical thought emerged. The Cynics preached the joy of a simple life. The Epicureans taught that pleasure is the chief good. Finally, the Stoics emphasized the importance of deeds well done. There was a good deal of rivalry as philosophers tried to demonstrate the superiority of their views, but in spite of all their differences the major branches of philosophy agreed on the necessity for making people self-sufficient. They all recognized the need to equip men and women to deal successfully with Tyche. The major schools of Hellenistic philosophy taught that people could be truly happy only when they had turned their backs on the world around them and focused full attention on one enduring thing. They differed chiefly on what that enduring thing was.

Cynics Undoubtedly the most unusual of the new philosophers were the Cynics, who urged a return to nature. They advised men and women to discard the old, accepted customs and conventions (which were in decline) and to live simply. The Cynics believed that by rejecting material things people become free and that nature will provide all necessities.

The founder of the Cynics was Antisthenes (b. ca 440 B.C.), but Diogenes (ca 412–323 B.C.), one of the most colorful men of the period, was responsible for the spread of the philosophy. Diogenes came to Athens to study philosophy and soon evolved his own ideas on the ideal life. He hit upon the solution that happiness was possible only by living according to nature and by forgoing luxuries. He attacked social conventions because he considered them contrary to nature. Throughout Greece he gained fame for the rigorous way in which he put his beliefs into practice. For instance, he felt that

nothing natural was dirty or shameful. Plutarch told how he drove the point home: "Diogenes rubbed his penis [and ejaculated] in public and said to those around him: 'I wish it were as easy to rub hunger from my stomach.'"[6]

Diogenes' disdain for luxury and social pretense also became legendary. Once when he was living at Corinth, he was supposedly visited by Alexander the Great: "While Diogenes was sunning himself in the area of Craneion [near Corinth] Alexander stood over him and said: 'Ask me whatever gift you like.' In answer Diogenes said to him: 'Get out of my sunlight.'"[7] The story underlines the essence of Diogenes' teachings: even a great, powerful, and wealthy conqueror like Alexander could give people nothing of any real value. Nature had already provided people with everything essential.

Diogenes did not establish a philosophical school in the manner of Plato and Aristotle. Instead, he and his followers took their teaching to the streets and marketplaces. They more than any other philosophical group tried to reach the common man. As part of their return to nature they often did without warm clothing, sufficient food, or adequate housing. To them these things were unnecessary. The Cynics also tried to break down political barriers by declaring that people owed no allegiance to any city or monarchy. Rather, they said, all people are cosmopolitan — that is, citizens of the world. The Cynics reached out beyond political boundaries to create a community of people, all sharing their humanity and living as close to nature as humanly possible. The Cynics set a striking example of how people could turn away from materialism. Although comparatively few men and women could follow such rigorous precepts, the Cynics influenced all the other major schools of philosophy.

Epicureans Epicurus (340–270 B.C.), who founded his own school of philosophy at Athens, based his view of life on scientific theories. Accepting Democritus' theory that the universe is composed of indestructible particles, Epicurus put forth a naturalistic theory of the universe. Although he did not deny the existence of the gods, he taught that they had no effect on human life. The essence of Epicurus' belief was that the principal good of human life is pleasure, which he defined as the absence of pain. He was not advocating drunken revels, orgies, and sensual dissipation, for he thought that they actually cause pain. Instead, Epicurus concluded that any violent emotion is undesirable. Drawing from the teachings of the Cynics, he advocated mild self-discipline. In his opinion, even poverty, if it is not grinding, is good as long as people have enough food, clothing, and shelter. Epicurus also taught that individuals can most easily find happiness by retiring within themselves. They can attain peace and serenity by ignoring the outside world and by looking into their personal feelings and reactions. Thus, Epicureanism led to quietism.

Epicureanism taught its followers to avoid politics and the great issues of the day, for politics led to tumult, which would disturb the soul. Although the Epicureans thought that the state originated through a social contract among individuals, they did not care about the political structure of the state. They were content to live in a democracy, oligarchy, monarchy, or whatever, and they never speculated about the ideal state. Their very ideals stood outside all political forms.

Stoics Opposed to the passivity of the Epicureans, Zeno (335–262 B.C.), a Hellenized Phoenician, put forth a different concept of human beings and the universe. When Zeno first came to Athens, he listened avidly to the Cynics. He thought, however, that the Cynics were extreme, and so he stayed in Athens to form his own school, the Stoa, named after the building where he preferred to teach.

Stoicism became the most popular philosophy of the Hellenistic world, and the one that captured the mind of Rome. Zeno and his followers considered nature to be an expression of god's will, and in their view people could be happy only when they lived in accordance with nature. They stressed the unity of man and the universe, and stated that all men were brothers. All people, they said, were obliged to help one another. Stoicism's science was derived from Heraclitus, but its broad and warm humanity was the work of Zeno and his followers.

Unlike the Epicureans, the Stoics taught that people should participate in politics and worldly affairs. Yet their ideas never led to the belief that individuals ought to change the order of things. Time and again the Stoics used the image of an actor appearing in a play: the Stoic plays an assigned part and never tries to change the play. To the Stoics the important goal was not whether they achieved anything, but whether they lived virtuous lives. In that way they could triumph over Tyche, for even though Tyche could destroy their achievements, it could never destroy the goodness and nobility of their lives.

Even though the Stoics evolved the concept of a world order, they thought of it in terms of the individual. Like the Epicureans, they were indifferent to specific political forms. They believed that people should do their duty to the state in which they found themselves. The universal state they preached about was ethical, not political. The most significant practical achievement of the Stoics was the creation of the concept of natural law. The Stoics concluded that since all men were brothers, since all men partook of divine reason, and since all good men were in harmony with the universe, one law, a part of the natural order of life, governed them all.

The Stoic concept of a universal state under natural law is one of the finest heirlooms the Hellenistic world passed on to Rome. The Stoic concept of natural law, of one law for all people, became a valuable tool when the Romans began to deal with many different peoples having different laws. The ideal of the universal state gave the Romans the reason for extending their empire to the farthest reaches of the world. The duty of individuals to their fellows gave the citizens of the Roman Empire the philosophical justification for doing their duty. In this respect, the real fruit of Hellenistic effort was to ripen only under the cultivation of Rome.

HELLENISTIC SCIENCE

The area in which Hellenistic culture made its greatest triumphs was science, and here too the ancient Near East made its contributions to Greek thought. The patient observations of the Babylonians, who for generations had scanned the skies, had provided the raw material for Thales' speculation, and they were the foundation of Hellenistic astronomy. The most notable of the Hellenistic astronomers was Aristarchus of Samos (ca. 310–230 B.C.), who was educated in Aristotle's school. Aristarchus concluded that the sun is far larger than the earth and that the stars are separated from the earth by enormous distances. He argued against Aristotle's view that the earth is the center of the universe. Instead, he propounded the heliocentric theory — that is, that the earth and the planets revolve around the sun. His work is all the more impressive because he lacked even a rudimentary telescope. Aristarchus had only the human eye and the human brain, but they were more than enough.

In geometry Hellenistic thinkers discovered little that was new, but Euclid (ca 300 B.C.), a mathematician who lived in Alexandria, compiled a valuable textbook of existing knowledge. His book, *The Elements of Geometry,* has exerted immense influence on Western civilization, for it rapidly became the standard introduction to geometry. Generations of students, from the Hellenistic period to the present day, have learned the essentials of geometry from it.

The greatest thinker of the Hellenistic period was Archimedes (ca 287–212 B.C.), who was also a clever inventor. He lived in Syracuse in Sicily and watched Rome emerge as a power in the Mediterranean. When the Romans laid siege to Syracuse in the Second Punic War (see Chapter 4), he invented a number of machines to thwart the Roman army. His catapults threw rocks large enough to sink ships and disrupt battle lines. His grappling devices lifted warships out of the water. The Romans developed a healthy respect for Archimedes, as Plutarch reports: "At last the Romans were so terrified . . . that if a small piece of rope or a small timber was seen protruding from the walls, they bellowed 'There's the thing; Archimedes is unleashing some machine against us,' and turned around and fled."[8]

In the Hellenistic period the practical use of the principles of mechanics was primarily military, for the building of artillery and siege engines. Archimedes built such machines out of necessity, but they were of little real interest to him. In a more peaceful vein, he invented the Archimedean screw, a device used to pump water into irrigation ditches and out of mines. He also invented the compound pulley. Plutarch described his dramatic demonstration of how easily it could move huge weights with little effort:

A three-masted merchant ship of the royal fleet had been hauled on land by hard work and many hands.

Archimedes put aboard her many men and the usual freight. He sat far away from her; without haste, but gently working a compound pulley with his hand, he drew her towards him smoothly and without faltering, just as though she were running on the surface of the sea.[9]

Archimedes was far more interested in pure mathematics than in his practical inventions. His mathematical research, which covered many fields, was his greatest contribution to Western thought. In his book *On Plane Equilibriums* he dealt for the first time with the basic principles of mechanics, including the principle of the lever. He once said that if he were given a lever and a suitable place to stand, he could move the world. In his treatise *Sand-Counter* Archimedes devised a system to express large numbers, a difficult matter considering the deficiencies of Greek numerical notation. In *Sand-Counter* he also discussed the heliocentric theory of Aristarchus. With his treatise *On Floating Bodies* he founded the science of hydrostatics. He concluded that whenever a solid floats in a liquid, the weight of the solid is equal to the volume of liquid displaced. His other works include *On the Measurement of a Circle, On the Sphere and Cylinder, On Conoids and Spheroids,* and *On Spirals.*

Archimedes was willing to share his work, and one of those with whom he communicated was Eratosthenes (285–ca 204 B.C.), a man of almost universal interests. From his native Cyrene in North Africa, Eratosthenes traveled to Athens, where he studied philosophy and learned mathematics. He refused to join any of the philosophical schools, for he was interested in too many things to follow any particular dogma. Hence, his thought was eclectic: he took his doctrines from many schools of thought. For instance, in philosophy he was influenced by Zeno, but Stoicism could not satisfy his mathematical and geographical interests. Besides his scientific work, he devoted time to poetry, in which he showed genuine talent, and he wrote a book on Attic comedy.

ARCHIMEDEAN MILL. Archimedes' invention of the screw was put to practical use in the Archimedean mill. The mill was used extensively in mining to pump water out of shafts and galleries. It was also used in irrigation projects, such as the one shown here, where the laborer turns the pump with his feet, and thus pumps water into fields or ponds. (Photo: Caroline Buckler)

Around 245 B.C., King Ptolemy invited him to Alexandria. The Ptolemies had done much to make Alexandria an intellectual, cultural, and scientific center. They had established a lavish library and museum, undoubtedly the greatest seat of learning in the Hellenistic world. The Ptolemies maintained at the crown's expense a number of distinguished scholars and poets. Eratosthenes came to Alexandria to become the librarian of the royal library, a position of great prestige. While there he continued his mathematical work and by letter struck up a friendship with Archimedes. Eratosthenes solved the problem of how to double a cube, built a machine to illustrate his proof, and in a short poem dedicated his work to King Ptolemy.

Unlike his friend Archimedes, Eratosthenes did not devote his life entirely to mathematics, although he never lost interest in it. He used his mathematics to further geographical studies, for which he is most famous. He calculated geometrically the circumference of the earth and estimated that it was 28,000 miles. He was not wrong by much, for the earth is actually 24,860 miles in circumference. He concluded that the earth is a spherical globe, that the landmass is roughly four-sided, and that the land is surrounded by ocean. He discussed the shapes and sizes of land and ocean and the irregularities of the earth's surface. He drew a map of the earth and used his own system of explaining the divisions of the earth's landmass.

Using geographical information gained by Alexander the Great's scientists, Eratosthenes tried to fit the East into Greek geographical knowledge. Even though for some reason he ignored the western Mediterranean and Europe, he declared that a ship could sail from Spain either around Africa to India or directly westward to India. Not until the great days of Western exploration did sailors such as Vasco da Gama and Magellan actually prove Eratosthenes' theories.

In his life and work Eratosthenes exemplifies the range and vitality of Hellenistic science. His interests were varied and included the cultural and humanistic as well as the purely scientific. Although his chief interest was in the realm of speculative thought, he did not ignore the practical. He was willing to deal with old problems and to break new ground.

In the Hellenistic period the scientific study of botany found its start. Aristotle's pupil Theophrastus (ca 372–288 B.C.), who became head of the Lyceum, the school established by Aristotle, studied the botanical information made available by Alexander's penetration of the East. Aristotle had devoted a good deal of his attention to zoology, and Theophrastus extended his work to plants. He wrote two books on the subject, *History of Plants* and *Causes of Plants*. He carefully observed phenomena and based his conclusions on what he had actually seen. He classified plants and accurately described their parts. He detected the process of germination and realized the importance of climate and soil to plants. Some of Theophrastus' work found its way into agricultural handbooks, but for the most part Hellenistic science did not carry the study of botany any further.

HELLENISTIC MEDICINE

The study of medicine flourished during the Hellenistic period, and Hellenistic physicians carried the work of Hippocrates into new areas. Herophilus, who lived in the first half of the third century B.C., worked at Alexandria and studied the writings of Hippocrates. He accepted Hippocrates' theory of the four humors, and he approached the study of medicine in a systematic, scientific fashion.

He dissected dead bodies and measured what he observed. He discovered the nervous system and concluded that two types of nerves, motor and sensory, exist. He also studied the brain, which he considered the center of intelligence, and discerned the cerebrum and cerebellum. His other work dealt with the liver, lungs, and uterus. His younger contemporary, Erasistratus, also conducted research on the brain and the nervous system, and he improved on Herophilus' work. He too followed in the tradition of Hippocrates and preferred to let the body heal itself by means of diet and air.

Both Herophilus and Erasistratus were members of the Dogmatic school of medicine at Alexandria. In this school speculation played an important part in research. So too did the study of anatomy. To learn more about human anatomy Herophilus and Erasistratus dissected corpses and even vivisected criminals whom King Ptolemy contributed for the purpose. Vivisection, cutting into the body of a living animal or person, was seen as a necessary cruelty: the knowledge gained from the suffering of a few evil men benefited many others — so the Dogmatists argued. Nonetheless, the practice of vivisection seems to have been short-lived, although dissection continued. Better knowledge of anatomy led to improvements in surgery. Because of these advances the Dogmatists were able to invent new surgical instruments and new techniques.

In about 280 B.C., Philinus and Serapion, two pupils of Herophilus, led a reaction to the Dogmatists. Believing that the Dogmatists had become too speculative, they founded the Empiric school of medicine at Alexandria. They claimed that the Dogmatists' emphasis on anatomy and physiology was misplaced. They concentrated instead on the observation and cure of illnesses. They also laid heavier stress on the use of drugs and medicine to treat illnesses. Heraclides of Tarentum (perhaps first century B.C.) carried on the Empirical tradition and dedicated himself to observation and use of medicines. He discovered the benefits of opium and worked with other drugs that relieved pain. He also steadfastly rejected magic and sorcery as pertinent to the application of drugs and medicines.

Hellenistic medicine had its dark side, for many physicians were moneygrubbers, fools, and quacks. One of the angriest complaints comes from the days of the Roman Empire:

Of all men only a physician can kill a man with total impunity. Oh no, on the contrary, censure goes to him who dies and he *is guilty of excess, and furthermore* he *is blamed. . . . Let me not accuse their* [physicians'] *avarice, their greedy deals with those whose fate hangs in the balance, their setting a price on pain, and their demands for down payment in case of death, and their secret doctrines.*[10]

Abuses such as these existed already in the Hellenistic period. As is true today, many Hellenistic physicians did not take the Hippocratic oath very seriously.

Besides incompetent and greedy physicians, the Hellenistic world was plagued by people who claimed to cure illnesses through incantations and magic. Their potions included such concoctions as blood from the ear of an ass mixed with water to cure fever, or the liver of a cat, killed when the moon was waning, and preserved in salt. Broken bones could be cured by applying the ashes of a pig's jawbone to the break. The dung of a goat mixed with old wine was good for healing broken ribs. One charlatan claimed that he could cure epilepsy by making the patient drink, from the skull of a man who had been killed but not cremated, water drawn from a spring at night. These quacks even claimed that they could cure mental illness with their remedies. The treatment for a person suffering from melancholy was calf dung boiled in wine. No doubt the patient became too sick to be depressed.

Quacks who prescribed such treatments were very popular, but they did untold harm to the sick and injured. Nor did they and competent, but greedy, physicians help the reputation of dedicated doctors who honestly and intelligently tried to heal and alleviate pain. The medical abuses that arose in the Hellenistic period were so huge that when the Romans entered the Hellenistic world, they developed an intense dislike and distrust of physicians. The Romans considered the study of Hellenistic medicine beneath the dignity of a Roman, and even as late as the Roman Empire few Romans undertook the study of Greek medicine. Nonetheless, the work of men like Herophilus and Serapion made valuable contributions to the knowledge of medicine, and the fruits of their work were preserved and handed on to the West.

HELLENISTIC ECONOMICS

Alexander's conquest of the Persian Empire not only changed the political face of the ancient world; it also brought the East fully into the sphere of Greek economics. Yet the Hellenistic period did not see a revolution in the way people lived and worked. The material demands of Hellenistic society remained as simple as those of Athenian society in the fifth century B.C. Clothes and furniture were essentially unchanged, as were household goods, tools, and jewelry. The real achievement of Alexander and his successors was the linking of East and West in a broad commercial network. The spread of Greeks throughout the East created new markets and stimulated trade. The economic unity of the Hellenistic world, like its cultural unity, would later prove valuable to the Romans, who took it over and extended it.

Agriculture

Hellenistic farmers seem to have tilled their land in pretty much the same way as Hellenic farmers. There seem to have been no innovations in plowing, preparing the land for sowing, in methods of reaping and threshing grain. Hellenistic farmers continued the traditional Greek practice of alternating the land under cultivation: the year after sowing a field and raising a crop they would leave the field fallow so that the soil would not become worn out and unable to produce crops. In some cases, farmers sowed the fallow land with leguminous plants, such as peas and beans, to replenish the fertility of the soil.

Hellenistic kings paid special attention to agriculture. Much of their revenue was derived from it: from the produce from royal lands, rents paid by the tenants of royal land, and taxation of agricultural land. Some Hellenistic kings sought out and supported agricultural experts. The Ptolemies, for instance, conducted experiments on seed grain. They selected seeds that seemed hardy and productive and tried to improve their characteristics. Hellenistic authors wrote handbooks that discussed how farms and large estates could be most profitably run. These handbooks described soil types, covered the proper times for planting and reaping, and discussed care of farm animals. Whether these efforts had any major impact on the average farmer is difficult to determine.

Hellenistic kings, who had vast tracts of land under their control, and owners of large estates experimented in cattle breeding to improve the size, strength, and usefulness of cattle. Because they used large herds, they needed a large staff of workers, dogs, and overseers. Clearly, such experimentation was impossible for the average farmer, and the practical results of selective breeding were slight.

The same is true of poultry farming. The monarchs and other owners of considerable amounts of land had extensive poultry farms to provide the table with a steady supply of chicken and pheasant, but there is little reason to think that any new techniques discovered on these farms affected the typical farmer.

Perhaps the Ptolemies made the greatest strides in agriculture, but a large part of their success was political. Egypt had a strong tradition of central authority that went back to the pharaohs, which the Ptolemies inherited and tightened. They could decree what Egyptian farmers would do, what crops would be planted, and what animals would be raised, and they had the power to carry out their commands. The Ptolemies recognized the need for well-planned and constant irrigation, and much native labor went into the digging and maintenance of canals and ditches. The Ptolemies claimed a great deal of land from the desert, including the Fayum, a dried lake bed. Although they improved strains of seed grain, they did not attempt to improve farm tools or invent agricultural machinery.

The centralized authority of the Ptolemies explains why agricultural advances in Egypt occurred at the local level. But such progress was not possible in any other Hellenistic monarchy. Despite the increased interest in agriculture and a more studied approach to it in the Hellenistic period, it is impossible to say what real progress was made. There is no evidence to suggest that agricultural productivity increased, and whether Hellenistic agricultural methods had any influence on Eastern practices is unknown.

Industry

Comparatively little is known of industry and manufacturing during the Hellenistic period. Although demand for goods increased, there were apparently no new techniques of production. The technological discoveries of Hellenistic mathematicians and thinkers failed to produce any significant corresponding technological development. Manual labor, not machinery, continued to turn out the raw materials and the few manufactured goods the Hellenistic world used.

Pottery remained an important commodity, and most of it was made locally. The pottery used in the kitchen, the coarse ware, did not change at all. Indeed, it is impossible to tell whether specimens of this type of pottery are Hellenic or Hellenistic. Fancier pots and bowls, decorated with a shiny black glaze, came into use during the Hellenistic period. This ware originated in Athens, but potters in other places began to imitate its style, heavily cutting into the Athenian market. In the second century B.C., a red-glazed ware, often called Samian, burst upon the market and soon dominated it. Athens still held its own, however, in the production of fine pottery. Despite the change in pottery styles, the method of production of all pottery, whether plain or fine, remained essentially unchanged.

In mining, perhaps only one technological innovation dates to the Hellenistic period — the introduction of the Archimedean screw for pumping water out of mines. Otherwise, machinery played no significant part in the mining industry.

A good idea of how metal was mined and processed can be gained from the industrial establishment at Thoricus in Attica. Miners dug the ore by hand and hauled it from the mines for processing. This was grueling work, and invariably miners were slaves, criminals, or forced laborers. The conditions under which they worked were frightful. At Laurium, which provided silver ore for the processing plant at Thoricus, one can still crawl into the labyrinthine shafts. They are narrow and have very low ceilings. The miners dug out the ore on their hands and knees; never did they have a chance to stand upright. Once a miner passed the entrance of the mine and crawled inside, his only light came

ORE-WASHING ESTABLISHMENT AT THORICUS. This building was part of an industrial complex which processed silver and lead. The ore was allowed to settle in the large basins, which were filled with water. Afterward, the silver-bearing ore was removed and smelted. (Photo: Caroline Buckler)

from the oil lamp that he carried. Ventilation was poor, and the air must have been foul and stifling.

After the miners dug the ore, other workers hauled it to a plant where it was washed and processed. The conventional washery was rectangular in shape, with large, rectangular settling pools. Workers crushed the ore and let it settle, so that the rich ore could be separated from the poorer. Workers then gathered the rich ore and gave it to others, who loaded it into a smelting furnace. When the fire had separated the metal from the slag, the workers removed the metal from the furnace.

The Ptolemies ran their gold mines along the same harsh lines. One historian gave a grim picture of the miners' lives:

The kings of Egypt condemn [to the mines] those found guilty of wrong-doing and those taken prisoner in war, those who were victims of false accusations and were put into jail because of royal anger. . . . The condemned — and they are very many — all of them are put in chains, and they work persistently and continually, both by day and throughout the night, getting no rest, and carefully cut off from escape.[11]

The Ptolemies even condemned women and children to work in the mines. The strongest men lived and died swinging iron sledgehammers to break up the gold-bearing quartz rock. Others worked underground following the seams of quartz, men who labored with lamps bound to their foreheads and who were whipped by overseers if they slacked off. Once the diggers had cut out blocks of quartz, young boys gathered up the blocks and carried them outside. All of them — men, women, and boys — worked until they died. Because human labor was so cheap and so abundant, people like the Ptolemies had no incentive to encourage the invention and manufacture of laborsaving machinery.

Apart from gold and silver, which were used primarily for coins and jewelry, iron was the most important metal, and saw the most varied use. Even so, the method of its production never became very sophisticated. The Hellenistic Greeks did manage to produce a low-grade steel by adding carbon to iron, heating them, and then cooling the mixture suddenly in water.

Although new techniques of production and wider use of machinery in industry did not occur, the volume of goods produced increased in the Hellenistic period. Whenever possible, these goods were made locally. Manufacturing establishments, though usually small, existed in nearly all parts of the Hellenistic world.

Commerce

Alexander's conquest of the Persian Empire had immediate effects on trade. In the Persian capitals Alexander had found vast sums of gold, silver, and other treasure. This wealth financed the creation of new cities, the building of roads, and the development of harbors. Most of the great monarchies coined their money on the Attic standard, which meant that much of the money used in the Hellenistic kingdoms had the same value. Traders were less in need of moneychangers than in the days when each major power coined money on a different standard. As a result of Alexander's conquest, geographical knowledge of the East increased dramatically, making the East far better known to the Greeks than previously. The Greeks themselves spread their law and their methods of transacting business throughout the East. Whole new fields lay open to Greek merchants, and they eagerly took advantage of the new opportunities.

The Seleucid and Ptolemaic dynasties traded as far as India, Arabia, and Africa. Overland trade with India and Arabia was conducted by caravan and was largely in the hands of Easterners. The caravan trade never dealt in bulk items or essential commodities, for only luxury goods were transported in this very expensive fashion. Once the goods reached the Hellenistic monarchies, Greek merchants took a hand in the trade. In the early Hellenistic period the Seleucids and Ptolemies saw that the caravan trade proceeded efficiently. Later in the period — a time of increased war and confusion — they left the caravans unprotected. Taking advantage of this situation, Palmyra in the Syrian desert and Nabataean Petra in Arabia arose as caravan states. They protected the caravans from bandits and marauders, and they served as dispersal areas for caravan goods. The Ptolemies established a direct maritime link with India by using the prevailing winds of the monsoons, but this sea route never replaced the caravan traffic.

HARBOR AND WAREHOUSES AT DELOS. During the Hellenistic period Delos became a thriving trading center. Shown here is the row of warehouses at water's edge. From Delos cargoes were shipped to virtually every part of the Mediterranean. (Photo: Caroline Buckler)

More important than this exotic trade were commercial dealings in essential commodities like raw materials, grain, and industrial products. The Hellenistic monarchies usually raised enough grain for their own needs as well as a surplus for export. For the cities of Greece and the Aegean the trade in grain was essential, because many of them could not grow enough of their own. Fortunately for them, abundant supplies of wheat were available nearby in Egypt and in the Crimea in southern Russia.

The large-scale wars of the Hellenistic period often interrupted both the production and the distribution of grain. This was especially true when the successors of Alexander were trying to carve out their kingdoms. In addition, natural calamities, such as excessive rain or drought, frequently damaged harvests. Throughout the Hellenistic period famine or severe food shortage remained a grim possibility.

Most trade in bulk commodities was seaborne, and the Hellenistic merchant ship was the workhorse of the day. The merchant ship had a broad beam and relied on sails for its propulsion. A small crew of experienced sailors could handle it easily. It was far more seaworthy than the contemporary warship, which was long, narrow, and built for speed. Maritime trade gave rise to other industries and trades: sailors and shipbuilders, dock workers, merchants, accountants, teamsters, and pirates. Piracy was always a factor in the Hellenistic world and remained so until Rome extended its power throughout the East.

The Greek cities paid for their grain by exporting olive oil and wine. When agriculture and oil production developed in Syria, Greek products began to meet competition from the Seleucid monarchy. Later in the Hellenistic period Greek oil and wine found a lucrative market in Italy. Another significant commodity was fish, which for export was either salted, pickled, or dried. This trade was doubly important because fish provided poor people with an essential element of their diet. Salt too was often imported, and there was some very slight trade in salted meat, which was a luxury item. Far more important was the trade in honey, dried fruit, nuts, and vegetables.

Among raw materials wood ranked high in demand. Not only was timber necessary for building, but it was also essential in the military sphere. Machinery and siege artillery were made mostly of wood with metal fittings. Hellenistic warships and merchant ships were wooden. The building industry required great quantities of wood, both for domestic housing and for public buildings. The chief producers of timber were the Antigonid and Seleucid monarchies.

Extensive trade in manufactured goods, other than pottery, did not occur in the Hellenistic period. The great monarchies were generally rich in raw materials and had the essentials for most manufacturing within their borders. The exception was trade in luxury goods, but the volume of this commerce cannot have been very great.

A good part of Hellenistic trade involved slaves. The wars provided prisoners for the slave market and to a lesser extent so did kidnapping or capture by pirates. The number of slaves involved cannot be estimated, but there is no doubt that slavery flourished. Both the old Greek states and the new Hellenistic kingdoms were ready markets for slaves, as was Rome when it emerged triumphant from the Second Punic War (see Chapter 4). The war had taken a huge toll of Italian manpower, and Rome bought slaves in vast numbers to replace them in the fields.

Throughout the Mediterranean world, slaves were almost always in demand. Only the Ptolemies discouraged both the trade and slavery itself, but only for economic reasons. Their system had no room for slaves, who would only have competed with free labor. Otherwise, slave labor was to be found in the cities and temples of the Hellenistic world, in the factories and fields, and in the homes of wealthier people. In Italy and some parts of the East, slaves provided the manual labor for the large estates, and they worked the mines. They were vitally important to the Hellenistic economy.

❧

The Hellenistic period was one of broad horizons, a period that spread Hellenism throughout the East. Though often called degenerate and stagnant, it could boast of considerable advances, especially in the sciences and medicine. More importantly, perhaps, the period prepared the way for Rome. Although the Hellenistic monarchies, like the Greek city-states, fought each other to a standstill and seriously weakened each other, they made something new of the East. Greek and Easterner alike changed the East, and into this world Rome moved. Rome brought political stability and its law, but it built upon the society and culture created by Hellenistic men and women.

NOTES

1. Diodorus 17.1.4.

2. U. Wilcken, *Alexander the Great,* G. C. Richards, trans., W. W. Norton, New York, 1967, p.3.

3. Plutarch, *Moralia* 328E.

4. Quoted in W. W. Tarn and G. T. Griffith, *Hellenistic Civilisation,* Meridian Books, Cleveland and New York, 1961, p. 199.

5. Plutarch, *Lives of Agis and Cleomenes,* 22.5.

6. Plutarch, *Moralia* 1044B.

7. Diogenes Laertius 6.38.

8. Plutarch, *Life of Marcellus* 17.4.

9. Ibid., 14.13.

10. Pliny the Elder, *Natural History* 29.8.18, 21.

11. Diodorus 3.12.2–3.

SUGGESTED READING

General treatments of Hellenistic political, social, and economic history can be found in S. A. Cook, et. al., *The Cambridge Ancient History,* vol. 7 (1928), and in the shorter and handier works of M. Cary, *A History of the Greek World 323–146 B.C.** (2nd ed., 1951), and W. W. Tarn and G. T. Griffith, *Hellenistic Civilisation,** (3rd ed., 1951; paperback ed., 1961). The undisputed classic in this field is M. Rostovtzeff, *The Social and Economic History of the Hellenistic World,* 3 vols. (1941).

Each year brings a new crop of biographies of Alexander the Great. The best, however, is J. R. Hamilton, *Alexander the Great** (1973). Wilcken's biography, cited in the Notes, has had a considerable impact on scholars and students alike. On the topic of Alexander's place in history, see A. R. Burn, *Alexander the Great and the Hellenistic World* (1947), a lively and sane treatment. Newer is C. B. Welles, *Alexander and the Hellenistic World.** (1970).

On the spread of Hellenism throughout the Near East, see F. E. Peters, *The Harvest of Hellenism** (1970), and most recently, A Momigliano, *Alien Wisdom: The Limits of Hellenization* (1975).

A. H. M. Jones, *The Greek City from Alexander to Justinian* (1940), deals with urban life during the Hellenistic, Roman, and early Byzantine periods. P. M. Fraser, *Ptolemaic Alexandria,* 3 vols. (1972), covers the life, history, and culture of the most flourishing and prominent of the Hellenistic cities. G. Downey, *A History of Antioch in Syria from Seleucus to the Arab Conquest* (1961), gives a good account of a major city in Asia Minor. Hellenistic Athens is described by C. Mossé, *Athens in Decline, 404–86 B.C.* (1973).

Two general studies of religion within the Hellenistic world are F. Grant, *Hellenistic Religion: The Age of Syncretism** (1953), and H. J. Rose, *Religion in Greece and Rome** (1959). For the effects of Hellenistic religious developments on Christianity, see A. D. Nock, *Early Gentile Christianity and Its Hellenistic Background** (1964). V. Tscherikover, *Hellenistic Civilization and the Jews* (1959), treats the impact of Hellenism on Judaism, and R. E. Witt, *Isis in the Graeco-Roman World* (1971), which is illustrated, studies the origins and growth of the Isis cult.

Hellenistic philosophy and science have attracted the attention of a number of scholars, and the various philosophical schools are especially well covered. A convenient survey of Hellenistic philosophy is A. A. Long, *Hellenistic Philosophy* (1974). F. Sayre, *The Greek Cynics* (1948), focuses on Diogenes' thought and manners, while C. Bailey, *Epicureans* (1926), although dated, is still a useful study of the origins and nature of Epicureanism. Two recent treatments of Stoicism are J. Rist, *Stoic Philosophy* (1969), and F. H. Sandbach, *The Stoics** (1975). A good survey of Hellenistic science is G. E. R. Lloyd, *Greek Science after Aristotle** (1963), and specific studies of major figures can be found in T. L. Heath's solid work, *Aristarchus of Samos* (1920), still unsurpassed, and E. J. Dijksterhuis, *Archimedes* (1956).

*Available in paperback.

Chapter 4

THE RISE OF ROME

"**W**ho is so thoughtless and lazy that he does not want to know in what way and with what kind of government the Romans in less than 53 years conquered nearly the entire inhabited world and brought it under their rule—an achievement previously unheard of?"[1] This question was first asked by Polybius, a Greek historian who lived in the second century B.C. With keen awareness Polybius realized that the Romans were achieving something unique in world history.

What was that achievement? Was it simply the creation of a huge empire? Hardly. The Persians had done the same thing. For that matter, Alexander the Great had conquered vast territories in a shorter time. Was it the creation of a superior culture? Even the Romans admitted that in matters of art, literature, philosophy, and culture they learned from the Greeks. Rome's achievement lay in the ability of the Romans not only to conquer peoples but to incorporate them into the Roman system. Rome succeeded where the Greek polis had failed. Unlike the Greeks, who refused to share citizenship, the Romans extended their citizenship first to the Italians and later to the peoples of the provinces. With that citizenship went Roman government and Roman law. Rome created a world state that embraced the entire Mediterranean.

Nor was Rome's achievement limited to the ancient world. Rome's law, language, and administrative practices were a precious heritage to medieval and modern Europe. London, Paris, Vienna, and many other modern European cities began as Roman colonies or military camps. When the Founding Fathers created the American Republic they looked to Rome as a model. On the darker side, Napoleon and Mussolini paid their own tribute to Rome by aping its forms. Whether Founding Father or modern autocrat, they were all acknowledging their admiration for the Roman achievement.

Roman history is usually broken into two periods: the Republic, the age in which Rome went from a small city-state to ruler of an empire, and the Empire, the period when the republican constitution gave way to constitutional monarchy. How did Rome rise to greatness? What effects did the conquest of the Mediterranean have on the Romans themselves? Finally, why did the republic collapse? These are the questions this chapter will attempt to answer.

THE LAND AND THE SEA

To the west of Greece the boot-shaped peninsula of Italy, with Sicily at its toe, occupies the center of the Mediterranean basin. Italy and Sicily thrust southward toward the African coast (see Map 4.1). At one point the distance between southwestern Sicily and Cape Bon near modern Tunis is roughly one hundred miles. Italy and Sicily literally divide the Mediterranean into two basins and form the focal point between the halves.

Like Greece and other Mediterranean lands, Italy enjoys a genial, almost subtropical, climate. The winters are rainy, but the summer months are dry. Because of the climate the rivers of Italy usually carry little water during the summer, and some go dry entirely. The low water level of the Arno, one of the principal rivers of Italy, at Florence once led Mark Twain to describe it as "a great historical creek with four feet in the channel and some scows floating around. It would be a very plausible river if they would pump some water into it."[2] The Arno at least is navigable. Most of Italy's other rivers are not. Clearly, these small rivers were unsuitable for regular, large-scale shipping. Italian rivers, unlike Twain's beloved Mississippi, never became major thoroughfares for commerce and communications.

Geography discouraged maritime trade as well. Italy lacks the numerous good harbors that are such a prominent feature of the Greek landscape. Only in the south are there good harbors, and Greek colonists had early claimed those ports for themselves. Yet geography gave rise to and the rivers nourished a bountiful agriculture that sustained a large population. The strength of Italy lay in the land and its produce.

Geography encouraged Italy to look to the Mediterranean. In the north Italy is protected by the Apennine Mountains, which break off from the Alps and form a natural barrier. The Apennines retarded, but did not prevent, peoples from penetrating Italy from the north. Throughout history, in modern times as well as ancient, various invaders have entered Italy by this route. From the north the Apennines run southward the entire length of the Italian boot. As they do, they virtually cut off access to the Adriatic Sea, which further induced Italy to look west to Spain and Carthage rather than east to Greece. Even though most of the land is mountainous, the hill country is not as inhospitable as are the Greek highlands. In antiquity the general fertility of the soil provided the basis for a large population. Nor did the mountains of Italy so carve up the land that they prevented the development of political unity. Geography proved kinder to Italy than to Greece.

In their southward course the Apennines leave two broad and fertile plains, those of Latium and Campania. These plains attracted settlers and invaders from the time when peoples began to move into Italy. Among these peoples were the Romans, who established their city on the Tiber River in Latium.

This site enjoyed several advantages. The Tiber provided Rome with a constant source of water.

ROME

0   500   1000 m.
0   1500   3000 Ft.

Field of Mars

QUIRINAL

VIMINAL

Tiber

CAPITOLINE   Senate House

JANICULUM   Forum

Temple of   Regia
Jupiter

ESQUILINE

PALATINE

CAELIAN

Circus Maximus

AVENTINE

ALPS

Po

Trebia

Trebia River ✕

A P P E N N I N E S

Arno

UMBRIA

ETRURIA ✕

L. Trasimene

PICENUM

A D R I A T I C

S E A

Tiber

Veii •

Rome

LATIUM   SAMNIUM

CAMPANIA   APULIA

Cannae ✕

CORSICA

SARDINIA

CALABRIA

Tarentum •

LUCANIA

T Y R R H E N I A N   S E A

BRUTTIUM

Messana •

SICILY

Carthage •

Cape Bon

✕

Zama

—————— Roman boundary before Augustus

- - - - - - Roman boundary before the Punic wars

✕   Major battle

—————— Major road

0   50   100   150 Km.

0   50   100   150 Mi.

STATUETTE OF AN ESTRUSCAN WARRIOR.   The warrior shows the Etruscan military debt to Greece. He wears Greek armor and carries the spear of the Greek heavy infantryman. The artistic rendering of the warrior, however, shows that Italic artists were moving away from Greek models and were creating a style of their own. (Collection of the University Museum, University of Pennsylvania)

MAP 4.1   PHYSICAL ITALY

Since Rome stood astride an easy crossing point of the river, the Tiber was not an obstacle to the main avenue of communications between northern and southern Italy. The famous seven hills of Rome were defensible and safe from the floods of the Tiber. Rome was in an excellent position to develop the resources of Latium and maintain contact with the rest of Italy.

THE ETRUSCANS AND ROME
(750–500 B.C.)

In recent years archaeologists have found traces of numerous early peoples in Italy. Often the origins of these cultures and their precise relations with one another are not well understood. In fact, no clear idea of the prehistory of Italy is yet possible. Of the period before the arrival of the Etruscans (1200–750 B.C.) one fundamental fact is indisputable: peoples probably moving in small groups and speaking Indo-European languages were moving into Italy from the north (see Chapter 1). They were part of the awesome, but imperfectly understood, movement of peoples that spread the Indo-European family of languages from Spain to India.

Only with the coming of the Greeks does Italy enter the light of history. As was seen in Chapter 2, a great wave of Greek immigration swept into southern Italy and Sicily during the eighth century B.C. The Greeks brought their urban life to these regions, spreading cultural influence far beyond the walls of their city-states. In the north the Greeks encountered the Etruscans, one of the truly mysterious peoples of antiquity. Who the Etruscans were, where they came from, and what language they spoke are not known. Nonetheless, this fascinating people was to leave an indelible mark on the Romans. The Etruscans were skillful metal workers, and they amassed extensive wealth by trading their manufactured goods in Italy and beyond. The strength of their political and military institutions enabled them to form a loosely organized league of cities whose dominion extended as far north as the Po valley and as far south as Latium and Campania (see Map 4.1). In Latium they founded cities and they took over control of Rome. Like the Greeks, the Etruscans promoted urban life, and one of the places that benefited from Etruscan influence was Rome.

The Etruscans found the Romans settled on three of Rome's seven hills. The site of the future Forum Romanum, the famous public square and center of political life, was originally the cemetery of the small community. According to Roman legend, Romulus and Remus founded Rome in 753 B.C. Romulus built his settlement on the Palatine Hill, while Remus chose the Aventine (see inset, Map 4.1). Jealous of his brother's work, Remus ridiculed it by jumping over Romulus's unfinished wall. In a rage, Romulus killed him and vowed, "So will die whoever else shall leap over my walls." In this instance legend preserves some facts. Archaeological investigation has confirmed that the earliest settlement at Rome was situated on the Palatine and that it dates to the first half of the eighth century B.C. The legend also shows traces of Etruscan influence on Roman customs. The inviolability of Romulus's walls involves the Etruscan concept of the *pomerium,* a sacred boundary intended to keep out anything evil or unclean.

Etruscan power and influence at Rome were so strong and important that Roman traditions preserved the memory of Etruscan kings who ruled the city. Under the Etruscans, Rome enjoyed contacts with the larger Mediterranean world, and the city began to grow. In the years 575–550 B.C., temples and public buildings began to grace the city. The Capitoline Hill became the religious center of the city when the temple of Jupiter Optimus Maximus (Jupiter the Best and Greatest) was built there. The forum ceased to be a cemetery and started its history as a public meeting place, much like the agora of a Greek city. Metalwork became common, and the wealthier classes began to import large numbers of fine Greek vases. The Etruscans had found Rome a collection of villages and had made of it a city.

During the years 753–509 B.C., the Romans picked up many Etruscan customs. They adopted the Etruscan alphabet, which the Etruscans themselves had adopted from the Greeks. The Romans later handed this alphabet on to medieval Europe and thence to the modern Western world. The Romans also adopted the symbols of political authority from the Etruscans. The symbol of the Etruscan king's right to execute or scourge his subjects was a bundle of rods and an ax, called in Latin the *fasces,* which the king's retainer carried before him on official occasions. When the Romans expelled the Etruscan kings, they created special attendants called lictors to carry the fasces before their new magistrates, the consuls. Even the toga, the white woolen robe worn by citizens, came from the Etruscans. In engineering and architecture the Romans adopted from the Etruscans the vault and the arch. Above all, it was thanks to the Etruscans that the Romans truly became urban dwellers.

THE ROMAN CONQUEST OF ITALY (509–290 B.C.)

Early Roman history is an uneven mixture of fact and legend. Roman traditions often contain a kernel of truth — which is important — but that does not make them history. In many cases they are really significant because they illustrate the ethics, morals, and ideals that Roman society considered valuable. Rome's early history also presents the historian with another problem. Historical writing did not begin among the Romans until the third century B.C., hundreds of years after the founding of Rome.

THE ROMAN FORUM. The forum was the center of Roman political life. From simple beginnings it developed into the very symbol of Rome's imperial majesty. (Italian Government Travel Office)

Much later still, around the time of Christ, the historian Livy (59 B.C.–A.D. 17) gave the final form to these legends.

How much genuine information about the early years did Romans like Livy have? Or did they simply take what they knew and try to make of it an intelligible story? Livy gave his own answer to these questions: "Events before Rome was born or thought of have come down to us in old tales with more of the charm of poetry than of sound historical record, and such traditions I propose neither to affirm nor refute."[3] Livy also admitted that these legends and tales depicted men and women not necessarily as they were, but as Romans should be. For him, the story of early Rome was an impressive moral tale. Today, historians would say that Livy took these legends and made of them a sweeping epic. But they would also admit that the epic preserved the broad outlines of the Roman conquest of Italy and the development of Rome's internal affairs. Both parts of the epic — legend and fact — are worth examining for what they can say about the Romans.

According to Roman tradition, in 509 B.C. the Romans expelled from Rome the Etruscan king Tarquin the Proud and founded the republic. In the years that followed, the Romans fought numerous wars with their neighbors on the Italian peninsula. They became soldiers, and the grim fighting bred tenacity, a prominent Roman trait. War also led to diplomacy, at which the Romans became masters. At an early date they learned the value of alliances and how to provide leadership for their allies. Their alliances with the Latin towns around them provided them with a large reservoir of manpower. Their alliances also involved them in still other wars and took them farther and farther afield in the Italian peninsula.

One of the earliest wars was with two nearby peoples, the Aequi and the Volsci, and from this contest came the legend of Cincinnatus. At one point, when the Aequi had launched a serious invasion, the Romans called upon Cincinnatus to assume the office of dictator. The Roman dictator in this period, unlike modern dictators, was a legitimate magistrate given ultimate powers for a definite and limited period of time. The Roman officials found Cincinnatus working his three-acre farm. Wiping the sweat from himself, he listened to the appeal of his countrymen and accepted the office. Fifteen days later, after he had defeated the Aequi, he returned to his farm. Cincinnatus personified the ideal of the Roman citizen — a man of simplicity, a man who put his duty to Rome before any consideration of personal interest or wealth.

Roman tradition tells of grand campaigns and continuous Roman successes in these wars. In reality, however, most campaigns were neither grand nor always victorious. A good idea of what the fighting was like comes from the legend of the Fabii, one of Rome's noblest families. On one occasion 306 members of the Fabii set out toward Etruscan territory on what was nothing more than a cattle raid. What could be more patriotic than to reduce the enemy's wealth while increasing your own? The Etruscans, however, ambushed the Fabii and surrounded them. One boy escaped from the fighting, but the rest of the Fabii died to the last man, as good Romans were supposed to do. The excessive losses belong to the realm of legend, but the Fabii's type of combat was no doubt typical of the hard-fought border skirmishes and raids, in which the Romans at times took a beating. But Roman tenacity and numbers gradually exhausted the strength of the enemy. The conflicts also taught the Romans to bounce back from defeat and to modify their institutions to deal effectively with changing problems and situations.

The growth of Roman power was slow but steady. Not until 405 B.C., roughly a century after the founding of the republic, did the Romans try to drive the Etruscans entirely out of Latium. They laid siege to Veii, the last neighboring Etruscan city. Ten years later they captured it. The story of the siege of Veii is in some ways the Roman equivalent to the Greek siege of Troy. But again tradition preserves a kernel of truth, confirmed now by archaeological exploration of Veii. This was an important Roman victory, for the land of Veii went to the Romans and provided additional resources for Rome's growing population. Rome's concentrated landholdings formed a strong, unified core in central Italy. After the destruction of Veii, Rome overshadowed its Latin allies and its enemies alike.

Although the Romans slowly but steadily advanced their power in central Italy, they suffered a major setback about 390 B.C. A new people, the Celts, or Gauls as the Romans called them, had been spreading their culture throughout the regions of modern France, Belgium, and southern Germany.

By about 550 B.C., they were trading with the Greek colony of Massilia (modern Marseilles) and with Etruscan cities in the Po valley. Lured by the wealth of northern Italy, bands of Gauls began to push into the Po valley. Around 390 B.C., one band struck as far south as Latium. The Gauls swept aside a Roman army and sacked Rome itself. More intent on loot than land, the Gauls agreed to abandon Rome in return for a large sum of gold.

These events gave rise to a number of legends as the Romans tried to put the best face on their defeat and humiliation. One of the most famous of these legends involves the nobility and fortitude of Rome's gray-bearded senators. On the approach of the Gauls, most Romans abandoned their homes and fortified themselves on the Capitoline Hill. The old senators refused to leave and instead offered themselves as a sacrifice for the state. Dressed in their ceremonial robes with all their magisterial trappings, they seated themselves on their chairs of state and awaited the Gauls. At first the Gauls were amazed and a little frightened by the sight of these solemn men seated in a deserted city. To see whether they were real men, one Gaul cautiously touched the beard of a senator, who in turn struck the Gaul on the head with his ceremonial staff. That set off a slaughter of the senators, who died without a whimper. These senators were ever after an example of Roman determination to die honorably rather than accept defeat.

Another legend concerns Dorsuo, a young man of the Fabii, who had fled to the Capitoline with the others. The Fabii had the duty of performing an annual sacrifice on the Quirinal Hill, and Dorsuo was determined that siege or no siege he would fulfill his religious duty. He gathered his toga in ceremonial fashion, took the sacred vessels for the sacrifice, and marched down the slopes through the enemy pickets. The threats and shouts of the Gauls did not stop him, and he walked through their lines to the Quirinal, where he performed the sacrifice. That done, he walked solemnly back through the lines of the Gauls to the Capitoline. His deed epitomized the ideal of Roman courage and piety to the gods even in the face of death.

The legend that the Romans most took to heart dealt with their decision to buy off the Gauls. The Gauls offered to lift the siege if the Romans paid them one thousand pounds of gold. The Romans agreed to the deal, but were disagreeably surprised when the Gauls produced their own weights. When the Romans complained about the scales, the Gallic chieftain threw his sword on the scale and exclaimed "Vae victis!" — "Woe to the conquered." Those words, legend though they were, became a challenge to the Romans. Thereafter they made it their policy never to accept peace, much less to surrender, as long as the enemy were still in the field.

Although the Gauls left Rome in rubble — another fact confirmed by modern archaeology — they had also helped the Romans. On their way to central Italy they broke forever the power of the Etruscans. When they took their gold and returned to the Alps, they left the north open to Roman expansion.

During the years 390–290 B.C., the Romans rebuilt their city and recouped their losses. They also reorganized their army to create the mobile legion, a flexible unit capable of fighting on either broken or open terrain. They finally brought Latium and their Latin allies fully under their control, and they conquered Etruria. In 343 B.C., they grappled with the Samnites in a series of bitter wars for the possession of Campania and southern Italy. The Samnites were a formidable enemy, and they inflicted some serious losses on the Romans. But the superior organization, institutions, and manpower of the Romans won out in the end. Although Rome had yet to subdue the whole peninsula, for the first time in history the city stood unchallenged in Italy.

Rome's success in diplomacy and politics was as important as its military victories. Unlike the Greeks, the Romans did not simply conquer and then dominate. Instead, they shared with other Italians both political power and degrees of Roman citizenship. Although Roman practice can be reduced to several categories, the Romans did not start out to build a system. They were always a practical people — that was one of their greatest strengths. When they found a treaty or a political arrangement that worked, they used it wherever possible. When it did not, they turned to something else. Consequently, Rome had a network of alliances and treaties with other peoples and states.

With many of their oldest allies, such as the Italian cities, they shared full Roman citizenship. In other instances they granted citizenship without the franchise (*civitas sine suffragio*). The allies who held this status enjoyed all the rights of Roman citizenship except that they could not vote or hold Roman offices. They were subject to Roman taxes and calls for military service, but they ran their own local affairs. They could obtain full Roman citizenship by moving to Rome.

By their willingness to extend their citizenship the Romans took Italy into partnership. Here the political genius of Rome triumphed where Greece had failed. Rome proved itself superior to the Greek polis because it both conquered and shared the fruits of conquest with the conquered. Rome could consolidate where Greece could only dominate. The unwillingness of the Greek polis to share its citizenship condemned it to a limited horizon. Not so with Rome. The extension of Roman citizenship strengthened the state, gave it additional manpower and wealth, and laid the foundations of the Roman Empire itself.

THE ROMAN STATE

The Romans summed up their political existence in a single phrase: *senatus populusque Romanus,* the Roman senate and the people. The real genius of the Romans lay in the fields of politics and law. Unlike the Greeks, they did not often speculate on the ideal state or on political forms; instead, they realistically met actual challenges and created institutions, magistracies, and legal concepts to deal with practical problems. Consequently, change was a common feature of Roman political life, and the constitution of 509 B.C. was far simpler than that of 27 B.C. Nonetheless, the principal magistracies and political organs of the state can be sketched briefly.

In the early republic the social divisions of the state determined the shape of politics. Political power was in the hands of the aristocracy, the patricians, who were wealthy landowners. Patrician families formed clans, as did aristocrats in early Greece. They dominated the affairs of state, provided military leadership in time of war, and monopolized knowledge of law and legal procedure. The common people of Rome were the plebeians, who had few of the advantages of the patricians. Some plebeians formed clans of their own, and rivaled the patricians in wealth. Many plebeian merchants increased their wealth in the course of Roman expansion, but most plebians were poor. They were the artisans, the small farmers, and the landless urban dwellers. The plebeians, rich and poor alike, were free citizens, who had a voice in politics. Nonetheless, they were overshadowed by the patricians.

Perhaps the greatest institution of the republic was the senate, which had originated under the Etruscans as a council of noble elders who advised the king. During the republic the senate advised the consuls and the other magistrates. Because the senate sat year after year, while magistrates changed annually, it provided stability and continuity. It also served as a reservoir of experience and knowledge. Technically, the senate could not pass legislation; it could only offer its advice. But increasingly because of the senate's prestige its advice came to have the force of law.

The Romans created several assemblies through which the people elected magistrates and passed legislation. The earliest of these assemblies was the *comitia centuriata,* a warrior assembly of those who defended the state. Since the patricians shouldered most of the burden of defense, they dominated the assembly and could easily outvote the plebeians. In 471 B.C., the plebeians won the right to meet in an assembly of their own, the *concilium plebis,* and pass ordinances of their own. In 287 B.C., the bills passed in the concilium plebis were recognized as binding on the entire population, patrician and plebeian alike.

The chief magistrates of the republic were the two consuls, elected for one-year terms. At first the consulship was open only to the patricians. The consuls commanded the army in battle, administered state business, convened the comitia centuriata, and supervised financial affairs. In effect, they, together with the senate, ran the state. The consuls appointed quaestors to assist them in their duties, and in 421 B.C. the quaestorship became an elective office open to the plebeians. The quaestors took charge of the public treasury and prosecuted criminals in the popular courts.

In 367 B.C., the Romans created a new office, that of praetor, and in 227 B.C. the number of praetors was increased to four. When the consuls were away from Rome, the praetor could act in their place. The praetor dealt primarily with the administration of justice. When he took office, the praetor issued a proclamation that declared the principles along which he would interpret the law. These proclamations became very important because they usually covered areas where the law was vague. Thus, they helped clarify the law.

The lowest officials were the aediles, four in number, who supervised streets and markets and presided over public festivals.

After the age of overseas conquest (282–146 B.C.), the Romans divided the Mediterranean area into provinces, which were governed by ex-consuls and ex-praetors. Because of their experience in Roman politics, they were well suited to administer the affairs of the provincials and to fit Roman law and custom into new contexts.

One of the most splendid achievements of the Romans was their development of law. Roman law began as a set of rules that regulated the lives and relations of citizens. This civil law, or *ius civile,* consisted of statutes, customs, and forms of procedure. Roman assemblies added to the body of law, and praetors interpreted it. The spirit of the law aimed at protecting the property, the lives, and the reputations of citizens, at redressing wrongs, and at giving satisfaction to the victims of injustice.

As the Romans came into more frequent contact with foreigners, they had to devise laws to deal with disputes either between Romans and foreigners or between foreigners under Roman jurisdiction. In these instances there was no precedent to guide the Romans. Under these conditions the legal decisions of the praetors proved to be of immense importance. The praetors adopted aspects of other legal systems, and they resorted to the law of equity — what they thought was right and just to all parties. Thus, the praetors were in effect free to determine law, and they were left with a great deal of flexibility. This situation illustrates the practicality and the genius of the Romans. By meeting specific, actual circumstances the praetors developed a body of law, the *ius gentium,* that included Romans and foreigners, and that laid the foundation for a universal conception of law. By the time of the late republic Roman jurists were using the Stoic concept of *ius naturae,* natural law, a universal law that could be applied to all societies.

SOCIAL CONFLICT IN ROME

War was not the only part of Rome's early history. In Rome itself a great social conflict, usually known as the Struggle of the Orders, developed between the patricians and the plebeians. What the plebeians wanted was real political representation and safeguards against patrician domination. The efforts of the plebeians to obtain recognition of their rights is the crux of the Struggle of the Orders.

Rome's early wars gave the plebeians the leverage they needed. Rome's survival depended on the army, and the army needed the plebeians. In 494 B.C., according to tradition, came the first showdown between the plebeians and the patricians. To force the patricians to grant concessions the plebeians seceded from the state. They literally walked out of Rome and refused to serve in the army. Livy tells how Menenius Agrippa, acting as spokesman for the senate, persuaded them to return by relating the story of the belly and the limbs.

Agrippa said that the limbs of the body once went on strike against the stomach because it did nothing but enjoy all the good things it received from the limbs. Yet the limbs found that by starving the stomach they also starved themselves. (In the same vein Benjamin Franklin once told the Founding Fathers that unless they all hung together they would all hang separately.) Livy's story is legend, but here once again the legend preserves truth. The Struggle of the Orders was marked by hard bargaining, but also by compromise and concession. Throughout the conflict plebeian and patrician alike were sincerely concerned for the welfare of Rome. Only this true patriotism prevented the conflict from becoming civil war.

The general strike of the plebeians worked. Because of it the patricians made important concessions. They recognized the right of the plebeians to elect their own officials, the tribunes. The tribunes in turn had the right to protect the plebeians from the arbitrary conduct of patrician magistrates. The tribunes brought plebeian complaints and grievances to the senate for resolution. In 471 B.C., the plebeians won the right to hold their own assembly, the concilium plebis, and to enact ordinances that concerned only themselves. The plebeians had become a state within a state. This situation could have led to chaos, but Rome was not a house divided against itself. The plebeians were not bent on undermining the state. Rather, they used their gains only to win full equality under the law.

The law itself was the next target of the plebeians. Only the patricians knew what the law was, and only they could argue cases in court. All too often they had used the law for their own benefit. The plebeians wanted the law codified and published. The result of their agitation was the Law of the Twelve Tables, so called because the laws were inscribed on large bronze plaques, which covered civil and criminal matters. Like Dracon's law code, the Law of the Twelve Tables seems stiff and even harsh. For instance, Table IV commands, "A seriously deformed child should be quickly killed." Table VIII deals handily with slander: "If anyone has sung or composed a song which caused dishonor or disgrace to another, he should be beaten to death with clubs." But at least all Romans could learn their rights and guard against arbitrary judgments. Later still, the plebeians forced the patricians to publish legal procedures as well. They had broken the patricians' legal monopoly. Henceforth, they enjoyed full protection under the law.

The decisive plebeian victory came with the passage of the Licinio-Sextian rogations (or laws) in 366 B.C. Licinius and Sextus were two plebeian tribunes who led a ten-year fight for further reform. Rich plebeians, like Licinius and Sextus themselves, joined the poor to mount a sweeping assault on patrician privilege. Wealthy plebeians wanted the opportunity to provide political leadership for the state. They demanded that the patricians allow them access to all the magistracies of the state. If they could hold the consulship, they could also sit in the senate and advise the senate on policy. The two tribunes won approval from the senate for a law that stipulated that one of the two annual consuls had to be a plebeian.

Licinius and Sextus also protected the interests of the plebeian poor, those who owned little or no land and whose poverty had driven them into debt. These plebeians wanted access to public land so that they could have a new start. The two tribunes sponsored legislation that limited the amount of public land an individual could hold. This restriction struck hard at the patricians, many of whom had used large tracts of public land for their own profit. The new law allowed magistrates to parcel out land in small lots, which plebeians could claim and work for themselves.

The Struggle of the Orders resulted in a Rome stronger and better united than before. It could have led to anarchy, but again the Roman political genius triumphed. Resistance and confrontation never exploded into class warfare. Instead, both sides resorted to compromises to hammer out a realistic solution. Important too were Roman patience and tenacity — and a healthy sense of the practical. These qualities enabled both sides to keep working until they had resolved the crisis. The Struggle of the Orders ended in 266 B.C. with a new concept of Roman citizenship. All citizens shared equally under the law. Theoretically, all could aspire to the highest political offices. Patrician or plebeian, rich or poor, Roman citizenship was equal for all.

THE AGE OF OVERSEAS CONQUEST (282–146 B.C.)

In 282 B.C., Rome embarked on a series of wars that left it the ruler of the Mediterranean world. There was nothing ideological about these wars. Unlike Napoleon or Hitler, the Romans did not map out grandiose strategies for world conquest. In 282 B.C., they had no idea of what lay in store for them. If they could have looked into the future, they would have stood amazed. In many instances the Romans did not even initiate action; rather, they responded to situations as they arose. Nineteenth-century Englishmen were fond of saying, "We got our empire in a fit of absence of mind." The Romans could not go quite that far. Even though they sometimes declared war reluctantly, they nonetheless felt the need to dominate, to eliminate any state that could threaten them.

Rome was imperialistic, and its imperialism took two forms. In the barbarian West, the home of fierce tribes, Rome resorted to bald aggression to conquer new territory. In areas like Spain, and later in Gaul, the fighting was fierce and savage, and gains came slowly. In the civilized East, the world of Hellenistic states, Rome tried to avoid annexing territory. The East was already heavily populated, and those people would have become Rome's responsibility. New responsibilities produced new problems, and such headaches the Romans shunned. In the East the Romans preferred to be patrons rather than masters. Only when that policy failed did they directly annex land. But in 282 B.C., all this lay in the future.

The Samnite wars had drawn the Romans into the political world of southern Italy. In 282 B.C., alarmed by the powerful newcomer, the Greek city of Tarentum in southern Italy called upon Pyrrhus, king of Epirus, in western Greece, for help. A relative of Alexander the Great and an excellent general, Pyrrhus landed in Italy with an experienced army. He won two furious battles but suffered heavy casualties — thus the phrase "Pyrrhic victory." Roman bravery and tenacity led Pyrrhus to comment: "If we win one more battle with the Romans, we'll be completely washed up." Against Pyrrhus's army the Romans threw new legions, and in the end Roman manpower proved decisive. In 275 B.C., the Romans drove Pyrrhus from Italy and extended their sway over southern Italy. Once they did, the island of Sicily became important to them.

Sicily is the steppingstone to Italy, and the Romans could not let it fall to an enemy. Pyrrhus once described Sicily as a future "wrestling ground for the Carthaginians and Romans." The Phoenician city of Carthage, located in North Africa near modern Tunis, had for centuries dominated the western Mediterranean. Sicily had long been a Carthaginian target. In 264 B.C., Carthage and Rome came to blows over the city of Messina, which commanded the straits between Sicily and Italy. This conflict, the First Punic War, lasted for twenty-three years. The Romans quickly learned that they could not conquer Sicily unless they controlled the sea. Yet they lacked a fleet and hated the sea as fervently as cats hate water. Nevertheless, with grim resolution the Romans built a navy and challenged the Carthaginians at sea. The Romans fought seven major naval battles with the Carthaginians and won six. Twice their fleet went down in gales. But finally the Romans wore down the Carthaginians. In 241 B.C., the Romans defeated them and took possession of Sicily, which became their first real province. Once again Rome's resources, manpower, and determination proved decisive.

The First Punic War was a beginning, not an end. In Carthage, Rome still had a formidable enemy. After the First Punic War the Carthaginians expanded their power to Spain and turned the Iberian Peninsula into a rich field of operations. By 219 B.C., Carthage had found its avenger — Hannibal. In Spain, Hannibal learned how to lead armies and to wage war on a large scale. A brilliant general, he realized the advantages of swift, mobile forces, and he was an innovator in tactics.

In 219 B.C., he defied the Romans by laying siege to the small city of Saguntum in Spain. When in the following year the Romans declared war, Hannibal gathered his forces and led them on one of the most spectacular marches in ancient history. Hannibal carried the Second Punic War to the very gates of Rome. Starting in Spain he led his troops — infantry, cavalry, and elephants — over the Alps and into Italy on a march that covered more than a thousand miles. Once in Italy he defeated one Roman army at the battle of Trebia and later in 217 B.C. another at the battle of Lake Trasimene. At the battle of Cannae in 216 B.C. he inflicted some forty thousand casualties on the Romans. Hannibal spread devastation throughout Italy, but he failed to crush Rome's iron circle of Latium, Etruria, and Samnium. The wisdom of Rome's political policy of extending rights and citizenship to its allies showed itself in these dark hours. Italy stood solidly with Rome against the invader. And Rome fought back.

The Roman general Scipio Africanus copied Hannibal's methods of mobile warfare. He streamlined the legions by making their components capable of independent action and by introducing new weapons. He gave his new army combat experience in Spain, which he wrested from the Carthaginians. Meanwhile, the Roman fleet dominated the western Mediterranean and interfered with Carthaginian attempts to reinforce Hannibal.

In 204 B.C., the Roman fleet landed Scipio in Africa, which prompted the Carthaginians to recall Hannibal from Italy to defend the homeland.

In 202 B.C., near the town of Zama, Scipio Africanus defeated Hannibal in one of the world's truly decisive battles. Scipio's victory meant that the world of the western Mediterranean would henceforth be Roman. Roman language, law, and culture, fertilized by Greek influences, would in time permeate this entire region. The victory at Zama meant that Rome's heritage — not Carthage's — would be passed on to the Western world.

The Second Punic War contained the seeds of still others wars. Unabated fear of Carthage led to the Third Punic War, a needless, unjust, and savage conflict that ended in 146 B.C. when Scipio Aemilianus, grandson of Scipio Africanus, destroyed the old, hated rival. As the Roman conqueror watched the death pangs of that great city, he turned to his friend Polybius with the words: "I fear and foresee that someday someone will give the same order about my fatherland." It would, however, be centuries before an invader would stand before the gates of Rome.

During the war with Hannibal the Romans had invaded Spain, a peninsula rich in material resources and the home of fierce warriors. When the Roman legions tried to reduce Spanish tribesmen, they met with bloody and determined resistance. Not until 133 B.C., after years of brutal and ruthless warfare, did Scipio Aemilianus finally conquer Spain.

When the Romans intervened in the Hellenistic East, they went from triumph to triumph. The Romans dealt with the Greeks in a civilized fashion. There were hard-fought battles in the East, but the bloodletting and carnage that marked the battles in the West were not repeated in the cultured East. Even so, the results were essentially the same. The kingdom of Macedonia fell to the Roman legions, as did Greece and the Seleucid monarchy. By 146 B.C., the Romans stood unchallenged in the eastern Mediterranean, and they had turned many

MODEL OF A ROMAN WARSHIP. This rare ancient model was found off the southern coast of the Peloponnesus near Sparta. The bow of the warship is capped by a ram, behind which run the seats for the rowers. At the stern is the poop, the station of the officers and steersmen. (Photo: Caroline Buckler)

states and kingdoms into provinces. In 133 B.C., the king of Pergamum in Asia Minor left his kingdom to the Romans in his will. The Ptolemies of Egypt meekly obeyed Roman wishes. The following years would bring the Romans new victories, and they would establish their system of provincial administration. But by 146 B.C., the work of conquest was largely done. The Romans had turned the entire Mediterranean basin into *mare nostrum* — "our sea."

OLD VALUES AND GREEK CULTURE

Rome had conquered the Mediterranean world, but some Romans considered that victory a misfortune. The historian Sallust (86–34 B.C.), writing from hindsight, complained that the acquisition of an empire was the beginning of Rome's troubles:

But when through labor and justice our Republic grew powerful, great kings defeated in war, fierce nations and mighty peoples subdued by force, when Carthage the rival of the Roman people was wiped out root and branch, all the seas and lands lay open, then fortune began to be harsh and to throw everything into confusion. The Romans had easily borne labor, danger, uncertainty, and hardship. To them leisure, riches — otherwise desirable — proved to be burdens and torments. So at first money, then desire for power grew great. These things were a sort of cause of all evils.[4]

Sallust was not alone in his feelings. At the time, some senators opposed the destruction of Carthage on the grounds that fear of their old rival would keep the Romans in check. Did Rome gain the whole world only to lose its soul? Sallust obviously thought so, and he could have made a good case. It is true that the new empire provided many Romans with golden opportunities to amass fortunes wrung

from the conquered. It is true that numerous generals, provincial governors, and other magistrates oppressed the vanquished for their personal gain. But it is also true that Rome continued to produce patriotic, noble, and hardworking men and women, just as it had in the past. Rome did not suddenly become weak and evil, but Roman society was undergoing a fundamental change. Rome's early period became the "good old days," a golden age of virtue the early Romans themselves would never have recognized.

In the second century B.C., Romans learned that they could not return to what they fondly considered a simple life. They were world rulers. The responsibilities they faced were complex and awesome. They had to change their institutions, their social patterns, and their way of thinking to meet the new era. They were in fact building the foundations of a great imperial system. It was an awesome challenge, and there were failures along the way. Roman generals and politicians would destroy each other. Even the republican constitution would eventually be discarded. But in the end Rome triumphed here just as it had on the battlefield, for out of the turmoil would come the pax Romana — the Roman peace.

How did the Romans of the day meet these challenges? How did they lead their lives and cope with these momentous changes? Obviously, there are as many answers to these questions as there were Romans living during this period. Yet two men can be taken to represent the major trends of the second century B.C. Cato the Elder shared the mentality of those who longed for the "good old days," those who idealized the traditional agrarian way of life. Scipio Aemilianus led those who embraced the new, urban life with its eager acceptance of Greek culture. Cato and Scipio were both aristocrats and neither of them was really typical, even of the aristocracy. But they do symbolize the opposing sets of attitudes that marked Roman society and politics in the age of conquest.

BATTLE BETWEEN THE ROMANS AND THE GAULS. All the brutality and fury of Rome's wars with the barbarians of western Europe come to life in this Roman sarcophagus of 225 B.C. Even the bravery and strength of the Gauls were no match for the steadiness and discipline of the Roman legions. (Alinari/Scala)

Cato and the Traditional Ideal

Marcus Cato was born a plebeian, but his talent and energy brought him to Rome's highest offices. He cherished the old virtues and consistently imitated the old ways. He had inherited an estate north of Rome and began his career as a man of moderate means. Near his estate were the fields and cottage of Manius Curius, the general who had driven Pyrrhus from Italy. Curius had been another Cincinnatus. Although Curius had held the consulship and commanded armies, he worked his small farm alone. He once refused a large bribe, saying that a man of his simple tastes did not need gold. It was the example of Curius that Cato constantly held before his eyes.

In Roman society ties within the family were very strong. In that sense Cato and his family were typical. Cato was paterfamilias, a term that meant far more than merely "father." The paterfamilias was the oldest dominant male of the family. He held nearly absolute power over the lives of his wife and children so long as he lived. He could kill his wife for adultery or divorce her at will. He could kill his children or sell them into slavery. He could force them to marry against their will. Until the paterfamilias died, his sons could not legally own property.

Despite his immense power, the paterfamilias did not necessarily act alone or arbitrarily. To deal with important family matters he usually called a council of the adult males. In that way the leading members of the family aired their views. They had the opportunity to give their support to the paterfamilias or to dissuade him from harsh decisions. In these councils the women of the family had no formal part, but it can safely be assumed that they played an important behind-the-scenes role. Although the possibility of serious conflicts between a paterfamilias and his grown sons is obvious, no one in ancient Rome ever complained about the institution. Perhaps in practice the paterfamilias preferred to be lenient rather than absolute.

Cato's wife (whose name is unknown) was the matron of the family, a position of authority and respect. The virtues expected of a Roman matron were those of Lucretia, a legendary figure from the early republic. In Livy's account, the son of the last Etruscan king wanted to sleep with Lucretia. One night while her husband was away, the king's son slipped into her room and tried to seduce her. When she refused him, he threatened to kill her and then he raped her. When he had gone, she sent for her father and husband and told them the whole story. They tried to console her, telling her that she had been helpless and was free from any shame. Her answer was short: "Never shall Lucretia provide a precedent for unchaste women to escape what they deserve." She demanded vengeance, the death of the king's son. Then, innocent though she was, she drew a knife and killed herself. Clearly, Lucretia was the ideal, but numerous funerary inscriptions testify

that the virtues of chastity and modesty were highly valued. The tribute of one husband to his wife is typical of many:

Here is laid a woman dutiful, temperate, pure, chaste, Sempronia Moschis, to whom thanks are returned by her husband for her merits.[5]

Like most Romans, Cato and his family started the day early in the morning. The Romans divided the period of daylight into twelve hours and the darkness into another twelve. In the summer the first hour of the day might begin as early as half past four, in winter as late as half past seven. Because Mediterranean summers are invariably hot, the farmer and his wife liked to take every advantage of the cool mornings. Cato and his family, like modern Italians, ordinarily started the morning with a light breakfast, usually consisting of nothing more than some bread and cheese. After breakfast the family went about its work.

Because of his political aspirations Cato often used the mornings to plead law cases. He walked to the marketplace of the nearby town and defended anyone who wished his help. He received no fees for these services, but he did put his neighbors in his debt. In matters of law and politics Roman custom was very strong. It demanded that his clients give Cato their political support or their votes in repayment whenever he asked for them. These clients knew and accepted their obligations to Cato for his help.

Cato's wife shared her husband's love for the old ways. While he was in town, she ran the household. She spent the morning spinning and weaving, preparing the wool for the clothes they wore. She supervised the domestic slaves and planned the meals. She devoted a good deal of attention to her son. In wealthy homes during this period the matron had begun to employ a slave for a wet nurse. The wife of Cato refused to neglect her maternal duties. Like most ordinary Roman women, she nursed her son herself. She also bathed and swaddled him daily. Later, the boy was allowed to play with toys and terra cotta dolls. Roman children, like children everywhere, kept pets. Dogs were especially popular, and they were valuable as house guards. Children played all sorts of games, and games of chance were very popular. Until the age of seven the child was under the matron's care. During this time the mother began to educate her daughter in the management of the household. After the age of seven, the son — and in many wealthy households the daughter too — began his formal education.

In the country, Romans like Cato continued to take their main meal at midday. This meal included either coarse bread made from the entire husk or porridge made with milk or water. The meal also included turnips, cabbage, olives, and beans. When Romans ate meat, they preferred pork. Unless the farm was located by the sea, the average farm family did not eat fish, which was expensive and a real delicacy. Cato once complained that Rome was a place where a fish could cost more than a cow. With this meal the family drank an ordinary wine mixed with water. After the main meal any Roman who could took a nap. This was especially true in the summer, when the Mediterranean heat can be fierce. Slaves, artisans, and hired laborers, however, went about their work. In the evening the Romans ate another light meal and went to bed about nightfall.

Agriculture was dear to Cato's heart. He spoke of it in glowing terms: "From the farms come the strongest men and the most vigorous soldiers, and their occupation is the most upright and steady."[6] Most Romans would have agreed with him that agriculture was the backbone of the state. Most of them would have been ready and willing to argue

with Sallust, who called farming "a slavish occupation." Agriculture shaped Rome's soldiers and supported the aristocracy. Nothing gave a family respectability like owning a farm, and the bigger the farm the better.

The agricultural year followed the sun and the stars. These were the farmer's calendar. Like Hesiod in Boeotia, the Roman farmer looked to the sky to determine when to plant, weed, shear sheep, and perform other chores. For instance, Varro (116–27 B.C.), one of the most famous writers on agriculture, did everything by the sun and stars. He advised farmers in Italy to harvest their grain crops between the summer solstice and the rising of the Dog Star. He suggested that they sow at the setting of the Pleiades. Varro's book on agriculture owed much to Hellenistic Greek manuals, but it also reflected actual Roman practice. Besides, the farmer could not depend on the civil calendar. The lunar year is 354 days long, and the solar year is $365\frac{1}{4}$ days long. So the civil calendar had to be adjusted to both lunar and solar years. To make matters worse politicans often tampered with the calendar. In 46 B.C., when Julius Caesar reformed the civil calendar, it was some $2\frac{1}{2}$ months out of step with the solar year. Obviously, farmers had to depend on something more reliable than this. Their solution was the sun, moon, and stars.

Spring was the season for plowing. Roman farmers plowed their land at least twice and preferably three times. The third plowing was to cover the sown seed in ridges and to use the furrows to drain off excess water. The Romans used a variety of plows. Some had detachable shares. Some were heavy for thick soil, others light for thin, crumbly soil. Farmers used oxen and donkeys to pull the plow. They collected the dung of their animals in heaps for fertilizer. Besides spreading manure, some farmers fertilized their fields by planting lupines and beans. When these began to pod, farmers plowed them under. The main money crops, at least for rich soils, were wheat and flax. Forage crops included

ROMAN PLOWING. This bronze statuette, which actually dates to the time of the Roman Empire, nonetheless shows the basic tools of Roman plowing. A team of oxen are yoked over their shoulders, and from the yoke the beam extends to the plowshare. This farmer wears heavier dress than Cato and his neighbors would have needed in sunny Italy. (The British Museum)

clover, vetch, and alfalfa. Prosperous farmers like Cato raised olive trees chiefly for the oil. They also raised grapevines for the production of wine.

Cato and his neighbors harvested their cereal crops in summer and their grapes in autumn. Harvests varied depending on the soil, but farmers could usually expect yields of 5½ bushels of wheat or 10½ bushels of barley per acre. In the early republic the master of the household worked the farm himself. By the second century B.C., however, Cato was noticeably old-fashioned because he stripped to the waist in summer and sweated alongside his slaves and day laborers.

One result of Rome's wars and conquests was an influx of slaves. Prisoners from Spain, Africa, the Hellenistic East, even some blacks from Hannibal's army, came to Rome as the spoils of war. The Roman attitude toward slaves and slavery had little in common with modern views. To the Romans slavery was a misfortune that befell some people. But slavery did not entail any racial theories. Races were not enslaved because the Romans thought them inferior. The black African slave was treated no worse—and no better—than the Spaniard. Indeed, some slaves were valued because of their physical differences: black Africans and blond Germans were particular favorites. For the talented slave, the Romans always held out the hope of eventual freedom. The Roman custom of manumission became very common, so common that it had to be limited by law. Not even the Christians questioned the institution of slavery. It was just a fact of life.

Slaves were entirely the property of their master, and they might be treated with great cruelty. Many Romans were practical enough to realize that they got more out of their slaves by kindness than by severity. Yet in Sicily slave owners treated their slaves viciously. They bought slaves in huge numbers, branded them for identification, put them in irons, and often made them go without food and clothing. In 135 B.C., these conditions gave rise to a major slave revolt, during which many of the most brutal masters died at the hands of their slaves. Italy too had trouble with slave unrest, but conditions there were generally better than in Sicily.

Cato urged his countrymen to treat slaves humanely. Varro suggested that masters should control slaves by knowledge and not by whips. Yet even Cato could be hardhearted. Although he worked and ate with them, he never forgot their money value. When they grew too old to work he sold them to save the expense of feeding them. Not all Romans were Catos, however. Between many slaves and masters there developed genuine bonds of affection. On numerous occasions slaves risked or gave their lives to protect kind masters.

Part of the reason for such good relations probably stems from the fact that many slaves came from the Hellenistic East. They were certainly not barbarians. Many of them were often more cultured than their owners. Greek male slaves frequently became the tutors of the master's children. These men especially were likely to receive their freedom. When slaves gained their freedom they also became Roman citizens. Freedmen and freedwomen often continued to live with their previous owners. And it was not unusual for Romans to permit their ex-slaves to be buried with them.

For Cato and most other Romans religion played an important part in life. Originally, the Romans thought of the gods as invisible and shapeless natural forces. Only through Etruscan and Greek influence did Roman deities take on human form. Jupiter, the sky god, and his wife, Juno, became equivalent to the Greek Zeus and Hera. Mars was the god of war, but he was also the god who guaranteed the fertility of the farm and protected it from danger. Cato habitually sacrificed a pig, a ram, and a bull to Mars to obtain his help and protection. Cato or one of his farmhands led the animals around the boundaries of the farm and then called upon Mars the Father

that you hold back, repel, and turn away disease seen and unseen, blight and devastation; that you allow my crops, grain, vines, and thickets to increase and flourish; that you keep my shepherd and flocks safe; that you watch over and give good health and strength to me, my house, and household.[7]

Cato then sacrificed the animals to Mars and offered the god small cakes. The Romans used a similar ritual, the Robigalia, to protect the grain crops from mildew. The Robigalia gave rise to the Christian practice of purifying farms on Rogation Days. During these days, the priest and his congregation marched in procession around the farms while calling upon Jesus and the saints for protection. Cato would have approved.

These two religious practices are illustrative of Roman religion in general. The gods of the Romans were not loving and personal. They were stern, powerful, and aloof. But as long as the Romans honored the cults of their gods, they could expect divine favor.

Along with the great gods the Romans believed in spirits who haunted fields, forests, crossroads, and even the home itself. Some of these deities were hostile, and only magic could ward them off. The spirits of the dead, like ghosts in modern horror films, frequented the places where they had lived. They too had to be placated, but they were ordinarily benign. As the poet Ovid (43 B.C.– A.D. 17) put it:

The spirits of the dead ask for little.
They are more grateful for piety than for an expensive gift—
Not greedy are the gods who haunt the Styx below.

A rooftile covered with a sacrificial crown,
Scattered kernels, a few grains of salt,
Bread dipped in wine, and loose violets —
These are enough.
Put them in a potsherd and leave them in the middle
of the road.[8]

A good deal of Roman religion consisted of such rituals as those Ovid describes. These practices lived on long after the Romans had lost interest in the great gods. Even Christianity could not entirely wipe them out. Instead, Christianity would incorporate many of these rituals into its own style of worship.

Scipio: Greek Culture and Urban Life

The old-fashioned ideals that Cato represented came into conflict with the new spirit of wealth and leisure. The conquest of the Mediterranean world and the spoils of war made Rome a great city. Some, like the historian Velleius Paterculus (first century A.D.), viewed these developments with distaste:

Scipio Africanus opened the way for Roman power. Scipio Aemilianus opened the way for luxury. Indeed, when Rome was free of the fear of Carthage, and its rival in empire was removed, Rome fell, not gradually but in headlong course from virtue towards vice. The old discipline was deserted and the new introduced. The state turned from vigilance to sleep, from military affairs to pleasures, from work to leisure.[9]

Roman life, especially in the cities, *was* changing and becoming less austere. The spoils of war went to the building of baths, theaters, and other places of amusement. Romans and Italian townsmen began to spend more of their time in leisure pursuits. But simultaneously the new responsibilities of governing the world produced in Rome a sophisticated society. Romans developed new tastes and a liking for Greek culture and literature. They began to

MANUMISSION OF SLAVES. During the Republic some Roman masters began to free slaves in public ceremonies. Here two slaves come before their master or a magistrate, who is in the process of freeing the kneeling slave by touching him with a manumission-rod. The other slave shows his gratitude and his good faith with a handshake. (Collection Waroque, Mariemont, Belgium. ©A. C. L. Brussels)

learn the Greek language. It became common for an educated Roman to speak both Latin and Greek. Hellenism dominated the cultural life of Rome. Even diehards like Cato found a knowledge of Greek essential for political and diplomatic affairs. The poet Horace (65–8 B.C.) summed it up well when he wrote: "Captive Greece captured her rough conqueror and introduced the arts into rustic Latium."

One of the most avid devotees of Hellenism and the new was Scipio Aemilianus. The destroyer of Carthage, Scipio was also the man whom Velleius had accused of introducing luxury into Rome. Scipio realized that broad and worldly views had to replace the old Roman narrowness. The new situation called for new ways. Rome was no longer a small city on the Tiber. It was the capital of the world, and Romans had to adapt themselves to that fact. Scipio was ready to become an innovator both in politics and in culture. He broke with the past in the conduct of his political career. He embraced Hellenism wholeheartedly. Perhaps more than anyone else of his day Scipio represented the new Roman — imperial, cultured, and independent.

Scipio even dared to be independent in his political career, which differed from that of traditional politicians. Usually, Roman aristocrats rose at dawn and for the first two hours of the day received callers. During this time patrons advised their clients on legal matters. Politicians consulted one another about current issues. Social climbers tried to ingratiate themselves with the rich and powerful. When the patron left his house for the law courts, the forum, or the public assemblies, his clients accompanied him. The bigger his entourage the more prestigious was the patron. Once the patron arrived, his clients gave him any support that he might demand of them. He might call upon them to vote for himself or a friend, if either of them happened to be running for office. Or he might instruct them to vote for or against a particular piece of legislation. In this way aristocrats built up powerful political followings and furthered their political careers.

Scipio Aemilianus took a somewhat different course. After rising early, he ordered his slave to shave him. Shaving itself was a new custom just becoming fashionable at Rome. Then he ate a light breakfast. On some mornings he might greet his clients as others did. But often he went hunting — a sport more Greek than Roman. His prowess at hunting won him considerable fame. This was all part of his plan to increase his popular appeal. Scipio was unwilling to rely solely on the prestige and influence of his family. Instead, he was intensely interested in winning the support of a new group, the growing body of people who owed nothing to patrons. He intended to cut a dashing figure, to become renowned among the voters for his courage, wealth, and skill. He was setting off on the course of personal politics. He was determined to carve out a career for himself on the strength of his own merits. In doing so he set an example for future politicians. One of the most successful of his imitators would be Julius Caesar.

In his education and interests, too, Scipio broke with the past. At first, while still a boy, he received the traditional Roman training. He learned to read and write Latin, and he became acquainted with the law. He mastered the fundamentals of rhetoric. He learned how to throw the javelin, fight in armor, and ride a horse. But later Scipio also learned Greek and became a fervent Hellenist. As a young man he formed a lasting friendship with the historian Polybius, who actively encouraged him in his study of Greek culture and in his intellectual pursuits. In later life Scipio's love of Greek learning, rhetoric, and philosophy became legendary. Scipio also promoted the spread of Hellenism in Roman society.

He became the center of the Scipionic Circle, a small group of Greek and Roman artists, philosophers, historians, and poets. Conservatives like Cato tried to stem the rising tide of Hellenism, but men like Scipio carried the day and helped make the heritage of Greece an abiding factor in Roman life.

The new Hellenism profoundly stimulated the growth and development of Roman art and literature. The Roman conquest of the Hellenistic East resulted in the wholesale confiscation of Greek paintings and sculpture to grace Roman temples, public buildings, and private homes. Roman artists copied many aspects of Greek art, but their emphasis on realistic portraiture carried on a native tradition.

In the field of history, Fabius Pictor (second half of the third century B.C.), a senator, wrote the first *History of Rome* in Greek. Other Romans translated Greek classics into Latin. Still others, like the poet Ennius (239–169 B.C.), the Father of Latin Poetry, studied Greek philosophy, wrote comedies in Latin, and adapted many of Euripides' tragedies for the Roman stage. He also wrote a history of Rome in Latin verse. Plautus (ca 254–184 B.C.) specialized in rough humor. He too decked out Greek plays in Roman dress, but he was no mere imitator. Indeed, his play *Amphitruo* was itself copied by the French playwright Molière (1622–1673) and the English poet John Dryden (1631–1700). The Roman dramatist Terence (ca 195–159 B.C.), a member of the Scipionic Circle, wrote comedies of refinement and grace that owed their essentials to Greek models. His plays lacked the energy and the slapstick of Plautus's rowdy plays. All of early Roman literature was derived from the Greeks, but it managed in time to speak in its own voice and to flourish because it had something of its own to say.

The conquest of the Mediterranean world brought the Romans leisure, and Hellenism influenced how they spent their free time. During the second century B.C., the Greek custom of bathing became a Roman passion and an important part of the day. In the early republic Romans bathed infrequently, especially in the winter. Now large buildings containing pools of water and exercise rooms went up in great numbers, and the baths became an essential part of the Roman city. Architects built an intricate system of aqueducts to supply the bathing establishments with water. Once again conservatives railed at this Greek custom, calling it a waste of time and an encouragement to idleness. The conservatives were correct in that bathing establishments were more than just places to take a bath. They included gymnasia, where men exercised and played ball games. Women had places of their own to bathe, generally sections of the same baths used by men; yet for some unknown reason, women's facilities lacked gymnasia. The baths contained hot-air rooms to induce a good sweat and pools of hot and cold water to finish the actual bathing. They also contained halls, where people chatted or read, and snack bars selling food and drink. The baths were socially important places where men and women went to see and be seen: social climbers tried to talk to "the right people" and wangle invitations to dinner; politicians took advantage of the occasion to discuss the affairs of the day. Despite the protests of the conservatives and moralists, the baths at least provided people—rich and poor—with places for clean and healthy relaxation.

This period also saw a change in the eating habits of urban dwellers. The main meal of the day shifted from midday to evening. Dinner usually became more elaborate than previously. Most Roman families normally dined alone, but dinner parties became fashionable. Although Scipio Aemilianus detested fat people, more and more Romans began to eat excessively. Dinner was a three-course meal.

BATHS OF CARACALLA. Once introduced into the Roman world, social bathing became a passion. These baths, which date to the Roman Empire, are the ultimate development of sophistication and size. (Italian Government Travel Office)

COIN OF JULIUS CAESAR. Immediately after Caesar's death, Augustus had to defend his position as Caesar's heir. As part of his propaganda campaign to publicize his position, he minted this coin with a crude portrait of Caesar on one side. His own portrait was on the other side. (Courtesy, World Heritage Museum. Photo: Caroline Buckler)

Rich men and women displayed their wealth by serving exotic dishes and gourmet foods. After a course of vegetables and olives came the main course, which consisted of meat, fish, or fowl. Pig was a favorite dish, and a whole suckling pig might be stuffed with sausage or other foods. A lucky guest might even dine on peacock and ostrich, each served with rich sauces. The last course was dessert. As in Italy today, it usually consisted of fruit. With the meal the Romans served wine, and during this period vintage wines became very popular. While the meal was in progress household slaves sometimes read poetry or performed music. People of more vulgar tastes hired jesters. Dwarves were in great demand, and the evening's entertainment consisted of buffoonery and coarse jokes. After dinner the party drank wine and talked, often late into the night.

Although the wealthy gorged themselves whenever they could, poor artisans and workers could rarely afford rich meals. Their dinners resembled those of Cato. Yet they too occasionally spent generously on food, especially during the major festivals. Love of food and drink was a characteristic of the average Roman, whether rich or poor.

Did Hellenism and the new social customs corrupt the Romans? Perhaps the best answer is simply this: the Roman state and the empire it ruled continued to exist for some six more centuries. Rome did not collapse because of the new developments. Instead, the state continued to prosper. The golden age of literature was still before it. The high tide of its prosperity still lay in the future. The Romans did not like change, but they took it in stride. That was part of their practical turn of mind and part of their genius.

THE LATE REPUBLIC
(133–27 B.C.)

The wars of conquest created many serious problems for the Romans. Some of the most pressing were political. The republican constitution suited the needs of a simple city-state, but it was inadequate to meet the requirements of Rome's new position in international affairs (see Map 4.2). Sweeping changes and reforms were necessary to make it serve the demands of empire. A whole system of provincial administration had to be established. Officials had to be created to govern the provinces and to administer the law. These officials and administrative organs had to find their places within the constitution. Armies had to be provided to defend the provinces, and a system of tax collection had to be created.

Other political problems were as serious. During the wars Roman generals commanded huge numbers of troops for long periods of time. Men such as Scipio Aemilianus were on the point of becoming too mighty for the state to control. Although Rome's Italian allies had borne a large part of the fighting, they received fewer rewards than did Roman officers and soldiers. Italians began to agitate for full Roman citizenship and a voice in politics.

There were serious economic problems, too. Hannibal's operations and the warfare in Italy had left the countryside a shambles. The movements of numerous armies had disrupted agriculture. The prolonged fighting had also drawn untold numbers of Roman and Italian men from their farms for long periods. The families of these soldiers could not keep the land in full cultivation. The people who defended Rome and conquered the world for Rome became impoverished for having done their duty.

These problems, complex and explosive, in large part account for the turmoil of the closing years of the republic. The late republic was one of the most dramatic eras of Roman history. It produced some of Rome's most famous figures: Marius, Sulla, Cicero, Pompey, and Julius Caesar, among others. In one way or another each of these men attempted to solve Rome's problems.

When the legionaries returned to their farms in Italy, they encountered an appalling situation. All too often their farms looked like the farms of people they had conquered. Two courses of action were open to them. They could rebuild as their forefathers had done. Or they could take advantage of an alternative not open to their ancestors: they could sell their holdings. The wars of conquest had made some men astoundingly rich. These men wanted to invest their wealth in land. They bought up small farms to create huge estates, which the Romans called latifundia.

MAP 4.2   ROMAN CONQUESTS DURING THE REPUBLIC

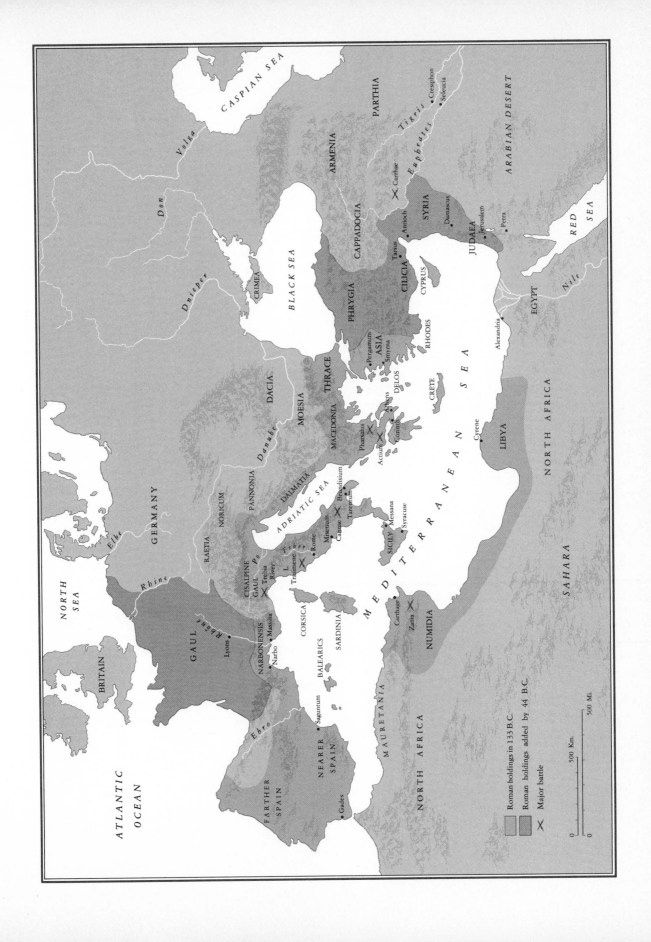

CASPIAN SEA

Volga

Don

Dnieper

ATLANTIC
OCEAN

NORTH
SEA

BRITAIN

GERMANY

Elbe

Rhine

BLACK SEA

CRIMEA

DACIA

Danube

MOESIA

THRACE

MACEDONIA

NORICUM

PANNONIA

RAETIA

DALMATIA

ADRIATIC SEA

GAUL

Rhône

Lyons

CISALPINE
GAUL ✕ Trebia
River
Lake
Trasimene ✕
Tiber
Rome ●

NARBONENSIS
Narbo ● Massilia

CORSICA

SARDINIA

BALEARICS

Ebro

Saguntum ●

NEARER
SPAIN

FARTHER
SPAIN

Gades ●

PARTHIA

Tigris
Ctesiphon ●
Seleucia ●

ARMENIA

CAPPADOCIA

Euphrates

ARABIAN DESERT

Carrhae ● ✕

SYRIA
Damascus ●
Antioch ●
JUDAEA
Jerusalem ●
Petra ●

CILICIA
Tarsus ●

CYPRUS

PHRYGIA
Pergamum ●
ASIA
Smyrna ●

RHODES

RED
SEA

EGYPT

Nile

Alexandria ●

DELOS

CRETE

Athens ●
Corinth ●
Pharsalus ✕
Actium ✕

Brundisium ●
Tarentum ●

Misenum ●
Cannae ● ✕
Po

MEDITERRANEAN SEA

Cyrene ●

LIBYA

NORTH AFRICA

SAHARA

SICILY
Messana ●
Syracuse ●

Carthage ● ✕
Zama ✕

NUMIDIA

MAURETANIA

NORTH AFRICA

Roman holdings in 133 B.C.

Roman holdings added by 44 B.C.

Major battle ✕

500 Mi.

500 Km.

The purchase offers of the rich landowners appealed to the veterans for a variety of reasons. Many veterans had seen service in the East, where they had tasted the rich city life of the Hellenistic states. They were reluctant to return home and settle down to a dull life on the farm. Often their farms were so badly damaged that rebuilding hardly seemed worth the effort. Besides, it was hard to make big profits from small farms. Nor could the veterans supplement their income by working on the latifundia. Although the owners of the latifundia occasionally hired free men as day laborers, they preferred to use slaves to work their land. Slaves could not go on strike, and they could not be drafted into the army. Confronted by these conditions, veterans and their families opted to sell their land. They took what they could get for their broken farms and tried their luck elsewhere.

Most veterans migrated to the cities, especially to Rome. Although some found work, most did not. Industry and small manufacturing were generally in the hands of slaves. Even when there was work, slave labor kept the wages of free men low. Instead of a new start, veterans and their families encountered slum conditions that matched those of modern American cities. Sanitation was virtually nonexistent. Housing was frequently shabby and structurally unsound, but expensive nonetheless. Fire and police protection were things of the future. These conditions were especially true of Rome and some larger cities. Within a brief period of time Rome was the home of a large body of urban poor.

This trend held ominous consequences for the strength of Rome's armies. The Romans had always believed that only landowners should serve in the army for only they had something to fight for. Landless men, even if they were Romans and lived in Rome, could not be conscripted into the army. These landless men may have been veterans of major battles and numerous campaigns; they may have won distinction on the battlefield. But once they

sold their land they became ineligible for further military service. A major pool of experienced manpower was going to waste. The landless ex-legionaries wanted a new start, and they were willing to support any leader who would provide it.

One man who recognized the plight of Rome's peasant farmers and urban poor was an aristocrat, Tiberius Gracchus (163–133 B.C.). Appalled by what he saw, Tiberius warned his countrymen that the legionaries were losing their land even while fighting Rome's wars:

The wild beasts that roam over Italy have every one of them a cave or lair to lurk in. But the men who fight and die for Italy enjoy the common air and light, indeed, but nothing else. Houseless and homeless they wander about with their wives and children. And it is with lying lips that their generals exhort the soldiers in their battles to defend sepulchres and shrines from the enemy, for not a man of them has an hereditary altar, not one of all these many Romans an ancestral tomb, but they fight and die to support others in luxury, and though they are styled masters of the world, they have not a single clod of earth that is their own.[10]

From that moment until his death, Tiberius Gracchus sought a solution to the problems of the veterans and the urban poor.

After his election as tribune of the people, Tiberius in 133 B.C. proposed that public land be given to the poor in small lots. His was an easy and sensible plan, but it angered many of the wealthy and noble. These people had usurped large tracts of public land for their own use. They had no desire to give any of it back, and they bitterly resisted Tiberius's efforts. Violence broke out in Rome when a large body of senators killed Tiberius in cold blood. It was a black day in Roman history. The very people who directed the affairs of state and administered the law had taken the law into their own hands. The death of Tiberius was the beginning of an era of political violence. In the end that violence would bring down the republic.

Although Tiberius was dead, his land bill became law. Furthermore, Tiberius's brother Gaius took up the cause of reform. Gaius Gracchus (153–121 B.C.), who also became tribune, demanded even more extensive reform than had his brother. To help the urban poor Gaius pushed legislation to provide them with cheap grain for bread. He defended his brother's land law and suggested other measures for helping the landless. He proposed that Rome send many of its poor and propertyless people out to form colonies in southern Italy. The poor would have a new start and could lead productive lives. The city of Rome would immediately benefit because excess and nonproductive families would leave for new opportunities abroad. Rome would be less crowded, sordid, and dangerous.

Gaius went a step further and urged that all Italians be granted full rights of Roman citizenship. This measure provoked a storm of opposition, and it was not passed in Gaius's lifetime. Yet in the long run he proved wiser than his opponents. In 91 B.C., many Italians revolted from Rome over the issue of full citizenship. After a brief but hard-fought war the senate gave Roman citizenship to all Italians. Had the senate listened to Gaius earlier, it could have spared a great deal of bloodshed. Instead, reactionary senators rose against Gaius and murdered him and three thousand of his supporters. Once again the cause of reform had met with violence. Once again Rome's leading citizens were the ones who discarded the law.

More trouble for Rome came from an unexpected source. In 112 B.C., war broke out in North Africa, when a Numidian king named Jugurtha rebelled against Rome. The Roman legions made little headway against him until 107 B.C., when Gaius Marius, an Italian "new man" (a politician not from the traditional Roman aristocracy), became consul. To prepare for the war with Jugurtha, Marius reformed the Roman army. He was the first Roman officer to recruit an army by permitting landless men to serve in the legions. He thus tapped Rome's vast reservoir of idle manpower. His volunteer army was a professional force, not a body of draftees. Marius also reorganized the Roman legion into smaller units, the cohorts, which made the legion more mobile and flexible. He rearmed the legion by making the sword and javelin the standard weapons of the legionaries.

There was, however, a disturbing side to Marius's reforms, one that would henceforth haunt the republic. Marius promised land to his volunteers after the war to encourage enlistments. Poor and landless veterans flocked to him, and together they handily defeated Jugurtha. When Marius proposed a bill to grant land to his veterans, the senate refused to act, in effect turning its back on the soldiers of Rome. This was a disastrous mistake. Henceforth, the legionaries expected their commanders—not the senate—to protect their interests. Through Marius's reforms the Roman army became a professional force, but it owed little allegiance to the state. By failing to keep the loyalty of Rome's troops, the senate set the stage for military rebellion and political anarchy.

Nor was trouble long in coming. The senate's refusal to honor Marius's promises to his soldiers and the brief, but bitter, war between the Romans and their Italian allies (91–88 B.C.), set off serious political disturbances in Rome. In 88 B.C., the Roman general and conqueror Sulla marched on Rome with his army to put an end to the turmoil. He made himself dictator—a far cry from Cincinnatus's dictatorship. He put his enemies to death and confiscated their land. The constitution thus disrupted was never effectively put back together.

In 79 B.C., Sulla voluntarily abdicated as dictator and permitted the republican constitution to function normally once again. Yet his dictatorship cast a long shadow over the late republic. Civil war was the constant lot of Rome until 27 B.C., when the republican constitution gave way to the empire of Augustus. The history of the late republic is the story of the power struggles of some of Rome's most famous figures: Julius Caesar and Pompey, Augustus and Marc Antony. One figure who stands apart is Cicero (106–43 B.C.), a practical politician whose greatest legacy to the Roman world and to Western civilization is his mass of political and oratorical writings.

A pompous, vain, and sometimes silly man, Cicero nonetheless was one of the few men of the period to urge peace and public order. As consul in 63 B.C. he put down a conspiracy against the republic, but he refused to participate in the scramble for power. Instead, he developed the idea of "concord of the orders," a permanent balance of the elements that constituted the Roman state, and in his writings he explored the underlying principles of statecraft. Cicero was a truly brilliant master of Latin prose and undoubtedly Rome's finest orator. He used his vast literary ability to urge various political and social reforms. Yet Cicero commanded no legions, and only legions commanded respect.

The real political heirs of Sulla were Pompey and Julius Caesar. Pompey, a man of boundless ambition, began his career as one of Sulla's lieutenants. He commanded a large army, which put down a rebellion in Spain and then he himself threatened to rebel unless the senate allowed him to run for consul. He and another ambitious politician, M. Crassus, pooled their political resources, and both won the consulship. They dominated Roman politics until the rise of Julius Caesar, who became consul in 59 B.C. Together the three of them concluded a political alliance, the First Triumvirate, in which they agreed to advance each other's interests.

In 58 B.C., Caesar became governor of Gaul, the region of modern France, a huge area he had conquered in the name of Rome. Caesar himself wrote an account of his operations, his *Commentaries* on the Gallic wars, which became a classic in Western literature and most schoolchildren's introduction to Latin. By 49 B.C., the First Triumvirate had fallen apart. Crassus had died in battle, and Caesar and Pompey, each suspecting the other of treachery, came to blows. The result was a long and bloody civil war, which raged from Spain across northern Africa to Egypt. Although Pompey enjoyed the official support of the government, Caesar finally defeated Pompey's forces in 45 B.C. He had overthrown the republic and made himself dictator.

Julius Caesar was not merely another victorious general. He was politically brilliant, and he was determined to reform the republic. He took the first long step to break down the barriers between Italy and the provinces, extending citizenship to many of the provincials who had supported him. Caesar also took measures to cope with Rome's burgeoning population. By Caesar's day perhaps 750,000 people lived in Rome. Caesar drew up plans to send his veterans and some 80,000 of the poor and unemployed to colonies throughout the Mediterranean. He founded at least twenty colonies, most of which were located in Gaul, Spain, and North Africa. These colonies were important agents in spreading Roman culture in the western Mediterranean. Caesar's work would eventually lead to a Roman empire composed of citizens, not subjects.

In 44 B.C., a group of conspirators assassinated Caesar and set off another round of civil war. Caesar had named his eighteen-year-old grandnephew,

Octavian—or Augustus as he is better known to history—as his heir. Augustus joined forces with two of Caesar's lieutenants, Marc Antony and Lepidus, in a pact known as the Second Triumvirate, and together they hunted down and defeated Caesar's murderers. In the process, however, Augustus and Antony came into conflict, and in 33 B.C., Augustus branded Antony as a traitor and a rebel. Augustus painted lurid pictures of Antony lingering in the eastern Mediterranean, a romantic and foolish captive of the seductive Cleopatra, queen of Egypt and bitter enemy of Rome. In 31 B.C., with the might of Rome at his back Augustus met and defeated the army and navy of Antony and Cleopatra at the battle of Actium in Greece. Augustus's victory put an end to an age of civil war that had lasted from the days of Sulla.

❧

The final days of the republic, even though filled with war and chaos, should not obscure the fact that much of the Roman achievement survived the march of armies. The Romans had conquered the Mediterranean world only to find that conquest demanded that they change their way of life. Socially, they imbibed Greek culture and adjusted themselves to the superior civilization of the Hellenistic East. Politically, their city-state constitution broke down and expired in the wars of the late republic. Even so, men like Caesar and later Augustus sought new solutions to the problems confronting Rome. The result, as will be seen in the next chapter, was a system of government capable of administering an empire with justice and fairness. Out of the failure of the republic came the pax Romana of the empire.

NOTES

1. Polybius, *The Histories* 1.1.5.
2. Mark Twain, *The Innocents Abroad,* Signet Classics, New York, 1966, p. 176.
3. Livy, *History of Rome,* Preface 6.
4. Sallust, *War with Catiline* 10.1–3.
5. *Corpus Inscriptionum Latinarum,* vol. 6, G. Reimer, Berlin, 1882, no. 26192.
6. Cato, *On Agriculture,* Preface 4.
7. Ibid. 141.2–3.
8. Ovid, *Fasti* 2.535–539.
9. Velleius Paterculus, *History of Rome* 2.1.1.
10. Plutarch, *Life of Tiberius Gracchus* 9.5–6.

SUGGESTED READING

H. H. Scullard covers much of Roman history in a series of books: *The Etruscan Cities and Rome* (1967), *A History of the Roman World 753–146 B.C.** (3rd ed., 1961), and *From the Gracchi to Nero** (4th ed., 1976). Roman expansion is the subject of J. Heurgon, *The Rise of Rome to 264 B.C.* (English trans., 1973), and R. M. Errington, *The Dawn of Empire* (1971). H. C. Boren, *The Gracchi* (1968), treats the work of the two brothers, and A. E. Astin, *Scipio Aemilianus* (1967), gives a good biography of that statesman. Very important are the works of E. Badian, *Roman Imperialism in the Late Republic** (1968) and *Publicans and Sinners* (1972). The crisis of the late republic receives careful treatment from R. Syme, *The Roman Revolution** (revised ed., 1952); P. A. Brunt, *Social Conflicts in the Roman Republic** (1971); A. J. Toynbee, *Hannibal's Legacy,* 2 vols. (1965); and A. W. Lintott, *Violence in the Roman Republic* (1968).

K. D. White, *Roman Farming* (1970), deals with agriculture, and J. P. V. D. Balsdon covers social life of the republic and the empire in two works: *Life and Leisure in Ancient Rome* (1969) and *Roman Women* (revised ed., 1974). F. Schulz, *Classical Roman Law* (1951), is a useful introduction to an important topic.

*Available in paperback.

Chapter 5

THE PAX ROMANA

*H*ad the Romans conquered the entire Mediterranean world only to turn it into their battlefield? Would they, like the Greeks before them, become their own worst enemies, destroying each other and wasting their strength until they perished? At Julius Caesar's death in 44 B.C. it must have seemed so to many. Yet finally, in 31 B.C., Augustus restored peace to a tortured world, and with peace came prosperity, new hope, and a new vision of Rome and Rome's destiny. The Roman poet Virgil (70–19 B.C.) said it most nobly:

You, Roman, remember — these are your arts:
To rule nations, and to impose the ways of peace,
To spare the humble and to war down the proud.[1]

In the place of the republic, Augustus established a constitutional monarchy. He attempted to achieve a lasting cooperation in government and a balance among the people, the magistrates, the senate, and the army. His efforts were not always successful. His settlement of Roman affairs did not permanently end civil war. Yet he carried on Caesar's work. Augustus created the structure that the modern world calls the Roman Empire. He did his work so well, and his successors so capably added to it, that Rome realized Virgil's hope. For the first and second centuries A.D. the lot of the Mediterranean world was peace — the pax Romana, a period of security, order, and harmony, of flourishing culture and expanding economy. It was a period that saw the wilds of Gaul, Spain, Germany, and eastern Europe introduced to Greco-Roman culture. By the third century A.D., when the empire gave way to the medieval world, the greatness of Rome and the blessings of Roman culture had left an indelible mark on the yet unseen ages to come.

How did the Roman emperors govern the empire, and how did they spread Roman influence into northern Europe? What were the fruits of the pax Romana? Finally, how did the empire meet the grim challenge of barbarian invasion and economic decline? These are the main questions with which this chapter will be concerned.

AUGUSTUS'S SETTLEMENT
(31 B.C.–A.D. 14)

When Augustus put an end to the civil wars that had raged since 83 B.C., he faced the monumental problems of reconstruction. Rome and the entire Mediterranean world were in his power, and the legions were obedient to his word. Sole ruler as no Roman had ever been, he had a rare opportunity to shape the future. But how was that to be accomplished?

Augustus could easily have declared himself dictator as Caesar had done, but the thought was repugnant to him. Augustus was neither an autocrat nor a revolutionary. His solution was to restore the republic. But was that possible? Some eighteen years of anarchy and civil war had shattered the republican constitution. It could not be rebuilt in a day. Augustus recognized these problems, but he did not let them stop him. From 29 to 23 B.C., he toiled to heal Rome's wounds. The first problem facing him was to rebuild the constitution and the organs of government. Next he had to demobilize the army and care for the welfare of the provinces. Last, he had to meet the danger of barbarians at Rome's European frontiers. Augustus was highly successful in meeting these challenges; his gift of peace to a war-torn world sowed the seeds of a literary flowering that produced some of the finest fruits of the Roman mind.

The Principate and the Restored Republic

Restoring the republic and creating a place for himself in it proved to be the biggest challenges to Augustus. Typically Roman, he preferred not to create anything new; rather, he intended to modify republican forms and offices to meet new circumstances. Augustus planned for the senate to take upon itself a serious burden of duty and responsibility. He expected it to administer some of the provinces, to continue as the chief deliberative body of the state, and to act as a court of law. Yet he did not give the senate enough power to become his partner in government. As a result, the senate failed to live up to its responsibilities, and increasingly its prerogatives went to Augustus by default.

Augustus's own position within the restored republic was something of an anomaly. He could not simply surrender the reins of power, for someone else would only have seized them. But how was he to fit into a republican constitution? Again Augustus had his own answer. He became *princeps civitatis,* "the First Citizen of the State." This prestigious title carried no power; it indicated instead that Augustus was the most distinguished of all Roman citizens. In effect, it designated Augustus as the first among equals and a little more equal than anyone else in the state. His real power came from the magistracies he held, the powers granted him by the senate, and his control of the army. Clearly, much of the principate, as the position of First Citizen is known, was a legal fiction. Yet that need not imply that Augustus, like a modern dictator, tried to clothe himself with constitutional legitimacy. In an inscription known as *Res Gestae (The Deeds of Augustus)* Augustus described his constitutional position in these terms:

In my sixth and seventh consulships [28–27 B.C.]. I had ended the civil war, having obtained through universal consent total control of affairs. I transferred the Republic from my power to the authority of the Roman people and the senate. . . . After that time I stood before all in rank, but I had power no greater than those who were my colleagues in any magistracy.[2]

Augustus was not being a hypocrite. As consul he had no more constitutional and legal power than his fellow consul. Yet in addition to the consulship Augustus held many other magistracies, while his fellow consul did not. Constitutionally, his ascendancy within the state stemmed from the number of magistracies he held and the power granted him by the senate. He either held the consulship annually, or the senate voted him consular power. The senate also voted him *tribunicia potestas* — the full power of the tribunes. Tribunician power gave him the right to call the senate into session, present legislation to the people, and defend their rights. He held either high office or the powers of the chief magistrate year in and year out. No other magistrate could do the same. In 12 B.C., he became *pontifex maximus,* chief priest of the state, a position of great honor. By assuming it he became the chief religious official within the state.

The main source of Augustus's power came from the fact that he commanded the Roman army. His title *imperator,* which Romans customarily gave to a general after a major victory, came to mean "emperor" in the modern sense of the term. Augustus governed the provinces where troops were needed for defense. The frontiers were his special concern. There Roman legionaries held the German barbarians at arm's length. The frontiers were also the areas where fighting could be expected to break out. Augustus made sure that Rome went to war only at his command. He controlled the deployment of the Roman army and paid its wages. He granted it bonuses and gave veterans retirement benefits. Thus, he avoided the problems with the army that the old senate had created for itself. Augustus never shared control of the army, and no Roman found it easy to defy him militarily.

The very size of the army was a special problem confronting Augustus. Rome's legions included thousands of men, far more than were necessary to maintain peace. What was Augustus to do with so many soldiers? This sort of problem had constantly

COIN OF AUGUSTUS. This portrait shows Augustus as a mature *princeps*. Like many of his coins, this one too has a propaganda value. On the reverse is his grandson Gaius. Augustus may have minted this coin to publicize Gaius's participation in Tiberius's campaign against the Germans. (Courtesy, World Heritage Museum. Photo: Caroline Buckler)

AUGUSTUS AS IMPERATOR. Here Augustus, dressed in breastplate and uniform, emphasizes the imperial majesty of Rome and his role as *imperator.* The figures on his breastplate represent the restoration of peace, one of Augustus's greatest accomplishments and certainly one that he frequently stressed. (Vatican Museum. Alinari/Scala)

plagued the late republic, whose leaders never found a solution to it. Augustus gave his own answer in the *Res Gestae:* "I founded colonies of soldiers in Africa, Sicily, Macedonia, Spain, Achaea, Gaul, and Pisidia. Moreover, Italy has 28 colonies under my auspices."[3]

At least forty new colonies arose, most of them in the western Mediterranean. Augustus's veterans took abroad with them their Roman language and culture. His colonies, like those of Julius Caesar, were a significant tool in the further spread of Roman culture throughout the West. In addition, Roman colonies differed from the Greek colonies of Archilochus' time (see Chapter 2). Greek colonies were independent. Once founded, they went their own way. Roman colonies were part of a system, the Roman Empire, that linked East with West in a mighty political, social, and economic network. The glory of the Roman Empire was its success in uniting the Mediterranean world and spreading Greco-Roman culture throughout it. Roman colonies played a crucial part in that process, and deservedly did Augustus boast of his foundations.

What is to be made of Augustus's constitutional settlement? Despite his claims to the contrary, Augustus had not restored the republic. In fact, he would probably have agreed with the words of John Stuart Mill, the nineteenth-century English philosopher: "When society requires to be rebuilt, there is no use in attempting to rebuild it on the old plan." Augustus had created a constitutional monarchy, something completely new in Roman history.

The title princeps, "First Citizen," came to mean in Rome, just as it does today, "prince" in the sense of a sovereign ruler. Furthermore, Augustus failed to solve a momentous problem. He never found a way to institutionalize his position with the army. The ties between the princeps and the army were always personal. The army was loyal to the princeps but not necessarily to the state. The Augustan Principate worked well at first, but by the third century A.D., the army would make and break

emperors at will. Nonetheless, it is a measure of Augustus's success that his settlement survived as long and as well as it did.

Augustus's Administration of the Provinces

Augustus cared for the welfare of the provinces. In his day the population of the Roman empire reached between 70 and 100 million people, 75 percent of whom lived in the provinces. In the areas under his immediate jurisdiction Augustus put provincial administration on an ordered basis. He improved its functioning as well. Believing that the cities of the empire should look after their own affairs, he encouraged and fostered local self-government and urbanism. Augustus respected local customs and ordered his governors to do the same. The lengths that he was willing to go to can be seen in Judaea.

Augustus wished to avoid antagonizing the Jews. As early as 40 B.C., long before he had put an end to the civil war, he and Antony had prevailed upon the senate to give the Jews their own king, Herod the Great, as an added gesture of good will. Also, when the Roman legionaries stationed outside of Jerusalem entered the city, they left their standards behind them because on the standards were graven images. This was a magnanimous gesture, the equivalent of a modern army leaving its national flags behind. Augustus saw no reason to interfere with the customs, institutions, and traditions of cities as long as they functioned peacefully and effectively.

As a spiritual bond between the provinces and Rome, Augustus encouraged the cult of Roma, the goddess and guardian of the state. In the Hellenistic East, where king worship was an established custom, the cult of Roma et Augustus grew up and spread rapidly. Augustus introduced it in the West. By the time of his death in A.D. 14, nearly every province could boast an altar or shrine to Roma et Augustus. In the West the person of the emperor was not worshiped but rather his *genius* — his guardian spirit. In praying for the good health and welfare of the emperor Romans and provincials were praying for the empire itself. The cult became a symbol of Roman unity.

Roman Expansion into Northern and Western Europe

For the history of Western civilization one of the most important aspects of Augustus's reign was Roman expansion into the wilderness of northern and western Europe. In this he followed in Julius Caesar's footsteps. From 58 to 51 B.C., Caesar had subdued Gaul and unsuccessfully attacked Britain. Carrying on his work, Augustus pushed Rome's frontier into the region of modern Germany. The Germanic tribes were tough opponents, and the Roman legions saw much bitter fighting in the north.

For the common soldier this fighting must have been exceptionally grim. Forests were believed to be the haunts of evil spirits, places of dim light and unidentifiable sounds. As early as the third century B.C. comes evidence that Roman armies habitually skirted the forests of Etruria. The vast forests of central Germany, with their thick, impenetrable gloom, must have oppressed even veteran legionaries. The thought of coming suddenly onto a war party of tall, bearded Germans was not particularly pleasing either. Even so, the Roman legionary was stouthearted, and these obstacles did not stop Roman expansion.

Augustus began his work in the north by completing the conquest of Spain. In Gaul, apart from minor campaigns, most of his work was peaceful. He founded twelve new towns and spread urban life through the area. The Roman road system linked new settlements with one another and with Italy. But the German frontier, anchored on the Rhine River, was the scene of hard fighting (see Map 5.1). In 12 B.C., Augustus ordered a major invasion of Germany beyond the Rhine. Roman legions advanced to the Elbe River, and a Roman fleet explored the North Sea and Jutland. The area north of the Main River and west of the Elbe was on the point of becoming Roman. But in 9 B.C., Augustus's general Varus lost some twenty thousand troops at the battle of the Teutoburger Forest. Thereafter, the Rhine remained the Roman frontier.

Meanwhile, more successful generals pushed the Roman standards as far as the Danube. Roman legions penetrated the area of modern Austria and western Hungary. The regions of modern Serbia, Bulgaria, and Rumania fell to Roman troops. Within this area the legionaries built fortified camps. Roads linked these camps with one another, and around the camps settlements began slowly to grow. Traders began to frequent the frontier and traffic with the barbarians. Thus, gradually, Roman culture, even the rough and ready kind found in military camps, spread into the northern wilderness.

Augustus's achievements in the north were monumental. For the first time in history, Greco-Roman culture left the sunny Mediterranean and advanced north into the heart of Europe. Amid the wilds and the vast expanse of forests, Roman towns, trade, language, and law began to exert a civilizing influence on the barbarians. The Roman way of life attracted the barbarians, who soon recognized the benefits of assimilating Roman culture. The military camps themselves often became towns, and many modern European cities in this area owe their origins to the forts of the Roman army. For the first time, the barbarian north came into direct, immediate, and continuous contact with Mediterranean culture.

MAP 5.1 THE ROMAN EMPIRE UNDER AUGUSTUS AND HADRIAN

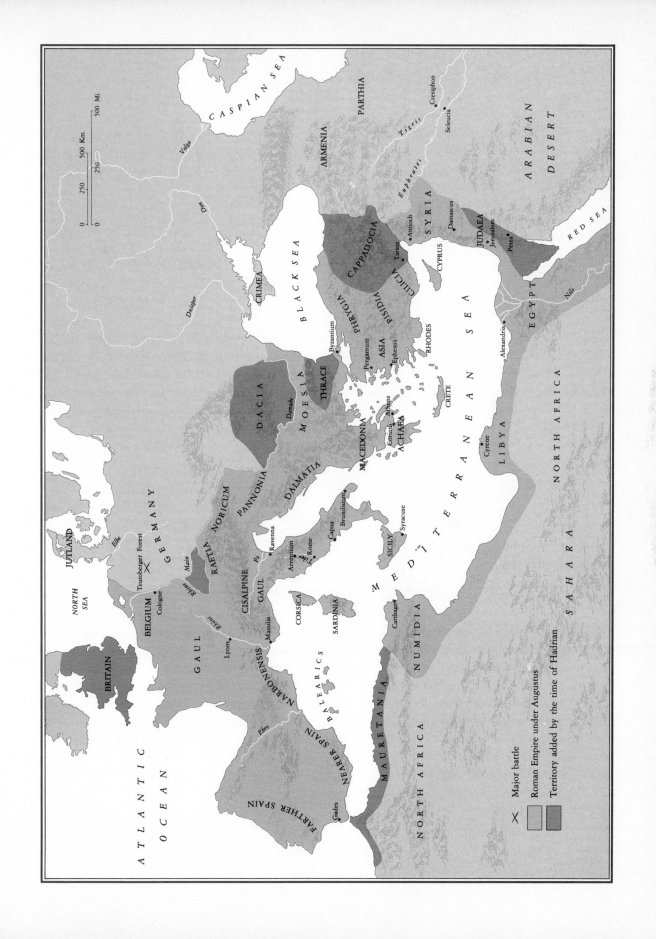

CASPIAN SEA

PARTHIA

ARMENIA

Ctesiphon
Seleucia

Tigris

ARABIAN

DESERT

500 Mi.

500 Km.

250

250

Volga

Don

Euphrates

SYRIA

Antioch
Damascus

CAPPADOCIA

Dnieper

CRIMEA

BLACK SEA

CILICIA
Tarsus

CYPRUS

JUDAEA
Jerusalem
Petra

RED SEA

EGYPT

Alexandria

Nile

PHRYGIA

PISIDIA

RHODES

Byzantium

Pergamum
ASIA
Ephesus

DACIA

MOESIA

THRACE

Danube

MACEDONIA
ACHAEA
Corinth Athens

CRETE

MEDITERRANEAN SEA

Cyrene

LIBYA

NORTH AFRICA

DALMATIA

PANNONIA

NORICUM

RAETIA

CISALPINE
GAUL

Po
Ravenna
Arretium
Rome
Capua

Brundisium

Syracuse
SICILY

SAHARA

GERMANY

Teutoberger Forest

Main

Rhine

Elbe

JUTLAND

NORTH
SEA

BELGIUM
Cologne

GAUL

Lyons

Rhone

NARBONENSIS

Massilia

CORSICA

SARDINIA

BALEARICS

Ebro

NEARER SPAIN

Carthage

NUMIDIA

MAURETANIA

NORTH AFRICA

FARTHER SPAIN

Gades

BRITAIN

ATLANTIC

OCEAN

✕ Major battle

Roman Empire under Augustus

Territory added by the time of Hadrian

Literary Flowering

The Augustan settlement's gift of peace nourished a literary flowering unparalleled in Roman history. With good reason this period is known as the "golden age" of Latin literature. Augustus and many of his friends actively encouraged poets and writers. Virgil, Rome's greatest poet, summed up Augustus and his era:

Here is the man, here is he whom you often hear
    promised to you,
Augustus Caesar, offspring of the deified [Julius
    Caesar], who will establish
Once more a golden age in Latium.[4]

Virgil was not alone in this sentiment. The poet Horace (65–8 B.C.) felt the same:

With Caesar [Augustus] the guardian of the state
Not civil rage nor violence shall drive out peace,
    Nor wrath which forges swords
    And turns unhappy cities against each other.[5]

These lines are not empty flattery. To a generation that had known only vicious civil war Augustus's settlement was an unbelievable blessing.

The tone and ideal of Roman literature, like that of the Greeks, was humanistic and worldly. Roman poets and prose writers celebrated the dignity of humanity and the range of its accomplishments. They stressed the physical and emotional joys of a comfortable, peaceful life. Their works were highly polished, elegant in style, and intellectual in conception. Roman poets referred to the gods and treated mythological themes, but always the core of their work was human, not divine.

Virgil celebrated the new age in the *Georgics,* four books of poems on agriculture. Virgil delighted in his own farm, and his poems sing of the pleasures of peaceful farm life. The *Georgics* are also a manual of agriculture written in meter. The poet tells how to keep bees, to grow grapes and olives, to plow, and to manage the farm. Throughout the *Georgics* Virgil wrote about the things he had seen, not drawing his inspiration from the writings of others. For instance, he describes the worker bees returning to the hive at nightfall:

The weary young bees come back late at night,
Their legs full of thyme. Far and wide they feed on
    arbutus and grey-green willows and red crocus
And rich linden and rust-colored hyacinth.[6]

He could be vivid and graphic as well as pastoral. Even a small event could be a drama for him. A farmer working his land and the death of a bull while plowing are hardly epic material; yet Virgil captured the sadness of the event. Very real is the scene of the farmer unyoking the remaining animal and leading it away from the plow;

Look, the bull, shining under the rough plough,
    falls to the ground
    and vomits from his mouth blood mixed with foam,
    and releases his dying groan.
Sadly moves the ploughman, unharnessing the
    young steer grieving for the death of his brother
    and leaves in the middle of the job
    the plough stuck fast.[7]

Virgil's poetry is robust yet graceful. A sensitive man who delighted in simple things, Virgil left in his *Georgics* a charming picture of Italian agriculture in a period of peace.

Virgil's masterpiece is the *Aeneid,* an epic poem that is the Latin equivalent to the Greek *Iliad* and *Odyssey.* In it Virgil expressed his admiration for Augustus's work. He depicted the shining ideal of a world blessed by the pax Romana. Virgil told of the founding of Rome and the early years of the city. He gave final form to the legend of Aeneas, the Trojan hero who escaped to Italy at the fall of Troy. The principal Roman tradition held that Romulus was the founder of Rome, but the legend of Aeneas

ARA PACIS.   This scene from the Ara Pacis, the Altar of Peace, celebrates Augustus's restoration of peace and the fruits of peace. Here Mother Earth is depicted with her children. The cow and the sheep under the goddess represent the prosperity brought by peace, especially the agricultural prosperity so highly cherished by Virgil. (Alinari/Scala)

was also very old and was known by the Etruscans in the fifth century B.C. Although Rome could not have two founders, Virgil linked the legends of Aeneas and Romulus and kept them both. In that way he also connected Rome with Greece's heroic past. Virgil added the story of Aeneas and Dido, the queen of Carthage. He made their ill-fated love affair the cause of the Punic wars. But above all, the *Aeneid* is the expression of Virgil's passionate belief in Rome's greatness. It is a vision of Rome as the protector of the good and noble against the forces of darkness and disruption.

In its own way Livy's history of Rome, entitled simply *Ab Urbe Condita* (*From the Founding of the City*), is the prose counterpart of the *Aeneid.* Livy (59 B.C.–A.D. 17) received training in Greek and Latin literature, rhetoric, and philosophy. He even urged the future emperor Claudius to write history.

He loved and admired the heroes and the great deeds of the republic, but he was also a friend of Augustus and a supporter of the principate. He especially approved of Augustus's efforts to restore the old republican virtues and morality.

Livy's history began with the legend of Aeneas and ended with the reign of Augustus. His theme of the greatness of the republic fitted admirably with Augustus's program of restoring the republic. Livy's history was colossal, consisting of 142 books of which only 25 percent is extant. Livy was a sensitive writer, and something of a moralist. Like Thucydides he felt that history should be applied to the present. His history later became one of Rome's legacies to the modern world. During the Renaissance the *Ab Urbe Condita* found a warm admirer in the poet Petrarch, and it left its mark on Machiavelli, who read it avidly.

The poet Horace went from humble beginnings to friendship with Augustus. The son of an ex-slave and tax collector, Horace nonetheless received an excellent education. He loved Greek literature and finished his education in Athens. After Augustus's victory he returned to Rome and became Virgil's friend. Horace obtained a small farm north of Rome, which delighted him. He was as content as Virgil on the farm, and he expressed his joy in a few lines:

Strive to add nothing to the myrtle plant!
The myrtle befits both you, the servant,
And me the master, as I drink under the
Thick-leaved vine.[8]

Horace recognized the value of Augustus's work. He happily turned his pen to celebrating the newly won peace and prosperity. One of his finest odes commemorates Augustus's victory over Cleopatra at Actium in 31 B.C. He depicted Cleopatra as a frenzied queen, drunk with desire to destroy Rome.

He saw in Augustus's victory the triumph of West over East, of simplicity over oriental excess. One of the truly moving aspects of Horace's poetry, like that of Virgil's, is his deep and abiding gratitude for the pax Romana.

For Rome, Augustus's age was one of hope and new beginnings. Augustus had put the empire on a new foundation. Constitutional monarchy was firmly established, and government was to all appearances a partnership between the princeps and the senate. The Augustan settlement was a delicate structure, and parts of it would in time be discarded. Nevertheless, it worked, and by building on it, later emperors would carry on Augustus's work.

JUDAISM AND THE RISE OF CHRISTIANITY

During the reign of the emperor Tiberius (A.D. 14–37), perhaps in A.D. 29, Pontius Pilate, prefect of Judaea, condemned Jesus of Nazareth to death. At the time it was a rather minor event, but it has become one of the best known moments in history. How did these two men come to their historic meeting? The question is not idle, for Rome was as important as Judaea to Christianity. Jesus was born in a troubled time, when Roman rule aroused hatred and unrest among the Jews. This climate of hostility affected the lives of all who lived in Judaea, Roman and Jew alike. It forms the backdrop of Jesus' life, and it had a fundamental impact on his ministry. Without an understanding of this age of anxiety in Judaea, Jesus and early Christianity cannot properly be appreciated.

The entry of Rome into Jewish affairs was certainly not peaceful. The civil wars that destroyed the republic wasted the prosperity of Judaea and the entire eastern Mediterranean world. Jewish leaders took sides in the fighting, and Judaea suffered its share of ravages and military confiscations. Peace brought little satisfaction to the Jews. Although

Augustus treated Judaea generously, the Romans won no popularity by making Herod king of Judaea. King Herod gave Judaea prosperity and security, but the Jews hated his acceptance of Greek culture. He was also a bloodthirsty prince, who murdered his wife and sons. Upon his death, the Jews broke out in revolt. For the next ten years his successor waged almost constant war against the rebels. Added to the horrors of civil war were years of crop failure, which caused famine and plague. Men who called themselves prophets proclaimed that the end of the world and the coming of the Messiah, the savior of Israel, were approaching.

At length the Romans intervened to restore order. Augustus put Judaea under the charge of a prefect answerable directly to the emperor. Religious matters and local affairs became the responsibility of the Sanhedrin, the highest Jewish judicial body. Although most prefects tried to perform their duties scrupulously and conscientiously, some were rapacious and indifferent to Jewish culture. Especially hated were the Roman tax collectors, many of whom pitilessly gouged the Jews. Publicans and sinners — the words became synonymous. Clashes between Roman troops and Jewish guerrillas inflamed the anger of both sides.

Among the Jews two movements were under way. First was the rise of the Zealots, extremists who worked and fought to rid Judaea of the Romans. They were resolute in their worship of Yahweh, and they refused to pay any but the tax levied by the Jewish temple. Their battles with the Roman legionaries were marked by savagery on both sides. As usual, the innocent were caught in the middle and suffered grievously. As Roman policy grew tougher, even moderate Jews began to hate the conquerors. Day by day Judaea came to resemble a tinderbox, ready to burst into flames at a single spark.

The second movement was the growth of militant apocalyptic sentiment — the belief that the coming of the Messiah was near. This belief was an old one among the Jews. But by the first century A.D. it had become stronger and more widespread than ever before. Typical was the Apocalypse of Baruch, which foretold the destruction of the Roman Empire. First would come a period of great tribulation, misery, and injustice. At the worst of the suffering, the Messiah — a superhuman individual — would appear. The Messiah would destroy the Roman legions and all the kingdoms that had ruled Israel. Then the Messiah would inaugurate a period of happiness and plenty.

This was no abstract notion among the Jews. As the ravages of war became ever more widespread and conditions worsened, more and more people prophesied the imminent coming of the Messiah. One such was John the Baptist, "the voice of one crying in the wilderness, prepare ye the way of the lord."9 Many Jews did just that in their own way. The sect described in the Dead Sea Scrolls readied itself for the end of the world. Its members were probably Essenes, and their social organization closely resembled that of the early Christians. Like the early Christians, the members of this group shared their possessions, precisely what John the Baptist urged people to do. Yet this sect, unlike the Christians, also made military preparations for the day of the Messiah.

Into this climate of Roman severity, Zealotry, and Messianic hope came Jesus of Nazareth (ca 3 B.C. – A.D. 29). He was born in Galilee, the stronghold of the Zealots. Yet Jesus himself was a man of peace. His teachings are strikingly similar to those of Hillel (30 B.C.–A.D. 9), the great rabbi and interpreter of the Scriptures. Hillel taught the Jews to love one another as they loved God. He taught them to treat others as they themselves wished to be treated. Jesus' preaching was in this same serene tradition.

Jesus' teachings were entirely and thoroughly Jewish. He declared that he would change not one jot or tittle of the Jewish law. His orthodoxy enabled him to preach in the synagogue and the temple. His only deviation from orthodoxy was his insistence that he taught in his own name, not in the name of Yahweh. Was he then the Messiah? A small band of followers thought so, and Jesus revealed himself to them as the Messiah. Yet Jesus had his own conception of the Messiah. Unlike the Messiah of the Apocalypse of Baruch, Jesus would not destroy the Roman Empire. He told his disciples flatly that they were to "render unto Caesar the things that are Caesar's." Jesus would establish a spiritual kingdom, not an earthly one. Repeatedly he told his disciples that his kingdom was "not of this world."

Of Jesus' life and teachings Pontius Pilate knew little and cared even less. All he was concerned about was the maintenance of peace and order. Christian tradition has made much of Pontius Pilate. In the medieval West he was considered a monster. In the Ethiopian church he is considered a saint. Neither monster nor saint, Pilate was simply a hard-bitten Roman official. He did his duty, and he at times did it harshly. In Judaea his duty was to enforce the law and to keep the peace. These were the problems on his mind when Jesus stood before him. Jesus as King of the Jews did not worry him. The popular outcry against Jesus did. To avert a riot and bloodshed Pilate condemned Jesus to death.

Once Pilate's soldiers had carried out the sentence, the entire matter seemed to be closed. There were rumors that Jesus had risen from the dead or that his disciples had stolen his body, but otherwise all the tumult subsided. Jesus' followers lived quietly and peacefully, unmolested by Roman or Jew. Pilate had no quarrel with them, and Judaism already had many minor sects. Peter (d. A.D. 67?), the first of Jesus' followers, became the head of the sect, which continued to observe Jewish law and religious customs. Peter was a man of traditional Jewish beliefs, and he felt that Jesus' teachings were meant exclusively for the Jews. Only in their practices of baptism and the Lord's Supper did the sect differ from normal Jewish custom. Meanwhile, they awaited the return of Jesus.

Christianity might have remained a purely Jewish sect had it not been for Paul of Tarsus (A.D. 5?–67?). The conversion of Hellenized Jews and of Gentiles, non-Jews, to Christianity caused the sect grave problems. Were the Gentiles subject to the law of Moses? If not, was Christianity to have two sets of laws? The answer to these questions was Paul's momentous contribution to Christianity. Paul was unlike Jesus or Peter. Born in a thriving and busy city filled with Romans, Greeks, Jews, Syrians, and others, he was at home in the world of Greco-Roman culture. After his conversion to Christianity he taught that his native Judaism was the preparation for the Messiah, and that Jesus by his death and resurrection had fulfilled the prophesy of Judaism and initiated a new age. Paul taught that Jesus was the Son of God, the beginning of a new law, and he preached that Jesus' teachings were to be proclaimed to all people, whether Jew or Gentile.

Paul's influence was far greater than that of any other early Christian. He traveled the length and breadth of the eastern Roman world, spreading his doctrine and preaching of Jesus. To little assemblies of believers in cities as far removed as Rome and Corinth he taught that Jesus had died to save all people. Paul's vision of Christianity won out over Peter's traditionalism. Christianity broke with Judaism and embarked on its own course.

What was Christianity's appeal to the Roman world? What did this obscure sect give to people that other religions did not? Christianity possessed many different attractions. One of its leading assets was its willingness to embrace both men and women, slaves and nobles. Many of the Eastern mystery religions with which Christianity competed were exclusive in one way or another. For instance,

Mithraism, a mystery religion born in Persia, spread throughout the entire empire, yet it permitted only men to become devotees. Pretty much the same was true of the ancient Eleusinian mysteries of Greece, which were open only to Greeks and Romans.

Christianity also appealed to common people and to the poor. Its communal celebration of the Lord's Supper gave men and women a sense of belonging. Christianity offered its adherents the promise of salvation. Christians believed that Jesus on the cross had defeated evil, and he would reward his followers with eternal life after death. Christianity also offered the possibility of forgiveness. Human nature was weak, and even the best Christians would fall into sin. But Jesus loved sinners and forgave those who repented. In its doctrine of salvation and forgiveness alone Christianity had a powerful ability to give solace and strength to those who believed.

Christianity was attractive to many because it gave the Roman world a cause. Hellenistic philosophy, as was seen in Chapter 3, had attempted to make men and women self-sufficient: people who became indifferent to the outside world could no longer be hurt by it. That goal alone ruled out any cause except the attainment of serenity. The Romans, who were never innovators in philosophy, merely elaborated this lonely and austere message. Instead of passivity Christianity stressed the ideal of striving for a goal. Each and every Christian, no matter how poor or humble, worked to realize the triumph of Christianity on earth. This was God's will, a sacred duty to every Christian. By spreading the word of Christ, the Christian played his or her part in God's plan. No matter how small a part each Christian played, that part was important. Since this duty was God's will, the Christian believed that sooner or later the goal would be achieved. The Christian was not to be discouraged by temporary setbacks, believing Christianity to be invincible.

Christianity gave its devotees a sense of community. The Christian was not alone in fulfilling God's plan. All members of the Christian community strived toward the same goal. Each individual community was in turn a member of a greater community. And that community, the Church General, was indestructible. After all, Jesus himself had promised, "Thou art Peter, and upon this rock I will build my church; and the gates of hell shall not prevail against it."[10]

So Christianity's attractions were many, from forgiveness of sin to an exalted purpose for each individual. Its insistence on the importance of the individual brought solace and encouragement, especially to the poor and meek. Its claim to divine protection produced hope in the eventual success of the Christian community. Christianity made participation in the universal possible for each and every person. The ultimate reward promised by Christianity was eternal bliss after death. Though at first the educated and wealthy scoffed at this message, they too fell to its charm. It was unlike anything the average man and woman had ever known.

THE JULIO-CLAUDIANS AND THE FLAVIANS (27 B.C.–A.D. 96)

The solidity of Augustus's work became obvious at his death in A.D. 14. Since the principate was not technically an office, Augustus could not legally hand it to a successor. Augustus had recognized this problem, and long before his death had found a way to solve it. He shared his consular and tribunician powers with his adopted son Tiberius, thus grooming him for the principate. In his will Augustus left most of his vast fortune to Tiberius, and the senate formally requested Tiberius to assume the burdens of the principate. All the formalities aside, Augustus had succeeded in creating a dynasty.

For the next fifty years this dynasty, known as the Julio-Claudians because they were all members of the Julian and Claudian clans, which were closely related, provided the emperors of Rome. Some of the Julio-Claudians, like Tiberius and Claudius, were sound rulers and able administrators. Others, like Caligula and Nero, were weak and frivolous men who exercised their power stupidly and brought misery to the empire. Writers such as the biting and brilliant historian Tacitus (ca A.D. 55–ca 116) and the gossipy Suetonius (ca A.D. 75–150) have left unforgettable—and generally hostile—pictures of these emperors that are literary masterpieces. Yet the venom of Tacitus and Suetonius cannot obscure the fact that Julio-Claudians were responsible for some notable achievements and that during their reigns the empire on the whole prospered.

One of the most momentous of achievements of the Julio-Claudians was Claudius's creation of an imperial bureaucracy. Even the most energetic emperor could not run the empire alone. The numerous duties and immense responsibilities of the emperor prompted Claudius to delegate power. He began by giving the freedmen of his household official duties, especially in the field of finances. It was a simple, workable system. Claudius knew his ex-slaves well and could discipline them at will. The effect of Claudius's innovations was to enable the emperor to rule the empire more easily and efficiently.

During the Julio-Claudian period, one of the worst defects of Augustus's settlement became obvious—the army's ability to interfere in politics. Augustus had created a special standing force, the Praetorian Guard, as an imperial bodyguard. In A.D. 14 one of the praetorians murdered Caligula, while others hailed Claudius as the emperor. Under the

threat of violence the senate ratified the praetorians' choice. It was a story repeated frequently, for during the first three centuries of the empire the Praetorian Guard all too often murdered emperors they were supposed to protect and saluted emperors of their own choosing.

In A.D. 69, Nero's rule led to an extensive military uprising that caused widespread disruption. No fewer than four men became emperor that year, because of which 69 is known as the "Year of the Four Emperors." Roman armies in Gaul, on the Rhine, and in the East marched on Rome to make their commanders emperor. The man who emerged triumphant was Vespasian, commander of the eastern armies, who entered Rome in 70 and restored order. Nonetheless, the "Year of the Four Emperors" proved that the Augustan settlement had failed to end civil war.

Not a brilliant politican, Vespasian did not institute reforms as had Augustus or tackle the problem of the army in politics. To prevent usurpers from claiming the throne Vespasian designated his sons Titus and Domitian as his successors. By establishing the Flavian (the name of Vespasian's clan) dynasty Vespasian turned the principate into an open and admitted monarchy. He also expanded the power of the emperor by increasing the size of the budding bureaucracy Claudius had created.

The Flavians carried on Augustus's work on the frontiers. Domitian, the last of the Flavians, was especially active in this sphere, and he created a new frontier in Germany. He won additional territory and consolidated it in two new provinces. He defeated barbarian tribes on the Danube frontier and strengthened that area as well. Despite his good work, Domitian was one of the most hated of Roman emperors, and he fell victim to an assassin's dagger. Nevertheless, the Flavians had given the Roman world peace and had kept the legions in line. Their work paved the way for the era of the "five good emperors," the golden age of the empire.

PERIODS OF ROMAN HISTORY

Period	Important Emperors	Significant Events
Julio-Claudians, 27 B.C.–A.D. 68	Augustus, 27 B.C.–A.D. 14 Tiberius, 14–37 Caligula, 37–41 Claudius, 41–54 Nero, 54–68	Augustan settlement Beginning of the principate Birth and death of Jesus Expansion into northern and western Europe Creation of the imperial bureaucracy
"Year of the Four Emperors," 68–69	Nero Galba Otho Vitellius	Civil war Major breakdown of the concept of the principate
Flavians, 69–96	Vespasian, 69–79 Titus, 79–81 Domitian, 81–96	Growing trend toward the concept of monarchy Defense and further consolidation of the European frontiers
Antonines, 96–192	Nerva, 96–98 Trajan, 98–117 Hadrian, 117–138 Antoninus Pius, 138–161 Marcus Aurelius, 161–180 Commodus, 180–192	The "golden age" – the era of the "five good emperors" Economic prosperity Trade and the growth of cities in northern Europe Beginning of the barbarian menace on the frontiers
Severi, 193–235	Septimius Severus, 193–211 Caracalla, 211–217 Elagabalus, 218–222 Severus Alexander, 222–235	Military monarchy All free men within the empire given Roman citizenship
"Barracks Emperors," 235–284	Twenty different emperors in forty-nine years	Civil war Breakdown of the Empire Barbarian invasions Severe economic decline
Tetrarchy, 284–337	Diocletian, 284–305 Constantine, 306–337	Political recovery Autocracy Legalization of Christianity Transition to the Middle Ages in the West Birth of the Byzantine Empire in the East

THE AGE OF THE "FIVE GOOD EMPERORS" (A.D. 96–180)

In the second century of the Christian era, the Empire of Rome comprehended the fairest part of the earth, and the most civilised portion of mankind. The frontiers of that extensive monarchy were guarded by ancient renown and disciplined valour. The gentle but powerful influence of laws and manners had gradually cemented the union of the provinces. Their peaceful inhabitants enjoyed and abused the advantages of wealth and luxury. The image of a free constitution was preserved with decent reverence: the Roman senate appeared to possess the sovereign authority, and devolved on the emperors all the executive powers of government. During a happy period (A.D. 96–180) of more than fourscore years, the public administration was conducted by the virtue and abilities of Nerva, Trajan, Hadrian, and the two Antonines.[11]

Thus Edward Gibbon (1737–1794) began his monumental *History of the Decline and Fall of the Roman Empire.* He saw the era of Nerva, Trajan, Hadrian, Antoninus Pius, and Marcus Aurelius—the "five good emperors"—as the happiest period of human history, the last burst of summer before the autumn of failure and barbarism. Gibbon recognized a great truth: the age of the Antonines, as the "five good emperors" are often called, was one of almost unparalleled prosperity. Wars were minor and confined to the frontiers. Even the serenity of Augustus's day seemed to pale in comparison. The emperors were among the noblest, most dedicated, and ablest men in Roman history. Fundamental political and military changes had taken place since Augustus's day, however.

The Antonine Monarchy

The age of the Antonines was the age of full-blown monarchy. Gibbon wrote:

The obvious definition of a monarchy seems to be that of a state, in which a single person, by whatsoever name he may be distinguished, is entrusted with the execution of the laws, the management of the revenue, and the command of the army.[12]

Augustus clearly fits Gibbon's definition of a monarch in all essentials. But there is a significant difference between Augustus's position and that of an Emperor like Hadrian.

Augustus claimed that his influence came from the collection of offices the senate had bestowed upon him. However, there was in law no position or office of "emperor." Augustus was merely the "First Citizen." Under the Flavians the principate had become a full-blown monarchy, and by the time of the Antonines the principate had become an office with definite rights, powers, and prerogatives. As the eminent historian M. Rostovtzeff observed:

The rule of one man had now been recognized by all classes of the population as a fact and a necessity. Without a single will the Roman Empire was bound to fall to pieces.[13]

Augustus had been monarch in fact but not in theory; the Antonines were monarchs in both.

The Antonines were not power-hungry autocrats. The concentration of power was the result of empire and, as the American historian M. Hammond pointed out:

Monarchy was indeed an inescapable result of the existence of the empire; the more efficient the imperial government became, the more it assumed new functions; and the more that increasing pressure made its task heavier, so much the more it became monarchical.[14]

In short, the easiest and most efficient way to run the Roman Empire was to invest the emperor with vast powers. Furthermore, Roman emperors on the whole proved to be effective rulers and administrators. As capable and efficient emperors took on new tasks and functions, the hand of the emperor was felt in more and more areas of life and government.

COIN OF HADRIAN. The emperor Hadrian not only energetically ruled the Roman Empire, he also helped to set a new fashion in Rome by sporting a full beard. Since Scipio Aemilianus's day, Romans had ordinarily been clean-shaven. (Courtesy, World Heritage Museum. Photo: Caroline Buckler)

Increasingly, the emperors became the source of all authority and guidance within the empire. The "five good emperors" were benevolent and exercised their power intelligently, but they were absolute kings all the same. Lesser men would later throw off the façade of constitutionality and use this same power in a despotic fashion.

Typical of the "five good emperors" is the career of Hadrian, who became emperor in A.D. 117. He was born in Spain, and that fact alone illustrates the increased importance of the provinces in Roman politics. Hadrian received his education at Rome and became an ardent admirer of Greek culture. He caught the attention of his elder cousin Trajan — the future emperor — who started him on a military career. At age nineteen Hadrian served on the Danube frontier, where he learned the details of how the Roman army lived and fought and saw for himself the problems of defending the frontiers. When Trajan became emperor in A.D. 98, he began giving Hadrian high military and administrative positions in which he learned how to defend and run the empire. At Trajan's death in 117, Hadrian assumed the reins of power.

Roman government had changed since Augustus's day. One of the most significant changes was the enormous growth of the imperial bureaucracy created by Claudius. Hadrian reformed this system by putting the bureaucracy on an organized, official basis. He established imperial administrative departments to handle the work formerly done by the imperial freedmen. Hadrian also separated civil service from military service. Men with little talent or taste for the army could instead serve the state as administrators. Hadrian's bureaucracy demanded professionalism from its members. Administrators made a career of the civil service. These innovations made for more efficient running of the empire, but they also increased the authority of the emperor, for he was the ruling power of the bureaucracy.

Changes in the Army

The Roman army had also changed since Augustus's time. The Roman legion had once been a mobile unit, but its duties under the empire no longer called for mobility. The successors of Augustus called a halt to further conquests. The army was expected to defend what had already been won. Under the Flavian emperors (A.D. 69–96) the frontiers became firmly fixed. Forts and watch stations guarded the borders. Behind the forts the Romans built a system of roads, which allowed the forts to be quickly supplied and reinforced in times of trouble. The army had evolved into a garrison force, with legions guarding specific areas for long periods.

The personnel of the legions was changing too. Italy could no longer supply all the recruits needed for the army. Increasingly, only the officers came from Italy and from the more Romanized provinces. The legionaries were mostly drawn from the less civilized provinces, especially the ones closest to the frontiers. A major trend was already obvious in Hadrian's day: fewer and fewer Roman soldiers were really "Roman." In the third century A.D., the barbarization of the army would result in an army that was indifferent to Rome and its traditions. In the age of the Antonines, however, the army was still a source of economic stability and a Romanizing agent. Provincials and even barbarians joined the army to learn a trade and to gain Roman citizenship. Even so, the signs were ominous. Julius Caesar's veterans would have had trouble recognizing Hadrian's troops as Roman legionaries.

LIFE IN THE "GOLDEN AGE"

If a man were called to fix the period in the history of the world, during which the condition of the human race was most happy and prosperous, he would without hesitation, name that which elapsed from the death of Domitian to the accession of Commodus.[15]

Thus, according to Gibbon, the age of the "five good emperors" was a "golden age" in human history. How does Gibbon's picture correspond to the popular image of Rome as a city of bread, brothels, and gladiatorial games? If the Romans were degenerates who spent their time carousing, who kept Rome and the empire running? Can life in Rome be taken as representative of life in other parts of the empire?

There is truth and exaggeration both in Gibbon's view and in the popular image of Rome. Rome and the provinces must be treated separately. Rome is no more typical of a provincial city like Cologne than New York is typical of Keokuk, Iowa. Rome was unique and must be treated as such. Only then can one turn to the provinces to obtain a full and reasonable picture of the empire under the Antonines.

Rome

Rome was truly an extraordinary city, especially by ancient standards. It was also an enormous city, with a population somewhere between 500,000 and 750,000. Although Rome could boast of stately palaces, noble buildings, and beautiful residential areas, most people lived in jerrybuilt apartment houses. Fire and crime were perennial problems, even after Augustus created fire and urban police forces. Streets were narrow and drainage inadequate. During the republic sanitation had been a common problem. Numerous inscriptions record prohibitions against the dumping of human refuse and even cadavers within the grounds of sanctuaries and cemeteries. Under the empire this situation improved. By comparison with medieval and early modern European cities, Rome was a healthy enough place to live.

APARTMENT HOUSES AT OSTIA. At heavily populated places such as Rome and Ostia, which was the port of Rome, apartment buildings housed urban dwellers. The brick construction of this building is a good example of solid Roman work. In Rome some apartment buildings were notoriously shoddy and unsafe. (Italian Government Travel Office)

Rome was such a huge city that the surrounding countryside could not feed it. Because of the danger of starvation, the emperor, following republican practice, provided the citizen population with free grain for bread, and later included oil and wine. By feeding the citizenry the emperor prevented bread riots caused by shortages and high prices. For the rest of the urban population who did not enjoy the rights of citizenship, the emperor provided grain at low prices. This measure was designed to prevent speculators from forcing up the price of grain in times of crisis. By maintaining the grain supply the emperor kept the favor of the people and insured that Rome's poor and idle did not starve.

The emperor also entertained the Roman populace, often at vast expense. The most popular forms of public entertainment were gladiatorial contests and chariot racing. Gladiatorial fighting originally was an Etruscan funerary custom, a blood sacrifice for the dead. Even a humane man like Hadrian staged extravagant contests. In A.D. 126, he sponsored six days of such combats, during which 1,835 pairs of gladiators dueled, usually with swords and shields. Many gladiators were criminals, some of whom were sentenced to be slaughtered in the arena. These convicts were given no defensive weapons and stood little real chance of survival. Other criminals were sentenced to fight in the arena as fully armed gladiators. Some gladiators were the slaves of gladiatorial trainers; others were prisoners of war. Still others were free men who volunteered for the arena. Even women at times engaged in gladiatorial combat. What drove these men and women on? Some obviously had no other choice. For a criminal condemned to death, the arena was preferable to the imperial mines, where convicts worked digging ore and died under wretched conditions. At least in the arena the gladiator might fight well enough to win his or her freedom. Others no doubt fought for the love of danger and fame. Although some Romans protested against gladiatorial fighting, most delighted in it — one of their least attractive sides. Not until the fifth century did Christianity put a stop to it.

The Romans were even more addicted to chariot racing than to gladiatorial shows. Under the empire four permanent teams competed against one another. Each team had its own color — red, white, green, or blue. Some Romans claimed that people cared more about their favorite team than about the race itself. Two-horse and four-horse chariots ran a course of seven laps, about five miles. A successful driver could be the hero of the hour. One charioteer, Gaius Appuleius Diocles, raced for twenty-four years. During that time he drove 4,257 starts and won 1,462 of them. His admirers honored him with an inscription that proclaimed him the champion of all charioteers.

But people like the charioteer Diocles were no more typical of the common Roman than Babe Ruth is of the average American. Ordinary Romans have nonetheless left their mark, if only in the inscriptions that grace their graves. These inscriptions give a glimpse of Roman life. Ordinary Romans were proud of their work and accomplishments. They were affectionate toward their families and friends, and they were eager to be remembered after death. They did not spend their lives in idleness, watching gladiators or chariot races. They had to make a living. They dealt with everyday problems and rejoiced over small pleasures. Some idea of them and their cares can be gained from their epitaphs. The funerary inscription of Paprius Vitalis to his wife is particularly engaging:

If there is anything good in the lower regions — I, however, finish a poor life without you — be happy there too, sweetest Thalassia . . . married to me for 40 years.[16]

As moving is the final tribute of a patron to his ex-slave:

To Grania Clara, freedwoman of Aulus, a temperate freedwoman. She lived 23 years. She was never vexatious to me except when she died.[17]

In another epitaph the wife of a merchant honored her husband for his honest dealings. Even the personal philosophy of typical Romans has come down from antiquity. Marcus Antonius Encolpus erected a funerary inscription to his wife that reads in part:

Do not pass by my epitaph, traveler.
But having stopped, listen and learn, then go your way.
There is no boat in Hades, no ferryman Charon,
no caretaker Aiakos, no dog Cerberus.
All we who are dead below
have become bones and ashes, but nothing else.
I have spoken to you honestly, go on, traveler,
lest even while dead I seem loquacious to you.[18]

Others put it more simply: "I was, I am not, I don't care." "To each his own tombstone." These Romans went about their lives much as people have always done. They had their fondness for brutal spectacles, but they also had their loves and their dreams.

The Provinces

In the provinces and even on the frontiers many men and women would have agreed with Gibbon's opinion of the second century. The age of the Antonines was one of extensive prosperity, especially in western Europe. The Roman army had beaten back the barbarians and had even exposed them to the civilizing effects of Roman traders. The resulting peace and security opened the areas of Britain, Gaul, Germany, and the lands of the Danube to immigration. Agriculture flourished as large tracts of land came under cultivation. Most of this land was in the hands of free tenant farmers. From the time of Augustus slavery had declined in the empire, as had the growth of latifundia (see Chapter 4). Augustus and his successors encouraged the rise of free farmers. Under the Antonines this trend continued, and the holders of small parcels of land thrived as never before. The Antonines provided loans on easy terms to farmers. These loans enabled them to rent land previously worked by slaves. It also permitted them to cultivate the new lands that were being opened up. Consequently, the small tenant farmer was becoming the backbone of Roman agriculture.

In continental Europe the army was largely responsible for the new burst of expansion. The areas where the legions were stationed readily became Romanized. When legionaries retired from the army, they often settled in the locality where they had served. Since they had usually learned a trade in the army, they brought essential skills to areas that badly needed trained men. These veterans took their retirement pay and used it to set themselves up in business.

Since the time of Augustus towns had gradually grown up around the camps and forts. The roads that linked the frontier with the rearward areas served as commercial lifelines for the new towns and villages. Part Roman, part barbarian, these towns were truly outposts of civilization, much like the raw towns of the American West. In the course of time many of them grew to be Romanized cities. As they did, emperors gave them the status of full Roman municipalities, with charters and constitutions. This development was very pronounced along the Rhine and Danube frontiers. Thus, while defending the borders, the army also spread Roman culture. This process would go so far that in A.D. 212 the emperor Caracalla would grant Roman citizenship to every free man within the empire.

The eastern part of the empire also participated in the boom. The Roman navy had swept the sea of pirates, and Eastern merchants traded their wares throughout the Mediterranean. The flow of goods and produce in the East matched that of the West. Venerable cities, such as Corinth, Antioch, and Ephesus, flourished as they rarely had before. The cities of the East built extensively, bedecking themselves with new amphitheaters, temples, fountains, and public buildings. For the East, the age of the Antonines was the heyday of the city. Urban life there grew ever richer and more comfortable.

Trade among the provinces increased dramatically. Britain and Belgium became prime producers of grain. Much of their harvests went to the armies of the Rhine. Britain's famous wool industry probably got its start under the Romans. Italy and southern Gaul produced wine in huge quantities. The wines of Italy went principally to Rome and the Danube, while Gallic wines were shipped to Britain and the Rhineland. Roman colonists had introduced the olive to southern Spain and northern

Africa. The experiment was so successful that these regions produced most of the oil consumed in the western empire. In the East, Syrian farmers continued to cultivate the olive, and the production of oil reached an all-time high. Egypt was the prime grain producer of the East, and tons of Egyptian wheat went to feed the populace of Rome. The Roman army in Mesopotamia consumed a high percentage of the raw materials and manufactured products of Syria and Asia Minor. The spread of trade meant the end of isolated and self-contained economies. By the time of the Antonines the empire had become an economic as well as political fact.

One of the most striking features about this period was the growth of industry in the provinces. Cities in Gaul and Germany eclipsed the old Mediterranean manufacturing centers. Italian cities were particularly hard hit by this development. Cities like Arrentium and Capua had dominated the production of glass, pottery, and bronze ware. Yet in the second century A.D. cities in Gaul and Germany took over the pottery market. Lyons in Gaul became the new center of the glassmaking industry. The technique of glass blowing spread to Britain and Germany. Later in the second century, Cologne replaced Lyons in glass production. The cities of Gaul were nearly unrivaled in the manufacture of bronze and brass. Gallic craftsmen invented a new technique of tin-plating, and they decorated their work with Celtic motives. Their wares soon drove Italian products out of the northern European market. For the first time in history northern Europe was able to rival the Mediterranean as a producer of manufactured goods. Europe had entered fully into the economic and cultural life of the Mediterranean world.

The age of the Antonines was generally one of peace, progress, and prosperity. The work of the Romans in northern and western Europe was a permanent contribution to the history of Western society. The cities that grew in Britain, Belgium, Gaul, Germany, Austria, and elsewhere survived the

SCENE FROM TRAJAN'S COLUMN. From 101 to 107 Trajan fought the barbarian tribes along the Danube. This scene depicts Roman soldiers unloading supplies at a frontier city, which forms the background. Not only did such walled cities serve as Roman strong points, they were also centers of Roman civilization, with their shops, homes, temples, and amphitheaters. (Alinari/Scala)

civil wars that racked the empire in the third century A.D. Likewise, they survived the barbarian invasions that destroyed the western empire. They handed on a precious heritage, both cultural and material, to the medieval world. The period of the Antonine monarchy was also one of consolidation. Roads and secure sea-lanes linked the empire in one vast web. The empire had become a commonwealth of cities, and urban life was the hallmark of this civilization. By no means a perfect age, it was at least a serene and generally happy one.

CIVIL WARS AND INVASION IN THE THIRD CENTURY

The age of the Antonines gave way to a period of chaos and stress. During the third century A.D., the empire was stunned by civil wars and barbarian invasions. By the time peace was restored, the economy was shattered, cities had shrunk in size, and agriculture was becoming manorial (see Chapter 9). In the disruption of the third century and the reconstruction of the fourth the medieval world had its origins.

After the death of Marcus Aurelius, the last of the "five good emperors," his son Commodus came to the throne, a man who was totally unsuited to govern the empire. His misrule led to his murder and a renewal of civil war. After a brief, but intense, spasm of fighting, the African general Septimius Severus defeated other rival commanders and established the Severan dynasty (A.D. 193–235). Although Septimius Severus was able to stabilize the empire, his successors proved incapable of disciplining the legions. When the last of the Severi was killed by one of his own soldiers, the empire was plunged into still another grim, destructive, and this time prolonged, round of civil war.

In the forty-nine years between 235 and 284, twenty different emperors ascended the throne, while many rebels died in the attempt to seize power. At various times, parts of the empire were lost to rebel generals, one of whom, Postumus, set up his own empire in Gaul for about ten years (A.D. 259/60–268/69). Yet other men like the iron-willed Aurelian (A.D. 270 – 275), dedicated their energies and their lives to restoring order. So many military commanders seized the rule that the middle of the third century has become known as the age of the "barracks emperors." The Augustan Principate had become a military monarchy, and that monarchy was nakedly autocratic.

The disruption caused by civil war opened the way for widespread barbarian invasions. Throughout the empire, barbarian invasions and civil war devastated towns, villages, and farms and caused a catastrophic economic depression. Indeed, the Roman Empire seemed on the point of collapse.

Barbarians on the Frontiers

The first and most disastrous result of the civil wars was trouble on the frontiers. It was Rome's misfortune that this era of anarchy coincided with immense movements of barbarian peoples. Historians still dispute the precise reason for these migrations. Their immediate cause was pressure from tribes moving westward across Asia. In the sixth century A.D., Jordanes, a Christianized Goth, preserved the memory of innumerable wars among the barbarians. Goths fought Vandals, Huns fought Goths. Steadily, the defeated and displaced tribes moved toward the Roman frontiers. Finally in A.D. 258, like "a swarm of bees" — to use Jordanes's image — the Goths burst into Europe.

When the barbarians reached the Rhine and Danube frontiers, they often found huge gaps in the Roman defenses. Typical is the case of Decius, a general who guarded the Danube frontier in Dacia (modern Rumania). In A.D. 249, he revolted and invaded Italy to become emperor. He left the frontier deserted, and the Goths easily poured through looking for new homes. Through much of the third century A.D., bands of Goths devastated the Balkans as far south as Greece. They even penetrated Asia Minor. The Alamanni, a German people, swept across the Danube. At one point they entered Italy and reached Milan before they were beaten back. Meanwhile the Franks, still another German folk, hit the Rhine frontier. The Franks then invaded eastern and central Gaul and northeastern Spain. Saxons from Scandinavia entered the English Channel in search of loot. In the East the Sassanids, of Persian stock, overran Mesopotamia. If the army had been guarding the borders instead of creating and destroying emperors, none of these invasions would have been possible. The "barracks emperors" should be credited with one accomplishment, however. They fought barbarians when they were not fighting each other. Only that kept the empire from total ruin.

Turmoil in Farm and Village Life

How did the ordinary people cope with this period of iron and blood? What did it mean to the lives of men and women on farms and in villages? How did local officials continue to serve their emperor and their neighbors? Some ideas can be had from isolated examples. For some people, the answer was simple: they became outlaws. One such person was Bulla, who organized a robber band of six hundred men and plundered the Italian countryside. Most of his men joined him because of poverty. Bulla was resourceful and clever, and he escaped capture as much by bribing officials as by his wits. He also had a sense of style, once freeing two members of his band by masquerading as a provincial governor. His humor became almost legendary. At one point Bulla captured an imperial officer who had been dispatched to capture him. Bulla shaved the centurion's head and ordered him to

return to his masters and tell them to feed their slaves if they really wanted to stop brigandage. He could even face his captors with a bit of humor. When the prefect asked him why he was a robber, Bulla merely asked his captor why he was a prefect.

Other people lived their lives more prosaically. In some instances they voiced their grievances to the emperor, thereby leaving a record of the problems they faced. In a surprising number of cases the barbarians were not as much of a problem as the lawlessness of soldiers, imperial officials, and local agents. For many ordinary people official corruption was the tangible and immediate result of the breakdown of central authority. In one instance some tenant farmers in Lydia (modern Turkey) complained to the emperor about arbitrary arrest and the killing of prisoners. They claimed that police agents had threatened them and prevented them from cultivating the land. Tenant farmers in Phrygia (modern Turkey) voiced similar complaints. They suffered extortion and illegal exactions at the hands of public officials. Military commanders, soldiers, and imperial agents requisitioned their livestock and compelled the farmers to forced labor. The farmers were becoming impoverished, and many people deserted the land to seek safety elsewhere. The inhabitants of an entire village in Thrace (modern Bulgaria) complained that they were being driven from their homes. From imperial and local officials they suffered insolence and violence. Soldiers demanded to be quartered and given supplies. Many villagers had abandoned their homes to escape. The villagers warned the emperor that unless order was restored, they too would flee.

Local officials were sometimes unsympathetic or violent to the farmers and villagers because of their own plight. They were responsible for the collection of imperial revenues. If their area could not meet its tax quota, they paid the deficit from their own pockets. For instance, Aurelius Hermophilus complained that he could no longer perform public duties because he had gone bankrupt. When Aemilius Stephanus, a wealthy Roman in Egypt, learned that he had been nominated to the local council of his town, he surrendered all his property to the man who had nominated him. In one Egyptian municipality fistfights broke out among the officials. Finally the emperor had to forbid fighting in the council house. Because the local officials were so hard pressed, they squeezed whatever they could from the villagers and farmers.

RECONSTRUCTION UNDER DIOCLETIAN AND CONSTANTINE (A.D. 284–337)

In the final part of the third century A.D., the emperor Diocletian (284–305) put an end to the period of turmoil. Repairing the damage done in the third century was the major work of the emperor Constantine (306–337) in the fourth. But the price was high.

Under Diocletian, Augustus's polite fiction of the emperor as "first among equals" gave way to the emperor as absolute autocrat. The princeps became *dominus* — lord. The emperor claimed that he was "the elect of god" — that he ruled because of god's favor. In the fourth century, Constantine even claimed to be the equal of Jesus' first twelve followers. To underline the emperor's exalted position Diocletian and Constantine adopted the gaudy court ceremonies and trappings of the Persian Empire. People entering the emperor's presence prostrated themselves before him and kissed the hem of his robes. Constantine went so far as to import Persian eunuchs to run the palace. The Roman emperor had become an oriental monarch.

Not merely a soldier, Diocletian was a man who gave serious thought to the ailments of the empire. He recognized that the empire and its difficulties had become too great for one man to handle. He also realized that during the third century provincial governors had frequently used their positions to begin or participate in rebellions. To solve the first of these problems Diocletian divided the empire into a western half and an eastern half (see Map 5.2). Diocletian assumed direct control of the eastern part. He gave the rule of the western part to a colleague, to whom he gave the title *augustus,* which had become synonymous with emperor. Diocletian and his fellow augustus further delegated power by appointing two men to assist them. Each man was given the title of *caesar* to indicate his exalted rank. Although this system is known as the Tetrarchy because four men ruled the empire, Diocletian was the senior partner and the final source of authority.

Each half of the empire was split into two prefectures, governed by a prefect responsible to an augustus. Diocletian reduced the power of the provincial governors by dividing the old provinces into smaller units. He organized the prefects into smaller administrative units called dioceses, which in turn were subdivided into small provinces. Wherever possible Diocletian deprived provincial governors of their military power, leaving them only with civil and administrative duties.

Diocletian's division of the empire into two parts was a momentous step, for this division became permanent. Constantine and later emperors tried hard to keep the empire together, but without any success. Throughout the fourth century A.D., the East and the West drifted apart. In the following centuries the western part witnessed the fall of Roman government and the rise of barbarian kingdoms, while the eastern empire evolved into the majestic Byzantine Empire.

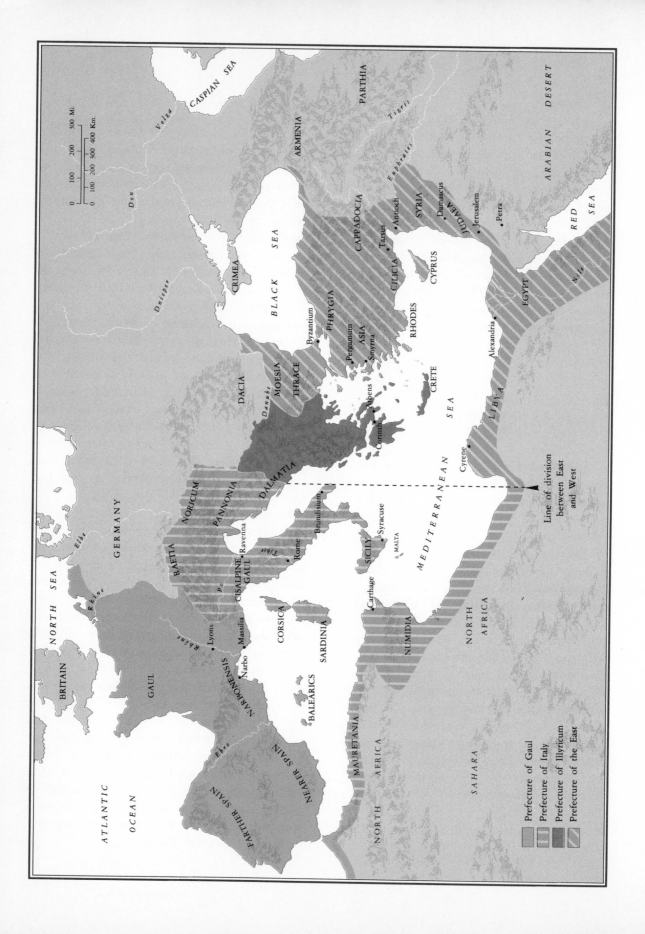

ATLANTIC
OCEAN

NORTH
SEA

BRITAIN

GERMANY

GAUL

CASPIAN SEA

Volga

Don

Dnieper

CRIMEA

BLACK
SEA

DACIA

MOESIA

THRACE

Danube

Byzantium

PHRYGIA

Pergamum
ASIA
Smyrna

Athens

Corinth

ARMENIA

PARTHIA

Tigris

CAPPADOCIA

Tarsus
CILICIA

RHODES

CYPRUS

CRETE

Antioch
SYRIA
Damascus
JUDEA
Jerusalem
Petra

Euphrates

ARABIAN   DESERT

RED

SEA

Nile

EGYPT

Alexandria

LIBYA

Cyrene

MEDITERRANEAN   SEA

NORICUM

PANNONIA

DALMATIA

RAETIA

Ravenna

CISALPINE
GAUL

Po

Tiber

Rome

Brundisium

Syracuse

SICILY

MALTA

Rhine

Elbe

Lyons

Massilia

Narbo

NARBONENSIS

CORSICA

SARDINIA

BALEARICS

Carthage

NORTH
AFRICA

NUMIDIA

Line of division
between East
and West

MAURETANIA

NORTH
AFRICA

SAHARA

Ebro

NEARER SPAIN

FARTHER SPAIN

Rhône

Prefecture of Gaul

Prefecture of Italy

Prefecture of Illyricum

Prefecture of the East

300 Mi.

200

100

0

400 Km.

300

200

100

0

THE ARCH OF CONSTANTINE.   To celebrate the victory which made him emperor, Constantine built this triumphal arch at Rome. Rather than decorate the arch with the inferior work of his own day, Constantine plundered other Roman monuments, including those of Trajan and Marcus Aurelius. (Italian Government Travel Office)

MAP 5.2   THE DIVISION OF THE ROMAN EMPIRE BY DIO-
CLETIAN

The most serious immediate matters confronting Diocletian and Constantine were economic, social, and religious. They needed additional revenues to pay for the army and the imperial court. Yet the wars and the barbarian invasions had caused widespread destruction and poverty. The fighting had struck a serious blow to Roman agriculture, which the emperors tried to revive. In the religious sphere Christianity had become too strong either to ignore or to crush. How Diocletian, Constantine, and their successors dealt with those problems helped create the economic and social patterns medieval Europe inherited.

Inflation and Taxes

The "barracks emperors" had dealt with economic hardship by depreciating the currency: they cut the silver content of the coins until the money was virtually worthless. As a result the entire monetary system fell into ruin. In Egypt governors had to order bankers to accept imperial money. The immediate result was a crippling inflation throughout the empire.

The empire was less capable of recovery than in earlier times. Wars and invasions had disrupted normal commerce and the means of production. Mines were exhausted in the attempt to supply much-needed ores, especially gold and silver. War and invasion had hit the cities especially hard. Markets were disrupted, and travel became dangerous. Craftsmen, artisans, and traders rapidly left devastated regions. The prosperous industry and commerce of Gaul and the Rhineland declined markedly. Those who owed their prosperity to commerce and the needs of urban life likewise suffered. Cities were no longer places where trade and industry thrived. The devastation of the countryside increased the difficulties of feeding and supplying the cities. The destruction was so extensive that many wondered whether the ravages could be repaired at all.

The response of Diocletian and Constantine to these problems was marked by compulsion, rigidity, and loss of individual freedom. Diocletian's attempt to curb inflation illustrates the methods of absolute monarchy. In a move unprecedented in Roman history, he issued an edict that fixed maximum prices and wages throughout the empire. The measure failed because it was unrealistic and unenforceable.

The emperors dealt with the tax system just as strictly and inflexibly. As in the past, local officials bore the responsibilities of collecting imperial taxes. Constantine made these officials into a hereditary class. Son followed father whether he wanted to or not. In this period of severe depression, many localities could not pay their taxes. In those cases the local officials had to make up the difference from their own funds. This system soon wiped out a whole class of moderately wealthy people.

With the monetary system in ruins most imperial taxes became payable in kind—that is, in goods or produce instead of money. The major problem with payment in kind is its demands on transportation. Goods have to be moved from where they are grown or manufactured to where they are needed. Accordingly, the emperors locked all those involved in the growing, preparation, and transportation of food and essential commodities into their professions. A baker or a shipper could not go into any other business, and his son took up the trade upon his father's death. The late Roman Empire had a place for everyone, and everyone had a place.

The Decline of Small Farms

The late Roman heritage to the medieval world is most obvious in agriculture. The disruption to agriculture fostered the growth of latifundia. Because of worsening conditions, free tenant farmers were reduced to serfdom. During the third century A.D., many were killed or fled the land to escape the barbarians, or they abandoned farms ravaged in the fighting. Consequently, large tracts of land lay deserted. Great landlords with ample resoures began at once to reclaim as much of this land as they could. Huge estates resulted, and these estates were the forerunners of medieval manors (see Chapter 9). Like manors, latifundia were self-sufficient. Since they often produced more than they consumed, they successfully competed with the declining cities by selling their surplus in the countryside. They became islands of stability in an unsettled world.

While the latifundia were growing, the small farmers who remained on the land barely held their own. They were too poor and powerless to stand against the tide of chaos. They were exposed to the raids of barbarians or brigands and to the tyranny of imperial officials. For relief they turned to the great landlords. After all, the landowners were men of considerable resources, lords in their own right. They were wealthy, and they had many people working their land. They were independent and capable of defending themselves. If need be, they could—and at times did—field a small force of their own. Already influential, they stood up to imperial officials.

In return for the protection and security that the landlords could offer, the small landholders gave them their lands. Free men and their families became clients of the landlords, and lost much of their freedom. To guarantee a steady supply of labor the landlords bound them to the soil. They could no longer decide to move elsewhere. Henceforth, they and their families worked the land of their patrons. Free men and women were in effect becoming serfs.

A LARGE ROMAN VILLA. During the third and fourth centuries, as the Roman Empire was breaking up, large villas such as this often became the focus of life. The villa was at once a fortress, as can be seen by the towers at the corner of the building, and the economic and social center of the neighborhood. (Courtesy, German Archeological Institute)

The Legalization of Christianity

In religious affairs Constantine took the decisive step of recognizing Christianity as a legitimate religion. No longer would Christians suffer persecution for their beliefs. Constantine himself died a Christian in 337.

Why had the pagans — those who believed in the Greco-Roman gods — persecuted Christians? Polytheism is by nature tolerant of new gods and accommodating in religious matters. Why was Christianity singled out for violence? These questions are still matters of scholarly debate, but some broad answers can be given.

Even an educated and cultured man like the historian Tacitus opposed the Christians. He believed that they hated the whole human race. As a rule, early Christians, like the Jews, kept to themselves. Romans distrusted and feared their exclusiveness, feeling there was something unsociable and subversive about it. Most pagans genuinely misunderstood Christian practices. They thought that the Lord's Supper, at which the Christians said they ate and drank the body and blood of Jesus, was an act of cannibalism. Pagans thought that Christians indulged in immoral and indecent rituals. In these respects pagans considered Christianity one of the worst of the oriental mystery cults, for one of the hallmarks of many of those cults was disgusting rituals.

Even these feelings of distrust and revulsion do not entirely account for the persecution, however. The main reason seems to have been the sincere religious conviction held by the pagans. Time and again they accused the Christians of atheism. Christians indeed denied the existence of pagan gods or else called them evil spirits. For this same reason many Romans hated the Jews, and Tacitus no doubt gave the common view when he said that Jews despised the gods. Christians went even further than Jews — they said that no one should worship pagan gods.

At first, some pagans were repelled by the fanaticism of these monotheists. They thought that no good could come from scorning the gods. The whole community might end up paying for the wickedness and blasphemy of the Christians. Besides — and this is important — pagans did not demand that Christians *believe* in pagan gods. Greek and Roman religion was never one of belief or ethics. It was purely a religion of ritual. One of the clearest statements of pagan theological attitudes comes from the Roman senator Symmachus:

We watch the same stars; heaven is the same for us all; the same universe envelops us: what importance is it in what way anyone looks for truth? It is impossible to arrive by one route at such a great secret.[19]

Yet Roman religion was inseparable from the state. An attack on one was an attack on the other. The Romans were being no more fanatical or intolerant than the eighteenth-century English judge who declared that "the Christian religion is part of the law of the land." All that the pagans expected was performance of the ritual act, a small token sacrifice. Any Christian who sacrificed went free, no matter what he or she personally believed. The earliest persecutions of the Christians were minor and limited. Even Nero's famous persecution was temporary and limited to Rome. Subsequent persecutions were sporadic and local.

As time went on, pagan hostility decreased. Pagans gradually realized that Christians were not working to overthrow the state and that Jesus was no rival of Caesar. The emperor Trajan forbade his governors from hunting down Christians. Trajan admitted that he thought Christianity an abomination, but he preferred to leave Christians in peace.

The stress of the third century, however, seemed to some emperors the punishment of the gods. What else could account for such anarchy? With the empire threatened on every side, a few emperors thought that one way to appease the gods was by offering them the proper sacrifices. The sacrifices would be a sign of loyalty to the empire, a show of Roman solidarity. Consequently, a new wave of persecutions began; yet even they were never very widespread or long-lived. By the late third century, pagans had become used to Christianity. They still did not like it, but at least they no longer found it subversive. Although a few emperors, including Diocletian, vigorously persecuted Christians, most pagans left them alone. Nor were they very sympathetic to the new round of persecutions. Pagan and Christian alike must have been glad when Constantine legalized Christianity.

Ironically enough, in time the Christian triumph would be complete. In 380, the emperor Theodosius made Christianity the official religion of the Roman Empire. At that point the Christians began to persecute the pagans for their beliefs. History had come full circle.

The Construction of Constantinople

The triumph of Christianity was not the only event that made Constantine's reign a turning point in Roman history. Constantine took the bold step of building a new capital for the empire. At the site of Byzantium, an old Greek city on the Bosporus, he built Constantinople, the New Rome. Throughout the third century, emperors had found Rome and the West hard to defend. The eastern part of the empire was more easily defensible. It also escaped the worst of the barbarian devastation. It was wealthy and its urban life still vibrant. Christianity was more widespread in the East than in the West, and Constantinople was intended to be a Christian city.

THE AWFUL REVOLUTION

On the evening of October 15, 1764, Edward Gibbon, a young Englishman, sat in Rome among the ruins of the Capitol listening to the chanting of some monks. As he heard the voices of the Christian present echo against the stones of the pagan past, he wondered how the Roman Empire had given way to the medieval world. His curiosity aroused, he dedicated himself to the study of what he considered the greatest problem in history.

Twelve years later, in 1776, he published *The History of the Decline and Fall of the Roman Empire,* one of the monuments of English literature, a brilliant work fashioned with wit, learning, humor, and elegance.

Gibbon's thesis is, as the title of his work indicates, that the Roman Empire, after the first two centuries of its existence, declined in strength, vitality, and prosperity and then fell into ruin. His concept of the "decline and fall," a process he called "the awful revolution," has dominated historical thought for two hundred years. Even those who disagree with Gibbon over various details have usually accepted his concept of the "decline and fall." What explanations did Gibbon give for the fate of the Roman Empire, and how have others responded to his views? Is Gibbon's concept valid, and is it the only way of looking at this problem?

Gibbon's Rationalistic Theories

Gibbon was a true son of the Enlightenment, the eighteenth-century mode of thought that honored reason and despised faith. He held Christianity in great contempt because he considered the faith, the myths, and the teachings of the Christian church nothing more than vile superstition. In his view the glory of the ancient world, with its learning, arts, manners, and philosophy, gleamed in comparison with the "Dark Ages" of the medieval period, when the church held Europe in the throes of ignorance and sorcery. Christianity emphasized the virtues of humility, patience, and piety — qualities hardly masculine or imperial and totally inadequate for the maintenance of a proud and vigorous empire. Christianity praised chastity and the monastic life, which, in Gibbon's interpretation, drained the empire of vitality and creativity. Nor did he have any admiration for the Germans who invaded and infiltrated the empire. Uncivilized and uncouth, they were, in Gibbon's eyes, even incapable of using reason. Although he acknowledged their hardiness and manly vigor, he scorned them as savages who ate horsemeat and lacked the refined graces suited to an eighteenth-century drawing room.

Despite the value of Gibbon's work, Christianity cannot reasonably be made the villain of the piece. True, many very able minds and forceful characters devoted their lives and energies to the Christian church and not to the empire. True, monasticism flourished and led to a passive and unproductive existence. Yet the numbers involved in these pursuits were small in proportion to the total population. Furthermore, the Byzantine Empire, which evolved from the eastern part of the Roman Empire, demonstrated that Christians could handle the sword and spear as well as the cross.

Gibbon also brought forward the idea that the empire had grown so large that it fell of its own weight. In his words, "the decline of Rome was the natural and inevitable effect of immoderate greatness. . . . The story of its ruin is simple and obvious; and instead of inquiring *why* the Roman empire was destroyed, we should rather be surprised that it had subsisted so long."[20] In effect, Gibbon begs the question, and instead chronicles the later history of the Roman world.

In slightly altered form, this view of natural decline has recently found supporters, who look at historical developments in biological terms. According to them, states and empires develop like living organisms, such as the human body, progressing through periods of birth, growth, and expansion into maturity and consolidation, and then to decrepitude, decline, and collapse. This argument is simply false analogy, unsupported by any scientific evidence.

Pseudoscientific Theories

Some twentieth-century writers have resorted to pseudoscientific theories to explain Rome's fate. They have blamed the "collapse" of the empire on racial corruption. As the physically strong, morally pure, and creatively intelligent Romans conquered inferior Asian and African peoples, so the explanation goes, they intermingled with them. The physical and intellectual traits of the less fit came to predominate. This "mongrelization" of the empire steadily sapped the physical and moral fiber of the Romans. When faced with a military crisis, Rome was too weak to cope. This theory can hardly be taken seriously. In the first place, science cannot prove one people "superior" and another "inferior." Even taken on its own terms, the theory is nonsense: The eastern half of the empire, the home of the "inferior" Asiatics, survived a thousand years longer than the western "superior" one.

A few historians of medicine have lately suggested that the Romans in fact slowly wiped themselves out. According to this view, many Romans died from lead poisoning contracted from the lead pipes that carried their water. If there were any value to this absurd explanation, one would expect to see the effects of lead poisoning show up long before the third century. That the Romans suffered from a certain, but unknown, amount of lead contamination is credible, but that they died from it in large numbers or that it blunted their energy and creativity has yet to be proved.

The Demographic Theory

Not all those who have used science to explain Rome's fate have been cranks. Some writers have tried to use statistical information and demographical arguments to explain "the fall." According to this view, a sharp decline in population diminishes the ability of a society to defend itself and weakens its economy and ultimately the entire civilization. In 167 A.D., they argue, the bubonic plague swept the empire and apparently killed large numbers of people. Yet it is a serious error to conclude that the ravages of disease in the second century were responsible for later catastrophes. Economic historians have demonstrated that even severe epidemics have only a short-term effect, after which conditions quickly normalize themselves. There was indeed ample time for the empire to recover from this plague.

Although the reasons are disputed, there was declining population in the third and fourth centuries, for which losses due to war and devastation provide the most likely explanation. Even so, the population of the Roman Empire outnumbered the invading barbarians, and there were more than enough people to defend the empire. Thus, the demographic theory does not explain the "decline."

The Socioeconomic Theories of Ferdinand Lot

The twentieth-century French scholar Ferdinand Lot relied on economics to explain "the awful revolution." He acknowledged that the causes of Rome's "decline" were many and interrelated, but maintained that the basic causes were socioeconomic. Lot pointed out that the Roman economy was badly adjusted; in fact, according to him, it never really developed. Although the Romans had technological skill, Rome never industrialized, only because there was an almost limitless supply of slaves that provided cheap labor and discouraged the development of laborsaving methods. Roman conquests brought a steady stream of slaves to the West. They worked the land on the latifundia and produced by human power what little was manufactured in the West. The Roman aristocracy lived on the revenues from their estates. The few people involved in trade and commerce served as middlemen, moneylenders, tax collectors, or civil bureaucrats. A commercial and industrial middle class failed to develop.

Western products—primarily, in Lot's view, raw materials—did not begin to equal the value of imports. Increasingly, the balance of trade within the empire worsened: the western part bought much more than it sold and paid for purchases with precious metals. The pressure of the German invasions made social and economic conditions worse. Once the West was cut off from sources of goods and without goods of its own to export, it reverted to an agrarian and isolated economy. The level of learning deteriorated and technical skills were lost. According to Lot, economic collapse accelerated political ruin. Moreover, great cities in the West drastically declined in population, and simultaneously trade and commerce slowed to a trickle. With the tax base gone, cultural movements and intellectual activities could not be maintained.

The force of Lot's theories is weakened by the fact that large-scale emancipation of slaves occurred during the empire. Roman emperors encouraged the growth of a prosperous class of small tenant farmers. Nor did slavery, which also existed in the East, prevent the West from industrializing. Cities in Gaul and Germany became centers of manufacturing, and even managed to dominate the production of glass, pottery, and bronze ware. Furthermore, these industries were usually in the hands of free labor, not slaves.

Lot's theories also make too little of political factors. The economic woes of the empire began during the civil wars and invasions of the middle of the third century, wars that left wide tracts of land desolate and manufacturing centers in shambles. Roman failure to create a stable form of government exposed the empire to serious disruption that could not fail to have dire economic effects. Though enlightening in many respects, Lot's theories are incapable of explaining the "decline and fall."

Political Explanations

Throughout the years political explanations for the "decline and fall" have won the widest acceptance. Historians have pointed out that the Roman imperial government never solved the problem of the succession: it never devised a peaceful and regular way to pass on the imperial power when an emperor died. Nor were the legions, which enjoyed too much power, sufficiently subordinated to the civil government. Too often they created and destroyed civil governments at will, and in the process disrupted the state. The assassinations of emperors and frequent changes of government produced chronic instability, weakening the state's ability to solve its problems.

From the late third century onward, successive approaches to Rome's economic difficulties proved disastrous. Emperors depreciated the coinage. The middle classes carried an increasingly heavy burden of taxation, and all the while the imperial bureaucracy grew bigger, though not more efficient. These factors combined to destroy the ordinary citizen's confidence in the state. Consequently, according to the political explanation, with the economy and society undermined, the empire was destroyed by its internal difficulties.

There is no question that the Roman Empire suffered from severe political problems, which were never solved. Energy that could have been spent defending the frontiers or policing the sea-lanes was all too often squandered in bloody and costly civil war. The same fate had overtaken the republic, but at least then there were no land-hungry barbarian tribes ready to turn Roman weakness to their own advantage. Political explanations, however, have their defects, for emperors such as Diocletian showed how the empire could survive even fearful ravages. Nor do political theories adequately explain why the West "fell" while the East survived for another millennium.

Continuity and Change

Some writers have rejected the whole idea of decline. As early as 1744, before Gibbon had contemplated writing the *Decline and Fall of the Roman Empire,* the Frenchman Abbé Galliani wrote: "The fall of empires? What can that mean? Empires being neither up nor down do not fall. They change their appearance."[21] The concept of change and development, instead of decline, has much to recommend it, inasmuch as many aspects of the Roman world survived to influence the medieval and eventually the modern world. Roman law left its traces on the legal and political systems of most European countries. Roman roads, aqueducts, bridges, and buildings continued in use, standing as constant reminders of the Roman past and its link with the present. The Latin language, with its rich vocabulary and its strict but rational grammatical rules, facilitated communication among individuals and allowed precision of expression. For almost two thousand years Latin language and literature lived and formed the core of all education in the West. Those who studied Latin came to some degree under the spell of Rome, as Roman attitudes and patterns of thought fertilized the intellectual lives of generation after generation of Europeans. Slowly, almost imperceptibly, the Roman Empire gave way to the medieval world.

࿏

Never before in Western history and not again until modern times did one state govern so many people over so much of the world for so long a span of time. Despite obvious defects, the true greatness of Rome is its long tradition of law and freedom. Under Roman law and government the West enjoyed relative peace and security over extensive periods of time. Under the auspices of Rome northern Europe entered the civilized world of the Mediterranean. Through Rome the best of ancient thought and culture was preserved to make its contribution to modern life. Perhaps no better epitaph for Rome can be found than the words of Virgil:

While rivers shall run to the sea,
While shadows shall move across the valleys of
mountains,
While the heavens shall nourish the stars,
Always shall your honor and your name and your .
fame endure.[22]

NOTES

1. Virgil, *Aeneid* 6.851–853.

2. Augustus, *Res Gestae* 6.34.

3. Ibid., 5.28.

4. Virgil, *Aeneid* 6.791–794.

5. Horace, *Odes* 4.15.

6. Virgil, *Georgics* 4.180–183.

7. Ibid., 3.515–519.

8. Horace, *Odes* 1.38.

9. Matthew 3.3.

10. Matthew 16.18.

11. Gibbon, *The History of the Decline and Fall of the Roman Empire,* Modern Library, New York, n.d., 1.1.

12. Ibid., 1.52.

13. M. Rostovtzeff, *The Economic and Social History of the Roman Empire,* Clarendon Press, Oxford, 1957, 1.121.

14. M. Hammond, *The Antonine Monarchy,* American Academy in Rome, Rome, 1959, p. x.

15. Gibbon, 1.70.

16. *Corpus Inscriptionum Latinarum,* vol. 6, G. Reimer, Berlin, 1882, no. 9792.

17. Ibid., vol. 10, no. 8192.

18. Ibid., vol. 6, no. 14,672.

19. Symmachus, *Relationes* 3.10.

20. *Gibbon,* 2.438.

21. Quoted in F. W. Walbank, *The Awful Revolution,* University of Toronto Press, Toronto, 1969, p. 121.

22. Virgil, *Aeneid* 1.607–609.

SUGGESTED READING

Of the works cited in the Notes those by Rostovtzeff and Hammond are classics in the field, and of course Gibbon's *Decline and Fall* is one of the masterpieces of English literature. Favorable to Augustus is M. Hammond, *The Augustan Principate* (1933), and G. W. Bowersock, *Augustus and the Greek World* (1965), is excellent intellectual history. C. M. Wells, *The German Policy of Augustus* (1972), uses archaeological findings to illustrate Roman expansion into northern Europe.

The commercial life of the empire is the subject of M. P. Charlesworth, *Trade Routes and Commerce of the Roman Empire* (2nd ed., 1926), and R. Duncan-Jones, *The Economy of the Roman Empire: Quantitative Studies* (1974), employs new techniques of historical inquiry.

Social aspects of the empire are the subject of R. Auguet, *Cruelty and Civilization: The Roman Games* (English trans., 1972); P. Garnsey, *Social Status and Legal Privilege in the Roman Empire* (1970); and A. N. Sherwin-White, *Racial Prejudice in Imperial Rome* (1967).

Christianity, paganism, and Judaism receive treatment in M. Grant, *The Jews in the Roman World* (1973); R. A. Markus, *Christianity in the Roman World* (1975); and A. D. Momigliano, *The Conflict between Paganism and Christianity in the Fourth Century* (1963).

A convenient survey of Roman literature is J. W. Duff, *Literary History of Rome from the Origins to the Close of the Golden Age* (1953) and *Literary History of Rome in the Silver Age** (3rd ed., 1964).

The fall of Rome continues to be a fertile field of investigation: A. H. M. Jones, *The Decline of the Ancient World** (1966); F. W. Walbank, *The Awful Revolution** (1969); and R. MacMullen's two books: *Soldier and Civilian in the Later Roman Empire* (1963) and *Enemies of the Roman Order: Treason, Unrest, and Alienation in the Empire* (1963).

*Available in Paperback.

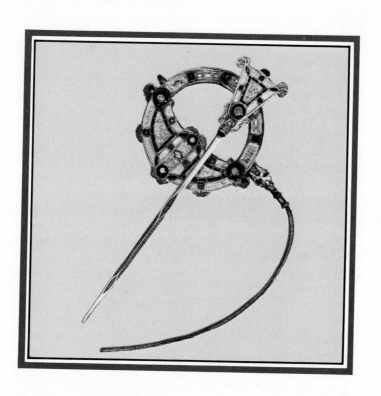

Chapter 6

THE MAKING OF EUROPE

he centuries between approximately 400 and 900 present the student with a paradox. On the one hand, these years witnessed the disintegration of the Roman Empire, which had been one of humanity's great political and cultural achievements. On the other hand, these five centuries were a creative and important period, in which Europeans laid the foundations for the development of medieval and modern Europe. This period saw the "making of Europe."

The basic ingredients that went into the making of a distinctly European civilization were the cultural legacy of Greece and Rome, the customs and traditions of the Germanic peoples, and the Christian faith. Of these, the most important was Christianity, because it absorbed and assimilated the other two. It interpreted the classics in a Christian sense. It instructed the Germanic peoples and gave them new ideals of living and social behavior. Christianity became the cement that held European society together.

The Byzantine Empire centered at Constantinople also contributed to the making of European culture. Byzantium served as a protective buffer between Europe and savage peoples to the east. The Greeks preserved the philosophical and scientific texts of the ancient world, which later formed the basis for study in science and medicine; and they produced a great synthesis of Roman law, the Justinian Code. In the urbane and sophisticated life led at Constantinople, the Greeks set a standard far above the primitive existence of the West.

In the seventh and eighth centuries, Arabic culture spread around the southern fringes of Europe—to Spain, Sicily, and North Africa, and to Syria, Palestine, and Egypt. The Arabs translated the works of such Greek thinkers as Euclid, Hippocrates, and Galen, and they made important contributions in mathematics, astronomy, and physics. In Arabic translation, Greek texts trickled to the West, and most later European scientific study rested on the Arabic work.

European civilization resulted from the fusion of Germanic traditions, the Greco-Roman heritage, and the Christian faith. How did these components act upon one another? How did they bring about the making of Europe? What influence did the Byzantine and Islamic cultures have on the making of European civilization? These are the questions discussed in this chapter.

THE MIGRATION OF THE GERMANIC PEOPLES

One of the dominant and continuing features of European history has been the migration of peoples from one area to another. Mass movements of Europeans occurred in the fourth through sixth centuries, in the ninth and tenth centuries, and in the twelfth and thirteenth centuries. From the sixteenth century to the present these movements have been almost continuous, and they have involved not only the European continent but all the rest of the world. The causes for each migration, or series of migrations, were different and are not thoroughly understood by scholars today. But there is no question that they profoundly affected both the regions to which peoples moved and the old ones from which they came.

An important factor in the "decline and fall of the Roman Empire" was the *völkerwanderungen,* or migrations of the Germanic peoples. Many twentieth-century historians and sociologists have tried to explain who the Germans were, why they emigrated, and the demographic problems related to their migrations. Yet, scholars have not had much success in answering these questions. The surviving evidence is primarily archaeological, scanty, and still not adequately explored. Conclusions are still tentative.

What answers do exist rest on archaeological evidence later found within the borders of the Roman Empire: bone fossils, cooking utensils, jewelry, instruments of war, and other surviving artifacts. Like the Vikings, who first terrorized and then settled in many sections of Europe in the ninth and tenth centuries, the Germans came from eastern Germany and the areas of modern Denmark, Sweden, and Norway (see Map 6.1). Ethnically they were Scandinavians.

Since about 250, Germanic tribes had pressed along the Rhine-Danube frontier of the Roman Empire. Depending upon their closeness to that border, they differed considerably from one another in level of civilization. Some tribes, such as the Visigoths and the Ostrogoths, led a settled existence, engaged in agriculture and trade, and accepted a heretical form of Christianity called Arianism. Long acquaintance with Roman ways made them very civilized, and some had been welcomed into the empire and had served as mercenaries in the imperial army. Tribes such as the Anglo-Saxons and the Huns, who lived far from the Roman frontiers, were not affected by the civilizing influences of Rome. They were primitive, nomadic, even barbaric peoples.

Historians do not know exactly when the Mongolian tribe called the Huns began to move westward from China, but about 370 they pressured the Goths living along the Rhine-Danube frontier. The Huns easily defeated the Ostrogoths, and the frightened Visigoths petitioned the emperor to be allowed to settle within the empire. Once inside, however, they revolted. In 378, a Visigothic army decisively defeated the emperor's army. This date marks the beginning of massive Germanic invasions; Germans flooded into the empire.

Why did the Germans emigrate? In the absence of literary evidence one can only speculate on the basis of later information. Perhaps overpopulation

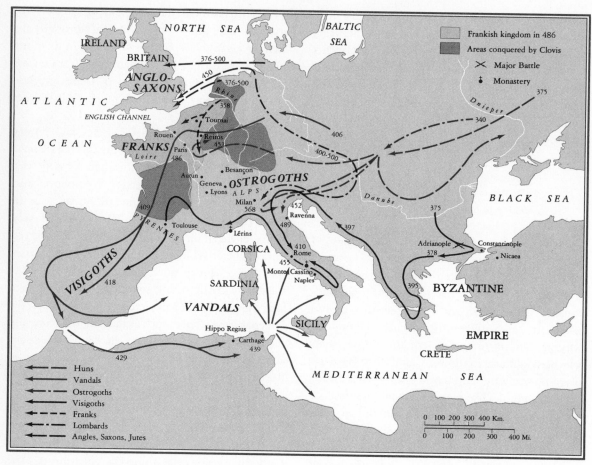

MAP 6.1   THE GERMANIC MIGRATION, FOURTH AND FIFTH CENTURIES

and food shortages resulting from polygamous (having several wives simultaneously) practices caused migration. Perhaps victorious tribes forced the vanquished ones to move south. Perhaps tales of the luxurious lifestyle of the cities of the Roman Empire attracted settlers. Perhaps the Germans migrated for a combination of all these reasons.

Some tribes that settled within the borders of the Roman Empire included perhaps no more than ten thousand individuals. Others, such as the Ostrogoths and the Visigoths, numbered about twenty or thirty times that figure. Because they settled near and quickly intermingled with Romans or Romanized peoples, it is impossible to specify numbers of the original migrators. Dense forests, poor soil, and inadequate equipment probably kept food production low. This meant that the Germans could not increase very rapidly in their new locations.

Except for the Lombards, whose conquests of Italy extended through the sixth and seven centuries, the movements of Germanic peoples ended around 600. Between 450 and 565, the Germans established a number of "kingdoms," but except for the Frankish kingdom, none of them lasted very long. Since the Germans did not think of their kingdoms as states with definite geographical boundaries, only approximate locations can be given. The Visigoths overran much of southwestern Gaul. They established their headquarters, or "capital," at Toulouse and exercised a weak domination over Spain until a great Muslim victory at Guadalete in 711 ended Visigothic rule. The Vandals, whose destructive ways are commemorated in the word "vandal," settled in North Africa. In northern and western Europe in the sixth century, the Burgundians established rule over lands roughly circumscribed by the Old Roman army camps at Lyons, Besançon, Geneva, and Autun.

In northern Italy, the Ostrogothic king Theodoric (489–526) pursued a policy of assimilation between Germans and Romans. He maintained close relations with the Roman emperor at Constantinople and drew Roman scholars and diplomats into the imperial civil service. He was a crude German, however, and his reign was disliked by the pagan Roman aristocrats. Moreover, he was an Arian Christian, so Roman Catholics hated him as heretical. His imperial administration fell apart during the reconquest of Italy by the Byzantine emperor Justinian (527–565). Weak power, war, and plague then made northern Italy ripe for the Lombard conquest in the seventh century.

VANDAL LANDOWNER. The adoption of Roman dress — short tunic, cloak, and sandals — reflects the way the Germanic tribes accepted Roman lifestyles. Likewise both the mosaic art form and the man's stylized appearance show the Germans' assimilation of Roman influences. (Notice that the rider has a saddle but not stirrups.) (The British Museum)

The most enduring Germanic kingdom was established by the Frankish chieftain Clovis (481–511). He was descended from the half-legendary chieftain Merovech; hence, the dynasty Clovis founded has been called Merovingian. Originally only a petty chieftain with headquarters in the region of Tournai in northwestern Gaul (modern Belgium), Clovis began to expand his territories in 486. His defeat of the Gallo-Roman general Syagrius extended his jurisdiction to the Loire. Clovis's conversion to orthodox Christianity in 496 won him the support of the papacy and the bishops of Gaul. As the defender of Roman Catholicism against heretical German tribes, he went on to conquer the Visigoths, increasing his domain as far as the Pyrenees and making Paris his headquarters. Clovis's sons subjugated the Burgundians in eastern Gaul and the Ostrogothic tribes living north of the Alps.

GERMANIC SOCIETY

The Germans replaced the Romans as rulers of most of the European continent, and German customs and traditions formed the basis of European society for centuries. The Germans constituted a major element in the making of Europe.

What patterns of social and political life did the Germans have? What kind of economy did they practice? Scholars are hampered in answering these questions because the Germans could not write, and so kept no written records before their conversion to Christianity. The earliest information about them comes from moralistic accounts produced by such Romans as the historian Tacitus, and he was acquainted only with the tribes living closest to the borders of empire. Tacitus wrote his *Germania* at the end of the first century A.D., and German practices in the fifth century differed from those of Tacitus's time. Our knowledge of the Germans depends on the information in records written in the sixth and seventh centuries and projected backward.

Kinship and Custom

The Germans had no notion of the state as people in the twentieth century use that concept; they thought in social, not political, terms. The basic social unit of the Germans was the tribe, or folk. Members of the folk believed that they were all descended from a common ancestor. Blood united them. Kinship protected them. Law was custom — unwritten, preserved in the minds of the elders of the tribe, and handed down by word of mouth from generation to generation. Custom regulated everything. Every tribe had its customs, and every member of the tribe knew what they were. Members took their tribe's customary law with them wherever they went, and friendly tribes respected one another's law.

The Germanic tribes were led by a king, or tribal chieftain. The chief was that member of the folk recognized as the strongest, the bravest in battle. The king was elected from among the male members of the strongest family. He led the tribe in war, settled disputes among tribal members, conducted negotiations with outside powers, and offered sacrifices to the gods. Closely associated with the king was the *gesith,* or war band (known in Latin as the *comitatus*). The members of the war band were usually the bravest young men in the tribe. They swore loyalty to the chief and fought with him in battle. They were not supposed to leave the battlefield without him; to do so implied cowardice and disloyalty and brought terrible disgrace.

Law

With custom determining all behavior, the early Germans had no need for written law. Beginning in the late sixth century, however, German tribal chieftains began to collect, write, and publish lists of their customs. Why at that time? First, Christian missionaries who were slowly converting the Germans to Christianity wanted to know the tribal customs, and they encouraged rulers to set them down in written form. Churchmen wanted to read about German ways in order to assimilate the tribes to Christianity. Moreover, by the sixth century the German kings needed rules and regulations for the Romans living under their jurisdiction as well as for their own people.

Today if a person holds up a bank, American law maintains that the robber attacks *both* the bank *and* the state in which it exists. That is a sophisticated notion involving the abstract idea of the state. In early German law, all crimes were regarded as crimes against a person.

The code of the Salian Franks reveals that every person had a particular monetary value to the tribe. This value was the wergeld, which literally means man-money, or money to buy off the spear. Men of fighting age had the highest wergeld, then women of child-bearing age, then children, and finally the aged. Everyone's value reflected his or her potential military worthiness. If a person accused of a crime agreed to pay the wergeld, and if the victim and his or her family accepted the payment, there was peace (hence the expression "money to buy off the spear"). Individuals depended on their kin for protection, and kinship served as a force of social control.

Historians and sociologists have difficulty using the early law codes, partly because they are patchwork affairs with additions made in later centuries. The Salic Law, for example, was issued by Clovis in the late fifth century and amended first in the eighth and again in the ninth century. This law code of the Salian Franks cannot be taken as an accurate representation of conditions in the sixth century. Nevertheless, it does give a general idea of Germanic life and problems in the early Middle Ages, and it is typical of the law codes of other tribes, such as the Visigoths, the Burgundians, the Lombards, and the Anglo-Saxons.

The most obvious problems facing the Germanic chieftains were theft, rape, assault, arson, and murder. The Salic Law lists the money fines to be paid to the victim or family for various injuries:

If any person strike another on the head so that the brain appears, and the three bones which lie above the brain shall project, he shall be sentenced to 1200 denars, which make 300 shillings.

But if it shall have been between the ribs or in the stomach, so that the wound appears and reaches to the entrails, he shall be sentenced to 1200 denars — which make 300 shillings — besides five shillings for the physician's pay.

If any one have hit a free woman who is pregnant, and she dies, he shall be sentenced to 2800 denars, which make 700 shillings.

If any one have killed a free woman after she has begun bearing children, he shall be sentenced to 2400 denars, which make 600 shillings.

If any one shall have drawn a harrow through another's harvest after it has sprouted, or shall have gone through it with a waggon where there was no road, he shall be sentenced to 120 denars, which make 3 shillings.

If any one shall have killed a free Frank, or a barbarian living under the Salic law, and it have been proved on him, he shall be sentenced to 8000 denars.

But if any one have slain a man who is in the service of the king, he shall be sentenced to 2400 denars, which make 600 shillings.

If any one have slain a Roman who eats in the king's palace, and it have been proved on him, he shall be sentenced to 1200 denars, which make 300 shillings.[1]

As can be seen, this collection is not really a code of law at all, but rather a list of tariffs or fines for particular offenses. German law aimed at the prevention or reduction of violence. It was not concerned with justice.

At first, Romans had been subject to Roman law, Germans to Germanic custom. As the German kings accepted Christianity, and as Romans and Germans increasingly intermarried, the distinction betwen the two laws blurred and, in the course of the seventh and eighth centuries, disappeared. The result of the fusion would be new feudal law, to which all people were subject.

Life in the Forests

How did the Germans live? Dark, dense forests dotted the continent of Europe. Life for the Germans who were not quickly Romanized must be seen against this background. Forests were the most important physical and psychological factor in the lives of the Germanic peoples. Forests separated one tribe from another. The pagan Germans believed that gods and spirits inhabited the forests. Trees were holy, and to cut them down was an act of grave sacrilege. Therefore, the Germans would not cut down the trees. They also feared to build a mill on a river or a bridge across a river, lest the river spirit be offended. This attitude prevented the clearing of land for farming and tended to keep the Germans isolated.

Within the forests the Germans lived in small villages of a few families. Individual families lived in huts made of mud, wood, or wattle (poles intertwined with twigs or reeds), and thatched with straw. Recent archaeological excavations at Thetford in East Anglia in England revealed a sixth-century village. Evidence from places on the Con-

tinent suggests that this English village was typical. It contained a number of one-room huts varying in length from 3.5 to 3.6 meters. Most had no fireplace. Uprights in the center of the gable supported the roof. These dwellings were scattered over a small cleared area, with no type of alignment or evidence of town planning.

Each German family owned its plot of land and passed it on to the next generation. All members of the small community worked together to cultivate the clearing. Apparently, the land farmed was adjacent to the dwellings. Farmers helped one another to plow and harvest, and all had to agree on the uniform rotation of crops. It is difficult to generalize about agricultural methods. The German plow dug deeper than the Roman plow, but turning it around at the end of the furrow was hard to do. The difficulty of this operation probably brought about the division of the arable into long, narrow strips.

With bread the basic food, oats and rye were the grains usually grown in the fifth and sixth centuries. Later, these cereals were held in low esteem, and wheat was raised everywhere it would grow. Peas and beans (a source of protein), turnips, onions, and cabbage supplemented the diet. Beside the field under cultivation, another stood fallow. Cattle grazed on it and fertilized it.

In the course of the sixth through eighth centuries, the Germans slowly adapted to Greco-Roman and Christian attitudes and patterns of behavior. The acceptance of Christianity and the end of animistic beliefs that spiritual forces live in natural objects had profound consequences. In fact, the decline of animistic beliefs marks a turning point in the economic and intellectual progress of the West. It encouraged a more settled and less nomadic way of life as people no longer feared to make use of natural resources like rivers and forests.

FRANKISH GLASSWARE. At various places along the Rhine River the Romans had manufactured glass for the army's use. After the Frankish occupation of the area, the glass industry continued, suggesting that rather than destroying everything, the Germans adapted many features of Roman culture to their own use. (Rheinisches Landesmuseum, Bonn)

Once animistic beliefs were dispelled, the forests were opened to use, and all members of the community had common rights in them. Trees provided everyone with wood for building and for fuel; the forests served as the perfect place for grazing animals through the Middle Ages. A major step in the agricultural development of Europe from the sixth through the thirteenth centuries was the steady reduction of forest land.

Anglo-Saxon England

In the first four centuries of the Christian era the island of Britain shared fully in the life of the Roman Empire. A military aristocracy governed. Towns were planned in the Roman fashion, with temples, public baths, theaters, and amphitheaters. In the countryside large manors controlled the surrounding lands. The official religion was the cult of the emperor. Roman merchants brought Eastern luxury goods and Eastern religions—including Christianity—into Britain. The native Britons, a gentle Celtic people, had become thoroughly Romanized. Their language was Latin. Their lifestyle was Roman. An event in distant Asia Minor changed all this.

In 378, the Visigoths crossed the Danube and inflicted a severe defeat on the emperor Valens at Adrianople. Britain felt the consequences. Rome was forced to retrench, and in 407, Roman troops were withdrawn from the island, leaving it unprotected. The savage Picts from Scotland began to harass the north. Teutonic tribes from Scandinavia and what is modern-day Belgium—the Angles, Saxons, and Jutes—stepped up their assaults. They attacked in a hit-and-run fashion. Their goal was plunder, and at first their invasions led to no permanent settlements. As more Germans arrived, however, they took over the best lands and enslaved the Britons. Increasingly, the natives fled to the west and settled in Wales. These sporadic raids continued for over a century and led eventually to

Germanic control of most of Britain. Historians have labeled the period from about 500 to 1066 as Anglo-Saxon.

Except for the Jutes, who probably came from Frisia (the area of modern Belgium), the Teutonic tribes came from the least Romanized and the least civilized parts of Europe. They destroyed Roman culture in Britain. As on the continent, tribal custom governed local societies.

The beginnings of the Germanic kingdoms in Britain are very obscure, but scholars suspect they came into being in the seventh and eighth centuries. Writing in the eighth century, the chronicler Bede (673–735), described seven kingdoms: the Jutish kingdom of Kent; the Saxon kingdoms of the East Saxons (Essex), the South Saxons (Sussex), and the West Saxons (Wessex); and the kingdoms of the Angles, Mercians, and Northumbrians (see Map 6.2). The names imply that these peoples thought of themselves in tribal, rather than in geographical, terms. They referred to the kingdom of the West Saxons, for example, rather than simply Wessex. Because of Bede's categorization, students refer to the Heptarchy, or seven kingdoms of Anglo-Saxon Britain. This division, however, is not entirely accurate. Germanic tribes never subdued Scotland, where the Picts remained strong, or Wales, where the Celts and native Britons continued to put up stubborn resistance.

The division of Anglo-Saxon England was racial and political. The Teutonic kingdoms in the south, east, and center opposed the British kingdoms in the west. The Britons wanted to get rid of the invaders. The Anglo-Saxon kingdoms also fought among themselves, with the result that boundaries shifted constantly. In the ninth century, under pressure of the Danish, or Viking, invasions, the Britons and the Germanic peoples were molded together under the leadership of King Alfred of Wessex (871–899).

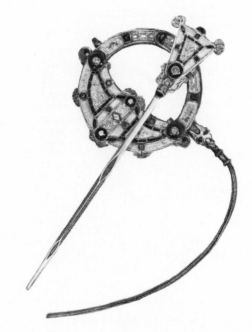

THE TARA BROOCH. Men and women of the Germanic tribes wore brooches to fasten their cloaks at the shoulder. This elaborately decorated brooch was worn by a person of the warrior aristocracy. Ordinary people used a thorn. (Courtesy, World Heritage Museum. Photo: Caroline Buckler)

MAP 6.2   ANGLO-SAXON ENGLAND

THE SURVIVAL AND GROWTH OF THE EARLY CHRISTIAN CHURCH

While many elements of the Roman Empire disintegrated, the Christian church survived and grew. The church gained the support of the fourth-century emperors, and it gradually adopted the Roman system of organization. Christianity had a dynamic missionary policy, and the church slowly succeeded in assimilating (or adapting) pagan peoples—both Germans and Romans—to Christian teaching. Moreover, within the church were able administrators and leaders and highly literate and creative thinkers. These factors help to explain the survival and growth of the early Christian church in the face of Germanic invasions.

The Church and the Roman Emperors

The early church benefited considerably from the support of the emperors. In return, the emperors expected the support of the Christian church in the maintenance of order and unity. In 312, Constantine had legalized the practice of Christianity within the empire, and although he was not baptized until he was on his deathbed, he encouraged Christianity throughout his reign. Constantine freed the clergy from imperial taxation. At the churchmen's request, he helped to settle theological disputes, and thus preserve doctrinal unity within the church. Constantine generously endowed the building of Christian churches, and one of his gifts—the Lateran Palace in Rome—remained the official residence of the popes until the fourteenth century. In 321, Constantine declared Sunday a public holiday, a day of rest for the service of God. As the result of its favored position within the empire, Christianity slowly became the leading religion.

At the end of the fourth century, the emperor Theodosius (379–395) went further than Constantine and made Christianity the official religion of the empire. Theodosius stripped Roman pagans' temples of their statues, made the practice of the old Roman state religion a treasonable offense, and persecuted Christians who dissented from orthodox doctrine. He allowed the church to establish its own courts. Church courts began to develop their own body of rules, called canon law. These courts, not the Roman government, had jurisdiction over the clergy and ecclesiastical disputes. At the death of Theodosius, the Christian church was completely independent of the authority of the Roman state. The basis for the power of the medieval church had been laid.

What was to be the church's relationship to secular powers? How was the Christian to render unto caesar the things that were his while returning to God his due? This problem had troubled the earliest disciples of Christ. The toleration of Christianity and the coming to power of Christian emperors in the fourth century did not make it any easier. Striking a balance between respect and responsibility to secular rulers and loyalty to spiritual duties was difficult.

In the fourth century, theological disputes arose within Christianity—disagreements about the nature of Christ, for example. At the bishop's request, Constantine intervened, for religious disagreement to him meant civil disorder. In 325, Constantine summoned a council of church leaders to Nicaea in Asia Minor, and he personally presided over it.

The council debated whether Christ was of a different substance from God, as Arius, a priest of Alexandria, maintained, or whether Christ was of the same substance, as Bishop Athanasius of Alexandria held. The council decided against the Arians and supported the doctrine that Christ was of the same substance as God. This became the orthodox position. Anxious to preserve the unity of the empire, Constantine insisted on its acceptance by all Christians. The participation of the emperor in a theological dispute within the church paved the way for later rulers to claim they could do the same.

So active was the emperor Theodosius's participation in church matters that he eventually came to loggerheads with Bishop Ambrose of Milan. Theodosius ordered Ambrose to hand over his cathedral church to the emperor. Ambrose's response contained important consequences for the future:

At length came the command, "Deliver up the Basilica"; I reply, "It is not lawful for us to deliver it up, nor for your Majesty to receive it. By no law can you violate the house of a private man, and do you think that the house of God may be taken away? It is asserted that all things are lawful to the Emperor, that all things are his. But do not burden your conscience with the thought that you have any right as Emperor over sacred things. Exalt not yourself, but if you would reign the longer, be subject to God. It is written, God's to God and Caesar's to Caesar. The palace is the Emperor's, the Churches are the Bishop's. To you is committed jurisdiction over public, not over sacred buildings."[2]

Ambrose's statement served as the cornerstone for the theory of state-church relations throughout the Middle Ages. Ambrose insisted that the church was independent of the state's jurisdiction. He maintained that the two powers were separate and autonomous. He insisted that in matters relating to the faith or to the church, the bishops were to be the judges of the emperors, not the other way around. In a Christian society, harmony and peace depended upon the agreement of the bishop and the secular ruler. If disagreement developed, the church was ultimately the superior power because the church was responsible for the salvation of all individuals (including the emperor).

Theodosius accepted Ambrose's argument and bowed to the church. In later centuries theologians, canonists, and propagandists repeatedly cited Ambrose's position as the basis for the relations of the two powers. The precedent set by Theodosius was repeatedly recalled by church leaders in the Middle Ages as proof that secular power had to yield to ecclesiastical authority.

Inspired Leadership

The early Christian church benefited from the considerable administrative abilities of some church leaders and from the identification of the authority and dignity of the bishop of Rome with the grand imperial traditions of the city. Some highly able Roman citizens accepted baptism and used their intellectual powers and administrative skills in the service of the church rather than the empire. Educated and experienced people entered the church and worked for it, because with the empire in decay they believed that the church was the one institution able to give leadership. Ambrose (339–397), for example, the son of the Roman prefect of Gaul, a trained lawyer and governor of a province, was baptized and became bishop of Milan. As such, he exercised considerable responsibility and influence in northern Italy, in temporal as well as ecclesiastical affairs.

In the reign of Diocletian (284–305), the Roman Empire had been divided for administrative purposes into geographical units called dioceses. Gradually, the church made use of this subdivision. The leaders of early Christian communities, called bishops, were popularly elected by the Christian people. Christian bishops established their headquarters, or sees, in the urban centers of the old Roman dioceses, and their jurisdiction extended throughout all parts of them. The center of the bishop's authority was his cathedral (the word derives from the Latin *cathedra,* meaning "chair"). Thus, church leaders capitalized on the Roman imperial method of organization and adapted it to ecclesiastical purposes.

After the removal of the capital and the emperor to Constantinople, the bishop of Rome exercised vast influence in the West because he had no real competitor there. Bishops of Rome, known as popes from the Latin word *papa,* meaning "father," began to identify their religious offices with the imperial traditions of the city. They stressed that Rome had been the capital of a worldwide empire, and they emphasized the special importance of Rome within the framework of that empire. Successive bishops of Rome reminded Christians in other parts of the world that Rome contained the tombs of Saint Peter and Saint Paul. Moreover, according to tradition, Saint Peter, the chief of Christ's first twelve followers, had lived and been executed in Rome. No other city in the world could make such claims.

In the fifth century, the bishops of Rome began to stress their supremacy over other Christian communities and to urge other churches to appeal to Rome for the resolution of complicated doctrinal issues. Thus, Pope Innocent I (401–417) wrote to the bishops of Africa:

[*We approve your action in following the principle of the Fathers*] *that nothing which was done even in the most remote and distant provinces should be taken as finally settled unless it came to the notice of this See, that any just pronouncement might be confirmed by all the authority of this See, and that the other churches might from thence gather what they should teach. . . .*[3]

The courage and leadership of the Roman bishops also enhanced the prestige of Rome and the early church as a whole. According to tradition, Pope Leo I (440–461) left Rome in 452 to meet the advancing army of Attila the Hun and, through his power of persuasion, saved the city from a terrible sacking. Three years later, Leo repeated this performance and secured concessions from the Vandal leader Gaiseric.

When Gregory I (590–604) became pope, there was no civic authority to handle the problems pressing the city. Flood, famine, plague, and an invasion of the Lombards presented an almost disastrous situation. Pope Gregory concluded a peace with the Lombards, organized relief services that provided water and food for the citizens, and established hospitals for the sick and dying. The fact that Christian leaders, rather than imperial administrators, responded to the dire needs of the times could not help but increase the prestige and influence of the church.

Missionary Activity

The word "catholic" derives from a Greek word meaning "general," "universal," or "worldwide." Early Christians believed that Christ's teaching was intended for all peoples, and they sought to make their faith catholic, that is, believed everywhere. This could be accomplished only through missionary activity. Between 61 and 63, Saint Paul had written to the Christian community at Colossae in Asia Minor:

You have stripped off your old behavior with your old self, and you have put on a new self which will progress towards true knowledge the more it is renewed in the image of its creator; and in that image there is no room for distinction between Greek and Jew, between the circumcised or the uncircumcised, or between barbarian or Scythian, slave and free man. There is only Christ; he is everything and he is in everything.[4]

Paul urged Christians to bring the "good news" of Christ to all peoples.

After 312, Christianity was tolerated throughout the Roman Empire. The Mediterranean Sea served as the highway over which Christianity spread to the cities of the empire. During the Roman occupation, there were scattered and isolated Christian communities in Gaul, Britain, and Ireland. They had no wide impact on the populations of their countries, however, and the migration of the German tribes in the fourth and fifth centuries virtually destroyed Christianity in remote and isolated Britain.

The Christianization of northern Europe really began in 597, when Pope Gregory I sent a delegation of monks under the Roman Augustine to Britain to convert the Britons. The pattern set by Augustine was followed by all subsequent missionaries. He succeeded in converting Ethelbert, king of Kent, and the baptism of Ethelbert's people took place as a matter of course. Augustine established his headquarters, or cathedral seat, at Canterbury, the capital of Kent.

In the course of the seventh century, two Christian forces competed for the conversion of the pagan Anglo-Saxons: Roman-oriented missionaries traveling north from Canterbury, and Celtic monks coming from Ireland and northwestern Britain. Monasteries were established at Iona, Lindisfarne, Jarrow, Whitby, and York.

In their forms of church organization, in their types of monastic life, and in their methods of arriving at the date of the central feast of the Christian calendar, Easter, the Roman and the Celtic traditions differed completely. At the Synod (ecclesiastical council) of Whitby in 664, the Roman tradition was completely victorious. The conversion of the English, with the English church attached closely to Rome, had wide consequences, because Britain later served as a base for the Christianization of the Continent.

Between the fifth and tenth centuries, the great majority of peoples living on the European continent and on the nearby islands accepted the Christian religion, that is, they received baptism, though baptism by itself did not automatically transform a person into a Christian.

Religion touched on all aspects of tribal life. It was a basic part of social existence. All members of the tribe participated in religious practices, because doing so was a social duty. Religion, then, was not a private or individual matter. The religion of the chieftain or king determined the religion of the people. So, missionaries concentrated their initial efforts not on the people but on kings or tribal chieftains. According to custom, tribal chiefs negotiated with all foreign powers, including the gods. Because the Christian missionaries represented a "foreign" power (the Christian God), the king naturally dealt with them. If the ruler accepted Christian baptism, then his people did so too. Mass baptism was the result.

Once a ruler had marched his people to the waters of baptism, however, the work of Christianization had only begun. Baptism involved either sprinkling of the head with or the immersion of the body in water. Conversion meant a turning toward, a mental and heartfelt acceptance of the beliefs of Christianity. What does it mean to be a Christian? This question has troubled sincere people from the time of Saint Paul down to the present. The problem rests in part in the basic teaching of the Gospel:

Then fixing his eyes on his disciples he said:

"How happy are you who are poor: yours is the kingdom of God. Happy you who are hungry now: you shall be satisfied. Happy you who weep now: you shall laugh.

"Happy are you when people hate you, drive you out, abuse you, denounce your name as criminal, on account of the Son of man. Rejoice when that day comes and dance for joy, then your reward will be great in heaven. This was the way their ancestors treated the prophets."

THE CURSES

"But alas for you who are rich: you are having your consolation now. Alas for you who have your fill now: you shall go hungry. Alas for you who laugh now: you shall mourn and weep.

"Alas for you when the world speaks well of you: This was the way their ancestors treated the false prophets."

LOVE OF ENEMIES

"But I say this to you who are listening: Love your enemies, do good to those who hate you, bless those who curse you, pray for those who treat you badly. To the man who slaps you on one cheek, present the other cheek too; to the man who takes your cloak from you, do not refuse your tunic. Give to everyone who asks you, and do not ask of your property back from the man who robs you. Treat others as you would like them to treat you."[5]

These ideas are the most radical and revolutionary the world has heard, and it has proved very difficult to get people fully to accept them.

The German peoples were warriors who idealized the military virtues of physical strength, ferocity in battle, and loyalty to the leader. They had trouble identifying with the Christian precepts of "love your enemies" and "turn the other cheek." Victors in battle enjoyed the spoils of success and plundered the vanquished. The greater the fighter, the more trophies and material goods he collected. How could a person be poor and happy at the same time, as Christians claimed?

Sin in Christian thought meant disobedience to the will of God as revealed in the Ten Commandments and the teachings of Christ. To the Germanic tribes notions of sin and repentance were virtually incomprehensible. Good or "moral" behavior to the barbarians meant the observance of tribal customs and practices. Dishonorable behavior caused social ostracism. The inculcation of Christian ideals took a very long time.

Pagan's Acceptance of Christianity

How did missionaries and priests get masses of pagan and illiterate peoples to understand and live by Christian ideals and teachings? Through preaching, through assimilation, and through the penitential system. Preaching aimed at instruction and

THE PANTHEON (EXTERIOR). The Pantheon represents one of the greatest Roman architectural triumphs: the enclosure of a vast circular space flooded with light that enters the building through a round window in the dome. (Italian Government Travel Office)

edification. Instruction presented the basic teachings of Christianity. Edification was intended to strengthen the newly baptized in their faith through stories about the lives of Christ and the saints. Deeply ingrained pagan customs and practices could not be stamped out by words alone, or even by imperial edicts. Christian missionaries often followed a policy of assimilation, easing the conversion of pagan men and women by stressing similarities between their customs and beliefs and those of Christianity. A letter that Pope Gregory I wrote to Augustine of Canterbury beautifully illustrates this policy. The pope intended that pagan buildings and practices be given a Christian significance. The letter (601) was carried to Augustine in Britain by one Mellitus:

To our well beloved son Abbot Mellitus: Gregory servant of the servants of God. . . . Therefore, when by God's help you reach our most reverent brother, Bishop Augustine, we wish you to inform him that we have been giving careful thought to the affairs of the English, and have come to the conclusion that the temples of the idols among that people should on no account be destroyed. The idols are to be destroyed, but the temples themselves are to be aspersed with holy water, altars set up in them, and relics deposited there. For if these temples are well-built, they must be purified from the worship of demons and dedicated to the service of the true God. In this way, we hope that the people, seeing that their temples are not destroyed, may abandon their error and, flocking more readily to their accustomed resorts, may come to know and adore the true God. And since they have a custom of sacrificing many oxen to demons, let some other solemnity be substituted in its place, such as a day of Dedication or the Festivals of the holy martyrs whose relics are enshrined there. On such occasions they might well construct shelters of boughs for themselves around the churches that were once temples, and celebrate the solemnity with devout feasting. . . . For it is certainly impossible to eradicate all errors from obstinate minds at one stroke, and whoever wishes to climb to a mountain top climbs gradually step by step, and not in one leap.[6]

THE PANTHEON (INTERIOR) Originally a temple for the gods, the Pantheon later served as a Christian church. As such, it symbolizes the adaptation of pagan elements to Christian purposes. (Alinari/Scala)

How assimilation works can perhaps be appreciated through the example of an annual festival familiar to all Americans, Saint Valentine's Day. There were two Romans named Valentine. Both were Christian priests, and both were martyred for their beliefs around the middle of the month of February in the third century. Since about 150 B.C., the Romans had celebrated the festival of Lupercalia, at which they asked the gods for fertility for themselves, their fields, and their flocks. This celebration occurred in mid-February, shortly before the beginning of the Roman New Year and the arrival of spring on March 1.

The early church reinterpreted the old festival of Lupercalia in terms of Saint Valentine. Nothing in the history of the two Christian martyrs connects them with lovers or the exchange of messages and gifts. (That practice began in the later Middle Ages.) The association lies only in the date, mid-February, the time of Lupercalia, and the martyrdoms. Lupercalia was "converted" into Saint Valentine's Day. February 14 was still celebrated as a festival, but it had Christian meaning.

Assimilation is a slow process. The penitential system probably had a more immediate impact on the unconverted masses. Penitentials were manuals for the examination of conscience. Irish priests wrote the earliest ones, and English missionaries carried them to the Continent. The illiterate penitent knelt beside the priest, who asked questions from the penitential about sins he or she might have committed. The recommended penance (or satisfaction) was then imposed. Penance usually meant fasting for three days each week on bread and water, which served as a "medicine" for the soul. Here is a section of the penitential prepared by Archbishop Theodore of Canterbury (668–690). It circulated widely in the eighth and ninth centuries:

If anyone commits fornication with a virgin he shall do penance for one year. If with a married woman, he shall do penance for four years, two of these entire, and in the other two during the three forty-day periods and three days a week.

A male who commits fornication with a male shall do penance for ten years.

If a woman practices vice with a woman, she shall do penance for three years.

Whoever has often committed theft, seven years is his penance, or such a sentence as his priest shall determine, that is, according to what can be arranged with those whom he has wronged. And he who used to steal, when he becomes penitent, ought always to be reconciled to him against whom he has offended and to make restitution according to the wrong he has done to him; and [in such case] he shall greatly shorten his penance.

If a layman slays another with malice aforethought, if he will not lay aside his arms, he shall do penance for seven years; without flesh and wine, three years.

If one slays a monk or a cleric, he shall lay aside his arms and serve God, or he shall do penance for seven years.

He who defiles his neighbor's wife, deprived of his own wife, shall fast for three years two days a week and in the three forty-day periods.

If [the woman] is a virgin, he shall do penance for one year without meat and wine and mead.

If he defiles a vowed virgin, he shall do penance for three years, as we said above, whether a child is born of her or not.

Women who commit abortion before [the fetus] has life, shall do penance for one year or for the three forty-day periods or for forty days, according to the nature of the offense; and if later, that is, more than forty days after conception, they shall do penance as murderesses, that is for three years on Wednesdays and Fridays and in the three forty-day periods. This according to the canons is judged [punishable by] ten years.

If a mother slays her child, if she commits homicide, she shall do penance for fifteen years, and never change except on Sunday.

If a poor woman slays her child, she shall do penance for seven years. In the canon it is said that if it is a case of homicide, she shall do penance for ten years.[7]

As this sample suggests, writers of penitentials were preoccupied with varieties of sexual transgressions. Penitentials are much more akin to the Jewish law of the Old Testament than to the spirit of the New Testament. They provide an enormous amount of information about the ascetic ideals of early Christianity and about the crime-ridden realities of Celtic and Germanic societies. Penitentials reveal the ecclesiastical foundations of such modern issues as sexual attitudes, birth control, and abortion. And, most important of all, the penitential system led to the growth of a different attitude toward religion. Where religious observances had always been public, corporate, and social, they gradually developed into private, personal, and individual affairs.[8]

CHRISTIAN ATTITUDES TOWARD CLASSICAL CULTURE

Probably the major dilemma the early Christian church faced concerned Greco-Roman culture. The Roman Empire as a social, political, and economic force gradually disintegrated. Its culture, however, survived. In Greek philosophy, art, and architecture, in Roman law, literature, education, and engineering, the legacy of a great civilization continued. The Christian religion had begun and spread within this intellectual and psychological milieu. What was to be the attitude of the Christian to the Greco-Roman world of ideas?

Hostility

Christians of the first and second centuries believed that the end of the world was near. Christ had promised to return, and Christians expected to witness that return. Therefore, they considered knowledge useless and learning a waste of time. The important duty of the Christian was to prepare for the Second Coming of the Lord.

Early Christians had a great hatred of pagan Roman culture — in fact, of all Roman civilization. Had not the Romans crucified Christ? Had not the Romans persecuted the Christians and subjected them to the most horrible and exquisite tortures? Did not the Book of Revelation in the New Testament call Rome the great whore of the world, filled with corruption, sin, and every kind of evil? Roman culture was sexual, sensual, and materialistic. The sensual poetry of Ovid, the pornographic descriptions of the satirist Petronius, the political poetry of Virgil, even the rhetorical brilliance of Cicero represented a threat, in the eyes of serious Christians, to the spiritual aims and ideals of Christianity. Good Christians who sought the Kingdom of Heaven through the imitation of Christ believed they had to disassociate themselves from the filth that Roman culture embodied.

Saint Paul had written, "The wisdom of the world is foolishness, we preach Christ crucified." Tertullian (ca 160–220), an important African Christian writer, condemned all secular literature as foolishness in the eyes of God. He called the Greek philosophers, such as Aristotle, "hucksters of eloquence" and compared them to "animals of self-glorification." "What has Athens to do with Jerusalem," he demanded, "the Academy with the Church? We have no need for curiosity since Jesus Christ, nor for inquiry since the gospel." Tertullian insisted that, in order to fulfill its mission, the church had to disassociate itself from the classical culture of Rome. Christians would find in the Bible all the wisdom they needed.

Compromise and Adjustment

On the other hand, Christianity encouraged adjustment to the ideas and institutions of the Roman world. Some biblical texts clearly urged Christians to accept the existing social, economic, and political establishment. In a letter specifically addressed to the Christians living in the hostile environment of Rome and among non-Christians, Saint Peter had written about the obligations of Christians:

TOWARDS PAGANS
Always behave honourably among pagans, so that they can see your good works for themselves and, when the day of reckoning comes, give thanks to God for the things which now make them denounce you as criminals.

TOWARDS CIVIL AUTHORITY
For the sake of the Lord, accept the authority of every social institution: the emperor, as the supreme authority, and the governors as commissioned by him to punish criminals and praise good citizenship. God wants you to be good citizens. . . . Have respect for everyone and love for your community; fear God and honour the emperor.[9]

Christians really had little choice. Greco-Roman culture, albeit pagan, was the only culture they knew. Only men received a formal education, and they went through the traditional curriculum of grammar and rhetoric. They learned to be effective public speakers in the forum or the law courts. No other system of education existed. Many early Christians had grown up as pagans; they were converted as adults. Even had they wanted to give up their classical ideas and patterns of thought, they would have had great difficulty in doing so. Therefore, they had to adapt or adjust their Roman education to their Christian beliefs. Saint Paul had believed there was a good deal of truth in pagan thought, as long as it was correctly interpreted and properly understood.

The result was a compromise. Christians gradually came to terms with Greco-Roman culture. Saint Jerome (340–419), a distinguished theologian and linguist, remains famous for his translation of the Old and New Testaments from the Hebrew and Greek into vernacular Latin. Called the Vulgate, his edition of the Bible served as the official translation until the sixteenth century, and even today scholars rely on that text. Saint Jerome was also familiar with the writings of such classical authors as Cicero, Virgil, and Terence. He believed that Christians should study the best of ancient thought, because it would direct their minds to God. He maintained that the best ancient literature should be interpreted in light of the Christian faith.

Synthesis: Saint Augustine

The finest representative of the blending of classical and Christian ideas, and indeed one of the most brilliant thinkers in the history of the Western world, was Saint Augustine of Hippo (354–430). Aside from the scriptural writers, no one has had a greater impact on Christian thought in every century than Saint Augustine. He was born into an urban family in what is now Algeria in North

THE ANTIOCH CHALICE. This earliest surviving Christian chalice, which dates from the fourth century A.D., combines the typical Roman shape with Christian motifs. The chalice is decorated with figures of Christ and the apostles, leaves, and grapes, which represent the sacrament of the Eucharist. (The Metropolitan Museum of Art; the Cloisters Collection; purchase, 1950)

Africa. His father was a pagan, his mother a devout Christian. Because his family was poor — his father was a minor civil servant — the only avenue to success in a highly competitive world was a classical education.

Augustine's mother believed that a good classical education, though pagan, would make her son a better Christian, so Augustine's father worked extremely hard to scrape together the money to educate him. The child received his basic education in the local school. By modern or even medieval standards, that education was extremely narrow: the textual study of the writings of the poet Virgil, the orator-politician Cicero, the historian Sallust, and the playwright Terence. Learning meant memorization. Education in the late Roman world aimed at an appreciation of words and the production of eloquent orators.

At the age of seventeen, Augustine went to nearby Carthage to continue his education. There he took a mistress with whom he lived for fifteen years. At Carthage, Augustine entered a difficult psychological phase and began an intellectual and spiritual pilgrimage that led him through experiments with several philosophies and heretical Christian sects. In 383, he traveled to Rome, where he endured illness and disappointment in his teaching because his students fled when their bills were due.

Finally, in Milan in 387, through his friendship with Ambrose and through the insights he received from reading Saint Paul's Letter to the Romans, Augustine was converted and received Christian baptism. He later became bishop of the seacoast city of Hippo Regius in his native North Africa. He was a renowned preacher to Christians there, a vigorous defender of orthodox Christianity, and the author of over ninety-three books and treatises.

Augustine produced in his autobiography, *The Confessions,* a literary masterpiece and one of the most influential books of Europe. Written in the form of a prayer to God, its language is often incredibly beautiful:

Great are thou, O Lord, and exceedingly to be praised: great is thy power and of thy wisdom there is no reckoning. And man, indeed, one part of thy creation, has the will to praise thee: yea, man, though he bears his mortality about with him . . . even man, a small portion of thy creation, has the will to praise thee. Thou dost stir him up, that it may delight him to praise thee, for thou hast made us for thyself, and our hearts are restless till they find repose in thee.[10]

Too late have I loved thee, O beauty ever ancient and ever new, too late have I loved thee! And behold! Thou wert within and I without, and it was without that I sought thee. Thou wert with me, and I was not with thee. Those creatures held me far from thee which, were they not in thee, were not at all. Thou didst call, thou didst cry, thou didst break in upon my deafness; thou didst gleam forth, thou didst shine out, thou didst banish my blindness; thou didst send forth thy fragrance, and I drew breath and yearned for thee; I tasted and still hunger and thirst; thou didst touch me, and I was on flame to find thy peace.[11]

The Confessions describes Augustine's moral struggle, the conflict between his spiritual and intellectual aspirations and his sensual and material self. It tells the eternally human story of a man constantly tempted by sin but aware also of the providence of God. *The Confessions* reveals the change and development of a human mind and personality steeped in the philosophy and culture of the ancient world.

Greek and Roman philosophers had taught that knowledge and virtue are the same thing: a person who really knows what is right will do what is right. Augustine rejected this idea. He believed that a person may know what is right but be powerless to act because of the innate weakness of the human will. People do not always act on the basis of rational knowledge. Here Augustine made a profound contribution to the understanding of human nature. He demonstrated that a very learned person can also be corrupt and evil. *The Confessions,* written in the rhetorical style and language of late Roman antiquity, marks the synthesis of Greco-Roman forms and Christian thought.

The first serious Germanic assault on Rome was led by the Visigothic chieftain Alaric, and his conquest of the Eternal City in 410 horrified the civilized world. Pagans blamed the disaster on the Christians, and in response Augustine wrote *City of God.* This profoundly original work contrasts Christianity with the secular society in which it existed. *City of God* presents a moral interpretation of the Roman government, and in fact of all history. Written in Latin and filled with references to ancient history and mythology, it is the best statement of the Christian philosophy of history.

In the Christian view, history is the account of God acting in time. All of human history reveals that there are two kinds of people: those who live according to the flesh in the city of Babylon and those who live according to the spirit in the City of God. In other words, humanity is divided between individuals who live entirely according to their selfish desires and inclinations and individuals who live according to the Word of God. The former will endure eternal hellfire, the latter eternal bliss.

Augustine maintained that states came into existence as the result of Adam's fall and people's inclination to sin. The state is a necessary evil, responsible only for providing the peace and order that the Christians need in order to pursue their pilgrimage to the City of God. The particular form of government — whether monarchy, aristocracy, or democracy — is basically irrelevant. Any civil government that fails to provide order, law, and justice is no more than a band of gangsters.

Since the state results from moral lapse, from sin, it follows that the church, which is concerned with salvation, is responsible for everyone, including Christian rulers. Churchmen in the Middle Ages used Augustine's theory to defend their belief in the ultimate superiority of the spiritual power over the temporal. This remained the dominant political theory until the late thirteenth century.

Augustine used the evidence of Roman history to defend Christian theology. He had assimilated Roman history, and indeed all of classical culture, into Christian teaching.

MONASTICISM AND THE RULE OF SAINT BENEDICT

Christianity began and spread as a city religion. Since the time of the first century, however, some especially pious Christians felt that the only alternative to the decadence of urban life was complete separation from the world. The all-consuming pursuit of material things, the gross sexual promiscuity, and the general political corruption disgusted them. They believed that the Christian life as set forth in the Gospel could not be lived in the midst of such immorality. They rejected the established values of Roman society and were the first real nonconformists in the church.

At first individuals or small groups left the cities and went to live in caves or rude shelters in the desert or on the mountains. These people were called hermits, from the Greek word *eremos,* meaning "desert." There is no way of knowing how many there were in the fourth and fifth centuries, partly because their conscious aim was a secret and hidden life known only to God.

Several factors worked against the eremitical variety of monasticism in western Europe. First was the climate. The cold, snow, ice, and fog that covered much of Europe for many months of the year discouraged isolated living. Dense forests filled with wild animals and wandering barbaric German tribes presented obvious dangers. Then, church leaders did not really approve of the eremitical life. Hermits sometimes claimed to have mystical experiences, direct communications with God. No one could verify these experiences. But if hermits could communicate directly with the Lord, what need had they for the priest and the institutional church? The church hierarchy, or leaders, encouraged coenobitic monasticism, that is, communal living of groups in monasteries.

In the fifth and sixth centuries, many experiments in communal monasticism were made in Gaul, Italy, Spain, Anglo-Saxon England, and Ireland. John Cassian, after studying both eremitical and coenobitic mysticism in Egypt and Syria, established around 415 two monasteries near Marseilles in Gaul. One of his books, *Conferences,* based on conversations he had had with holy men in the East, discussed the dangers of the isolated hermit life. The abbey or monastery of Lérins in the Mediterranean Sea near Cannes (ca 410) also had significant contacts with the monastic centers in the Middle East and North Africa. Lerins encouraged the severely penitential and extremely ascetic behavior, such as long hours of prayer, fasting, and self-flagellation, that were common in the East. It was this tradition of harsh self-mortification that the Roman-British monk Saint Patrick (ca 389–461) carried from Lérins to Ireland. Church organization in Ireland became closely associated with the monasteries, and Irish monastic life followed the ascetic Eastern form.

Around 540, the Roman senator Cassiodorus (480–575) retired from public service and established a monastery, the Vivarium, on his estate in Italy. He enlisted highly educated and sophisticated men for it. Cassiodorus wanted the Vivarium to become an educational and cultural center, and he set the monks to copying both sacred and secular manuscripts. He intended this to be their sole occupation. Cassiodorus started the association of monasticism with scholarship and learning. This developed into a great tradition in the medieval and modern worlds. But Cassiodorus's experiment did not become the most influential form of monasticism in European society. The fifth and sixth centuries witnessed the appearance of many monastic lifestyles.

In 529, Benedict of Nursia (480–543), who had experimented with both the eremitical and the communal forms of monastic life, wrote a brief set of regulations, or rules, for the monks who had gathered around him at Monte Cassino between Rome and Naples. This guide for monastic life slowly replaced all others. *The Rule of Saint Benedict* has influenced all forms of organized religious life in the Roman church.

The Rule of Saint Benedict

Saint Benedict conceived of his *Rule* as a simple code for ordinary men. It outlined a monastic life of regularity, discipline, and moderation. Each monk received ample food and an adequate amount of sleep. Self-destructive acts of mortification were forbidden. In an atmosphere of silence, the monk spent part of the day in formal prayer, which was called the Work of God. This consisted of chanting psalms and other prayers from the Bible in the monastery church, called the choir. The rest of the day was passed in study and manual labor. After a year of probation, the monk made a profession of his future life.

Profession consisted of three vows. First, the monk vowed stability: he promised to live his entire life in the monastery of his profession. The vow of stability was Saint Benedict's major contribution to Western monasticism; his object was to prevent the wandering so common in his day. Second, the monk vowed conversion of manners, that is, to strive to improve himself and to come closer to God. Third, he promised obedience, the most difficult vow because it meant the complete surrender of his will to the abbot, or head of the monastery. The first sentence of the *Rule* encouraged the monk, by the labor of obedience, to return to God, from whom he had departed "by the sloth of disobedience."

The Rule of Saint Benedict shows the assimilation of the Roman spirit into Western monasticism. It reveals the logical mind of its creator and the Roman concern for order, organization, and respect for law. Its spirit of moderation and flexibility is reflected in the patience, wisdom, and understanding with which the abbot is to govern, and, indeed, the entire life is to be led. The *Rule* could be used in vastly different physical and geographical circumstances, in damp and cold Germany as well as in warm and sunny Italy. The *Rule* was quickly adapted for women, and many monasteries of nuns were established in the early Middle Ages.

The attitude of Saint Benedict's *Rule* toward newcomers implies that a person who wants to become a monk or nun need have no previous ascetic experience or even a particularly strong bent toward the religious life. Thus, it allowed for the admission of individuals of different backgrounds and personalities. This flexibility helps to explain the attractiveness of Benedictine monasticism throughout the centuries. *The Rule of Saint Benedict* is a superior example of the way in which the Greco-Roman heritage and Roman patterns of thought were preserved.

At the same time, the *Rule* no more provides a picture of actual life within a Benedictine abbey of the seventh or eighth (or twentieth) century than the American Constitution of 1789 reveals living conditions in the United States today. A code of laws cannot do that. Monasteries were composed of individuals, and human beings defy strict classification according to rules, laws, or statistics. *The Rule of Saint Benedict* had one fundamental purpose. The exercises of the monastic life were designed to draw the person, slowly but steadily, away from attachment to the world and away from love of self to the love of God.

The Success of Benedictine Monasticism

Why was the Benedictine form of monasticism so successful? Why did it eventually replace other forms of Western monasticism? The answer lies partly in its spirit of flexibility and moderation and partly in the balanced life it provided. Early Benedictine monks and nuns spent part of the day in prayer, part in study or some other form of intellectual activity, and part in manual labor. The monastic life as conceived by Saint Benedict did not lean too heavily in any one direction; it struck a balance between asceticism and idleness. It opened opportunities for persons of entirely different abilities and talents — from mechanics to gardeners to literary scholars. Benedict's *Rule* contrasts sharply with Cassiodorus's narrow concept of the monastery as a place for aristocratic scholars and bibliophiles.

Benedictine monasticism suited the social circumstances of early medieval society. The German invasions had fragmented European life: the rural, self-sufficient estate replaced the city as the basic unit of civilization. A monastery had to be economically self-sufficient. It was supposed to produce from its lands and properties all that was needed for food, clothing, buildings, and the liturgical service of the altar. The monastery fit in, indeed represented, the trend toward localism.

Finally, Benedictine monasticism succeeded because it was so materially successful. In the seventh and eighth centuries, monasteries pushed back forest and wasteland, drained swamps, and experimented with crop rotation. For example, the abbey of Saint Wandrille, founded in 645 near Rouen in northwestern Gaul, sent squads of monks to clear the forests that surrounded it. Within seventy-five years it was immensely wealthy. The economic development of Jumièges, also in the diocese of Rouen, followed much the same pattern. Such Benedictine houses made a significant contribution to the agricultural development of Europe. The socialistic nature of their organization, whereby property was held in common and profits pooled and reinvested, made this contribution possible.

At the same time, monasteries conducted schools for the education of the young people of the neighborhood. Some learned about prescriptions and herbal remedies for disease. They provided medical treatment for their localities. A few copied manuscripts and wrote books. These abilities did not go unobserved in a society desperately in need of them. Local and royal governments drew upon the services of the literate men, the able administrators whom the monasteries produced. This was not what Saint Benedict had intended, but the effectiveness of the institution he designed made it perhaps inevitable.

THE BYZANTINE EAST
(CA 400–988)

Constantine (306–337) had tried to maintain the unity of the Roman Empire, but during the fifth and sixth centuries the western and eastern halves drifted apart. Later emperors worked to hold the empire together. Justinian (527–565) waged long and hard-fought wars against the Ostrogoths and temporarily regained Italy and North Africa. But his conquests had disastrous consequences. Justinian's wars exhausted the resources of the Byzantine state. They destroyed Italy's economy and killed a large part of its population. The wars paved the way for the easy conquest of Italy by another Germanic tribe, the Lombards, shortly after Justinian's death. In the late sixth century, the territory of the western Roman Empire came under Germanic sway, while in the East the Byzantine Empire continued the traditions and institutions of the caesars.

Latin Christian culture was only one legacy the Roman Empire bequeathed to the Western world. The Byzantine culture centered at Constantinople—Constantine's New Rome—was another. The Byzantine Empire maintained a high standard of living, and for centuries the Greeks were the most civilized people in the Western world. The Byzantine Empire held at bay, or at least hindered, barbarian peoples who could have otherwise wreaked additional devastation on western Europe, thus retarding its development. Most important, however, is the role of Byzantium as preserver of the wisdom of the ancient world. Through the long years when barbarians in western Europe trampled down the old and then painfully built something new, Byzantium protected and then handed on to the West the intellectual heritage of Greco-Roman civilization.

Byzantine East and Germanic West

As imperial authority disintegrated in the West during the fifth century, civic functions were performed first by church leaders and then by German chieftains. For example, in 452, when Attila the Hun invaded Italy, Pope Leo I negotiated with the barbarians and persuaded them to withdraw. There was no other authority in Rome to do so. The death of the Roman emperor Romulus

Augustus in 476 signaled the end of the empire in the West. Thereafter, German chieftains held power.

Meanwhile, in the East, the Byzantines preserved the forms and traditions of the Old Roman Empire, and they even called themselves Romans. Byzantine emperors traced their lines back past Constantine to Augustus. The senate that sat in Constantinople carried on the traditions and preserved the glory of the old Roman senate. The army that defended the empire was the direct descendant of the old Roman legions. Even the chariot factions of the Roman Empire lived on under the Byzantines, who cheered their favorites as enthusiastically as had the Romans of Hadrian's day.

The Byzantine East and the Germanic West differed considerably with respect to the position of the church in the two areas. The fourth-century emperors Constantine and Theodosius had wanted the church to act as a unifying force within the empire, but the Germanic invasions made that impossible. The bishops of Rome repeatedly called upon the emperors at Constantinople for military support against the invaders. Rarely could the emperors send it. The Church in the West steadily grew away from the empire and became involved in the social and political affairs of Italy and the West. Nevertheless, until the eighth century, the popes, who were selected by the clergy of Rome, continued to send to the emperors at Constantinople announcements of their elections—a sign that the Roman popes long thought of themselves as bishops of the Roman Empire.

In Constantinople, on the other hand, the emperor nominated the patriarch, as the highest prelate of the church in the East was called. The emperor looked upon religion as a branch of the state. Religion was such a vital aspect of the social life of the people that the emperor devoted considerable attention to it. He considered it his duty to protect the faith, not only against heathen enemies but also against heretics from within the empire. In case of doctrinal disputes, the emperor, following Constantine's example at Nicaea, summoned councils of bishops and theologians to settle problems.

In the East, Christianity was the established religion. All citizens of the Byzantine Empire were Christians; to be Byzantine meant to be Christian. The Greek church was an imperial state church subject to and guided by the emperor. The clergy were well organized. The level of theological debate was high. Fine points of Christian theology held the attention of the leaders of the Greek church.

In the West, conditions were quite different. The popes were preoccupied with the conversion of the Germanic peoples, with the Christian attitude toward classical culture, and with relations with the German rulers. The church concentrated on its missionary function. Most of the Germanic tribes were pagan, and only gradually and imperfectly were they converted to Christianity. It took time for the clergy to be organized and for the papacy to get in touch with all clerics. Most of the theology of the church in the West came from the East, and the overwhelming majority of the popes were themselves of Eastern origin.

In the West, tensions occasionally developed between church officials and secular authorities. The dispute between Bishop Ambrose of Milan and the emperor Theodosius is a good example. A century later, Pope Gelasius I (492–496) insisted that bishops, and not civil authorities, were responsible for the administration of the church. Gelasius maintained that two powers governed the world, the sacred authority of the popes and the royal power of kings. Because priests have to answer to God even for kings, the sacred power was the greater. Such an assertion was virtually unheard of in the East, where the emperor's jurisdiction over the church was fully acknowledged.

JUSTINIAN AND HIS COURT. The Emperor Justinian (center) with ecclesiastical and court officials personifies the unity of the Byzantine state and the orthodox church in the person of the emperor. Just as the emperor was both king and priest, so all his Greek subjects belonged to the orthodox church. (Alinari/Scala)

The expansion of the Arabs in the Mediterranean in the seventh and eighth centuries contributed to the increasing separation of the churches. Separation bred isolation. Isolation, combined with prejudice on both sides, bred hostility. Finally, in 1054, a theological disagreement led the bishop of Rome and the patriarch of Constantinople to excommunicate each other. A permanent schism, or split, between the Roman Catholic and the Greek Orthodox churches was the outcome.

In spite of religious differences, the Byzantine Empire served as a bulwark for the West, protecting it against invasions from the east. The Greeks stopped the Persians in the seventh century. They blunted—although they could not stop—Arab attacks in the seventh and eighth centuries, and they fought courageously against Turkish invaders until the fifteenth century, when they were finally over-whelmed. In Europe, Byzantine Greeks slowed the impetus of the Slavic incursions in the Balkans and held the Russians at arm's length.

Turning from war to the arts of peace, the Byzantines set about civilizing the Slavs, both in the Balkans and in Russia. Byzantine missionaries spread the word of Christ, and one of their triumphs was the conversion of the Russians. The Byzantine missionary Cyril adapted the Greek alphabet to the Russian language, and this script (called the Cyrillic alphabet) is still in use today. Cyrillic script made possible the birth of Russian literature. Similarly, Byzantine art and architecture became the basis and inspiration of Russian forms. The Byzantines were so successful that the Russians claimed to be the successors of the Byzantine Empire. For a time Moscow was known as the "Third Rome" (the second Rome being Constantinople).

The Law Code of Justinian

One of the most splendid achievements of the Byzantine emperors was in the field of law: the Byzantine Empire preserved Roman law for the medieval and modern worlds. Roman law had developed from many sources — decisions by judges, edicts of the emperors, legislation passed by the senate, and the opinions of jurists expert in the theory and practice of law. By the fourth century, Roman law had become a huge and bewildering mass. Its sheer bulk made it almost unusable. To make matters worse, some laws had become out-dated, some repeated others, and some contradicted others. Faced with this vast, complex, and often confusing hodgepodge, the emperor Theodosius decided to clarify and codify the law. He explained the need to do so:

When we consider the enormous multitude of books, the diverse modes of process and the difficulty of legal cases, and further the huge mass of imperial constitutions, which hidden as it were under a rampart of gross mist and darkness precludes men's intellects from gaining a knowledge of them, we feel that we have met a real need of our age, and dispelling the darkness have given light to the laws by a short compendium. . . . Thus having swept away the clouds of volumes, on which many wasted their lives and explained nothing in the end, we established a compendious knowledge of the Imperial constitutions since the time of the divine Constantine.[12]

Theodosius's work was only a beginning. He left centuries of Roman law untouched.

A far more sweeping and systematic codification took place under the emperor Justinian. Justinian intended to simplify the law and to make it known to everyone. He appointed a committee of eminent jurists to sort through and organize the laws. In 529, Justinian published the *Code,* which distilled the legal genius of the Romans into a coherent whole, eliminated outmoded laws, removed con-tradictions, and clarified the law itself. Not content with the *Code,* Justinian set about bringing order to the equally huge body of Roman jurisprudence, the science or the philosophy of law.

During the second and third centuries, the foremost Roman jurists, at the request of the emperors, had expressed learned opinions on com-plex legal problems, but often these opinions dif-fered from one another. To harmonize this body of knowledge, Justinian directed his jurists to clear up disputed points and to give definitive rulings. Accordingly, in 533 his lawyers published the *Digest,* which codified Roman legal thought. Fi-nally, Justinian's lawyers compiled a handbook of civil law, the *Institutes.*

These three works — *Code, Digest,* and *Insti-tutes* — are the backbone of the *corpus juris civilis,* the body of civil law, which is the foundation of law for nearly every modern European nation. Even England, which developed its own common law, has been influenced by it. The work of Justinian and his dedicated band of jurists still affects the life of the modern world nearly fifteen hundred years later.

Byzantine Intellectual Life

Among the Byzantines education was highly prized, and because of them many masterpieces of ancient Greek literature survived to fertilize the intellectual life of the modern world. The literature of the Byzantine Empire was predominantly Greek, although Latin was long spoken among top politicians, scholars, and lawyers. Indeed, Justinian's *Code* was first written in Latin. Among the reading public, which was quite large, history was a favorite subject. Generations of Byzantines read the historical works of Herodotus, Thucydides, and others. Some Byzantine historians abbreviated long histories, such as those of Polybius, while others left detailed narratives of their own days.

The most remarkable Byzantine historian was Procopius (ca 500–ca 562), who left a rousing account of Justinian's reconquest of North Africa and Italy. Proof that the wit and venom of ancient writers like Archilochus and Aristophanes still lived in the Byzantine era can be found in Procopius's *Secret History,* a vicious and uproarious attack on Justinian and his wife, the empress Theodora. Although the Byzantines are often depicted as dull and lifeless, such opinions are hard to defend in the face of Procopius's descriptions of Justinian's character:

For he was at once villainous and amenable; as people say colloquially, a moron. He was never truthful with anyone, but always guileful in what he said and did, yet easily hoodwinked by any who wanted to deceive him. His nature was an unnatural mixture of folly and wickedness.[13]

Procopius even accused Justinian of being a demon who possessed strange powers:

And some of those who have been with Justinian at the palace late at night, men who were pure of spirit, have thought they saw a strange demoniac form taking his throne and walked about, and indeed he was never wont to remain sitting for long, and immediately Justinian's head vanished, while the rest of his body seemed to ebb and flow; whereat the beholder stood aghast and fearful, wondering if his eyes were deceiving him. But presently he perceived the vanished head filling out and joining the body again as strangely as it had left it.[14]

The *Secret History* may not be great history, but it is robust literature.

Later Byzantine historians chronicled the victories of their emperors and the progress of their barbarian foes. Like Herodotus before them, they were curious about foreigners. They have left striking descriptions of the Turks, who eventually overwhelmed Byzantium. They painted unflattering pictures of the uncouth and grasping princes of France and England, who saw in the Crusades the perfect combination of faith and piety, bloodshed and profit.

In other fields the achievements of the Byzantines are less noteworthy. In mathematics and geometry they discovered nothing new. Yet they were exceptionally important as catalysts, for they passed Greco-Roman learning on to the Arabs, who assimilated it and made remarkable advances upon it. The Byzantines were equally uncreative in astronomy and natural science, but they at least faithfully learned what the ancients had to teach.

Only when science could be put to military use did the Byzantines make any advances. The best-known Byzantine scientific discovery was chemical—"Greek fire," a combustible liquid that was the medieval equivalent of the flame thrower. In mechanics the Byzantines continued the work of Hellenistic and Roman inventors of artillery and siege machinery. Just as Archimedes had devised machines to stop the Romans (see Chapter 3), so Byzantine scientists improved and modified devices for defending their empire.

The Byzantines devoted a great deal of attention to medicine. The general level of medical competence was far higher in the Byzantine Empire than it was in the medieval West. The Byzantines assimilated the discoveries of Hellenic and Hellenistic medicine but added very little of their own. The basis of their medical theory was Hippocrates' concept of the four humors of the body. Byzantine physicians emphasized the importance of diet and rest, and they relied heavily on drugs made from herbs. Perhaps their chief weakness was their excessive use of bleeding and burning, which often succeeded only in further weakening an already weak patient. Byzantine hospitals were a prominent feature of life, and the army too had its medical corps.

THE ARABS AND ISLAM

Around 610, in the obscure town of Mecca in what is now Saudi Arabia, a merchant of only moderate commercial success called Mohammed began to have religious visions. By the time he died in 632, all Arabia had accepted his creed. A century later his followers controlled Syria, Palestine, Egypt, all of North Africa, Spain, and part of France. This Arabic expansion profoundly affected the development of a distinct European culture.

Another significant influence on the creation of European civilization was Arabic learning. Arabic scholars, together with Byzantine ones, preserved the scientific, philosophical, and medical writings of the ancient world, and through centers at Salerno in southern Italy and Toledo in central Spain, Arabic and Greek learning reached the West. Arabic mathematicians not only preserved ancient learning but also made original contributions. Western

knowledge, especially in medicine, mathematics, and engineering, rests heavily on Arabic achievements.

The Arabs

In the early seventh century, Arabia was inhabited by Semitic tribes, most of whom were Bedouins. These primitive and warlike peoples grazed their goats and sheep on the sparse patches of grass that dotted the vast semi-arid peninsula. Other Arabs, called Hejaz, lived in the southern valleys and coastal towns along the Red Sea—in Yemen, Mecca, and Medina. The Hejaz led a more sophisticated life and supported themselves by agriculture and trade. Their caravan routes crisscrossed Arabia and carried goods to Byzantium, Persia, and Syria. The Hejaz had wide commercial dealings, but they avoided cultural contacts with their Jewish, Christian, and Persian neighbors. The wealth produced by business transactions led to luxurious and extravagant living in the towns.

Although the nomadic Bedouins condemned the urbanized lifestyle of the Hejaz as immoral and corrupt, Arabs of both types deeply respected each other's local tribal customs. They had no political unity beyond their tribal bonds. Tribal custom regulated their lives. Custom demanded the rigid observance of family obligations and the performance of religious rituals. Custom insisted that an Arab be proud, generous, swift to take revenge. Custom required manly courage in public and the avoidance of shameful behavior that could bring social disgrace.

Although there were wide differences among the various tribes, they did have certain religious rules in common. For example, all Arabs kept three months of the year as sacred, and during that time fighting was stopped so that everyone could attend the holy ceremonies in peace. The city of Mecca was accepted as the religious center of the Arab world, and fighting was never tolerated there. All Arabs prayed at the Kaaba, the sanctuary in Mecca. Within the Kaaba was a sacred black stone that Arabs revered because they believed it had fallen from heavan.

What eventually molded the diverse Arab tribes into a powerful political and social unity was the religion founded by Mohammed.

Mohammed and the Faith of Islam

Except for a few vague autobiographical remarks in the Koran (the sacred book of Islam), Mohammed (ca 571–632) left no account of his life. Arab tradition, however, accepts as sacred and historically true some of the legends that developed about him. Those legends were not written down until about a century after his death. Orphaned at the age of six, Mohammed was brought up by his grandfather. As a young man he became a merchant in the caravan trade. Later he entered the service of a wealthy widow, and his subsequent marriage to her brought him financial independence. The Koran reveals him as an extremely devout man, ascetic, self-disciplined, literate but not educated.

Since childhood Mohammed had had strange seizures, or fits, during which he became completely unconscious and had visions. After 610, these attacks and the accompanying visions apparently became more frequent. He described the visions in verse form and used these verses as his Qur'an (Koran) or prayer recitation. For a time unsure of what he should do, Mohammed recognized his mission after a vision in which the angel Gabriel instructed him to preach.

The religion established by Mohammed is called Islam; a believer in that faith is called a Muslim. Mohammed's religion eventually attracted great numbers of people, probably because it is based on simple doctrines that ordinary people can understand. Islam lacked the subtle and complex reasoning Christianity had acquired by the seventh century. Nor did Islam place emphasis on study and learning, as did Judaism.

The theology outlined in the Koran has only a few basic tenets. Islam is strictly monotheistic, and Allah (the Muslim god) is all-powerful and all-knowing. Mohammed, Allah's prophet, preached his word and carried his message. He described himself as the successor both of the Jewish patriarch Abraham and of Christ, and he claimed that his teachings replaced theirs. Mohammed invited and secured converts from Judaism and Christianity.

Because Allah is all-powerful, believers must submit themselves to him. ("Islam" literally means "submission to the word of God.") This part of Islamic belief is closely related to the central feature of Muslim doctrine, the coming Day of Judgment. Muslims need not be concerned about *when* judgment will occur, but they must believe with absolute and total conviction that the Day of Judgment *will* come. Consequently, all of a Muslim's thoughts and actions during every hour of every day should be oriented toward the Last Judgment.

The Islamic Day of Judgment will be very similar to the Christian one: on that day God will separate the saved and the damned. Mohammed described in lengthy detail the frightful tortures with which Allah will punish the damned: scourgings, beatings with iron clubs, burnings, and forced drinking of boiling water. The prophet's depiction of the heavenly rewards of the saved and the blessed are just as graphic but different in kind from those of Christian theology. The Muslim vision of heaven entails lush green gardens surrounded by refreshing streams. There, the saved, clothed in rich silks, lounge about on soft cushions and couches, nibbling ripe fruits, sipping delicious beverages served by handsome youths, and enjoying the companionship of plump, black-eyed maidens. It is not difficult to understand how these particular sensual delights would appeal to a people living in or near the hot, dry desert.

In order to merit the rewards of heaven, Mohammed prescribed a strict code of morality and behavior. The Muslim must recite a profession of faith in Allah and in Mohammed as God's prophet: "There is no god but Allah and Mohammed is his prophet." The believer must pray five times a day, fast and pray during the sacred month of Ramadan, make a pilgrimage to the holy city of Mecca once during his or her lifetime, and give alms to the poor. The Koran forbids alcoholic beverages and gambling. It condemns usury in business, that is, lending money at high interest rates or taking advantage of the market demands for products by charging high prices for them. Some foods, such as pork, are forbidden. The Koran sets forth an austere code of sexual morality, but the man who can afford them may have four wives. The Koran implies the social inferiority of women to men, but in law women are given some rights of inheritance. The widespread Arab practice of infanticide was prohibited by Islam. The Muslim who faithfully observed the laws of the Koran could hope for salvation. The believer who suffered and died for his faith in battle was assured the sensual rewards of the Muslim heaven immediately.

According to the Koran, salvation is by Allah's grace and choice alone. A Muslim will not "win" salvation as a reward for good behavior. Because Allah is all-knowing and all-powerful, he knows from the moment of a person's conception whether or not that person will be saved. Nevertheless, Mohammed maintained, predestination gave the believer the will and the courage to try to achieve the impossible. Devout Muslims came to believe that the mechanical performance of the basic rules of the faith would automatically gain them salvation.

Historians and ecumenically minded theologians have pointed out many similarities among Islam, Christianity, and Judaism. All three religions are monotheistic. Like the orthodox Jews, Muslims are forbidden to eat pork. Like the Christians, Muslims are urged to practice charity and to be generous to the poor and the weak. Like the Christians, also, the Muslims believe in the Last Judgment. Mohammed probably had a general familiarity with the Old and New Testaments, and he must have learned something of Jewish and Christian cultures on his commercial travels.

In the Koran, Mohammed gave his believers a holy book of revelation, moral principles, and history on a par with the Old and New Testaments. Like Jews and Christians, Muslims became people with a sacred book. The Koran was not only a sacred book, however. It was written with great eloquence and poetic charm, qualities the Arabs of Mohammed's day especially praised.

Muslim Expansion

Mohammed's preaching at first did not appeal to many people. Legend holds that for the first three years, he attracted only fourteen believers. One explanation for the slow acceptance of Islam is that Mohammed urged the destruction of the idols in the sanctuary at Mecca. This site drew thousands of devout Arabs annually and thus brought important revenue to the city. The townspeople turned against him, and Mohammed and his followers were forced to flee to Medina. This Hegira, or flight, occurred in 622, and Muslims subsequently dated the beginning of their era from that event. At Medina, Mohammed attracted increasing numbers of believers, and his teachings began to have an impact.

ISLAMIC RELIGIOUS HERITAGE. In these two miniature paintings a Muslim artist acknowledges the Islamic debt to Judaism and to Christianity. Above, Samson destroys the temple of the Philistines (Judges 16: 28–30). Below, Christ at a window watches Mohammed's flight from Mecca. (Edinburgh University Library)

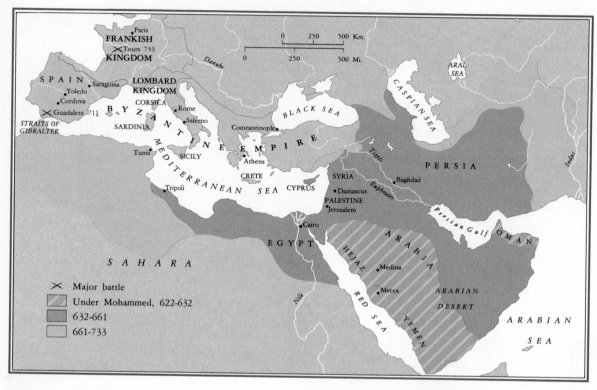

MAP 6.3   THE EXPANSION OF ISLAM TO 733

The real significance of Islam rests in its social and political effects. Mohammed destroyed the communal and tribal quality of Arab life. Individuals could perform the religious rituals, such as the five daily prayers, alone. Although Muslims were accustomed to worship together at sundown on Fridays, no assembly or organized church was essential. Islam lacked the public and corporate aspects of tribal religion. Every Muslim hoped that by following the simple requirements of Islam he or she could achieve salvation. For the believer, the significance of the petty disputes and conflicts of tribal society paled before the simple teachings of Allah. On this basis Mohammed united the nomads of the desert and the merchants of the cities. The doctrines of Islam, instead of the ties of local custom, bound all Arabs.

The faith of Allah, having united the Arabs, redirected their warlike energies. Hostilities were launched outward. By the time Mohammed died in 632, he had welded together all the Bedouin tribes. The crescent of Islam, the Muslim symbol, controlled the entire Arabian peninsula. In the following century, between 632 and 733, one rich province of the old Roman Empire after another came under Muslim domination—first Syria, then Egypt and Persia, and then all of North Africa (see Map 6.3). The seat of government, or headquarters, of this vast new empire was established at Damascus in Syria by the ruling Omayyad family. A contemporary proverb speaks of the Mediterranean as a Muslim lake.

In 711, a Muslim force crossed the Straits of Gibraltar and at Guadalete easily defeated the weak Visigothic kingdom in Spain. The Muslims swept across Spain in seven years (711–718), and one scholar has written, "What was lost in seven years, it took seven hundred to regain."[15] A few Christian princes supported by the Frankish rulers held out in northern mountain fortresses, but in actual fact the Muslims controlled most of Spain until the twelfth century. The political history of Spain in the Middle Ages is the history of the *reconquista,* or Christian reconquest of that country.

In 719, the Arabs pushed beyond the Pyrenees into the kingdom of the Franks. At the battle of Tours in 733, the Frankish ruler Charles Martel defeated the Arabs and halted their further expansion. Charlemagne ultimately expelled them from France.

Arab political influence was felt almost exclusively in Spain. A member of the Omayyad dynasty, Abdurrahman (756–788), established the Moorish kingdom of Spain with the capital at Cordova. (The Spanish kingdom and Spanish culture were called Moorish after the Berber-Arabs, the dark-skinned Moors of North Africa who had conquered the Iberian Peninsula.) Jewish people there were generally well treated, and Christians were tolerated as long as they paid a small tax.

Toledo became an important center of learning, and through Toledo, Arab intellectual achievements entered and influenced western Europe. Arabic knowledge of science and mathematics, derived from the Chinese, the Greeks, and the Hindus, was highly sophisticated. The Muslim mathematician Al-Khwarizmi (d. 830) wrote the important treatise *Algebra.* It is the first work in which the word "algebra" is used mathematically, meaning the transposing of negative terms of an equation to the opposite side. Al-Khwarizmi used Arabic numerals in *Algebra,* and he applied mathematics to problems of physics and astronomy. Muslims also instructed Westerners in the use of the zero, which permitted the execution of complicated problems of multiplication and long division. The use of the zero marked an enormous advance over the clumsy Roman numerals.

Muslim medical knowledge was also much superior to that of Westerners. By the ninth century, Arab physicians had translated most of the treatises of Hippocrates and Galen. Unfortunately, these Greek treatises came to the West by way of translations from Greek to Arabic to Latin, and inevitably lost a great deal in translation. Nevertheless, in the ninth and tenth centuries, Arabic knowledge and experience in anatomy and pharmaceutical prescriptions much advanced Western knowledge.

There is no question that Islam was a significant ingredient in the making of Europe. Muslim expansion meant that Mediterranean civilization would be divided into three spheres of influence, the Byzantine, the Arabic, and the Western. Arabic mathematics, medicine, philosophy, and science, beginning in the ninth century, played a decisive role in the formation of European culture. A few words that came into English from the Arabic illustrate the extent of Arabic influence: alcohol, admiral, algebra, almanac, candy, cipher, coffee, damask, lemon, orange, sherbet, zero.

❧

Saint Augustine died in 430 as the Vandals approached the coastal city of Hippo. Scholars have sometimes described him as standing with one foot in the ancient world and one in the Middle Ages. Although the image, taken literally, is rather ridiculous, Augustine does symbolize the end of ancient culture and the birth of what has been called the Middle Ages. A new and different kind of society was gestating in the mid-fifth century. The world of the Middle Ages combined Germanic practices and institutions, classical ideas and patterns of thought, Christianity, and a significant dash of Islam. Of these elements, Christianity, because it creatively and energetically fashioned the Germanic and the classical legacies, was the most powerful agent in the making of Europe. It is significant that Saint Augustine of Hippo, dogmatic thinker and Christian bishop, represents the coming world-view.

NOTES

1. E. F. Henderson, ed., *Select Historical Documents of the Middle Ages,* G. Bell & Sons, London, 1912, pp. 176–189.

2. R. C. Petry, ed., *A History of Christianity: Readings in the History of Early and Medieval Christianity,* Prentice-Hall, Englewood Cliffs, N.J., 1962, p. 70.

3. H. Bettenson, ed., *Documents of the Christian Church,* Oxford University Press, Oxford, 1947, p. 113.

4. Colossians 3.9–11 (*Jerusalem Bible*).

5. Luke 6.20–32 (*Jerusalem Bible*).

6. L. Sherley-Price, trans., *Bede: A History of the English Church and People,* Penguin Books, Baltimore, 1962, pp. 86–87.

7. J. T. McNeill and H. Gamer, trans., *Medieval Handbooks of Penance,* Octagon Books, New York, 1965, pp. 184–197.

8. L. White, "The Life of the Silent Majority," in R. S. Hoyt, ed., *Life and Thought in the Early Middle Ages,* University of Minnesota Press, Minneapolis, 1967, p. 100.

9. I Peter 2.11–20 (*Jerusalem Bible*).

10. F. J. Sheed, trans., *The Confessions of St. Augustine,* Sheed & Ward, New York, 1953, book 1, pt. 1, p. 3.

11. Ibid., book 10, pt. 27, p. 236.

12. Quoted by J. B. Bury, *History of the Later Roman Empire,* Dover Publications, New York, 1958, 1.233–234.

13. R. Atwater, trans., *Procopius: The Secret History,* University of Michigan Press, Ann Arbor, 1963, book 8.

14. Ibid., book 12.

15. J. H. Elliott, *Imperial Spain,* 1469–1716, Mentor Books, St. Martin's Press, London, 1966, p. 26.

SUGGESTED READING

In addition to the studies listed in the Notes, this chapter leans on the following works, which students may consult for a broader treatment of the characteristics of the early Middle Ages.

P. Brown, *The World of Late Antiquity,* A.D. 150–750* (1971), is a well-illustrated and lucidly written introduction to the entire period, with an emphasis on social and cultural change. B. Lyon, *The Origins of the Middle Ages: Pirenne's Challenge to Gibbon** (1972), is an excellent bibliographical essay with extensive references. For the Germans, see J. M. Wallace-Hadrill, *The Barbarian West, The Early Middle Ages* A.D. 400–1000* (1962), and A. Lewis, *Emerging Europe,* A.D. 400–1000* (1967), both of which describe German customs and society and the Germanic impact on the Roman Empire. F. Lot, *The End of the Ancient World** (1965), emphasizes the economic and social causes of Rome's decline.

There is a rich literature on the Christian church and its role in the transition between ancient and medieval civilizations. F. Oakley, *The Medieval Experience: Foundations of Western Cultural Singularity** (1974), stresses the Christian roots of Western cultural uniqueness. J. Danielou and H. Marrou, *The Christian Centuries,* vol. 1: *The First Six Hundred Years** (1964), is a clearly written and comprehensive history. G. Le Bras, "The Sociology of the Church in the Early Middle Ages," in S. L. Thrupp, ed., *Early Medieval Society** (1967), discusses the Christianization of the barbarians. Students interested in the synthesis of classical and Christian cultures should see C. N. Cochrane, *Christianity and Classical Culture** (1957), a deeply learned monograph. T. E. Mommsen, "Saint Augustine and the Christian Idea of Progress: The Background of the City of God," in *Journal of the History of Ideas* 12 (1951): 346–374, and G. B. Ladner, *The Idea of Reform* (1959), treat ideas of history and progress among the early fathers of the Christian church. The best biography of St. Augustine is P. Brown, *Augustine of Hippo* (1967), which pictures him as a symbol of change.

Monasticism has attracted the interest of Western peoples from sixth-century Germans to twentieth-century hippies. L. Doyle, trans., *St. Benedict's Rule for Monasteries** (1957), presents the monastic guide in an accessible pocket-size form; a more scholarly edition is J. McCann, ed. and trans., *The Rule of Saint Benedict* (1952). Two beautifully illustrated syntheses by distinguished authorities are D. Knowles, *Christian Monasticism** (1969), which sketches monastic history through the middle of the twentieth century, and G. Zarnecki, *The Monastic Achievement** (1972), which focuses on the medieval centuries. L. J. Daly, *Benedictine Monasticism** (1965), stresses the day-to-day living of the monks, and H. B. Workman, *The Evolution of the Monastic Ideal** (1962), concentrates on monasticism as a spiritual and intellectual ideal.

For Byzantium and the Arabs, see J. Hussey, *The Byzantine World** (1961); A. A. Vasiliev, *History of the Byzantine Empire** (1968); S. Runciman, *Byzantine Civilization* (1956); B. Lewis, *The Arabs in History** (1966); T. Andrae, *Mohammed: The Man and His Faith** (1970); M. Rodinson, *Mohammed** (1974); and G. E. von Grunebaum, *Medieval Islam** (1961), which are all excellent treatments.

*Available in paperback.

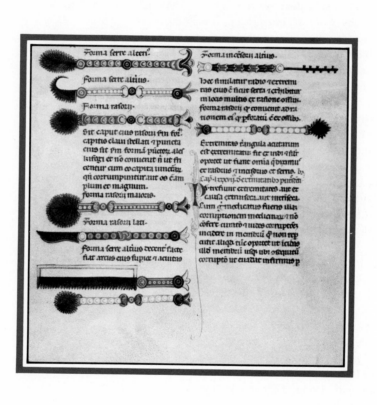

Chapter 7

THE CAROLINGIAN WORLD:
EUROPE IN THE EARLY
MIDDLE AGES

n 733, the Frankish chieftain Charles Martel defeated the Muslim invaders at the battle of Tours in central France. At the time it was only another skirmish in the struggle between Christians and Muslims, but in retrospect it looms as one of the great battles of history: this Frankish victory halted Arab expansion in Europe. In 843, Charles Martel's three great-great-grandsons, after a bitter war, concluded the Treaty of Verdun, which divided the European continent among themselves.

Between 733 and 843, a society emerged that was distinctly European. A new kind of social and political "organization," later called feudalism, appeared. For the first time since the collapse of the Roman Empire, most of western Europe was united under one government. That government reached the peak of development under Charles Martel's grandson, Charlemagne. Christian missionary activity among the Germanic peoples continued, and strong ties were forged with the Roman papacy. Under Charlemagne a revival of study and learning, sometimes styled the Carolingian Renaissance, occurred.

This chapter will explore the following questions: what was feudalism and how did it come about? How did Charlemagne acquire and govern his vast empire? What were the features of the Carolingian Renaissance? What was the significance of the relations between Carolingian rulers and the church? The culture that existed within the Carolingian Empire has been described as "the first European civilization." What is meant by this term?

THE PIRENNE THESIS

Many scholars believe that the fifth century marks the end of the ancient world and the beginning of the medieval. But others do not consider the fifth century a crucial turning point at all. In fact, one of the most distinguished historians of the twentieth century, the Belgian Henri Pirenne, has argued that the eighth century was the real turning point in Western civilization.

Pirenne's thesis focuses on the Mediterranean Sea. Rome had controlled the Mediterranean from the Bosporus in the east to the Straits of Gibraltar in the west. The empire had surrounded the Mediterranean. Roman trade, Roman armies, and Greco-Roman ideas had been carried by way of the Mediterranean. It was the highway that united the empire. Although the German tribes had conquered the western provinces in the fifth and sixth centuries, they continued many Roman ways. The Germans were gradually converted to Christianity, and with Christianization came Romanization. German rulers in the West continued trade and economic relations with the East, and the Germans shared in the economic and cultural unity the Mediterranean provided.

But, according to Pirenne, the Muslim conquests of the seventh and eighth centuries stopped all this. The Mediterranean Sea, long the thoroughfare of the Greco-Roman world, became a Muslim lake. By the time of Charlemagne in the late eighth century, the Muslims controlled the Mediterranean and the land bordering three sides of it. Their control meant the real end of the ancient world, which had centered on the Mediterranean. In the eighth century, western Europe, which had been relying on Eastern imports, was cut off from its sources of supply. An isolated and agrarian economy developed. Charlemagne's capital at Aix-la-Chapelle was a sign of the shift of political and military power to the north, away from the Mediterranean. For the next five hundred years, northern Europe, rather than Rome and Italy, was the center of culture and civilization. Likewise, the imperial coronation of Charlemagne by Pope Leo III on Christmas Day in the year 800 represented the end of the ancient world and the start of the medieval.

EQUESTRIAN STATUE OF CHARLEMAGNE. A medieval king was expected to be fierce (and successful) in battle, to defend the church and the poor, and to give justice to all. This majestic and idealized figure of Charlemagne conveys these qualities. The horse is both the symbol and the means of his constant travels. (French Embassy Press and Information Division)

Pirenne's thesis has provoked a great deal of discussion. Historians have questioned his facts and vigorously disputed his interpretation. For example, considerable evidence suggests that trade between the East and the West continued through the eighth and ninth centuries and was not shut off by Muslim control of the Mediterranean. Pirenne's argument rests heavily on Mohammed; indeed, as Pirenne put it, "It is therefore strictly correct to say that without Mohammed, Charlemagne would have been inconceivable."[1] By this he meant that the empire of Charlemagne was centered in northern Europe and was oriented to the West as the direct consequence of Muslim expansion.

TOWARD A FEUDAL SOCIETY

In the period of the Germanic invasions the Roman imperial government had been compelled to retrench. Roman troops and Roman administrators were withdrawn from the provinces. Local leaders, Gallo-Romans in Gaul and Romanized natives in Britain, were forced to cope as best they could. No authority was strong enough to provide peace and order over a very wide area.

Men who could fight, or who owned horses, or who were wealthy enough and had the time to learn how to fight and ride could join a local band of warriors. But the vast and defenseless majority, compelled to work the land for their livelihood, had little choice but to seek out some local strong man and ask that "lord" for protection. Local strong men replaced Roman administrators. Western Europe was governed by the simple law that he should take who has the power, and he should keep who can.

The lord, of course, demanded some quid pro quo, some service in return for his protection. The free peasant who secured protection (or the promise of it) surrendered himself and his land to the lord's jurisdiction. The land was given back, but the peasant was obliged to turn over a percentage of his annual harvest to the lord. Other services were usually required also, such as labor on the lord's own land for a set number of days per year.

In entering into this relationship, the free farmer lost status. His position became servile, and he became a serf. He was bound to the land and could not leave it without the lord's permission. He was also subject to the jurisdiction of the lord's court.

In the sixth through eighth centuries, European society slowly evolved toward a condition in which economic and political power were in the hands of a military elite. Scholars have traditionally described this condition as feudalism. The economic power of the elite was based on estates worked by serfs. The political power of the elite rested on the ability to raise an army of fighting men, to coin money, to hold courts, and to conduct relations and make agreements with outside powers. These powers were held by many lords, both lay and ecclesiastical, not just by rulers.

Although a great amount of research has been done on the emergence of feudalism, many details about it are still not known. The transition from freedom to serfdom was slow; its speed was closely related to the level of political order in a given geographical area. Even in the late eighth century there were still many free men. And within the legal category of serfdom there were many economic steps, ranging from the highly prosperous to the desperately poor. Nevertheless, a social and legal revolution was taking place.

Around the year 800, perhaps 60 percent of the population of western Europe, which a century before had been completely free, had been reduced to serfdom. The Viking assaults on Europe in the ninth century gave rise to an additional loss of personal freedom. Although the later Middle Ages witnessed a great deal of upward social mobility, serfdom was the condition of most Europeans, in fact if not in law, for almost a thousand years.

The fundamental strength of the feudal elite rested in its military might. The ethos, the values—indeed, the entire culture of feudal society—was military. Almost everything was determined by war or the preparation for war. Thus, loyalty was the highest virtue. It was the cement that held a warring society together.

In order to insure the support of his fighters, a lord would give them land in exchange for their loyalty. Charles Martel got land to distribute to his men simply by confiscating church property. Lesser lords, as they defeated weaker neighbors and seized their property, divided it among their followers. Early feudalism resulted from the fusion of the Germanic custom of swearing allegiance to the warrior leader and the granting of an estate or of some of the booty of war. The mounted warrior became the vassal (from the Celtic word meaning "a well-born young man") of the lord, and he was obliged to perform services, usually military ones, in return for holding land—the *feud,* or fief. In the process, the vassal lost nothing in social status.

The ceremony by which a man became the vassal of another involved the use of religious objects, such as the Bible or relics of the saints, and the presence of a priest. The vassal knelt, placed his folded hands between those of the lord, and declared his intention to become the lord's man. By this he meant he would fight for the lord. The vassal then rose and swore his faith (or fidelity) on the Bible or the relics. The religious elements served to Christianize this Germanic ritual.

Because feudal society was a military society, men held the dominant positions in it. A high premium was placed on physical strength, fighting skill, and bravery. The legal and social position of women was not as insignificant as might be expected, however. Charters recording gifts to the church indicate that women owned land in many areas. Women frequently endowed monasteries, churches, and other religious establishments. The possession of land obviously meant economic power. Moreover, women inherited fiefs. For example, in southern France and in Catalonia in Spain, women inherited feudal property as early as the tenth century.

Other kinds of evidence attest to the status of women. In parts of northern France, children sometimes identified themselves in legal documents by their mother's name rather than by their father's name. This shows that the mother's social position in the community was better than the father's. The son or daughter wanted the superior social and legal position, and the customary law allowed the taking of the mother's name.

In 822, Archbishop Hincmar of Reims wrote a treatise on the organization of the royal household. He placed the treasurer directly below the queen. She was responsible for giving the knights their annual salaries. She supervised the manorial accounts. Thus, in the management of large households, with many knights to oversee and with complicated manorial records to supervise, the lady of the manor had highly important responsibilities. With responsibility, came power and influence.[2]

THE RISE OF THE CAROLINGIAN DYNASTY

In the seventh century, the kingdom of the Franks steadily deteriorated. Weak and incompetent rulers lost power to local strong men. Central authority collapsed in the face of brute force. The administrative agencies of the Merovingian kings slipped into the hands of local powers.

The rise of the Carolingian family—the word "Carolingian" derives from the Latin *Carolus,* meaning "Charles"—began with the efforts of Pippin I in the mid-seventh century. He made himself mayor of the palace of Austrasia, which meant that he was head of the Frankish administration. His grandson, Pippin II (d. 714), also gained the title of mayor of the palace, and from that position he worked to reduce the power of the Frankish aristocracy.

In 733, Pippin's son, Charles Martel (714–741), defeated the Muslims at Tours in what is now central France and thus checked Arab expansion into Europe. Charles's wars against the Saxons, the Burgundians, and the Frisians broke those weakening forces. His victory over the infidels and his successful campaigns within the Frankish kingdom added to the prestige of his family the reputation of great military strength. Charles Martel had the real power in the Frankish kingdom; the Merovingians were king in name only.

The rise of the Carolingian dynasty was also aided by the church. In the early eighth century, while Charles Martel and his son, Pippin III, were attempting to bring the various Germanic tribes under their jurisdiction, they gained the support of two Anglo-Saxon missionaries, Willibrord and Wynfrith. The Northumbrian monk Willibrord crossed the English Channel and preached to the pagans on the Frisian Islands and in the area roughly of the modern Netherlands, Belgium, and Luxembourg. With enormous zeal Willibrord organized the church of Friesland, established the see of Utrecht, and acted as the first archbishop. He founded the abbey of Echternach (in what is now Luxembourg), and it subsequently became an important missionary center.

Even more spectacular were the achievements of Wynfrith, or Boniface (680–754), as he was later called. A native of Devonshire in England, Boniface preached in Bavaria and Hesse in southern Germany. There, assisted by other monks from Britain, his many conversions attracted the attention of both Charles Martel and Pope Gregory II (715–731). Boniface traveled to Rome several times and was made a bishop. He became an enthusiastic champion of ecclesiastical principles and of papal authority in the Frankish kingdom.

Given the semibarbarous peoples with whom he was dealing, Boniface's achievements were remarkable. He founded the see of Mainz, the primatial (or chief) see of Germany, and the abbey of Fulda, which became one of the great centers of Christian culture in the ninth century. He built churches. He established the *Rule of Saint Benedict* in all the monasteries he founded or reformed. With the full support of Pippin III, Boniface held several councils that reformed the Frankish church. He even succeeded in cutting down the famous Oak of Thor, the center of a pagan cult.

Saint Boniface preached against divorce, polygamous unions, and incest throughout Germany. On these matters German custom and ecclesiastical law completely disagreed. The Germanic peoples practiced polygamy and incest (sexual relations between brothers and sisters or between parents and their children) on a wide scale. (Incest, in fact, is a major theme of a seventh-century German legend about the twins Sigmund and Siglinda. Their tragic love and the life of their son Siegfried were immortalized in three operas by the nineteenth-century composer Richard Wagner.) The Germans allowed divorce simply by the mutual consent of both parties. Church councils in the sixth and seventh centuries repeatedly condemned incest, which shows that it

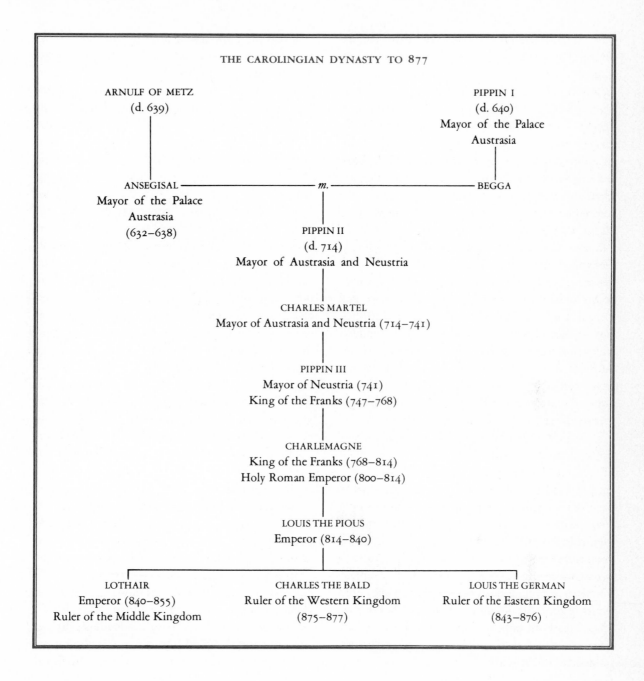

THE CAROLINGIAN DYNASTY TO 877

ARNULF OF METZ
(d. 639)

PIPPIN I
(d. 640)
Mayor of the Palace
Austrasia

ANSEGISAL ——————— *m.* ——————— BEGGA
Mayor of the Palace
Austrasia
(632–638)

PIPPIN II
(d. 714)
Mayor of Austrasia and Neustria

CHARLES MARTEL
Mayor of Austrasia and Neustria (714–741)

PIPPIN III
Mayor of Neustria (741)
King of the Franks (747–768)

CHARLEMAGNE
King of the Franks (768–814)
Holy Roman Emperor (800–814)

LOUIS THE PIOUS
Emperor (814–840)

LOTHAIR
Emperor (840–855)
Ruler of the Middle Kingdom

CHARLES THE BALD
Ruler of the Western Kingdom
(875–877)

LOUIS THE GERMAN
Ruler of the Eastern Kingdom
(843–876)

was common. And theologians since Saint Augustine of Hippo had stressed that marriage, validly entered into, could not be ended.

The immediate results of Boniface's preaching are not known. But his words were not without impact, for in 802 Charlemagne prohibited incest, and he decreed that a husband might separate from an adulterous wife. The woman could be punished, and the man could not remarry in her lifetime. Charlemagne encouraged severe punishment for the adulterous male. In so doing, he contributed to the dignity of marriage, the family, and women.

Saint Boniface is known as the Apostle of Germany, but he is actually one of the most important figures in early European history. In all of his missionary activity he promoted peace and respect for legally established civil authorities. Charles Martel and Pippin III protected Boniface, and he preached Christian obedience to the rulers. At the same time, because of his staunch adherence to Roman ideas, Roman traditions, and the Roman pope, the Romanization of Europe accompanied Christianization.

Charles Martel had been king of the Franks in fact if not in title. His son Pippin III (747–768) made himself king in title as well as in fact. In Germanic custom (and custom was law) the kingship had to pass to someone with royal blood. Pippin did not want to do away with the ineffectual Merovingian king, but he did want the kingship. Because the missionary activity of Boniface had spread Christian ideals and enhanced papal influence in the Frankish kingdom, Pippin decided to consult the pope about the kingship. Accordingly, Pippin sent Boniface to Rome to ask the pope whether the man who has the power is entitled to be king. Pope Zacharias, guided by the Augustinian principle that the real test of kingship is whether it provided order and justice, responded in 751 that he who has the power should also have the title. This answer constituted recognition of the Carolingians.

Just as the emperors Constantine and Theodosius in the fourth century had taken actions that would later be cited as precedents in the relations between church and state, so Pippin III in the eighth century took papal confirmation as the official approval of his title. In 752, Pippin III was formally elected king of the Franks by the great lords, or magnates, of the Frankish territory. Two years later the pope came to Gaul and personally anointed Pippin king at Paris.

An important alliance between the papacy and the Frankish ruler was struck. In 754, Pope Stephen gave Pippin the title of protector of the Roman church. As such, Pippin agreed to restore to the papacy territories in northern Italy recently seized by the Lombards. Pippin marched into Italy and defeated the Lombards. The Carolingian family had received official recognition and anointment from the leading spiritual power in Europe. The papacy had gained a military protector.

On a second successful campaign in Italy in 756, Pippin made a large donation to the papacy. The gift was estates in central Italy that technically belonged to the Byzantine emperor at Constantinople. Known as the Papal States, they existed until 1870, when the newly formed kingdom of Italy abolished them.

Because of his anointment, Pippin's kingship took on a special spiritual and moral character. Before Pippin, only priests and bishops had received anointment: Pippin became the first lay person to be anointed with the sacred oils. His person was considered sacred. He was acknowledged as *rex et sacerdos* (king and priest). Pippin also cleverly eliminated possible threats to the Frankish throne, and the pope promised him support in the future. When Pippin died, his son Charlemagne succeeded him.

THE EMPIRE OF CHARLEMAGNE

Charles the Great (768–814) built on the military and diplomatic foundations of his ancestors. Charles's secretary and biographer, the Saxon Einhard, wrote a lengthy description of this warrior-ruler. It has serious flaws, partly because it is modeled directly on the Roman author Suetonius's *Life of the Emperor Augustus*. Still, it is the earliest medieval biography of a layman, and historians consider it generally accurate:

Charles was large and strong, and of lofty stature, though not disproportionately tall . . . the upper part of his head was round, his eyes very large and animated, nose a little long, hair fair, and face laughing and merry. Thus his appearance was always stately and dignified . . . although his neck was thick and somewhat short, and his belly rather prominent; but the symmetry of the rest of his body concealed these defects. His gait was firm, his whole carriage manly, and his voice clear, but not so strong as his size led one to expect. His health was excellent, except during the four years preceding his death. . . . Even in those years he consulted rather his own inclinations than the advice of physicians, who were almost hateful to him, because they wanted him to give up roasts, to which he was accustomed, and to eat boiled meat instead. In accordance with the national custom, he took frequent exercise on horseback and in the chase, accomplishments in which scarcely any people in the world can equal the Franks. He enjoyed the exhalations from natural warm springs, and often practiced swimming, in which he was such an adept that none could surpass him; and hence it was that he built his palace at Aix-la-Chapelle, and lived there constantly during his latter years until his death. He used not only to invite his sons to his bath, but his nobles and friends, and now and then a troop of his retinue or bodyguard. . . .

He used to wear the national, that is to say, the Frank, dress — next his skin a linen shirt and linen breeches, and above these a tunic fringed with silk; while hose fastened by bands covered his lower limbs, and shoes his feet, and he protected his shoulder and chest in winter by a close-fitting coat of otter or marten skins. Over all he flung a blue cloak, and he always had a sword girt about him, usually one with a gold or silver hilt and belt; he sometimes carried a jeweled sword, but only on great feastdays or at the reception of ambassadors from foreign nations.[3]

Crude and brutal, Charlemagne was still a man of enormous intelligence. He appreciated good literature, such as Saint Augustine's *City of God*, and Einhard considered him an unusually effective speaker. On the other hand, he could not really write, not even his own name.

For all his concern for moderation in food and wine, he apparently had very strong sexual appetites: he had three wives, one after the other, and after they died, three concubines simultaneously. The austere code of sexual morality he published for the empire reflects the attitude of the clerics who wrote it more than the actual behavior of the warrior-king. The most striking feature of Charlemagne's character was his phenomenal energy, which helps to account for his great military achievements.

Territorial Expansion

Charlemagne was the greatest warrior of the early Middle Ages. Continuing the expansionist policies of his ancestors, he fought more than fifty campaigns. In what is now France, he subdued all of the north. In the south, the lords of the mountainous ranges of Aquitaine — what is now called Basque country — limited his efforts toward total conquest. The Muslims in northeastern Spain were checked by the establishment of strongly fortified areas known as marches.

Charlemagne's greatest successes were in what is today called Germany. There, his concerns were basically defensive. In the course of a thirty-year war against the semibarbaric Saxons, he added most of the northwestern German tribes to the Frankish kingdom. The story goes that because of their repeated rebellions, Charlemagne ordered more than four thousand Saxons slaughtered on one day.

To the south, he achieved spectacular results. In 773–774, the Lombards in northern Italy once again threatened the papacy. Charlemagne marched south, overran the fortresses at Pavia and Spoleto, and incorporated Lombardy—including Venetia, Istria, and Dalmatia—into the Frankish kingdom. To his title of king of the Franks, he added king of the Lombards. This victory ended all serious attempts at the unification of Italy until the nineteenth century.

Around the year 805, the Frankish kingdom included all of continental Europe except for Spain, Scandinavia, southern Italy, and the Slavic fringes of the east (see Map 7.1). Not since the third century A.D. had any ruler controlled so much of the Western world. Not until Napoleon Bonaparte in the early nineteenth century was the feat to be repeated.

The Government of the Carolingian Empire

Charlemagne ruled over a vast rural world dotted with isolated estates and characterized by constant, petty violence. His empire was definitely not a "state" as people today understand that term. It was a collection of primitive peoples and semibarbarian tribes. Apart from a small class of warrior-aristocrats and clergy, almost everyone engaged in agriculture. Trade and commerce played only a small part in the economy. Cities served as the headquarters of bishops and as ecclesiastical centers.

By constant travel, personal appearances, and the sheer force of his personality, Charlemagne sought to awe his conquered peoples with his fierce presence and his terrible justice. He confiscated the estates of the great territorial magnates. In this way he got land with which to gain the support of lesser lords.

Charles divided his kingdom into counties, which served as administrative units. Two or three hundred counts were appointed as the king's representatives. They had full military and judicial powers to maintain law and order and to do justice at the local level. They held their offices for life. As a link between local authorities and the central government of the emperor, Charles established, in 802, officials called *missi dominici,* agents of the lord king. The empire was divided into visitorial districts. Each year, beginning in 802, two missi, usually a count and a bishop or abbot, visited certain areas. They held courts and investigated the judicial, financial, and clerical activities of the district. They held commissions (sometimes called capitularies), which sought to regulate crime, moral conduct, the clergy, education, the poor, and many other subjects. The missi checked up on the counts and worked to prevent the counts' positions from becoming hereditary. Strong counts, holding hereditary estates, weakened the power of the emperor.

In especially barbarous areas, such as the Spanish and Danish borders, Charles set up areas called marks. There, royal officials called margraves had extensive powers to meet the needs of their dangerous localities.

The immense conglomeration of peoples over whom Charlemagne presided was no state in any meaningful modern sense. A modern state has institutions of government, such as a civil service, courts of law, financial agencies for the collection and apportionment of taxes, and police and military powers with which to maintain order internally and to protect it from foreign attack. These simply did not exist in Charlemagne's empire. What held

MAP 7.1   THE CAROLINGIAN WORLD

CAROLINGIAN SILVER COIN. While a severe shortage of currency existed in the early Middle Ages, coins never completely disappeared as a medium of exchange. Carolingian rulers divided a pound of silver into 240 parts, from which coins called *denarii* or pennies were minted. This penny was probably minted at Cologne in the early tenth century. (Courtesy, World Heritage Museum. Photo: Caroline Buckler)

society together were relationships of dependence cemented by other oaths promising faith and loyalty.

Although the empire lacked viable institutions, some of the Carolingians involved in governing did have important political ideas. The abbots and bishops who served as Charlemagne's advisers worked out what was for their time a sophisticated political ideology. In letters and treatises they set before the emperor high ideals of behavior and of government. They wrote that a ruler may hold power from God, but he is responsible to the law. Just as all subjects of the empire were required to obey him, so too was he obliged to respect the law. They envisioned a unified Christian society presided over by a king who was responsible for the maintenance of peace, which would let Christians pursue their pilgrimage to the City of God. They encouraged the emperor to maintain law and order and to do justice, without which neither the ruler nor the "state" has any justification. These views derived basically from Saint Augustine's theories of kingship. Inevitably, they could not be realized in an illiterate, half-Christianized, and preindustrial society. But they were the seeds from which medieval and even modern ideas of government were to develop.

The Imperial Coronation of Charlemagne (800)

In the autumn of the year 800, Charlemagne paid a visit to Rome. Here are two accounts of what happened.

According to the Frankish *Royal Annals,* a year-by-year description of events:

On the very day of the most holy nativity of the Lord [Christmas], when the king at Mass had risen from prayer before the tombs of Blessed Peter the Apostle, Pope Leo placed the crown on his head, and by all the people of Rome he was acclaimed: Long Life and Victory to the August Charles, the Great and Peace-Giving Emperor, crowned by God. And after the ovations, the pope did obeisance to him according to the custom observed before the ancient emperors, and the title of Patricius [Protector] being dropped, he was called Emperor and Augustus.[4]

Einhard wrote:

His last journey there [to Rome] was due to another factor, namely that the Romans, having inflicted many injuries on Pope Leo—plucking out his eyes and tearing out his tongue, he had been compelled to beg the assistance of the king. Accordingly, coming to Rome in order that he might set in order those things which had exceedingly disturbed the condition of the Church, he remained there the whole winter. It was at the time that he accepted the name of Emperor and Augustus. At first he was so much opposed to this that he insisted that although that day was a great [Christian] feast, he would not have entered the Church if he had known beforehand the pope's intention. But he bore very patiently the jealousy of the Roman Emperors [that is, the Byzantine rulers] who were indignant when he received these titles. He overcame their arrogant haughtiness with magnanimity, a virtue in which he was considerably superior to them, by sending frequent ambassadors to them and in his letters addressing them as brothers.[5]

Charlemagne became *Holy* Roman emperor, adding the sacred authority of the Christian church to the universal authority of the Roman emperor. Einhard says that Charlemagne seldom used the imperial title. The fact that he did sometimes use it illustrates a significant point. Charlemagne governed most of continental Europe. He considered himself a Christian king ruling a Christian people. The title expressed his connection with the Rome of the caesars and the Rome of the popes. By using it, Charlemagne was consciously continuing the old Roman imperial notions, while at the same time identifying with the new Rome of the Christian church. Charlemagne and his government represent a combination of German feudal practices and Christian ideals. These two elements were basic constituents of Europe in the early Middle Ages.

For centuries scholars have debated the significance of the imperial coronation of Charlemagne. The questions remain: Did Charles plan the coronation in St. Peter's on Christmas Day? What did he have to gain from the imperial title? Did Pope Leo III arrange the coronation in order to identify the Frankish monarchy with the papacy and papal policy? Did a coronation actually happen, or are accounts of it later inventions?

Although final answers probably will never be given to these questions, two facts are certain. First, later German rulers were anxious to gain the imperial title and to associate themselves with the legend of Charlemagne and with ancient Rome. They wanted to use the ideology of imperial Rome to strengthen their own positions. Second, ecclesiastical authorities continually cited the event as proof that the dignity of the imperial crown could be granted only by the pope. The imperial coronation of Charlemagne, event or nonevent, was to have a profound effect on the course of German history and on the later history of Europe.

THE CAROLINGIAN INTELLECTUAL REVIVAL

It is somewhat ironic that the most enduring legacy of Charlemagne was the stimulus he gave to scholarship and learning. Barely literate himself, preoccupied with the control of vast territories, much more of a warrior than a thinker, he nevertheless set in motion a cultural revival that had "international" and long-lasting consequences. The revival of learning associated with Charlemagne and his court at Aix-la-Chapelle drew its greatest inspiration from seventh- and eighth-century intellectual developments in the Anglo-Saxon kingdom of Northumbria, situated on the northernmost tip of the old Roman world.

Northumbrian Culture

The victory of the Roman forms of Christian liturgy and monastic life at the Synod of Whitby in 664 marked the official end of the Celtic church in Britain. But Whitby did not stop the Celtic influence on Christianity in Northumbria. Rather, Irish-Celtic culture — through such monasteries as Lindisfarne and York — permeated the Roman church in Britain and resulted in a flowering of artistic and scholarly activity.

Northumbrian creativity owes a great deal to the intellectual curiosity and collecting zeal of Saint Benet Biscop (ca 628–689). Descended from a noble Northumbrian family, he became a monk at Lérins, an island monastery in the Mediterranean that had valuable contacts with the Eastern monastic tradition of Syria and Egypt. Benet Biscop returned to Britain in the company of the Syrian archbishop of Canterbury, Theodore of Tarsus. Between 674 and 682, Benet Biscop founded the monasteries of Wearmouth and Jarrow. A strong supporter of Benedictine monasticism, he introduced the Roman form of ceremonial into the new religious houses and encouraged it in older ones. He made five dangerous trips to Italy, raided the libraries, and brought back to Northumbria manuscripts, relics, paintings, and other treasures. These books and manuscripts formed the libraries on which much later study was based.

Northumbrian monasteries produced scores of missals (used for the celebration of the mass), psalters (which contained the 150 Psalms and other prayers used by the monks in their devotions), commentaries on the Scriptures, illuminated manuscripts, law codes, and collections of letters and sermons. The finest product of Northumbrian art is probably the Gospel book produced at Lindisfarne

THE IMPERIAL CORONATION OF CHARLEMAGNE. Contemporary evidence for Charlemagne's coronation by Pope Leo III is literary and contradictory. This fifteenth-century illustration supports the ecclesiastical view that Charlemagne (kneeling) humbly accepted the crown, which the papacy could grant or withhold. The presence of two cardinals (in broad-brimmed hats) and the dress of all show this is a late medieval interpretation of the event. (Musée Condé, Chantilly/Giraudon)

around 700. Because of the incredible expense involved in the publication of such a book — for paper, coloring, gold leaf — it reflects an aristocratic display of wealth. The script, called uncial, is a Celtic version of contemporary Greek and Roman handwriting. The illustrations have a strong Eastern quality. They combine the abstract style of the Christian Middle East and the narrative approach of classical Roman art. Likewise, the use of geometrical decorative designs shows the influence of Syrian art. Many scribes, artists, and illuminators must have participated in its preparation.

The Venerable Bede (ca 673–735) is the finest representative of Northumbrian and indeed all Anglo-Saxon scholarship. The simplicity of his life illustrates his greatness. Given by his parents when he was seven years old as an oblate or "offering," to Benet Biscop's monastary at Wearmouth, he was later sent to the new monastery at Jarrow five miles away. There, surrounded by the books Benet Biscop had brought from Italy, Bede spent all of his life.

As a monk, Bede's scrupulous observance of the *Rule of Saint Benedict* revealed his deep piety. His days were punctuated only by the bells for choir and other religious duties. As a scholar, his patience and diligence reflected his deep love for learning. Contemporaries revered Bede for his learned commentaries on the Scriptures and for the special holiness of his life, which earned him the title "Venerable." He was the most widely read author in the entire Middle Ages.

Modern scholars praise Bede for his book *The Ecclesiastical History of the English Nation,* which is actually broader in scope than the title suggests. It is the chief source of information about early Britain. Bede searched far and wide for his information, discussed the validity of his evidence, compared various sources, and exercised a rare critical judgment. For these reasons, he has been called "the first scientific intellect among the Germanic peoples of Europe."

Bede was probably the greatest master of chronology of the Middle Ages. He began the system of dating events from the birth of Christ, instead of from the foundation of the city of Rome, as the Romans had done, or from the regnal years of kings, as the Germans did. Thus, Bede was the first person to use the term "anno Domini," in the year of the Lord, or simply the letters A.D. He fit the entire history of the world into this new dating method. (The reverse, or diminishing, dating system of B.C. before Christ, does not seem to have been widely used before 1700.) Under the influence of the Anglo-Saxon missionary Wynfrith (Saint Boniface), this system of reckoning time was carried throughout the Frankish empire of Charlemagne.

At the very time that monks at Lindisfarne were producing their Gospel book, and Bede at Jarrow was writing his *History,* another Northumbrian monk was at work on a nonreligious epic poem. Literature is usually a good hallmark of the psychology of an age. It also provides considerable information about the society that produced it. The poem *Beowulf* is perhaps the finest expression of the secular literature of the eighth century. Scholars have hailed it as a masterpiece of Western heroic literature, but the tale is almost childish in its simplicity.

The great hall (or palace) of the Danish king Hrothgar has been ravaged for twelve years by a half-human monster called Grendel. Hrothgar and his men cannot stop Grendel's attacks and depredations. Finally, Beowulf, a relative of the Swedish royal house, hears of Grendel's murderous destructions. With a bodyguard of fourteen trusted warriors, Beowulf sails to Denmark and in a brutal battle destroys Grendel. Hrothgar and his queen,

THE SCRIBE EZRA. Monks at Bede's monastery at Jarrow made this copy of an early Christian manuscript showing the Jewish scribe Ezra writing his chronicle. The backless bench on which he works appears very uncomfortable. Books were stored against theft and climate in heavy chests or cabinets. (Scala/Editorial Photocolor Archives)

Wealhtheow, give a great banquet for Beowulf and his followers. Afterward, Grendel's mother enters the hall and carries off one of Hrothgar's closest advisers in revenge for her son's death. Beowulf ultimately catches and destroys her. This victory is followed by more feasting. Beowulf returns home to Sweden laden with rich gifts.

Beowulf later becomes king of the Geats (a Swedish tribe) and rules them for fifty years. When his country is ravaged by a terrible dragon, the aged Beowulf challenges him. In the ensuing battle, Beowulf is overwhelmed by the dragon's fiery breath, and all but one of his followers flee. Although Beowulf succeeds in defeating the dragon, he is mortally wounded and dies.[6]

The story appears to be a rather ordinary Norse legend, but actually it is permeated with classical, Germanic, and Christian elements. The poem was written in England, but all the action takes place in Scandinavia. This reflects the "international" quality of the culture of the age, or at least the close ties between England and the Continent in the eighth century. (Britain exported wool, and the settlements in Frisia that later developed into the flourishing commercial centers at Ypres and Bruges produced cloth.)

Beowulf's entire life was devoted to fighting and war. His values are military and aristocratic: the central institution in the poem is the *gesith,* or Germanic band of warriors united to fight with Beowulf. Their highest virtue is loyalty to him, and loyalty is maintained by the giving of gifts. Yet, the author was a Christian monk, and the basic theme of the poem is the conflict between good and evil. Beowulf, however, does not show any of the Christian virtue of humility. Never one to hide his light under a bushel, he is as quick as a twentieth-century Mohammed Ali to boast of his exploits and to tell all that he is the greatest. In this, he embodies the classical idea of fame, the notion that fame is the greatest achievement because it is all that a person leaves behind.

Pagan and Germanic symbols and practices suffuse the lives and even the deaths of these warrior heroes. For example, the aristocratic warriors indulge in a great deal of feasting and drinking throughout the poem. Their lives are devoted, it appears, either to fighting or to feasting. There is no glimpse of those who raised and prepared all the food that is consumed. The author did not think what the peasants did deserved mention. In a famous scene Hrothgar's beautiful queen Wealhtheow enters the great hall, dispensing grace and gifts. The scene suggests that women of the upper class served a decorative function in aristocratic society. But Wealhtheow may have been handing out presents to the warriors because she had custody of and responsibility for her husband's treasure.

In another scene the body of a dead king, along with considerable treasure, is put on a ship and floated out to sea. That this was a typical method of burial for Scandinavian kings is known from the ship burial uncovered at Sutton Hoo in England in 1939. Such customs are far removed from the traditional Christian method of burial in the ground. A monk may have composed Beowulf, but this practice indicates that conversion was still imperfect in much of Europe.

Reading this story, one enters a world of darkness, cold, gloom, and pessimism, pierced by a weak ray of Christian hope. *Beowulf* is a sign of the psychological complexities and spiritual contradictions of what has been called the heroic age of Scandinavia—the eighth and ninth centuries.

Another literary genre, less serious than the epic poem but highly popular in Anglo-Saxon England and Carolingian Europe, was the riddle. Riddles were more than a guessing game for children; in the riddle a poet took on the characteristics or personality of someone or something. Riddles were intended to instruct and to entertain:

Swings by his thigh a thing most magical!
Below the belt, beneath the folds
of his clothes it hangs, a hole in its front end,
stiff-set & stout, but swivels about.

Levelling the head of this hanging instrument,
its wielder hoists his hem above the knee:
it is his will to fill a well-known hole
that it fits fully when at full length.

He has often filled it before. Now he fills it again.[7]

The answer is a key.

The physical conditions of life in the seventh and eighth centuries make the Northumbrian cultural achievements all the more remarkable. Learning took place and works of art were produced under circumstances that were terribly primitive. Monasteries such as Jarrow and Lindisfarne stood on the very fringes of the European world. The barbarian Picts, just an afternoon's walk away from Jarrow, were likely to attack at any time.

Food, perhaps, was not the greatest problem. The North Sea and the nearby rivers, the Tweed and the Tyne, yielded abundant salmon and other fish, which could be salted or smoked for winter. Fish provided a nutritious, if monotonous, diet. Climate was another matter. Winter, as in 664, could be extremely harsh. That year, deep snow was hardened by frost from early winter until mid-spring. When it melted away, many animals, trees, and plants were found dead. To make matters worse, disease and sickness could take terrible tolls. Bede described events in the year 664:

In the same year of our Lord 664 there was an eclipse of the sun on the third day of May at about four o'clock in the afternoon. Also in that year a sudden pestilence first depopulated the southern parts of Britain and then attacked the kingdom of the Northumbrians as well. Raging far and wide for a long time with cruel devastation it struck down a great multitude of men. . . . This same plague oppressed the island of Ireland with equal destruction.[8]

Damp cold with bitter winds blowing across the North Sea must have pierced everyone and everything, even the stone monasteries. Inside, only one room, the calefactory, or warming room, had a fire. Scribes in the scriptorium, or writing room, had to stop frequently to rub the circulation back into numb hands. These monk-artists and monk-writers paid a very high physical price for what they gave to posterity.

Had they remained entirely insular, the Northumbrian culture achievements would have been of slight significance. As it happened, an Englishman from Northumbria played a decisive role in the transmission of English learning to the Carolingian Empire and continental Europe.

The Carolingian Renaissance

Charlemagne's empire disintegrated shortly after his death in 814. But the support he gave to education and learning preserved the writings of the ancients and laid the foundations for all subsequent medieval culture. Charlemagne promoted a revival that scholars have named the "Carolingian Renaissance."

He assembled at his court learned men from all over Europe. From Visigothic Spain came Theodulf, the best writer of Latin verse of the day. From Pavia in Lombardy came the monk-historian Paul the Deacon, who later wrote the invaluable *History of the Lombards,* still the chief source for the history of the sixth and seventh centuries. From the abbey of Fulda came Einhard, who served as a royal administrator and Charlemagne's closest adviser and as the emperor's biographer.

The most important scholar and the leader of the palace school at Aix-la-Chapelle was the Northumbrian Alcuin. He was born about a year after Bede's death (ca 735) and educated at the cathedral school at York. On a visit to Italy in 781, Alcuin met Charlemagne, who invited him to his court. From then until his death in 804, Alcuin remained the emperor's major adviser on religious and educational matters.

Alcuin was an unusually prolific scholar. He prepared some of the emperor's official documents. He wrote many moral *exempla,* or models, which set high standards for royal behavior and constitute a treatise on kingship. Alcuin's letters to Charlemagne set forth political theories on the authority, power, and responsibilities of a Christian ruler.

What did the scholars at Charlemagne's court do? They copied books and manuscripts and built up libraries. They devised the beautifully clear handwriting known as Carolingian minuscule, from which modern Roman type is derived. (This script is called minuscule because it has lower-case letters; the Romans had only capitals.) They established schools all across Europe, attaching them to monasteries and cathedrals. They placed great emphasis on the education of priests, trying to make all of them at least able to read, write, and do simple arithmetical calculations. The scholars at Aix-la-Chapelle made their greatest contribution not so much in the originality of their ideas as in the hard work of salvaging and preserving the thought and writings of the ancients. Thus, the Carolingian Renaissance was a rebirth of interest in, and the study and preservation of, the ideas and achievements of classical Greece and Rome.

Language has been called "the nourishing mother of history." It is the core, the center, of all culture and civilization. Without the ability to communicate ideas, grammatically and effectively, orally and in writing, an individual or a society is barbaric. The revival of learning inspired by Charlemagne and directed by the Northumbrian Alcuin halted the dangers of barbaric illiteracy on the European continent. Although hardly widespread by later standards, basic literacy was established among the clergy and even among some of the nobility. The small group of scholars at Aix-la-Chapelle preserved Greek and Latin culture from total extinction in the West.

With basic literacy once established, monastic and other scholars went on to more difficult work. By the middle years of the ninth century there was a great outpouring of more sophisticated books. Collections of canon law, illustrated manuscripts, codes of Frankish law, commentaries on the Bible and on the church fathers flowed from monastic and cathedral scriptoria. Ecclesiastical writers, imbued with the legal ideas of ancient Rome and with the theocratic ideals of Saint Augustine of Hippo, instructed the semibarbarian rulers of the West. Likewise, it is no accident that important medical study in the West, at Salerno in southern Italy, began in the late ninth century, *after* the Carolingian Renaissance.

Alcuin completed the work of his countryman Boniface — the Christianization of northern Europe. Latin Christian attitudes penetrated deeply into the consciousness of European peoples. By the tenth century, the patterns of thought and lifestyles of educated western Europeans were those of Rome and Latin Christianity. Even the violence and destruction of the great invasions of the late ninth and tenth centuries could not destroy the strong foundations laid by the Northumbrian Alcuin and his colleagues.

BINDING OF THE LINDAU GOSPELS. This splendid example of the Carolingian revival combines the geometric forms of Anglo-Irish art with the Roman portrait tradition. The strong face of Christ shows no suffering. The semiprecious stones around the border are raised to catch the light. (The Pierpont Morgan Library)

DIVISION AND DISINTEGRATION OF THE CAROLINGIAN EMPIRE (814–887)

Charlemagne left his vast empire to his only surviving son, Louis the Pious (814–840), who had actually been crowned emperor in his father's lifetime. Deeply religious he was, and well educated, but Louis was no soldier. Thus, he could not retain the respect and loyalty of the warrior-aristocracy on whom he depended for troops and for the administration of his territories. Disintegration began almost at once.

The basic reason for the collapse of the Carolingian Empire is simply that it was too big. In Charlemagne's lifetime it was held together by the sheer force of his personality and by his driving energy. After his death, it began to fall apart. The empire lacked a bureaucracy — the administrative machinery necessary for continuing and strong government. It was a collection of tribes held together at the pleasure of warrior-aristocrats, men most interested in strengthening their own local positions and insuring that they could pass on to their sons the offices and estates they had amassed. Counts, abbots, bishops — lay and ecclesiastical magnates needed estates in order to support themselves and to reward their followers. In their localities, they simply assumed judicial, military, and financial functions. Why should they obey an unimpressive distant ruler who represented a centralizing power, a power that threatened their localistic interests? What counted was strength in one's own region and the preservation of a family's possessions.

Bad roads filled with thugs and rivers swarming with pirates made communication within the empire very difficult. Add to this the Frankish custom of dividing estates among all male heirs. Between 817 and his death in 840, Louis the Pious made several divisions of the empire. Dissatisfied with their portions and anxious to gain the imperial title, Louis's sons, Lothair, Louis the German, and Charles the Bald, fought bitterly among themselves. Finally, in the Treaty of Verdun of 843, the brothers agreed to partition the empire (see Map 7.2).

MAP 7.2   THE DIVISION OF THE CAROLINGIAN EMPIRES, 843. The treaty of Verdun (843), which divided the empire among Charlemagne's grandsons, is frequently taken as the start of the separate development of Germany, France, and Italy. The "Middle Kingdom" of Lothair, however, lacking defensive borders and any political or linguistic unity, soon broke up into several territories.

Lothair, the eldest, received the (now empty) title of emperor and the "middle kingdom," which included Italy and the territories bordered by the Meuse, Saône, and Rhône rivers on the west and the Rhine in the east. Almost immediately this "kingdom" broke up into many petty principalities extending diagonally across Europe from Flanders to Lombardy. When the French and German monarchs were trying to build strong central governments in the twelfth and thirteenth centuries, this area was constantly contested between them. Even in modern times, the "middle kingdom" of Lothair has been blood soaked.

The eastern and most Germanic part of the Carolingian Empire passed to Louis the German. The western kingdom went to Charles the Bald. It included the provinces of Aquitaine and Gascony and formed the basis of medieval and modern France. The descendants of Charles the Bald held on in the west until 987, when the leading magnates elected Hugh Capet as king. The heirs of Louis the German ruled the eastern kingdom until 911, but the real power was in the hands of local chieftains. Everywhere in the tenth century fratricidal warfare among the descendants of Charlemagne meant the acceleration of feudalism.

HEALTH AND MEDICAL CARE

In a society devoted to fighting, warriors and civilians alike faced the strong chance of wounds from sword, spear, battle-axe, or some blunt instrument. Trying to eke a living from poor soil with poor tools, perpetually involved in pushing back forest and wasteland, the farmer and his family daily ran the risk of accidents. Poor diet weakened everyone's resistance to disease. People bathed rarely. Low standards of personal hygiene increased the danger of infection. This being the case, what medical or surgical attention was available to medieval people?

Much remains to be learned about medical treatment in the early Middle Ages. Scholars' careful examination of medical treatises, prescription (or herbal) books, manuscript illustrations, and archaeological evidence, however, has recently revealed a surprising amount of information.

The Germanic peoples all across Europe had no rational understanding of the causes of and cures for disease. They believed that sickness was due to one of three factors: elf-shot, in which elves hurled darts that produced disease and pain; wormlike creatures in the body; and the number nine. Treatment involved the use of charms, amulets, priestly incantations, and potions. For example, drinks prepared from mistletoe, it was thought, served as an antidote to poison and made women fertile.

Medical practice consisted primarily of drug and prescription therapy. Through the monks' efforts and through the recovery of Greek and Arabic manuscripts, a large body of the ancients' prescriptions was preserved and passed on. For almost any ailment, several recipes were likely to exist in the prescription lists. Balsam was recommended for coughs. For asthma an ointment combining chicken, wormwood, laurel berries, and oil of roses was to be rubbed on the chest. The scores of prescriptions to rid the body of lice, fleas, and other filth reflect the frightful standards of personal hygiene. The large number of prescriptions for eye troubles implies that they too must have been very common. This is understandable, given the widespread practice of locating the fireplace in the center of the room. A lot of smoke and soot filtered into the room, rather than going up the chimney. One remedy calls for bathing the eyes in a solution of herbs mixed with honey, balsam, rainwater, saltwater, or wine.

Poor diet caused frequent stomach disorders and related ailments such as dysentery, constipation, and diarrhea. The value of dieting and the avoidance of greasy foods was recognized. For poor circulation, a potion of meadow wort, oak rind, and lustmock was recommended. Pregnant women were advised to abstain from eating the flesh of almost all male animals, because their meat might deform the child. Men with unusually strong sexual appetites were advised to fast and to drink at night the juice from agrimony (an herb of the rose family) boiled in ale. But if a man suffered from a lack of drive, the same plant boiled in milk gave him "courage."

Most of these "remedies" seem to be more of a danger to health than a cure for disease. The "physician" was not concerned with the treatment of specific diseases or illnesses. He did not examine the patient. The "physician," or leech, as he was known in Anglo-Saxon England, tried to treat only what he could see or deduce from the patient's obvious symptoms. Treatment consisted of the application of herbal, animal, or superstitious remedies to these symptoms. The physician knew little of the pathology of disease or of physiological functions. He knew little of internal medicine. He had no accurate standards of weights and measures. Prescriptions called for "a pinch of" or "a handful" or "an eggshell full."

Given the brutal nature of warfare and the dangers inherent in working the land, broken bones, wounds, and burns must have been common. All wounds and open injuries presented a grave risk to the victim. Dirty bodies invited infection, and infection invited gangrene.

Several remedies were known for wounds. Physicians appreciated the antiseptic properties of honey, and prescriptions recommended that wounds be cleaned with it. When an area or limb had become gangrenous, a good technique of amputation existed. The physician was instructed to cut above the diseased flesh, that is, to cut away some healthy tissue and bone, in order to hasten

MEDICAL INSTRUMENTS. Medieval physicians invented hundreds of instruments for surgical operations. This page shows a number of knives and saws. The accompanying text explains which instrument to use for various operations. (Yale Medical Library)

cure. The juice from white poppy plants, the source of heroin, could be added to wine and drunk as an anesthetic. White poppies, however, grew only in southern Europe and North Africa. If a heavy slug of wine was not enough to dull the patient for his operation, then he had to be held down forcibly while the physician cut. Butter and egg whites, which have a soothing effect, were the recommended prescriptions for burns.

Medical science today stresses the importance of good dental hygiene for general body health. Recently uncovered archaeological evidence proves that medieval people knew little about it. Teeth survive long periods of burial and give reasonably good information about disease. Evidence from early medieval England shows that the incidence of tooth decay was very low. In the adult population, the rate of cavities was only one-sixth that of the present day. Cavities below the gum line, however, were very common. As the result of eating coarse foods containing many carbohydrates and a lot of starch, the wear on teeth was severe. Because of the lack of oral hygiene, food was trapped at the neck of the teeth, just below the gum line. The result was abscesses of the gums. These and other forms of periodontal disease were widespread after the age of thirty.[9]

The spread of Christianity under the Carolingian dynasty had a beneficial effect on medical knowledge and treatment. Several of the church fathers expressed serious interest in medicine. Some of them even knew something about it. The church was deeply concerned about human suffering, whether physical or mental. Christian teaching vigorously supported concern for the poor, sick, downtrodden, and miserable. Churchmen taught that while all knowledge came from God, he had supplied it so that people could use it for their own benefit.

In the period of the bloodiest violence, the sixth and seventh centuries, medical treatment was provided by the monasteries. No other places offered the calm and quiet atmosphere necessary for treatment and recuperation. Monks took care of the sick. They collected and translated the ancient medical treatises. They cultivated herb gardens from which medicines were prepared. Monks practiced medicine throughout the Middle Ages. So also did lay people.

A major development encouraged the study of medicine by lay people. The foundation of a school at Salerno in southern Italy sometime in the ninth century gave a tremendous impetus to medical study. Its location attracted Arabic, Greek, and Jewish physicians from all over the Mediterranean region. Students flocked there from northern Europe. The Jewish physician Shabbathai Ben Abraham (931–982) left behind pharmacological notes that were widely studied in later centuries.

By the eleventh century, the medical school at Salerno enjoyed "international" fame. Its most distinguished professor then was Constantine the African. A native of Carthage, he had studied medicine throughout the Middle East and, because of his thorough knowledge of oriental languages, served as an important transmitter of Arabic culture to the West. Constantine taught and practiced medicine at Salerno for some years before becoming a monk at Monte Cassino.

Several women physicians also contributed to the celebrity of the school. One, Trotula, wrote a book called *On Female Disorders,* which suggests that she was an authority on gynecological problems. (Although not connected with the Salerno medical school, the abbess Hildegard [1098–1179] of Rupertsberg in Hesse, Germany, reputedly treated the emperor Frederick Barbarossa. Hildegard's treatise *On the Physical Elements* shows a remarkable degree of careful scientific observation. She was probably the most famous woman physician of the twelfth century.)

How available was medical treatment? Almost all people lived on rural estates, considerably isolated from outside influences. They had to take such advice and help as was available locally. Physicians were very few. They charged a fee, which only the rich could afford. Most illnesses, apparently, simply took their course. People had to develop a stoical attitude. Death came early. A person of forty was considered old. Poor health, poor diet, frequent ailments for which there was no probable cure contributed to a fatalistic acceptance of death at an early age. Early medical literature shows that attempts to relieve pain and suffering were primitive and crude. Still, it is significant that serious attempts *were* made.

GREAT INVASIONS OF THE NINTH CENTURY

After the Treaty of Verdun and the division of Charlemagne's empire among his grandsons, continental Europe presented an easy target for foreign invaders. All three kingdoms were torn by domestic dissension and disorder. No political power was strong enough to put up effective resistance to external attacks. The frontier and coastal defenses erected by Charlemagne and maintained by Louis the Pious were completely neglected.

From the moors of Scotland to the mountains of Sicily there arose in the ninth century the Christian prayer "Save us, O God, from the violence of the Northmen." The Northmen, or Normans, or Vikings, came from Norway, Sweden, and Denmark. They were Germanic peoples, who had remained outside of the Christianizing and civilizing influences of the Carolingian Empire. They are often referred to simply as Vikings. Some scholars believe that the name "Viking" derives from the Old Norse word *vik,* meaning creek. A Viking, then, was a pirate who waited in a creek or bay to attack passing vessels.

Charlemagne had established marches, fortresses, and watchtowers along his northern coasts to defend his territory against Viking raids. Their assaults began around 787, and by the mid-tenth century they had brought large chunks of continental Europe and Britain under their sway. In the East they pierced the rivers of Russia as far as the Black Sea. In the West they sailed as far as Greenland and even to the coast of North America, perhaps as far south as Boston.

The Vikings were superb seamen. Their advanced methods of boatbuilding gave them great speed and maneuverability. Propelled either by oars or sails, deckless, about sixty-five feet long, a Viking ship could carry between forty and sixty men—quite enough to harass effectively an isolated monastery or village. These boats, navigated by thoroughly experienced and utterly fearless sailors, moved through the most complicated rivers, estuaries, and waterways in Europe. They could move swiftly, attack, and get away quickly—before help could arrive.

Scholars disagree about the reasons for these migrations. Some maintain that because the Vikings practiced polygamy, their countries were vastly overpopulated. Since the property of a family passed to the oldest son, other sons had to emigrate. Others argue that climatic conditions and crop failures forced migration. Still others insist that the Northmen were looking for trade and new commercial contacts. What better targets for plunder, for example, than the mercantile centers of northern France and Frisia?

Plunder they did. Viking attacks were bitterly savage. At first, they attacked and sailed off laden with booty. Later, they returned, settled down, and colonized the areas they had conquered. For example, they overran a large part of northwestern France and called the territory Norsemanland, from which the word "Normandy" is derived.

VIKING SHIP MODEL. The Norwegian original was built entirely of oak, weighed over twenty tons, and could carry a sizable contingent of men and horses. With fleets of these ships, the Vikings conducted piratical raids, territorial conquests, and colonizing ventures. (Courtesy, World Heritage Museum. Photo: Caroline Buckler)

Scarcely had the savagery of the Viking assaults begun to subside when Europe was hit from the east and the south (see Map 7.3). Beginning around 862, Magyar, or Hungarian, tribes crossed the Danube and pushed steadily to the west. They subdued northern Italy, compelled Bavaria and Saxony to pay tribute, and penetrated even into the Rhineland and Burgundy. Roving bandits, they attacked isolated villages and monasteries, taking prisoners and selling them in the Eastern slave markets. The Magyars were not colonizers; their sole object was booty and plunder.

The Magyars and Vikings depended upon fear. In their initial attacks on isolated settlements, every man, woman, and child was put to the sword. The few attractive women who might be spared satisfied the lusts of the conquerors or were sold into slavery. Thus, the Hungarians and Scandinavians struck such terror in rural and defenseless peoples that they often gave up without a struggle. Many communities bought peace by paying tribute.

From the south the Muslims began new encroachments. They concentrated on the two southern peninsulas, Italy and Spain. Their goal was plunder. In Italy the monks of Monte Cassino were forced to flee. The Muslims drove northward and sacked Rome in 846. Most of Spain had remained under their domination since the sixth century (see Chapter 6). Having long been expert seamen, they sailed around the Iberian Peninsula, braved the notoriously dangerous shoals and winds of the Atlantic coast, and attacked the settlements along the coast of Provence. Muslim attacks on the European continent in the ninth and tenth centuries were less destructive, primarily because in comparison to the rich and sophisticated culture of the Arab capitals, northern Europe was primitive, backward, and offered little.

MAP 7.3   THE GREAT INVASIONS OF THE NINTH CENTURY

What effect did these invasions have on the structure of European society? Viking, Magyar, and Muslim attacks accelerated the development of feudalism. Lords capable of rallying fighting men, supporting them, and putting up resistance to the invaders did so. They also assumed political power in their territories. Weak and defenseless people sought the protection of local strong men. Free men sank to the level of serfs. Consequently, European society became further fragmented. Public power became increasingly decentralized.

FEUDALISM AND HISTORY

Scholars agree that feudalism is a persistent feature of European culture, but they disagree about when it first appeared and when it finally disappeared. They even disagree on what it was. When the philosophers and thinkers of the eighteenth century sought to bring about a more egalitarian and democratic society, they insisted that feudalism had to be abolished. The destruction of feudalism and of feudal elements in society was among the main goals of the French Revolution and of all the eighteenth-century democratic revolutions. Even today the adjective "feudal" is used in a negative sense, suggesting something antiquated, barbaric, and long out-of-date. But many twentieth-century scholars have demonstrated that when medieval feudalism developed it served the needs of contemporary society. Consequently, for the Middle Ages, the word "feudal" connotes "progressive" and "modern."

The term "feudalism" was not invented in the Middle Ages. It was first coined in the late seventeenth century. The men who coined it meant a type of government in which political power was treated as a private possession and divided among a large number of lords. At first, then, the word had political implications, but it was not thought to be related to the broad mass of the people. Although "feudalism" referred to a large number of lords, they constituted a small part of the entire European population.

More recently, historians and sociologists have used "feudalism" sweepingly to describe all the important social and political aspects of European life from the ninth to the eighteenth centuries. This approach is unsatisfactory because in those centuries society was constantly changing and evolving. A definition of feudalism that is suitable for one time and place may be virtually meaningless for another period and territory. For example, the feudalism developing in the ninth-century Frankish kingdom of Charlemagne was vastly different from the feudalism of thirteenth-century France under King Louis IX. The feudalism of eleventh-century Normandy was considerably different from that of eleventh-century Anglo-Saxon England just twenty-six miles away.

Today, under the influence of Marxist thought, it has become fashionable to treat feudalism entirely in economic terms. Some students describe feudalism as a system that let a small group of lazy military leaders exploit the producing class, the tillers of the soil. This too is not a very useful approach. Many societies, from ancient Greece to the American South before the Civil War to some twentieth-century Latin American countries, have been sharply divided between "exploiters" and "exploited." Writers who used the word "feudal" to describe all preindustrial societies strip the term of significant meaning.

A political interpretation of feudalism — focusing entirely on government and law — is concerned only with a small number of men, the tiny minority who exercised political power. A political interpretation tends to ignore the mass of people who constituted

European society. On the other hand, if feudalism is defined strictly in social and economic terms—with respect to the ordinary people—then the great political power and responsibilities that lords had within their localities are ignored or downplayed.

The word "feudalism" itself calls too much attention to the feud, the land given by a lord to a vassal in return for his promise to fight or to perform some other kind of service. In the eighth century, for example, lords maintained their vassals in their own households. The giving of land was largely a tenth-century development, though in the tenth century most vassals in France held no land. Sometimes lords never gave their vassals land; instead, they gave cash.

Historians trying to make sense of complicated social and political phenomena have coined the phrase "feudal system." They have discussed the subject in terms of a pyramid with weak men at the bottom, ever more important lords in the middle, and the king at the top. This social structure is easy to discuss, but unfortunately the lords and king never arranged themselves so neatly. Many men became the vassals of *several* lords in order to acquire more land or money and thus improve their economic position. Feudal lords everywhere were out for themselves, and everywhere they tended to oppose the centralizing ambitions of kings. The word "system" implies organization, regularity, and rational connections. In many ways these characteristics were entirely lacking in medieval European feudalism.

"Feudalism" refers to a society in which economic and political power was in the hands of military leaders. These lords provided protection for the peasants who worked the land. The lords also had political and judicial authority over the dependent serfs. When the lord was also a bishop or abbot, he had ecclesiastical, as well as civil, jurisdiction over his peasants. Because almost all communities were rural, isolated, and liable to attack, the basic need of society was physical security. Successful lords provided that. Consequently, the military virtues and values of the feudal nobility infused all aspects of the culture.

∾

The culture that emerged in Europe between 733 and 843 has frequently been called the first European civilization. The civilization had definite characteristics: it was feudal, Christian, and infused with Latin ideas and models. A military elite controlled most forms of economic and political power. Almost all peoples were baptized Christians. Latin was the common language of educated people everywhere; what was written was written in Latin. In spite of the disasters of the ninth and tenth centuries, these features remained basic aspects of European culture for centuries to come.

NOTES

1. H. Pirenne, *Mohammed and Charlemagne,* Barnes & Noble, New York, 1955, pp. 234–235.
2. See D. Herlihy, "Land, Family, and Women in Continental Europe, 701–1200," in S. M. Stuart, ed., *Women in Medieval Society,* University of Pennsylvania Press, Philadelphia, 1976, pp. 13–45.
3. Einhard, *The Life of Charlemagne,* with a foreword by S. Painter, University of Michigan Press, Ann Arbor, 1960, pp. 50–51.
4. B. D. Hill, ed., *Church and State in the Middle Ages,* John Wiley & Sons, New York, 1970, p. 45.

5. Ibid., pp. 46–47.

6. D. Wright, trans., *Beowulf,* Penguin Books, Baltimore, 1957, pp. 9–19.

7. M. Alexander, trans., *The Earliest English Poems,* Penguin Books, Baltimore, 1972, p. 99.

8. L. Sherley-Price, trans., *Bede: A History of the English Church and Peoples,* Penguin Books, Baltimore, 1962, book 3, chap. 27, p. 191.

9. See S. Rubin, *English Medieval Medicine,* Barnes & Noble, New York, 1974.

SUGGESTED READING

In spite of centuries of war, violence, and destruction, a sizable literature survives from the period once inaccurately described as the "Dark Ages." Scholars have devoted considerable attention to that literature because it was produced in such a crucial period, and the enterprising student who seeks further information about it may find the following works useful.

Chapters 4, 5, and 6 of J. B. Russell, *A History of Medieval Christianity: Prophecy and Order** (1968), describe the mind of the Christian church and show how it gradually made an impact on pagan Germanic peoples, while C. Dawson, *Religion and the Rise of Western Culture** (1958), emphasizes the religious origins of Western culture. C. H. Talbot, ed., *The Anglo-Saxon Missionaries in Germany* (1954), gives a good picture, through biographies and correspondence, of eighth-century religious life.

Einhard's *Life of Charlemagne** is probably the best starting point for the study of the great chieftain. There is no easily accessible and thorough treatment of the man and his government, but the advanced student with a knowledge of French should see L. Halphen, *Charlemagne et L'Empire Carolingien** (1949), the standard scholarly treatment. Recent research has been incorporated in E. Perroy, "Carolingian Administration," in S. Thrupp, ed., *Early Medieval Society** (1967). J. Brondsted, *The Vikings** (1960), is an excellently illustrated study of many facets of the culture of the Northmen.

In addition to the references to Bede, Beowulf, and Anglo-Saxon poetry given in the Notes to this chapter, D. L. Sayers, trans., *The Song of Roland** (1957), provides an excellent key, in epic form, to the values and lifestyles of the feudal classes. For the eighth-century revival of learning, see W. Levison, *England and the Continent in the Eighth Century* (1946); M. L. W. Laistner, *Thought and Letters in Western Europe, 500–900* (1931); and the beautifully written evocation by P. H. Blair, *Northumbria in the Days of Bede* (1976). E. S. Duckett, *Alcuin, Friend of Charlemagne* (1951), makes light and enjoyable reading, while L. Wallach, *Alcuin and Charlemagne* (rev. ed., 1968), is a technical study of Alcuin's treatises for the advanced student. The best treatment of the theological and political ideas of the period is probably K. F. Morrison, *The Two Kingdoms: Ecclesiology in Carolingian Political Thought* (1964), a difficult book.

Those interested in the role of women and children in early medieval society should see two articles: D. Herlihy, "Land, Family, and Women in Continental Europe, 701–1200," and E. Coleman, "Infanticide in the Early Middle Ages," which are both in S. M. Stuart, ed., *Women in Medieval Society** (1976).

For health and medical treatment, the curious student should consult S. Rubin, *Medieval English Medicine, A.D. 500–1300* (1974), especially pp. 97–149; W. H. McNeill, *Plagues and Peoples* (1976); A. Castiglioni, *A History of Medicine,* E. B. Krumbhaar, trans. (1941); and the important article by J. M. Riddle, "Theory and Practice in Medieval Medicine," *Viator* 5 (1974): 157–184.

A good introduction to the thorny problem of feudalism is F. L. Ganshof, *Feudalism** (1961), while M. Bloch, *Feudal Society,* L. A. Manyon, trans. (1961), is the standard scholarly study. J. R. Strayer, "Feudalism in Western Europe," in R. Coulborn, ed., *Feudalism in History* (1956), is a masterpiece. The finest recent study of peasant life and conditions of work is G. Duby, *Rural Economy and Country Life in the Medieval West,* C. Postan, trans. (1968).

*Available in paperback.

Chapter 8

REVIVAL, RECOVERY,

AND REFORM

*T*he century and a half after the death of Charlemagne witnessed a degree of disintegration, destruction, and disorder unparalleled in Europe before the twentieth century. The Viking, Magyar, and Muslim invasions made a frightful situation absolutely disastrous. The Carolingian Empire was split into several parts, each tending to go its own way. No civil or religious authority could maintain stable government over a very wide area. Local strong men provided what small security existed. Commerce and long-distance trade were drastically reduced. The leadership of the church became the political football of Roman aristocratic families. The result was that society underwent feudalization. The rich became warriors; the poor sought protection.

By the last quarter of the tenth century, after a long and bitter winter of discontent, the first signs of European spring were appearing. The European springtime lasted from the early eleventh century to the end of the thirteenth century. The period from about 1050 to 1300 has often been called the High Middle Ages. By that term scholars have marked off a time of crucial growth and development between two eras of economic, political, and social crisis. The phrase "High Middle Ages" also refers to a time of remarkable cultural achievement.

What were the signs of revival? How did they come about? What impact did the recovery of Europe have on social and economic change? How did the reform of the Christian church affect relations between the church and civil authorities? These are the questions discussed in this chapter.

POLITICAL REVIVAL

The eleventh century witnessed the beginnings of political stability in western Europe. Foreign invasions gradually declined, and domestic disorder subsided. This development gave people security in their persons and property. Security and political stability, supported by the peace movements of the church, contributed to a slowly increasing population. Political order and stability paved the way for economic recovery.

The Decline of Invasion and Civil Disorder

The most important factor in the revival of Europe after the disasters of the ninth century was the gradual decline of foreign invasions and the reduction of domestic violence. In 911, the Norwegian leader Rollo subdued large parts of what was later called Normandy. The West Frankish ruler Charles the Simple, unable to oust the Northmen, went along with that territorial conquest. He recognized Rollo as duke of Normandy on the condition that Rollo swear allegiance to him and hold the territory as a sort of barrier against future Viking assaults. This agreement, embodied in the treaty of Saint-Clair-sur-Epte, marks the beginning of the rise of Normandy.

Rollo kept his word. He exerted strong authority over Normandy and in troubled times supported the weak Frankish king. Rollo and his men were baptized as Christians. Although additional Viking settlers arrived, they were easily pacified. The tenth and eleventh centuries saw the steady assimilation of Normans and French. Major attacks on France had ended.

Rollo's descendant, Duke William I (1035–1087), made feudalism work as a system of government in Normandy. William attached specific quotas of military or knight service to the lands he distributed. Vassals who defaulted on their military obligations or refused attendance at the duke's court were ruthlessly executed. William forbade the construction of private castles, always the symbol of feudal independence. He limited private warfare

and vigorously supported a peace movement sponsored by the church. He kept strict control over the coinage and maintained strong supervision over the church, actively participating in church councils and in the selection of abbots and bishops. By 1066, the duchy of Normandy was the strongest, and the most peaceful, territory in Western Europe.

Recovery followed a somewhat different pattern in England. Between 960 and 1040, England was part of a vast Scandinavian empire that stretched from Normandy to Britain to Iceland and even to the eastern coast of North America. The Danish ruler Canute, king of England (1016–1035) and after 1030 king of Norway as well, made England the center of his empire. Canute started a policy of assimilation and reconciliation between Anglo-Saxons and Vikings.

Canute governed with the help of a witan — literally, a council of wise men — composed of Anglo-Saxons and Danes. He republished the laws of tenth-century Anglo-Saxon kings to show the continuity of his government with theirs. Canute and his followers accepted Christianity and Christian ideas of the responsibilities of a good and just king. Slowly the two peoples were molded together. King Edward the Confessor (1042–1066), the son of an Anglo-Saxon father and a Norman mother who had taken Canute as her second husband, personified the assimilation of Viking and Anglo-Saxon.

In the East the German king Otto I (936–973) inflicted a crushing defeat on the Hungarians on the banks of the Lech River in 955. The battle of Lechfeld halted the Magyars' westward expansion and threat to Germany, and made Otto a great hero to the Germans. It also signified the revival of the German monarchy and demonstrated that Otto was a worthy successor to Charlemagne.

When Otto had been chosen king, he had selected Aix-la-Chapelle as the site of his coronation. He did this to symbolize his intention to continue the work and tradition of Charlemagne.

The basis of his power was to be an alliance with, and the control of, the church. Otto asserted the right to invest bishops and abbots with the symbols of their office — the ring, which symbolized the bishop's union with his dioceses, and the staff, which was the symbol of his pastoral authority. This assertion gave Otto effective control over ecclesiastical appointments. Before receiving religious consecration, bishops and abbots had to perform feudal homage for the lands that went with the church office. (This practice, later known as lay investiture, created a grave crisis in the eleventh century.) Otto knew that he had to use the financial and military resources of the church to halt feudal anarchy. He used the higher clergy extensively in his administration, and the bulk of his army came from monastic and other church lands. Between 936 and 955, Otto succeeded in breaking the territorial power of the great German dukes.

In 962, Otto was crowned Holy Roman emperor by the pope. The imperial coronation had important results. It revived the Holy Roman Empire and its traditions, and it showed that Otto had the full support of the church in Germany and Italy. The uniting of the kingship with the imperial crown advanced German interests. Otto filled a power vacuum in northern Italy and brought about peace among the great aristocratic families. He established stable government there for the first time in over a century. Peace and political stability in turn promoted the revival of northern Italian cities, such as Venice.

By the start of the eleventh century, the maritime cities were seeking a place in the rich Mediterranean trade. Pisa and Genoa fought to break Muslim control of the trade and shipping with the Byzantine Empire and the Orient. Once the Muslim fleets had been destroyed, the Italian cities of Venice, Genoa, and Pisa embarked on the road to prosperity. The eleventh century witnessed their steadily rising strength and wealth. Freedom from invasion and domestic security made economic growth possible all over western Europe.

The Peace Movements of the Church

The church also worked to end arson, rape, homicide, and wanton destruction. In the last quarter of the tenth century, councils of bishops met in Burgundy. The place is significant, for Burgundy was the part of the Carolingian Empire where anarchy was the worst and where the clergy and the poor had no defenders whatsoever. The knights were developing a class consciousness, and the social gap between knight and serf was widening. Attacks on churches were common because local lords ignored all laws and restraints. Physical assaults on the peasants and the devastation of their fields caused terrible suffering.

The bishops proclaimed the Peace of God. It placed certain persons — the monks who lived in monasteries, the clergy who lived in villages and cathedral cities, and the poor — and certain places — church buildings and peasant fields — under ecclesiastical protection. Those who attacked such persons and places were anathematized, which meant that they were to be totally excluded from contact with all Christians. The bishops got their aristocratic relatives to try to enforce the peace.

In 1027, a council published the Truce of God, which attempted to regulate the times of fighting. An agreement was sworn that, "in order to enable every man to show respect for the Lord's Day," no one was to attack an enemy between Saturday evening and Monday morning. Before 1050, the number of restricted days was increased. Thursday, Friday, and Saturday were added as reminders of the Last Supper, the Crucifixion, and the Entombment. Gradually, some saints' days were added and then the seasons of Advent (the four weeks before Christmas) and Lent (the six weeks before Easter). Lords and knights were urged to form groups to preserve the peace. How effective they were is not known, but without strong and determined lay support they would not have been very successful.

The chief importance of the peace movements lies in the idea they gave to secular rulers. Around 1050, Duke William of Normandy compelled his vassals to join the movement. His backing, and eventually that of other leaders, was an important element in the promotion of peace.

Increasing Population and Mild Climate

A steady growth of population contributed to the general recovery of Europe. The decline of foreign invasions and of internal civil disorder reduced the number of people killed or maimed. Feudal armies in the eleventh through thirteenth centuries continued their destruction, but they were very small by modern standards and fought few pitched battles. Most medieval warfare consisted of the besieging of castles or fortifications. As few as twelve men could defend a castle. With sufficient food and an adequate water supply, they could hold out for a long time. Monastic chroniclers, frequently bored and almost always writing from hearsay evidence, tended to romanticize medieval warfare (as long as it was not in their neighborhood). Most conflicts were petty skirmishes with slight loss of life. The survival of more young people, those most often involved in warring activities and those usually the most sexually active, meant a population rise.

Nor was there any "natural," or biological, hindrance to population expansion. Between the tenth and the fourteenth centuries, Europe was not hit by any major plague or other medical scourge, though leprosy and malaria did strike down some people. Leprosy had entered Europe in the early Middle Ages. Although it was caused by a virus, the disease was not very contagious and, if contracted, worked slowly. Lepers presented a frightful appearance: the victim's arms and legs rotted away, and gangrenous sores emitted a horrible smell. Physicians had no cure. For these reasons, and because of the command, mentioned in the thirteenth chapter of Leviticus, that lepers be isolated, medieval lepers were segregated in hospitals called leprosaria.

Malaria, spread by protozoa-carrying mosquitoes that infested swampy areas, also caused problems. Malaria is characterized by alternate chills and fevers, and leaves the afflicted person extremely weak. Peter the Venerable, the ninth abbot of the monastery of Cluny (1122–1156), suffered for many of his later years from recurring bouts of malaria contracted on a youthful trip to Rome. Still, relatively few people caught malaria or leprosy. Crop failure and the ever-present danger of starvation were much more pressing threats.

The weather cooperated with the revival. Meteorologists believe that between the ninth and the eleventh centuries there was a slow but steady retreat of polar ice. A significant warming trend occurred and continued until around 1200. The climate was generally mild, milder even than in the early to mid-twentieth century. The century between 1080 1180 witnessed exceptionally clement weather in England, France, and Germany, with mild winters and dry summers.

Good weather helps to explain the advances made in population growth, land reclamation, and agricultural yield. Increased agricultural output had a profound impact on society. It affected Europeans' health, commerce, trade, industry, and general lifestyle.

ECONOMIC RECOVERY

In the eighteenth and nineteenth centuries, towns, together with commerce and manufacturing, transformed Europe from a rural and agricultural society into an industrial and urban society. The foundations for this change, which had global implications, were laid in the Middle Ages. The greatest manifestation of the recovery of Europe was the rise of towns and the development of a new business and commercial class.

Why did these developments occur when they did? What sorts of people first populated the towns and where did they come from? What is known of town life in the High Middle Ages? What relevance did towns have for the broad medieval culture? Part of the answer to at least one of these questions has already been given. Without an increased agricultural output, there would not have been an adequate food supply for new town dwellers. Without a rise in population, there would have been no one to people the towns. Without a minimum of peace and political stability, merchants could not have transported and sold goods (merchants dislike nothing more than domestic disorder).

The Rise of Towns

Medieval society was traditional, agricultural, and rural. The emergence of a new class that was none of these constituted a social revolution. The new class—artisans and merchants—came from the peasantry. They were landless. They were younger sons of large families, driven away by land shortage. Or they were forced by war and famine to seek new possibilities. Or they were unusually enterprising and adventurous, curious and willing to take a chance.

One of the most exciting aspects of the study of history is that facts or evidence may be explained in a variety of ways. There is no final or "definitive"

interpretation. Serious investigation of the origin of European towns began only in the twentieth century. Historians have suggested a number of hypotheses, which can be reduced to three basic theories. Some scholars believe that towns began as boroughs—that is, as forts or fortifications erected during the ninth-century Viking invasions. According to this view, towns at first were places of defense or security into which farmers from the surrounding countryside moved when their area was attacked. Later, merchants were attracted to the fortifications because they had something to sell and wanted to be where the potential customers were. Most of the residents of the early towns, however, made their living by farming outside the town.

A second theory was set forth by the great Belgian historian Henri Pirenne. He maintained that towns sprang up when merchants who engaged in long-distance trade gravitated toward attractive or favorable spots, such as near a fort. Usually the traders settled just outside the walls, in the *faubourgs* or *suburbs*—both of which mean "outside," or "in the shelter of the walls." As their markets prospered and as their number outside the walls grew, the merchants built a wall around themselves. This construction might be necessary every century or so. According to Pirenne, then, a medieval town consisted architecturally of a number of concentric walls, and the chief economic pursuit of its residents was trade and commerce.

A third explanation calls attention to some of the great cathedrals and monasteries. The large numbers of clergy attached to a cathedral or monastery represented a demand for goods and services. Cathedrals, such as Notre Dame in Paris, conducted schools, which drew students from far and wide. Consequently, traders and merchants

THE CITY WALL OF YORK, ENGLAND. Town walls protected citizens from theft and physical attack. Upkeep of the walls was usually the town's heaviest expense. (Royal Commission on Historical Monuments, England)

settled near the religious establishments to cater to the residents' economic needs. Concentrations of people accumulated, and towns came into being.

All three theories have some validity, but none of them explains the origins of *all* medieval towns. Many towns of the tenth and eleventh centuries were not "new" in the sense that American towns and cities were new in the seventeenth and eighteenth centuries. They were not carved out of forest and wilderness. Some medieval towns, which in the mid-twelfth century were flourishing centers of trade, had originally been Roman army camps: York in northern England, Bordeaux in west central France, and Cologne in west central Germany are good examples of ancient towns that underwent revitalization in the eleventh century. Some Italian seaport cities, such as Pisa and Genoa, had been centers of shipping and commerce in earlier times. Muslim attacks and domestic squabbles had cut their population and drastically reduced the volume of their trade in the early Middle Ages, but trade with Constantinople and the Orient had never stopped entirely. The restoration of order and political stability promoted rebirth and new development. Pirenne's interpretation works well for the Flemish towns of Bruges and Ypres. It does not fit the course of development in the Italian cities or in such centers as London.

Whether evolving from a newly fortified place or an old Roman army camp, from a cathedral site or a site at the junction of rivers, or from a place where several overland routes met, all medieval towns had a few common characteristics. Walls enclosed the town. (The terms "burgher" and "bourgeois" derive from the Old English and Old German words *burg, burgh, borg,* and *borough,* meaning a walled or fortified place. Thus, a burgher or bourgeois originally was a person who lived or worked inside the walls.) The town had a marketplace. It often had a mint for the coining of money and a court to settle disputes.

In each town a sizable number of inhabitants lived in a small, cramped area. Census records do not exist for most of Europe before the early eighteenth century, but tax returns give the population of many English towns in 1377. The largest city, London, had 23,314 persons. The second largest city, Cambridge, had only 6,345 citizens. Some continental cities, such as Paris, were probably much bigger. Size was not important, however. The real strength of the medieval towns rested in their people.

In their backgrounds and their abilities, townspeople represented diversity and change. They constituted an entirely new element in medieval society. They were "middle" class. They fit into none of the traditional categories. Their occupations, their preoccupations, their very lives were different from those of the feudal nobility and the laboring peasantry.

The aristocratic nobility glanced down with contempt and derision at the moneygrubbing townspeople. But the nobles were not above borrowing from them. The rural peasantry peered up with suspicion and fear at the town dwellers. What was the point, the farmer wondered, of making money? "You can't take it with you." Only the land had real permanence.

Nor did the new commercial classes make much sense initially to the churchmen. The immediate goal of the middle class obviously was not salvation. It was a good while before churchmen developed a theological justification for the new classes.

Town Liberties

In the words of the Greek poet Alcaeus, "Not houses finely roofed or well built walls, nor canals or dockyards make a city, but men able to use their opportunity."[1] Men and opportunity. That is fundamentally what medieval towns meant — concentrations of people and varieties of chances. No matter where groups of traders congregated, they settled on someone's land and had to secure from king or count, abbot or bishop, permission to live and trade. Aristocratic nobles and churchmen were suspicious of and hostile to the middle class. They soon realized, however, that profits and benefits came to them and their territories from the markets set up on their land.

The history of towns in the eleventh through thirteenth centuries consists in great part of the efforts of merchants to acquire "liberties." In the

Middle Ages "liberties" connoted special privileges. For the town dweller, liberties included the privilege of living and trading on the lord's land. The most important privilege a medieval townsperson could gain was freedom. An individual who lived in a town for a year and a day was free of servile obligations and status. More than anything else, perhaps, the "liberty" of personal freedom that came with residence in a town contributed to the emancipation of the serfs in the High Middle Ages. "Liberty" meant citizenship, and citizenship in a town implied the right to buy and sell goods there. Unlike foreigners or outsiders of any kind, the full citizen did not have to pay taxes and tolls in the market. Obviously, this increased profits.

In the twelfth and thirteenth centuries, towns fought for, and slowly gained, legal and political rights. Since the tenth century, some English boroughs had held courts with jurisdiction over members of the town in civil and criminal matters. In the twelfth century, such English towns as London and Norwich developed courts that applied a special kind of law, called law merchant. It dealt with commercial transactions, debt, bankruptcy, proof of sales, and contracts. Law merchant was especially suitable to the needs of the new bourgeoisie. Around 1116, the count of Flanders granted to the burgesses of Ypres the right to hold a municipal court that alone could judge members of the town. Gradually, other towns across Europe acquired the same right. In effect it gave them judicial independence.[2]

In the acquisition of full rights of self-government, the merchant guilds played a large role. Medieval men were long accustomed to communal enterprises. In the late tenth and early eleventh centuries, men who were engaged in foreign trade joined together in merchant guilds; united enterprise provided them greater security and smaller loss than did individual action. At about the same time, the artisans and craftsmen of particular trades formed guilds of their own. They were the butchers, the bakers, and the candlestick makers. Members of the craft guilds determined the quality, quantity, and price of the goods produced and the number of apprentices and journeymen affiliated with the guild. (Terrible conflicts arose between the craft guilds and the merchant guilds in the thirteenth and fourteenth centuries, but that is a later story.)

By the late eleventh century, the leading men in the merchant guilds, especially in the towns of the Low Countries (present-day Belgium and Holland) and in northern Italy, were quite rich and powerful. Constituting an oligarchy in their towns, they controlled economic life and bargained with kings and lords for political independence. Full rights of self-government included the right to hold a town court, the right to select the mayor and other municipal officials, and the right to tax and collect taxes. Kings often levied on their serfs and unfree townspeople arbitrary taxes called tallage, or the taille. Such taxes (also known as customs) called attention to the fact that men were not free. Citizens of a town much preferred to levy and collect their own taxes.

A charter that King Henry II of England granted to the merchants of Lincoln around 1157 nicely illustrates the town's rights. The romanized phrases clearly suggest that the merchant guild had been the governing body in the city for almost a century and that anyone who lived in Lincoln for a year and a day was considered free:

Henry, by the grace of God, etc., to the bishop of Lincoln, and to the justices, sheriffs, barons, servants and all his liegemen, both French and English, of Lincoln, greeting. Know that I have granted to my citizens of Lincoln all their liberties and customs and laws which they had in the time of Edward [King Edward the Confessor] and William and Henry, kings of England. And I have granted them their gild-merchant, comprising men of the city and other merchants of the shire, *as well and freely as they had it in the time of our aforesaid predecessors, kings of England. And all the men who live within the four divisions of the city and attend the market, shall stand in relation to gelds [taxes] and customs and the assizes [ordinances or laws] of the city as well as ever they stood in the time of Edward, William and Henry, kings of England. I also confirm to them that* if anyone has lived in Lincoln for a year and a day without dispute from any claimant, *and has paid the customs, and if the citizens can show by the laws and customs of the city that the claimant has remained in England during that period and has made no claim,* then let the defendant remain in peace in my city of Lincoln as my citizen, *without [having to defend his] right.*[3]

Kings and lords were reluctant to grant towns self-government, because they feared loss of authority and revenue if they gave the merchant guilds full independence. But the lords discovered that towns attracted increasing numbers of people to an area — people whom the lords could tax. Moreover, when burghers bargained for a town's political independence, they offered sizable amounts of ready cash. Consequently, feudal lords ultimately agreed to self-government.

Town Life

Protective walls surrounded almost all medieval towns and cities. The valuable goods inside a town presented too much of a temptation to marauding bands for the town to be without the security of bricks and mortar. The walls were pierced by gates, and visitors waited at the gates to gain entrance to the town. When the gates were opened, early in the morning, guards inspected the quantity and quality of the goods brought in and collected the customary taxes. Part of the taxes went to the king or lord on whose land the town stood, part went to the town

council for a variety of civic purposes. Constant repair of the walls was usually the town's greatest expense.

Peasants coming from the countryside and merchants traveling from afar set up their carts as stalls just inside the gates. The result was that the road nearest the gate was the widest thoroughfare. It was the ideal place for a market, because everyone coming in or going out used it. Most streets in a medieval town were as much marketplaces as passages for transit. They were narrow, just wide enough to transport goods through.

Medieval cities served, above all else, as markets. In some respects the entire city was a marketplace. Merchants lived close to their businesses. The place where a product was made and sold was also the merchant's residence. Usually, the ground floor was the scene of production. A window or door opened from the main workroom directly onto the street. The window displayed the finished product, and passersby could look in and see the goods being produced. The merchant and his family lived in rooms just above the business on the first or second floor above the ground. As his business and his family expanded, he built additional stories on top of his house.

Space within the walls of the town was limited. Expansion, therefore, was upward. Second and third stories were built to jut out over the ground floor and thus over the street. Neighbors on the opposite side of the road did the same. Since streets were narrow to begin with, the amount of air and light entering all houses was considerably reduced. Initially, houses were erected of wood and thatched with straw. Fire thus represented a constant danger, and, because houses were built so close together, fires spread rapidly. Municipal governments, consequently, vigorously urged construction in stone or brick.

MEDIEVAL STREET SCENE. Merchants displayed their goods from shop windows on the ground floor: tailors, furriers, a barber, and a grocer. Merchants with shops on the street that linked the two main town gates naturally profited more than did those on side streets which were blocked by the town wall. (Bibliothèque Nationale, Paris)

Most medieval cities developed gradually. There was little town planning. As the population increased, space became more and more limited. Air and water pollution presented serious problems. Many families raised pigs for household consumption in sties next to the house. Horses and oxen, the chief means of transportation and power, dropped tons of dung on the streets every year. The universal practice existed in the early towns of dumping household waste, both animal and human, into the

A FIFTEENTH-CENTURY HOUSE. Medieval merchants conducted their business on the ground floor and lived with their families on the floors above. As additional stories were added on, they jutted out one over the other. Since this form of building was done on both sides of the street, streets received little light during the day and were dangerously dark at night. (Royal Commission on Historical Monuments, England)

road in front of one's house. The stench must have been abominable. The possibility of disease was everywhere. In 1298, the burgesses of the town of Boutham in Yorkshire, England, received the following order:

To the bailiffs of the abbot of St. Mary's York, at Boutham. Whereas it is sufficiently evident that the pavement of the said town of Boutham is so very greatly broken up and that all the singular passing and going through that town sustain immoderate damages and grievances, and in addition the air is so corrupted and infected by the pigsties situated in the king's highways and in the lanes of that town and by the swine feeding and frequently wandering about in the streets and lanes and by dung and dunghills and many other foul things placed in the streets and lanes, that great repugnance overtakes the king's ministers staying in that town and also others there dwelling and passing through, the advantage of more wholesome air is impeded, the state of men is grievously injured, and other unbearable inconveniences and many other injuries are known to proceed from such corruption, to the nuisance of the king's ministers aforesaid and of others there dwelling and passing through, and to the peril of their lives, and to the manifest shame and reproach of the bailiffs and other the inhabitants of that town: the king, being unwilling longer to tolerate such great and unbearable defects there, orders the bailiffs to cause the pavement to be suitably repaired within their liberty before All Saints next, and to cause the pigsties, aforesaid streets and lanes to be cleansed from all dung and dunghills, and to cause them to be kept thus cleansed hereafter, and to cause proclamation to be made throughout their bailiwick forbidding any one, under pain of grievous forfeiture, to cause or permit their swine to feed or wander outside his house in the king's streets or the lanes aforesaid.[4]

A great deal of traffic passed through Boutham in 1298, because of the movement of the English troops to battlefronts in Scotland. Conditions probably were not typical. Still, this document provides a good glimpse of the kinds of problems towns had. Difficulties of space, air pollution, and sanitation bedeviled medieval urban people just as they do modern ones today.

The church took a great interest in the towns-people as Christians. Parish clergy catered to their spiritual needs. As the bourgeoisie gained in wealth, they expressed their continuing Christian faith by refurbishing old churches, constructing new ones, and giving stained-glass windows, stat-ues, and carvings. The twelfth-century chronicler William of Newburgh, writing about 1170, could proudly boast that the city of London had 126 parish churches, in addition to 13 monastic churches and the great cathedral of St. Paul's.

Some literary descriptions of medieval cities survive, but they do not tell all that we would like to know. Most illustrations of walls, streets, and houses date only from the fifteenth century. Medi-eval cities, like modern ones, changed a great deal in the course of decades and even more over a couple of centuries. A fifteenth-century picture is not a very accurate representation of twelfth-century condi-tions. William of Newburgh, however, left a detailed description of the city of London around 1175:

Among the noble and celebrated cities of the world that of London, the capital of the kingdom of the English, is one which extends its glory farther than all the others and sends its wealth and merchandise more widely into distant lands. Higher than all the rest does it lift its head. . . .

It has on the east the Palatine castle [the Tower of London], very great and strong: the keep and walls rise from very deep foundations and are fixed with a mortar tempered by the blood of animals. On the west there are two castles very strongly fortified, and from these there *runs a high and massive wall with seven double gates and with towers along the north at regular intervals. London was once also walled and turreted on the south, but the mighty Thames, so full of fish, has with the sea's ebb and flow washed against, loosened, and thrown down those walls in the course of time. Upstream to the west there is the royal palace [the Palace of Westmin-ster]. . . .*

Everywhere outside the houses of those living in the suburbs, and adjacent to them, are the spacious and beautiful gardens of the citizens, and these are planted with trees. Also there are on the north side pastures and pleasant meadow lands through which flow streams wherein the turning of mill-wheels makes a cheerful sound. Very near lies a great forest with woodland pastures in which there are the lairs of wild animals: stags, fallow deer, wild boars and bulls. . . .

Those engaged in business of various kinds, sellers of merchandise, hirers of labour, are distributed every morning into their several localities according to their trade. Besides, there is in London on the river bank among the wines for sale in ships and in the cellars of the vintners a public cook-shop. There daily you may find food according to the season, dishes of meat, roast, fried and boiled, large and small fish, coarser meats for the poor and more delicate for the rich, such as venison and big and small birds. If any of the citizens should unexpectedly receive visitors, weary from their journey, who would fain not wait until fresh food is bought and cooked, or until the servants have brought bread or water for washing, they hasten to the river bank and there find all they need. . . .

Immediately outside one of the gates there is a field [Smithfield] which is smooth both in fact and in name. On every sixth day of the week, unless it be a major feast-day, there takes place there a famous exhibition of fine horses for sale. Earls, barons and knights, who are in the town, and many citizens come out to see or to buy. It is pleasant to see the high-stepping palfreys with their gleaming coats, as they go through their paces, putting down their feet alternately one one side together. . . .

By themselves in another part of the field stand the goods of the countryfolk: implements of husbandry, swine with long flanks, cows with full udders, oxen of immense size, and woolly sheep. There also stand the mares fit for plough, some big with foal, and others with brisk young colts closely following them.

To this city from every nation under heaven merchants delight to bring their trade by sea. The Arabian sends gold; the Sabaean spice and incense. The Scythian brings arms, and from the rich, fat lands of Babylon comes oil of palms. The Nile sends precious stones; the men of Norway and Russia, furs and sables; nor is China absent with purple silk. The Gauls come with their wines. . . .

We now come to speak of the sports of the city, for it is not fitting that a city should be merely useful and serious-minded, unless it be also pleasant and cheerful. . . .

Furthermore, every year on the day called Carnival — to begin with the sports of boys (for we were all boys once) — scholars from the different schools bring fighting-cocks to their masters, and the whole morning is set apart to watch their cocks do battle in the schools, for the boys are given a holiday that day. After dinner all the young men of the town go out into the fields in the suburbs to play ball. The scholars of the various schools have their own ball, and almost all the followers of each occupation have theirs also. The seniors and the fathers and the wealthy magnates of the city come on horseback to watch the contests of the younger generation, and in their turn recover their lost youth: the motions of their natural heat seem to be stirred in them at the mere sight of such strenuous activity and by their participation in the joys of unbridled youth.

Every Sunday in Lent after dinner a fresh swarm of young men goes forth into the fields on war-horses, steeds foremost in the contest, each of which is skilled and schooled to run in circles. From the gates there sallies forth a host of laymen, sons of the citizens, equipped with lances and shields, the younger ones with spears forked at the top, but with the steel point removed. They make a

pretence at war, carry out field-exercises and indulge in mimic combats. Thither too come many courtiers, when the king is in town, and from the households of bishops, earls and barons come youths and adolescents, not yet girt with the belt of knighthood, for the pleasure of engaging in combat with one another. Each is inflamed with the hope of victory. . . .

On feast-days throughout the summer the young men indulge in the sports of archery, running, jumping, wrestling, slinging the stone, hurling the javelin beyond a mark and fighting with sword and buckler. . . .

Others, more skilled at winter sports, put on their feet the shin-bones of animals, binding them firmly around their ankles, and, holding poles shod with iron in their hands, which they strike from time to time against the ice, they are propelled swift as a bird in flight or a bolt shot from an engine of war. . . .[5]

People wanted to get into medieval cities because they represented a means of economic advancement, social mobility, and definite improvement in legal status. For the adventurous, the ambitious, and the shrewd, cities offered tremendous opportunities.

The Revival of Long-Distance Trade

The eleventh century witnessed a remarkable revival of trade as artisans and craftsmen manufactured goods for local and foreign consumption (see Map 8.1). Most trade was centered in towns and controlled by professional traders. Because long-distance trade was risky and required great investment of capital, it could be practiced only by professionals. The transportation of goods involved serious risks. Shipwrecks were common. Pirates infested the sea-lanes, and robbers and thieves roamed virtually all of the land routes. Since the risks were so great, merchants preferred to divide them. A group of men would pool some of their capital to finance an expedition to a distant place.

MAP 8.1   TRADE AND MANUFACTURING IN MEDIEVAL EUROPE

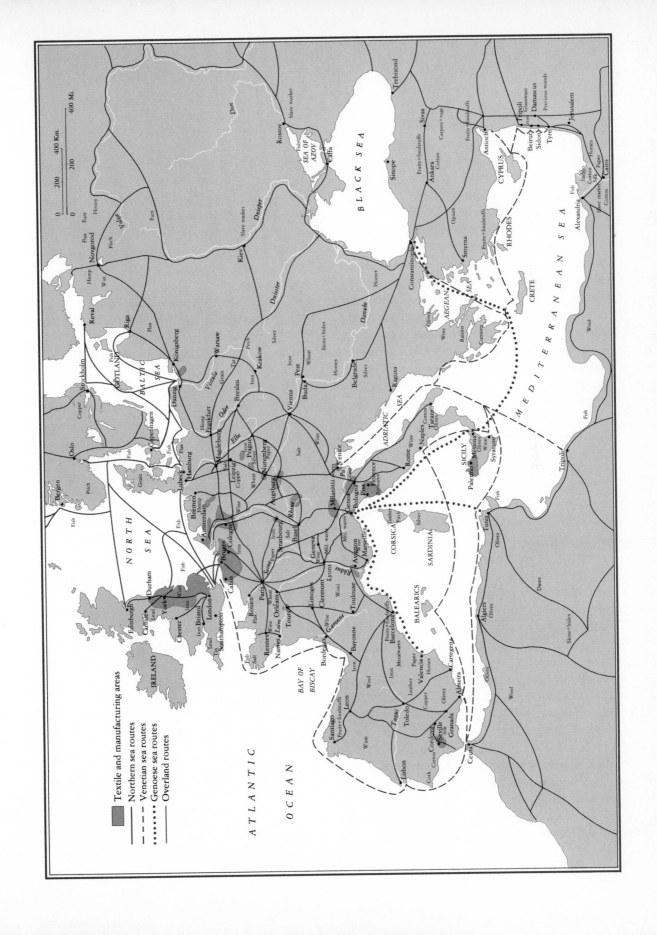

When the ship or caravan returned and the goods brought back were sold, the investors would share the profits. If some kind of disaster struck the caravan, the investors' loss was limited to the amount of their investment.

What goods were exchanged? What towns took the lead in medieval "international" trade? Venice in the south and the Flemish towns in the north present typical case studies. In the late eleventh century, the Italian cities, especially Venice, led the West in trade in general and completely dominated the oriental market. Ships carried salt from the Venetian lagoon, pepper and other spices from North Africa, and silks and purple textiles from the Orient to northern and western Europe. Venetian caravans brought slaves from the Crimea and Chinese silks from Mongolia to the town markets and regional fairs of France, Flanders, and England. (Fairs were periodic gatherings that attracted buyers, sellers, and goods from all over Europe.) Flanders controlled the cloth industry. The towns of Bruges, Ghent, and Ypres built up a vast industry in the manufacture of cloth. Italian merchants exchanged their products for Flemish tapestries, fine broadcloths, and various other textiles.

Two developments help to explain the lead Venice and the Flemish towns gained in long-distance trade. Both enjoyed a high degree of peace and political stability. Geographical factors were equally if not more important. Situated at the northwestern end of the Adriatic Sea, with easy access to both the transalpine land routes and the Adriatic and Mediterranean sea-lanes, Venice was ideally located. The markets of North Africa, Byzantium, and Russia and the great fairs of Ghent in Flanders and Champagne in France provided commercial opportunities Venice quickly seized. Likewise, the geographical situation of Flanders offered unusual possibilities. Just across the Channel from England, Flanders had easy access to English wool. Indeed, Flanders and England developed a very close economic relationship.

Sheep had been raised for their wool in England since Roman times. The rocky soil and damp climate of Yorkshire and Lincolnshire, while poorly suited for agriculture, were excellent for sheep farming. Beginning in the early twelfth century, but especially after the arrival of Cistercian monks around 1130, the size of the English flocks doubled and then tripled. Scholars have estimated that by the end of the twelfth century roughly 6 million sheep grazed on the English moors and downs. They produced fifty thousand sacks of wool a year.[6] Originally, a "sack" of wool was the burden one packhorse could carry, and eventually that amount was fixed at 364 pounds; fifty thousand sacks, then, represented huge production.

Most of the English wool was exported to Flanders. Thus, the production of English wool stimulated Flemish manufacturing, and the growth of the Flemish cloth industry stimulated the production of English wool. The textiles of the Flemish towns were shipped to all parts of Europe and the Middle East.

The Commercial Revolution

The steadily expanding volume of foreign trade in the late eleventh through the thirteenth centuries was the sign of a great economic surge, but it was not the only one. In cities all across Europe trading and transportation firms opened branch offices. Credit was widely extended, considerably facilitating exchange. Merchants devised the letter of credit, which made unnecessary the slow, and dangerous, shipment of coin for payment.

A new capitalistic spirit developed. Professional merchants were always on the lookout for new markets, new opportunities. They invested their surplus capital in new enterprises to make more

A FLEMISH DOCK SCENE. Flemish towns early developed commercial ties with neighboring countries. The Flemish purchased wool from England and manufactured excellent textiles, which they sold to merchants from all over Europe. This print shows bales of cloth being loaded at dockside for transport abroad. (Bodleian Library)

money. They diversified their interests and got involved in a wide variety of operations. The typical prosperous merchant of the mid-thirteenth century might well be involved in buying and selling, in shipping, in lending some capital at interest, and in other banking practices. Medieval merchants were fiercely competitive.

Some scholars believe that capitalism is a modern phenomenon, beginning in the fifteenth or sixteenth century. But what is "modern"? In their use of capital to make more money, in their speculative practices and willingness to gamble, in their competitive spirit, and in the variety of their interests and operations, medieval businessmen displayed the essential traits of capitalists.

These developments added up to a remarkable commercial revolution, which has been called by a scholar who knows it well "probably the greatest turning point in the history of our civilisation."[7] That is not an extravagant statement. In the long run the commercial revolution of the High Middle Ages brought about a radical change in European society and culture. One remarkable aspect of this change is that the commercial classes did not constitute a large part of the population — never more than 10 percent. They exercised an influence far in excess of their actual numbers.

The commercial revolution created a great deal of new wealth. Wealth meant a higher standard of living. The new availability of something as simple as spices, for example, allowed for variety in food. Dietary habits gradually changed. Taste became more sophisticated. Contact with Eastern civilizations introduced Europeans to eating utensils such as forks. Table manners improved. People learned to eat with forks and knives, instead of tearing the meat from the roast with their hands. They began to use napkins, instead of wiping their greasy fingers on the dogs lying under the table.

The existence of wealth did not escape the attention of kings and other rulers. Wealth could be taxed, and through taxation kings could create strong and centralized states. In the years to come, through alliances with the middle classes, kings would defeat feudal powers and aristocratic interests and build the states that came to be called modern.

The commercial revolution also provided the opportunity for thousands of serfs to improve their social position. The slow but steady transformation of European society from an almost completely rural

and isolated one to a relatively more sophisticated one constituted the greatest effect of the commercial revolution that began in the eleventh century.

REVIVAL AND REFORM IN THE CHRISTIAN CHURCH

The eleventh century also witnessed the beginnings of a remarkable religious revival. The monasteries, always the leaders in ecclesiastical reform, remodeled themselves under the leadership of the Burgundian abbey of Cluny. Subsequently, new religious orders, such as the Cistercians, were founded and became a broad spiritual movement.

The papacy itself, after a century of corruption and decadence, was cleaned up. The popes worked to clarify church doctrine and to codify church law. They and their officials sought to communicate with all the clergy and peoples of Europe through a clearly defined and obedient hierarchy of bishops. The popes wanted the basic loyalty of all members of the clergy. Pope Gregory VII (1073–1085) tried to enforce an entirely new theory of Christian kingship, and his assertion of papal power caused profound changes and serious conflicts between secular and religious authorities. The revival in the Christian church was manifested in the twelfth and thirteenth centuries by a flowering of popular piety, reflected in the building of magnificent cathedrals.

Monastic Revival

In the early Middle Ages the best Benedictine monasteries had been citadels of good Christian living and centers of education and learning. Between the seventh and ninth centuries, religious houses like Bobbio in northern Italy, Luxeuil in France, and Jarrow in England copied and preserved manuscripts, maintained schools, and set high standards of monastic observance. Charlemagne encouraged and supported these monastic activities, and the collapse of the Carolingian Empire had disastrous effects.

The Viking and Muslim invaders attacked and ransacked many monasteries across Europe. Some communities fled and were dispersed. In the period of political disorder that followed the disintegration of the Carolingian Empire, many religious houses fell under the control and domination of local feudal lords. Powerful laymen appointed themselves or their relatives abbots, while retaining their wives and/or mistresses. They took for themselves the lands and goods of monasteries. They spent monastic revenues and sold monastic offices. Temporal powers all over Europe dominated the monasteries. The level of spiritual observance and intellectual activity declined.

In 909, William the Pious, duke of Aquitaine, established the abbey of Cluny near Mâcon in Burgundy. This was to be a very important event. In his charter of endowment Duke William stated that Cluny was to have complete independence from all feudal or secular lordship. The new monastery was to be subordinate only to the authority of Saints Peter and Paul as represented by the pope. Then the duke renounced his own possession of, and influence over, Cluny.

This monastery and its foundation charter came to exert vast religious influence. The first two abbots of Cluny, Berno (910–927) and Odo (927–942), set very high standards of religious behavior. They stressed the strict observance of the *Rule of Saint Benedict,* the development of a personal spiritual life by the individual monk, and the importance of the liturgy. In the church as a whole, Cluny gradually came to stand for clerical celibacy and the suppression of simony (the sale of church offices). Within a generation neighboring monasteries sought the help of Cluny and were reformed along Cluniac lines.

In the course of the eleventh century, Cluny was fortunate in having a series of extremely able abbots,

who all ruled for a long time. They paid careful attention to sound economic management and to the principle of independence from lay influence. In the Holy Roman Empire, Cluniac reform had the strong and significant support of the emperor Henry III (1039–1056). He aided the religious houses in their struggle for independence from the lay aristocracy. Hundreds of monasteries across Europe, in France, Germany, Italy, Spain, and England, placed themselves under Cluny's jurisdiction. By the reign of Abbot Hugh (1049–1109) the Cluniac reforming spirit was felt everywhere.

Success for an institution, as for an individual, is measured by the degree to which it lives up to the goals it sets for itself. In religion nothing leads to failure like material success. By the last quarter of the eleventh century, some monasteries enjoyed wide reputations for the beauty and richness of their chant and the piety of the monks' lives. Deeply impressed laymen showered gifts upon them. Jewelry, rich vestments and elaborately carved sacred vessels, lands and properties poured in to some houses. With this wealth came the influence of laymen. As the monasteries became richer, the lifestyle of the monks became luxurious, and monastic observance and spiritual fervor declined.

Once again the ideals of the pristine Benedictine life were threatened. Fresh demands for reform were heard, and the result was the appearance of new religious orders. These emerged in the late eleventh and early twelfth centuries. The Cistercians became the best representatives of the new reforming spirit and monastic piety of the twelfth century.

In 1098, a group of monks left the rich abbey of Molesmes in Burgundy and founded a new house in the swampy forest of Cîteaux. They had specific goals and high ideals. They planned to avoid all involvement with secular and feudal society. They decided to accept only uncultivated lands far from regular habitation. They intended to refuse all gifts of mills, serfs, tithes, ovens—the traditional manorial sources of income. The early Cistercians determined to avoid elaborate liturgy and ceremony and to keep their chant simple. Finally, they refused to allow the presence of high and powerful laymen in their monasteries, because they knew that such an influence was usually harmful to careful observance.

To the Cistercian reformers the older Benedictine monasteries represented power, wealth, and luxurious living, which violated the spirit of the *Rule of Saint Benedict*. The Cistercian life was to be a new kind of commune. It was to be simple, isolated, austere, and purified of all the economic and religious complexities found in the Benedictine houses.

These Cistercian goals coincided perfectly with the needs of twelfth-century society. The late eleventh and early twelfth centuries were times of agricultural expansion and land reclamation all across Europe. The early Cistercians wanted to farm only land that had previously been uncultivated, or swampland, or fenland, and that was exactly what needed to be done. They thus became the great pioneers of the twelfth century. Their churches had to be plain, and they wanted their daily lives to be simple. A pioneer existence in a commune where all had to work hard and all resources were pooled obviously had enormous economic and social possibilities. The Cistercian life could and did bring wealth, and wealth brought power and influence.

The first monks at Cîteaux experienced serious sickness, a dearth of recruits, and terrible privations. Their obvious sincerity and high idealism eventually attracted attention. In 1112, a twenty-three-year-old nobleman called Bernard, together with thirty of his aristocratic friends and companions, joined the community at Cîteaux. Thereafter, this reforming movement gained wide impetus. Cîteaux founded hundreds of new monasteries in the course of the twelfth century, and its influence on European society was profound.

Reform of the Papacy

Some scholars believe that the monastic revival spreading from Cluny influenced the reform of the Roman papacy and eventually that of the entire Christian church. Certainly, Abbot Odilo of Cluny (994–1048) was a close friend of the German emperor Henry III, who promoted reform throughout the empire. Pope Gregory VII, who carried the ideals of reform to extreme lengths, had spent some time at Cluny. And the man who consolidated the reform movement and established the medieval papal monarchy, Pope Urban II (1088–1099), had been a monk and prior at Cluny. The precise degree of Cluny's impact on the reform movement, however, cannot be proven. Nevertheless, the broad goals of the Cluniac movement and those of the Roman papacy were the same.

In the tenth century, the papacy provided little leadership to the Christian peoples of western Europe. Factions in Rome sought to control the papacy for their own material gains. Descended from the great aristocratic families of the city, the popes were appointed to advance the political ambitions of their families, not because of special spiritual qualifications. The office of pope, including its spiritual powers and influence, was frequently bought and sold, although this grave crime, called simony, had been condemned by Saint Peter (Acts 8.9–24). The licentiousness and debauchery of the papal court scandalized people. According to a contemporary chronicler, for example, Pope John XII (955–963), who secured the papal office at the age of eighteen, had worn himself out from sexual excesses before he was twenty-eight. Such conditions weakened the religious prestige and moral authority of the pope.

At the local, or parish, level there were many married priests. Taking Christ as the model for the priestly life, the Roman church had always encouraged clerical celibacy, but only since the fourth century had it been an obligation for ordination. In the tenth and eleventh centuries, probably a majority of the priests of Europe were married or living with a woman. Such priests were called Nicolaites from a reference in the Book of Revelation to early Christians who advocated a return to pagan sexual practices.

Several factors may account for the uncelibate state of the clergy. Perhaps the explanation lies in the basic need for warmth and human companionship. Perhaps the village priests could not survive economically on their small salaries and needed the help of a mate. Perhaps in the tenth century the tradition of a married clergy was so deep-rooted that each generation simply followed the practice of its predecessor. In any case, the disparity between the law and the reality shocked people and caused disrespect for the clergy.

Serious efforts at reform began under Pope Leo IX (1049–1054). Not only was he related to Emperor Henry III, but as bishop of Toul and a German, he was an outsider and owed nothing to any Roman faction. Leo traveled widely and held councils at Pavia, Reims, and Mainz, which issued decrees against simony, Nicolaism, and violence. Leo's representatives held church councils across Europe, pressing for moral reform. They urged individuals who could not secure justice at home to appeal to the pope, the ultimate source of justice.

Leo himself was a man of deep humility and great pastoral zeal. By his character and his actions, he set high moral standards for the West. The reform of the papacy had legal as well as moral aspects. During Leo's pontificate a new collection of ecclesiastical law was prepared—the Collection of 74 Titles. Based on letters of popes and the decrees of councils, the Collection of 74 Titles laid great emphasis on papal authority. It stressed the rights, the legal position, and the supreme spiritual prerogatives of the bishop of Rome as the successor of Saint Peter.

POPE LEO IX. Called the "founder of the medieval papal monarchy," Leo IX stood for the ideal of the papacy as a moral force throughout Europe. A strong supporter of the Cluniac reform movement, Leo is portrayed here blessing an abbey church. (Burgerbibliothek, Bern. Cod. 292, fol. 73)

Papal reform continued after Leo IX. In the short reign of Nicholas II (1058–1061), a council held in the ancient church of St. John Lateran in 1059 reached a momentous decision. A new method was devised for electing the pope. Since the eighth century, the priests of the major churches in and around Rome had constituted a special group (or college) that advised the pope. These chief priests were called cardinals from the Latin word *cardo,* meaning "hinge." The cardinals were the "hinges" on which the church turned. When the pope summoned them to meetings, they acted as his advisers. A decree of the Lateran Synod of 1059 stated that the authority and power to elect the pope rested solely in this college of cardinals.

The object of the decree was to remove this crucial decision from the secular squabbling of Roman aristocratic factions. When the office of pope was vacant, the cardinals were responsible for the government of the church. (In the Middle Ages the college of cardinals numbered around twenty-five or thirty, most of them drawn from Italy. In 1586, the figure was set at seventy. In the 1960s, Pope Paul VI virtually doubled that number, appointing men from the remotest parts of the globe to reflect the international character of the church.) By 1073, the progress of reform in the Christian church was well advanced. The election of Cardinal Hildebrand as Pope Gregory VII changed the direction of reform from a moral to a political one.

THE GREGORIAN REVOLUTION

The papal reform movement of the eleventh century has frequently been named the Gregorian reform movement, after Pope Gregory VII. That label is not accurate, however, because reform began long before his pontificate and continued after it. Gregory's reign did, however, inaugurate a radical or revolutionary phase that had important political and social consequences.

Pope Gregory VII's Ideas

In contrast to his predecessors and successors in the eleventh century, Cardinal Hildebrand, who took the name Gregory when he was elected pope, was not of aristocratic descent but the son of poor Tuscan peasants. Because of this genealogical fact, some historians have argued that the bitter clash between Pope Gregory VII and the German emperor Henry IV was the result of the desire of a lowborn upstart to humble the chief secular power in Europe. This idea is intriguing, if not thoroughly convincing. Education probably had more influence on Gregory's mature attitudes than his social origins did. He received a good education at Rome and spent some time at Cluny, where his strict views of clerical life were strengthened. Hildebrand served in the papal secretariat under Leo IX, and after 1065 he was probably the chief influence there.

Hildebrand was dogmatic, inflexible, and unalterably convinced of the truth of his own views. He believed that the pope, as the successor of Saint Peter, was the Vicar of God on earth and that papal orders were the orders of God. His ideas of kingship were even more notorious — and dangerous — to his contemporaries. He believed that in a Christian society the king was responsible for providing peace and order so that Christians could pursue their pilgrimage to the City of God.

The king was obliged to act righteously. If he did not, he was by that fact alone a tyrant, to whom *no one* owed allegiance. Who was to decide if a ruler was a tyrant, an unjust king? The pope, as the Vicar of God, would make that decision and, Hildebrand maintained, could release subjects from their duty of obedience. Much of this view of kingship had been part of Christian theory since the time of Saint Augustine. But Hildebrand wanted to put the theory into practice, and in that respect he was very much a radical.

Once Hildebrand became pope the reform of the papacy took on a new dimension. Its goal was not only the moral regeneration of the clergy and the centralization of the church under papal authority. Gregory and his assistants began to insist upon "the freedom of the church." By this they meant the freedom of all churchmen to obey the newly codified canon law and freedom from lay control and interference by laymen.

"Freedom of the church" pointed to the end of lay investiture. Lay investiture meant the selection and appointment of church officials by secular authority, and ecclesiastical opposition to it was not new in the eleventh century. It had been part of church theory for centuries. Gregory's attempt to put theory into practice was a radical departure from tradition. Since feudal monarchs depended for the operation of their governments upon churchmen, Gregory's program seemed to spell disaster for stable royal administration. It provoked a terrible crisis.

The Controversy over Lay Investiture

In February 1075, Pope Gregory held a council at Rome. It published decrees not only against Nicolaism and simony, but also, and for the first time, against lay investiture:

If anyone henceforth shall receive a bishopric or abbey from the hands of a lay person, he shall not be considered as among the number of bishops and abbots. . . . Likewise if any emperor, king . . . or any one at all of the secular powers, shall presume to perform investiture with bishoprics or with any other ecclesiastical dignity . . . he shall feel the divine displeasure as well with regard to his body as to his other belongings.[8]

In short, clerics who accepted investiture from laymen were to be deposed, and laymen who invested clerics were to be excommunicated, that is, cut off from contact with other Christians.

The church's penalty of excommunication relied for its effectiveness on the support of public opinion. Since most Europeans favored Gregory's

moral reforms, he believed that excommunication would compel rulers to abide by his changes. Immediately, Henry IV in the German Empire, William the Conqueror in England, and Philip I in France protested, however.

The strongest reaction came from Germany. Henry IV (1056–1106) had strongly supported the moral aspects of church reform within the empire. In fact, they would not have achieved much success without his support. But of all the countries of Europe, the Holy Roman Empire most depended upon the services of churchmen. Governing a vast territory that contained a mixture of half Christianized and half pagan peoples, the emperor relied heavily upon the assistance of churchmen. His fledgling bureaucracy could not survive without the literacy and the administrative know-how of bishops and abbots. Naturally, then, he had selected and invested most of them.

Over and beyond the subject of lay investiture, however, a more fundamental issue was at stake. Gregory's decree raised the question of the proper role of the monarch in a Christian society. Did a king have ultimate jurisdiction over all his subjects, including the clergy? For centuries tradition had answered this question in favor of the ruler; so it is no wonder that Henry vigorously protested the papal assertions about lay investiture. By implication they undermined imperial power and sought to make papal authority supreme.

An increasingly bitter exchange of letters ensued. Gregory accused Henry of lack of respect for the papacy and insisted that disobedience to the pope was disobedience to God. Henry protested in a now-famous letter beginning, "Henry King not by usurpation, but by the pious ordination of God, to Hildebrand, now not Pope, but false monk."

Within the empire, those who had most to gain from the dispute quickly took advantage of it. In January 1076, in the southwestern German city of Worms on the Rhine, the German bishops who had been invested by Henry withdrew their allegiance from the pope. Gregory replied by excommunicating them and the emperor. The lay nobility delighted in the bind the emperor had been placed in. With Henry IV excommunicated and cast outside the fold of the Christian faithful, they did not have to obey him and could advance their own interests. Gregory hastened to support them. The Christmas season of 1075 witnessed an ironical situation within Germany: the greater clergy supported the emperor, while the great nobility favored the pope.

Henry outsmarted Gregory, however. Crossing the Alps in January, he approached the pope's lodgings at Canossa in northern Italy. According to legend, Henry stood for three days in the snow begging forgiveness. As a priest, Pope Gregory was obliged to grant forgiveness and readmit the emperor to the Christian fold. Henry's going to Canossa is often described as the most dramatic event in the High Middle Ages. Some historians claim that it marked the peak of papal power because the most powerful ruler in Europe, the Holy Roman emperor, had bowed before the pope. Actually, the victory went to Henry. When the sentence of excommunication was lifted, Henry regained the kingship and his authority over his rebellious subjects.

Dramatic though it was, the incident at Canossa settled nothing. The controversy over lay investiture and over the position of the king in Christian society continued. In 1080, Gregory VII again excommunicated and deposed the emperor, but this time it appeared to public opinion that Henry was being persecuted. The papal edicts had little effect. Moreover, Henry invaded Italy, captured Rome, and controlled the city when Gregory died in 1085, in exile. Henry won no lasting victory, however. Gregory's successors encouraged the revolt of Henry's sons against their father. With lay investiture the ostensible issue, the conflict between the papacy and the successors of Henry IV continued into the twelfth century.

TWELFTH-CENTURY ROMANESQUE CROZIER   This ivory crozier or staff shows Saint John baptizing Christ in the Jordan River, while the Holy Spirit in the form of a dove descends and God the Father blesses the event. Old Testament prophets with scrolls surround the head of the crozier. (Courtesy, World Heritage Museum. Photo: Caroline Buckler)

The kings of England and France were just as guilty of lay investiture as the German emperor. William the Conqueror (1066–1087) ignored papal decrees against the practice. He selected bishops and counted them among his most important tenants-in-chief. He presided over church councils and refused to allow papal letters or legates to enter England without his permission. He did work to achieve in England the moral goals of reform. Under the Conqueror's sons, William Rufus and Henry I, however, disagreement with the popes over lay investiture was long and violent. Philip I (1060–1108) of France also quarreled with Gregory, but the subject of their dispute was more Philip's adulterous marriage than lay investiture. Philip enjoyed the profits he received from the sale of church offices. And he probably thought that a church independent of royal control would be a real threat to the French monarchy. The conflict between the western rulers and Rome never reached the proportions of the dispute with the German emperor. Gregory VII and his successors had the diplomatic sense to avoid creating three enemies at once.

A long and exhausting propaganda campaign followed the events of 1075–76. Finally, in 1122, at a conference held at Worms, the issue was settled by compromise. The terms, as it happened, were the same as those agreed upon by the papacy and the English king Henry I in 1107. Bishops were to be chosen according to canon law, that is, by the clergy, in the presence of the emperor or his delegate. The emperor surrendered the right of investing bishops with the ring and staff. But, since lay rulers were permitted to be present at ecclesiastical elections and to accept or refuse feudal homage from the new prelates, they still possessed an effective veto over ecclesiastical appointments. At the same time, the papacy achieved technical success, because rulers could no longer invest. Papal power was enhanced. Neither side won a clear victory, however. The real winners in Germany were the great princes and the lay aristocracy.

The long controversy had tremendous social and political consequences in Germany. For half a century, between 1075 and 1125, civil war was chronic within the empire. Preoccupied with Italy and the quarrel with the papacy, there was little the emperors could do about it. To control their lands, great lords built castles, symbolizing their increased power and growing independence. (In no European country do more castles survive today.) The castles were both military strongholds and centers of administration for the surrounding territories. The German aristocracy subordinated the knights and reinforced their dependency with strong feudal ties. They reduced freemen and serfs to an extremely humble and servile position. Henry IV and Henry V (1106–1125) were compelled to surrender rights and privileges to the nobility. Particularism, localism, and feudal independence characterized the Holy Roman Empire in the High Middle Ages. The investiture controversy had a catastrophic effect there, severely retarding the development of a strong centralized monarchy.

The Papacy in the High Middle Ages

In the late eleventh century and throughout the twelfth, the papacy pressed Gregory's campaign for reform of the church. Pope Urban II laid the real foundations for the papal monarchy: he reorganized the papal writing office (the chancery) and papal finances. He recognized the college of cardinals as a definite consultative body. These agencies, together with the papal chapel, constituted the papal court, or curia. Urban II was the first pope to use the word "curia" to designate the central government of the Roman church. The term referred both to the papacy's administrative bureaucracy and to its court of law. The papal curia, although not fully developed until the mid-twelfth century, was the first well-organized institution of monarchial authority in medieval Europe.

The Roman curia had its greatest impact as a court of law. The highest ecclesiastical tribunal, it formulated canon law for all of Christendom. It was the instrument with which the popes pressed the goals of reform and centralized the church. The curia sent legates to hold councils in various parts of Europe. Councils published decrees and sought to enforce the law. When individuals in any part of Christian Europe felt they were being denied justice in their local church courts, they could appeal to Rome. Slowly but surely, in the High Middle Ages the papal curia developed into the court of final appeal for all of Christian Europe.

In the course of the twelfth century, the number of appeals to the curia steadily increased. The majority of cases related to disputes over church property or ecclesiastical elections and above all to questions of marriage and annulment. Significantly, most of the popes in the twelfth and thirteenth centuries were themselves canon lawyers. The most famous of them, the man whose pontificate represents the height of medieval papal power, was Innocent III (1198–1216).

Innocent judged a vast number of cases. He compelled King Philip Augustus of France to take back his wife, Ingeborg of Denmark. He arbitrated the rival claims of two disputants to the imperial crown of Germany. He forced King John of England to accept as archbishop of Canterbury a man whom John did not really want. Innocent exerted papal authority in the Iberian Peninsula, in Norway and Sweden, in the Balkans, and even in distant Cyprus and Armenia.

By the early thirteenth century, papal efforts for reform begun more than a century before had attained a phenomenal success. The popes themselves were men of high principles and strict moral behavior. The frequency of clerical marriage had declined considerably. The level of violence had dropped sharply. Simony was much more the exception than the rule. The church enjoyed a huge success in most places and provided leadership for Christian Europe.

Yet the seeds of future difficulties were being planted. As the volume of appeals to Rome multiplied, so did the size of papal bureaucracy. As the number of lawyers increased, so did concern for legal niceties and technicalities, fees, and church offices. As early as the mid-twelfth century, John of Salisbury, an Englishman working in the papal curia, had written a blistering critique of the expanding curial bureaucracy. The people, he wrote, condemned the curia for its greed and its indifference to human suffering. Nevertheless, the trend continued.

Thirteenth-century popes, a long series of canon lawyers, devoted their attention to the bureaucracy and to their conflicts with the German emperor Frederick II (1215–1250). Some, like Gregory IX (1227–1241), abused their prerogatives to such an extent that their moral impact was seriously weakened. Even worse, Innocent IV (1243–1254) used secular weapons, including military force, to maintain his leadership. These badly damaged papal prestige and influence. By the early fourteenth century, the seeds of disorder would grow into a vast and sprawling tree, and once again cries for reform would be heard.

NOTES

1. Quoted by R. S. Lopez, "Of Towns and Trade," in R. S. Hoyt, ed., *Life and Thought in the Early Middle Ages,* University of Minnesota Press, Minneapolis, 1967, p. 33.

2. H. Pirenne, *Economic and Social History of Medieval Europe,* Harcourt Brace, New York, 1956, p. 53.

3. D. Douglas and G. W. Greenaway, eds., *English Historical Documents,* Eyre & Spottiswoode, London, 1961, 2.969.

4. H. Rothwell, ed., *English Historical Documents,* Eyre & Spottiswoode, London, 1975, 3.854.

5. Douglas and Greenaway, 2.956–961.

6. M. M. Postan, *The Medieval Economy and Society: An Economic History of Britain in the Middle Ages,* Penguin Books, Baltimore, 1975, pp. 213–214.

7. R. S. Lopez, "The Trade of Medieval Europe: The South," in M. M. Postan and E. E. Rich, eds., *The Cambridge Economic History of Europe,* Cambridge University Press, Cambridge, 1952, 2.289.

8. B. D. Hill, ed., *Church and State in the Middle Ages,* John Wiley & Sons, New York, 1970, p. 68.

SUGGESTED READING

In addition to the references given in the Notes, the curious student will find a fuller treatment of many of the topics raised in this chapter in the following works.

Both C. D. Burns, *The First Europe* (1948), and G. Barraclough, *The Crucible of Europe: The Ninth and Tenth Centuries in European History** (1976), survey the entire period and emphasize the transformation from a time of anarchy to one of great creativity; Barraclough also stresses the importance of stable government. His *The Origins of Modern Germany** (1963) is essential for central and eastern Europe. For the social significance of the peace movements, see H. E. J. Cowdray, "The Peace and the Truce of God in the Eleventh Century," *Past and Present* 46 (1970): 42–67.

The role of climate as it affected population and the economic growth of Europe is discussed in the remarkable work of E. L. Ladurie, *Times of Feast, Times of Famine: A History of Climate since the Year 1000,* B. Bray, trans. (1971). R. Latouche, *The Birth of the Western Economy: Economic Aspects of the Dark Ages** (1966), traces the development of economic activities through the end of the eleventh century in fascinating detail. An excellent account of agricultural changes and their sociological implications is given in G. Duby, *The Early Growth of the European Economy: Warriors and Peasants from the Seventh to the Twelfth Century* (1974).

Students interested in the beginnings of medieval towns and cities will discover how historians use the evidence of numismatics, archaeology, tax records, and geography, as well as laws, in J. F. Benton, ed., *Town Origins: The Evidence of Medieval England** (1968). H. Pirenne, *Medieval Cities** (1956), is an important and standard work. H. Saalman, *Medieval Cities** (1968), provides a fresh description of the layout of medieval cities and shows how they were places of production and exchange. All will enjoy the highly readable account of J. and F. Gies, *Life in a Medieval City** (1973).

For the Christian church, the papacy, and ecclesiastical developments, G. Barraclough's richly illustrated *The Medieval Papacy** (1968) is a good general survey that emphasizes the development of administrative bureaucracy. The advanced student may tackle W. Ullmann, *A Short History of the Papacy in the Middle Ages* (1972). S. Williams, ed., *The Gregorian Epoch: Reformation, Revolution, Reaction?** (1964), contains significant interpretations of the eleventh-century reform movements. Ullmann's *The Growth of Papal Government in the Middle Ages* (rev. ed., 1970) traces the evolution of papal law and government, while G. Tellenbach, *Church, State, and Christian Society at the Time of the Investiture Contest* (1959), emphasizes the revolutionary aspects of the Gregorian reform program. The relationship of the monks to the ecclesiastical crisis of the late eleventh century is discussed by N. F. Cantor, "The Crisis of Western Monasticism," *The American Historical Review* 66 (1960), and by H. E. J. Cowdray, *The Cluniacs and the Gregorian Reform* (1970), an impressive but difficult study. J. B. Russell, *A History of Medieval Christianity: Prophecy and Order** (1968) is an important and sensitively written work.

*Available in paperback.

Chapter 9

LIFE IN CHRISTIAN EUROPE IN THE

HIGH MIDDLE AGES

he revival of trade and commerce in the eleventh century brought into being a new class of merchants and businessmen. Traders, merchants and city dwellers, however, were not typical of medieval society. They may have represented the wave of the future, but in the twelfth century that future was far in the distance. Some historians, trying to show the links between medieval and modern urban and industrialized society, have concentrated their attention on the medieval commercial classes. In doing so, they have presented a distorted and anachronistic picture of medieval society. Other scholars have painted medieval society as static and unchanging. This picture also is inaccurate, because there was a good deal of movement, change, and migration.

In his biography of the Anglo-Saxon king Alfred (871–899), the monk Asser described Christian society as divided among those who pray (the monks), those who fight (the nobles), and those who work (the peasants). This description was widely accepted and frequently repeated by other writers in the High Middle Ages. It set forth the basic sociological division of the medieval world. This division does not take into consideration the emerging commercial classes. But medieval people were usually contemptuous (at least officially) of profit-making activities, and long after the appearance of commercial and urban groups, the general medieval view of Christian society remained the one formulated by Asser in the tenth century.

The most representative figures of Christian society in the High Middle Ages were the peasants, the monks, and the nobles. How did these people actually live? What were their major preoccupations and lifestyles? To what extent was social mobility possible for them? These are the questions this chapter seeks to answer.

THE THREE CLASSES. Medieval people believed that their society was divided among warriors, clerics, and workers, here represented by a monk, a knight, and a peasant. The new commercial class had no recognized place in the agrarian military world. (The British Museum)

According to Asser, the most important service was performed by the monks. But the largest and economically most productive group was the peasants. The peasantry of Europe, the men and women who worked the land in the twelfth and thirteenth centuries, made up the overwhelming majority of the population, probably more than 90 percent. Yet is is difficult to form a coherent picture of them. The records that form the historical sources were written by and for the aristocratic classes. Since the farmers did not perform what were considered "noble" deeds, the aristocratic monks and clerics did not waste time or precious paper and ink on them. When the peasants were mentioned, it was usually with contempt or in terms of the services and obligations they owed. Usually — but not always.

In the early twelfth century, Honorius, a monk and teacher at Autun who composed a popular handbook of sermons, wrote: "What do you say about the agricultural classes? Most of them will be saved because they live simply and feed God's people by means of their sweat."[1] This sentiment circulated widely. Honorius's comment suggests that the peasant workers may have been appreciated and in a sense respected more than is generally believed.

In the last twenty-five years, historians have made remarkable advances in their knowledge of the medieval European peasantry. They have been able to do this by bringing fresh and different questions to old documents, by paying greater attention to such natural factors as geography and climate, and by studying demographic changes. Nevertheless, the new information raises additional questions, and a good deal is still unknown.

In 1932, a distinguished economic historian wrote, "The student of medieval social and economic history who commits himself to a generalization is digging a pit into which he will later assuredly fall and nowhere does the pit yawn deeper than in the realm of rural history."[2] This remark is virtually as true today as when it was written. It is, therefore, important to remember that peasants' conditions varied widely across Europe, that geographical and climatic features as much as human initiative and local custom determined the peculiar quality of rural life. The problems that faced the farmer in Yorkshire, England, where the soil was rocky and the climate rainy were very different from those of the Italian peasant in the sun-drenched Po valley.

Another difficulty in the study of the peasants has been historians' tendency to group them all into one social class. That is a serious mistake. It is true that medieval theologians who made the divisions today called sociological simply lumped everyone who worked the land into the category of "those who work." In actual fact, however, there were many gradations, classes, and levels of peasants, ranging all the way from complete slaves to free and very rich farmers. The period from 1050 to 1250 was one of considerable fluidity with no little social mobility. The status of the peasantry varied widely all across Europe.

Slavery, Serfdom, and Upward Mobility

Slaves were found in western Europe in the High Middle Ages, but in steadily declining numbers. The word "slave" derives from "Slav," revealing the widespread trade in men and women from the Slavic areas in the early Middle Ages. Around the year 1200, there were in aristocratic and upper-middle-class households in Provence, Catalonia, Italy, and Germany a few slaves — blond Slavs from the Baltic, olive-skinned Syrians, and blacks from Africa.

Since the time of the ancient world, it had been a universally accepted practice to reduce conquered peoples to slavery. The church had long taught that all baptized Christians were brothers in Christ and that all Christians belonged to one "international"

community. Although the church never issued a blanket condemnation of slavery, it did vigorously oppose the enslaving of Christians. In attacking the enslavement of Christians and in criticizing the reduction of pagans and infidels, the church made a contribution to the development of human liberty.

In western Europe during the Middle Ages legal language differed considerably from place to place, and the distinction between the slave and the serf was not always clear. Both lacked freedom and were subject to the arbitrary will of one man, the lord. Freedom meant the power to do as one wished, and that neither the serf nor the slave could do. A serf, however, could not be bought and sold like an animal or an inanimate object, as the slave could.

The serf was required to perform labor services on the lord's land. The number of workdays varied, but it was usually three days a week, except in the planting or harvest seasons, when it would be more. Serfs frequently had to pay arbitrary taxes. When a man married, he had to pay his lord a fee. When he died, his son or heir had to pay an inheritance tax to inherit his parcels of land. The precise amounts of taxes paid to the lord on these important occasions depended upon local custom and tradition. Every manor had its particular obligations.

A free person had to do none of these things. For his or her landholding, rent had to be paid to the lord, and that was often the sole obligation. A free person could move and live as he or she wished. Serfs were tied to the land, and serfdom was a hereditary condition. A person born a serf was likely to die a serf, though many did secure their freedom. About 1187, Glanvill, an official of King Henry II and an expert on English law, described the ways in which villeins (literally, inhabitants of small villages) — as English serfs were called — could be made free:

A person of villein status can be made free in several ways. For example, his lord, wishing him to achieve freedom from the villeinage by which he is subject to him, may quit-claim him from himself and his heirs; or he may give or sell him to another with intent to free him. It should be noted, however, that no person of villein status can seek his freedom with his own money, for in such a case he could, according to the law and custom of the realm, be recalled to villeinage by his lord, because all the chattels of a villein are deemed to such an extent the property of his lord that he cannot redeem himself from villeinage with his own money, as against his lord. If, however, a third party provides the money and buys the villein in order to free him, then he can maintain himself for ever in a state of freedom as against his lord who sold him. . . . If any villein stays peaceably for a year and a day in a privileged town and is admitted as a citizen into their commune, that is to say, their gild, he is thereby freed from villeinage.[3]

Many energetic and hardworking serfs acquired their freedom in the High Middle Ages. More than anything else, the economic revival beginning in the eleventh century advanced the cause of individual liberty. The revival saw the rise of towns, increased land productivity, the growth of long-distance trade, and the development of a money economy.

Another opportunity for increased personal freedom, or at least for a reduction in traditional manorial obligations and dues, was provided by the waste and forest land reclaimed in the eleventh and twelfth centuries. Immigration and resettlement on newly cleared land offered unusual possibilities for younger sons and for those living in areas of acute land shortage or on overworked, exhausted soil. Historians still do not know very much about this movement: how the new frontier territory was advertised, how men were recruited, how they and their households were transported, and how the new lands were distributed. It is certain, however, that there was significant migration and that only a lord with considerable authority over a wide territory could support and sponsor such a movement.

As land long considered poor was brought under cultivation, there was a steady nibbling away at the wasteland on the edge of old villages. Clearings were made in forests. Marshes and fens were drained and slowly made arable. This type of agricultural advancement frequently improved the peasants' social and legal condition. A serf could clear a patch of fen or forest land, make it productive, and, through prudent saving, buy more land and eventually purchase his freedom. There were in the thirteenth century many free tenants on the lands of the bishop of Ely in eastern England, tenants who had moved into the area in the twelfth century and drained the fens. Likewise, settlers on the low lands of the abbey of Bourbourg in Flanders, who had erected dikes and extended the arable, possessed hereditary tenures by 1159. They secured personal liberty and owed their overlord only small payments.

The condition of peasants who remained in the villages of their birth often was made easier because landlords, threatened with the loss of serfs, relaxed ancient obligations and duties. While it would be unwise to exaggerate the degree of social advancement offered by the settling of new territories, frontier lands in the Middle Ages did provide opportunities for upward mobility.

The Manor

In the High Middle Ages, most European peasants, free and unfree, lived on estates called manors. The word "manor" derives from a Latin term meaning "dwelling," "residence," or "homestead." In the twelfth century it meant the estate of a lord and his dependent tenants.

The manor was the basic unit of medieval rural organization and the center of rural life. All other generalizations about manors and manorial life have to be limited by the quality of the soil, local climatic conditions, and different methods of cultivation. Some manors were vast, covering several thousand acres of farmland; others were quite small, no more than 120 acres. A manor might include several villages or none at all, but usually it comprised a single village and was subject to one lord (see Figure 9.1). Village life differed greatly from town life: villagers lived in a rural world and worked the land; townspeople lived in an urban environment and were involved in the production and exchange of goods.

The arable land of the manor was divided into two sections. The demesne, or home farm, was cultivated for the lord. The other part was held by the peasantry. Usually, the peasants' portion was the larger amount, held on condition that they cultivate the lord's demesne. All the arable, both lord's and peasants', was divided into strips, and the strips of any individual were scattered throughout the manor. All peasants cooperated in the cultivation of the land, working it as a group. This meant that all shared in any disaster as well as in any large harvest.

A manor usually included pasture or meadow-land for the grazing of cattle, sheep, and sometimes goats. Often the manor had some forest land. Forests had enormous economic importance: they were the source of wood for building and resin for lighting; ash for candles, and ash and lime for fertilizers and all sorts of sterilizing products; wood for fuel and bark for the manufacture of rope. From the forests came the wood for the construction of barrels, vats, and all sorts of storage containers. Last but hardly least, the forests were used for the feeding of pigs, cattle, and domestic animals on nuts, roots, and wild berries. If the manor was intersected by a river, then it had a welcome source of fish and eels.

Agricultural Methods

The fundamental objective of all medieval agriculture was the production of an adequate food supply. According to the method historians have called the open-field system, at any one time half the manorial land was under cultivation and the other half lay fallow. The length of the fallow period was usually one year. Every peasant farmer had strips scattered in both halves. One part of the land under cultivation was sown with winter cereals, such as wheat and rye, the other with spring crops, such as peas, beans, and barley. What was planted in a particular field varied each year when the crops were rotated.

Local needs, the fertility of the soil, and dietary customs determined what was planted and the method of crop rotation. Where one or several manors belonged to a great aristocratic establishment, such as the abbey of Cluny, where the need for oats for horses was great, then more of the arable land would be planted in oats than in other cereals. Where the land was extremely fertile, such as the Alsace region of France, a biennial cycle was used: one crop of wheat was sown and harvested every other year, and in alternate years all the land lay fallow. The author of an English agricultural treatise advised his readers to stick to a two-field method of cultivation and insisted that a rich harvest every second year was preferable to two mediocre ones every three years. Farmers everywhere obviously sought to use the land in the most productive way and to get the greatest output.

Nor were they ignorant of the value of animal fertilizers. Chicken manure, because of its high nitrogen content, was the richest but came in small quantities. Sheep manure was also valuable. Frequently, gifts to English Cistercian monasteries were given on condition that the monks' sheep be allowed to graze at certain periods on the benefactor's demesne. Because cattle were fed on the common pasture and were rarely stabled, gathering

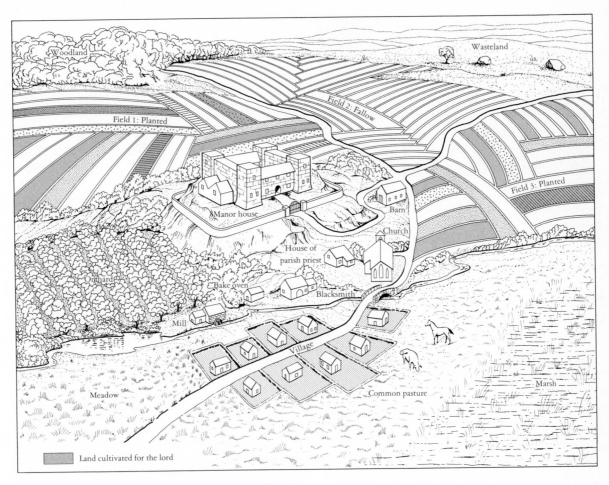

Field 1: Planted

Field 2: Fallow

Field 3: Planted

Woodland

Wasteland

Manor house

Barn

Church

House of
parish priest

Orchard

Bake oven

Blacksmith

Mill

Village

Meadow

Common pasture

Marsh

Land cultivated for the lord

FIGURE 9.1 A MEDIEVAL MANOR. The basic unit of rural organization and the center of life for most people, the manor constituted the medieval peasants' world. Since manors had to be economically self-sufficient, life meant endless toil.

their manure was laborious and time-consuming. Nevertheless, whenever possible, animal manure was gathered and thinly spread. So also was house garbage—eggshells, fruit cores, onion skins—that had disintegrated on a compost heap.

Tools and farm implements are often shown in medieval manuscripts. There is a major problem in accepting such representations at face value, however. Rather than going out into a field to look at a tool, medieval artists simply copied drawings from classical and other treatises. Thus, a picture of a plow or harrow in a book written in the Ile-de-France may actually show a tool or method of

SHEEPSHEARING. After the sheep was tied up, the farmer clipped the wool and bagged it. English wool was internationally famous for its fine quality, and the English and the Flemish economies depended upon the wool trade. (The British Museum)

farming used in England or Italy a half century before.

In the early twelfth century there was a great increase in the production of iron. There is considerable evidence for the manufacture of iron plowshares (the part of the moldboard that cuts the furrow into and grinds up the earth). In the thirteenth century the wooden plow continued to be the basic instrument of agricultural production, but its edge was strengthened with iron. Only after the start of the fourteenth century, when lists of manorial equipment began to be kept, is there evidence for pitchforks, spades, axes, and harrows. Harrows were used to smooth out the soil after it had been broken up. A crude harrow is illustrated in the picture of the month of October in the *Très riches heures du duc de Berry,* completed in the mid-fifteenth century. The harrow is made of wood and weighted down with a large stone to force it to cut more deeply into the earth.

The harrow was drawn by horses. The use of horses rather than oxen in the agricultural economy increased in the later thirteenth century. Horses were expensive because they had to be shod (another indication of increased iron production) and because the oats they ate were costly. They represented an important element in the improvement of the medieval agricultural economy. Indeed, some scholars believe that the use of the horse in agriculture is one of the decisive ways in which western Europe advanced over the rest of the world. Because of their greater strength, horses brought far greater efficiency to farming than oxen. But horses were a large investment, perhaps comparable to a modern tractor. Nor were they universally adopted. For example, the Mediterranean countries did not use horsepower. And, at the same time, tools remained pitifully primitive.

Agricultural yields varied widely from place to place and from year to year. Even with good iron tools, horsepower, and careful use of seed and fertilizer, medieval peasants were at the mercy of the

LATE MEDIEVAL WHEELLESS PLOW.   This plow has a sharp-pointed colter, which cut the earth while the attached mold-board lifted, turned, and pulverized the soil. As the man steers the plow, his wife prods the oxen. The caption reads, "God speed the plow, and send us corn (wheat) now." (Trinity College Library, Cambridge)

weather, just as farmers are today, despite their sophisticated machinery. Even today, lack of rain or too much rain can be disastrous and cause terrible financial loss and extreme hardship. How much more vulnerable was the medieval peasant with his primitive tools! By twentieth-century standards medieval agricultural yields were very low. The inadequate preparation of the soil, the poor selection of seed, the lack of sufficient manure — all made this virtually inevitable. Yet there was striking improvement over time.

Between the ninth and early thirteenth centuries, it appears that the yield of cereals approximately doubled, and on the best-managed estates, for every bushel of seed planted, the farmer harvested five bushels of grain. This is a very tentative conclusion. Because of the great scarcity of manorial inventories before the thirteenth century, the student of medieval agriculture has great difficulty determining how much the land produced. The author of a treatise on land husbandry, Walter of Henley, who lived in the mid-thirteenth century, wrote that the land should yield three times its seed; that amount was necessary for sheer survival. The surplus would be sold to grain merchants in the nearest town. Townspeople were wholly dependent on the surrounding countryside for food, which could not be shipped a long distance. A poor harvest meant that both town and rural people suffered.

Grain yields were probably greatest on the large manorial estates, where there was more professional management. For example, on the estates of Battle Abbey in Sussex, England, there was a very high yield of wheat, rye, and oats in the century and a half between 1350 and 1499. This was due to heavy seeding, good crop rotation, and the use of manure from the monastery's sheep flocks. Battle Abbey's yields seem to have been double those of smaller, less efficiently run farms. In contrast, a modern Illinois farmer expects to get 40 bushels of soybeans for every bushel of seeds planted. The farmer expects a yield of 150 bushels of corn and 50 bushels of wheat for every one planted. Of course, modern costs of production in labor, seed, and fertilizer are quite high, but this yield is at least ten times that of the farmer's medieval ancestor. The average manor probably got a yield of 5:1 in the thirteenth century.[4] As low as that may seem by current standards, it marked a rise in the level of productivity equal to that of the years just before the great agricultural revolution of the eighteenth century.

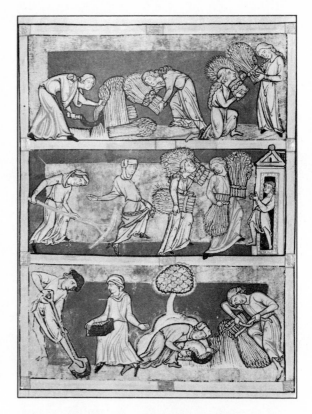

WORKING IN THE FIELDS. Women shared with men all the difficult agricultural work. These farm scenes show women hoeing, sowing seed, cutting and tying the grain, and carrying it to the mill. Although the sickles and the spade appear to have an iron tip, the hoe is entirely wooden. (Rheinisches Landesmuseum, Bonn)

Life on the Manor

Life for most people in medieval Europe meant country life. A person's horizons were largely restricted to the manor on which he or she was born. People rarely traveled more than twenty-five miles beyond their villages. Everyone's world was small, narrow, and provincial in the original sense of that word: limited by the extents of the province. This way of life did not have entirely unfortunate results. A farmer had a strong sense of family and the certainty of its support and help in time of trouble. People knew what their life's work would be — the same as their mother's or father's. They had a sense of geographical place, and pride in that place was reflected in the adornment of the village church. Religion and the village gave a sure sense of identity and with it psychological peace. Modern people — urban, isolated, industrialized, rootless, and thoroughly secular — have lost many of these reinforcements.

On the other hand, even aside from the unending physical labor, life on the manor was dull. Medieval men and women must have had a crushing sense of frustration. They lived lives of quiet desperation. Often they sought escape in heavy drinking. English judicial records of the thirteenth century reveal a surprisingly large number of deaths labeled "accidental." Strong, robust, and commonsensical farmers do not ordinarily fall down on their knives and stab themselves, or slip out of a boat and drown, or get lost in the woods on a winter's night, or fall from their horses and get trampled. They were probably drunk. Many of these accidents occurred, so the court records say, "coming from an ale." Brawls and violent fights were frequent at taverns. They reflect in part the drudgery of life and simple human frustration.

Women played a significant role in the agricultural life of medieval Europe. This obvious fact is often overlooked by historians. Women shared with their fathers and husbands the backbreaking labor in the fields, work that was probably all the more difficult for them because of weaker muscular development and frequent pregnancies. The adage from the Book of Proverbs (19.14) — "Houses and riches are the inheritances of fathers: but a prudent wife is from the lord" — was seldom more true than in an age when the wife's prudent management was often all that separated a household from starvation in a year of crisis — and starvation was a very real danger to the peasantry until the eighteenth century.

Women managed the house. The size and quality of the peasants' houses varied according to their relative prosperity, and that prosperity usually depended upon the amount of land held. Poorer peasants lived in windowless cottages built of wood and clay or wattle and thatched with straw. These cottages consisted of one large room that served as the kitchen and living quarters for all. Everyone slept there. The house had an earthen floor and a fireplace. The lack of windows meant that the room was very sooty. A trestle table, several stools, one or two beds, and a chest for storing clothes constituted the furniture. A shed attached to the house provided storage for tools and shelter for animals. A prosperous peasant added rooms and furniture as they could be afforded, and some wealthy peasants in the early fourteenth century had two-story houses with separate bedrooms for the parents and the children.

Every house had in front or back a small clearing of land used for a garden and an outbuilding. Onions, garlic, turnips, and carrots were grown. All these vegetables could be stored through the winter months, either in the main room of the dwelling or in the shed attached to it. Cabbage was raised almost everywhere and, after being shredded, salted, and packed in vats in hot water, was turned into kraut. Peasants ate vegetables not necessarily because they appreciated their importance for good health but because there was usually little else. Some manors were fortunate in having fruit trees — apple, cherry, and pear in northern Europe; lemon, lime, and olive in the south. These yielded their produce in the spring and summer months, but because of the high price of sugar, when it was available, fruit could not be preserved. Preserving and storing other foods were the basic responsibility of the women and children.

Women had to know something about the production of beer — the universal drink of the common people in northern Europe. The housewife had to know the correct proportions of barley, water, yeast, and hops that went into the manufacture of beer. By modern American standards the rate of beer consumption was heroic. Each monk of Abingdon Abbey in England in the twelfth century was allotted three gallons a day, and a man working in the fields for ten or twelve hours a day probably drank much more.

The mainstay of the diet for peasants everywhere — and for all other classes — was bread. It was a hard, black substance made of barley, millet, and oats — rarely of expensive wheat flour. The housewife usually baked the supply for the household once a week. Where sheep, cows, or goats were raised, she also made cheese. In places like the Bavarian Alps region of southern Germany, where hundreds of sheep grazed on the mountainsides, or at Cheddar in southwestern England, cheese was a large and valuable supplement to the diet.

The diet of those living in an area with access to a river, lake, or stream would be supplemented with fish, which could be preserved by salting. In many places there were severe laws against hunting and trapping in the forests. Deer, wild boars, and other game were strictly reserved for the king and nobility. Those laws were flagrantly violated, however, and stolen rabbits and wild game often found

their way to the peasants' tables. Woods and forests also provided nuts, which the housewives and small children would gather in the fall.

The list of peasant obligations and services to the lord, such as the one below from a manor in Battle Abbey in England, commonly included the payment of chickens and eggs:

John of Coyworth holds a house and thirty acres of land, and owes yearly 2 p at Easter and Michaelmas; and he owes a cock and two hens at Christmas, of the value of 4 d.[5]

Chickens and eggs must have been a valuable source of protein in the prudently managed household. Indeed, some scholars believe that by the mid-thirteenth century there was a great increase in the consumption of meat generally. If so, this improvement in the diet is further evidence of a better standard of living.

Breakfast, which was eaten at dawn before the farmer departed for his work, might well consist of bread, an onion (easily stored through the winter months), and a piece of cheese, all of it washed down with milk or beer. Farmers then as now ate their main meal around noon. This was often soup — a thick *potage* of boiled cabbage, onions, turnips, and peas, seasoned with a bone or perhaps a sliver of meat. The evening meal, taken at sunset, consisted of leftovers from the noon meal, with perhaps bread, cheese, milk, or beer. Except for the rare chicken or the illegally caught wild game, meat appeared on the table only on the great feast days of the Christian year: Christmas, Easter, and Pentecost. Then, the meat was likely to be pork from the pig that had been slaughtered in the fall and salted for the rest of the year.

Children, once they were able to walk, helped their parents in the hundreds of chores that had to be done. Small children were set to collecting eggs, if the family possessed chickens, or gathering twigs and sticks for firewood. As they grew older, children had more responsible tasks, such as weeding the family vegetable garden, milking the cows, shearing the sheep, cutting wood for fires, helping with the planting or harvesting, and assisting their mothers in the endless tasks involved in baking, cooking, and preserving. Because of poor diet, terrible sanitation, and the lack of medical care, the death rate of children was phenomenally high.

Popular Religion

Apart from the land and the weather and the peculiar conditions that existed on each manor, the Christian religion had the greatest impact on the daily lives of ordinary people in the High Middle Ages. Religious practices varied widely from country to country and even from province to province. Nowhere was religion a one-hour-on-Sunday or High Holy Days affair. Rather, Christian practices and attitudes shaded and permeated virtually all aspects of everyday life.

In the ancient world participation in religious rituals was a public and social duty. As the Germanic and Celtic peoples were Christianized, their new religion became a fusion of Jewish, pagan, Roman, and Christian practices. In the High Middle Ages, religious rituals and practices represented a synthesis of many elements, and all people shared as a natural and public duty in the religious life of the community.

The village church was the center of manorial life—social, political, and economic, as well as religious. Most of the important events of a person's life took place in or around the church. A person was baptized there, within hours of birth. Men and women confessed their sins to the village priest there and received, usually at Easter and

THIRTEENTH-CENTURY CRUCIFIX. Christian teaching in the High Middle Ages stressed the humanity, compassion, and understanding of Christ, as the face of Christ on this richly enamelled crucifix suggests. (Courtesy, World Heritage Museum. Photo: Caroline Buckler)

Christmas, the sacrament of the Eucharist. In front of the church, the bishop reached down from his horse and confirmed a person as a Christian by placing his hands over the candidate's head and making the sign of the cross on the forehead. (Bishops Thomas Becket of Canterbury and Hugh of Lincoln were considered especially holy men, because they got down from their horses to confirm.) A young man courted his girl in the churchyard and, so the sermons of the priests complained, made love to her in the church cemetery. They were married before the altar in the church.

The stone in the church altar contained relics of the saints, often a local saint to whom the church itself had been dedicated. In the church women and men could pray to the Virgin and the local saints. The saints had once lived on earth and thus could well understand human problems. They could be helpful intercessors with Christ or God the Father. According to official church doctrine, the center of the Christian religious life was the mass, the re-enactment of Christ's sacrifice on the cross. Every Sunday and on holy days, the villager stood at mass or squatted on the floor (there were no chairs), breaking the painful routine of work. Finally, people wanted to be buried in the church cemetery, close to the holy place and the saints believed to reside there.

The church served as the center for village social life. The feasts that accompanied baptisms, weddings, funerals, and other celebrations were commonly held in the churchyard. From the liturgy, drama developed. Medieval drama originated within the church. Mystery plays, based on biblical episodes, were performed first in the sanctuary, then on the church porch, finally in the village square, which was often in front of the west door.

From the church porch the priest read to his parishioners orders and messages from royal and ecclesiastical authorities. Royal judges traveling on circuit opened their courts on the church porch. The west front of the church, with its scenes of the

Last Judgment, was the background against which the justices disposed of civil and criminal cases. Farmers from outlying districts pushed their carts to the marketplace in the village square near the west front. In busy mercantile centers, such as London, business agreements and commercial exchanges were made in the aisles of the church itself, as at St. Paul's.

Popular religion consisted largely of rituals heavy with symbolism. Shortly after a woman had successfully delivered a child, she was "churched." This was a ceremony of thanksgiving, based on the Jewish rite of purification. When a child was baptized, a few grains of salt were dropped on its tongue. Salt had been the symbol of purity, strength, and incorruptibility for the ancient Hebrews, and the Romans had used it in their sacrifices. It was used in Christian baptism both to drive away demons and to strengthen the infant in its new faith.

Before slicing a loaf of bread, the good wife tapped the sign of the cross on it with her knife. Before the planting, the village priest customarily went out and sprinkled the fields with water, symbolizing refreshment and life. The system of dating, the entire calendar, was designed with reference to the great festivals of the Christian year—Easter, Christmas, and Pentecost. Saints' days were legion. Everyone participated in village processions. The colored vestments the priests wore at mass gave the villagers a sense of the changing seasons of the church's liturgical year. The signs and symbols of Christianity were everywhere.

Was popular religion entirely a matter of ritualistic formulas and ceremonies? What did the peasants actually *believe?* They accepted what family, customs, and the clergy ingrained in them. They learned the fundamental teachings of the church from the homilies given by the village priests. They grasped the meaning of biblical stories and church doctrines from the paintings on the village church wall. If their parish were wealthy, the scenes in the church's stained-glass windows instructed them. Illiterate and uneducated, they certainly could not reason out the increasingly sophisticated propositions of clever theologians. Still, scriptural references and proverbs sprinkled everyone's language. Christianity was a basic element in the common people's culture; indeed, it was their culture.

At the same time, they had a strong sense of the universal presence of God. The peasants believed that God intervened directly in human affairs and could reward the virtuous and bring peace, health, and material prosperity. They believed, too, that God punished men and women for their sins with disease, poor harvests, and the destructions of war. Sin was caused by the Devil, who lurked everywhere. The Devil constantly incited people to evil deeds and sin, especially sins of the flesh. Sin frequently took place in the dark. Thus, evil and the Devil were connected in the peasant's mind with darkness or blackness. In medieval literature the Devil often appears as a Negro, an identification that has had a profound and sorry impact on Western racial attitudes.

There were many things the peasants could not understand. They saw that life was not only hard but short. Few lived much beyond the age of forty. They had a great fear of nature: storms, thunder, and lightning terrified them. They had a terror of hell, whose geography and awful tortures they knew from sermons. And they certainly saw that the virtuous were not always rewarded but sometimes suffered considerably on earth. These things, which they could not explain, bred in them a deep pessimism.

No wonder, then, that pilgrimages to shrines of the saints were so popular. They brought hope in a world of gloom. They satisfied a strong emotional need. They meant change, adventure, excitement. The church granted indulgences to those who

BURIAL OF CHRIST. Carved in a piece of ivory 5″ × 2½″, this detailed scene of Christ's burial reflects both the profound faith of the age and the incredible skill of medieval artists. (Courtesy, World Heritage Museum. Photo: Caroline Buckler)

visited the shrines of great saints. Indulgences provided only a reduction of the priest-imposed penalties for sin, but people equated them with salvation. They generally believed that the indulgence received from a pilgrimage reduced the amount of time that one would spend in hell. Pilgrimages promised salvation. Vast numbers embarked on pilgrimages to the shrines of St. James at Santiago de Compostella in Spain, Thomas Becket at Canterbury, St.-Gilles de Provence, and Saints Peter and Paul at Rome. Pilgrimages are a striking aspect of medieval popular religion.

THOSE WHO FIGHT

In the High Middle Ages members of the nobility were those who fought. From the nobility also came the vast majority of monks and clerics, and from the nobility came the opinions, attitudes, and behavior that, to a considerable extent, shaped the lifestyles of other classes.

The word "nobility" refers to a legal status that a person acquired automatically at birth or received from a king or ruler as a reward for outstanding fighting skill or unusual services. The word "aristocrat" derives from a Greek term meaning "the best." Nobles considered themselves aristocrats, but only toward the end of the twelfth century did the European nobility begin to develop a definite class consciousness. Nobles had a way of life based on a chivalric code and the observance — at least among those they considered social equals — of ideals of courtesy, generosity, graciousness, and hospitality. Most monks came from noble families, and the opinions they expressed were aristocratic.

The aristocratic nobility, although a small part of the total population, strongly influenced all aspects of culture — political, economic, religious, educational, and artistic. For that reason European society in the twelfth and thirteenth centuries may be termed aristocratic. In spite of scientific, industrial,

and political revolutions, the nobility held the real political and social power in Europe down to the nineteenth century. In order to account for this continuing influence in later centuries, it is important to understand its development in the High Middle Ages.

The noble was almost always a military man, and he frequently used the Latin title *miles,* or knight, to designate his nobility. He possessed a horse and a sword. These, together with the leisure time in which to learn how to use them in combat, were the visible signs of his nobility.

Members of the nobility enjoyed a special legal status. The noble was free personally and in his possessions. He had immunity from almost all outside authorities. He was limited only by his military obligation to king, duke, or prince. As the result of his liberty, he had certain rights and responsibilities. He raised troops and commanded them in the field. He held courts that dispensed a sort of justice. Sometimes he coined money intended to circulate within his territories. He conducted relations with outside powers. He was the political, military, and judicial lord of the people who settled on his lands. He made political decisions affecting them, he resolved disputes among them, and he protected them in time of attack. The liberty of the noble and the privileges that went with his liberty were inheritable; they were perpetuated by blood and not by wealth alone.

Women whose fathers or husbands were noble were considered noble too, but not in their own right. Noble ladies often performed the political and military obligations of the men of their class, but there is no evidence of a woman being raised to the nobility. The values of a society are largely determined by its needs, and in the High Middle Ages needs were military. Fighting was usually done by men, and so men were given noble status.

In the course of the twelfth century, the aristocratic knights slowly evolved into a distinct and closely knit class with feelings of superiority and an attitude of exclusivity. They had a common culture based on a consciousness of family, the veneration of ancestors, and a sense of their own worth. Nobles almost always married within their class. Those who were or who aspired to be aristocrats wanted to possess a castle, the symbol of feudal independence and of a military lifestyle.

By the twelfth century, all men who legally and socially were noble had been formally knighted and could use the titles *dominus* and *messire,* which mean "lord." The ceremony of knighthood was one of the most important in a man's life. Once knighted, the young man was supposed to be courteous, generous, and if possible handsome and rich. Above all, he was to be loyal to his lord and brave in battle. Loyalty was the greatest, the most important, virtue. In a society lacking strong institutions of government, loyalty was the cement that held aristocratic society together. That is why the greatest crime was called a felony, which meant treachery to one's lord.

Infancy and Childhood

According to psychologists and pediatricians, the future mental and physical health of a child is strongly influenced by the pre- and postnatal care it receives. Some very exciting research has been done on childbirth in the Middle Ages. Most information comes from manuscript illuminations. They reveal the birth process from the moment of coitus and orgasm through pregnancy to delivery.

An interesting thirteenth-century German miniature from Vienna shows a woman in labor. She is sitting on a chair or stool surrounded by four other women, who are present to help her in the delivery. They could be relatives or neighbors. If they are midwives, the woman in labor is probably noble or rich, since midwives charged a fee. Delivery seems

MIDWIVES HASTENING DELIVERY. Relatives or midwives assist the woman in childbirth by shaking her up and down. Significantly, no physician is present. With such treatment, the death-rate for both mothers and infants was high. (Bildarchiv der Österreichischen Nationalbibliothek)

to be slow, because two midwives seem to be shaking the mother up and down to hasten it. One of the women is holding a coriander seed near the mother's vagina. Coriander is an herb of the carrot family, and its seeds were used for cleaning purposes. They were thought to be helpful for expelling gas from the alimentary canal — hence their value for speeding up delivery.

The rate of infant mortality in the High Middle Ages must have been staggering. Such practices as jolting the pregnant woman up and down and inserting a seed into her surely contributed to the death rate of both the newborn and the mother. "Natural" causes — disease and poor or insufficient food — also resulted in many deaths. Infanticide, however, which was common in the ancient world, seems to have declined in the High Middle Ages. Ecclesiastical pressure worked steadily against it. Foreign invasions and the generally violent and unstable conditions of the ninth and tenth centuries also made unnecessary the deliberate killing of one's own children. On the other hand, English court records from the counties of Warwickshire, Staffordshire, and Gloucestershire for 1221 reveal a suspiciously large number of children dying from what were classified as "accidental deaths" — drowning, falling from carts, disappearing into the woods, falling into the fire. Still, accidental deaths in rural conditions are more common than is usually thought. Until more research is done, students cannot be certain about the prevalence of infanticide in the High Middle Ages.

Noble women did not nurse their own children but sent them out to wet nurses — women who had recently had a baby and therefore had milk. When Richard Plantagenet was born to Henry II and Eleanor on September 8, 1157, his mother immediately gave him to a woman of St. Alban's to nurse.

The wet nurse also had had a son on September 8. How long the infant Richard and other medieval children were nursed is not known.

Swaddling was probably common in the Middle Ages. Strips of cloth were wrapped tightly around the child's arms, legs, and entire body until it was immobile. The infant was often strapped to a board, which could be set down in a corner or hung up in an out-of-the-way spot. Swaddling reduced the bodily functions. The heartbeat slowed, the child slept more and cried less. Theoretically, this practice arose from adult fears that the child would harm or damage itself if the limbs were free. Probably, too, swaddling was a convenience to the nurse or parent. A swaddled child could be ignored for hours.[6] Any number of unfortunate things could happen to the inert infant, not the least of which was lying for a long time in its own filth. Swaddling surely led to body rashes, disease, and death.

For persons of aristocratic birth the years from infancy to around the age of seven or eight were primarily years of play. Infants had their rattles, as the twelfth-century monk Guibert of Nogent reports, and young children their special toys. Of course, then as now, children would play with anything handy — balls, rings, pretty stones, horns, any small household object. Gerald of Wales, who later became a courtier of King Henry II, describes how as a child he built monasteries and churches in the sand, while his brothers were making castles and palaces. Vincent of Beauvais, who composed a great encyclopedia around 1250, recommended that children be bathed twice a day, fed well, and given ample playtime.

Guibert of Nogent speaks in several places in his autobiography of "the tender years of childhood" — the years from six to twelve. Describing the severity of the tutor whom his mother assigned to him, Guibert wrote:

Placed under him, I was taught with such purity and checked with such honesty from the vices which commonly spring up in youth that I was kept from ordinary games and never allowed to leave my master's company, or to eat anywhere else than at home, or to accept gifts from anyone without his leave; in everything I had to show self-control in word, look, and deed, so that he seemed to require of me the conduct of a monk rather than a clerk. While others of my age wandered everywhere at will and were unchecked in the indulgence of such inclinations as were natural at their age, I, hedged in with constant restraints and dressed in my clerical garb, would sit and look at the troops of players like a beast awaiting sacrifice. Even on Sundays and saints' days I had to submit to the severity of school exercises. At hardly any time, and never for a whole day, was I allowed to take a holiday; in fact, in every way and at all times I was driven to study. Moreover, he devoted himself exclusively to my education, since he was allowed to have no other pupil.[7]

Guibert's mother had intended him for the church. Other boys and girls had more playtime and more freedom.

Aristocrats deliberately had large families in order to insure the continuation of the family. Although many women died in childbirth and many children died before they reached the age of seven, the survival of four or five children was not uncommon. Parents decided upon the future of their children when they were born or when they were just toddlers. Sons were prepared for one of the two positions considered suitable to their birth and position. Careers for the youngest sons might well be found in the church. For the rest, a suitable position meant a military career. Likewise, parents determined early which daughters would be married — and to whom — and which would become nuns.

Youth

At about the age of seven a boy of the noble class was placed in the household of one of his father's friends or relatives. There he became a servant to the lord and received his formal training in arms. As a page to the lord he was expected to serve him at the table, to assist him as a private valet when called upon to do so, and, as he gained experience, to care for the lord's horses and equipment. The boy might have a great amount of work to do, depending upon the size of the household and the personality of the lord. The work children did, medieval people believed, gave them experience and preparation for later life.

Training was in the arts of war. The boy learned to ride and to manage a horse. He had to acquire skill in wielding a sword, which sometimes weighed as much as twenty-five pounds. He had to be able to hurl a lance, to shoot with a bow and arrow, and to care for armor and other equipment. In the eleventh and twelfth centuries, noble youths rarely were taught to read and write. Thousands of charters from that period show that the nobles signed with a cross (+) or some other mark. Literacy for the nobility becomes a little more common in the thirteenth century. Formal training was concluded around the age of eighteen with the ceremony of knighthood.

Knighthood, however, did not mean adulthood, power, and responsibility. Unless the young man's father was dead, he was still considered a "youth," and he remained a youth until he was in a financial position to marry. That might not happen until he was in his late thirties, and marriage at forty was not uncommon. A famous English soldier of fortune, William Marshal, had to wait until he was forty-five to take a wife. One factor — the inheritance of land and the division of properties — determined the lifestyle of the aristocratic nobility. Sons were completely dependent upon their fathers for support, and the result was tension, frustration, and sometimes violence.

Once he had been knighted, the young man traveled. His father selected a group of friends to accompany, guide, and protect him. The band's chief pursuit was fighting. They meddled in local conflicts. Sometimes they departed on crusades. They did the tournament circuit. The tournament, in which a number of men competed from horseback (in contrast to the joust, which involved only two competitors), gave the bachelor knight experience in pitched battle. Since the horses and equipment of the vanquished were forfeited to the victors, the knight could also gain a reputation and a profit. The group hunted. They took great delight in spending money on horses, armor, gambling, drinking, and women. Everywhere these bands of youths went they stirred up trouble. It is no wonder that kings supported the Crusades. Those foreign excursions rid their countries of considerable violence caused by bands of footloose young knights.

The period of traveling lasted two or three years. Although some young men met violent death and others were maimed or received serious injury, many returned home, still totally dependent upon their fathers for support. Serious trouble frequently developed at this stage, for the father was determined to preserve intact the properties of the lordship, and he also wanted to maintain his power and position within the family. Young men could not marry and set up a household on their own without the father's approval. When fathers survived until advanced years, marriage and independence had to be long postponed.

Parents often wanted to settle their daughters' future as soon as possible. Men, even older men, tended to prefer young brides. Marrying a woman in her late twenties or thirties would reduce the years of her married fertility, limit the number of children that she could produce, and thus threaten the survival of the family. Therefore, aristocratic girls in the High Middle Ages were married at around the age of sixteen.

The future of many young women was not enviable. For a sweet young girl of sixteen, marriage to a man in his thirties was not the most attractive prospect, and marriage to a widower in his forties and fifties would be even less so. If there were a large number of marriageable young girls in a particular locality, then their market value was reduced. In the early Middle Ages it had been the custom for the groom to present a dowry to the bride and her family, but by the late twelfth century the process was reversed. Thereafter, the size of the marriage portions offered by brides and their families rose higher and higher.

Many girls of aristocratic families did not marry at all, although there were few professions a well-born lady could honorably enter. She certainly could not be apprenticed to a trader or artisan. Even less did her blood and dignity allow her to perform any manual labor. The sole alternative was the religious life. Benedictine abbeys for women provided "career opportunities" for some unmarriageable girls. Parents commonly decided upon this option, especially if there were several daughters in the family, when the child was under ten. If a girl thought she felt no particular inclination toward becoming a nun, her mother changed her mind quickly enough. The girl of eleven or twelve years was taken to the childbed of a relative or neighbor, there to observe the pain and blood that brought life into the world. It was an event she would not quickly forget. This traumatic experience made her willing to go along with her parents' wishes.

In England in the later Middle Ages there were 138 nunneries, the residents of which were overwhelmingly women from the nobility and the upper middle classes. Most convents were small, however, and did not have places for everyone desiring entrance. The new religious orders of the thirteenth century, the Franciscan and the Dominican, provided some relief for a serious situation. They established many convents for girls and women of the upper class.

Within noble families and within medieval society as a whole, paternal control of the family property and wealth led to serious difficulties. Because marriage was long delayed for men, a considerable age difference existed between husbands and their wives and between fathers and their sons. Because of this generation gap, as one scholar has written, "the father became an older, distant, but still powerful figure. He could do favors for his sons, but his very presence, once his sons had reached maturity, blocked them in the attainment and enjoyment of property and in the possession of a wife."[8] Consequently, disputes between the generations were common in the twelfth and thirteenth centuries. Older men held on to property and power. Younger sons wanted a "piece of the action." This explains in great part the conflicts and rebellions between Henry II of England and his sons Geoffrey, Richard, and John. Their case was quite typical.

At the same time, the relationship between the mother and her sons was affected. She was closer in years to her children than her husband. She was perhaps more able to understand their needs and frustrations. She often served as a mediator between conflicting male generations. One authority, discussing the rule of the mother in French epic poetry, has written, "In extreme need, the heroes betake themselves to their mother, with whom they always find love, counsel and help. She takes them under her protection, even against their father."[9]

Sexual tensions also arose when society included so many married young women and unmarried young men. The young male noble, unable to marry for a long time, could satisfy his lust with peasant girls or prostitutes. But what was a young woman unhappily married to a much older man to

do? The literature of courtly love is filled with stories of young bachelors in love with young married women. How hopeless their love was is not known. The cuckolded husband is a stock figure in such masterpieces as *The Romance of Tristan and Isolde,* Chaucer's *The Merchant's Tale,* and Boccaccio's *Fiammetta's Tale.*

In the High Middle Ages, because of economic reasons, a man might remain a bachelor knight—a "youth"—for a very long time. The identification of bachelorhood with youth has survived into modern times, and the social attitude persists that marriage makes a man mature—an "adult." Marriage is no guarantee of that, however.

Power and Responsibility

A member of the nobility became an "adult" when he came into the possession of his property. He then had vast authority over lands and people. With it went responsibility. The first obligation of the noble was to fight. He was supposed to be the protector and the defender of Christian society against its enemies. In the words of Honorius of Autun:

Soldiers: You are the arm of the Church, because you should defend it against its enemies. Your duty is to aid the oppressed, to restrain yourself from rapine and fornication, to repress those who impugn the Church with evil acts, and to resist those who are rebels against priests. Performing such a service, you will obtain the most splendid of benefices from the greatest of Kings.[10]

Nobles rarely lived up to this ideal, and there are countless examples of nobles attacking the church. In the early thirteenth century, Peter of Dreux, count of Brittany, spent so much of his time attacking the church that he was known as the "Scourge of the Clergy."

FRENCH CASTLE UNDER SIEGE. Most medieval warfare consisted of small skirmishes and the besieging of castles. If surrounded by a moat and supplied with food and water, a few knights could hold a castle against large armies for a long time. Notice the use of engines to hurl missiles. (The British Museum)

The nobles' conception of rewards and gratification did not involve the kind of postponement envisioned by the clergy. They wanted rewards immediately. Since by definition a military class is devoted to war, those rewards came through the pursuit of arms. When they were not involved in local squabbles with neighbors—usually disputes over property or over real or imagined slights—they participated in tournaments.

The complete jurisdiction over his properties allowed the noble, at long last, to gratify his desire for display and lavish living. Since his status in medieval society depended upon the size of his household, he would be anxious to increase the number of household retainers. The elegance of his clothes, the variety of the foods and the richness of his table, the number of his horses and followers, the freedom with which he spent money—all these things were indications to the public of his social standing. The aristocratic lifestyle was luxurious and extravagant. Often nobles had to borrow to maintain it. At the same time they had a great deal of work to do.

The responsibilities of a noble in the High Middle Ages depended upon the size and extent of his estates, the number of his dependents, and his position in his territory relative to others of his class and to the king. First of all, as a vassal he was required to fight for his lord or with the king when called upon to do so. By the mid-twelfth century this service was limited to forty days a year in most parts of western Europe. He might have to perform guard duty at his lord's castle for a certain number of days a year. He was obliged to attend his lord's court on important occasions, times when the lord wanted to put on great displays, such as at Easter, Pentecost, and Christmas. When the lord knighted his eldest son or married off his eldest daughter, he called his vassals to his court, and they were expected to come and to present a contribution known as a gracious aid.

Throughout the year a noble had to look after his own estates. He had to appoint prudent and honest overseers and make sure that they paid him the customary revenues and services. Since the estates of a great lord were usually widely scattered, he had to travel frequently to all parts of them.

Until the late thirteenth century, when royal authority in France and England intervened, a noble had great power over the knights and peasants on his estates. He maintained order among them and dispensed justice to them. Holding the manorial court, which punished criminal acts and settled disputes, was one of his gravest obligations. The quality of justice varied widely: some lords were vicious tyrants who exploited and persecuted their peasants; others were reasonable and evenhanded. In any case, the quality of life on the manor and its productivity were related in no small way to the temperament and decency of the lord — and his lady.

Women played a large and important role in the functioning of the estate. They were responsible for the practical management of the household's "inner economy" — cooking, brewing, spinning, weaving, overseeing servants, caring for yard animals. The lifestyle of the medieval warrior nobles required constant travel, both for purposes of war and for the supervision of distant properties. When the lord was away for long periods, the women frequently had the care of the herds, barns, granaries, and outlying fields as well.

Frequent pregnancies and the reluctance to expose women to hostile conditions kept the lady at home and therefore able to assume supervision over the family's fixed properties. When a husband went away on crusade — and his absence could last anywhere from two to five years, if he returned at all — his wife was often the sole manager of the family properties. When, between 1060 and 1080 her husband went to the Holy Land, the lady Hersendis was the sole manager of the family properties in the Vendomois region in northern France.

CHAIN MAIL. This long shirt of interlinked metal rings, though heavy and uncomfortable, was flexible and allowed movement. Knights wore it because before the manufacture of plate armor, chain mail provided a fair degree of protection. (Courtesy, World Heritage Museum. Photo: Caroline Buckler)

Nor were the activities of women confined to managing family households and estates in the absence of their husbands. Medieval warfare was largely a matter of brief skirmishes, and in any one encounter not many men were killed. But all together, the number slain ran high, and there was a large number of widows. Aristocratic widows frequently controlled family properties and fortunes and exercised great authority. Although the evidence is scattered and sketchy, there are indications that women performed many of the functions of men. In Spain, France and Germany, they bought, sold, and otherwise transferred property. In Saxony, Gertrude, labeled "Saxony's almighty widow" by the chronicler Ekkehard of Aaura, took a leading role in the conspiracies against the emperor Henry V. Sophia, wife of Berthold of Zohringer, assisted her brother Henry the Proud with eight hundred knights at the siege of Falkenstein in 1129. And Eilika Billung, the widow of Count Otto of Ballenstedt, built a castle at Burgwerben on the Saale River and, as advocate of the monastery of Goseck, removed one abbot and selected his successor. From her castle at Bernburg, the countess Eilika was also reputed to ravage the countryside.

THOSE WHO PRAY

In the Middle Ages prayer was looked upon as a vital social service, one that was just as important as the agricultural labor of the farmers and the military might of the nobles. Just as the knights protected and defended society with the sword, and just as the peasants provided food and sustenance through their toil, so the monks with their prayers and chants worked to secure God's blessing for society as a whole.

Monasticism represented some of the finest aspirations of medieval civilization. The monasteries were devoted to prayer, and their standards of Christian behavior influenced the entire church.

The monasteries produced the educated elite that was continually drawn into the administrative services of kings and great lords. Monks kept alive the remains of classical culture and experimented with new styles of architecture and art. They introduced new techniques of estate management and land reclamation. Although relatively small in numbers in the High Middle Ages, the monks played a significant role in medieval society.

Recruitment

Toward the end of his *Ecclesiastical History of England and Normandy,* when he was a man well into his sixties, Orderic Vitalis, a monk of the Norman abbey of St. Evroul, interrupted his narrative to explain the way he happened to become a monk:

It was not thy will, O God, that I should serve thee longer in that place, for fear that I might be less attentive to thee among kinsfolk, who are often a burden and an impediment to thy servants, or might in any way be distracted from obeying the law through human affection for my family. And so, O glorious God, you didst inspire my father Odeleric to renounce me utterly and submit me in all things to thy goverance. So, weeping, he gave me, a weeping child, into the care of the monk Reginald, and sent me away into exile for love of thee, and never saw me again. And I, a mere boy, did not presume to oppose my father's wishes, but obeyed him in all things, for he promised me for his part that if I became a monk I should taste of the joys of Heaven with the Innocents after my death. . . . And so, a boy of ten, I crossed the English channel and came into Normandy as an exile, unknown to all, knowing no one. Like Joseph in Egypt I heard a language which I could not understand. But thou didst suffer me through thy grace to find nothing but kindness among strangers. I was received as an oblate in the abbey of St. Evroul by the venerable abbot Mainier in the eleventh year of my life. . . . The name of Vitalis was given me in place of my English name, which sounded harsh to the Normans.[11]

Orderic Vitalis (ca 1075–ca 1140) was one of the leading scholars of his times. As such, he is not a representative figure or even a typical monk. Intellectuals, those who earn their living or spend most of their time working with ideas, are never typical figures of their times. In one respect, however, Orderic was quite representative of the monks of the High Middle Ages: although he had no doubt that God wanted him to be a monk, the decision was actually made by his parents who gave him to a monastery as a child-oblate. Orderic was the third son of Odeleric, a knight who fought for William the Conqueror at the battle of Hastings (1066). For his participation in the Norman conquest of England, Odeleric was rewarded with lands in western England. Concern for the provision of his two older sons probably led him to give his youngest to the monastery.

Medieval monasteries were religious institutions whose organization and structure fulfilled the social needs of the feudal nobility. Between the tenth and thirteenth centuries, economic necessities compelled great families, or aspiring ones, to seek a life in the church for some members. There simply were not sufficient resources, or career opportunities, to provide suitable, honorable positions in life for all the children in aristocratic families. The monasteries provided these children with an honorable and aristocratic life and with opportunities for ecclesiastical careers.[12]

Until long into modern times, and certainly in the Middle Ages, almost everyone believed in and accepted the thorough subjection of children to their parents. This belief was the logical consequence of the fact that young men were not expected to work and therefore were totally dependent on their fathers. Some men did become monks

MONKS IN CHOIR. Seven times during the day and once during the night monks went to the church to chant the psalms and other prayers, performing what everyone believed to be a valuable service for the rest of society. (The British Museum)

as adults, and apparently for a wide variety of reasons: belief in a direct call from God, disgust with the materialism and violence of the secular world, the encouragement and inspiration of others, economic failure or lack of opportunity, poverty, sickness, the fear of hell. However, most men who became monks, down to about the early thirteenth century, seem to have been given as child-oblates by their parents.

In the thirteenth century, the older Benedictine and Cistercian orders had to compete with the new orders of the friars — the Franciscans and the Dominicans. More and more monks had to be recruited from the middle class, that is, from small landholders or traders in the district near the abbey. As medieval society changed economically, and as European society ever so slowly developed middle-class traits, the monasteries almost inevitably drew their manpower, when they were able, from the middle classes. Until that time, they were preserves of the aristocratic nobility.

Prayer and Other Work

The pattern of life within individual monasteries varied widely from house to house and from region to region. Each monastic community was a family, shaped by the circumstances of its foundation and endowment, by tradition, by the interests of its abbots and members, and by local conditions. It would therefore be a mistake to think that Christian monasticism in the High Middle Ages was everywhere the same. One central activity, however, the work of God, was performed everywhere. Daily life was centered around the liturgy.

Seven times a day and once in the night, the monks went to choir to chant the psalms and other prayers prescribed by Saint Benedict. Those prayers were offered for benefactors, local authorities, peace, good harvests, rain, and an end to foreign invasion. Through their prayers, everyone believed, the monks performed a valuable service for all of society.

The rest of the monks' day was devoted to other work of one kind or another. The operation of a large establishment, such as Cluny in Burgundy or Bury St. Edmunds in England, which by 1150 had several hundred monks, involved planning, prudence and wise management. Although the abbot or prior had absolute authority in making assignments, common sense advised that tasks be allotted according to the ability and talents of individual monks.

The administration of the abbey's estates and properties consumed considerable time. The usual method of economic organization was the manor. Many monastic manors were small enough and close enough to the abbey to be supervised directly by the abbot. But if a monastery held and farmed vast estates, the properties were divided into administrative units under the supervision of one of the monks of the house. The lands of the German abbey of St. Emmeran at Regensburg, for example, were divided into thirty-three manorial centers.

Because the choir monks were aristocrats, they did not till the land themselves. In each house one of the monks was responsible for supervising the peasants, or lay brothers, who did the actual agricultural labor. This was the duty of the cellarer, the general financial manager. He had to see to it that the estates of the monastery produced enough income to cover such necessities as food, fuel, and clothing. One monk, the almoner, was responsible for feeding and caring for the poor of the neighborhood. At the French abbey of St.-Requier in the eleventh century, 110 persons were fed every day.

MONK HARVESTING GRAIN. Saint Benedict wrote, "they are truly monks when they live by the labor of their hands" (*Rule,* chapter 48). The isolated and localized nature of life in the early Middle Ages required that monasteries be entirely self-supporting. (Bibliothèque Publique de Dijon)

MONK INSTRUCTING ILLUMINATOR. All monks had to learn to read in order to perform the religious services. A few of the intellectually and artistically gifted were often taught to copy and to illuminate manuscripts. (The Pierpont Morgan Library)

At Corbie, fifty loaves of bread were distributed daily to the poor.

The precentor, or cantor, was responsible for the library and the careful preservation of books. The sacristan of the abbey had in his charge all the materials and objects connected with the liturgy — vestments, candles, incense, sacred vessels, altar cloths, and hangings. The novice master was responsible for the training of recruits; he had to instruct them in the *Rule,* the chant, the Scriptures, and the history and traditions of the house. For a few of the monks, work involved some form of intellectual activity, such as the copying of books and manuscripts, the preparation of manuals, and the writing of letters.

Although the law of the church forbade monks to study law and medicine, that law was often ignored. In the twelfth and thirteenth centuries, many monks gained considerable reputations for their knowledge and experience in the practice of both the canon law of the church and the civil law of their countries. For example, the Norman monk Lanfranc (ca 1005–1089), because of his legal knowledge and administrative ability, became the chief adviser of William the Conqueror.

Although knowledge of medicine was primitive by twentieth-century standards, monastic practitioners were not as ignorant as one would suspect. Long before 1066, a rich medical literature had been produced in England. The most important of these treatises was *The Leech Book of Bald* ("leech" means medical). This work shows a wide knowledge of herbal prescriptions, familiarity with ancient authorities, and evidence based on empirical practice. Bald discusses diseases of the lungs and stomach together with their remedies and shows no little acquaintance with surgery. *The Leech Book of Bald* was copied and circulated widely in the eleventh through thirteenth centuries, and many monastic libraries both in England and on the Continent had a copy of it. Medical knowledge was sometimes rewarded. King Henry II of England made his medical adviser, the monk Robert de Veneys, abbot of Malmesbury.

The religious houses of medieval Europe usually took full advantage of whatever resources and opportunities their location offered. For example, the raising of horses could produce income in a world that depended on horses for travel and for warfare. Some monasteries, such as the Cistercian abbey of Jervaulx in Yorkshire, became famous for and quite wealthy from their production of prime breeds. In the eleventh and twelfth centuries, a period of considerable monastic expansion, large tracts of swamp, fen, forest, and wasteland were brought under cultivation — principally by the Cistercians.

The Cistercians, whose constitution insisted that they accept lands far from human habitation and forbade them to be involved in the traditional feudal-manorial structure, were ideally suited to the agricultural needs and trends of their times. In the Low Countries, they built dikes to hold back the sea, and the reclaimed land was put to the production of cereals. In the eastern parts of the Holy Roman Empire — in Silesia, Mecklenburg, and Pomerania — they took the lead in draining swamps and cultivating wasteland. Because of a labor shortage, they advertised widely all across Europe for monks and brothers. Because of their efforts, the rich, rolling land of French Burgundy was turned into lush vineyards. In northern and central England, the rocky soil and damp downs of Lincolnshire, poorly suited to agriculture, were turned into sheep runs, and by the third quarter of the twelfth century, the Cistercians were raising sheep and playing a very large role in the production of England's staple crop, wool.

Some monasteries got involved in iron and lead mining. In 1291, the Cistercian abbey of Furness operated at least forty forges. In the thirteenth century, the German abbeys of Königsbronn, Waldsassen, and Saarbegen also mined iron. The monks entered this industry first to fill their own needs, but in an expanding economy, they soon discovered a large market. Iron had hundreds of uses. Nails, hammers, plows, armor, spears, axes, stirrups, horseshoes, and many weapons of war were all made from this basic metal. When in 1189, King Richard of England was preparing to depart on crusade, he wanted to take fifty thousand horseshoes with him. Lead also had a great variety of uses. It could be used for the roofing of buildings, and as alloy for strengthening the silver coinage, for the framing of pane-glass windows in parish, monastery, and cathedral churches, and even for lavatory drainpipes.

Whatever work particular monks did and whatever economic activities individual monasteries were involved in, monks also performed social services and exerted an influence for the good. Monasteries often ran schools that gave primary education to young boys. Abbeys like St. Albans, situated north of London on a busy thoroughfare, served as hotels and resting places for travelers. Monasteries frequently operated "hospitals" and leprosaria, which provided care for and attention to the sick, the aged, and the afflicted — primitive care, it is true, but often all that was available. In short, they performed a variety of social services in an age when "the state" did not consider social welfare its responsibility.

Economic Difficulties

The monks fulfilled their social responsibility by praying. It was generally agreed that they could best carry out this duty if they were not distracted by worldly matters. Thus, great and lesser lords gave the monasteries lands that would supply the community with necessities. Each manorial unit was responsible for provisioning the abbey for a definite period of time, and the expenses of each manor were supposed to equal its income. Frequently, however, the monasteries spent more than they took in.

In the twelfth century, expenses in the older Benedictine monastic houses increased more rapidly than did income, and this led to a steadily worsening economic situation. Cluny provides a good example. There, the style of life was lavish and extravagant. There were large quantities of rich food. The monks' habits were made of the best cloth available. Cluny's abbots and priors traveled with sizable retinues, as great lords were required to do. The abbots worked to make the liturgy ever more magnificent, and large sums were spent on elaborate vestments and jeweled vessels. Abbot Hugh (1049–1109) embarked on an extraordinarily expensive building program. He entirely rebuilt the abbey church, and when Pope Urban II consecrated it on October 25, 1095, it was the largest church in Christendom. The monks lived like lords, which in a sense they were.

Yet, while Cluny's expenses increased, its income did not equal them. Revenue came from the hundreds of monasteries scattered across France, Italy, Spain, and England, which Cluny had reformed in the eleventh century; each year they paid Cluny a cash sum. Novices were expected to make a gift of land or cash when they entered. For reasons of security, knights departing on crusade often placed their estates under Cluny's authority. Still, this income was not enough. The management of Cluny's manors all across Europe was entrusted to bailiffs or wardens who were not monks and who were given lifetime contracts. Frequently, these bailiffs were poor managers and produced no profits. But they could not be removed and replaced. In order to meet expenses, Cluny had to rely on cash reserves. For example, Cluny's estates

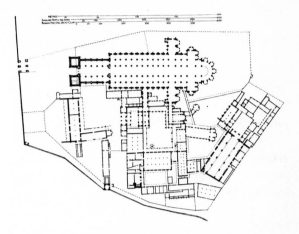

TWENTIETH-CENTURY RECONSTRUCTION OF THE ABBEY OF CLUNY AS IT WAS ca 1150. A community of several hundred monks, the headquarters of an "international" monastic empire, and a major European tourist attraction, Cluny was a microcosm of the feudal world. Cluny had facilities for guests, storage, the sick, work, and of course prayer. (Mediaeval Academy of America [by K. J. Conant])

produced only a small percentage of needed food supplies; the rest had to be bought and paid for from cash reserves.

Cluny had two basic alternatives—improve management to cut costs or borrow money. The abbey could have placed the monastic manors under the jurisdiction of monks, rather than hiring bailiffs who would grow rich as middlemen. It could have awarded annual rather than lifetime contracts, supervised all revenues, and tried to cut costs within the monastery. Cluny chose the second alternative—borrowing. Consequently, the abbey spent hoarded reserves of cash and fell into debt.

In contrast to the abbot of Cluny, the superior of the royal abbey of St.-Denis near Paris, Suger (1122–1151), was a shrewd manager. Although he too spared no expense to enhance the beauty of his monastery and church, Suger kept an eye on costs and made sure that his properties were soundly managed. The management of St.-Denis was unusual. Far more typical was the economic mismanagement at Cluny, and by the later twelfth century, small and great monasteries were facing comparable financial difficulties.

❧

It would be a grave mistake to underestimate the profound influence the monasteries had on matters of the spirit. In the chant and rich ceremonial, in the Gothic splendor of their buildings, in the example usually set by the very lives of the monks, the degree to which the monasteries moved and inspired Christian peoples is incalculable. And, in exercising a Christian influence, "those who prayed" also exercised a civilizing influence on "those who worked" and "those who fought."

NOTES

1. Honorius of Autun, "Elucidarium sive Dialogus de Summa Totius Christianae Theologiae," in J. P. Migne, ed., *Patrologia Latina,* Garnier Bros., Paris, 1854, vol. 172, col. 1149.

2. E. Power, "Peasant Life and Rural Conditions," in J. R. Tanner, et al., *The Cambridge Medieval History,* Cambridge University Press, Cambridge, 1958, 7.716.

3. Glanvill, "De Legibus Angliae," book 5, chap. 5, in G. G. Coulton, ed., *Social Life in Britain from the Conquest to the Reformation,* Cambridge University Press, London, 1956, pp. 338–339.

4. G. Duby, *Early Growth of the European Economy,* Cornell University Press, Ithaca, N.Y., 1977, pp. 213–219.

5. S. R. Scargill-Bird, ed., *Custumals of Battle Abbey in the Reign of Edward I and Edward II,* Camden Society, London, 1887, p. 19.

6. L. Demause, "The Evolution of Childhood," in L. Demause, ed., *The History of Childhood,* Psychohistory Press, New York, 1974, pp. 32–37.

7. J. F. Benton, ed. and trans., *Self and Society in Medieval France: The Memoirs of Abbot Guibert of Nogent,* Harper & Row, New York, 1970, p. 46.

8. D. Herlihy, "The Generation Gap in Medieval History," *Viator* 5 (1974): 360.

9. Cited in ibid., p. 361.

10. Honorius of Autun in *Patrologia Latina,* vol. 172, col. 1148.

11. M. Chibnall, ed. and trans., *The Ecclesiastical History of Orderic Vitalis,* Oxford University Press, Oxford, 1972, 2.xiii.

12. R. W. Southern, *Western Society and the Church in the Middle Ages,* Penguin Books, Baltimore, 1970, pp. 224–230, esp. p. 228.

SUGGESTED READING

The best short introduction to the material of this chapter is C. Brooke, *The Structure of Medieval Society** (1971), a beautifully illustrated book. The student interested in aspects of medieval slavery, serfdom, or the peasantry should begin with M. Bloch, "How Ancient Slavery Came to an End" and "Personal Liberty and Servitude in the Middle Ages, Particularly in France," in *Slavery and Serfdom in the Middle Ages: Selected Essays,* W. R. Beer, trans. (1975). There is an excellent discussion of these problems in the magisterial work of G. Duby, *Rural Economy and Country Life in the Medieval West,* C. Postan, trans. (1968). G. C. Homans, *English Villagers of the Thirteenth Century** (1975), is a fine combination of sociological and historical scholarship, while the older study of H. S. Bennett, *Life on the English Manor: A Study of Peasant Conditions** (1960), contains much useful information presented in a highly readable fashion. G. Duby, *The Early Growth of the European Economy: Warriors and Peasants from the Seventh to the Twelfth Century** (1977), is a superb synthesis by a leading authority.

For the nobility, see L. Genicot, "The Nobility in Medieval Francia: Continuity, Break, or Evolution?"; A. Borst, "Knighthood in the High Middle Ages: Ideal and Reality"; and two studies by G. Duby, "The Nobility in Eleventh and Twelfth Century Maconnais" and "Northwestern France: The 'Youth' in Twelfth Century Aristocratic Society": all these articles appear in F. L. Cheyette, ed., *Lordship and Community in Medieval Europe: Selected Readings* (1968). Social mobility among both aristocracy and peasantry are discussed in T. Evergates, *Feudal Society in the Bailliage of Troyes under the Counts of Champagne, 1152–1284* (1976). The standard treatment remains M. Bloch, *Feudal Society,** (1966).

E. Power, *Medieval Women,** (1976), is a nicely illustrated sketch of the several classes of women. For women, marriage, and the family in the High Middle Ages, J. McNamara and S. F. Wemple, "Sanctity and Power: The Dual Pursuit of Medieval Women," in R. Bridenthal and C. Koonz, eds., *Becoming Visible: Women in European History** (1977), and E. R. Coleman, "Medieval Marriage Characteristics: A Neglected Factor in the History of Medieval Serfdom," in T. K. Rabb and R. I. Rotberg, eds., *The Family in History: Interdisciplinary Essays** (1973), make interesting reading.

There is no dearth of good material on the monks in medieval society. The titles listed in the Suggested Reading for Chapter 6 of this book represent a useful starting point for study. L. J. Lekai, *The Cistercians: Ideals and Reality* (1977), is the best recent work on the Cistercians. Both W. Braunfels, *Monasteries of Western Europe: The Architecture of the Orders* (1972), and C. Brooke, *The Monastic World* (1974), are magnificently illustrated studies with texts that discuss every aspect of monastic life; they contain fine bibliographies.

*Available in paperback.

Chapter 10

THE CREATIVITY AND VITALITY OF

THE HIGH MIDDLE AGES

he High Middle Ages witnessed some of the most remarkable achievements in the entire history of Western society. Europeans displayed tremendous creativity, vitality, and energy in many realms of culture. In government, rulers tried to get in touch with all of their peoples, developed new legal and financial institutions, and slowly consolidated power in the hands of the monarchy. The kings of England and France succeeded in laying the foundations of the modern national state. In learning, a new educational institution, the university, came into being. The university is a uniquely Western contribution to civilization, and it is a superb expression of medieval creativity. In religion, Europeans showed their faith in many ways. For example, they created a splendid new architectural style for their churches. The Gothic cathedral manifested medieval peoples' deep Christian faith and their appreciation for the worlds of nature, man, and God. The Crusades, a series of holy wars to recover the Holy Land from the Muslims, also expressed European Christians' strong, even fanatical, religious faith. The Crusades demonstrated enormous vitality; they were not creative movements, however.

This chapter will discuss the following questions. How did medieval rulers in England, France, and the Holy Roman Empire work to solve their problems of government? How did universities develop, and what needs of medieval society did they serve? What does the Gothic cathedral reveal about the ideals, the attitudes, and the interests, of medieval people? What functions did the cathedral serve? Finally, what combination of motives inspired the Crusades, and what results did they have?

MEDIEVAL ORIGINS OF THE MODERN STATE

The modern state is an organized territory with definite geographical boundaries that are recognized by other states. It has a body of law and institutions of government. If the state claims to govern according to law, it is guided in its actions by the law. The modern national state counts on the loyalty of its citizens, or at least a majority of them. The modern state is so familiar an institution that it is usually taken for granted. It provides order so that citizens can go about their daily work and other activities. The state protects its citizens in their persons and property. The state tries to prevent violence and to apprehend and punish those who commit it. The state supplies a currency or medium of exhange that permits financial and commercial transactions. The state conducts relations with foreign governments. These are some of the state's minimal functions, but in order to accomplish even them, it must have officials, bureaucracies, laws and courts of law, soldiers, information, and money. States with these attributes are relatively recent developments.

Rome's great legacy to Western civilization had been the idea of the state and the law, but for almost five hundred years after the disintegration of the Roman Empire in the West, the state as a reality did not exist. Political authority was completely decentralized. Power was spread among many feudal lords, who gave such protection and security in their locality as their strength allowed. The fiefdoms, kingdoms, and territories that covered the continent of Europe did not have the qualities or provide the services of a modern state. They did not have jurisdiction over many people, and their laws affected a relative few. In the mid-eleventh century, there existed layers of authorities — earls, counts, barons, knights — between a king and the ordinary people.

In these circumstances, medieval kings had common goals. The rulers of England, France, and the Holy Roman Empire wanted to strengthen royal authority and extend it within their territories.

They wanted to establish a means of communication with all peoples in order to increase public order. They wanted more revenue and efficient state bureaucracies. The solutions found to these problems laid the foundations for modern national states.

Unification and Communication

Under the pressure of the Danish (or Viking) invasions of the ninth and tenth centuries, the seven kingdoms of Anglo-Saxon England united under one king. In the same period, and for reasons historians still cannot fully explain, England was divided into local units called shires, or counties, each one under the jurisdiction of a sheriff appointed by the king. The Danish king Canute (1016–1035) and his successor Edward the Confessor (1042–1066) exercised a broader authority than any contemporary ruler on the Continent. All the English thegns, or local chieftains, recognized the central authority of the kingship. The kingdom of England, therefore, had a political head start on the rest of Europe. When Edward the Confessor died in January 1066, his cousin, Duke William of Normandy, claimed the English throne and in October 1066, defeated the Anglo-Saxon claimant on the battlefield of Hastings. As William subdued the rest of the country, he distributed lands to his Norman followers and assigned to each estate specific military quotas. He also required all feudal lords to swear an oath of allegiance to him as king.

William the Conqueror (1066–1087) preserved the Anglo-Saxon institution of having sheriffs represent the king at the local level, but he replaced Anglo-Saxons in office with Normans. A sheriff, who always lived in the county where he worked, had heavy duties. He maintained order in the shire. He caught criminals and punished them in the shire court, over which he presided. He collected taxes and, when the king ordered him to do so, raised an army of foot soldiers. The sheriff also organized adult males in groups of ten, with each member

THE BAYEUX TAPESTRY. Measuring 231′ by 19½″, the Bayeux Tapestry gives a narrative description of the events surrounding the Norman Conquest of England. The tapestry provides an important historical source for the clothing, armor, and lifestyles of the Norman and Anglo-Saxon warrior class. (Tapissérie de la Reine Mathilde, Ville de Bayeux)

DOMESDAY BOOK. This document listed the land holdings of every lord in England. With this record the monarchy could apportion knight service and taxes. (The Master and Fellows of Balliol College, Oxford)

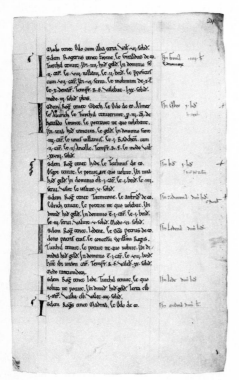

liable for the good behavior of the others. The Conqueror thus made local people responsible for order in their communities. For all his efforts, the sheriff received no pay. This system, in which unpaid officials governed the county, served as the basic pattern of English local government for many centuries.

In addition to the sheriffs, William retained another Anglo-Saxon device, the writ. This brief administrative order written in the vernacular (Anglo-Saxon) by a government clerk was the means by which the central government communicated with people at the local level. Sheriffs also were empowered to issue writs relating to matters in their counties.

In 1086, the Conqueror introduced into England a major innovation, the Norman inquest. At his Christmas court in 1085, William discussed with his vassals the state of the kingdom and decided to conduct a systematic investigation of the entire country. The survey was to be made by means of inquests, or general inquiries, held throughout England. William wanted to determine how much wealth there was in his new kingdom, to find out who held what land, and to discover what lands had been disputed among his vassals since the conquest of 1066. In 1086, groups of royal officials or judges were sent to every part of the country. In every village and farm, the priest and six ordinary people were put under oath to answer the questions asked of them by the king's commissioners. Everybody and everything was counted and listed. In the words of a contemporary chronicler:

He sent his men over all England into every shire and had them find out how many hundred hides there were in the shire, or what land and cattle the king himself had, or what dues he ought to have in twelve months from the shire. Also . . . what or how much everybody had who was occupying land in England, in land or cattle, and how much money it was worth. So very narrowly did he have it investigated, that there was no single hide nor yard of land, nor indeed . . . one ox nor one cow nor one pig was there left out, and not put down in his record: and all these records were brought to him afterwards.[1]

The resulting record, called *Domesday Book* from the Anglo-Saxon word *doom* meaning "judgment," still survives as an invaluable source of social and economic information about medieval England.

The Conqueror's scribes compiled *Domesday Book* in less than one year, using the evidence given by local people. *Domesday Book* provided William and his descendants with information vital for the exploitation and government of the country. For example, knowing the amount of wealth every area possessed, the king could tax accordingly. Knowing the amount of land his vassals had, the king could allot knight service fairly. *Domesday Book* was a unique document that included material about all of England. English kings could think of their country as a single unit and, as such, work to bind it together. Across the English Channel, in France, state building took a different course.

In the early twelfth century, France consisted of a number of virtually independent provinces. Each was governed by its local ruler; each had its own laws and customs; each had its own coinage; and each had its own dialect. Unlike the king of England, the king of France had jurisdiction over a very small area. Chroniclers called King Louis VI (1108–1137) *roi de St.-Denis,* king of St.-Denis, because the territory he controlled was limited to Paris and the St.-Denis area surrounding the city. This region was called the Ile-de-France, or royal domain, and it became the nucleus of the French state. The goal of the medieval French monarchy was to increase the royal domain and extend the power and authority of the king (see Map 10.1).

The work of unifying France began under Louis VI's grandson, Philip II (1180–1223). Rigord, Philip's biographer, gave him the title "Augustus" (from a Latin word meaning "to increase") because he vastly enlarged the territory of the kingdom of France. By defeating a baronial plot against the Crown, Philip Augustus acquired the northern counties of Artois and Vermandois. When King John of England, who was Philip's vassal for the rich province of Normandy, defaulted on his feudal obligation to come to the French court, Philip declared Normandy forfeit to the French crown. He enforced this declaration by war, and in 1204 Normandy fell to the French. Within two years, Philip also gained the prosperous farmlands of Maine, Touraine, and Anjou. By the end of his reign, Philip was effectively master of northern France.

In the thirteenth century, Philip Augustus's descendants made important acquisitions in the south. Louis VIII (1223–1226) added the county of Poitou to the kingdom of France by war. Louis IX (1226–1270) gained Toulouse and a vital interest in the Mediterranean province of Provence through his marriage to Margaret of Provence. Louis' son, Philip III (1270–1285), secured Languedoc through inheritance. By the end of the thirteenth century, most of the provinces of modern France had been added to the royal domain, through diplomacy, marriage, war, and inheritance, and the king of France was stronger than any group of antagonistic French nobles who might try to challenge his authority.

Philip Augustus devised a method of governing the provinces and established a means of communication between the central government in Paris and local communities. Philip decided that each province would retain its own institutions and laws. Royal agents called baillis in the north and seneschals in the south, however, were sent from Paris into the provinces as the king's official representatives with authority to act for him. Often middle-

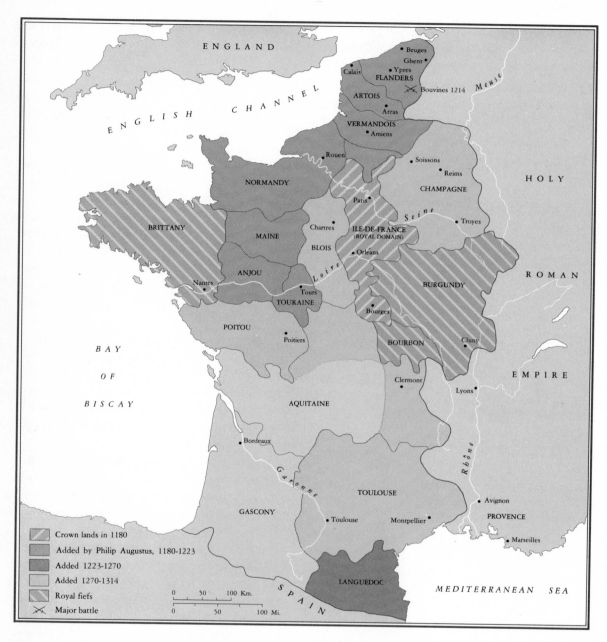

ENGLAND

ENGLISH CHANNEL

• Bruges
Ghent •
Calais • • Ypres
FLANDERS
• Bouvines 1214
ARTOIS
• Arras
VERMANDOIS
• Amiens
• Rouen

HOLY

NORMANDY
• Soissons
• Reims

CHAMPAGNE

Paris •

Seine

BRITTANY

MAINE
Chartres •
ILE-DE-FRANCE
(ROYAL DOMAIN)
• Troyes

BLOIS
• Orleans

Loire

ROMAN

ANJOU

BURGUNDY

Nantes •
TOURAINE
• Tours

BAY

POITOU
• Bourges

OF
• Poitiers
BOURBON
• Cluny

BISCAY

EMPIRE

• Clermont

AQUITAINE

• Lyons

• Bordeaux

Garonne

Rhône

TOULOUSE
• Avignon

GASCONY
• Toulouse
• Montpellier
PROVENCE

• Marseilles

Meuse

SPAIN
LANGUEDOC

MEDITERRANEAN SEA

Crown lands in 1180
Added by Philip Augustus, 1180-1223
Added 1223-1270
Added 1270-1314
Royal fiefs
✕ Major battle

0   50   100 Km.
0   50   100 Mi.

MAP 10.1   THE GROWTH OF THE KINGDOM OF FRANCE

class lawyers, these men possessed full judicial, financial, and military jurisdiction in their districts. The baillis and seneschals were appointed by, paid by, and responsible to the king. Unlike the English sheriffs, they were never natives of the provinces to which they were assigned, and they could not own land in their bailliages. A fundamental principle of French administration was that royal interests superseded local interests.

While English governmental administration was based on the services of unpaid local officials, the administration of France rested on a professional royal bureaucracy. Bureaucracy was the cornerstone of French royal government. As new territories came under royal control, the bureaucracy expanded. So great a variety of customs, laws, and provincial institutions existed that any attempt to impose uniformity would have touched off a rebellion. The French system was characterized by diversity at the local level and centralization at the top. Although it sometimes fell into disrepair, the basic system that Philip Augustus created worked so well that it survived until the Revolution of 1789.

The political problems of the Holy Roman Empire differed considerably from those of France and England. The eleventh-century investiture controversy between the German emperor and the Roman papacy left the empire shattered and divided. In the twelfth and thirteenth centuries, the Holy Roman Empire was split into hundreds of independent provinces, principalities, bishoprics, duchies, and free cities. Princes, dukes, and local rulers held power over small areas. Several difficulties prevented the development of a strong central government.

Unlike the French kings, the German rulers lacked a strong royal domain to use as a source of revenue and as a base from which to expand royal power. Within the empire, no accepted principle of succession to the throne existed, and as a result the death of the emperor was often followed by disputes, civil war, and anarchy. Moreover, the German rulers were continually attracted south by the wealth of the northern Italian cities or by dreams of the restoration of the imperial glory of Charlemagne. Time after time, the German emperors got involved in Italian affairs, and the papacy, fearful of a strong German power in northern Italy, interfered in German affairs. The German princes would take bribes from whichever authority — the emperor or the pope — best supported their own particular ambitions. Consequently, the centralization of authority in Germany, in contrast to that in France and England, occurred very slowly. In medieval Germany, power was in the hands of numerous princes, instead of being held by the emperor.

Through most of the first half of the twelfth century, civil war wracked the Holy Roman Empire, because the emperors tried to strengthen their position by playing off baronial factions against one another. When the emperor Conrad III died in 1152, the anarchy was so terrible that the electors, the seven princes responsible for choosing the emperor, decided that the only alternative to continued chaos was the selection of a strong ruler. They chose Frederick Barbarossa (1152–1190) of the house of Hohenstaufen.

Frederick Barbarossa tried valiantly to unify the empire. Just as the French rulers branched out from their compact domain in the Ile-de-France, so Frederick tried to use his family duchy of Swabia in southwestern Germany as a power base (see Map 10.2). Just as the king of England had done, Frederick required all the vassals in Swabia to take an oath of allegiance to himself as emperor, no matter who their immediate lord might be. He appointed officials called ministeriales, men of low social origin, to exercise the full imperial authority over administrative districts of Swabia. Ministeriales linked the emperor and local communities.

DENMARK

FRISIA

SAXONY

POMERANIA

• Lübeck

• Bremen

• Brandenburg

POLAND

LUSATIA

• Goslar

LOWER
LORRAINE

• Cologne

• Aix-la-Chapelle

THURINGIA

FRANCONIA

• Mainz

• Prague

• Trier

• Worms

BOHEMIA

UPPER
LORRAINE

MORAVIA

• Verdun

• Toul

BAVARIA

AUSTRIA

FRANCE

• Augsburg

SWABIA

• Salzburg

• Besançon

HUNGARY

BURGUNDY—ARLES

Legnano 1176

LOMBARDY

✕

• Milan

Venice •

• Pavia

• Roncaglia

REPUBLIC OF VENICE

• Avignon

• Florence

PROVENCE

• Arles

TUSCANY

PAPAL
STATES

• Marseilles

• Rome

APULIA

KINGDOM OF SICILY

Naples •

• Salerno

• Messina

• Palermo

SICILY

✕ Major battle

   Holy Roman Empire, ca 1200

   Kingdom of Sicily

   Republic of Venice

0   100   200 Km.

0   100   200 Mi.

Outside of Swabia, Frederick tried to make feudalism work as a system of government. The princes throughout the empire exercised tremendous power, and Frederick tried to subordinate them to the authority of the royal government. He had alliances with the great lay princes in which they acknowledged that their lands were fiefs of the emperor, and he in turn recognized their military and political jurisdiction over their territories. Frederick also compelled the great churchmen to become his vassals, so that when they died he could control their estates. Frederick solved the problem of chronic violence by making the princes responsible for the establishment of peace within their territories. At a great assembly held at Roncaglia in 1158, private warfare was forbidden, and severe penalties were laid down for violations of the peace.

Unfortunately, Frederick Barbarossa did not concentrate his efforts and resources in one area. He became embroiled in the affairs of Italy. He wanted to restore the Holy Roman Empire, combining Germany and Italy. In the eleventh and twelfth centuries, the northern Italian cities had grown rich on trade, and Frederick believed that if he could gain the imperial crown, he could cash in on Italian wealth. Frederick saw that although the Italian cities were populous and militarily strong, they lacked stable governments and were often involved in struggles with one another. The German emperor mistakenly believed that moneygrubbing infantrymen could not stand up against his tough, aristocratic knights. He did not realize that the merchant oligarchs who ran the city governments of Milan, Venice, and Florence considered themselves just as noble as he and prized their independence and were determined to fight for it. Frederick's desire to control the papacy and to end papal claims to suzerainty over the empire also attracted him southward. He did not know that the popes feared a strong German state in northern Italy even more than they feared the rich and (the popes suspected) slightly heretical Italian cities.

Between 1154 and 1188, Frederick made six expeditions into Italy. Using a scorched-earth policy, he was successful at first, making significant conquests in the north. The brutality of his methods, however, provoked revolts, and the Italian cities formed an alliance with the papacy. At Legnano in 1176, Frederick suffered a catastrophic defeat. This battle marked the first time a feudal cavalry of armed knights was decisively defeated by bourgeois infantrymen. Frederick was forced to recognize the independence of the northern Italian cities. Germany and Italy remained separate countries and followed separate courses of development.

Frederick Barbarossa's Italian ventures contributed nothing to the unification of the German states. Because the empire lacked a stable bureaucratic system of government, his presence was essential for the maintenance of peace. In Frederick's absences, the fires of independence and disorder spread. The princes and magnates consolidated their power, and the unsupervised royal ministeriales gained considerable independence. By 1187, Frederick had to accept again the reality of private warfare. The power of the princes grew at the expense of a centralized monarchy.

Finance

As medieval rulers expanded their territories and extended their authority, they required more officials, larger armies, and more and more money. Officials and armies had to be paid, and kings had to find ways to raise revenue.

In England, William the Conqueror's son Henry I (1100–1135) established a bureau of finance called the Exchequer (from the checkered cloth at which his officials collected and audited royal accounts). Henry's income came from a variety of sources: from taxes paid by peasants living on the king's

MAP 10.2   THE HOLY ROMAN EMPIRE, ca 1200

estates; from the Danegeld, an old tax originally levied to pay tribute to the Danes; from the *dona,* an annual gift from the church; from money paid to the Crown for setting disputes; and from fines paid by people found guilty of crimes. Henry also received income because of his position as feudal lord. For example, if one of his vassals died and the son wished to inherit the father's properties, the heir had to pay Henry a relief tax. The sheriffs in each county were responsible for collecting all these sums and for paying them twice a year to the king's Exchequer.

An accurate record of expenditures and income is needed to insure a state's solvency. Henry assigned a few of the barons and bishops at his court to keep careful records of the monies paid into the royal treasury and the monies spent by it. These financial officials, called barons of the Exchequer, gradually developed into a professional organization with its own rules, procedures, and esprit de corps. The Exchequer, which always sat in London, became the first institution of the governmental bureaucracy of England. Because of its work, an almost complete series of financial records for England dating back to 1130 survives.

The development of royal financial agencies in most continental countries lagged behind the English Exchequer. Twelfth-century French rulers derived their income from their royal estates in the Ile-de-France region. As Philip Augustus and his successors added provinces to the royal domain, the need for money became increasingly acute. Philip made the baillis and seneschals responsible for collecting taxes in their districts. This income came primarily from fines and confiscations imposed by the courts. Three times a year the baillis and seneschals reported to the king's court with the monies they had collected.

In the thirteenth century, French rulers found additional sources of revenue. They acquired some income from the church and some from people living in the towns. Townspeople paid tallage — a tax arbitrarily laid by the king. In all parts of the country feudal vassals owed military service to the king when he called for it. Louis IX converted this military obligation into a cash payment, called host tallage, and thus increased his revenues. Philip Augustus, Louis VIII, and Louis IX all taxed the Jews mercilessly.

Medieval people believed that a good king lived on the income of his own land and taxed only in time of a grave emergency — that is, a just war. Because the church, and not the state, performed what twentieth-century people call social services, such as education and care for the sick, the aged, and orphaned children, there was no ordinary need for the government to tax. Taxation meant war financing. The French monarchy could not continually justify taxing the people on the grounds of the needs of war. Thus, the French kings were slow to develop an efficient bureau of finance. Not until the fourteenth century, as a result of the demands of the Hundred Years' War, did a state financial bureau emerge — the Chamber of Accounts.

In the High Middle Ages, the one European government, apart from that of England, that developed an efficient financial bureaucracy was the kingdom of Sicily. Sicily is a good example of how strong government could be built by determined rulers using a feudal base.

Like England, Sicily had come under Norman domination. Between 1061 and 1091, a bold Norman knight, Roger de Hauteville, with a small band of mercenaries defeated the Muslims and Greeks who controlled the island. As William the Conqueror did in England, so Roger introduced Norman feudalism in Sicily and made it work as a system of government. Roger distributed scattered fiefs to his followers, so that no vassal had a centralized power base. He took an inquest of royal properties and rights, and he forbade private warfare. Roger adapted his Norman experience to Arabic and Greek governmental practices. Thus, he retained the Muslims' main financial agency, the *diwan,* a sophisticated bureau for record keeping.

His son and heir, Count Roger II (1130–1154), continued the process of state building. He subdued the province of Apulia in southern Italy, united it with his Sicilian lands, and had himself crowned king of Sicily (1130–1154). Roger II organized the economy in the interests of the state; for example, the Crown secured a monopoly on the sale of salt and lumber. With the revenues thus acquired, Roger hired mercenary troops. His judiciary welcomed appeals from local communities. The army, the judiciary, and the *diwan* were staffed by Greeks and Muslims, as well as Normans.

Under the grandson of Roger II, Frederick II Hohenstaufen (1212–1250), Sicily underwent remarkable development. Frederick, also the grandson and heir of Frederick Barbarossa, was a brilliant legislator and administrator, and he constructed the most advanced bureaucratic state in medieval Europe. The institutions of the kingdom of Sicily were harnessed in the service of the state as represented by the king.

Frederick banned private warfare, and he placed all castles and towers under royal administration. Frederick also replaced town officials with royal governors. In 1231, he published the Constitutions of Melfi, a collection of laws that vastly enhanced royal authority. Both feudal and ecclesiastical courts were subordinated to the king's courts. Each year royal judges visited all parts of the kingdom, and the supreme court at Capua heard appeals from all lesser courts. Thus, churchmen accused of crimes were tried in the royal courts. Royal control of the nobility, of the towns, and of the judicial system added up to great centralization, which required a professional bureaucracy and sound state financing.

In 1224, Frederick founded the University of Naples to train clerks and officials for his bureaucracy. University-educated administrators and lawyers emphasized the stiff principles of Roman law, such as the Justinian maxim that "what pleases the prince has the force of law." Frederick's financial experts regulated agriculture, public works, and even business. For example, his customs service carefully supervised all imports and exports, collecting taxes for the Crown on all products. Royal revenues increased tremendously. Moreover, Frederick strictly regulated the currency and forbade the export of gold and silver bullion.

Finally, Frederick secured the tacit consent of his people to regular taxation. This was an incredible achievement in the Middle Ages, when most people believed that taxes should be taken only in time of grave emergency, the just war. Frederick defined emergency broadly. For much of his reign he was involved in a bitter dispute with the papacy. Churchmen hardly considered the emperor's wars with the popes as "just," but Frederick's position was so strong that he could ignore criticism and levy taxes.

Frederick's contemporaries called him "The Transformer of the World." He certainly transformed the kingdom of Sicily, creating a state that was in many ways modern. But Frederick was highly ambitious: he wanted to control the entire peninsula of Italy. The popes, fearful of being encircled, waged a long conflict to prevent that. The kingdom of Sicily required constant attention, and Frederick's absences took their toll. Shortly after he died, the unsupervised bureaucracy he had built fell to pieces. The pope, claiming feudal suzerainty over Sicily, called in a French prince to rule.

Frederick showed little interest in Germany. He concentrated his attention on Sicily, rather than on the historic Hohenstaufen stronghold in Swabia, and the focus of imperial concerns shifted southward. When he visited the empire, in the expectation of securing German support for his Italian policy, he made sweeping concessions to the princes, bishops, duchies, and free cities. For example, in 1220, he exempted German churchmen from taxation and from the jurisdiction of imperial authorities. In 1231, he gave lay princes the same exemptions and even threw in the right to coin money. Frederick gave away so much that imperial authority was seriously weakened. In the later Middle Ages, lay and ecclesiastical princes held power in the Holy Roman Empire. The centralizing efforts of Frederick Barbarossa were destroyed by his grandson Frederick II.

Law and Justice

Throughout Europe, the form and application of laws depended upon local and provincial custom and practice. In the twelfth and thirteenth centuries, the law was a hodgepodge of Germanic customs, feudal rights, and provincial practices. Kings wanted to blend these elements into a uniform system of rules acceptable to all their peoples. In France and England kings made a contribution to the development of national states in the administration of their laws. Roman law strongly influenced legal developments in continental countries like France, while in England a unique and unwritten common law was slowly accepted.

The French king Louis IX was famous in his time for his concern for justice. Each French province, even after it had been made part of the kingdom of France, retained its unique laws and procedures, but Louis IX created a royal judicial system. He established the Parlement of Paris, a kind of "supreme court" that welcomed appeals from local administrators and from the courts of feudal lords throughout France. By the very act of appealing the decisions of feudal courts to the Parlement of Paris, French people in distant provinces were recognizing the superiority of royal justice. The Parlement of Paris reviewed the decisions of baronial courts and thus dispensed the king's justice to all French people.

Louis sent royal judges to all parts of the country to check up on the work of the baillis and seneschals and to hear complaints of injustice. He was the first French monarch to publish laws for the entire kingdom. The Parlement of Paris registered (or announced) the laws. These laws forbade private warfare, judicial duels, gambling, blaspheming, and prostitution. Louis sought to identify justice with the kingship, and gradually royal justice touched all parts of the kingdom.

Under Henry II (1154–1189), England developed and extended a common law, a law common to and accepted by the entire country. No other country did that in medieval Europe. Henry I had occasionally sent out circuit judges (royal officials who traveled a given circuit or district) to hear civil and criminal cases. Henry II made this way of extending royal justice an annual practice. Every year royal judges left London and set up court in the counties. Wherever the king's judges sat, there sat the king's court. Slowly, the king's court gained jurisdiction over all property disputes and criminal actions.

Henry made an important innovation in civil or property law. Disputes over land and movable property had caused a great deal of violence. Henry established a procedure whereby a person who felt unjustly deprived of possessions could get a remedy in the royal court. The aggrieved person could apply to the sheriff for help. The sheriff summoned a jury of local people before the king's judges, and there in the royal court the jury answered questions about rightful possession. On the basis of the jury's verdict, the disputed property was awarded. Thus, rather than attempting to get property back by force, English people had the assistance of the king's court.

Henry also improved procedure in criminal justice. In 1166, he instructed the sheriffs to summon local juries to conduct inquests and draw up lists of known or suspected criminals. These lists, sworn to by the juries, were to be presented to the royal judges when they arrived in the community. This accusing jury is the ancestor of the modern grand jury.

An accused person formally charged with a crime did *not* undergo trial by jury. He or she was tried by ordeal. The accused was tied hand and foot and dropped in a lake or river. People believed that water was a pure substance and would reject anything foul or unclean. Thus, a person who sank was considered innocent, and a person who floated was considered guilty. Trial by ordeal was a ritual that appealed to the supernatural for judgment. God determined innocence or guilt, and thus a priest had to be present to bless the water.

Henry II and others considered this ancient Germanic method irrational and a poor way of determining results, but they knew no alternative. In 1215, the Fourth Lateran Council of the church forbade the presence of the priest at trials by ordeal and thus effectively abolished them. Gradually, in the course of the thirteenth century, the king's judges adopted the practice of calling upon twelve people (other than the accusing jury) to answer the question of innocence or guilt. This became the jury of trial, but it was very slowly accepted because medieval people had more confidence in the judgment of God than in that of twelve ordinary people.

The innovations during the reign of Henry II in civil procedure, in the use of the accusing jury, and in regularizing visits by circuit judges marked a decisive step forward. Since the judges pushed the notion that any serious crime belonged under the

king's jurisdiction, crime was no longer considered a violent act against an individual to be avenged by the victim and his or her family. Rather, criminal acts became deeds against the state, or against the king as the embodiment of the state.

One aspect of Henry's judicial reforms encountered stiff resistance from an unexpected source. Opposition came from a friend and former chief adviser whom Henry had made archbishop of Canterbury — Thomas Becket. In 1162, Henry selected Becket to be archbishop, because he believed he could depend on Becket's support. Henry wanted to bring all persons in the kingdom under the jurisdiction of the royal courts. Thomas Becket's opposition led to another dramatic conflict between temporal and spiritual powers.

In the 1160s, many literate persons accused of crimes claimed "benefit of clergy," even though they were not clerics and often had no intention of being ordained. "Benefit of clergy" gave the accused the right to be tried in church courts, which meted out mild punishments. A person found guilty in the king's court might suffer mutilation — the loss of a hand or foot, or castration — or even death. Ecclesiastical punishments tended to be an obligation to say certain prayers or to make a pilgrimage. In 1164, Henry II insisted that everyone, including clerics, be subject to the royal courts.

Becket vigorously protested that church law required that clerics be subject to church courts. When he proceeded to excommunicate one of the king's vassals, the issue became more complicated. Because no one was supposed to have any contact with an excommunicated person, it appeared that the church could arbitrarily deprive the king of necessary military forces. The disagreement between Henry II and Becket dragged on for years.

Becket maintained that as archbishop he had to defend the rights of the church. Henry insisted that the Crown should have full jurisdiction over all its subjects. The king grew increasingly bitter that his appointment of Becket had proved to be such a mistake. Late in December 1170, in a fit of rage Henry expressed the wish that Becket be destroyed. Four knights took the king at his word, went to Canterbury, and killed the archbishop in his cathedral as he was leaving evening services.

What Thomas Becket could not achieve in life, he gained in death. The assassination of an archbishop in his own church during the Christmas season turned public opinion in England and throughout western Europe against the king. Moreover, within months miracles were recorded at Becket's tomb, and in a short time Canterbury Cathedral became a major pilgrimage and tourist center. Henry had to back down. He did public penance for the murder and gave up his attempts to bring clerics under the authority of the royal court.

Henry II's sons, Richard I (the "Lion-Hearted") (1189–1199) and John (1199–1216), lacked their father's interest in the work of government. Handsome, athletic, and with an international reputation for military prowess, Richard looked upon England as a source of revenue for his military enterprises. Soon after his accession, he departed on crusade to the Holy Land. During his reign he spent only six months in England, and the government was run by ministers trained under Henry II. Unlike Richard, King John was hopelessly incompetent as a soldier and unnecessarily suspicious that the barons were plotting against him. His basic problems, however, were financial.

King John inherited a heavy debt from his father and brother. The country had paid dearly for Richard's crusading zeal. Returning from the Holy Land, Richard had been captured, and England had paid an enormous ransom to secure his release. In 1204, John lost the rich province of Normandy to Philip Augustus of France and then spent the rest of

THE MARTYRDOM OF THOMAS BECKET. Becket's murder evoked many illustrations in the thirteenth century. This illumination faithfully follows the manuscript sources: while one knight held off the archbishop's defenders, the other three attacked. With a powerful stroke, the crown of his head was slashed off and his brains scattered on the cathedral floor. (Walters Art Gallery)

his reign trying to get it back. To finance that war, he got in deeper and deeper trouble with his barons. John squeezed as much money as possible from his position as feudal lord. He took scutage, a tax paid by his vassals in lieu of the performance of knight service. Each time John collected it, he increased the amount due. He forced widows to remarry when they did not wish to do so. He sold young girls who were his feudal wards to the highest bidder. These actions antagonized the nobility.

John also alienated the church and the English townspeople. He rejected Pope Innocent III's nominee to the see of Canterbury. And he infuriated the burghers of the towns by extorting money from them and by threatening to revoke their charters of self-government.

All the money John raised did not bring him success. In July 1214, a coalition including the emperor Frederick II and Philip Augustus of France crushed the English at Bouvines in Flanders. This defeat ended English hopes for the recovery of territories from France. The battle of Bouvines also strengthened the barons' opposition to John. On top of his heavy taxation, his ineptness as a soldier in a society that idealized military glory was the final straw. Rebellion begun by a few hotheaded northern barons eventually grew to involve a large number of the English nobility, including the archbishop of Canterbury and the earl of Pembroke, the leading ecclesiastical and lay peers. After lengthy negotiations in the spring of 1215, John met the barons at Runnymede, a meadow along the Thames River. There he was forced to sign the treaty called Magna Carta, which became the cornerstone of English justice and law.

Magna Carta implies the principle that the king and the government shall be under the law, that everyone, including the king, must obey the law. It includes clauses to protect the rights and property of all English people. It defends the interests of widows, orphans, townspeople, and freemen. Some clauses contain the germ of the ideas of due process of law and of the right to a fair and speedy trial. Every English king in the Middle Ages reissued Magna Carta as evidence of his promise to observe the law. Because it was reissued frequently, and because later generations appealed to Magna Carta as a written statement of English liberties, it acquired an almost sacred importance as a guarantee of law and justice.

In the thirteenth century, the judicial precedents set under Henry II slowly evolved into permanent institutions. The king's judges asserted the royal authority and applied the same principles everywhere in the country. English people found the king's justice more rational and more evenhanded than the justice meted out in the baronial courts. The royal courts gained popularity, and the baronial courts lost rights and business. Respect for the king's law and the king's courts promoted loyalty to the Crown. By the time of Henry's great-grandson, Edward I (1272–1307), one law, the common law, operated all over England.

MEDIEVAL UNIVERSITIES

Just as the first strong secular states emerged in the thirteenth century, so did the first universities. This development was not coincidental. The new bureaucratic states needed educated administrators, and universities were a response to this need. The word "university" derives from the Latin *universitas,* meaning "corporation" or "guild." Medieval universities were educational guilds that produced educated and trained individuals. They were also signs of the tremendous vitality and creativity of the High Middle Ages. They developed a form of organization, methods of instruction, and educational goals that continue to influence institutionalized learning in the Western world.

Origins

In the early Middle Ages, anyone who received any education got it from a priest. He instructed the clever boys on the manor in the Latin words of the mass, and he taught them the rudiments of reading and writing. Few boys acquired elementary literacy, however, and girls did not even obtain that. The peasant who wished to send his son to school had to secure the permission of his lord, because the result of formal schooling tended to be a career in the church or in some trade. If a young man were to pursue either profession, he had to leave the manor and gain free status. Because the lord stood to lose the services of educated peasants, he carefully limited the number of serfs who were sent to school.

Few schools were available, anyway. Society was organized for war and defense and gave slight support to education. By the late eleventh century, however, social conditions had markedly improved. There was greater political stability, and favorable economic conditions had advanced many people beyond the bare subsistence level. The curious and the able felt the lack of schools and teachers.

Since the time of the Carolingian Empire, monasteries and cathedral schools offered the only formal instruction available. The monasteries were geared to religious needs, and the monastic curriculum consisted of the study of the Scriptures and the writings of the church fathers. Monasteries wished to maintain an atmosphere of seclusion and silence and were unwilling to accept large numbers of noisy lay students. In contrast, schools attached to cathedrals and run by the bishop and his clergy were frequently situated in bustling urban environments, and in Italian cities like Bologna wealthy businessmen had established municipal schools. Inhabited by peoples of many backgrounds and "nationalities," cities had the stimulating atmosphere necessary for the growth and exchange of ideas. In the course of the twelfth century, universities grew out of cathedral schools in France and municipal schools in Italy (see Map 10.3).

The school at Chartres Cathedral in France became famous for its studies of the Latin classics and for the broad literary interests it fostered in its students. The most famous graduate of Chartres was the Englishman John of Salisbury (d. 1180), who wrote *The Statesman's Book,* an important treatise on the corrupting effects of political power. But Chartres, situated in the center of rich farmland remote from the currents of commercial traffic and intellectual ideas, did not develop into a university. The first European universities appeared in Italy, at Bologna in the north and at Salerno in the south.

The growth of the University of Bologna coincided with a revival of interest in Roman law. The study of Roman law as embodied in the Justinian Code had never completely died out in the West, but the sudden burst of interest seems to have been inspired by Irnerius (d. 1125), a great teacher at Bologna. His fame attracted students from all over Europe. Irnerius not only explained the Roman law of the Justinian Code, he applied it to difficult practical situations. Although an important school of civil law was founded at Montpellier in southern France, Bologna remained the greatest law school throughout the Middle Ages.

At Salerno, interest in medicine had persisted for centuries. Greek and Muslim physicians had studied the possibilities of herbs as cures for diseases, and they had experimented with surgery. In the early twelfth century, there was a new interest in Greek medical texts and in the work of Arab and Greek doctors. Students of medicine poured into Salerno, and their study soon attracted royal attention. In 1140, King Roger II of Sicily took the practice of medicine under royal control. His ordinance stated:

Who, from now on, wishes to practice medicine, has to present himself before our officials and examiners, in order to pass their judgment. Should he be bold enough to disregard this, he will be punished by imprisonment

MAP 10.3   INTELLECTUAL CENTERS OF MEDIEVAL EUROPE

BALTIC
SEA

SCOTLAND

St. Andrews

Glasgow

NORTH

SEA

DENMARK

Copenhagen

Jarrow

Durham

Rivaulx

York

IRELAND

ENGLAND

HOLY

Magdeburg

Leipzig

Peterborough

Bury
St. Edmunds

Cambridge

Louvain

Cologne

Fulda

Prague

Oxford

Mainz

Bamberg

ROMAN

Salisbury

Winchester

Canterbury

Heidelberg

Salisbury

Jumièges

Laon

Regensburg

Mont St.
Michel

Bec

Reims

St.-Denis

Hirsau

Lorch

ATLANTIC

Notre Dame

Paris

Vienna

OCEAN

Savigny

Chartres

Clairvaux

Orléans

Fleury

Citeaux

St.-Gall

Tours

Basel

Bourges

Cluny

EMPIRE

Poitiers

Padua

FRANCE

Pavia

Bordeaux

Grenoble

Piacenza

Bologna

Cahors

Florence

Vallombrosa

Montpellier

Avignon

CORSICA

Perugia

Toulouse

Valladolid

Salamanca

Rome

Coimbra

SPAIN

Monte Cassino

Naples

Toledo

SARDINIA

Salerno

Seville

Palermo

MEDITERRANEAN SEA

SICILY

■ University

✝ Monastery school

♜ Cathedral school

0   100   200   300 Km.

0   100   200   300 Mi.

and confiscation of his entire property. In this way we are taking care that our subjects are not endangered by the inexperience of the physicians.

Nobody dare practice medicine unless he has been found fit by the convention of the Salernitan masters.[2]

King Roger sought to protect the people of the kingdom of Sicily from incompetent doctors.

In the first decades of the twelfth century, students converged upon Paris. They crowded into the cathedral school of Notre Dame and spilled over into the area later called the Latin Quarter — a name that reflects the Italian origin of many of the students attracted to Paris by the surge of interest in the classics, logic, and theology. The cathedral school's international reputation had already brought to Paris scholars from all over Europe. One of the most famous teachers was Peter Abélard.

The son of a minor Breton knight, Peter Abélard (1079–1142) studied in Paris, quickly absorbed a large amount of material, and set himself up as a teacher. Abélard was fascinated by logic, which he believed could be used to solve most of the world's problems. He had a brilliant mind and, although orthodox in his philosophical teaching, appeared to challenge ecclesiastical authorities. His book *Sic et Non (Yes and No)* was a list of apparently contradictory propositions drawn from the Bible and the writings of the church fathers. For example, one proposition stated that sin is pleasing to God, and sin is not pleasing to God. Abélard used a method of systematic doubting in his writing and teaching. As he put it in the preface to *Sic et Non,* "By doubting we come to questioning, and by questioning we perceive the truth." While other scholars merely asserted theological principles, Abélard discussed and analyzed them. Through reasoning he even tried to describe the attributes of the three persons of the Trinity, the central mystery of the Christian faith. He was severely censured by a church council, but his cleverness, boldness, and imagination made him highly popular with students.

The influx of students eager for learning, together with dedicated and imaginative teachers, created the atmosphere from which universities grew. In northern Europe — at Paris and later at Oxford and Cambridge in England — associations or guilds of professors organized universities. They established the curriculum, set the length of time for study, and determined the form and content of examinations. In 1200, King Philip Augustus officially recognized the University of Paris, and in 1208, Pope Innocent III, who had studied there, designated the community of students and scholars a *universitas.*

Instruction and Curriculum

University faculties grouped themselves according to the various academic disciplines, called schools — law, medicine, philosophy, and theology. Professors were called schoolmen, or scholastics. They developed a method of thinking, reasoning, and writing in which questions were raised and authorities cited on both sides of the question. The scholastic method was used in teaching as well as in writing. The goal of the scholastic method was to arrive at definitive answers and, so the schoolmen believed, a deeper understanding of the Christian faith.

Some scholastic philosophers relied on Latin translations of Greek and Arabic texts to explore the natural world. Gradually, natural science emerged as a discipline separate from philosophy. Medieval science, however, was based on some authority, such as the Bible, the Justinian Code, or a treatise of Aristotle (rather than on observation and experimentation, as modern science is), and the conclusions of medieval scientists were often wrong. Nevertheless, scholastics made two important contributions. They preserved the Greek and Arabic texts that contained the body of ancient scientific knowledge and that otherwise would have been lost. And, in asking questions about nature and the universe, scholastics laid the foundations for later scientific work.

Thirteenth-century scholastics devoted an enormous amount of time to collecting and organizing knowledge on all topics. These collections were published as *summa,* or reference books. There were *summa* on law, philosophy, vegetation, animal life, and theology. Saint Thomas Aquinas (1225–1274), a professor of theology at Paris, produced the most famous collection, the *Summa Theologica,* which deals with a vast number of theological problems. His work later became the fundamental text of Roman Catholic doctrine.

At all universities, the standard method of teaching was the lecture, that is, a reading. The professor read a passage from the Bible, the Justinian Code, or one of Aristotle's treatises and then commented on it. He explained and interpreted the passage; the interpretation was called a gloss. Students wrote down everything. Texts and glosses were sometimes collected and reproduced as textbooks. For example, the Italian Peter Lombard (d. 1160), a professor at Paris, wrote what became the standard textbook in theology, *Sententiae (The Sentences),* which was a compilation of basic theological principles.

Because books had to be copied by hand, they were extremely expensive, and few students could afford them. Students therefore depended for study on their own or friends' notes accumulated over a period of years. The choice of subjects was narrow. The syllabus at all universities consisted of a core of ancient texts that everyone studied and, if they wanted to get ahead, mastered.

There were no examinations at the end of a series of lectures. Examinations were given after three, four, or five years of study—when the student applied for a degree. Professors determined the amount of material students had to know for each degree, although students frequently insisted that the professors specify precisely what that material was. When the candidate for a degree believed himself prepared, he presented himself to a committee of professors for examination.

Examinations were oral and very difficult. (Not only did paper and ink cost a great deal, the examination was designed to test the student's ability to think quickly on his feet and to express his thoughts in an effective fashion.) If the candidate passed, he was awarded the first, or bachelor's, degree. Further study, about as long, arduous, and expensive as it is today, enabled the graduate to try for the master's and doctor's degrees. All degrees certified competence in a given subject, and, technically, degrees were licenses to teach. Most students, however, did not become teachers.

Student Power

The people who made up medieval universities, the students and the faculties—those responsible for instruction and government—were from the middling rungs of society, very much like many of the students and teachers at American state universities today. Most students (and they were all male) came from families of lesser knights, burgesses of the towns, merchants, and artisans—the group that today would be called middle class. Undergraduates were usually in their twenties or thirties, poor, ambitious, and aggressively upwardly mobile. They wanted, and received, an education that was practical, utilitarian, and vocational.

Students wanted to acquire as quickly as possible the knowledge necessary for a secure, well-paying job in the service of the church or secular government. Consequently, once the first degree had been

A UNIVERSITY LECTURE.   Some students doze, some chat, and
some are attentive to the lecturer. All students appear much
older than undergraduates today. (Bildarchiv Preussischer
Kulturbesitz)

attained, law was the subject most often taken for an
advanced degree. Students studied law because governments needed the expertise of lawyers. Philip
Augustus of France employed law graduates as
baillis and seneschals. Frederick II, when he established the University of Naples, had clearly stated
in the university's charter that the school's purpose
was to train men who would dispense the law
throughout his kingdom.

Medieval students exercised more power in their
universities than do students today. In the Middle
Ages students often traveled long distances to work

with great scholars. They arrived as foreigners in the countries where they studied, and, fearful of the natives, they formed associations for mutual security. Some guilds were set up for sheer physical protection; others sought to defend students from the high rates charged by local boarding houses and innkeepers. Student guilds, especially in southern Italy, hired the professors, paid their fees, and demanded that teachers cover the syllabus within an agreed-upon time. If they became dissatisfied with incompetent professors or the financial gouging of townspeople, students did not hesitate to boycott lectures or to leave the town entirely. Cambridge University, for example, began when students at Oxford got fed up with conditions at the university there.

Municipal court records of towns like Paris, Oxford, and Cambridge reveal that in the thirteenth and fourteenth centuries student riots and rebellions were common. Townspeople resented what they considered the wasteful lives of students. Students protested the high costs of living in university towns or what they felt were the unfair decisions of professors or university officials. Friction between students and townspeople or between students and university authorities was common. But the aim of medieval student movements was never to reform society as a whole. Medieval students had no interest in changing the basic social system. Rather, they wanted to get into the system; they wanted a "piece of the action."

Medieval universities did not have luxurious dormitories, semiprofessional athletic teams, vast administrations, or even classrooms. The first professors lectured in rented halls. In the later thirteenth century, first at Paris and then at Oxford, noblemen or wealthy businessmen established colleges, or residence halls, and endowed scholarships for poor students. Most students lived in abject poverty, and before the sixteenth century they led a cold, uncomfortable, and hand-to-mouth existence. Nevertheless, in establishing the lecture system, textbooks, faculties, examinations, and degrees, medieval universities laid the foundations for modern institutional learning. Universities are a uniquely important contribution of the Middle Ages to Western society.

GOTHIC CATHEDRALS

Medieval churches stand as the most spectacular manifestations of the vitality and creativity of the High Middle Ages. It is difficult for twentieth-century people to appreciate the incredible amount of energy, imagination, and money involved in building them. Between 1180 and 1270, in France alone, eighty cathedrals, about five hundred abbey churches, and tens of thousands of parish churches were constructed. This construction represents a remarkable investment for a country of scarcely 18 million people. More stone for churches was quarried in medieval France than had been mined in ancient Egypt, where the Great Pyramid alone consumed 40.5 million cubic feet of stone. All these churches displayed a new architectural style. Fourteenth-century critics called the new style "Gothic" because they mistakenly believed the Goths of the fifth century had invented it. Actually, it developed partly in reaction to an earlier style named Romanesque, which supposedly resembled ancient Roman architecture.

Gothic cathedrals were built in towns, and they reflect bourgeois wealth and enormous civic pride. The manner in which a society spends its wealth indicates its values. Cathedrals, abbeys, and village churches testify to the deep religious faith and piety of medieval people. If the dominant aspect of medieval culture had not been the Christian faith, the builder's imagination and the merchant's money would have been used in other ways.

From Romanesque Gloom to "Uninterrupted Light"

The beginnings of relative political stability and the increase of ecclesiastical wealth in the eleventh century encouraged the arts of peace. After the year 1000, church building increased on a wide scale. In the ninth and tenth centuries, the Vikings and Magyars had burned hundreds of wooden churches. In the eleventh century, abbots wanted to rebuild in a more permanent fashion. Because fireproofing was essential, the ceiling had to be made of stone. Therefore, builders replaced wooden roofs with arched stone ceilings called vaults. The stone ceilings were heavy; only thick walls would support them. Because the walls were so thick, windows were small, allowing little light into the interior of the church. The basic features of Romanesque architecture, as this style is called, are stone vaults in the ceiling, a rounded arch over the nave (the central part of the church), and thick, heavy walls. In northern Europe, twin bell towers often crowned the Romanesque churches, giving them a powerful, fortresslike appearance. Built primarily by the monasteries, Romanesque churches reflect the quasi-military, aristocratic, and pre-urban society that built them.

Eleventh-century Romanesque architecture evolved from Roman, early Christian, and Carolingian models. The inspiration for the Gothic style originated in the brain of one monk, Suger, abbot of St.-Denis (1122–1151). His life is a remarkable medieval success story. Born of very poor parents, he was given as a child-oblate to the abbey of St.-Denis. St.-Denis was a royal abbey, closely associated with the French monarchy, the custodian of the royal insignia, and the burial place of the French kings. Suger became the chief adviser of Louis VI and Louis VII; and when Louis VII was away on crusade, he served as the regent of France. When Suger became abbot, he decided to reconstruct the old Carolingian abbey church at St.-Denis. Work

ROMANESQUE AND GOTHIC ARCHES. The round barrel vault characterizes the Romanesque style. Cross vaults built on arches and supported by buttresses typify the Gothic.

began in 1137. On June 11, 1144, King Louis VII and a large crowd of bishops, dignitaries, and common people witnessed the solemn consecration of the first Gothic church in France.

Art historians described the basic features of Gothic architecture as the pointed arch, the ribbed vault, and the flying buttress. None of these features was unknown before 1137. What was without precedent was the interior lightness they made possible. Since the ceiling of a Gothic church weighed less, the walls could be thinner because they had less to support. Windows were cut into the stone, allowing the church to be flooded with light. The combination of the pointed arch, ribbed vault, flying buttress, and stained-glass windows created the Gothic style. But the bright interior was the most astounding feature. Suger, describing his achievement, exulted:

Moreover, it was cunningly provided that — through the upper columns and central arches which were to be placed upon the lower ones built in the crypt — the central nave of the old nave should be equalized, by means of geometrical and arithmetical instruments, with the central nave of the new addition; and, likewise, that the dimensions of the old side-aisles should be equalized with the dimensions of the new side-aisles, except for that elegant and praiseworthy extension, in [the form of] a circular string of chapels, by virtue of which the whole [church] would shine with the wonderful and uninterrupted light of most sacred windows, pervading the interior beauty.[3]

Thirteenth-century people referred to Gothic architecture as "the new style," or as "the Frankish work." Begun in the Ile-de-France and strongly supported by the royal family, Gothic architecture spread throughout France with the expansion of royal power. French architects were soon invited to design and supervise the construction of churches in other parts of Europe. For example, William of Sens, an experienced architect, was commissioned to rebuild Canterbury Cathedral after a disastrous fire in 1174. The distinguished scholar John of Salisbury was then in Canterbury and observed William's work. After John became bishop of Chartres, he wanted William of Sens to assist in the renovation of Chartres Cathedral. Through personal contacts "the new style" traveled rapidly all over Europe.

The Creative Outburst

The construction of a Gothic cathedral represented a gigantic investment of time, money, and corporate effort. The bishop and the clergy of the cathedral made the decision to build, but they depended on the support of all the social classes. Bishops raised revenue from contributions made by people in their dioceses, and the clergy appealed to the king and the nobility. The French rulers were generous benefactors of many cathedrals. Louis IX endowed so many churches in the Ile-de-France, most notably Sainte Chapelle — a small chapel he built to house the crown of thorns — that scholars speak of a "court style" of Gothic. Noble families often gave in order to have their crests in the stained-glass windows. Sometimes, in return for a contribution to the building of a church, churchmen granted indulgences, cancellations of vows made to go on crusade. Above all, the church relied on the financial help of those with the greatest amount of ready cash, the commercial classes.

Money was not the only need. A great number of craftsmen had to be assembled: quarrymen, sculptors, stonecutters, masons, mortar makers, carpenters, blacksmiths, glassmakers, roofers. Each master craftsman had his own apprentices, and unskilled laborers had to be recruited for the heavy work. Workshops and tools had to be provided. The construction of a large cathedral took a long time and was rarely completed in one lifetime; many were never finished at all. Generation after generation of craftsmen added to the building, which explains why many Gothic churches show the architectural influences of two or even three centuries.

The surge of church building in the twelfth and thirteenth centuries is intimately associated with the growth of towns and the increase of commercial wealth. The medieval cathedrals are monuments to the interest and support of the business classes. Townspeople had secured their independence from feudal authorities, and they celebrated that freedom by building splendid cathedrals. A large and magnificent church also reflected the wealth and prosperity of the townspeople — and the cleverness and industry needed to acquire that wealth. What better way to display that wealth than in the house of God?

Since cathedrals were symbols of bourgeois civic pride, towns entered into competition to build the largest and most splendid church. In northern France in the late twelfth and early thirteenth centuries, cathedrals grew progressively taller. In 1163, the citizens of Paris began Notre Dame cathedral, intending it to reach a height of 114 feet, 8 inches. Reconstruction on Chartres Cathedral was begun in 1194: it was to be 119 feet, 9 inches. The people of Beauvais exceeded everyone: their church, started in 1247, reached 157 feet, 3 inches; unfortunately, the weight imposed on the vaults was too great, and the building collapsed in 1284. Medieval people built cathedrals to glorify God — and if mortals were impressed, so much the better.[4]

Cathedrals served secular as well as religious purposes. The sanctuary contained the altar and the bishop's chair and belonged to the clergy, but the rest of the church belonged to the people. In addition to the ceremonies connected with marriages, baptisms, and funerals, there were scores of feast days on which the entire town gathered in the cathedral for festivities. Amiens Cathedral, covering 208,000 square feet, could hold the entire town

WEST FRONT OF NOTRE DAME CATHEDRAL. In this powerful vision of the Last Judgment, Christ sits in judgment surrounded by angels, the Virgin, and Saint John. Scenes of paradise fill the arches on Christ's right, scenes of hell on the left. In the lower lintel, the dead arise incorruptible, and in the upper lintel (below Christ's feet), the saved move off to heaven, while devils push the damned to hell. Below, the twelve apostles line the doorway. (Alinari/Scala)

of ten thousand people. Local guilds, which fulfilled the economic, fraternal, and charitable functions of modern labor unions, met in the cathedrals. Guild members arranged business deals, planned recreational events, and undertook the support of disabled members in the cathedral. Magistrates and municipal officials held political meetings there. Some towns never built town halls, because all civic functions took place in the cathedral. Pilgrims slept there, lovers courted there, traveling actors staged plays there. The cathedral belonged to all.

The structure of the Gothic cathedral mirrored the interests and support of all classes of medieval society. The clergy planned the design of the building along orderly theological principles. Churchmen put into practice the axiom of the fifth-century mystical writer Dennis the Areopagite, who wrote, "Through the senses man may rise to the contemplation of the divine." The cathedral was intended to teach the people the doctrines of the Christian faith through visual images.

Architecture became the servant of theology. Accordingly, the ground plan was oriented from west to east. The main altar was in the east end, which pointed toward Jerusalem, the city of peace. The west front of the cathedral faced the setting sun, and its wall was usually devoted to scenes of the Last Judgment. The north side, which received the least amount of sunlight, displayed events from the Old Testament. The south side, washed in warm sunshine for much of the day, depicted scenes from the New Testament. This symbolism implied that the Jewish people of the Old Testament lived in darkness and the gospel brought by Christ illuminated the world. In the same way, every piece of sculpture, stained glass, and furniture had some religious significance.

Contributors to the cathedral and the workmen left their imprint upon it. The stonecutter cut his mark on every block of stone, partly so that he would be paid, partly, too, so that his work would be remembered. At Chartres Cathedral the craft and merchant guilds—drapers, furriers, haberdashers, tanners, butchers, bakers, fishmongers, and wine merchants donated money and are memorialized in the stained-glass windows. The carpenters' window shows carpenters with the tools of their trade. In the bakers' window, two bakers carry loaves of bread. The incredibly beautiful window of the wine merchants reveals their business in three central medallions: the bottom medallion shows a wine merchant and his cart; the central medallion depicts a man pouring wine from a cask; and the top medallion reveals the wine being used at the mass. Around the border of this window small figures hold little wine cups.

Thousands of scenes in the cathedral celebrate nature, country life, and the activities of ordinary people. All the members of medieval society had a place in the City of God, which the Gothic cathedrals represented. No one, from kings to milkmaids, was excluded.

THE CRUSADES

In the late eleventh and early twelfth centuries, a crusade was a holy war, under the theoretical leadership of the papacy, for the recovery of the Holy Land from the Muslim Arabs or the Turks. In the later twelfth and through the thirteenth centuries, crusades were sometimes directed against heretics and other Christian peoples.

The Crusades were another manifestation of the tremendous vitality of the High Middle Ages. Between 1096 and 1270, there were at least eight official campaigns to wrest the Holy Land from the infidels, and through this period Christian individuals and groups left Europe for the Middle East in a

THE WINE MERCHANT'S WINDOW. Chartres Cathedral contained over 5,000 square yards of stained glass, an incredible achievement given the limitations of medieval technology. The various guilds that donated individual windows are represented by some aspect of their work. This medallion shows a wine merchant with a cask of wine on a wagon. (Giraudon)

ENGLISH MASONS' MARKS. Masons showed their responsibility for, and their pride in, their work with their marks, which passed from father to son. (John Harvey)

steady trickle. The Crusades were an expression of Europeans' religious zeal. Although peoples of all ages and classes participated in them, so many knights departed for the Holy Land that crusading became a feature of the upper-class lifestyle. In an aristocratic, militaristic society, men coveted the reputation of being a Crusader, and the Christian knight enjoyed great prestige. These expeditions reflected the religious, military, and chivalric ideals of medieval aristocratic society.

The Crusades of the High Middle Ages grew out of the earlier conflict between Christians and Muslims in Spain. The concept of a holy war originated in the Spanish peninsula and gradually influenced all parts of western Europe. In the eighth century, the Arabs had overrun the peninsula, and Christian lords fled into the mountains in the north. In the tenth century, Christians started the *reconquista,* or holy war of reconquest. Christian warriors made slow progress — not until 1492 did Isabella and Ferdinand finally succeed in expelling the Arabs — but by about 1100, Christian kings had regained about a fourth of the peninsula. The *reconquista* dominates the history of medieval Spain.

The Roman papacy supported the holy war in Spain and by the late eleventh century had strong reasons for wanting to launch an expedition against Muslim infidels in the Middle East as well. The papacy had been involved in a bitter struggle over investiture with the German emperors. If the pope could muster a large army against the enemies of Christianity, then his claim to be the leader of Christian society in the West would be strengthened.

Moreover, in 1054, a serious theological disagreement had split the Greek church of Byzantium and the Roman church of the West. The pope believed that a crusade would lead to the establishment of strong Roman influence in Greek territories and eventually the reunion of the two churches. Then, in 1071 at Manzikert in eastern Anatolia, Turkish soldiers in the pay of the Arabs defeated a

Greek army and occupied much of Asia Minor. The emperor at Constantinople appealed to the West for support. Shortly afterward, the holy city of Jerusalem, the scene of Christ's preaching and burial, fell to the Turks. Pilgrimages to holy places in the Middle East became very dangerous, and the papacy was outraged because the holy city was in the hands of infidels.

In 1095, Pope Urban II journeyed to Clermont in France and called for a great Christian holy war against the infidels. He stressed the sufferings and persecution of Christians in Jerusalem. He urged Christian knights who had been fighting one another to direct their energies against the true enemies of God, the Muslims. Urban proclaimed an indulgence, or remission of sin, to those who would fight for and regain the holy city of Jerusalem. Few speeches in history have had such a dramatic effect as Urban's call at Clermont for the First Crusade.

The response was fantastic. Godfrey of Bouillon, Geoffrey of Lorraine, and many other great lords from northern France immediately had the cross of the Crusader sewn on their tunics. Encouraged by popular preachers like Peter the Hermit, and by papal legates in Germany, Italy, and England, thousands of people of all classes joined the crusade. Although most of the Crusaders were French, pilgrims from all countries streamed southward from the Rhineland, through Germany and the Balkans. No development in the High Middle Ages better reveals Europeans' religious zeal and emotional fervor, and the influence of the reformed papacy, than this incredible outpouring of support for the First Crusade.

Religious convictions inspired many, but mundane motives were also involved. Except for wives, who had to remain at home to manage estates, many people expected to benefit from the crusade. For the curious and the adventurous, it offered the chance for foreign travel and excitement; it promised escape from the dullness of everyday life. The crusade provided kings, who were trying to establish order and to build states, the perfect opportunity to get rid of troublemaking knights. It gave land-hungry younger sons a chance to acquire fiefs in the Middle East. Even some members of the middle class who stayed at home profited from the crusade. Nobles often had to borrow money from the middle class to pay for their expeditions, and they put up part of their land as security. If a noble did not return home or could not pay the interest on the loan, the middle-class creditor took over the land.

The First Crusade was successful, mostly because of the dynamic enthusiasm of the participants. The Crusaders had little more than religious zeal. They knew nothing about the geography or climate of the Middle East. Although among the host there were several counts with military experience, the Crusaders could never agree upon a leader, and the entire expedition was marked by disputes among the great lords. Lines of supply were never set up. Starvation and disease wracked the army, and the Turks slaughtered hundreds of noncombatants. Nevertheless, convinced that "God wills it" — the war cry of the Crusaders — the army pressed on and in 1099 captured Jerusalem. Although the Crusaders fought bravely, Arab disunity was a chief reason for their victory. At Jerusalem, Edessa, Tripoli, and Antioch, Crusader kingdoms on the Western feudal model were set up (see Map 10.4).

Between 1096 and 1270, the crusading ideal was expressed in eight official, papally approved expeditions to the East. (In addition to those eight, the papacy in 1208 proclaimed a crusade against heretics in southern France. In the same year, two expeditions of children set out on a crusade to the Holy Land; one contingent turned back, the other was captured and sold into slavery. And, in 1227 and 1239, the pope launched a crusade against the emperor Frederick II.) None of the "official"

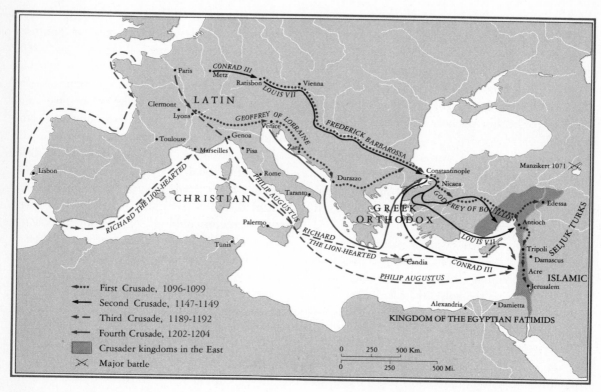

MAP 10.4   THE ROUTES OF THE CRUSADERS

crusades against the Muslims achieved very much. The third one (1189–1192) was precipitated by the recapture of Jerusalem by the sultan Saladin in 1187. Frederick Barbarossa of the Holy Roman Empire, Richard the Lion-Hearted of England, and Philip Augustus of France participated in it, and it was better financed than previous ones, but disputes among the leaders and strategic problems prevented any lasting results.

During the Fourth Crusade (1198–1204), careless preparation and inadequate financing led to disastrous consequences for Byzantine-Latin relations. Hoping to receive material support from the Greeks, the leaders of the crusade took the expedition to Constantinople before advancing to Jerusalem. But once there, they sacked the city and established the Latin Empire of Constantinople.

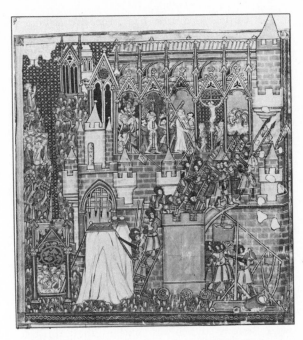

THE CAPTURE OF JERUSALEM IN 1099. As engines hurl stones to breach the walls, crusaders enter on scaling ladders. Scenes from Christ's passion (above) identify the city as Jerusalem. (Bibliothèque Nationale, Paris)

This assault of one Christian people on another, when one of the goals of the crusade was the reunion of the Greek and Latin churches, helped to discredit the entire crusading movement. Two later crusades undertaken by King Louis IX of France added to his prestige as a pious ruler. Apart from that, the last of the official crusades accomplished nothing at all.

The Crusades brought few cultural changes to western Europe. By the late eleventh century, strong economic and intellectual ties with the East had already been made. The Crusades testify to the religious enthusiasm of the High Middle Ages. But, as Steven Runciman, a distinguished scholar of the Crusades, concluded in his three-volume history:

The triumphs of the Crusade were the triumphs of faith. But faith without wisdom is a dangerous thing. . . . In the long sequence of interaction and fusion between Orient and Occident out of which our civilization has grown, the Crusades were a tragic and destructive episode. . . . There was so much courage and so little honour, so much devotion and so little understanding. High ideals were besmirched by cruelty and greed, enterprise and endurance by a blind and narrow self-righteousness; and the Holy War itself was nothing more than a long act of intolerance in the name of God, which is the sin against the Holy Ghost.[5]

❧

Societies, like individuals, cannot maintain a high level of energy indefinitely. In the later years of the thirteenth century, Europeans seemed to run out of steam. The crusading movement gradually fizzled out. No new cathedrals were constructed, and if one had not been completed by 1300, the chances were that it never would be. The strong rulers of France and England, building on the foundations of their predecessors, increased their authority and gained the loyalty of all their subjects. The vigor of those kings, however, did not pass to their immediate descendants. The church, which for two centuries had guided Christian society, began to face grave difficulties. A violent dispute between the papacy and the kings of France and England badly damaged papal prestige.

In 1296, King Edward I of England and Philip the Fair (1285–1314) of France declared war upon each other. To finance this war both kings laid taxes on the clergy. Kings had been taxing the church for decades. Pope Boniface VIII (1294–1303) a staunch defender of papal supremacy, forbade churchmen to pay the taxes. But Edward and Philip refused to accept this decree, partly because it hurt royal finances, partly because the papal order threatened royal authority within their countries. Edward immediately denied the clergy the protection of the law, which meant that they could be attacked with impunity. Philip halted the shipment of all ecclesiastical revenue to Rome. Boniface had to back down.

Philip the Fair and his ministers continued their attack on all powers in France outside royal authority. Philip arrested a French bishop who was also the papal legate. When Boniface defended the ecclesiastical status and the diplomatic immunity of the bishop, Philip replied with the trumped-up charge that the pope was a heretic. Both the papacy and the French monarchy waged a bitter war of propaganda. Finally, in 1302, in a letter entitled *Unam Sanctam* (because its opening sentence spoke of one holy Catholic church), Boniface insisted that Philip, like everyone else, submit to papal authority. Philip's university-trained advisers responded with an argument drawn from Roman law: they maintained that the king of France was completely sovereign in his kingdom and responsible to God alone. French mercenary troops went to Italy and arrested the aged pope at Anagni. Although Boniface was soon freed, he died shortly afterward. The incident at Anagni marked a decisive turning point.

The Christian church had been the strongest influence in medieval society, and the French attack on the leadership of the church signaled the weakening of religious authority. A new power, the national secular state, had emerged in western Europe. Boniface's successors not only retracted *Unam Sanctam* but apologized for it. This retraction illustrates the power of the French state. The centralized power of the French monarchy, which had been growing for over a century, scored a victory over the papacy. Then, the presence of King Philip the Fair at the coronation of Pope Clement V at Lyons in 1305 was symbolic. Clement was a Frenchman, and he established the papal court at Avignon, which although within the borders of the Holy Roman Empire, was very much a French city. For the next sixty years, the Roman papacy was strongly influenced by France. Anagni foreshadowed serious difficulties within the Christian church, but additional difficulties awaited Western society in the fourteenth century.

NOTES

1. D. C. Douglas and G. W. Greenaway, eds., *English Historical Documents,* Eyre & Spottiswoode, London, 1961, 2.853.

2. Quoted by H. E. Sigerist, *Civilization and Disease,* University of Chicago Press, Chicago, 1943, p. 102.

3. E. Panofsky, trans., *Abbot Suger on the Abbey Church of St.-Denis and Its Art Treasures,* Princeton University Press, Princeton, 1946, p. 101.

4. See J. Gimpel, *The Cathedral Builders,* Grove Press, New York, 1961, pp. 42–49.

5. S. Runciman, *A History of the Crusades,* vol. 3: *The Kingdom of Acre,* Cambridge University Press, Cambridge, 1955, p. 480.

SUGGESTED READING

The achievements of the High Middle Ages have attracted considerable scholarly attention, and the curious student will have no difficulty finding exciting material on the points raised in this chapter. Three general surveys of the period 1050–1300 are especially recommended: J. R. Strayer, *Western Europe in the Middle Ages** (1955), a masterful synthesis; J. W. Baldwin, *The Scholastic Culture of the Middle Ages** (1971), which stresses the intellectual features of medieval civilization; and F. Heer, *The Medieval World** (1963).

G. O. Sayles, *The Medieval Foundations of England** (1961), traces English conditions to the end of the thirteenth century, while R. Fawtier, *The Capetian Kings of France** (1962), shows how the French monarchy built a nation. G. Barraclough, *The Origins of Modern Germany** (1963), provides the best explanation of the problems and peculiarities of the Holy Roman Empire; this is a fine example of a Marxist interpretation of medieval history. A good comparative study of English and French conditions is given in the older work of C. Petit-Dutailles, *Feudal Monarchy in France and England** (1964), while J. R. Strayer, *On the Medieval Origins of the Modern State** (1972), is an excellent recent treatment of the political and bureaucratic development of European states, also with emphasis on France and England. Students interested in approaching the High Middle Ages through biographies of leading political figures will find D. C. Douglas, *William the Conqueror** (1964); W. L. Warren, *Henry II* (1974); and E. Kantorowicz, *Frederick II* (1931) interesting and thorough.

For the new currents of thought in the High Middle Ages, see C. Brooke, *The Twelfth Century Renaissance**(1970), a splendidly illustrated book with copious quotations from the sources; E. Gilson, *Héloise and Abélard** (1960) which treats the medieval origins of modern humanism against the background of Abélard the teacher; D. W. Robertson, Jr., *Abélard and Héloise* (1972), which is highly readable, commonsensical, and probably the best recent study of Abélard and the love affair he supposedly had; and C. W. Hollister, ed., *The Twelfth Century Renaissance** (1969), a well-constructed anthology with source materials on many aspects of twelfth-century culture. N. Orme, *English Schools in the Middle Ages* (1973), focuses on the significance of schools and literacy in English medieval society, while J. Leclercq, *The Love of Learning and the Desire of God** (1974), discusses monastic literary culture.

On the medieval universities, C. H. Haskins, *The Rise of the Universities** (1959), is a good introduction, while H. Rashdall, *The Universities of Europe in the Middle Ages,* (1936), is the standard scholarly work. G. Leff, *Paris and Oxford Universities in the Thirteenth and Fourteenth Centuries** (1968), gives a fascinating sketch and includes a useful bibliography.

Students will find a good general introduction to Romanesque and Gothic architecture in N. Pevsner, *An Outline of European Architecture** (1963), a standard work. D. Grivot and G. Zarnecki, *Gislebertus, Sculptor of Autun* (1961), is the finest appreciation of Romanesque architecture written in English. For the actual work of building, see D. Macaulay, *Cathedral: The Story of Its Construction* (1973), a prizewinning, simply written, and cleverly illustrated re-creation of the problems and duration of cathedral building. J. Gimpel, *The Cathedral Builders** (1961), explores the engineering problems involved in cathedral building and places the subject within its social context. Advanced students will enjoy E. Mâle, *The Gothic Image: Religious Art in France in the Thirteenth Century** (1958), which contains a wealth of fascinating and useful detail. For the most important cathedrals in France, architecturally and politically, see A. Temko, *Notre Dame of Paris, the Biography of a Cathedral** (1968); G. Henderson, *Chartres* (1968); and A. Katzenellenbogen, *The Sculptural Programs of Chartres Cathedral** (1959), by a distinguished art historian. E. Panofsky, *Abbot Suger on the Abbey Church of St.-Denis and Its Art Treasures* (1946), provides a contemporary background account of the first Gothic building. G. Holt, ed., *A Documentary History of Art** (1957), contains source materials useful for writing papers. J. Gimpel, *The Medieval Machine: The Industrial Revolution of the Middle Ages** (1977), discusses the mechanical and scientific problems involved and shows how construction affected the medieval environment; this is an extremely useful book.

*Available in paperback.

Chapter 11

THE CRISIS OF THE LATER

MIDDLE AGES

n the later Middle Ages, the last book of the New Testament, the Book of Revelation, formed the basis for thousands of sermons and hundreds of religious tracts. The Book of Revelation deals with visions of the end of the world, with disease, war, famine, and death. It is no wonder this part of the Bible was so popular. Between 1300 and 1450, Europeans experienced a frightful series of shocks: economic dislocation, plague, war, social upheaval, and increased crime and violence. Death and the preoccupation with death make the fourteenth century one of the gloomiest periods in Western civilization.

The miseries and disasters of the later Middle Ages bring to mind a number of questions. What are the social and psychological effects of repeated attacks of plague and disease? Some scholars maintain that war is often the catalyst for political, economic, and social change. Does this theory have validity for the fourteenth century? Finally, what provoked the division in the church in the fourteenth century? What other ecclesiastical difficulties was the schism a sign of, and what impact did it have on the faith of the common people? This chapter seeks to answer these questions.

PRELUDE TO DISASTER

The fourteenth century began with serious economic problems. In the first decade, the countries of northern Europe experienced a considerable price inflation. The costs of grain, livestock, and dairy products rose sharply. The weather made a serious situation worse. An increasing number of storms brought torrential rains. Almost everywhere, heavy rains ruined the wheat, oats, and hay crops on which people and animals depended. The long-distance transportation of food was not only expensive but difficult. Most urban areas, consequently, depended for bread and meat on an area no more than a day's journey away. Poor harvests — and one in four was likely to be poor — led to scarcity and starvation. For example, almost all of northern Europe suffered a terrible famine in the years 1315–1317.

Hardly had western Europe begun to recover from this disaster when another struck. An epidemic of typhoid fever carried away thousands. In 1316, perhaps as many as 10 percent of the population of the city of Ypres in Belgium may have died between May and October alone. Then, in 1318, diseases hit cattle and sheep, drastically reducing the herds and flocks. Another bad harvest in 1321 brought famine, starvation, and death.

The large province of Languedoc in southern France presents a classic example of agrarian crisis. For over 150 years, Languedoc had witnessed continual land reclamation, steady agricultural expansion, and enormous population growth. Then, the fourteenth century opened with four years of bad harvests, 1302 through 1305. Torrential rains in 1310 ruined the harvest and brought terrible famine. Harvests failed again in 1322 and 1329. In 1332, desperate peasants survived the winter on raw herbs. In the entire half-century from 1302 to 1348, poor harvests occurred twenty times, bringing starvation and death. The undernourished population was ripe for the Grim Reaper, who appeared in 1348 in the form of the Black Death.

These catastrophes had inevitable social consequences. Poor harvests meant that marriage had to be postponed. Coming on top of the deaths caused by famine and disease, later marriages meant a further reduction in population. Thus, after the steady population growth of the twelfth and thirteenth centuries, western Europe suffered a gradual decline in the first third of the fourteenth century. The international character of trade and commerce meant that a disaster in one country had serious implications elsewhere. For example, the sheep murrain that attacked English sheep in 1318 caused a sharp decline in wool exports in the following years. Without wool, Flemish weavers could not work, and thousands were laid off. Without woolen cloth, the businesses of Flemish, French, and English merchants suffered. Unemployment encouraged many men to turn to crime with the result that violence and lawlessness increased.

To none of these problems did governments have any solutions. In fact, they even lacked policies. After the death of Edward I in 1307, England was governed by the incompetent and weak Edward II (1307–1327), and his reign was dominated by a series of baronial conflicts. In France the three sons of Philip the Fair who followed their father on the French throne between 1314 and 1328 showed no interest in the increasing economic difficulties. In the Holy Roman Empire power drifted into the hands of the many German local rulers. The only actions taken by the governments tended to be in response to the demands of the upper classes. Economic and social problems were aggravated by the appearance in western Europe of a frightful disease.

THE BLACK DEATH

Around 1331, the bubonic plague attacked regions of China. In the course of the next fifteen years, merchants, traders, and soldiers carried the disease across the Asian caravan routes until, in 1346, it reached the Crimea region in southern Russia. From there the plague had easy access to the Mediterranean lands and western Europe.

In 1291, Genoese sailors had defeated the Moroccans and thereby opened the Straits of Gibraltar to Italian shipping. Then, shortly after 1300, important advances were made in the design of Italian merchant ships. A square rig was added to the mainmast, and ships began to carry three masts instead of just one. Additional sails better utilized wind power to propel the ship. The improved design of ships permitted, for the first time, year-round shipping, and Venetian and Genoese merchant ships could sail the dangerous Atlantic coast even in the winter months. With ships continually at sea, the rats that bore the disease spread beyond the Mediterranean to Atlantic and North Sea ports.

Thus, in October 1347, Genoese ships brought the plague to Messina, from which it spread to Sicily. Venice and Genoa were hit in January 1348, and from the port of Pisa the disease spread south to Rome and north to Florence and all Tuscany. By late spring southern Germany was attacked. Frightened French authorities chased the galley bearing the disease from the port of Marseilles, but not before plague had infected the city, from which it spread into Languedoc and Spain. In June 1348, two ships entered the Bristol Channel and introduced it into England. All Europe felt the scourge of this horrible disease (See Map 11.1).

Pathology

Modern knowledge of the bubonic plague rests on the researches of two bacteriologists, one French and one Japanese, who in 1894 independently identified *Pasteurella pestis,* the bacillus that causes the plague. (The bacillus was labeled *Pasteurella pestis* after the French scientist's teacher, Louis Pasteur.) The bacillus liked to live in the bloodstream of an animal or, ideally, in the stomach of a flea. The flea resided in the hair of a rodent, sometimes a squirrel but preferably the hardy, nimble, and vagabond black rat. Why the host black rat moved so much, scientists still do not know, but it often traveled by ship. There the black rat could feast for months on a cargo of grain or live snugly among bales of cloth. Fleas bearing the bacillus also had no trouble nesting in saddlebags.[1]

Comfortable, well fed, and often having greatly reproduced, the black rats ended their ocean voyage and descended upon the great cities of Europe.

Although by the fourteenth century urban authorities from London to Paris to Rome had begun to try to achieve a primitive level of sanitation, urban conditions remained ideal for the spread of disease. Narrow streets filled with mud, refuse, and human excrement were as much cesspools as thoroughfares. Dead animals and sore-covered beggars greeted the traveler. Houses constructed with each story projecting over the one below eliminated light and air. And within the houses terrible overcrowding existed everywhere. When all members of an aristocratic family lived and slept in one room, it should not be surprising that six or eight persons in a middle-class or poor household slept in one bed — if they had one. Closeness, after all, provided warmth. Houses were beginning to be constructed of brick, but many remained of wood, clay, and mud. A determined rat had little trouble tearing and entering such a house.

Standards of personal hygiene remained frightfully low. Since water was considered dangerous, and partly for good reasons, people rarely bathed. Skin infections, consequently, were common. The lack of personal cleanliness, combined with any number of temporary ailments such as diarrhea and the common cold, naturally weakened the body's resistance to serious disease. Fleas and body lice were univeral afflictions. Everyone from peasants to archbishops had them. One more bite did not cause much alarm. But if that nibble came from a bacillus-bearing flea, an entire household or area was doomed.

The symptoms of the bubonic plague started with a growth the size of a nut or an apple in the armpit, the groin, or on the neck. This was the boil, or *buba,* that gave the disease its name and caused agonizing pain. If the *buba* was lanced and the pus thoroughly drained, the victim had a chance of recovery. The secondary stage was the appearance of

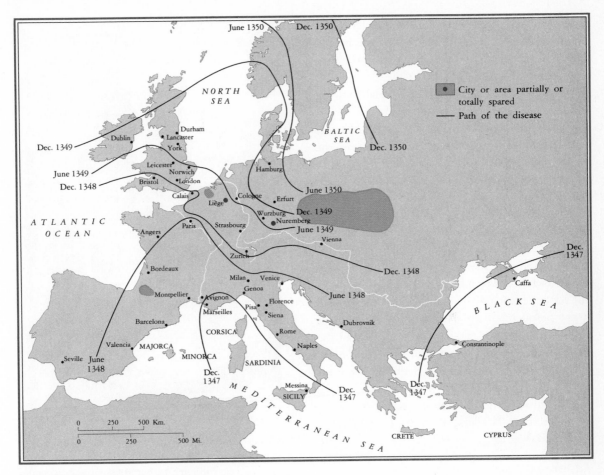

MAP II.I THE COURSE OF THE BLACK DEATH IN FOUR-
TEENTH-CENTURY EUROPE

black spots or blotches caused by bleeding under the skin. (This syndrome did not give the disease its common name; contemporaries did not call the plague the Black Death. Sometime in the fifteenth century the Latin phrase *atra mors,* meaning "terrible" or "dreadful death" was translated "black death," and the phrase has stuck.) Finally, the victim began to cough violently and spit blood. This stage, indicating the presence of thousands of bacilli in the bloodstream, signaled the end, and death followed in two or three days. Rather than evoking compassion for the sick, a French scientist has written that everything about the bubonic plague provoked horror and disgust: "All the matter which exuded from their bodies let off an unbearable stench; sweat, excrement, spittle, breath, so fetid as to be overpowering; urine turbid, thick, black or red."[2]

Medieval people had no rational explanation for the disease nor any effective medical treatment for it. Fourteenth-century medical literature indicates that while the physicians could sometimes ease the pain, they had no cure. The overwhelming majority of people — lay, scholarly, and medical — believed that the Black Death was caused by some "vicious property in the air" that carried the disease from place to place. All authorities took it for granted that some corruption of the atmosphere caused the disease. (Still, one should be cautious in condemning medieval "backwardness and superstition." In July 1977, a New York City blackout was described by the president of a powerful utility company as "an act of God." In the same week a leader of the Mormon church laid responsibility for the severe drought in the western United States on the great prevalence of homosexuality there.)

The Italian writer Giovanni Boccaccio (1313–1375) described the course of the disease in Florence in the preface to his tales, *The Decameron*. He pinpointed the cause of the spread:

Moreover, the virulence of the pest was the greater by reason that intercourse was apt to convey it from the sick to the whole, just as fire devours things dry or greasy when they are brought close to it. Nay, the evil went yet further, for not merely by speech or association with the sick was the malady communicated to the healthy with consequent peril of common death, but any that touched the clothes of the sick or aught else that had been touched or used by them, seemed thereby to contract the disease.[3]

The bubonic plague, as is known from its twentieth-century appearances in Hong Kong, Bombay, and Uganda, is highly infectious. In the fourteeth century, its transmission from person to person was

THE PLAGUE STRICKEN. Even as the dead were wrapped in shrouds and collected in carts for mass burial, the disease struck others. The man collapsing has the symptomatic buba on his neck. As Saint Sebastian pleads for mercy (above), a winged devil, bearer of the plague, attacks an angel. (Walters Art Gallery)

accelerated by the filthy and overcrowded conditions of living. A few sophisticated Arabs recognized this. When the disease struck the town of Salé in Morocco, the Muslim Ibu Abu Madyan shut in his household with sufficient food and water and allowed no one to enter or leave until the plague had passed. Madyan was entirely successful. In European cities, those who could afford to fled to the countryside, which generally suffered less. Few were so wise or so lucky, however, and the plague took a staggering toll.

The mortality rate cannot be specified, because population figures for most countries and cities for the period before the arrival of the plague do not exist. The largest amount of material survives for England, but it is difficult to use and, after enormous scholarly controversy, only educated guesses can be made. In a total population of perhaps 4.2 million persons, probably 1.4 million died of the Black Death in its several visits.[4] Densely populated Italian cities endured incredible losses. Florence lost between half and two-thirds of its 1347 population of 85,000 when the plague visited in 1348. In general, it is fair to say that rural areas suffered much less than urban ones. The disease recurred intermittently in the 1360s and 1370s and, in fact, reappeared several times down to 1700.

Social and Psychological Consequences

Predictably, the poor died more rapidly than the rich, because the rich enjoyed better health to begin with; but the powerful were not unaffected. In England two archbishops of Canterbury became victims of the plague in 1349, King Edward III's daughter Joan died, and many of the leading members of the London guilds followed her to the grave.

It is noteworthy that in an age of mounting criticism of clerical wealth and luxury, the behavior of the clergy during the plague was often exemplary. Priests, monks, and nuns cared for the sick and buried the dead. In places like Venice, where even the physicians ran away, priests remained to give what ministrations they could. Consequently, their mortality rate was phenomenally high. The German clergy, especially, suffered a severe decline in personnel in the years after 1350. With the ablest killed off, the wealth of the German church fell into the hands of the incompetent and weak. The situation was already ripe for reform.

The plague accelerated the economic decline that had begun in the early part of the fourteenth century. In many parts of Europe there was not enough work for people to do. The Black Death was a grim remedy to this problem. The population decline, however, led to an increased demand for labor and to considerable mobility among the peasant and working classes. Wages rose sharply. The shortage of labor and steady requests for higher wages put landlords on the defensive. They retaliated with such measures as the English Statute of Laborers (1351), which attempted to freeze salaries and wages at pre-1347 levels. The statute could not be enforced and was largely unsuccessful.

Even more frightening than the social effects were the psychological consequences. The knowledge that once the disease was contracted, no cure existed, and death almost surely followed provoked the most profound pessimism. Everyone experiences at some time the sense that he or she is the victim of uncontrollable social or psychological pressures. A healthy person overcomes this depression by concentrating on good qualities and by constructive activities. But imagine an entire society in the grips of the belief that it was at the mercy of a frightful affliction about which nothing could be done, a disgusting disease from which family and friends would flee, leaving one to die in agony and alone. It is not surprising that some sought release in orgies and gross sensuality while others turned to the severest forms of asceticism and frenzied religious fervor. Some extremists joined groups of flagellants, who, armed with leather straps tipped with metal, collectively whipped and scourged themselves as penance for their and society's sins. Flagellants believed the Black Death was God's punishment for humanity's wickedness.

Both the literature and the art of the fourteenth century reveal a terribly morbid concern with death. One highly popular artistic motif, the "Dance of Death," shows a dancing skeleton leading away a living person. No wonder that survivors experienced a sort of shell shock and a terrible crisis of faith. Lack of confidence in the leaders of society, lack of hope for the future, defeatism, and malaise wreaked enormous anguish and contributed to the decline of the Middle Ages. A long international war added further misery to the frightful disasters of the plague.

PROCESSION OF FLAGELLANTS. The horrors of the Black Death provoked terrible excesses. People believed that the disease was God's punishment for humanity's sins, which could be atoned for only through severe penances. In this procession of robed and hooded flagellants, two of the men flog those ahead of them. (Bibliothèque Royale Albert I, Brussels)

THE HUNDRED YEARS' WAR
(CA 1337–1453)

In January 1327, Queen Isabella of England, her lover Mortimer, and a group of barons, having deposed and murdered Isabella's husband, the incompetent King Edward II, proclaimed his fifteen-year-old son king as Edward III. In February 1328, Charles IV, the last surviving son of the French king Philip the Fair, died and with him ended the Capetian dynasty. An assembly of French barons, intending to exclude Isabella (daughter of Philip the Fair) and her son Edward III from the French throne, proclaimed that "no woman nor her son could succeed to the [French] monarchy." The

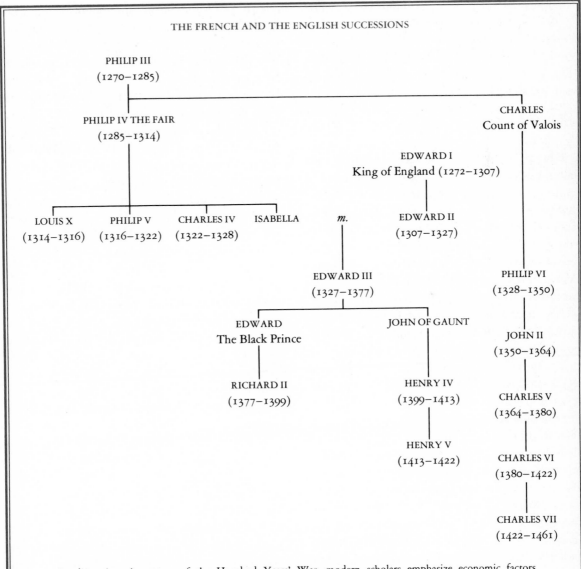

THE FRENCH AND THE ENGLISH SUCCESSIONS

In discussing the causes of the Hundred Years' War, modern scholars emphasize economic factors or the French-English dispute over the province of Gascony. Fourteenth-century Englishmen, however, believed they were fighting because King Edward III was denied his legal right to the French crown. He was the eldest surviving male descendant of Philip the Fair.

barons passed the crown to Philip VI of Valois (1328–1350), a nephew of Philip the Fair. In these actions lie the origins of another phase of the centuries-old struggle between the English and the French monarchies, one that was fought intermittently from 1337 to 1453.

Causes

Edward III, as the eldest surviving direct male descendant of Philip the Fair of France, believed he was entitled to the French throne. He maintained that since God had given him the French kingdom, it was his special duty to claim it. King Edward of England was also duke of Aquitaine, and in 1329 he did homage to Philip VI for the duchy. Although Edward was a vassal of the French ruler, his interests were often diametrically opposed to those of Philip VI. Moreover, the dynastic argument had feudal implications. In order to increase their independent power, French vassals of Philip VI used the excuse that they had to transfer their loyalty to a more legitimate overlord, Edward III. This position resulted in widespread conflicts.

Economic factors involving the wool trade, the ancient dispute over Aquitaine, control of the Flemish towns — for centuries these had served as justifications for war between France and England. The causes of the conflicts labeled the Hundred Years' War were dynastic, feudal, political, and economic. Recent historians have stressed the economic factors. The wool trade between England and Flanders served as the cornerstone of the economy of both countries; they were closely interdependent. Flanders was a fief of the French crown, and the Flemish aristocracy was highly sympathetic to the monarchy in Paris. But the wealth of the Flemish merchants and cloth manufacturers depended on English wool, and the Flemish burghers strongly supported the claims of Edward III. The disruption of their commerce with England threatened their prosperity.

It is impossible to measure the precise influence of the Flemings on the cause and course of the war. Certainly, Edward could not ignore that influence, however, because it represented money he needed to carry on the war. Although the impact of the war on commerce fluctuated, over the long run the war badly hurt the wool trade and the cloth industry.

Governments manipulated public opinion in the fourteenth century as they do in the twentieth. Whatever significance modern students ascribe to the economic factor, public opinion in fourteenth-century England held that the war was waged for one reason: to secure for King Edward the French crown he had been denied.[5]

Why did the struggle last so long? One historian has written in jest that if Edward III had been locked away in a castle with a pile of toy knights and archers to play with, he would have done far less damage.[6] The same might be said of Philip VI. Both rulers glorified war and saw in it the perfect arena for the realization of their chivalric ideals. Neither king possessed any sort of policy for dealing with his kingdom's social, economic, or political ills. Both sought military adventure as a means of diverting attention from domestic problems.

The Popular Response

The governments of both England and France worked to mold public opinion to support the war. Edward III issued letters to the sheriffs describing in graphic terms the evil deeds of the French and listing the royal needs. Royal letters instructed the clergy to deliver sermons filled with patriotic sentiment. Frequent assemblies of Parliament — where, theoretically, representatives of the entire nation were present — spread royal propaganda for the war. All the information coming from the royal courts sensationalized the wickedness of the other side and stressed the great fortunes to be made from the war. Philip VI sent agents to warn local communities about the dangers of invasion and to stress the Crown's need for revenue to meet the attack.

The royal campaign to rally public opinion was highly successful, at least in the early stage of the war. Edward III gained widespread support in the 1340s and 1350s. The English developed a deep hatred of the French and feared that King Philip intended "to have seized and slaughtered the entire realm of England." As England was successful in the field, pride in the country's military proficiency increased.

Most important of all, the war was popular because it presented unusual opportunities for wealth and advancement. Poor and unemployed knights were promised regular wages. Criminals who enlisted were granted pardons. The great nobles had the expectation of great estates. Royal exhortations to the troops before battles repeatedly stressed that, if victorious, the men might keep whatever they seized. The French chronicler Jean Froissart (1337–1410) wrote that at the time of Edward III's expedition of 1359, men of all ranks flocked to the king's banner. Some came to acquire honor, but many came "to loot and pillage the fair and plenteous land of France."[7]

The Indian Summer of Medieval Chivalry

The period of the Hundred Years' War witnessed the final flowering of the aristocratic code of medieval chivalry. Indeed, the enthusiastic participation of the nobility in both France and England was in response primarily to the opportunity that war provided to display the qualities of chivalric behavior. Chivalry was a code of conduct originally devised by the clergy to improve the crude and brutal behavior of the knightly class. A knight was supposed to be brave, anxious to win praise,

FIFTEENTH-CENTURY ARMOR. This kind of expensive plate armor was worn by the aristocratic nobility in the fifteenth and sixteenth centuries. The use of gunpowder gradually made armor outmoded. (Courtesy, World Heritage Museum. Photo: Caroline Buckler)

courteous, loyal to his commander, gracious, and generous in the giving of gifts. What better place to display these qualities than on the field of battle?

War was considered an ennobling experience; there was something elevating, manly, fine, and beautiful about it. When Shakespeare in the sixteenth century wrote of "the pomp and circumstance of glorious war," he was echoing the fourteenth- and fifteenth-century chroniclers who had glorified the trappings of war. Describing the French army before the battle of Poitiers (1356), a contemporary said, "Then you might see banners and pennons unfurled to the wind, whereon fine gold and azure shone, purple, gules and ermine. Trumpets, horns and clarions — you might hear sounding through the camp; the Dauphin's great battle made the earth ring."[8]

The chronicler Froissart repeatedly speaks of the "beauty" of an army assembled for battle. Writing of the French army before the battle of Bergues in 1383, Froissart reflected the attitudes of the aristocratic classes: it was "a great beauty to see the banners, pennons, and basinets glittering against the sun, and such a great multitude of men-at-arms that the eye of man could not take them in, and it seemed that they bore a veritable forest of lances." At Poitiers, it was a marvelous and terrifying thing to hear the thundering of the horses' hooves, the cries of the wounded, the sound of the trumpets and clarions, and the shouting of the war cries. The tumult was heard at a distance of more than three leagues. And it was a great grief to see and behold the flower of all the nobility and chivalry of the world go thus to destruction, to death, and to martyrdom on both sides.

This romantic and "marvelous" view of war holds little appeal to modern men and women, who are more conscious of the slaughter, the brutality, the dirt, and the blood that war inevitably involves.

Modern thinkers are usually conscious of the broad mass of people; the chivalric code, however, applied only to the aristocratic military elite. Chivalry had no reference to those outside the knightly class.

The knight was supposed to show courtesy, graciousness, and generosity to his social equals, but he was certainly not obliged to display these qualities to his social inferiors. English knights fought French ones, but they were social equals fighting according to a mutually accepted code of behavior. The infantry troops were looked upon as inferior beings. When a peasant force at Longueil destroyed a contingent of English knights, their comrades mourned them because "it was too much that so many good fighters had been killed by mere peasants."[9]

The Course of the War to 1419

Armies in the field were commanded by rulers themselves, by princes of the blood, such as Edward III's son Edward, the Black Prince — so called because of the color of his armor — or by great aristocrats. Knights formed the cavalry; the despised peasantry served as infantrymen, pikemen, and archers. Edward III set up recruiting boards in the counties to enlist the strongest peasants. Perhaps 10 percent of the adult population of England was involved in the actual fighting or in supplying and supporting the troops. The French contingents were even larger. By medieval standards, the force was astronomically large, especially considering the problems of transporting men, weapons, and horses across the English Channel. The costs of these armies stretched French and English resources to the breaking point.

The war was fought almost entirely in France and the Low Countries. It consisted mainly of a series of random sieges and cavalry raids. The French began in 1335 by supporting Scottish incursions into northern England, by ravaging the countryside in Aquitaine, and by sacking and burning English

THE BATTLE OF CRÉCY, 1346.   Pitched battles were unusual in the Hundred Years' War. At Crécy, however, the English (on the right with lions on their royal standard) scored a spectacular victory. The longbow proved a more effective weapon than the French crossbow, and the low-born English archers withstood a charge of the aristocratic French knights. (Photo: Larousse)

coastal towns, such as Southampton. Naturally, such activities lent weight to Edward III's propaganda campaign. More significantly, royal propaganda on both sides contributed to a kind of early nationalism.

In the early stages, England was highly successful. At Crécy in northern France in 1346, English longbowmen scored a great victory over French knights and crossbowmen. Although the fire of the longbow was not very accurate, it allowed for rapid reloading, and the English archers could send off three arrows to the French crossbowmen's one. The result was a blinding shower of arrows that unhorsed the French knights and caused mass confusion. The firing of cannon in what was probably the first use of artillery in the West created further panic. Thereupon the English horsemen charged and butchered the French. This was not war according to the chivalric rules that Edward III would have preferred. The English victory at Crécy rests on the skill and swiftness of the despised peasant archers, who had nothing at all to do with the chivalric ideals for which the war was being fought.

Ten years later, Edward the Black Prince, following the same tactics as at Crécy, smashed the French at Poitiers, captured the French king, and held him for ransom. Again at Agincourt near Arras in 1415, the chivalric English soldier-king Henry V (1413–1422) gained the field over vastly superior numbers. Henry followed up his triumph at Agincourt with the reconquest of Normandy (see Map 11.2). By 1419, the English had advanced to the walls of Paris.

The French cause was not lost, however. England won the initial victories, but France won the war.

Joan of Arc and France's Victory

The ultimate French success rests heavily on the actions of an obscure French peasant girl, Joan of Arc (1412–1431), whose vision and work revived French fortunes and led to victory. A great deal of pious and popular legend surrounds Joan the Maid, because of her peculiar appearance on the scene, her astonishing success, her matryrdom, and her canonization by the Catholic church. The historical fact is that she saved the French monarchy, which was the embodiment of France.

Born in the village of Domrémy in Champagne of well-to-do peasants, Joan of Arc grew up in a religious household. During adolescence she began to hear voices, which she later said belonged to Saint Michael, Saint Catherine, and Saint Margaret. In 1428, these voices spoke to her with great urgency, telling her that the dauphin (the uncrowned King Charles VII) had to be crowned and the English expelled from France. Joan went to the French court, persuaded the king to reject the rumor that he was illegitimate, and secured his support for her relief of the besieged city of Orléans.

The astonishing thing is not that Joan the Maid overcame serious obstacles to seeing the dauphin, nor even that Charles and his advisers listened to her. What is amazing is the swiftness with which they were convinced. French fortunes had been so low for so long that the court believed only a miracle could save the country. Because Joan cut her hair short and dressed like a man, she scandalized the court. But hoping she would provide the necessary miracle, Charles allowed her to accompany the army that was preparing to raise the English siege of Orléans.

In the meantime, Joan (herself illiterate) dictated the following letter, calling upon the English to withdraw:

JHESUS MARIA

King of England, and you Duke of Bedford, calling yourself regent of France, you William Pole, Count of Suffolk John Talbot, and you Thomas Lord Scales,

MAP 11.2 ENGLISH HOLDINGS IN FRANCE DURING THE HUNDRED YEARS' WAR

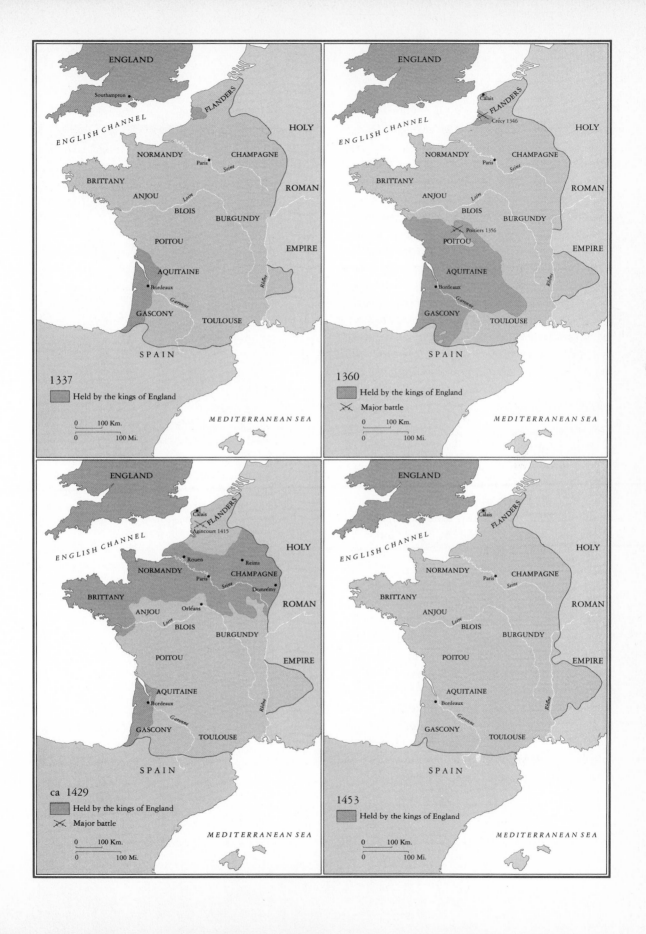

ENGLAND

Southampton •

ENGLISH CHANNEL

FLANDERS

HOLY

NORMANDY

CHAMPAGNE

Paris •   Seine

BRITTANY

ROMAN

ANJOU

Loire

BLOIS

BURGUNDY

POITOU

EMPIRE

AQUITAINE

Rhône

Bordeaux •

Garonne

GASCONY   TOULOUSE

SPAIN

1337

Held by the kings of England

0   100 Km.

0   100 Mi.

MEDITERRANEAN SEA

ENGLAND

Calais

ENGLISH CHANNEL

FLANDERS

Crécy 1346

HOLY

NORMANDY

CHAMPAGNE

Paris •   Seine

BRITTANY

ROMAN

ANJOU

Loire

BLOIS

Poitiers 1356

BURGUNDY

POITOU

EMPIRE

AQUITAINE

Rhône

Bordeaux •

Garonne

GASCONY   TOULOUSE

SPAIN

1360

Held by the kings of England

✕ Major battle

0   100 Km.

0   100 Mi.

MEDITERRANEAN SEA

ENGLAND

Calais

ENGLISH CHANNEL

FLANDERS

Agincourt 1415

Rouen •

Reims •

NORMANDY

CHAMPAGNE

Paris •

Seine

Domrémy •

BRITTANY

ROMAN

ANJOU

Orléans •

Loire

BLOIS

BURGUNDY

POITOU

EMPIRE

AQUITAINE

Rhône

Bordeaux •

Garonne

GASCONY   TOULOUSE

SPAIN

ca 1429

Held by the kings of England

✕ Major battle

0   100 Km.

0   100 Mi.

MEDITERRANEAN SEA

ENGLAND

Calais

ENGLISH CHANNEL

FLANDERS

HOLY

NORMANDY

CHAMPAGNE

Paris •   Seine

BRITTANY

ROMAN

ANJOU

Loire

BLOIS

BURGUNDY

POITOU

EMPIRE

AQUITAINE

Rhône

Bordeaux •

Garonne

GASCONY   TOULOUSE

SPAIN

1453

Held by the kings of England

0   100 Km.

0   100 Mi.

MEDITERRANEAN SEA

calling yourselves Lieutenants of the said Duke of Bedford, do right in the King of Heaven's sight. Surrender to The Maid *sent hither by God the King of Heaven, the keys of all the good towns you have taken and laid waste in France. She comes in God's name to establish the Blood Royal, ready to make peace if you agree to abandon France and repay what you have taken. And you, archers, comrades in arms, gentles and others, who are before the town of Orléans, retire in God's name to your own country. If you do not, expect to hear tidings from* The Maid *who will shortly come upon you to your very great hurt. And to you, King of England, if you do not thus, I am a chieftain of war, and whenever I meet your followers in France, I will drive them out; if they will not obey, I will put them all to death. I am sent here in God's name, the King of Heaven, to drive you body for body out of all France.*[10]

This message suggests that Joan thought of herself as an agent of God.

Joan arrived before Orléans on April 28, 1429. She knew little of warfare and believed that if she could keep the French troops from swearing and out of the whorehouses, victory would be theirs. On May 8, the English, weakened by disease and lack of supplies, withdrew from Orléans. Ten days later, Charles VII was crowned king at Reims. These two events marked the turning point in the war.

Joan herself was ignored by the French court, sold to the English, tried and condemned as a heretic (who else but a witch or a heretic would wear short hair and dress like a man?), and in 1431 burned at the stake in the marketplace in Rouen. A fresh trial in 1456 rehabilitated her. In 1920, she was canonized and declared a holy maiden and today is revered as the second patron saint of France. The nineteenth-century French historian Jules Michelet extolled Joan of Arc as a symbol of the vitality and strength of the peasant classes of France.

JOAN OF ARC. Later considered the symbol of the French state in its struggle against the English, Joan of Arc here carries a sword in one hand and a banner with the royal symbol of fleur-de-lis in the other. Her face, which scholars believe to be a good resemblance, shows inner strength and calm determination. (Archives Nationales, Paris/Giraudon)

The relief of Orléans stimulated French pride and rallied French resources. In England, as the war dragged on, as the loss of life mounted, as money appeared to be flowing into a bottomless pit, demands for an end increased. The clergy and the intellectuals pressed for peace. Parliamentary opposition to additional war grants stiffened. Slowly, the French reconquered Normandy and finally ejected the English from Aquitaine. At the end of the war, in 1453, only the town of Calais remained in English hands.

Costs and Consequences

For both France and England, the struggle proved a disaster. In France, the English kings Edward III and Henry V and their commanders had slaughtered thousands of soldiers and civilians. In the years after the sweep of the Black Death, this additional killing meant a grave loss of population. The English had laid waste to hundreds of thousands of acres of rich farmland, leaving the rural economy of many parts of France in shambles. The war had disrupted trade and the great fairs, resulting in the drastic reduction of French participation in international commerce. Defeat in battle and heavy taxation contributed to widespread dissatisfaction and aggravated peasant grievances.

In England, only the southern coastal ports experienced much destruction; yet England fared little better than France. The costs of war were tremendous: England spent over £5 million in the war effort, a huge sum in the fourteenth and fifteenth centuries. The worst loss was in manpower. Between 10 and 15 percent of the adult male population between the ages of fifteen and forty-five fought in the army or navy. In the decades after the plague when the country was already suffering a severe manpower shortage, war losses made a bad situation frightful. Peasants serving in France as archers and pikemen were desperately needed to till the fields. The knights who ordinarily handled the work of local government as sheriffs, coroners, jurymen, and justices of the peace were abroad, and their absence contributed to the breakdown of order at the local level.

The English government attempted to finance the war effort by raising the taxes on the wool crop. Because of steadily increasing costs, the Flemish and Italian buyers could not afford English wool. Consequently, wool exports slumped drastically between 1350 and 1450. Many men of all social classes had volunteered for service in France in the hope of acquiring booty and becoming rich. The chronicler Walsingham, describing the period of Crécy, tells of the tremendous prosperity and abundance resulting from the spoils of war: "For the woman was of no account who did not possess something from the spoils of . . . cities overseas in clothing, furs, quilts, and utensils . . . table-cloths and jewels, bowls of murra [semiprecious stone] and silver, linen and linen cloths."[11] Walsingham is referring to 1348, in the first generation of war. As time went on, most fortunes seem to have been squandered as fast as they were made.

If English troops returned with cash, they did not invest it in land. In the fifteenth century, returning soldiers were commonly described as beggars and vagabonds, roaming about making mischief. Even the large sums of money received from the ransom of the great — such as the £250,000 paid to Edward III for the freedom of King John of France — and the monies paid as indemnities by captured towns and castles did not begin to equal the £5 million-plus spent. England suffered a serious net loss.[12]

The long war also had a profound impact on the political and cultural lives of the two countries. It stimulated the development of the English Parliament. Edward III's constant need for money to pay for the war compelled him to summon not only the great barons and bishops but knights of the shires and burgesses from the towns as well. Between the outbreak of the war in 1337 and the king's death in 1377, parliamentary assemblies met twenty-seven times. Parliament met in thirty-seven of the fifty years of Edward's reign.

The frequency of the meetings is significant. Representative assemblies were becoming a habit, a tradition. Knights and burgesses, or the Commons, as they came to be called, recognized their mutual interests and began to meet apart from the great lords. The Commons gradually realized that they held the country's purse strings, and a parliamentary statute of 1341 required that all nonfeudal levies have parliamentary approval. When Edward III signed the law, he acknowledged that the king of England could not tax without Parliament's consent. Increasingly, during the course of the war, money grants were tied to royal redress of grievances. If the government was to secure finances, it had to correct the wrongs subjects protested.

As the Commons met in a separate chamber — the House of Commons — so also it developed its own organization. The speaker came to preside over debates in the House of Commons and to represent the Commons before the House of Lords and the king. Clerks kept a record of what transpired during discussions in the Commons.

In England theoretical consent to taxation and legislation was given in one assembly for the entire country. In France there was no single assembly; instead, there were many regional or provincial assemblies. Why did a national representative assembly fail to develop in France? The initiative for developing assemblies rested with the king, who needed revenue almost as much as the English ruler.

But the French monarchy found the idea of representative assemblies thoroughly distasteful. The advice of a counselor to King Charles VI (1380–1422), "above all things be sure that no great assemblies of nobles or of *communes* take place in your kingdom,"[13] was accepted. Charles VII (1422–1461) even threatened to punish those who proposed a national assembly.

The English Parliament was above all else a court of law, a place where justice was done and grievances remedied. No French assembly (excepting the Estates of Brittany) had such competence. The national assembly in England met frequently. In France general assemblies were so rare that they never got the opportunity to develop precise procedures or to exercise judicial functions.

No one in France wanted a national assembly. Linguistic, geographical, economic, legal, and political differences were very strong. Through much of the fourteenth and early fifteenth centuries, weak monarchs lacked the power to call a national assembly. Provincial assemblies, highly jealous of their independence, did not want a national assembly. The costs of sending delegates to it would be high, and the result was likely to be increased taxation. Finally, the Hundred Years' War itself hindered the growth of a representative body. Violence on dangerous roads discouraged travel. As the fifteenth-century English jurist Sir John Fortescue wrote, "Englishmen made such war in France that the three Estates dared not come together."[14]

The war did, however, promote the growth of nationalist sentiment in both countries. Nationalism is a feeling of unity and identity among a people who speak the same language, have a common ancestry and social or religious customs, and live together in a specific geographical area. In the fourteenth century, nationalism took the form of xenophobia, or hostility to foreigners. Both Philip VI and Edward III drummed up support for the war by portraying the enemy as an alien, evil people.

Edward III linked his personal dynastic quarrel with England's national interests. The Parliament Roll of 1348 states:

The Knights of the shires and the others of the Commons were told that they should withdraw together and take good counsel as to how, for withstanding the malice of the said enemy and for the salvation of our said lord the King and his Kingdom of England . . . the King could be aided.[15]

After victories, each country experienced a surge of pride in its military strength. Just as English feeling and patriotism ran strong after Crécy and Poitiers, so French national confidence rose after Orléans. French national feeling demanded the expulsion of the enemy not merely from Normandy and Aquitaine but from French soil. Perhaps no one expressed this national consciousness better than Joan of Arc, when she said that the enemy had been "driven out of *France.*"

THE DECLINE OF THE CHURCH'S PRESTIGE

In times of crisis or disaster, peoples of all faiths have sought the consolation of religion. In the fourteenth century, however, the official Christian church offered very little solace. In fact, the leaders of the church, it can be said, added to the sorrow and misery of the times.

The Babylonian Captivity

From 1309 to 1372, the popes lived in the city of Avignon in southeastern France. Philip IV (the Fair) of France (1285–1314), in order to control the church and its policies, pressured Pope Clement V (1305–1314) to settle in Avignon, and Clement,

because he was critically ill with cancer, lacked the will to resist Philip. This period in church history is often called the Babylonian Captivity (the term refers to the seventy years the ancient Hebrews were held captive in Mesopotamian Babylon). The Avignon papacy reformed its financial administration and centralized its government. The seven popes at Avignon concentrated on bureaucratic matters to the exclusion of spiritual objectives.

The Babylonian Captivity badly damaged papal prestige. Although some of the popes led austere lives at Avignon, the general atmosphere was one of luxury, splendor, and extravagance. The leadership of the church was cut off from its historical roots and the source of its ancient authority, the city of Rome. In the absence of the papacy, the Papal States in Italy lacked stability and good government. The economy of Rome had long been based on the presence of the papal court and the rich tourist trade the papacy attracted. The Babylonian Captivity left Rome poverty-stricken. As long as the French crown dominated papal policy, papal influence in England (with whom France was intermittently at war) and in Germany declined.

Many devout Christians urged the popes to return to Rome. The Dominican mystic Catherine of Siena (1347?–1380), for example, made a special trip to Avignon to plead with the pope to return. In 1377, Pope Gregory XI (1370–1378) brought the papal court back to Rome. Unfortunately, he died shortly after the return. At Gregory's death, Roman citizens demanded an Italian pope who would remain in Rome. Determined to influence the papal conclave (the assembly of cardinals to choose the new pope) and to force the election of an Italian, a Roman mob surrounded St. Peter's Basilica, blocked the roads leading out of the city, and seized all boats on the Tiber River. Between the time of Gregory's death and the opening of the conclave, great pressure was put on the cardinals to elect an Italian. At the time, none of them protested this pressure.

Sixteen cardinals — eleven Frenchmen, four Italians, and one Spaniard — entered the conclave on April 7, 1378. After two ballots they unanimously chose a distinguished administrator, the archbishop of Bari, Bartolomeo Prignano, who took the name Urban VI. Each of the cardinals swore that Urban had been elected "sincerely, freely, genuinely, and canonically."

Urban VI (1378–1389) had excellent intentions for church reform: he wanted to abolish simony, pluralism (holding several church offices at the same time), absenteeism, clerical extravagance, and ostentation. These were the very abuses increasingly criticized by Christian peoples across Europe. Unfortunately, Pope Urban went about the work of reform in a tactless, arrogant, and bullheaded manner. The day after his coronation he delivered a blistering attack on cardinals who lived in Rome while drawing their income from benefices elsewhere. His criticism was well founded but ill timed, because he provoked opposition among the hierarchy before he had consolidated his authority.

In the weeks that followed he stepped up attacks on clerical luxury, denouncing individual cardinals by name. He threatened to strike the cardinal archbishop of Amiens. Urban even threatened to excommunicate certain cardinals, and when he was advised that such excommunications would not be lawful unless the guilty had been warned three times, he shouted, "I can do anything, if it be my will and judgment."[16] Urban's quick temper and irrational behavior have led scholars to question his sanity. Whether today he would be considered medically insane or just drunk with power is a moot point. In any case, Urban's actions brought on disaster.

In groups of two and three, the cardinals slipped away from Rome and met at Anagni. They declared Urban's election invalid because it had been made under threats from the Roman mob, and they asserted that Urban himself was excommunicated. The cardinals then proceeded to the city of Fondi between Rome and Naples and elected Cardinal Robert of Geneva, the brother of King Charles V of France, as pope. Cardinal Robert took the name of Clement VII. There were then two popes — Urban at Rome and the anti-pope Clement VII (1378–1394), who set himself up at Avignon in opposition to the legally elected Urban. So began the Great Schism, which divided Western Christendom and lasted until 1417.

The Great Schism

The powers of Europe aligned themselves with Urban or Clement along strict political lines. France naturally recognized the French anti-pope, Clement. England, France's historic enemy, recognized Pope Urban. Scotland, subsidized by France for attacks on England, followed the French and supported Clement. Aragon, Castile, and Portugal hesitated before deciding for Clement at Avignon. The German emperor, who enjoyed the title of king of the Romans and bore ancient hostility to France, recognized Urban VI. At first, the Italian city-states recognized Urban; but when he alienated them, they opted for Clement.

John of Spoleto, a professor at the law school at Bologna, summed up intellectual opinion of the schism:

The longer this schism lasts, the more it appears to be costing, and the more harm it does: scandal, massacres, ruination, agitations, troubles and disturbances . . . this dissension is the root of everything: divers tumults, quarrels between kings, seditions, extortions, assassinations, acts of violence, wars, rising tyranny, decreasing freedom, the impunity of villains, grudges, error, disgrace, the madness of steel and of fire given license.[17]

The scandal of competing popes "rent the seamless garment of Christ," as the church was called, and provoked horror and vigorous cries for reform. The common people, wracked by inflation, wars, and plague, were thoroughly confused about which pope was legitimate. The schism weakened the religious faith of many Christians and gave rise to instability and religious excesses. It brought the leadership of the church into serious disrepute. At a time when ordinary Christians needed the consolation of religion and confidence in religious leaders, church officials were fighting among themselves for power.

The Conciliar Movement

Calls for the reform of the church were not new. A half-century before the Great Schism, in 1324, Marsiglio of Padua (1275–1342), then rector of the University of Paris, had published his *Defensor Pacis* (*The Defender of the Peace*). Dealing with questions of the authority of the state and the church, *Defensor Pacis* proved to be one of the most controversial works written in the Middle Ages.

Marsiglio argued that the state was the great unifying power in society and that the church was subordinate to the state. He put forth the revolutionary ideas that the church had no inherent jurisdiction and should own no property. Authority in the Christian church, according to Marsiglio, rested in a general council, made up of laymen as well as priests, which was superior to the pope. These ideas contradicted the medieval notion of a society governed by the church and the state with the church ultimately supreme.

Defensor Pacis was condemned by the pope and Marsiglio excommunicated. But the idea that a general council representing all of the church had a higher authority than the pope was repeated by John Gerson (1363–1429), a later chancellor of the University of Paris and influential theologian.

Even more earthshaking than the theories of Marsiglio of Padua were the ideas of the English scholar and theologian John Wyclif (1329–1384). Wyclif's views had broad social and economic significance. He urged that the church be stripped of its property. His idea that every Christian free of mortal sin possessed lordship was seized upon by peasants in England during a revolt in 1381 and used to justify their goals. Wyclif wrote that papal claims of temporal power had no foundation in the Scriptures and that the Scriptures alone should be the standard of Christian belief and practice. He urged the abolition of such practices as the veneration of saints, pilgrimages, pluralism, and absenteeism. Every sincere Christian, according to Wyclif, should read the Bible for himself.

In advancing these views, Wyclif struck at the roots of medieval church structure and religious practices. Consequently, he has been hailed as the precursor of the Reformation of the sixteenth century. Although Wyclif's ideas were vigorously condemned by ecclesiastical authorities, they were widely disseminated by humble clerics and enjoyed great popularity in the early fifteenth century. Wyclif's followers were called Lollards. After the Czech king Wenceslaus's sister Anne married Richard II of England, members of Queen Anne's household carried Lollard principles back to Bohemia, where they were spread by John Hus, rector of the University of Prague.

While John Wyclif's ideas were being spread, at the University of Paris, two German scholars, Henry of Langenstein and Conrad of Gelnhausen, produced treatises urging the summoning of a general council. Conrad wrote that the church, as the congregation of all the faithful, was superior to the pope and that although canon law held that only a pope might call a council, a higher law existed, the common good. The common good of Christendom required the convocation of a council.

In response to continued and Europe-wide calls, the two colleges of cardinals — one at Rome, the other at Avignon — summoned a council at Pisa in Italy in 1409. A distinguished gathering of prelates and theologians deposed both popes and selected another. Unfortunately, neither the Avignon pope nor the Roman pope would resign, and the appalling situation of a threefold schism existed.

Finally, through the pressure of the German emperor Sigismund, a great council met at Constance in Switzerland (1414–1418). It had three objectives: to end the schism, to reform the church "in head and members" (from top to bottom), and to wipe out heresy. The council condemned the Lollard ideas of John Hus, and he was burned at the stake. The council eventually deposed both the Roman pope and the successor of the pope chosen at Pisa, and it isolated the Avignonese anti-pope. A conclave elected a new leader, who took the name of Martin V (1417–1431).

Martin proceeded to dissolve the council. Nothing was done about reform. The schism was over, and the conciliar movement in effect ended. For a time thereafter, the papacy concentrated on Italian problems to the exclusion of universal Christian interests. The schism and the conciliar movement had exposed the crying need for ecclesiastical reform, however, laying the foundations for the great reform efforts of the sixteenth century.

THE LIFE OF THE PEOPLE

In the fourteenth century, economic and political difficulties, disease, and war profoundly affected the lives of European peoples. Decades of slaughter and destruction, punctuated by the decimating visits of the Black Death, made a grave economic situation virtually disastrous. In many parts of France and the Low Countries fields lay in ruin or untilled for lack of manpower. In England, as taxes increased, criticism of government policy and mismanagement multiplied. Crime, which is always a factor in social history, aggravated economic troubles, and throughout Europe the frustrations of the common people erupted into widespread revolts. For most people, marriage and the local parish church continued to be the center of their lives.

Fur-Collar Crime

The Hundred Years' War had provided employment and opportunity for thousands of idle and fortune-seeking knights. But during periods of truce and after the war finally ended, many nobles once again had little to do. The international inflation hurt them. Although many were living on fixed incomes, their chivalric code with its feature of lavish generosity demanded that they maintain an aristocratic lifestyle. Many nobles turned to crime as a way of raising money. The fourteenth and fifteenth centuries witnessed a great deal of "fur-collar crime," so called from the miniver fur the nobility alone were allowed to wear on their collars. England provides a good case study of upper-class crime.

Fur-collar crime differed from the felonies of homicide, robbery, rape, and arson. The nobles used their superior social status to rob and extort from the weak and then to corrupt the judicial process. Groups of noble brigands roamed the English countryside stealing from both rich and poor. Sir John de Colseby and Sir William Bussy led a gang of thirty-eight knights who stole goods worth £3,000 in various robberies. Operating exactly like modern urban racketeers, knightly gangs demanded that peasants pay "protection money" or else have their hovels burned and their fields destroyed. Members of the household of a certain Lord Robert of Payn beat up a victim and then demanded money for protection from future attack.

Attacks on the rich often took the form of kidnaping and extortion. Individuals were grabbed in their homes, and wealthy travelers were seized on the highways and then held for ransom. In northern England a gang of gentry led by Sir Gilbert de Middleton abducted Sir Henry Beaumont, his brother and the bishop-elect of Durham, and two Roman cardinals in England on a peacemaking visit. Only after a ransom was paid were the victims released.[18]

Fur-collar criminals were terrorists, and just like some twentieth-century corporation executives who commit white-collar (but nonviolent) crimes, medieval aristocratic criminals got away with their outrages. When accused of wrongdoing, fur-collar criminals intimidated witnesses. They threatened jurors. They used "pull" or influence or cash to bribe the judges. As a fourteenth-century English judge wrote to a young nobleman, "For the love of your father I have hindered charges being brought against you and have prevented execution of indictment actually made."[19]

The ballads of Robin Hood, a collection of folk legends from late medieval England, describe the adventures of the outlaw hero and his band of followers, who lived in Sherwood Forest and attacked and punished those who violated the social system and the law. Most of the villains in these simple tales were fur-collar criminals — grasping landlords, wicked sheriffs, such as the famous sheriff of Nottingham, and mercenary churchmen. Robin and his merry men performed a sort of retributive justice. Robin Hood was a popular figure, because he symbolized the deep resentment against aristocratic corruption and abuse; he represented the struggle against tyranny and oppression.

Criminal activity by nobles continued decade after decade because governments were not strong enough to stop it. Then, too, much of the crime was directed against a lord's own serfs, and the line between a noble's legal jurisdiction over his peasants and criminal behavior was a very fine one indeed. The persecution of lords, coming on top of war, disease, and natural disasters, eventually drove long-suffering peasants all across Europe to revolt.

Peasant Revolts

Peasant revolts occurred often in the Middle Ages. Early in the thirteenth century, the French preacher Jacques de Vitry asked rhetorically, "How many serfs have killed their lords or burnt their castles?"[20] Social and economic conditions in the fourteenth and fifteenth centuries caused a great increase in peasant uprisings.

In 1358, the frustrations of the French peasantry exploded in a massive uprising, called the *Jacquerie*, after the nickname of a supposedly happy agricultural laborer, Jacques Bonhomme (Good Fellow). Peasants in Picardy and Champagne went on the rampage. Crowds swept through the countryside slashing the throats of the nobles, burning their castles, raping their wives and daughters, killing or maiming their horses and cattle. Peasants blamed the nobility for oppressive taxes, for the criminal brigandage of the countryside, for defeat in war, and for the general misery. Artisans, small merchants, and parish priests joined the peasants. Urban and rural groups committed terrible destruction, and for several weeks the nobles were on the defensive. Then, the upper classes united to repress the revolt with savage and merciless ferocity. Thousands of the "Jacques," innocent as well as guilty, were cut down.

This forcible suppression of social rebellion, without some attempt at removing its underlying causes, could only serve as a stopgap measure and

THE JACQUERIE. Because revolt seemed to threaten the natural order of Christian society, the upper classes everywhere exacted terrible vengeance on peasants and artisans. In this scene some *jacques* are cut down, some beheaded, and others drowned. (Bibliothèque Nationale, Paris)

drive protest underground. Between 1363 and 1484, serious peasant revolts swept the Auvergne; in 1380, uprisings occurred in the Midi; and in 1420, they erupted in the Lyonnais region of France.

The Peasants' Revolt in England in 1381, involving perhaps a hundred thousand people, was probably the largest single uprising of the entire Middle Ages. The causes were complex and varied from place to place. The thirteenth century had witnessed the steady commutation of labor services for cash rents. The Black Death drastically cut the labor supply. As a result, peasants demanded higher wages and a reduction in the amount of manorial obligations. The parliamentary Statute of Laborers (1351) declared:

Whereas to curb the malice of servants who after the pestilence were idle and unwilling to serve without securing excessive wages, it was recently ordained . . . that such servants, both men and women, shall be bound to serve in return for salaries and wages that were customary . . . five or six years earlier.[21]

It was an attempt by landlords to freeze wages and social mobility.

The statute could not be enforced. As a matter of fact, the condition of the English peasantry steadily improved in the course of the fourteenth century. Some scholars believe that the peasantry in most places was better off in the period 1350–1450 than it had been for centuries before or was to be for four centuries after.

Why then was the outburst in 1381 so serious? It was provoked by a crisis of rising expectations. The improved position of the peasants, the relative prosperity of the laboring classes, led to demands that the upper classes were unwilling to grant. Unable to climb higher, the peasants' frustration found release in revolt. Economic grievance combined with other factors. Decades of aristocratic violence, much of it perpetrated against the weak peasantry, had bred hostility and bitterness. In France frustration over the lack of permanent victory increased. In England the social and religious agitation of the popular preacher John Ball fanned the embers of discontent. Such couplets as Ball's famous

When Adam delved and Eve span
Who was then the gentleman?

reflect real revolutionary sentiment. But, the lords of England believed that God had permanently fixed the hierarchical order of society and that nothing man could do would change that order.

Moreover, the south of England, where the revolt broke out, had been subjected to frequent and destructive French raids. The English government did little to protect the south, and villagers grew increasingly scared and insecure. Fear erupted into violence.

The straw that broke the camel's back in England was a head tax on all adult males. Although it met widespread opposition in 1380, the royal council ordered the sheriffs to collect it again in 1381 on penalty of a huge fine. Beginning with assaults on the tax collectors, the uprising in England followed much the same course as the Jacquerie had in France. Castles and manors were sacked; manorial records were destroyed. Many nobles, including the archbishop of Canterbury, who had ordered the collection of the tax, were murdered.

Although the center of the revolt was the highly populated and economically advanced south and east, considerable parts of the north and the Midlands also witnessed rebellions. These took different forms in different places. The townspeople of Cambridge expressed their hostility to the university by sacking one of the colleges and building a bonfire of academic property. In towns containing skilled Flemish craftsmen, fear of competition led to their attack and murder. Urban discontent merged with rural, agrarian violence. Apprentices and journeymen, frustrated because the highest positions in the guilds were closed to them, rioted.

The boy-king Richard II (1377–1399) met the leaders of the revolt, agreed to charters insuring peasants' freedom, tricked them with false promises, and then proceeded to crush the uprising with terrible ferocity. Although the nobility tried to restore ancient duties of serfdom, virtually a century of freedom had elapsed, and the commutation of manorial services continued. Rural serfdom had disappeared in England by 1550.

Conditions in England and France were not unique. In Florence in 1378, the *ciompi,* the poorest workmen, revolted. Serious social trouble occurred in Lübeck, Brunswick, and other cities of the Holy Roman Empire. In Spain in 1391, aristocratic attempts to impose new forms of serfdom combined with demands for tax relief led to massive working-class and peasant uprisings in Seville and Barcelona. These took the form of vicious attacks on Jewish communities. The rebellions and uprisings everywhere reveal deep peasant and working-class frustration and the general socioeconomic crisis of the times.

Marriage

Marriage and the family provided a great part of such peace and satisfaction as most people attained. In fact, life for those who were not clerics or nuns meant marriage. Apart from the sexual and emotional urgency, the community expected people to marry. For a woman, girlhood was a preparation for marriage, and she learned, in addition to the thousands of chores involved in running a household, obedience, or at least subordination. Adulthood meant living as a wife or widow. Marriages in the Middle Ages, however, were between two individuals, and sweeping statements about marriage in general have limited validity. Most of the peasants were illiterate and left slight record about their feelings toward their spouses or about marriage as an institution. The gentry, however, often could write, and the letters exchanged between Margaret and John Paston, upper-middle-class people who lived in Norfolk, England, in the fifteenth century, provide important evidence of the experience of one couple.

John and Margaret Paston were married about 1439, after an arrangement concluded entirely by their parents. John spent most of his time in London fighting through the law courts to increase his family properties and business interests; Margaret remained in Norfolk to supervise the family lands. Her enormous responsibilities involved managing the Paston estates, hiring workers, collecting rents, ordering supplies for the large household, hearing complaints and settling disputes among tenants, and marketing her crops. In these duties she proved herself a remarkably shrewd businessperson. Moreover, when an army of over one thousand men led by the aristocratic thug Lord Moleyns attacked her house, she successfully withstood the siege. When the Black Death entered her area, Margaret moved her family to safety.

Margaret Paston did all this on top of bearing and raising eight children (there were probably other children who did not survive childhood). Her husband died before she was forty-three, and she conducted the negotiations for the children's marriages. Her children's futures, like her estate management, were planned with an eye toward economic and social advancement. When one daughter secretly married the estate bailiff, an alliance considered beneath her, the girl was cut off from the family as if she were dead.[22]

The many letters surviving between Margaret and John reveal slight tenderness towards their children. They seem to have reserved their love for each other, and during many of his frequent absences, they wrote to express mutual affection and devotion. How typical the Paston relationship was modern historians cannot say, but the marriage of John and Margaret, although completely arranged by their parents, was based on respect, responsibility, and love.[23]

In the later Middle Ages, as earlier — and, indeed, until the late nineteenth century — economic factors, rather than romantic love or physical attraction, determined whom and when a person married. The young agricultural laborer on the manor had to wait until he had sufficient land. Thus, most men had to wait until their fathers died or yielded the holding. The age of marriage was late, which in turn affected the number of children a couple had. The journeyman craftsman in the urban guild faced the same material difficulties. Prudent young men selected (or their parents selected for them) girls who would bring the most land or money to the union. Once a couple married, the union ended only with the death of one partner.

Divorce — the complete dissolution of the contract between a woman and man lawfully married — simply did not exist in the Middle Ages. The church held that a marriage validly entered into could not be dissolved. A valid marriage consisted of the oral consent or promise of the two parties made to each other. Church theologians urged that the marriage be publicized by banns, or announcements in the parish church, and that the union be celebrated and witnessed in a church ceremony and blessed by a priest.

A great number of couples did not observe the church's regulations, however. Some treated marriage as a private act — they made the promise and spoke the words of marriage to each other without witnesses and then proceeded to enjoy the sexual pleasures of marriage. This practice led to a great number of disputes, because one or the other of the two parties could later deny having made a marriage agreement. The records of the ecclesiastical courts reveal many cases arising from privately made contracts. Here is a typical case heard by the ecclesiastical court at York in England in 1372:

[The witness says that] one year ago on the feast day of the apostles Philip and James just past, he was present in the house of William Burton, tanner of York. . . . when and where John Beke, saddler . . . called the said Marjory to him and said to her, "Sit with me." Acquiescing in this, she sat down. John said to her, "Marjory, do you wish to be my wife?" And she replied, "I will if you wish." And taking at once the said Marjory's right hand, John said, "Marjory, here I take you as my wife, for better or worse, to have and to hold until the end of my life; and of this I give you my faith." The said Marjory replied to him, "Here I take you John as my husband, to have and to hold until the end of my life, and of this I give you my faith." And then the said John kissed the said Marjory. . . . [24]

This was a private arrangement, made in secret and without the presence of the clergy. Evidence survives of marriages contracted in a garden, in a blacksmith's shop, at a tavern, and, predictably, in a bed. Church courts heard a great number of similar cases. The records of those courts that relate to marriage reveal that rather than suits for divorce, the great majority of petitions asked the court to enforce the marriage contract that one of the parties believed she or he had validly made. Divorces were granted only in extraordinary circumstances, such as male impotence.

Parish Life and Recreation

In the later Middle Ages, the land and the parish remained the focus and the center of the life of the peasantry of Europe. Work on the land continued to be a collective responsibility of all on the manor. All men, for example, cooperated in the annual tasks of planting and harvesting. The close association of the cycle of agriculture and the liturgy of the Christian calendar endured. The parish priest blessed the fields before the annual planting, offering prayers on behalf of the people for a good crop.

If the harvest was a rich one, the priest led the processions and celebrations of thanksgiving.

How did the common people feel about their work? Since the vast majority were illiterate and inarticulate, it is difficult to say. It is known that the peasants hated the ancient services and obligations on the lords' lands and tried to get them commuted for a money rent. When lords attempted to re-impose service duties, the peasants revolted.

In the thirteenth century, the craft guilds pro-vided the small minority of men living in towns and cities with the psychological satisfaction of involvement in the manufacture of a superior product. The guild member also had economic security. The craft guilds set high standards for their merchandise. The guilds looked after the sick, the poor, the widowed, and the orphaned. Master and journeymen worked side by side.

In the fourteenth century, those ideal conditions began to change. The fundamental objective of the craft guild was to maintain a monopoly of its product, and to do that recruitment and promotion were carefully restricted. Some guilds required a large entrance fee for apprentices; others admitted only the sons or relatives of members. Apprentice-ship increasingly lasted a long time, seven years. Even after the young man had satisfied all the tests for full membership in the guild and had attained the rank of master, other hurdles had to be crossed, such as finding the funds with which to open his own business or special connections just to get in a guild. Restrictions limited the number of appren-tices and journeymen to the anticipated openings for masters. The larger a particular business was, the greater was the likelihood that the master was separated from and did not know his employees.

The divorce of master and journeyman and the decreasing number of openings for master craftsmen created serious frustrations. Strikes and riots oc-curred in the Flemish towns, in France, and in England.

The recreation of all classes reflected the fact that late medieval society was organized for war and that violence was common. The aristocracy engaged in tournaments or jousts; archery and wrestling held great popularity among ordinary people. Everyone enjoyed the cruel sports of bullbaiting and bearbait-ing. As the great French scholar Marc Bloch wrote, "Violence was an element in manners. Medieval men had little control over their immediate im-pulses; they were emotionally insensitive to the spectacle of pain, and they had small regard for human life . . . "[25] Thus, the hangings and mu-tilations of criminals were exciting and well-at-tended events, with all the festivity of a university town before a Saturday football game. Chroniclers exulted in their descriptions of executions, murders, and massacres. Here a monk gleefully describes the gory execution of the notorious criminal William Wallace in 1305:

Wilielmus Waleis, a robber given to sacrilege, arson and homicide . . . was condemned to most cruel but justly deserved death. He was drawn through the streets of London at the tails of horses, until he reached a gallows of unusual height, there he was suspended by a halter; but taken down while yet alive, he was mutilated, his bowels torn out and burned in a fire, his head then cut off, his body divided into four, and his quarters transmitted to four principal parts of Scotland. Behold the end of the merciless man, who himself perished without mercy.[26]

Violence was as English as roast beef and plum pudding, as French as bread, cheese, and *potage*.

Alcoholic consumption, primarily beer or ale, provided solace to the poor, and the frequency of drunkenness reflects their terrible frustrations.

MASKED MUMMERS.   People of all classes enjoyed mummers' shows, performed by groups of masked actors who burlesqued some well-known event or person. Sometimes mummers accompanied their shows with primitive musical instruments, such as drums or tambourines. (Bibliothèque Nationale, Paris)

In the fourteenth and fifteenth centuries, the laity began to exercise increasing influence and control over the affairs of the parish. Churchmen were criticized. The constant quarrels of the mendicant orders (the Franciscans and Dominicans), the mercenary and grasping attitude of the parish clergy, the scandal of the Great Schism and a divided Christendom — all these did much to weaken in the popular mind the spiritual mystique of the clergy. The laity steadily took responsibility for the management of parish lands. Laymen and laywomen developed associations for the voting on and expenditure of money for furnishings for the church. And, ordinary lay people secured jurisdiction over the structure of the church building, its vestments, books, and furnishings. These new responsibilities of the laity reflect the increased dignity of the parishioners in the late Middle Ages.[27]

✤

Late medieval preachers likened the crises of their times to the "Four Horsemen of the Apocalypse" in the Book of Revelation who brought famine, war, disease, and death. The crises of the fourteenth and fifteenth centuries were acids that burned deeply into the fabric of traditional medieval European society. Natural factors, such as the bad weather, brought poor harvests, which contributed to the international economic depression. Disease, over which people also had little control, added to the widespread psychological depression and dissatisfaction. Population losses caused by the Black Death and the Hundred Years' War encouraged the working classes to try to profit from the labor shortage by selling their services higher: they wanted to move up the economic ladder. The socialistic ideas of thinkers like John Wyclif and John Hus fanned the flames of social discontent, and when peasant frustrations exploded in uprisings, the frightened nobility and upper middle class crushed the revolts and condemned heretical preachers as agitators of social rebellion. But the war had contributed to a heightened social consciousness among the poor and weak.

The Hundred Years' War served as a catalyst for the development of representative government in England. The royal policy of financing the war through Parliament-approved taxation gave the middle classes an increased sense of their economic power. They would pay taxes in return for some influence in shaping royal policies.

ALBRECHT DÜRER: THE FOUR HORSEMEN OF THE APOCALYPSE. From right to left, representatives of war, strife, famine, and death gallop across Christian society leaving thousands dead or in misery. The horrors of the age made this subject extremely popular in art, literature, and sermons. (Courtesy, Museum of Fine Arts, Boston)

In France, on the other hand, the war stiffened opposition to national assemblies. The disasters that wracked France decade after decade led the French people to believe that the best solutions to complicated problems lay not in an assembly but in the hands of a strong monarch. France became the model for continental countries in the evolution toward royal absolutism.

In addition, the war stimulated technological experimentation, especially with artillery. After about 1350, the cannon, although highly inaccurate, was commonly used all over Europe.

Religion remained the cement that held society together. European culture was a Christian culture. But the Great Schism weakened the prestige of the church and people's faith in papal authority. The conciliar movement, by denying the church's universal sovereignty, strengthened the claims of secular governments to jurisdiction over all their peoples. The later Middle Ages witnessed a steady shift of basic loyalty from the Christian church to the emerging national states.

Life, for people of most classes and countries, meant the land, work, marriage, and the village or parish church.

NOTES

1. W. H. McNeill, *Plagues and Peoples*, Anchor Press/Doubleday, New York, 1976, pp. 151–168.

2. Quoted by P. Ziegler, *The Black Death*, Pelican Books, Harmondsworth, England, 1969, p. 20.

3. J. M. Rigg, trans., *The Decameron of Giovanni Boccaccio*, Everyman's Library, J. M. Dent & Sons, London, 1903, p. 6.

4. Ziegler, pp. 232–239

5. J. Barnie, *War in Medieval English Society: Social Values and the Hundred Years' War*, Cornell University Press, Ithaca, N.Y., 1974, p. 6

6. N. F. Cantor, *The English: A History of Politics and Society to 1760*, Simon & Schuster, New York, 1967, p. 260.

7. Quoted by Barnie, p. 34.

8. Ibid., p. 73.

9. Ibid., pp. 72–73.

10. W. P. Barrett, trans., *The Trial of Jeanne d'Arc*, George Routledge, London, 1931, pp. 165–166.

11. Quoted by Barnie, pp. 36–37.

12. M. M. Postan, "The Costs of the Hundred Years' War," *Past and Present* 27 (April 1964):34–53.

13. Quoted by P. S. Lewis, "The Failure of the Medieval French Estates," *Past and Present* 23 (November 1962): 6.

14. Ibid., p. 10.

15. C. Stephenson and G. F. Marcham, eds., *Sources of English Constitutional History*, rev. ed., Harper & Row, New York, 1972, p. 217.

16. Quoted by J. H. Smith, *The Great Schism 1378: The Disintegration of the Papacy*, Weybright & Talley, New York, 1970, p. 141.

17. Ibid., p. 15.

18. B. A. Hanawalt, "Fur Collar Crime: The Pattern of Crime Among the Fourteenth-Century English Nobility," *Journal of Social History* 8 (Spring 1975):1–14.

19. Ibid., p. 7.

20. Quoted by M. Bloch, *French Rural History*, Janet Sondheimer, trans., University of California Press, Berkeley, 1966, p. 169.

21. Stephenson and Marcham, p. 225.

22. A. S. Haskell, "The Paston Women on Marriage in Fifteenth Century England," *Viator* 4 (1973):459–469.

23. Ibid., p. 471.

24. Quoted by R. H. Helmholz, *Marriage Litigation in Medieval England*, Cambridge University Press, Cambridge, 1974, pp. 28–29.

25. M. Bloch, *Feudal Society*, L. A. Manyon, trans., Routledge & Kegan Paul, London, 1961, p. 411.

26. A. F. Scott, ed., *Everyone a Witness: The Plantagenet Age*, Thomas Y. Crowell Co., New York, 1976, p. 263.

27. See E. Mason, "The Role of the English Parishioner, 1000–1500," *Journal of Ecclesiastical History* 27:1 (January 1976):17–29.

SUGGESTED READING

Students who wish further elaboration of the topics covered in this chapter should consult the following studies, on which the chapter leans extensively. For the Black Death and health generally, see W. H. McNeill, *Plagues and Peoples* (1976), a fresh, challenging, and comprehensive study; F. F. Cartwright, *Disease and History* (1972), which contains an interesting section on the Black Death; P. Ziegler, *The Black Death** (1969), a fascinating and highly readable book; and H. E. Sigerist, *Civilization and Disease** (1970), which treats many of the social implications of disease.

The standard study of the long military conflicts of the fourteenth and fifteenth centuries remains that of E. Perroy, *The Hundred Years' War** (1959), J. Henneman, *Royal Taxation in Fourteenth Century France: The Development of War Financing, 1322–1356* (1971), is an important technical work by a distinguished historian. J. Barnie's *War in Medieval English Society: Social Values and the Hundred Years' War* (1974), treats the attitude of patriots, intellectuals, and the general public. The best treatment of the financial costs of the war is probably M. M. Postan, "The Costs of the Hundred Years' War," *Past and Present* 27 (April 1964):34–53. E. Searle and R. Burghart, "The Defense of England and the Peasants' Revolt," *Viator* 3 (1972), is a fascinating study of the peasants' changing social attitudes.

For political and social conditions in the fourteenth and fifteenth centuries, the following studies are all useful: P. S. Lewis, *Later Medieval France: The Polity* (1968) and "The Failure of the French Medieval Estates," *Past and Present* 23 (November 1962); L. Romier, *A History of France** (1962); G. O. Sayles, *The King's Parliament of England** (1974); M. Bloch, *French Rural History** (1966); I. Kershaw, "The Great Famine and Agrarian Crisis in England, 1315–1322," *Past and Present* 59 (May 1973); B. A. Hanawalt, "Fur Collar Crime: The Pattern of Crime Among the Fourteenth-Century English Nobility," *Journal of Social History* 8 (Spring 1975): 1–17 — a fascinating discussion; K. Thomas, "Work and Leisure in Pre-Industrial Society," *Past and Present* 29 (December 1964); M. Keen, *The Outlaws of Medieval Legend* (1961) and "Robin Hood — Peasant or Gentleman?," *Past and Present* 19 (April 1961):7–18; P. Wolff, "The 1391 Pogrom in Spain, Social Crisis or Not?," *Past and Present* 50 (February 1971):4–18; and R. H. Helmholz, *Marriage Litigation in Medieval England* (1974). Students are especially encouraged to consult the brilliant achievement of E. L. Ladurie, *The Peasants of Languedoc,** John Day, trans., (1976).

Many of the preceding titles treat the religious history of the period. In addition, the following contain interesting and valuable information: G. Barraclough, *The Medieval Papacy** (1968), which is splendidly illustrated; W. Ullmann, *A Short History of the Papacy in the Middle Ages* (1972); E. Mason, "The Role of the English Parishioner, 1000–1500," *Journal of Ecclesiastical History* 27:1 (January 1976):17–29; and J. H. Smith, *The Great Schism 1378: The Disintegration of the Medieval Papacy* (1970).

*Available in paperback.

Chapter 12

EUROPEAN SOCIETY IN THE AGE

OF THE RENAISSANCE

While the "*Four Horsemen of the Apocalypse*" carried war, plague, famine, and death across the Continent, a new culture was emerging in southern Europe. The fourteenth century witnessed the beginnings of remarkable changes in many aspects of Italian society. In the fifteenth century, these phenomena spread outside of Italy and gradually influenced society in northern Europe. These cultural changes have been labeled the Renaissance. The sculptors, painters, and writers of the Renaissance spoke contemptuously of their medieval predecessors and identified themselves with the thinkers and artists of Greco-Roman civilization. What does the term "Renaissance" mean? How did the Renaissance manifest itself in the areas of politics, government, and social organization? Did the Renaissance involve shifts in religious attitudes? This chapter is concerned with these questions.

THE IDEA OF THE RENAISSANCE

The Renaissance was an intellectual movement that began in Italy in the fourteenth century. It was characterized by hostility to the culture of the Middle Ages and a fascination with the ancient world. Writers and artists of the Renaissance displayed great concern for individualism, a serious interest in human nature based on the study of the Greek and Latin classics, and a new excitement about life in this world. The cultural movement scholars have called the Renaissance involved a small, self-conscious, educated elite; it never directly involved the masses of people.

The realization that something new and unique was happening first came to men of letters of the fourteenth century, especially to the poet and humanist Francesco Petrarch (1304–1374). Petrarch thought that he was living at the start of a new age, a period of light coming after a long night of Gothic gloom. He believed that the first and second centuries of the Roman Empire represented the peak in the development of human civilization. The Germanic invasions had caused a sharp cultural break with the glories of Rome and had inaugurated what he called the "Dark Ages." Medieval people had believed that they were continuing the glories that had been ancient Rome and that no cultural division existed between the world of the emperors and their own times. But for Petrarch and many of his contemporaries, the thousand-year period between the fourth and the fourteenth centuries constituted a barbarian, or Gothic, or middle age. Petrarch believed he was witnessing a new golden age of intellectual achievement — a "rebirth" or, to use the French word that came into English, "renaissance." The division of time into historical periods is often arbitrary and made for the convenience of historians. As far as the way in which most people lived and thought, no sharp division exists between the "Middle Ages" and the "Renaissance." Nevertheless, Petrarch's distinction of time periods has had great influence. Most scholars accept the word "Renaissance" to mean the artistic and cultural developments that occurred in western Europe beginning in the fourteenth century and lasting to sometime in the seventeenth.

ITALIAN ORIGINS OF THE RENAISSANCE

The Renaissance began in Italy. Why was there a brilliant flowering of artistic and intellectual creativity in Italy in the fourteenth through sixteenth centuries? This question has troubled scholars for a long time, and they still have not arrived at a definite answer. Some have emphasized economic features — that the cornerstone of northern Italian economic activity was international trade, commerce, and banking. The northern Italian cities had led the way in the commercial revival of the eleventh century. By the middle of the twelfth century, Venice, Genoa, Florence, and Milan were carrying on a great volume of trade with the Middle East and with northern Europe. These Italian cities fully exploited their geographical position as natural places for exchange between the East and the West. Venice profited tremendously from the Fourth Crusade. In the early fourteenth century, Genoa and Venice made important strides in shipbuilding, which allowed their ships for the first time to sail all year long. Improvements in the construction of cargo ships also enabled the Venetians and Genoese to carry more bulk and to navigate the dangerous Atlantic Ocean. Most goods were purchased directly from the producers and sold a good distance away. For example, Italian merchants bought fine English wool directly from the Cistercian abbeys of Yorkshire in northern England. The wool was transported to the bazaars of North Africa either overland or by ship through the Straits of Gibraltar. The risks in such an operation were great, but the profits were enormous. These profits were continually reinvested.

It is generally agreed that the first manifestations of the Italian Renaissance — in art, architecture, and literary creativity — appeared in Florence. Florence possessed enormous wealth, and money, without which the arts cannot flourish, supported talent and genius. Geography did not help Florence. It was an inland city without easy access to water transportation. But toward the end of the thirteenth century, Florentine merchants and bankers acquired control of papal banking. From their position as tax collectors for the papacy, Florentine mercantile families began to dominate European banking on both sides of the Alps. These families had offices in Paris and London, Barcelona and Marseilles, Tunis and the North African ports, and, of course, Naples

BUSINESS ACTIVITIES IN A FLORENTINE BANK. The Florentines early developed new banking devices. One man (left)
presents a letter of credit or a bill of exchange, forerunners of
the modern check, which allowed credit in distant places. A
foreign merchant (right) exchanges one kind of currency for
another. The bank profited from the fees it charged for these
services. (Prints Division; New York Public Library; Astor,
Lenox and Tilden Foundation)

and Rome. The profits from loans, investments,
and money exchanges that poured back to Florence
were pumped into urban industries. Such profits
contributed to the city's economic worth.

The Florentine wool industry, however, was the
major factor in the city's financial expansion and
population increase. Florence purchased the best-
quality wool from England and Spain, developed
remarkable techniques for its manufacture, and
employed thousands of workers to turn it into
cloth. Florentine weavers produced immense quantities of superb woolen cloth, which brought the
highest prices in the fairs, markets, and bazaars of
Europe, Asia, and Africa.

By the first quarter of the fourteenth century,
the economic foundations of Florence were so strong
that two severe crises did not destroy the city. In
1344, King Edward III of England repudiated his
huge debts to Florentine bankers and forced them
into bankruptcy. Florence also suffered frightfully
from the Black Death, losing perhaps half of its
population. Still, the basic Florentine economic
structure remained stable. Driving enterprise, technical know-how, and competitive spirit saw Florence
through the difficult economic period of the late
fourteenth century.[1]

One difficulty with this economic explanation of
the origins of the Renaissance in Florence lies in the
fact that in the middle of the fourteenth century the
Florentine wool and banking industries experienced
a serious depression. Trade, affected by the Black
Death and the international business slump, declined. Moreover, such cities as Genoa, which had at
one time enjoyed considerable prosperity, made no
profound contribution to the Renaissance. It is
possible, however, that Florentine businessmen who
found foreign markets closed and could not make
profits in commerce invested in art. They expected a
financial return from the art works as they increased
in value.

A leading interpretation of the Italian Renaissance today traces it to the development of civic
humanism, or public pride, in Florence. In the

1380s, Florence was severely threatened by the conquests of Gian Galeazzo Visconti, duke of Milan. The Florentines put up a heroic and successful resistance, and in so doing, came to appreciate the special virtues of their republican form of government — in contrast to the tyranny represented by Visconti. Awareness of their unique political heritage, which they traced back to the time of the Roman Empire, led the Florentines to take great pride in their city. Accordingly, civic humanism took the form of public respect for Florence's achievements, whether in trade or architecture, education or the arts. They embarked upon a policy of beautification. This civic self-consciousness eventually spread to the other city-states of Italy.

Unlike the countries of northern Europe, Italy had never been heavily feudalized. Italian feudal lords rarely exercised the vast, independent powers held by the barons of France, England, and the Holy Roman Empire. Although the volume of urban trade and the size of urban populations severely declined in the early Middle Ages, cities survived as commercial centers. In the twelfth and thirteenth centuries, northern Italian cities like Venice and Milan gained control of their surrounding territories. The wealth they steadily gained was used to acquire their independence. The Holy Roman emperors never fully exploited the wealth of the cities.

Moreover, the rural nobility of northern Italy began to strike military and marital contracts with the wealthy burghers of the urban centers. These alliances let the nobles maintain a high standard of living in a rising money economy and gave the cities military support and protection. When the rural nobility united with the rich merchants, two significant developments occurred: the possession of land gradually came into the hands of bankers and merchants, and as a result the cities obtained political as well as economic jurisdiction over the surrounding countryside. In no other part of Europe did cities acquire such political power,

primarily because the aristocratic ethos forbade feudal barons to unite with the moneygrubbing bourgeoisie. Elsewhere, too, cities did not have the commercial and financial strength of the Italian towns.

Italian society in the fourteenth century meant urban society. This fundamental fact helps to account for the Italian origin of the Renaissance. The cities of Milan, Venice, Florence, Genoa, and Pisa were visited by traders and businessmen from all parts of the Western world. Foreigners brought their own customs, traditions, and values with them, and considerable communication, social as well as business, inevitably took place. The merchant Francesco Datini, for example, was involved in commercial transactions with two hundred cities, from Alexandria and Beirut in the south to Stockholm in the north. Italians gained an awareness of different parts of the world. They grew more refined, more sophisticated in their tastes and lifestyles, more worldly and urbane. Although Italians remained devoted sons and daughters of the church, they grew more secular in their outlook and behavior. Class distinctions remained strong in Renaissance Italy, but those distinctions were based on wealth rather than birth. And enterprise, imagination, and hard work could lead to wealth in the urban environment.

Finally, the Renaissance started in Italy because Italian poets, sculptors, painters, and philosophers of the fifteenth and sixteenth centuries considered themselves the natural heirs of the ancient Romans. Italy still possessed the literary manuscripts, the architectural monuments, the roads that linked all parts of the peninsula. Above all, Italians retained the historical memory of Roman power and imperial grandeur. The national past of Italy was visible everywhere, and Italians became very

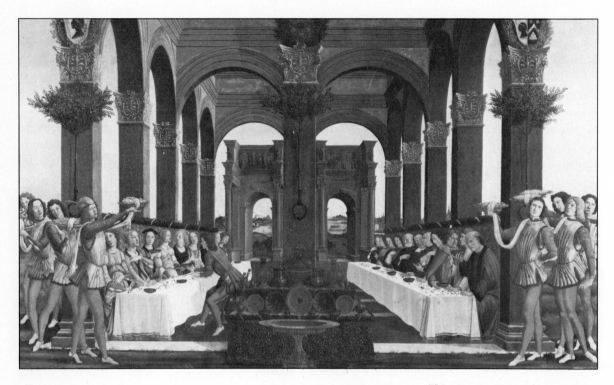

THE WEDDING FEAST.   This picture was one of a series Botticelli produced illustrating a story in Boccaccio's *Decameron*. The classical architecture with its vision of nature beyond, the pomp with which the meal is served, and the philosophical discussion at the tables – all represent the tastes and ideals of the Florentine aristocracy under the Medici. (Courtesy of Christie's)

interested in that past. No other country in Europe possessed so much of the physical heritage of Roman civilization. Fourteenth-century Italians looked back on Roman antiquity as the golden age, as an ideal to be restored and reborn.

A "foreign" element also played a significant role. Beginning in the late fourteenth century, a steady stream of educated Greek refugees came from Byzantium to Italy to escape Turkish domination. Greek scholars like Manuel Chrysolas, John Bessarion, and Jonus Lascaris taught the Greek language and translated important Greek literary classics into Latin. Venice became the chief center of Greek scholarship, but Florence and Rome also gained an international reputation for Greek learning. Greek emigration to Italy broadened the intellectual horizon and enriched Italian Renaissance culture.

The Renaissance, then, was an artistic and intellectual movement that began in the Italian cities and that was supported and sustained by urban wealth. Increased wealth afforded a greater amount of leisure time. By the middle of the fourteenth century, the commercial classes of Florence and other Italian cities had acquired enough money that they could finance non-moneymaking activities.

Wealth, by itself, is usually not sufficient to satisfy the human psyche. When the physical and material needs of life are fulfilled and there is a surplus, then the spirit can be enriched by esthetic and intellectual interests.

HALLMARKS OF THE RENAISSANCE

The Renaissance was characterized, first, by the self-conscious awareness among fourteenth- and fifteenth-century Italians that they were living in a new era and a different time. The Renaissance also manifested itself by a new attitude toward men and women and the world — an attitude that may be described as individualism. A form of humanism stemming from a deep interest in the Latin classics and the deliberate attempt to revive antique lifestyles also emerged, as did a bold new secular spirit.

Individualism

Scholars generally agree that a sense of individualism pervades the Renaissance. In the Middle Ages individuals thought of themselves as part of a group — as a member of a guild, as a resident of a particular area. The very few persons who considered themselves so unusual that they indulged in autobiography — Saint Augustine in the fifth century and Guibert of Nogent in the twelfth, for example — were unique for that very reason. Christian humility and the corporate structure of Western society encouraged people to define themselves in terms of a larger religious, economic, or social group.

This organic view of society deteriorated during the fourteenth and fifteenth centuries. The Renaissance witnessed the emergence of many distinctive personalities who gloried in their uniqueness. Italians of unusual abilities were self-consciously aware of their individuality; they were not afraid of singularity, of being unlike their neighbors. They had enormous confidence in their ability to achieve great things. Leon Battista Alberti (1404–1474), a writer, architect, and mathematician, remarked, "Men can do all things if they will."[2] Completely lacking in modesty, real or false, people of the Renaissance were proud of their abilities and believed everyone should know about them. The Florentine goldsmith and sculptor Benvenuto Cellini (1500–1574) prefaced his *Autobiography* with a sonnet that declares:

My cruel fate hath warr'd with me in vain:
Life, glory, worth, and all unmeasur'd skill,
Beauty and grace, themselves in me fulfill
That many I surpass, and to the best attain.[3]

Cellini was certain of his genius, and he wrote so that the whole world might appreciate it.

Individualism stressed personality, genius, uniqueness, and the fullest development of capabilities and talents. Artist, athlete, painter, scholar, sculptor, whatever — a person's potential should be stretched until fully realized. A thirst for fame, a driving ambition, a burning desire for success drove people to the complete achievement of their potential. The quest for glory was central to Renaissance individualism.

The Revival of Antiquity

One indication of the renewed interest in antiquity was Italians' enthusiastic investigation of the ruins of their national past. In the cities of Italy, and especially in Rome, civic leaders and the wealthy populace showed phenomenal archaeological zeal for the recovery of manuscripts, statues, and monuments. Pope Nicholas V (1447–1455), a distinguished scholar, planned the Vatican Library for the nine thousand manuscripts he had collected. Pope Sixtus IV (1471–1484) built that library, which remains one of the richest repositories of ancient and medieval documents.

Patrician Italians consciously copied the lifestyle of the ancients and even searched for pedigrees going back to ancient Rome. Aeneas Silvius Piccolomini, a native of Siena who became Pope Pius II (1458–1464), once pretentiously declared, "Rome is as much my home as Siena, for my House, the Piccolomini, came in early times from the capital to Siena, as is proved by the constant use of the names Aeneas and Silvius in my family."[4]

The revival of antiquity was also seen in the profound interest in and study of the Latin classics. This feature of the Renaissance became known as the "new learning," or simply as "humanism," the term of the Florentine rhetorician and historian Leonardo Bruni (1370–1444). The words "humanism" and "humanist" derive ultimately from the Latin *humanitas*, which Cicero used to mean the literary culture needed by anyone who would be considered educated and civilized. Humanists studied the Latin classics to learn what they reveal about human nature. Humanism emphasized human beings, their achievements, interests, and capabilities. Although churchmen supported the new learning, Italian humanism had a preponderantly lay influence.

Appreciation for the literary culture of the Romans had never died completely in the West.

Bede, Alcuin, and Einhard in the eighth century, and Ailred of Rievaulx, Bernard of Clairvaux, and John of Salisbury in the twelfth century, for example, all studied and imitated the writings of the ancients. Medieval writers, however, had studied the ancients in order to come to know God. Medieval thinkers held that human beings are the noblest of God's creatures, and that even though they have fallen, they are still capable of regeneration and thus deserving of respect. Medieval scholars interpreted the classics in a Christian sense and invested the ancient's poems and histories with Christian meaning.

Renaissance philosophers and poets also emphasized human dignity, but usually not in a Christian context. The Florentine writer Pico della Mirandola wrote a remarkable essay, "On the Dignity of Man," in which he maintained that man's place in the universe may be somewhere between the beasts and the angels but there are no limits to what he can accomplish.

Humanists tried to approach the classical texts with an open mind, to learn what the ancients had thought. They rejected the religious interpretations and systematic and formal scholastic works of the Middle Ages. They hated scholasticism because they believed it denied humanity and destroyed style.

The fourteenth- and fifteenth-century humanists loved the language of the classics and considered it superior to the corrupt Latin of the medieval schoolmen. Renaissance writers were very excited by the purity of ancient Latin. They became concerned more about form than about content, more about the way an idea was expressed than about the significance and validity of the idea. Literary humanists of the fourteenth century wrote highly stylized letters to each other, imitating ancient authors, and they held witty philosophical dialogues in conscious imitation of the Platonic

Academy of the fifty century B.C. Wherever they could, Renaissance humanists poured scorn on the "barbaric" Latin style of the medievalists. The leading humanists of the early Renaissance were rhetoricians, seeking effective and eloquent communication, both oral and written.

Secular Spirit

Secularism involves a basic concern with the world, with material objects instead of eternal and spiritual interests. A secular way of thinking tends to find the ultimate explanation of everything and the final end of human beings within the limits of what the senses can discover. In a religious society, such as the medieval, the focus is on the otherworldly, on life after death. In a secular society, attention is concentrated on the here and now, often on the acquisition of material things. The fourteenth and fifteenth centuries witnessed the slow but steady growth of secularism in Italy.

The economic changes and rising prosperity of the Italian cities in the thirteenth century worked a fundamental change in social and intellectual attitudes and values. In the Middle Ages the feudal nobility and the higher clergy had determined the dominant patterns of culture. The medieval aristocracy expressed disdain for moneymaking. Christian ideas and values infused literature, art, politics, and all other aspects of culture. In contrast, the business concerns of the urban bourgeoisie in the Renaissance required constant and rational attention.

Worries about shifting rates of interest, shipping routes, personnel costs, and employee relations did not leave too much time for thoughts about penance and purgatory. The busy bankers and merchants of the Italian cities calculated ways of making and increasing their money. Money allowed greater material pleasures, a more comfortable life, the leisure time to appreciate and to patronize the arts. Money could buy many sensual gratifications, and the rich and social-climbing patricians of Venice, Florence, Genoa, and Rome came to see life more as an opportunity to be enjoyed than as a painful pilgrimage to the City of God.

The humanist Lorenzo Valla (1406–1457), in the treatise *On Pleasure,* defended the pleasures of the senses as the highest good. Scholars praise Valla as the father of modern historical criticism. His study, *On the False Donation of Constantine* (1444), demonstrated by careful textual examination that the anonymous ninth-century document supposedly giving the papacy jurisdiction over vast territories in western Europe was a forgery. Medieval people had accepted the Donation of Constantine as a reality, and the proof that it was an invention seriously weakened the foundations of papal claims to temporal authority. Lorenzo Valla's work reflects the application of critical scholarship to old and almost sacred writings and the new secular spirit of the Renaissance. The tales in the *Decameron* by the Florentine Boccaccio (1313–1375), which describe ambitious merchants, lecherous friars, and cuckolded husbands, reveal a frankly acquisitive, sensual, and secular society. The "contempt of the world" theme, so pervasive in medieval literature, had disappeared. Renaissance writers justified the accumulation and enjoyment of wealth with references to ancient authors.

Nor did church leaders do much to combat the new secular spirit and set high moral standards. In the fifteenth and early sixteenth centuries, the papal court and the households of the cardinals were just as worldly as those of great urban patricians. Of course, most of the popes and the higher church officials had come from the bourgeois aristocracy.

The Medici pope Leo X (1513–1521), for example, supported artists and men of letters because patronage was an activity he had learned in the household of his father, Lorenzo the Magnificent. Renaissance popes beautified the city of Rome and patronized the arts. They spent an enormous amount of enthusiasm and huge sums of money on the re-embellishment of the city. A new papal chancellery, begun in 1483 and finished in 1511, stands as one of the architectural masterpieces of the High Renaissance (roughly, the period from 1500–1530). Pope Julius II (1503–1513) tore down the old St. Peter's Basilica and began work on the present structure in 1506. Michelangelo's dome for St. Peter's is still considered his greatest work. Papal interests and activities, removed from spiritual concerns, fostered rather than discouraged the new worldly attitude.

The broad mass of the people and even the intellectuals and leaders of society remained faithful to the Christian church, however. Few people questioned the basic tenets of the Christian religion. Italian humanists and their aristocratic patrons were antiascetic, antischolastic, and anticlerical, but they were not agnostics or skeptics The thousands of pious paintings, sculptures, processions, and pilgrimages of the Renaissance period indicate that strong religious feeling persisted.

THE RENAISSANCE IN THE NORTH

In the last quarter of the fifteenth century, Renaissance thought and ideals penetrated northern Europe. Students from the Low Countries, France, Germany, and England flocked to Italy, imbibed the "new learning," and carried it back to their countries. Northern humanists interpreted Italian ideas about and attitudes toward classical antiquity, individualism, and humanism in terms of their own traditions. The cultural traditions of northern Europe tended to remain more distinctly Christian,

or at least pietistic, than those of Italy. Thus, while the Renaissance in Italy was characterized by a secular and pagan spirit and focused on Greco-Roman motifs and scholarship, north of the Alps the Renaissance had a religious character and involved biblical and early Christian themes. Scholars have termed the northern Renaissance "Christian humanism."

Christian humanists were interested in the development of an ethical way of life. To achieve it they believed that the best elements of classical and Christian cultures should be combined. For example, the classical ideals of calmness, stoical patience, and broad-mindedness should be joined in human conduct with the Christian virtues of love, faith, and hope. Northern humanists also stressed the use of reason, rather than the acceptance of dogma, as the foundation for an ethical way of life. Like the Italians, they were extremely impatient with scholastic philosophy. Christian humanists had a profound faith in the power of the human intellect to bring about moral and institutional reform. They believed that although human nature had been corrupted by sin it was fundamentally good and capable of improvement through education, which would lead to piety and an ethical way of life.

This optimistic viewpoint found expression in scores of lectures, treatises, and collections of precepts. Treatises, such as Erasmus's *The Education of a Christian Prince,* express the naive notion that peace, harmony among nations, and the achievement of a truly ethical society will result from a new system of education. This hope has been advanced repeatedly in Western history — by the ancient Greeks, by the sixteenth-century Christian humanists, by the eighteenth-century philosophers of the Enlightenment, and by the nineteenth-century advocates of progress. The proposition remains highly debatable, but certainly each time the theory has reappeared education has been further democratized.

The work of the French priest Jacques Lefèvre d'Etaples (ca 1455–1536) is one of the early attempts to apply humanistic learning to religious problems. A brilliant thinker and able scholar, he believed that improved and critically accurate texts of the Bible would lead people to live better lives. According to him, a solid education in the Scriptures would increase piety and raise the level of behavior in Christian society. Lefèvre produced an edition of the Psalms and a commentary on Saint Paul's Epistles. In 1516, when Martin Luther lectured to his students at Wittenberg on Paul's Letter to the Romans, he relied on Lefèvre's texts.

Lefèvre's English contemporary, John Colet (1466–1519), also published lectures on Saint Paul's Epistles. Colet approached them in the new critical spirit. Unlike the medieval theologians, who studied the Bible for allegorical meanings, Colet, who was a priest, interpreted the Pauline letters historically, that is, within the social and political context of the times when they were written. Both Colet and Lefèvre d'Etaples were later suspected of heresy, as humanistic scholarship got entangled with the issues of the Reformation.

Colet's friend and countryman Thomas More (1472–1535) towers above other figures in sixteenth-century English social and intellectual history. More's political stance at the time of the Reformation, a position that in part flowed from his humanist beliefs, got him into serious trouble with King Henry VIII and has tended to obscure his contribution to the program of Christian humanism.

The early career of Thomas More presents a number of paradoxes that reveal the marvelous complexity of the man. Trained as a lawyer, he lived as a student in the London Charterhouse, a Carthusian monastery. Although he subsequently married and practiced law, he became deeply interested in the classics, and his household served as a model of warm Christian family life and as a mecca for foreign and English humanists. Following the career pattern of such Italian humanists as Petrarch, he entered government service under Henry VIII (1509–1547) and was sent as ambassador to Flanders. There More found the time to write a book, *Utopia* (1516), that presented a revolutionary view of society.

Utopia literally means "nowhere." It describes an ideal socialistic community on a South Sea island. All its children receive a good education, primarily in the Greco-Roman classics, and learning does not cease with the arrival of maturity, for the goal of all education is to develop rational faculties. Adults divide their days equally between manual labor or business pursuits (the Utopians were thoroughly familiar with advanced Flemish business practices) and various intellectual activities.

The profits made from business and property are held strictly in common. Consequently, there is absolute social equality. The Utopians use gold and silver to make chamber pots or to prevent wars by buying off their enemies. By this use of precious metals, More meant to suggest that the basic problems in society were caused by greed.

Utopian law exalts mercy above justice. Citizens of Utopia lead an ideal and nearly perfect existence because they live by reason. Their institutions are perfect.

More's ideas were profoundly original in the sixteenth century. Contrary to the long-prevailing view that vice and violence exist because women and men are basically corrupt, More maintained that *society's* flawed institutions are responsible for corruption and war. Today most people take this view so much for granted that it is difficult to appreciate how radical it was in the sixteenth century. According to More, the key to the improvement and reform of the individual was the reform of the social institutions that mold the individual.

Better known by his contemporaries than Thomas More was the Dutch humanist Desiderius Erasmus of Rotterdam (1469?–1536). Orphaned as a small boy, Erasmus was forced to enter a monastery, and although he intensely disliked the religious life, he developed there an excellent knowledge of the Latin language and a deep appreciation for the Latin classics. During a visit to England in 1499, Erasmus met John Colet. Colet decisively influenced his life's work: the application of the best humanistic learning to the study and explanation of the Bible. As a mature scholar with an international reputation stretching from Krakow to London, Erasmus could boast with truth, "I brought it about that humanism, which among the Italians . . . savored of nothing but pure paganism, began nobly to celebrate Christ."[5]

Erasmus's long list of publications includes *The Adages* (1500), a list of Greek and Latin precepts on ethical behavior; *The Education of a Christian Prince* (1504), which combines ideal and practical suggestions for the formation of a ruler's character through the careful study of Plutarch, Aristotle, Cicero, and Plato; *The Praise of Folly* (1509), a satire on monasticism and a plea for the simple and spontaneous Christian faith of children; and, most important of all, a critical edition of the Greek New Testament (1516). In the preface to the New Testament Erasmus explained the purpose of his great work:

Only bring a pious and open heart, imbued above all things with a pure and simple faith. . . . For I utterly dissent from those who are unwilling that the sacred Scriptures should be read by the unlearned translated into their vulgar tongue, as though Christ had taught such subtleties that they can scarcely be understood even by a few theologians. . . . Christ wished his mysteries to be published as openly as possible. I wish that even the weakest woman should read the Gospel — should read the epistles of Paul. And I wish these were translated into all languages, so that they might be read and understood, not only by Scots and Irishmen, but also by Turks and Saracens. To make them understood is surely the first step. It may be that they might be ridiculed by many, but some would take them to heart. I long that the husbandman should sing portions of them to himself as he follows the plough, that the weaver should hum them to the tune of his shuttle, that the traveller should beguile with their stories the tedium of his journey. . . .

Why do we prefer to study the wisdom of Christ in men's writings rather than in the writing of Christ himself? [6]

Two fundamental themes run through all of Erasmus's scholarly work. First, education was the means to reform, the key to moral and intellectual improvement. The core of education centered in the study of the Bible and the classics. Second, the essence of Erasmus's thought is, in his own phrase, "the philosophy of Christ." By this he meant that Christianity is an inner attitude of the heart or spirit. Christianity is not formalism, special ceremonies, law; Christianity is Christ — his life and what he said and did, not what theologians and commentators have written about him. The Sermon on the Mount, for Erasmus, expressed the heart of the Christian message.

ART AND THE ARTIST

No feature of the Renaissance evokes a greater shock of recognition or wider admiration than the artistic masterpieces. The 1400s (quattrocento) and

the 1500s (cinquecento) witnessed a dazzling creativity in painting, architecture, and sculpture. In all the artistic media, the city of Florence consistently led the way. According to the Renaissance historian of art Giorgio Vasari (1511–1574), the painter Perugino (ca 1450–1523) once asked why it was in Florence and not elsewhere that men achieved perfection in the arts. The first answer he received was, "There were so many good critics there, for the air of the city makes men quick and perceptive and impatient of mediocrity."[7]

Enthusiasm for Renaissance art, however, has led many people to hysterical excess. Some historians and art critics have maintained that the Renaissance "discovered" or "rediscovered" the world of nature and of human beings. This is nonsense, as a quick glance at a Gothic cathedral or an ancient artifact reveals. The enormous detail applied to the depiction of animals' bodies, the careful carving of leaves, flowers, and all kinds of vegetation, the fine sensitivity frequently shown in human faces — these clearly show medieval and ancient people's appreciation for nature in all its manifestations. Saint Francis of Assisi (1181–1226) encouraged throughout his entire life an awareness of nature. No historical period has a monopoly on the appreciation of nature or beauty; the problem has always been learning to look, to understand, to appreciate.

The Social Function of Art

In the fourteenth century, significant changes in the realm of art did occur. Art served the newly rich middle class as well as the institutional church. The patrons of Renaissance art were more frequently laymen and laywomen, not ecclesiastics. The patrician merchants and bankers supported the arts to display their wealth, as a means of self-glorification and self-perpetuation. Art may also have been a form of financial investment. Great families, such as the Medicis in Florence, used works of art as a means of gaining and maintaining public support for their rule. A magnificent style of living, enriched by works of art, seemed to prove the greatness of the rulers. As the fifteenth century advanced, the subject matter of art became steadily more secular. The study of classical texts and manuscripts brought deeper understanding of ancient ideas. Classical themes and classical motifs, such as the lives and loves of pagan gods and goddesses, figure in increasing numbers of paintings and sculptures. Religious topics, such as the Annunciation of the Virgin and the Nativity, remained popular for both patrons and artists, but frequently a patron had himself and his family memorialized by his appearance in some part of the picture. People were conscious of their physical uniqueness, and they wanted those individual characteristics immortalized. Paintings cost money and thus were also means of displaying wealth. Although many Renaissance paintings contain a classical or Christian theme, the appearance of the patron also reflects the new spirit of individualism and secularism.

The style of Renaissance art was decidedly different from that of the Middle Ages. The individual portrait as a distinct artistic genre appeared. Increasingly in the fifteenth century members of the newly rich middle class had themselves painted, often in a scene of romantic chivalry or in courtly society. Rather than reflecting a spiritual ideal, as medieval painting and sculpture tended to do, Renaissance portraits mirrored reality. The Florentine painter Giotto (1276–1337) led the way in the depiction of realism; his treatment of the human body and face replaced the formal stiffness and artificiality that for so long had characterized the representation of the human body. The sculptor Donatello (1386–1466) probably exerted the greatest influence of any Florentine artist before Michelangelo. His many statues showed an appreciation of the incredible varieties of human nature. For example, while the medieval artist had depicted the nude human body only in a spiritualized and moralizing context, Donatello revived the classical figure with its balance and self-awareness. The short-lived Florentine Masaccio (1401–1428), sometimes called the Father of Modern Painting, inspired a new style in painting characterized by great realism, narrative power, and remarkable effect through the use of light and dark.

Narrative artists depicted the body in a more scientific and natural manner. The female figure is voluptuous and sensual. The male body, as in Michelangelo's *David* and *The Last Judgment*, is strong and heroic. Renaissance glorification of the human body reveals the secular spirit of the age. Filippo Brunelleschi (1377–1446), together with Piero della Francesca (1420–1492), seems to have developed perspective in painting, the representation through mathematical lines of distance and space on a flat surface. *The Last Supper* of Leonardo da Vinci (1452–1519), with its stress on the psychological tension between Christ and the disciples, was an incredibly subtle interpretation for the fifteenth century.

The distinctly religious features that marked the literary works of the Renaissance in the north were also present in northern art and architecture. Some Flemish painters, notably Jan van Eyck (1366–1441), were the equals of Italian painters. One of the earliest artists successfully to use oil on wood panels, Jan van Eyck, in paintings such as the *Ghent Altarpiece* and the portrait of *Giovanni Arnolfini and His Bride,* shows the Flemish love for detail; the effect is great realism. Van Eyck's paintings also demonstrate remarkable attention to human personality, as do those of Hans Memling (d. 1494) in his studies of *Tommaso Portivari and His Wife.* Typical of northern piety, the Portivari are depicted in an attitude of prayer.

A quasi-spiritual aura, likewise, infuses architectural monuments in the north. The city halls of wealthy Flemish towns like Bruges, Brussels, Louvain, and Ghent strike the viewer more as shrines to house the bones of saints than as buildings to witness the mundane decisions of politicians and businessmen. Northern architecture was not much influenced by the classical revival so obvious in Renaissance Rome and Florence.

ADORATION OF THE MAGI. The Flemish artist who painted this biblical scene for Don Alfonso of Castile gave the figures elegant fifteenth century costumes and achieved a fair degree of perspective. The three kings are sometimes thought to represent the continents of Europe, Asia, and Africa. Like medieval manuscripts, the border has a rich variety of floral, animal, and hunting life. (The Pierpont Morgan Library)

The Status of the Artist

In the Renaissance the social status of the artist improved. The lower-middle-class medieval master mason had been viewed in the same light as any mechanic. The artist in the Renaissance was considered an independent intellectual worker. Some artists and architects achieved not only economic security but very great wealth. All aspiring artists received a practical (and not theoretical) education in a recognized master's workshop. For example, Michelangelo (1475–1564) was apprenticed at age thirteen to the artist Ghirlandaio (1449–1494), although he later denied the fact to make it appear he never had any formal training. The more famous the artist, the more he attracted assistants or apprentices. Lorenzo Ghiberti (1378–1455) had twenty assistants during the period he was working on the bronze doors of the Baptistery in Florence, his most famous achievement.

Ghiberti's salary of two hundred florins a year at that time compares very favorably with that of the head of the city government, who earned five hundred florins. Moreover, at a time when a man could live in a princely fashion on three hundred ducats a year, Leonardo da Vinci was making two thousand annually. Michelangelo was paid three thousand ducats for painting the ceiling of the Sistine Chapel. When he agreed to work on St. Peter's Basilica, he refused a salary; he was already a wealthy man.[8]

Renaissance society respected and rewarded the distinguished artist. In 1537, the prolific letter writer, humanist, and satirizer of princes, Pietro Aretino (1492–1556), wrote to Michelangelo while he was painting the Sistine Chapel:

TO THE DIVINE MICHELANGELO:

Sir, just as it is disgraceful and sinful to be unmindful of God so it is reprehensible and dishonourable for any man of discerning judgement not to honour you as a brilliant and venerable artist whom the very stars use as a target

HANS MEMLING: MARIA AND TOMMASO PORTINARI. A Florentine citizen, Tommaso Portinari earned a fortune as representative of the Medici banking interests in Bruges, Flanders. Husband and wife are dressed in a rich but durable black broadcloth; Maria's necklace displays their wealth. Although both faces show a sharp intelligence, there is a melancholy sadness about them, suggestive of the pessimism of northern religious piety. (The Metropolitan Museum of Art; Bequest of Benjamin Altman, 1913)

*at which to shoot the rival arrows of their favour. You
are so accomplished, therefore, that hidden in your hands
lives the idea of a new king of creation, whereby the most
challenging and subtle problem of all in the art of
painting, namely that of outlines, has been so mastered by
you that in the contours of the human body you express
and contain the purpose of art. . . . And it is surely
my duty to honour you with this salutation, since the
world has many kings but only one Michelangelo.*[9]

When the Holy Roman emperor Charles V
(1519–1556) visited the workshop of the great
Titian (1477–1576) and stooped to pick up the
artist's dropped paintbrush, the emperor demonstrated that the patron himself was honored in the
act of honoring the artist. The social status of the
artist of genius was immortally secured.

Renaissance artists were not only aware of their
creative power but boasted about it. The architect
Brunelleschi had his life written, and Ghiberti and
Cellini wrote their autobiographies. Many medieval
sculptors and painters had signed their own works;
Renaissance artists almost universally did so, and
many left self-portraits, usually as bystanders, in
their paintings. These actions reflect an acute
consciousness of creative genius.

The Renaissance witnessed the birth of the
concept of the artist as *genius*. In the Middle Ages
people believed that only God created, albeit
through individuals; the medieval conception recognized no particular value in artistic originality.
Renaissance artists and humanists came to think
that a work of art was the deliberate creation of a
unique personality, of an individual who goes
beyond traditions, rules, and theories. A genius has
a peculiar gift, which ordinary laws should not
inhibit. The creation of a genius is often impossible
to describe, because it surpasses traditional language, forms, and experience. Cosimo de' Medici
described a painter, because of his genius, as
"divine," implying that the artist shared in the
powers of God. The word "divine" was widely

applied to Michelangelo. The Renaissance bequeathed the idea of genius to the modern world.

The student must guard against interpreting
Italian Renaissance culture in twentieth-century
democratic terms. The culture of the Renaissance
was devised for a small mercantile elite, a business
patriciate with aristocratic pretensions. Renaissance
culture did not directly affect the broad middle
classes, let alone the vast urban proletariat. The
"typical" small tradesman or craftsman could not
read the sophisticated Latin essays of the humanists,
even if he had the time to do so. He could not
afford to buy the art works of the great masters. A
small, highly educated minority of literary humanists and artists created the culture of and for an
exclusive elite. They cared little for ordinary people. Castiglione, Machiavelli, and Vergerio, for
example, thoroughly despised the masses. Renaissance humanists were a smaller and narrower group
than the medieval clergy had ever been. High
churchmen had commissioned the construction of
the Gothic cathedrals, but, once finished, the
buildings were for all to enjoy. The modern visitor
can still see the deep ruts in the stone floors of
Chartres and Canterbury where the poor pilgrims
slept at night. Nothing like that existed in the
Renaissance. Insecure, social-climbing merchant
princes were hardly egalitarian.[10] The Renaissance
intelligentsia laid the foundation for the vast gulf
between the learned minority and the uneducated
multitude that has survived for many centuries.

SOCIAL CHANGE

The Renaissance changed many aspects of Italian,
and subsequently European, society. The new
developments brought about real breaks with the

medieval past. What impact did the Renaissance have on educational theory and practice, on political thought? Did "women have a Renaissance?" How did printing, the major technological discovery, affect fifteenth- and sixteenth-century society?

Education and Political Thought

One of the central preoccupations of the humanists was education and moral behavior. Humanists poured out treatises, often in epistolary form, on the structure and goals of education and the training of rulers. In one of the earliest systematic programs for the young, Peter Paul Vergerio (1370–1444) wrote Ubertinus, the ruler of Carrara:

The lives of men of position are passed, as it were, in public view; and are fairly expected to serve as witness to personal merit and capacity on the part of those who occupy such exceptional place amongst their fellow men. You therefore, Ubertinus, . . . the representative of a house for many generations sovereign in our ancient and most learned city of Padua, are peculiarly concerned in attaining this excellence in learning of which we speak. . . . Progress in learning . . . as in character, depends largely on ourselves.

For the education of children is a matter of more than private interest; it concerns the State, which indeed regards the right training of the young as, in certain aspects, within its proper sphere. . . . In order to maintain a high standard of purity all enticements of dancing, or suggestive spectacles, should be kept at a distance: and the society of women as a rule carefully avoided. A bad companion may wreck the character. Idleness, of mind and body, is a common source of temptation to indulgence, and unsociable, solitary temper must be disciplined, and on no account encouraged. Tutors and comrades alike should be chosen from amongst those likely to bring out the best qualities, to attract by good example, and to repress the first signs of evil. . . . Above all, respect for Divine ordinances is of

the deepest importance; it should be inculcated from the earliest years. Reverence towards elders and parents is an obligation closely akin. In this, antiquity offers us a beautiful illustration. For the youth of Rome used to escort the Senators, the Fathers of the City, to the Senate House: and awaiting them at the entrance, accompany them at the close of their deliberations on their return to their homes. In this the Romans saw an admirable training in endurance and in patience. This same quality of reverence will imply courtesy towards guests, suitable greeting to elders, to friends and to inferiors. . . .

We call those studies liberal which are worthy of a free man; those studies by which we attain and practise virtue and wisdom; that education which calls forth, trains and develops those highest gifts of body and of mind which ennoble men, and which are rightly judged to rank next in dignity to virtue only. . . .[11]

Part of Vergerio's treatise deals with specific subjects for the instruction of young men in public life: history teaches virtue by examples from the past; ethics focuses on virtue itself; and rhetoric or public speaking trains for eloquence.

No book on education achieved wider fame or broader influence than Baldassare Castiglione's *The Courtier* (1528). This treatise sought to train, discipline, and fashion the young man into the courtly ideal, the gentleman. The educated man of the upper class should have a broad background in many academic subjects, and his spiritual and physical, as well as his intellectual, capabilities should be trained. The courtier should have easy familiarity with dance, music, and the arts. Castiglione envisioned a man who could compose a sonnet, wrestle, sing a song and accompany himself on an instrument, ride expertly, solve difficult mathematical problems, and, above all, speak and write eloquently. With these accomplishments, he was the perfect "Renaissance man."

In contrast to the patterns of medieval education, the Renaissance courtier had the aristocrat's hostility to specialization and professionalism. Medieval higher education, as offered by the universities, had aimed at providing a practical grounding in preparation for a career. After exposure to the rudiments of grammar and rhetoric, which the medieval student learned mainly through memorization, he was trained for a profession — usually law — in the government of the state or the church. Education was very functional and, by later standards, middle class.

In manner and behavior also, the Renaissance courtier had traits his medieval predecessor probably had not had time to acquire. The gentleman was supposed to be relaxed, controlled, always composed and "cool," elegant but not ostentatious, doing everything with a casual and seemingly effortless grace. In the sixteenth and seventeenth centuries, *The Courtier* was widely read. It influenced the social mores and patterns of conduct of elite groups in Renaissance and early modern Europe. The courtier became the model of the European gentleman.

No Renaissance book on any topic, however, has been more widely read and studied in all the centuries since its publication than the short political treatise *The Prince,* by Niccolò Machiavelli (1469–1527). Some political scientists maintain that Machiavelli was describing the actual competitive framework of the Italian states with which he was familiar. Other thinkers praise *The Prince*

because it revolutionized political theory and destroyed medieval views of the nature of the state. Still other scholars consider this work a classic because it deals with eternal problems of government and society.

Born to a modestly wealthy Tuscan family, Machiavelli received a good education in the Latin classics. He entered the civil service of the Florentine government and served on thirty diplomatic missions. When the exiled Medicis returned to power in the city in 1512, they expelled Machiavelli from his position as officer of the city government. In exile he wrote *The Prince.*

The subject of *The Prince* is political power: how the ruler should gain, maintain, and increase his power. In this, Machiavelli implicitly addresses the question of the citizen's relationship to the state. As a good humanist, he explores the problems of human nature and concludes that human beings are selfish, corrupt, and out to advance their own interests. This pessimistic view leads him to maintain that the prince should manipulate the people in any way he finds necessary:

The manner in which men live is so different from the way in which they ought to live, that he who leaves the common course for that which he ought to follow will find that it leads him to ruin rather than to safety. For a man who, in all respects, will carry out only his professions of good, will be apt to be ruined amongst so many who are evil. A prince therefore who desires to maintain himself must learn to be not always good, but to be so or not as necessity may require.[12]

The prince should combine the cunning of a fox with the ferocity of a lion to achieve his goals. Asking rhetorically whether it is better for a ruler to be loved or feared, Machiavelli wrote:

A prince, therefore, should not mind the ill repute of cruelty, when he can thereby keep his subjects united and loyal; for a few displays of severity will really be more merciful than to allow, by an excess of clemency, disorders to occur, which are apt to result in rapine and murder; for these injure a whole community, whilst the executions ordered by the prince fall only upon a few individuals. And, above all others, the new prince will find it almost impossible to avoid the reputation of cruelty, because new states are generally exposed to many dangers. . . .

. . . This, then, gives rise to the question "whether it be better to be loved than feared, or to be feared than be loved." It will naturally be answered that it would be desirable to be both the one and the other; but as it is difficult to be both at the same time, it is much more safe to be feared than to be loved, when you have to choose between the two. For it may be said of men in general that they are ungrateful and fickle, dissemblers, avoiders of danger, and greedy of gain. So long as you shower benefits upon them, they are all yours. . . . And the prince who relies upon their words, without having otherwise provided for his security, is ruined; for friendships that are won by rewards, and not by greatness and nobility of soul, although deserved, yet are not real, and cannot be depended upon in time of adversity.[13]

Medieval political theory derives ultimately from Saint Augustine's view that the state arose as a consequence of Adam's fall and people's propensity to sin. The test of good government was whether it provided justice, law and order. Political theorists and theologians from Alcuin to Marsiglio of Padua had stressed the way government ought to be; they set high moral and Christian standards for the ruler's conduct.

Machiavelli totally divorced government from moral and ethical considerations. He was concerned not with the way things ought to be but with the way they actually are. Consequently, the sole test of a "good" government was whether it was effective, whether the ruler increased his power. The state Machiavelli envisioned was a dynamic, amoral force.

Scholars have debated whether Machiavelli was writing a satire, trying to ingratiate himself with the Medicis, objectively describing contemporary Italian events, or advocating a fierce Italian nationalism that would achieve the unification of the peninsula. In any case, political leaders from Henry VIII to Bismarck to Richard Nixon carefully studied the treatise. The word "Machiavellian" entered English as a synonym for devious, crafty, and corrupt politics in which the end justifies any means.

Women

The status of upper-class women declined during the Renaissance. If women in the High Middle Ages are compared with those of fifteenth- and sixteenth-century Italy with respect to the education they received, the kind of work they performed, their access to property and to political power, and the role they played in shaping the outlook of their society, it is clear that ladies in the Renaissance ruling classes generally had less power than comparable ladies of the feudal age.

In the urban centers of Renaissance Italy, girls received the same education as boys. Young ladies learned their letters and studied the classics. Many read Greek as well as Latin, knew the poetry of Ovid and Virgil, and could speak one or two "modern" languages, such as French or Spanish. In this respect, Renaissance humanism represented a real educational advance for women. Girls also received some training in painting, music, and dance. What were they to do with this training? They were to be gracious, affable, charming — in short, decorative. Renaissance women were better educated than their medieval counterparts. But, whereas education trained a young man to rule and to participate in the public affairs of the city, it prepared a woman for the social functions of the home. An educated lady was supposed to know how to attract artists and literati to her husband's court; she was to add grace to her husband's household.

TITIAN: THE RAPE OF EUROPA. According to Greek myth, the Phoenician princess Europa was carried off to Crete by the god Zeus disguised as a white bull. The story was highly popular in the Renaissance with its interests in the classics. In this masterpiece, the erotic and voluptuous female figure reveals the new interest in the human form and the secular element in Renaissance art. (Isabella Stewart Gardner Museum)

A striking difference also exists between the medieval literature of courtly love, the etiquette books and the romances, and the widely studied Renaissance manual on courtesy and good behavior, Castiglione's *The Courtier*. In the medieval books manners shaped the man to please the lady; in *The Courtier* the lady was to make herself pleasing to the man. With respect to love and sex, the Renaissance witnessed a downward shift in women's status. In contrast to the medieval tradition of relative sexual equality, Renaissance humanists laid the foundations for the bourgeois double standard. Men, and men alone, operated in the public sphere; women belonged in the home. Castiglione, the foremost spokesman of Renaissance love and manners, completely separated love from sexuality. For women, sex involved marriage, and sex was restricted entirely to marriage. Ladies were bound to chastity, to the roles of wife and mother in a politically arranged marriage. Men, however, could slake their passions in sensual indulgence outside marriage. The Italian Renaissance courts accepted, as the medieval courts did not, a dual sexual standard. Although some noble ladies were highly educated and some exercised considerable political power, Renaissance culture did little to advance the dignity of women. They usually served as decorative objects in a male society.[14]

Popular attitudes toward rape provide another index of the status of women in the Renaissance. A careful study of the legal evidence from Venice for the years 1338–1358 is informative. The Venetian shipping and merchant elite held economic and political power and made the laws. Those laws reveal that rape was not considered a particularly serious crime against either the victim or society. Noble youths committed a higher percentage of rapes than their small numbers in Venetian society would imply, even though government-regulated prostitution offered release from strong sexual tension. The rape of a young girl of marriageable age or of a child under twelve was considered a graver crime than the rape of a married woman. Still, the punishment for the rape of a noble marriageable girl was only a fine or about six months' imprisonment. In an age when theft and robbery were punished by mutilation, and forgery and sodomy by burning, this penalty was very mild indeed. When a youth of the upper class was convicted of the rape of a nonnoble girl, his punishment was even lighter.

Conversely, the sexual assault on a noblewoman by a man of working-class origin, which was extraordinarily rare, resulted in severe penalization because the crime had social and political overtones.

In the eleventh century, William the Conqueror had decreed that rapists should be castrated, thus implicitly according women protection and a modicum of respect. But, in the early Renaissance, rape was treated as a minor offense. Venetian laws and their enforcement show that the populace believed that rape damaged, but only slightly, men's property — women.[15]

Evidence from Florence in the fifteenth century reveals another serious social problem, infanticide. Early medieval penitentials and church councils had legislated against abortion and infanticide. Historians are only now beginning to study these problems in the Middle Ages and the Renaissance and while conclusions are still tentative, it is known that Pope Innocent III (1198–1216) was moved to establish an orphanage "because so many women were throwing their children into the Tiber."[16] In the fourteenth and early fifteenth centuries, a considerable number of children died in Florence under suspicious circumstances. Some were simply abandoned outdoors. Some were crushed to death while sleeping in the same bed with their parents. Some died from "crib death" or suffocation. These deaths occurred with too great a frequency to have all been accidental. And, a much greater number of girls than boys died in these ways, reflecting societal discrimination against girl children as inferior and less useful than boys. The dire poverty of parents led them to do away with unwanted children.

The gravity of the problem of infanticide, which violated both the canon law of the church and the civil law of the state, forced the Florentine government to build the Foundling Hospital. Supporters of the institution maintained that without public responsibility, "many children would soon be found dead in the rivers, sewers, and ditches, unbaptized."[17] The city fathers commissioned Filippo Brunelleschi, who had recently completed the dome over the Cathedral of Florence, to design the building. (Interestingly enough, the Foundling Hospital — completed in 1445 — is the very first building to use the revitalized Roman classic design that characterizes Renaissance architecture.) The unusually large size of the hospital suggests that great numbers of children were abandoned.

The Printed Word

Within the past twenty-five years, two inventions have revolutionized life for most Americans, television and the computer. By the late 1960s, the tired business executive or mechanic could return home in the evening, flip on "the tube," and while eating dinner watch battles in Vietnam or Israel that had occurred only a few hours before. The American tourist in Copenhagen or Florence or Tokyo who suddenly needs to draw on a bank account in New Orleans or Portland can have the account checked by computer in a matter of minutes. The impact of these relatively recent developments has been absolutely phenomenal. The invention of movable type likewise transformed European society in the sixteenth century.

Sometime in the thirteenth century, paper money and playing cards from China reached the West. They were block printed, that is, Chinese characters or pictures were carved into a wooden block, inked, and the words or illustrations put on paper. Since each word, phrase, or picture was on a separate block, this method of reproducing an idea was extraordinarily expensive and time-consuming.

Around 1455, and probably through the combined efforts of three men — Johan Gutenberg (ca 1395–1468), Johan Fust (ca 1400–1465), and Peter Schoffer (ca 1425–1502), all experimenting at Mainz — movable type came into being. The mirror image of each letter (rather than entire words or phrases) was carved in relief on a small block. Individual letters, easily movable, were put together to form words; words separated by low-cast blank spaces formed lines of type; and lines of type were brought together to make up a page. The printer placed wooden pegs around the type for a border, locked the whole in a chase (or frame), and the page was then ready for printing. Since letters could be arranged into any format, an infinite variety of texts could be printed by reusing and rearranging the pieces of type.

Paper, by the middle of the fifteenth century, was no problem. The technologically advanced but extremely isolated Chinese knew how to manufacture paper in the first century A.D. This knowledge reached the West in the twelfth century, when the Arabs introduced the process into Spain. Europeans quickly learned that old rags could be shredded, mixed with water, placed in a mold, squeezed, and dried to make a durable paper, far less expensive than the vellum (calfskin) or parchment (sheepskin) on which medieval scribes had relied for centuries.

The effects of the invention of printing from movable type were not felt overnight. Nevertheless, within a half-century of the publication of Gutenberg's Bible in 1456, movable type brought about radical changes. The costs of reproducing books were drastically reduced. It took less time and money to print a book by machine than to make

THE PRINT SHOP.   Sixteenth-century printing involved a division of labor. Two persons (left) at separate benches set the pieces of type. Another (center, rear) inks the chase (or locked plate containing the set type). Another (right) operates the press which prints the sheets. The boy removes the printed pages and sets them to dry. Meanwhile, a man carries in fresh paper on his head. (Radio Times Hulton Picture Library)

copies by hand. The press also cut the chances of error. If the type had been accurately set, then all copies would be correct no matter how many were reproduced. The greater the number of pages a scribe copied, the greater the chances for human error. Printing stimulated the literacy of the laity. Although most of the earliest books dealt with religious subjects, students, businessmen, and upper- and middle-class people sought books on all kinds of subjects. Thus, intellectual interests were considerably broadened. International communication was enormously facilitated. The invention of printing permitted writers and scholars of different countries to learn about one another's ideas and discoveries quickly. Intellectuals working in related fields got in touch with each other and cooperated in the advancement of knowledge.

The very process of learning was made easier by printing from movable type. In the past, students had to memorize everything because only the cathedral, monastery, or professor possessed the book. The greater availability of books meant that students could begin to buy their own. If information was not at the tip of the tongue, knowledge was at the tip of the fingers, in the book. The number of students all across Europe multiplied. It is not entirely accidental that between 1450 and 1517 seven new universities were established in Spain, three in France, nine in Germany, and six new colleges were set up at Oxford in England.

Printing also meant that ideas critical of the established order in state or church could be more rapidly disseminated. In the early sixteenth century, for example, the publication of Erasmus's *The Praise of Folly* helped pave the way for the Reformation. After 1517, the printing press played no small role in the spread of Martin Luther's political and social views. Consequently, cartoons and satirical engravings of all kinds proliferated. They also provoked state censorship, which had been very rare in the Middle Ages. The printed word eventually influenced every aspect of European culture: educational, economic, religious, political, and social.

The Environment

Historians and natural scientists are only today beginning to study the attitude of peoples in earlier centuries toward their natural environment. An enormous amount of exciting research, which could improve ecological knowledge and aid in the solution of present-day problems, waits to be done. The measures the city of Florence took against water pollution in the fifteenth century provide some interesting information.

In 1450, the Florentine governing body expressed concern that fishermen and others several miles southeast of the city were polluting the Arno River, which flowed through the city and which was the source of much of Florence's fish. Fewer fresh fish reached the city markets. Ecclesiastical law required Christians to abstain from meat during the Fridays of the year and during the seasons of Advent and Lent. Fish was an obvious substitute, and the fishing industry was large and influential. The law of 1450 states:

Whereas it often happens, especially in parts of the Casentino and areas near there, that poisons and toxic substances are put and inserted into the neighboring rivers and waters to capture and angle fish more easily and in greater number . . .

This is done where those fish are procreated and made which are called Trout, and truly noble and impressive fish they are. The result is that the said fish are destroyed and wasted.

And certainly if this were not so, our city and also other neighboring areas would continually and far more abound in the said fish. So that, therefore, the said genus of fish is preserved, and our city and the other said areas have a copious and abundant supply of such fish, the magnificent . . . lords priors . . . ordain . . . [18]

The citizens of Florence did not understand the ecological problem, and they apparently were not concerned about conservation. While they appreciated the beauty of the "noble trout," they realized only that if upstream waters were polluted and the fish there killed, there would be fewer fish caught and brought to market in Florence. Government officials did not see the damage to the river as a source of beauty, pleasure, and drinking water. Variations of the law of 1450 were put on the statute books in 1455, 1460, 1471, and 1477.[19] This suggests that these early conservation measures could not be enforced.

POLITICS AND THE STATE IN THE RENAISSANCE
(CA 1450–1521)

Renaissance political ideas found concrete expression in the aggressive methods rulers used in government. In the middle of the fifteenth century, first in Italy, and then in France, England, and Spain, rulers began the work of reducing violence, curbing unruly nobles and troublesome elements, and establishing domestic order. Within the Holy Roman Empire of Germany, the lack of centralization helps to account for the later German distrust of the Roman papacy. Divided into scores of independent principalities, Germany could not deal with the Roman church as an equal.

The dictators and oligarchs of the Italian city-states, however, together with Louis XI of France, Henry VII of England, and Ferdinand and Isabella of Spain, were tough, cynical, and calculating rulers. In their ruthless push for power and strong governments, they subordinated morality and considerations of right and wrong to the achievement of hard results. They preferred to be secure, if feared, rather than loved. Whether or not they actually read Machiavelli's *The Prince,* they acted as if they had.

Some historians have called Louis XI (1461–1483), Henry VII (1485–1509), and Ferdinand and Isabella of Spain (1474–1516) "new monarchs." The term is only partly appropriate. These monarchs were "new" in that they invested kingship with a strong sense of royal authority and national purpose. They stressed that monarchy was the one institution that linked all classes and peoples within definite territorial boundaries. Rulers emphasized the "royal majesty" and royal sovereignty and insisted that all must respect and be loyal to them. They ruthlessly suppressed opposition and rebellion, especially from the nobility. They loved the business of kingship and worked hard at it.

In other respects, however, the methods of these rulers, which varied from country to country, were not so new. They reasserted long-standing ideas and practices of strong monarchs in the Middle Ages. The Holy Roman emperor Frederick Barbarossa, the English Edward I, and the French King Philip the Fair had all applied ideas of Roman law in the High Middle Ages. Renaissance princes also did so. They seized upon the maxim of the Justinian Code, "What pleases the prince has the force of law," to advance their authority. Some medieval rulers, such as Henry I of England, had depended heavily upon middle-class officials. Renaissance rulers too tended to rely on civil servants of middle-class background. With tax revenues, medieval rulers had built armies to crush feudal anarchy. Renaissance townspeople with commercial and business interests naturally wanted a reduction of violence and usually were willing to be taxed in order to achieve domestic order.

Scholars have often described the fifteenth-century "new monarchs" as crafty, devious, and thoroughly Machiavellian in their methods. Yet, contemporaries of the Capetian Philip the Fair considered him every bit as devious and crafty as his Valois descendants, Louis XI and Francis I, were considered in the fifteenth and sixteenth centuries. Machiavellian politics were not new in the age of the Renaissance. What was new was a marked acceleration of politics, whose sole rationalization was the acquisition and expansion of power. Renaissance rulers spent precious little time seeking a religious justification for their actions. With these qualifications of the term "new monarchs" in mind, we shall consider the development of national states in Italy, France, England, and Spain in the period 1450 to 1521.

The Italian City-States

In the fourteenth century, several efforts had been made to impose imperial authority in Italy and continue the tradition begun by Charlemagne, but the German emperors, economically and militarily weak, could not defeat the powerful, though separate, city-states. The Italian city-states were entirely independent of the Holy Roman Empire.

In the fifteenth century, five powers dominated the Italian peninsula — Venice, Milan, Florence, the Papal States, and the Kingdom of Naples (see Map 12.1). Rulers of the city-states, whether despots in Milan, patrician elitists in Florence, or oligarchs in Venice, governed as monarchs. They crushed proletarian revolts, levied taxes, killed their enemies, and used massive building programs to employ, and the arts to overawe, the masses.

Venice, with enormous trade and a vast colonial empire, ranked as an international power. Although Venice had a sophisticated constitution and was a republic in name, an oligarchy of merchant-aristocrats actually ran the city. Milan also was called a republic, but despots of the Sforza family ruled harshly and dominated the smaller cities of the north. Likewise in Florence the form of government was republican, with authority vested in several councils of state. In reality, between 1434 and 1494, power in Florence was held by the great Medici banking family. Cosimo (1434–1464) and Lorenzo (1469–1492), although they did not hold public office, ruled from behind the scenes.

A republic is a state in which political power resides in the people and is exercised by them or their chosen representatives. The Renaissance nostalgia for the Roman form of republican government, combined with a calculating shrewdness, prompted leaders of Venice, Milan, and Florence to preserve the old forms: the people could be deceived into thinking they still possessed the decisive voice.

Central Italy consisted mainly of the Papal States, which during the Babylonian Captivity had come under the power of important Roman families. Pope Alexander VI (1492–1503), aided militarily and politically by his son Cesare Borgia, reasserted papal authority in the papal lands. Cesare Borgia became the hero of Machiavelli's *The Prince* because he began the work of uniting the peninsula by ruthlessly conquering and exacting total obedience from the principalities making up the Papal States.

South of the Papal States was the kingdom of Naples, consisting of virtually all of southern Italy and including, at times, Sicily. The kingdom of Naples had long been disputed by the Aragonese and by the French. In 1435, it passed to Aragon.

The major Italian city-states controlled the smaller ones, such as Siena, Mantua, Ferrara, and Modena, and they competed furiously among themselves for territory. The large cities used diplomacy, spies, paid informers, and any other means to get information that could be used to advance their ambitions. While the states of northern Europe moved toward national centralization and consolidation, the world of Italian politics resembled a jungle where the powerful dominated the weak. In one significant respect, however, the Italian city-states anticipated future relations among competing European states after 1500. Whenever one Italian state appeared to gain a position of predominant influence within the peninsula, other states combined to establish a balance of power against the major threat.

In 1450, for example, Venice went to war against Milan in protest against Francesco Sforza's acquisition of the title of duke of Milan. Cosimo de' Medici of Florence, a long-time supporter of a Florentine-Venetian alliance, switched his position and aided Milan. Florence and Naples combined

DUCHY
OF
SAVOY

Turin•

SALUZZO

DUCHY
OF
MILAN

Milan•
Pavia•   Lodi•
•

REP. OF GENOA

Genoa•

REP. OF LUCCA
Pisa• Arno
REP. OF
FLORENCE

Siena

REP. OF
SIENA

D. OF MODENA

D. OF
FERRARA

Bologna•   •Ravenna

Florence•

Urbino•

PAPAL
STATES

•Assisi

Tiber

Rome•

M. OF
MANTUA

Padua•
•
Venice

REPUBLIC OF VENICE

ADRIATIC SEA

DALMATIA

OTTOMAN
EMPIRE

CORSICA

SARDINIA

M E D I T E R R A N E A N

KINGDOM
OF
NAPLES

Naples•
Salerno•

•Bari

Palermo•

KINGDOM OF
SICILY

0   50   100 Km.

0   50   100 Mi.

S E A

MAP 12.1   THE ITALIAN CITY-STATES, CA 1494

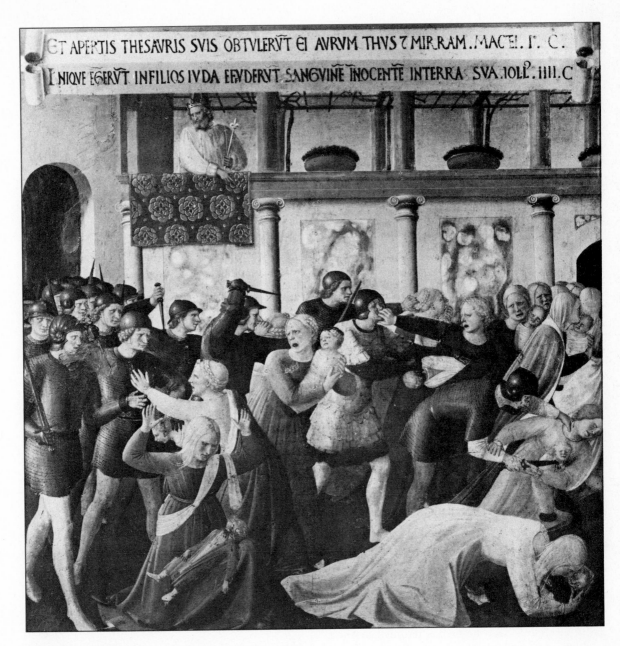

FRA ANGELICO: THE MASSACRE OF THE INNOCENTS. Piero
de Medici commissioned this painting as part of a series on the
life of Christ. Although based on the story of King Herod's
execution of all male infants, contemporary violence in
fifteenth-century Italy may have partly influenced Fra Angelico,
who composed the scene with great delicacy and realism.
Notice the swaddled infants. (Alinari/Editorial Photocolor
Archives)

with Milan against powerful Venice and the papacy. By the peace treaty signed at Lodi in 1454, Venice, in return for recognizing Sforza's right to the duchy, received territories. This pattern of shifting alliances continued until 1494.

At the end of the fifteenth century, Venice, Florence, Milan, and the papacy possessed great wealth and represented high cultural achievement. Their imperialistic ambitions against one another, however, and their inability to form a common alliance against potential foreign enemies, made Italy an inviting target for invasion. When Florence and Naples entered into an agreement to acquire Milanese territories, Milan called upon France for support.

The invasion of Italy in 1494 by the French king Charles VIII (1483–1498) inaugurated a new period in Italian and European power politics. Italy became the focus of international ambitions and the battleground of foreign armies. Charles swept down the peninsula with little opposition, and Florence, Rome, and Naples soon bowed before him. When Piero de' Medici, Lorenzo's son, went to the French camp seeking peace, the Florentines exiled the Medicis and restored republican government.

Charles's success simply whetted French appetites. In 1508, Charles's son Louis XII (1498–1515) formed the League of Cambrai with the pope and the German emperor Maximilian (1493–1519) with the purpose of stripping rich Venice of its mainland possessions. Pope Leo X soon found the French a dangerous friend and in a new alliance called upon the Spanish and Germans to expel the French from Italy. This anti-French combination was temporarily successful. But the French returned in 1522, and after Charles V succeeded his grandfather Maximilian as Holy Roman emperor, there began the series of conflicts called the Habsburg-Valois wars (named for the German and French dynasties) with Italy the battlefield.

In the sixteenth century, the political and social life of Italy was upset by the relentless competition between France and the empire for dominance. The Italian cities suffered severely from the continual warfare, especially in the frightful sack of Rome in 1527 by imperial forces under Charles V. The failure of the city-states to form some federal system, or to consolidate, or at least to establish a common foreign policy, led to the continuation of the centuries-old subjection of the peninsula by outside invaders. Italy did not achieve unification until 1870.

France

The Hundred Years' War left France badly divided, drastically depopulated, commercially ruined, and agriculturally weak. Nevertheless, the ruler whom Joan of Arc had seen crowned at Reims, Charles VII (1422–1461), revived the monarchy and France. He seemed an unlikely person to do so. Frail, ugly, feeble, hypochondriacal, mistrustful, and called "the son of a madman and a loose woman," Charles VII began the long recovery.

Through a treaty signed in 1435, Charles reconciled the conflicting Burgundians and Armagnacs, who had been waging civil war for thirty years. By 1453, French armies had expelled the English from French soil, except in Calais. Charles reorganized the royal council, giving increased influence to the middle-class men, and he strengthened royal finances through such taxes as the gabelle (on salt) and the taille (a land tax). These taxes remained the Crown's chief sources of state income until the Revolution of 1789.

Justice was reformed and the army remodeled. Through the establishment of regular companies of cavalry and archers, recruited, paid, and inspected by the state, Charles brought into existence the first permanent royal army. In 1438, Charles published the Pragmatic Sanction of Bourges. This asserted the superiority of a general council over the papacy, gave the French crown control over the appointment of bishops, and deprived the pope of French ecclesiastical revenues. The Pragmatic Sanction established the Gallican (or French) liberties, because it affirmed the autonomy of the French church from the Roman papacy.

Charles's son Louis XI, called "the Spider King" by his subjects because of his treacherous, tricky, and cruel character, was very much a Renaissance prince. He faced the perpetual French problems of the unification of the realm and the reduction of feudal disorder. Money was the answer. Louis promoted new industries, such as silk weaving at Lyons and Tours. He welcomed tradesmen and foreign craftsmen, and he entered into commercial treaties with England, Portugal, and the towns of the Hanseatic League, a group of cities which played an important role in the development of towns and commercial life in northern Germany. The revenues raised through these economic activities, and through severe taxation, were used to improve the army. With the army Louis stopped aristocratic brigandage and slowly cut into urban independence.

Luck favored his goal to expand royal authority and to unify the kingdom. In 1477, on the timely death of Charles the Bold, duke of Burgundy, Louis invaded Burgundy and gained some territories. Three years later, the extinction of the house of Anjou brought Louis the counties of Anjou, Bar, Maine, and Provence.

Some scholars have credited Louis XI with laying the foundations for later French royal absolutism. Louis summoned only one meeting of the Estates General, and the delegates requested that they not be summoned in the future. Thereafter, the king would decide. Building on the system begun by his father, Louis XI worked tirelessly to remodel the government following the debacle of the fourteenth and fifteenth centuries. To the extent that he relied on finances supplied by the middle classes to fight the feudal nobility, Louis is typical of the new monarchs of the period.

Two further developments strengthened the French monarchy. The marriage of Louis XII and Anne of Brittany added the large western duchy of Brittany to the state. Then, an agreement between the French king Francis I and Pope Leo X in 1516 nullified parts of the Pragmatic Sanction. The new treaty, the Concordat of Bologna, rescinded the assertion in the Pragmatic Sanction that upheld the superiority of a general council over the papacy and approved the pope's right to receive the first year's income of new bishops and abbots. In return, Leo X recognized the French ruler's right to select French bishops and abbots. French kings thereafter effectively controlled the appointment and thus the policies of church officials within the kingdom.

England

English society suffered severely from the disorders of the fifteenth century. The aristocracy dominated the government of Henry IV (1399–1413) and created mischievous violence at the local level. Population, decimated by the Black Death, continued to decline. While Henry V (1413–1422) gained chivalric prestige for his military exploits in France, he was totally dependent upon the feudal magnates who controlled the royal council and Parliament. Henry V's death, leaving a nine-month-old son as heir, the future Henry VI (1422–1461), gave the barons a perfect opportunity to entrench their power. Between 1455 and 1471, adherents of the ducal houses of York and Lancaster waged civil war, commonly called the Wars of the Roses because the symbol of the Yorkists was a white rose, that of the Lancastrians a red one. Although only a small minority of the nobility participated, the chronic disorder hurt trade, agriculture, and domestic industry. Under the pious but spineless Henry VI, the authority of the monarchy sank lower than it had been in centuries.

The reign of Edward IV (1461–1483) witnessed the beginnings of domestic tranquility. He succeeded in defeating the Lancastrian forces and after 1471 began to reconstruct the monarchy and consolidate royal power. Edward, his brother Richard III (1483–1485), and Henry VII of the Welsh house of Tudor worked to restore royal prestige, to crush the power of the nobility, and to establish order and law at the local level. All three rulers used methods and displayed qualities Machiavelli would have praised — ruthlessness, efficiency, and secrecy.

The Hundred Years' War had cost the nation dearly, and the money to finance it had been raised by Parliament. Dominated by various baronial factions, Parliament had been the arena where the nobility exerted its power. As long as the monarchy was dependent on the lords and the commons for revenue, the king had to call Parliament. Edward IV repeated the medieval ideal that he would "live of his own," meaning his own financial resources. He reluctantly established a policy the monarchy with rare exception followed down to 1603. Edward, and subsequently the Tudors, conducted foreign policy on the basis of diplomacy and avoided expensive wars. Thus, the English monarchy did not depend on Parliament for money, and the Crown undercut that source of aristocratic influence.

Henry VII did summon several meetings of Parliament in the early years of his reign, however. He used these assemblies primarily to confirm laws. Parliament remained the highest court in the land, and a statute registered (or approved) there by the lords, bishops, and commons gave the appearance of broad national support plus thorough judicial authority.

The center of royal authority was the royal council, which governed at the national level. There too Henry VII revealed his distrust of the nobility, because although they were not completely excluded, very few great lords were among the king's closest advisers. Regular representatives on the council numbered between twelve and fifteen men, and while many gained high ecclesiastical rank (the means, as it happened, by which the Crown paid them), in origin they came from the lesser landowning class and in education they had been trained in law. They were in a sense middle class.

The royal council handled any business the king put before it — executive, legislative, judicial. For example, the council conducted negotiations with foreign governments and secured international recognition of the Tudor dynasty through the marriage in 1501 of Henry VII's eldest son Arthur to Catherine of Aragon, the daughter of Ferdinand and Isabella of Spain. The council prepared laws for parliamentary ratification. The council dealt with real or potential aristocratic threats through a judicial offshoot, the court of Star Chamber, so called because of the stars painted on the ceiling of the room.

The court of Star Chamber applied principles of Roman law, and its methods were terrifying: the accused was not entitled to see evidence against him; sessions were secret; torture could be applied to extract confessions; and juries were not called. These procedures ran directly counter to English common law precedents, but they effectively reduced aristocratic troublemakers. Henry VIII (1509–1547) summoned rioters of all classes before this branch of the council, and Star Chamber served to promote peace.

Unlike the continental countries of Spain and France, England had no standing army or professional civil service (bureaucracy). The Tudors relied upon the support of unpaid local officials, the justices of the peace. These influential landowners in the shires handled all the work of local government. They apprehended and punished criminals, enforced parliamentary statutes, supervised conditions of service, fixed wages and prices, maintained proper standards of weights and measures, and even checked up on moral behavior. Justices of the peace were appointed and supervised by the council. From the royal point of view, they were an inexpensive method of government.

The Tudors won the support of the influential upper middle class because the Crown linked government policy with their interests. A commercial or agricultural upper class fears and dislikes few things more than disorder and violence. If the Wars of the Roses served any useful purpose, it was in killing off dangerous nobles, thus making the Tudors' work easier. The Tudors promoted peace and social order, and the gentry did not object if they used arbitrary methods like the court of Star Chamber, because the government had halted the long period of anarchy.

Grave, secretive, cautious, and always thrifty, Henry VII rebuilt the monarchy. He encouraged the cloth industry and built up the English merchant marine. English exports of wool and the royal export tax on that wool steadily increased. Henry crushed an invasion from Ireland and secured peace with Scotland through the marriage of his daughter Margaret to the Scottish king. When Henry VII died in 1509, he left a country at peace both domestically and internationally, a fat treasury, and the dignity of the royal majesty much enhanced.

Spain

Political development in Spain followed a pattern different from that in France and England. The central theme in the history of medieval Spain or, more accurately, of the separate kingdoms Spain comprised, was disunity and plurality. The various peoples who lived in the Iberian Pensinsula lacked a common cultural tradition. Different languages, different laws, and different religious communities made for a rich diversity. Complementing the legacy of Hispanic, Roman, and Visigothic peoples, Muslims and Jews had made significant contributions to Spanish society.

The centuries-long *reconquista,* the attempts of the northern Christian kingdoms to control the entire peninsula, combined military and religious objectives: the expulsion or conversion of Arabs and Jews and the political control of the south. By the middle of the fifteenth century, the kingdoms of Castile and Aragon dominated the weaker Navarre, Granada, and Portugal, and, with the exception of Granada, the Iberian Peninsula had been won for Christianity. The wedding in 1469 of the dynamic and aggressive Isabella, heiress of Castile, and the crafty and persistent Ferdinand, heir of Aragon, was the final major step in the unification and Christianization of Spain (see Map 12.2). This marriage constituted, however, a dynastic union of two royal houses, not the political union of two peoples. Although Ferdinand and Isabella pursued a common foreign policy, Spain under their rule remained a loose confederation of separate states. Each kingdom continued to maintain its own cortes (parliament), laws, courts, bureaucracies, and systems of coinage and taxation.

Isabella and Ferdinand determined to strengthen royal authority. In order to curb the rebellious and warring aristocracy, they revived an old medieval institution. Popular groups in the towns called *hermandades,* or brotherhoods, were given the authority to act both as local police forces and as judicial tribunals. Local communities were made responsible for raising troops and apprehending and punishing criminals of all types. The *hermandades* repressed violence with such savage punishments that by 1498 they could be disbanded.

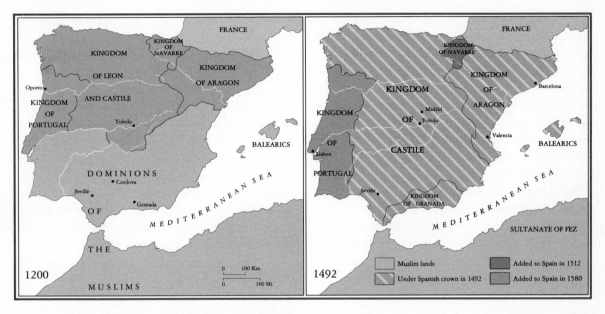

MAP 12.2 THE CHRISTIANIZATION AND UNIFICATION OF SPAIN, CA 1200–1580

The second step taken to curb aristocratic power was the restructuring of the royal council. Aristocrats and great territorial magnates were rigorously excluded from it. Thus, the influence of the nobility on state policy was greatly reduced. Ferdinand and Isabella intended the council to be the cornerstone of their governmental system, with full executive, judicial, and legislative power under the monarchy. The council was also to be responsible for the supervision of local authorities. The king and queen, therefore, appointed to the council only persons of middle-class background. The council and various government boards recruited men trained in Roman law, a system that exalted the power of the Crown as the embodiment of the state.

In the extension of royal authority and the consolidation of the territories of Spain, the church was the linchpin. The church possessed vast power and wealth, and churchmen enjoyed exemption from taxation. Most of the higher clergy were descended from great aristocratic families, controlled armies and strategic fortresses, and fully shared the military ethos of their families.

The major issue confronting Isabella and Ferdinand was the appointment of bishops. If the Spanish crown could select the higher clergy, then the Catholic rulers could influence ecclesiastical policy, wealth, and military resources. Through a diplomatic alliance with the papacy, especially with the Spanish pope Alexander VI, the Spanish monarchs secured the right to appoint bishops in Spain and in the Hispanic territories in America. This power enabled the "Catholic Kings of Spain," a title granted Ferdinand and Isabella by the papacy, to establish, in effect, a national church.[20]

The Spanish rulers used their power to reform the church, and they used some of its wealth for national purposes. For example, they appointed a learned and zealous churchman, Cardinal Jiménez (1436–1517), to reform the monastic and secular clergy. Jiménez not only proved effective in this task, he established the University of Alcalá in 1499 for the education of the clergy, although instruction did not actually begin until 1508. A highly astute statesman as well, Jiménez twice served as regent of Castile.

Revenues from ecclesiastical estates provided the means to raise an army to continue the *reconquista*. The victorious entry of Ferdinand and Isabella into Granada on January 6, 1492, signaled the culmination of eight centuries of Spanish struggle against the Arabs in southern Spain and the conclusion of the *reconquista*. Granada in the south was incorporated into the Spanish kingdom, and in 1512 Ferdinand conquered Navarre in the north.

Although the Arabs had been defeated, there still remained, in the view of the Catholic sovereigns, a sizable and potentially dangerous minority, the Jews. Since ancient times, governments had never tolerated religious pluralism; religious faiths that differed from the official state religion were considered politically dangerous. Medieval writers quoted the fourth-century Byzantine theologian Saint John Chrysostom, who had asked rhetorically, "Why are the Jews degenerate? Because of their odious assassination of Christ." Both John Chrysostom and his admirers in the Middle Ages chose to ignore two facts: first, that the Romans had killed Christ (because they considered him a *political* troublemaker), and second, that Christ had forgiven his executioners from the cross. France and England had expelled their Jewish populations in the Middle Ages, but in Spain Jews had been tolerated. In fact, Jews had played a decisive role in the economic and intellectual life of the several Spanish kingdoms. The anti-Semitic riots and pogroms of the late fourteenth century had led many Jews to convert; they were called *conversos*.

By the middle of the fifteenth century, many conversos held high positions in Spanish society as financiers, physicians, merchants, tax collectors, and even as officials of the church hierarchy. Numbering perhaps 200,000 in a total population of about 7.5 million, the Jews exercised an influence quite disproportionate to their numbers. Aristocratic grandees who borrowed heavily from Jews resented their financial dependence, and churchmen questioned the sincerity of Jewish conversions. At first, Isabella and Ferdinand continued the policy of royal toleration — a natural position, since Ferdinand himself had inherited Jewish blood from his mother. Many conversos apparently reverted to the faith of their ancestors, however, prompting Ferdinand and Isabella to secure Rome's permission to revive the Inquisition, a medieval judicial procedure for the punishment of heretics. It was controlled only by the Crown.

Although the Inquisition was a religious institution established to insure the Catholic faith, it served as a politically unifying force in Spain. (Because the Spanish Inquisition commonly applied torture to extract confessions first from lapsed conversos, then from Muslims, and later from Protestants, it gained a notorious reputation. Thus, the word "inquisition," meaning "any judicial inquiry conducted with ruthless severity," came into the English language. The methods of the Spanish Inquisition were cruel, though not as cruel as the investigative methods of some twentieth-century governments.) Ferdinand and Isabella, both deeply pious, introduced the Inquisition into their kingdoms to handle the problem of the backsliding conversos. They solved the problem of identifying Jews and backsliding conversos in a dire and drastic manner. Less than three months after the defeat of the Moors, Isabella and Ferdinand issued an edict expelling all practicing Jews from Spain. Of the community of perhaps 200,000 Jews, 150,000 fled. (Efforts were made through last-minute conversions to retain good Jewish physicians.) Absolute religious orthodoxy served as the foundation of the Spanish national state.

The diplomacy of the Catholic rulers of Spain achieved a success they never anticipated. Partly from hatred for the French and partly to gain international recognition for their new dynasty, Ferdinand and Isabella in 1496 married their second daughter, Joanna, heiress to Castile, to the archduke Philip, heir through his mother to the Burgundian Netherlands and through his father to the Holy Roman Empire. Philip and Joanna's son, Charles V (1519–1556), succeeded to a vast patrimony on two continents. When Charles's son Philip II united Portugal to the Spanish crown in 1580, the Iberian Peninsula was at last politically united.

NOTES

1. A. Brucker, *Renaissance Florence,* John Wiley & Sons, New York, 1969, chap. 2.

2. Quoted by J. Burckhardt, *The Civilization of the Renaissance in Italy,* Phaidon Books, London, 1951, p. 89.

3. *Memoirs of Benvenuto Cellini; A Florentine Artist; Written by Himself,* Everyman's Library, J. M. Dent & Sons Ltd., London, 1927, p. 2.

4. Quoted by Burckhardt, p. 111.

5. Quoted by E. H. Harbison, *The Christian Scholar and His Calling in the Age of the Reformation,* Charles Scribner's Sons, New York, 1956, p. 109.

6. Quoted by F. Seebohm, *The Oxford Reformers,* Everyman's Library, J. M. Dent & Sons Ltd., London, 1867, p. 256.

7. B. Burroughs, ed., *Vasari's Lives of the Artists,* Simon & Schuster, New York, 1946, pp. 164–165.

8. See chap. 3, "The Social Status of the Artist," in A. Hauser, *The Social History of Art,* vol. 2, Vintage Books, New York, 1959, esp. pp. 60, 68.

9. G. Bull, trans., *Aretino: Selected Letters,* Penguin Books, New York, 1976, p. 109.

10. Hauser, pp. 48–49.

11. Quoted by W. H. Woodward, *Vittorino da Feltre and Other Humanist Educators,* Cambridge University Press, Cambridge, 1897, pp. 96–97.

12. C. E. Detmold, trans., *The Historical, Political and Diplomatic Writings of Niccolò Machiavelli,* J. R. Osgood & Co., Boston, 1882, pp. 51–52.

13. Ibid., pp. 54–55.

14. This account rests on the excellent study of J. Kelly-Gadol, "Did Women Have a Renaissance?" in R. Blumenthal and C. Koonz, eds., *Becoming Visible: Women in European History,* Houghton Mifflin, Boston, 1977, pp. 137–161, esp. p. 161.

15. G. Ruggiero, "Sexual Criminality in the Early Renaissance: Venice 1338–1358," *Journal of Social History* 8 (Spring 1975):18–31.

16. Quoted by R. C. Trexler, "Infanticide in Florence: New Sources and First Results," *History of Childhood Quarterly* 1:1 (Summer 1973): 99.

17. Ibid., p. 100.

18. Quoted by R. C. Trexler, "Measures against Water Pollution in Fifteenth-Century Florence," *Viator* 5 (1974): 463.

19. Ibid., pp. 464–467.

20. See J. H. Elliott, *Imperial Spain 1469–1716,* Mentor Books, New York, 1963, esp. pp. 97–108 and p. 75.

SUGGESTED READING

There are scores of exciting studies available on virtually all aspects of the Renaissance. In addition to the titles given in the Notes, the curious student interested in a broad synthesis should see J. H. Plumb, *The Italian Renaissance** (1965), a superbly written book based on deep knowledge and understanding; this book is probably the best starting point. F. H. New, *The Renaissance and Reformation: A Short History** (1977), gives a concise, balanced, and up-to-date account. M. P. Gilmore, *The World of Humanism** (1962), is an older but sound study that recent scholarship has not superseded on many subjects. Students interested in the problems the Renaissance has raised for historians should see K. H. Dannenfeldt, ed., *The Renaissance: Medieval or Modern** (1959), an anthology with a variety of interpretations, and W. K. Ferguson, *The Renaissance in Historical Thought* (1948), a valuable but difficult book. For the city where much of it originated, G. A. Brucker, *Renaissance Florence** (1969), gives a good description of Florentine economic, political, social, and cultural history.

J. R. Hale, *Machiavelli and Renaissance Italy** (1966), is the best short biography of Machiavelli and broader in scope than the title would imply, while G. Bull, trans., *Machiavelli: The Prince** (1959), is a readable and easily accessible edition of the political thinker's major work. C. Singleton, trans., *The Courtier** (1959), presents an excellent picture of Renaissance court life.

The best introduction to the Renaissance in northern Europe and a book that has greatly influenced twentieth-century scholarship is J. Huizinga, *The Waning of the Middle Ages: A Study of the Forms of Life, Thought, and Art in France and the Netherlands in the Dawn of the Renaissance** (1954), while the leading northern humanist is sensitively treated in M. M. Phillips, *Erasmus and the Northern Renaissance** (1965), and in J. Huizinga, *Erasmus of Rotterdam* (1952), probably the best biography.

Renaissance art has understandably inspired vast researches. In addition to Vasari's volume of biographical sketches on the great masters referred to in the Notes, A. Martindale, *The Rise of the Artist in the Middle Ages and Early Renaissance** (1972), is a splendidly illustrated introduction. B. Berenson, *Italian Painters of the Renaissance** (1957), the work of an American ex-patriate who was an internationally famous art historian, has become a classic. W. Sypher, *Four Stages of Renaissance Style** (1956), relates drama and poetry to the visual arts of painting and sculpture. One of the finest appreciations of Renaissance art, written by one of the greatest art historians of this century, is E. Panofsky, *Meaning in the Visual Arts** (1955). Both Italian and northern painting are treated in the brilliant study of M. Meiss, *The Painter's Choice: Problems in the Interpretation of Renaissance Art** (1976), a collection of essays dealing with Renaissance style, form, and meaning.

The following works are not only useful for the political and economic history of the age of the Renaissance but also contain valuable bibliographical information: A. J. Slavin, ed., *The "New Monarchies" and Representative Assemblies** (1965), a collection of interpretations; R. Lockyer, *Henry VII** (1972), a biography with documents illustrative of the king's reign; J. H. Elliott, *Imperial Spain: 1469–1716** (1966), with a balanced treatment of Isabella and Ferdinand; and I. Origo, *The Merchant of Prato* (1957), a perceptive and detailed account of one busy Florentine businessman.

*Available in paperback.

INDEX

Germany: under Augustus, 146; Carolingian Empire, 219–235; feudal practices combined with Christianity in Holy Roman Empire, 227; Otto crowned Holy Roman emperor with church support, 247–248

Gerson, John, 357

Gertrude of Saxony, 296

Gesith, 182, 230

Ghiberti, Lorenzo, 386, 387

Ghirlandaio, 386

Gibbon, Edward, 156, 158, 171, 174

Giotto, 384

Glanvill, 276

Godfrey of Bouillon, 331

Gospel book of Lindisfarne, 228–229

Gothic cathedrals, 325–329

Goths, 163–164, 179

Government, Machiavelli's theories on, 390

Gracchus, Gaius, 137

Gracchus, Tiberius, 136

Granada, 404, 406

Great Schism, 356–357

Greco-Roman culture: under Augustus, 145; Christian attitude toward, 195–198; revival of in Renaissance, 376, 378–379

Greece: Hellenic, 39–75; land, 41–42; polis, 42–45; early Mycenaeans, 45–46; Bronze Age in, 45–47; periods of history, 46; Dark Age, 46–50; Heroic Age, 47–50; colonization of Mediterranean region, 50–52; Lyric Age, 50–58; growth of Sparta, 54–55; evolution of Athens, 55–58; wars with Persians, 58–62; classical period, 58–74; Peloponnesian War, 60; arts in Periclean Athens, 62–67; daily life in Athens, 67–70; philosophy in, 70–73; Hellenistic period, 78–107; Alexander's conquests and legacies, 79–84; Hellenism's spread, 84–106; religion, 92–94; philosophy, 94–97; science, 97–99; medicine, 99–101; economy, 101–106; Roman conquest of, 123–124

Greek Orthodox church: schism with Roman Catholic church 202–203; Crusaders attempt to unite with Roman Catholic church 330–333

Gregory I, pope, 190, 192

Gregory II, pope, 220

Gregory VII, pope, 262, 264–269

Gregory, IX, pope, 270

Gregory XI, pope, 355

Guibert of Nogent, 290–291, 377

Guilds, medieval, 253

Gutenberg, Johan, 393

Hadrian, 157–158, 160

Hammond, M., 156

Hammurabi, 14–22

Hammurabi's code, 35

Hannibal, 122–123, 134

Hanseatic League, 402

Hastings, battle of, 307

Health, in Middle Ages, 235–238, 249. *See also* Medicine

Hebrews: and Semitic migrations, 27; early history of, 32; kingdom splits into Israel and Judah, 32; influence on other religions, 34–36. *See also* Jews

Hejaz, 206

Heliocentric theory, 97, 98

Hellas, 41

Hellenism: defined, 40; influence on Roman life, 130–133. *See also* Greece

Helots, 54, 55

Heptarchy, 186

Henry III, Holy Roman emperor, 263–265

Henry IV, Holy Roman emperor, 266–269

Henry V, Holy Roman emperor, 269, 296

Henry I, king of England, 269, 313–316

Henry II, king of England: charter to town of Lincoln, 253; son Richard, 290; conflict with sons, 293; medical adviser, 300; judicial reforms and development of common law, 316–318

Henry IV, king of England, 402

Henry V, king of England, 350, 353, 402

Henry VI, king of England, 402

Henry VII, king of England, 403, 404

Henry VIII, king of England: and Thomas More, 381; studied Machiavelli, 390; use of Star Chamber, 403

Henry of Langenstein, 357

Henry the Proud, 296

Heraclides of Tarentum, 100

Heraclitus, 71, 96

Hermandades, 404

Hermits, 198–199

Herod, 145, 151

Herodotus, 22, 29, 47, 61

Herophilus, 99–100

Hesiod, 47–50

High Middle Ages, 246–335; life in, 274–302; vitality and creativity of, 305–335. *See also* Middle Ages

High Renaissance, 380. *See also* Renaissance

Hildegard, German abbess, 237

Hillel, 151

Hincmar, Archbishop, 219

Hippias, 57

Hippocrates, 71, 99